INTRODUCTORY PSYCHOLOGY
THROUGH
SCIENCE FICTION

INTRODUCTORY PSYCHOLOGY THROUGH THROUGH SCIENCE FICTION

Second Edition

Edited by

Harvey A. Katz
Suffolk University

Martin Harry Greenberg
University of Wisconsin, Green Bay

Patricia S. Warrick
University of Wisconsin

 RAND McNALLY COLLEGE PUBLISHING COMPANY • Chicago

77 78 79 10 9 8 7 6 5 4 3 2 1

preface

"Psychology and literature have like purposes: to better understand the individual and his society. Because the study of each discipline can add to the dimensions of understanding in the other, their marriage in a reader like this one hopefully will be productive. The specific genre of literature—science fiction—offers a model to examine modern man in a technological society."

These words expressed our hopes and beliefs in 1974, when we offered the introductory psychology community a different kind of reader. We are gratified that professors in many excellent schools saw the expansive vistas that the use of science fiction for introductory psychology promised. We are happy that a whole new audience could experience the imagination and human understanding with which our authors fill their stories. We are pleased that our introductions and other editing contributions has enabled students to learn introductory psychology in a new and interesting way. Hopefully, students have been able to take with them a feel for the psychological problems of modern man today and tomorrow. Finally, we are excited over the fact that the level of acceptance of our first edition has warranted a second one.

Our criteria for the inclusion of stories in our second edition remain as they were for the first edition: (1) each story has to contain material which makes it workable as a vehicle for exploring an important aspect of introductory psychology; (2) the science background of the story has to be essentially sound; and (3) the story has to be good literature. The stories offer particular people in particular situations. By identifying with these people and abstracting general principles which can apply to their own lives, students become active rather than passive learners.

We have tried to make improvements for our book in its

v

second edition without changing the essence of the first edition. We have had the benefit of using the book in introductory psychology classes, intuiting which stories worked better than others by student reactions as well as the constructive comments of our own critics and friends like Professor Charles Waugh. In addition different stories have come to our attention since our initial pool was created.

As a result we have changed the order of the chapters to better reflect typical chapter orders of popular introductory textbooks which might be used with our reader. However, there is still no one order used in textbooks, and while many professors will still have to make adjustments in their chapter assignments, we feel that there is little lost in assigning our chapters out of order. All chapters now have four stories in them rather than varying from three to five as in our first edition. Thus no area should feel slighted this time around. Within each chapter the stories have been reordered to give greater logic and impact to their presentation. We have dropped four stories while adding five new ones, have switched one story to a different chapter, and have rewritten some introductions. In general, we have given more emphasis to topics relating to cognition and less emphasis to those relating to instinct. As a result of these changes, we feel that the book has been strengthened academically, as well as having been improved in its intrinsic ability to provide pleasurable reading.

As in the first edition, we would like to acknowledge the many fine introductory psychology texts which were helpful in preparing the chapters and story introductions. Special acknowledgment is given to texts written by Ruch and Zimbardo, Hilgard and Atkinson, and Mussen et al.

We believe that this book, like the first edition, exemplifies the creative restructuring of old and new; business and pleasure; past, present, and future. It is forward looking, yet uses literary works, some of which were written more than thirty years ago. It aims to retain the foundation of psychology in solidly established knowledge while at the same time broadening its horizons with imaginative journeys into space and time. We have attempted to instill new life into the introductory psychology course and in this same spirit we dedicate this book to Joshua Lawrence Murphy–Katz, son of

the first editor. Like our book, Joshua represents the merging of past, present, and future. Hopefully, as in the biblical past, if impeding walls come tumbling down in the present, we can rise to the stars in the future.

Harvey A. Katz
Patricia Warrick
Martin Harry Greenberg

contents

Introduction: Psychology and Science Fiction **1**

1 Developmental Processes **11**

That Only a Mother *Judith Merril* 15
The First Men *Howard Fast* 26
The Examination *Felix Gotschalk* 57
The Playground *Ray Bradbury* 73

2 Psychobiology **91**

Flowers for Algernon *Daniel Keyes* 95
The Brain *Norbert Wiener* 125
Socrates *John Christopher* 141
Nine Lives *Ursula K. Le Guin* 157

3 Sensation, Perception, and Awareness **183**

Through Other Eyes *R. A. Lafferty* 187
And He Built a Crooked House *Robert A. Heinlein* 200
The Subliminal Man *J. G. Ballard* 221
Such Stuff *John Brunner* 241

4 Learning and Cognition 259

Learning Theory *James McConnell* 262
Susie's Reality *Bob Stickgold* 277
Rat in the Skull *Rog Phillips* 307
The Man Who Devoured Books *John Sladek* 332

5 Social Processes 341

All the Last Wars at Once *Geo. Alec Effinger* 345
Adjustment *Ward Moore* 361
Seventh Victim *Robert Sheckley* 382
Love, Incorporated *Robert Sheckley* 397

6 Personality 411

Mother *Philip Jose Farmer* 416
Dreaming is a Private Thing *Isaac Asimov* 446
Alter Ego *Hugo Correa* 464
The Man in the Rorschach Shirt *Ray Bradbury* 468

7 Abnormal Process and Therapy 481

And Now the News *Theodore Sturgeon* 486
The Plot *Tom Herzog* 508
The Yellow Pill *Rog Phillips* 517
Going Down Smooth *Robert Silverberg* 531

Bibliography 541

introduction

PSYCHOLOGY AND SCIENCE FICTION

Introductory Psychology Through Science Fiction is a collection of short stories selected and organized to explore the concepts of psychology as they function in fictional worlds. Both psychology and fiction grow out of the fact that man is a curious creature, endlessly asking questions and forever seeking answers. Of all the areas of the universe that he explores, nothing fascinates him more than man. He is curious about himself and about other men—individually and in groups. What makes me like I am? How much does my environment affect me? Do other people experience the world as I do: think like me, feel like me? In what ways are they different?

Both psychology and literature attempt to provide answers for these questions but they use different forms of expression. Psychology states concepts. Literature provides examples which demonstrate these concepts in action.

From the beginnings of mankind, man has looked at his own behavior and the behavior of those around him with curiosity and wonder. Shakespeare caught the essence of this wonder when, through Hamlet, he declared, "What a piece of work is a man! How noble in reason! How infinite in faculty . . . !" The systematic study of this complex "piece of work" is psychology: the science of the behavior of organisms. Psychology studies both the external behavior which we can observe others being engaged in, and the internal behavior which we experience as it occurs inside ourselves, and which we surmise is also occurring inside others.

Psychology as a science has developed only within the last hundred years, and it is a product of the scientific method. Francis Bacon, a sixteenth century Englishman, is credited with being the father of the scientific method of inquiry, and its first application was in the physical sciences like chemistry and physics. The steps in the method are (1) observation, (2) hypothesis, (3) experimentation, and (4) verification.

Scientific inquiry leads to the understanding of natural events and the cause-effect relationships which produce them. Once these relationships are understood, events can be predicted; and the possibility exists that they can be controlled. The results of scientific study in the natural sciences were so productive that during the late nineteenth and early twentieth centuries, the scientific method was applied to a systematic study of the individual and his society. The result was the social sciences: psychology, sociology, political science, economics, and anthropology.

Man has always attempted to understand himself and his behavior. Literary masters like Fedor Dostoevsky and William Shakespeare demonstrate in their writings enormously penetrating psychological insights. All of us who are interested in understanding ourselves arrive at conclusions about behavior, although they are probably less perceptive than those of someone like Shakespeare. But there is a fundamental difference between the layman and the professional psychologist. The layman looks at people around him and in attempting to understand their behavior appeals to his own experiences and insights. The layman uses *intuitive* methods.

Like the layman, the professional psychologist observes behavior, and he may also use his intuitive powers to suggest answers for his questions. However, in addition to these initial steps, the professional psychologist goes further. He suggests a cause for the behavior he observes (he forms a hypothesis), and then he tries to demonstrate that this cause and effect relationship actually exists (he tests the hypothesis). He uses *empirical* methods.

The two major approaches used to empirically test hypotheses have been the behavioristic or "experimental" method and the clinical method. The behaviorist approach was promoted in this country by John B. Watson. Impressed with the Russian psychologist Pavlov's work on conditioning, Watson insisted that the laboratory be the place to empirically test all of the psychologist's hypotheses. If the psychologist believed that specific conditions caused specific behaviors, he should try to create these conditions in the laboratory and systematically observe whether in fact individuals behaved in the suspected manner when exposed to the created conditions. Watson insisted that the only behavior that could be studied objectively was external behavior which could be observed by others, and he advised psychologists to forget about studying the internal aspects of observable behavior. In general, American psychologists adopted Watson's methods, leading to the scientific experimental approach which presently dominates psychological research in America.

The clinical approach originated with Sigmund Freud's psychoanalytic methods and theories. Here, the patient comes to the psychotherapist with behavior problems. Although the patient describes behavior, the therapist can only observe it when the patient is in his office. However, he also inquires about the patient's feelings (internal behavior), believing that feelings and emotions are very important in motivating external behavior.

After listening to the patient, the therapist hypothesizes as to the cause of the problem behavior. Therapists believing in different theories of behavior will look for different kinds of causes. Psychoanalysts go back to the patient's past for these causes: highly emotional incidents and relationships in the patient's childhood which were buried rather than properly dealt with at that time. The therapist helps and encourages the patient to discuss these childhood incidents and to experience again the strong emotions which accompanied them.

Constructive changes in the patient's behavior as a result of this process lend support to the therapist's hypothesis about what has been causing his patient's problem behavior. If the therapist has a continuing series of similar successes with his other patients, he can view these successes as empirical support for the theory of personality and method of therapy that he subscribes to. Of course, the general method of therapy used is transmitted and modified by the sensitivities and technical skills of the specific therapist. Thus the therapy is both empirical and intuitive.

The behaviorist and psychoanalytic approaches have traditionally been the two most important schools on the psychological scene. Recently, however, a third force—humanistic psychology—has appeared, speaking out for a new approach in the study of modern man. Men like Carl Rogers, Abraham Maslow, and Gordon Allport have criticized the two traditional approaches for being inadequate in psychology's search to fully understand what it means to be human in a technological society. They see the behavioristic approach, focusing on external behavior which can be observed only in the laboratory, as at best limited. Furthermore, they see the psychoanalytic approach, focusing on the childhood causes of adult neurotic behavior, as omitting the great majority of healthy adults who are not prisoners of the unfinished business of their childhoods. These healthy people can freely choose behaviors which enable them to grow and develop their individual potentialities; they *self-actualize*. The humanistic psychologists feel it is more fruitful to study the behavior of these emotionally healthy individuals than to study primarily disturbed individuals.

As one solution to the shortcomings of the traditional psychological approaches, the humanistic psychologists believe that there must be an integration of psychology and the humanities. This inclusion of the humanities would bring a new and much needed balance to the field of psychology. It has always had ties with the sciences—as a result of the behavioristic approach, and with medicine—as a result of the clinical approach. The new approach would make full use of fields like philosophy, theology, theater, and literature. It would tap these rich sources of insight about the human condition, even though they may be presently difficult to relate to the psychological laboratory or the analyst's couch. If these other fields in the humanities contain knowledge which can help people live meaningful lives today and tomorrow, then the humanistic psychologist wants them included in his bag. In addition to using concepts acquired by detached observation *of* life, he can also use the wisdom accrued from involvement and experience *in* life.

As the humanistic psychologists suggest, the understanding of the good fiction writer can help us explore important human problems today. This anthology of short stories uses a particular type of fiction—social science fiction—as the tool for that exploration. Social science fiction is defined by Isaac Asimov as "that branch of literature which is concerned with the impact of scientific advance upon human beings."[1] It does not limit itself to the real, but imaginatively explores all the possibilities that can be conceived.

Science fiction as a literary form came to full flower following World War II. It had its beginnings in the late nineteenth century in such writers as H. G. Wells, Jules Verne, and Ralph Bellamy. Its twentieth century development paralleled the flowering of our space age technological society which, following the second World War, turned the full power of its research and technological energies in all directions. The explosion in knowledge, in new technological developments, in consumer goods, in social change, was overwhelming. As Alvin Toffler points out in *Future Shock*,[2] we have not yet learned to cope with it. But science fiction is one attempt to understand this knowledge and the social change that is or might be a by-product of the new technology. It is uniquely the literature of the twentieth century, portraying as it does a world of science and technology.

Insights about man and his relationship to his world so fundamental that the meaning survives time can be found in the old biblical and Greek myths. One such myth, the story of the Greek architect and artist Daedalus, offers an image to help us see our condition today. Daedalus, an ingenious artificer, planned and built the labyrinth. Its numberless winding passages opening into one another seemed without beginning or end, like a river that returns upon itself. Although it was conceived by a human, a human could be trapped in it, unable to escape.

Daedalus, however, was not an ordinary human. When later in his life he did become trapped in a situation, he conceived of flight as an escape. He built wings and flew away from his prison and his captors.

Architect and artist—Daedalus was both, and this is what man must be to survive. He must be a builder, certainly, but he must also be able to rise above what he has built and view it objectively with artistic detachment. Twentieth century technological man has achieved too much as a builder and too little as an artist. He has created labyrinths of new intellectual awarenesses and technologi-

1. Issac Asimov, "Social Science Fiction" in *Science Fiction and the Future*, ed. Dick Allen (New York: Harcourt Brace Jovanovich, 1971), 272.

2. Alvin Toffler, *Future Shock* (New York: Random House, 1970).

cal structures which model and utilize the knowledge research has given him. But he wanders in a maze, unable to see his way out of the effects of plans which began as blueprints for utopia and ended by producing nightmare consequences. He needs the artistic awareness which he can find only by moving above his world to a detached overview. There he can discover the fundamental ecological truth that each part and its action affects the whole. There are no islands—in society, or in academic disciplines.

Science fiction provides the wings to fly to a distance for a long view. Indeed, one of the recurring images in science fiction is of flight through space. Because science fiction is always set in a situation, event, or time other than the one which is occurring or has occurred in the real world, it provides a fresh vantage point which is different from the conventional one. It creates aliens who come—without our cultural conditioning—to examine our society. It visits other worlds—with different sets of conditions—where societies nevertheless function. Devices like this make science fiction an effective tool for social criticism. This quality makes it a natural companion for any course in the social sciences, whose objective is to understand man and his social structures so that he can function more effectively.

Literature and psychology have a natural kinship. Literature—like Daedalus—creates a little world of labyrinthian complexities in which the characters move. Not only the exterior world but the interior worlds of the major characters are mazelike in their infinite patterns of complexity. Literature asks the reader to perform two acts simultaneously: to identify with the character and to move beyond the character to an objective understanding which the character himself may not be able to achieve. In a similar approach, psychology asks us both to experience ourselves—living organisms with perceptions, emotions, intelligence—and also like Daedalus, move above ourselves to a detached, objective understanding of what we are and how we behave.

More specifically, there are several ways in which science fiction literature can be a helpful supplement to a conventional text in learning the important aspects of psychology. First, it brings the abstractions to life by presenting a specific example. These abstractions—or psychological concepts—grew out of careful observation and study of the particular. Recreating this particular in a short story illuminates the principle being studied and makes it clear and meaningful in a sharply focused image. Images remain more vividly in the mind and so aid not only comprehension but also retention.

Closely related to the first is a second way in which science fiction can be an effective tool for learning. In contrast to the theoretical, which must analyze one aspect at a time, the story can present the individual in a social setting. We see him as life is really experienced—as a whole person in a living system. Certainly dissection to understand the parts, as theory must do, is necessary. But this crucifixion should be followed by a resurrection to maintain the vital awareness that beyond his complex and infinite parts man is a whole entity—not static and lifeless, but dynamic and moving in a social milieu.

This capability of presenting a dynamic view of man is the unique quality of literature. The supporting structure of good fiction is always a plot. Things happen; there is movement; conflicting elements oppose each other. Physicists tell us that matter is always in motion. To study the human, then, as he really is means to study him in motion. Fiction provides this dynamic view of man for our observation.

The third dimension of science fiction as a teaching tool is its capacity for reflecting new knowledge in research and the technology which has developed and may develop in the future. Good science fiction writers, who more often than not are part-time writers and full-time professionals in another field, are well aware of the forefront of developments in science and technology. These developments are reflected in the stories they write. For example, the possibility of alternate methods of reproduction is being studied in biological research. "Nine Lives" in this anthology reflects this research in a story about cloning. Certain areas of the brain, recent research indicates, produce pleasure sensations when stimulated. "Love, Incorporated" uses this research as one of its starting points and asks: How might this knowledge be exploited in a consuming, pleasure-seeking society? Increasingly the sophistication of computers is leading to their widespread utilization in our society. "Going Down Smooth" is a story of psychotherapy where the computer has replaced the therapist.

Not only the new developments in science and technology but

also the social changes which may occur as a result are reflected in science fiction. For example, communications technology makes it possible for an individual to know almost immediately any event which occurs any place in the world. A substantial part of the events reported are disasters. What effect does it have on a person to constantly be deluged with news of all the wars, floods, murders, and earthquakes occurring daily on earth? "And Now The News" explores this question. Are people provoked to more hostility because they are constantly bombarded through the news media with reports of unfair treatment of minority groups with which they may identify? "All the Last Wars at Once" creates an alternate society where this is exactly what happens.

The reader of science fiction becomes sharply aware of the social change produced by technology. He notes not only actual social changes, but he can also explore change which might result from certain uses of new technological knowledge. By considering and evaluating alternatives before they occur, the possibility exists that social change can be directed toward more constructive patterns than it has sometimes achieved in the past. The awareness of alternatives increases the possibility of a wise choice, and so the link between the present and the future becomes the human imagination.

A fourth function of science fiction is to provide a point of discussion for some of the ethical implications of research in psychology. Increasingly we are recognizing that science cannot be totally detached and divorced from concern for the effects of the new knowledge it produces, and also the means by which this new knowledge is acquired. The American Psychological Association in 1973 developed a code of principles governing psychological research with human beings. As research increasingly moves into areas that have immediate relevance for personal and social problems, it is clear that some kind of guide is necessary to determine what sorts of research techniques are ethical. The use of deception, the invasion of privacy, the induction of mental or physical stress, the administration of drugs—all these are procedures which must be questioned. Stories like "Flowers for Algernon," where intelligence is manipulated, and "Such Stuff," where questionable methods are used in dream research, allow an opportunity for discussion of the ethical aspects of psychological research.

Finally, reading science fiction encourages an active, creative response of the mind as it encounters new ideas. Dennis Livingston, commenting on the values of science fiction in the learning process, calls it "the laboratory of the imagination."[3] In science fiction, nothing is given; anything is possible. The author of a story takes an idea and playfully shakes It, looks at it from new angles, makes novel associations, and delightfully records the results of his mind play in fictional form.

The reader of science fiction becomes conditioned by this creative process. He begins to have a similar response as he encounters new ideas. He experiences the exhilarating potential of the imagination in synthesizing new forms. The sense of wonder which infuses science fiction is infectious. The reader tastes, savors, delights. Hopefully, he discovers his own store of wonder and begins to play with ideas himself. He has moved from the passive to the creative stance.

This book is organized into seven important areas of introductory psychology. Chapter 1 presents developmental psychology, which may be the organism's most fundamental general process. Chapters 2 and 3 explore the areas of the organism which are most closely associated with physical processes, while Chapters 4 and 5 cover the areas and processes most closely associated with the environment. Chapter 6 explores the whole product to which the previous processes contribute. Finally, Chapter 7 considers maladaptive behaviors engaged in by the individual personality and the efforts involved in correcting them.

Chapter 1: Developmental Processes

Chapter 2: Psychobiology

Chapter 3: Sensation, Perception, and Awareness

---

3. Dennis Livingston, "Science Fiction Taught as Futurology," *Extrapolation* 14 (May 1973): 154.

Chapter 4: Learning and Cognition

Chapter 5: Social Processes

Chapter 6: Personality

Chapter 7: Abnormal Processes and Therapy

Each of these chapters contains four stories, selected on the basis of the richness of the concepts embodied as well as their literary excellence. The short story is particularly well suited to the overall pedagogical purpose of this book. Unlike a novel, which may involve complicated subplots and subthemes, a good short story aims to produce *one single effect* by revealing a theme or a basic idea. The idea is dramatized by placing a *character* in a situation where a conflict exists. As the *plot* reveals and resolves the conflict, the idea becomes clear. The action takes place in a *setting* or background which harmonizes with and enriches the action and the characters. The writer of merit brings his idea or theme to life by skillful use of character, plot, and setting. He *shows* us rather than merely tells us about it. The aim of the editors has been to select stories of this quality.

We know the stories that appear on the following pages are sometimes comical, often shocking. They are always imaginative, fascinating, and absorbing. We challenge the student to not only experience the pleasure of reading these stories, but also to think about the psychological concepts they include, relating them to our present knowledge. We hope the professor sees the possibilities the book contains for motivating the student to seek and discover for himself the answers to life's questions which psychology can provide. If science fiction can energize the learning process, then the hope of the editors of this book will have been realized.

1

DEVELOPMENTAL PROCESSES

The major emphasis for developmental psychologists is their focus on growth over time as the major process which affects all others. They begin with conception and birth, studying how the fetus forms and grows, and then observe infancy and beyond: childhood, adolescence, adulthood, and the aged. In their quest for understanding, they continually assess the relative roles of inherent or built-in growth (maturation) and the role of experience (learning). Some developmentalists would emphasize the relative influence of one aspect more than the other, but all would agree that healthy growth depends on an interaction of the two.

As might be expected, the developmental age receiving the lion's share of interest is infancy and early childhood, the foundation for later growth. It is in this period that physical growth is fastest, where the brain, nervous system, muscles, and skeletal system push the child to one-half of his adult height by the age of two-and-a-half. The first three years of life comprise the period in which Sigmund Freud insisted that the adult's personality was basically formed, and it is the period which Head Start workers found crucial in their attempt to teach deprived preschoolers. The Head Start experience and other evidence suggest that it is the crucial period for the development of many abilities, the period in which some developmental systems become maximally ready for growth stimulation—their first and only chance because later on maximal growth switches to other systems.

The role of maturation in early development is programmed by genetics. Preprogrammed behavior patterns or instincts are extremely important in understanding the behavior of animals that, for example, can build specific kinds of nests or webs without previous experience or learning. The role of instincts in human development is less clear. Much of the physical and motor development would appear to be genetically preprogrammed for the order in which development occurs. The baby learns to walk in a series of relatively unchangeable stages, and physical changes like dental development occur in a genetically predetermined sequence.

The role of early experience is viewed in terms of the kind and amount of stimulation which the child receives. From virtually the time of birth, sustained stimulation of all kinds appears to enhance development, while deprivation of stimulation retards development. As might be expected, the role of the mother is extremely important for stimulating intellectual development, as well as personality development. Classic studies by Harlow with monkeys suggest that in the infancy stage, the mother serves as a vital security blanket for her child, enabling the child to venture out into the world without crippling fear and anxiety. Studies of children who spent their infancy without the stimulation and warmth of a mother indicate that they are apt to develop crippling depression and apathy, which is often accompanied by retarded physical development, physical illness, and only superficial social adjustment in later life.

Freud emphasized both the role of instincts and the role of the mother during the first three years of life in his theory of psychosexual development. He suggested that activities like feeding and toilet training had both psychological and sexual connotations, and further suggested that by the time the child reached the age of four, he had to learn to repress his instinctive drive to sexually possess his mother (the Oedipus Complex) in order for personality development to progress normally. Freud postulated stages of development corresponding to the maturational development of various areas of the child's body as erogenous or sexually sensitive zones. In the first year the infant passed through the Oral Stage, emphasizing the mouth area; at age two he entered the Anal Stage, emphasizing the rectal area. The Phallic Stage was next, emphasizing the area of the sex organs. If in this stage the above mentioned Oedipus Complex was resolved, the child would develop through adolescence and eventually enter the Genital Stage, where he would engage in the sexual activity and the responsibilities of adulthood.

Erik Erikson has modified Freud's stages of development into a "life cycle" of eight stages of man, beginning at infancy and reaching into the retirement years. Erikson changed the emphasis of his scheme from the psychosexual, where areas of the body played a primary role, to the psychosocial, where the basic social problems that the individual had to come to terms with throughout life became primary. Most important were the problems of establishing a basic trust in the world and in one's self (which occurs in the first year of life) and of establishing a sense of one's own individual identity. Perhaps the most interesting problem is that of establishing a sense of integrity rather than of despair at old age. According to Erikson, the individual who feels that he has lived a meaningful life develops integrity, while the individual who feels that his life has been wasted develops despair.

Another important developmentalist using stages of development in the area of cognitive development has been Piaget. Piaget, creatively working with Swiss children to determine the ages at which they can understand different kinds of concepts, had discovered important conceptual ways in which children progress in understanding their environment. Through various stages the child moves from reliance on physical manipulation of objects in order to understand them to more sophisticated and abstract conceptualizations. The child learns, among other things, what Piaget calls "conservations," realizing, for example, that liquids do not change volume by being moved from a container of one shape to a container with a different shape. Using Piaget's ideas about conceptual development, Kohlberg has formulated stages of moral

13

development. According to Kohlberg's scheme, the child begins at Level I, the premoral level, in which he simply acts to avoid punishments and obtain rewards. At Level II, he accepts and conforms to conventional conceptions of morality, while at Level III, he uses moral principles and individual conscience.

The development of perception and language are two more areas which developmental psychologists have thoroughly investigated. In perceptual studies of infant abilities to see and discriminate different forms and color, again the mutual dependence of the innate and the learned have been demonstrated. For example, when early visual deprivation has resulted in damage to the retina, permanent perceptual deficiencies can develop. In language development, research has reaffirmed the important differences between the capacity for complex speech by humans and the inability of other species to go beyond simple sign language. In a still raging controversy, learning approaches have suggested that the child learns language through the piecemeal rewarding and punishing of his utterances by parents and others. Linguistic approaches, in vehement opposition to the reward and punishment view, insist that the intelligence of the human infant is preprogrammed to relate to the implicit logic of language in sentences, and that language cannot be learned piecemeal. Here again we are left with the basic question, rather than a clear answer: Is it "nurture" or "nature"?

that only a mother

Judith Merril

Human development has the attribute of being reasonably consistent from child to child. Most children can be expected to walk and talk in their first years unless disease, injury, malnutrition, or other basically environmental influences retard growth. Other changes may occur because of birth defects or from prenatal influences, which are also basically environmental influences. Genetic influences may cause mental retardation, but basically genetic transmission can be relied upon to produce children with "standard equipment," which leads to development with few surprises.

"That Only A Mother" is a story about genetic mutations which alter normal development. Such mutations have been relatively rare; now, however, they are more frequent, occurring often after exposure to radiation. Usually mutations have been viewed as negative; in this story drastic changes, both positive and negative, occur. This presents enormous physical problems for the child in adjusting to the world and equally enormous psychological problems for the parents.

Margaret Marvell faces the birth of her first child with apprehension, knowing that her husband has been exposed to radiation. As she feared, her baby has a genetic mutation. However, Margaret chooses to face only the positive aspects: the mutation has greatly accelerated the baby's intellectual development, so that at ten months she has the intelligence of a four-year-old. How do child and parent cope with this situation? The child, not expectant of particularly different development, adjusts rather well, apparently because of her superior intelligence and understanding of the social implications of her different development.

The mother has a more difficult time adjusting because of her social expectations and hopes for normal development. In addition, the difficult social situation in which she finds herself makes her afraid to tell her husband, as there have been a number of mutant killings by fathers. To cope with the situation, the mother's psychological defenses force her to deny to her conscious processes that her child has a physical detriment (the defense mechanism is called "denial," perhaps the most primitive defense mechanism), and she compensates for this by overemphasizing the positive intellectual achievements. She does this only with respect to her child, not to other aspects of her life. She has lost reality testing thus in just this one area, but later we see her laughing about the situation, suggesting that she may be developing manic symptoms of a more general manic-depressive psychosis. These patients manifest a more general use of denial and overcompensation of the positive. The manic state is seen as an overcompensation (here technically a reaction-formation) for an underlying deep depression. This mother is deeply depressed about her child and has repressed her real feelings.

THAT ONLY A MOTHER   *Judith Merril*

Margaret reached over to the other side of the bed where Hank should have been. Her hand patted the empty pillow, and then she came altogether awake, wondering that the old habit should remain after so many months. She tried to curl up, cat-style, to hoard her own warmth, found she couldn't do it any more, and climbed out of bed with a pleased awareness of her increasing clumsy bulkiness.

Morning motions were automatic. On the way through the kitchenette, she pressed the button that would start breakfast cooking—the doctor had said to eat as much breakfast as she could—and tore the paper out of the facsimile machine. She folded the long sheet carefully to the "National News" section, and propped it on the bathroom shelf to scan while she brushed her teeth.

No accidents. No direct hits. At least none that had been offically released for publication. *Now, Maggie, don't get started on that. No accidents. No hits. Take the nice newspaper's word for it.*

The three clear chimes from the kitchen announced that breakfast was ready. She set a bright napkin and cheerful colored dishes on the table in a futile attempt to appeal to a faulty morning appetite. Then, when there was nothing more to prepare, she went for the mail, allowing herself the full pleasure of prolonged anticipation, because today there would *surely* be a letter.

There was. There were. Two bills and a worried note from her mother: "Darling, why didn't you write and tell me sooner? I'm thrilled, of course, but, well, one hates to mention these things, but are you *certain* the doctor was right? Hank's been around all that uranium or thorium or whatever it is all these years, and I know you say he's a designer, not a technician, and he doesn't get near anything that might be dangerous, but you know he used to, back at Oak Ridge. Don't you think . . . well, of course, I'm just being a foolish old woman, and I don't want you to get upset. You know much more about it than I do, and I'm sure your doctor was right. He *should* know. . . ."

Margaret made a face over the excellent coffee, and caught herself refolding the paper to the medical news.

Stop it, Maggie, stop it! The radiologist said Hank's job couldn't have exposed him. And the bombed area we drove past. . . . No, no. Stop it, now! Read the social notes or the recipes, Maggie girl.

A well-known geneticist, in the medical news, said that it was possible to tell with absolute certainty, at five months, whether the child would be normal, or at least whether the mutation was likely to produce anything freakish. The worst cases, at any rate, could be prevented. Minor mutations, of course, displacements in facial features, or changes in brain structure could not be detected. And there had been some cases recently of normal embryos with atrophied limbs that did not develop beyond the seventh or eighth month. But, the doctor concluded cheerfully, the *worst* cases could now be predicted and prevented.

17

*"Predicted and prevented." We predicted it, didn't we? Hank
and the others, they predicted it. But we didn't prevent it. We could
have stopped it in '46 and '47. Now. . . .*

Margaret decided against the breakfast. Coffee had been
enough for her in the morning for ten years; it would have to do for
today. She buttoned herself into the interminable folds of material
that, the salesgirl had assured her, was the *only* comfortable thing to
wear during the last few months. With a surge of pure pleasure, the
letter and newspaper forgotten, she realized she was on the next to
the last button. It wouldn't be long now.

The city in the early morning had always been a special kind of
excitement for her. Last night it had rained, and the sidewalks were
still damp-gray instead of dusty. The air smelled the fresher, to a
city-bred woman, for the occasional pungency of acrid factory
smoke. She walked the six blocks to work, watching the lights go out
in the all-night hamburger joints, where the plate-glass walls were
already catching the sun, and the lights go on in the dim interior of
cigar stores and dry-cleaning establishments.

The office was in a new Government building. In the rolovator,
on the way up, she felt, as always, like a frankfurter roll in the
ascending half of an old-style rotary toasting machine. She abandoned the air-foam cushioning gratefully at the fourteenth floor, and
settled down behind her desk, at the rear of a long row of identical
desks.

Each morning the pile of papers that greeted her was a little
higher. These were, as everyone knew, the decisive months. The war
might be won or lost on these calculations as well as any others. The
manpower office had switched her here when her old expediter's job
got to be too strenuous. The computer was easy to operate, and the
work was absorbing, if not as exciting as the old job. But you didn't
just stop working these days. Everyone who could do anything at all
was needed.

And—she remembered the interview with the psychologist—
*I'm probably the unstable type. Wonder what sort of neurosis I'd get
sitting home reading that sensational paper. . . .*

She plunged into the work without pursuing the thought.

February 18.

Hank darling,

Just a note—from the hospital, no less. I had a dizzy spell at
work, and the doctor took it to heart. Blessed if I know what I'll do

with myself lying in bed for weeks, just waiting—but Dr. Boyer seems to think it may not be so long.

There are too many newspapers around here. More infanticides all the time, and they can't seem to get a jury to convict any of them. It's the fathers who do it. Lucky thing you're not around, in case—

Oh, darling, that wasn't a very *funny* joke, was it? Write as often as you can, will you? I have too much time to think. But there really isn't anything wrong, and nothing to worry about.

Write often, and remember I love you.

Maggie.

SPECIAL SERVICE TELEGRAM

February 21, 1953
22:04 LK37G

From: Tech. Lieut. H. Marvell
    X47-016 GCNY
    To: Mrs. H. Marvell
    Women's Hospital
    New York City

HAD DOCTOR'S GRAM STOP WILL ARRIVE FOUR OH TEN STOP SHORT LEAVE STOP YOU DID IT MAGGIE STOP LOVE

HANK

February 25.

Hank dear,

So you didn't see the baby either? You'd think a place this size would at least have visiplates on the incubators, so the fathers could get a look, even if the poor benighted mommas can't. They tell me I won't see her for another week, or maybe more—but, of course, mother always warned me if I didn't slow my pace, I'd probably even have my babies too fast. Why must she *always* be right?

Did you meet that battle-ax of a nurse they put on here? I imagine they save her for people who've already had theirs, and don't let her get too near the prospectives—but a woman like that simply shouldn't be allowed in a maternity ward. She's obsessed with mutations, can't seem to talk about anything else. Oh, well, *ours* is all right, even if it was in an unholy hurry.

I'm tired. They warned me not to sit up so soon, but I *had* to write you. All my love, darling,

Maggie.

February 29.

Darling,

I finally got to see her! It's all true, what they say about new babies and the face that only a mother could love—but it's all there, darling, eyes, ears, and noses—no, only one!—all in the right places. We're so *lucky*, Hank.

I'm afraid I've been a rambunctious patient. I kept telling that hatchet-faced female with the mutation mania that I wanted to *see* the baby. Finally the doctor came in to "explain" everything to me, and talked a lot of nonsense, most of which I'm sure no one could have understood, any more than I did. The only thing I got out of it was that she didn't actually *have* to stay in the incubator; they just thought it was "wiser."

I think I got a little hysterical at that point. Guess I was more worried than I was willing to admit, but I threw a small fit about it. The whole business wound up with one of those hushed medical conferences outside the door, and finally the Woman in White said: "Well, we might as well. Maybe it'll work out better that way."

I'd heard about the way doctors and nurses in these places develop a God complex, and believe me it is as true figuratively as it is literally that a mother hasn't got a leg to stand on around here.

I *am* awfully weak, still. I'll write again soon. Love,

Maggie.

March 8.

Dearest Hank,

Well, the nurse was wrong if she told you that. She's an idiot, anyhow. It's a girl. It's easier to tell with babies than with cats, and *I know*. How about Henrietta?

I'm home again, and busier than a betatron. They got *everything* mixed up at the hospital, and I had to teach myself how to bathe her and do just about everything else. She's getting prettier, too. When can you get a leave, a *real* leave?

Love,
Maggie.

May 26.

Hank dear,

You should see her now—and you shall. I'm sending along a reel of color movie. My mother sent her those nighties with drawstrings all over. I put one on, and right now she looks like a snow-white potato sack with that beautiful, beautiful flower-face blooming on top. Is that *me* talking? Am I a doting mother? But wait till you *see* her!

July 10.

. . . Believe it or not, as you like, but your daughter can talk, and I don't mean baby talk. Alice discovered it—she's a dental assistant in the WACs, you know—and when she heard the baby giving out what I thought was a string of gibberish, she said the kid knew words and sentences, but couldn't say them clearly because she has no teeth yet. I'm taking her to a speech specialist.

September 13.

. . . We have a prodigy for real! Now that all her front teeth are in, her speech is perfectly clear and—a new talent now—she can sing! I mean really carry a tune! At seven months! Darling, my world would be perfect if you could only get home.

November 19.

. . . at last. The little goon was so busy being clever, it took her all this time to learn to crawl. The doctor says development in these cases is always erratic. . . .

SPECIAL SERVICE TELEGRAM

December 1, 1953
08:47 LK59F

From: Tech. Lieut. H. Marvell
    X47-016 GCNY
      To: Mrs. H. Marvell
      Apt. K-17
      504 E. 19 St.
      N.Y. N.Y.
WEEK'S LEAVE STARTS TOMORROW STOP WILL
AIRPORT TEN OH FIVE STOP DON'T MEET ME STOP
LOVE LOVE LOVE

HANK

Margaret let the water run out of the bathinette until only a few inches were left, and then loosed her hold on the wriggling baby.

"I think it was better when you were retarded, young woman," she informed her daughter happily. "You *can't* crawl in a bathinette, you know."

"Then why can't I go in the bathtub?" Margaret was used to her child's volubility by now, but every now and then it caught her unawares. She swooped the resistant mass of pink flesh into a towel, and began to rub.

"Because you're too little, and your head is very soft, and bathtubs are very hard."

"Oh. Then when can I go in the bathtub?"

"When the outside of your head is as hard as the inside, brainchild." She reached toward a pile of fresh clothing. "I cannot understand," she added, pinning a square of cloth through the nightgown, "why a child of your intelligence can't learn to keep a diaper on the way other babies do. They've been used for centuries, you know, with perfectly satisfactory results."

The child disdained to reply; she had heard it too often. She waited patiently until she had been tucked, clean and sweet-smelling, into a white-painted crib. Then she favored her mother with a smile that inevitably made Margaret think of the first golden edge of the sun bursting into a rosy pre-dawn. She remembered Hank's reaction to the color pictures of his beautiful daughter, and with the thought, realized how late it was.

"Go to sleep, puss. When you wake up, you know, your *Daddy* will be here."

"Why?" asked the four-year-old mind, waging a losing battle to keep the ten-month-old body awake.

Margaret went into the kitchenette and set the timer for the roast. She examined the table, and got her clothes from the closet, new dress, new shoes, new slip, new everything, bought weeks before and saved for the day Hank's telegram came. She stopped to pull a paper from the facsimile, and, with clothes and news, went into the bathroom, and lowered herself gingerly into the steaming luxury of a scented tub.

She glanced through the paper with indifferent interest. Today at least there was no need to read the national news. There was an article by a geneticist. The same geneticist. Mutations, he said, were increasing disproportionately. It was too soon for recessives; even the first mutants, born near Hiroshima and Nagasaki in 1946 and 1947, were not old enough yet to breed. *But my baby's all right*

Apparently, there was some degree of free radiation from atomic explosions causing the trouble. *My Baby's fine. Precocious, but normal.* If more attention had been paid to the first Japanese mutations, he said. . . .

There was that little notice in the paper in the spring of '47. That was when Hank quit at Oak Ridge. "Only two or three per cent of those guilty of infanticide are being caught and punished in Japan today. . . ." *But* MY BABY'S *all right.*

She was dressed, combed, and ready to the last light brush-on of lip paste, when the door chime sounded. She dashed for the door, and heard, for the first time in eighteen months, the almost-forgotten sound of a key turning in the lock before the chime had quite died away.

"Hank!"

"Maggie!"

And then there was nothing to say. So many days, so many months, of small news piling up, so many things to tell him, and now she just stood there, staring at a khaki uniform and a stranger's pale face. She traced the features with the finger of memory. The same highbridged nose, wide-set eyes, fine feathery brows; the same long jaw, the hair a little farther back now on the high forehead, the same tilted curve of his mouth. Pale . . . Of course, he'd been underground all this time. And strange, stranger because of lost familiarity than any newcomer's face could be.

She had time to think all that before his hand reached out to touch her, and spanned the gap of eighteen months. Now, again, there was nothing to say, because there was no need. They were together, and for the moment that was enough.

"Where's the baby?"

"Sleeping. She'll be up any minute."

No urgency. Their voices were as casual as though it were a daily exchange, as though war and separation did not exist. Margaret picked up the coat he'd thrown on the chair near the door, and hung it carefully in the hall closet. She went to check the roast, leaving him to wander through the rooms by himself, remembering and coming back. She found him, finally, standing over the baby's crib.

She couldn't see his face, but she had no need to.

"I think we can wake her just this once." Margaret pulled the covers down, and lifted the white bundle from the bed. Sleepy lids pulled back heavily from smoky brown eyes.

"Hello." Hank's voice was tentative.

"Hello." The baby's assurance was more pronounced.

He had heard about it, of course, but that wasn't the same as hearing it. He turned eagerly to Margaret. "She really can—?"

"Of course she can, darling. But what's more important, she can even do nice normal things like other babies do, even stupid ones. Watch her crawl!" Margaret set the baby on the big bed.

For a moment young Henrietta lay and eyed her parents dubiously.

"Crawl?" she asked.

"That's the idea. Your Daddy is new around here, you know. He wants to see you show off."

"Then put me on my tummy."

"Oh, of course." Margaret obligingly rolled the baby over.

"What's the matter?" Hank's voice was still casual, but an undercurrent in it began to charge the air of the room. "I thought they turned over first."

"This baby," Margaret would not notice the tension, "*This* baby does things when she wants to."

This baby's father watched with softening eyes while the head advanced and the body hunched up, propelling itself across the bed.

"Why the little rascal," he burst into relieved laughter. "She looks like one of those potato-sack racers they used to have on picnics. Got her arms pulled out of the sleeves already." He reached over and grabbed the knot at the bottom of the long nightie.

"I'll do it, darling." Margaret tried to get there first.

"Don't be silly, Maggie. This may be *your* first baby, but *I* had five kid brothers." He laughed her away, and reached with his other hand for the string that closed one sleeve. He opened the sleeve bow, and groped for an arm.

"The way you wriggle," he addressed his child sternly, as his hand touched a moving knob of flesh at the shoulder, "anyone might think you were a worm, using your tummy to crawl on, instead of your hands and feet."

Margaret stood and watched, smiling. "Wait till you hear her sing, darling—"

His right hand traveled down from the shoulder to where he thought an arm would be, traveled down, and straight down, over firm small muscles that writhed in an attempt to move against the pressure of his hand. He let his fingers drift up again to the shoulder. With infinite care, he opened the knot at the bottom of the

24

nightgown. His wife was standing by the bed, saying: "She can do 'Jingle Bells,' and—"

His left hand felt along the soft knitted fabric of the gown, up towards the diaper that folded, flat and smooth, across the bottom end of his child. No wrinkles. No kicking. *No. . . .*

"Maggie." He tried to pull his hands from the neat fold in the diaper, from the wriggling body. "Maggie." His throat was dry; words came hard, low, and grating. He spoke very slowly, thinking the sound of each word to make himself say it. His head was spinning, but he had to *know* before he let it go. "Maggie, why . . . didn't you . . . tell me?"

"Tell you what, darling?" Margaret's poise was the immemorial patience of woman confronted with man's childish impetuosity. Her sudden laugh sounded fantastically easy and natural in that room; it was all clear to her now. "Is she wet? I didn't know."

She didn't know. His hands, beyond control, ran up and down the soft-skinned baby body, the sinuous, limbless body. *Oh God, dear God*—his head shook and his muscles contracted, in a bitter spasm of hysteria. His fingers tightened on his child—*Oh God, she didn't know. . . .*

the first men

Howard Fast

The genesis of "The First Men" grows out of a question: What if the potential for a new and better race—man-plus—is present in children but never fulfills itself because they are trapped in and totally conditioned by their environment?

In this fictional world, anthropologist Jean Arbalaid theorizes that, given super-children who were raised in an ideal environment, man-plus could be produced. She designs and gets funding for an elaborate and long experiment which will allow a testing of her theory. To start the experiment—which must be kept secret— she asks her brother to aid her in collecting infants of superior intelligence from around the world. He finds the children for her, and the experiment begins.

Twenty years later she writes to tell him she has experienced "the strangest two decades that men ever lived through." She reports that the unexpected was what she and her co-researchers hoped and watched for—and it happened! Then all communication from her ceases. Her brother is left with the tantalizing question: What were the children like when they grew up? What unexpected things happened? In the climax of "The First Men" he finds the answer to his questions.

Some psychological background material will help orient us to the various aspects of the story. First, the general psychological position taken in the story is a combination of the humanistic and behavioristic schools. It is humanistic in its strong suggestion that mankind has not yet fulfilled itself but must continue to develop its full human potential. The emphasis on love, warmth, and acceptance as catalytic agents in bringing out this humaneness is very similar to the therapeutic position of Carl Rogers, emphasizing that with this atmosphere, the human spirit develops on its own, controlling its own destiny. The strong emphasis in the story on the importance of the environment and environmental control is basically behavioristic, almost reminiscent of B. F. Skinner's *Walden Two*. These two positions—behavioristic and humanistic—held by Rogers and Skinner mix like oil and water; but in the story they seem to merge quite nicely—a triumph for science fiction over the rigidified schools too prevalent in psychology.

In the story, author Howard Fast posits an ideal environment for raising children which is much more socialistic or communistic than traditional American. There is a group family rather than the nuclear family; there is no religion; and there is a version of free love rather than the traditional middle-class mores for sexual behavior. Is there any evidence in the real world to suggest that these methods are successful? If the Israeli kibbutz life is a good test, then the evidence suggests that the methods work well in some ways, but not so well in others. Children raised in the kibbutz are hard working, highly efficient, very assertive, and highly achieving, and they see their colleagues as brothers and sisters, rather than as sexual objects. However, some less desirable traits are reported to develop, such as a lack of creativity. Communes in the United States have had difficulties staying together for more than short periods of time. A recent one in Virginia, consciously based on Skinnerian principles, reports a great deal of difficulty and only moderate success.

The story takes a very strong environmental position in the longstanding heredity versus environment and nature versus nurture controversy. It uses as its "scientific" backing the cases of the wolfchildren reported in the literature in the forties. Few cases were actually reported and even fewer well documented; today they are held in relatively low esteem in the field. They seem somewhat overused and glorified in the story.

Reference is made in "The First Men" to the difficulties experienced by children with IQs over 150, and this material is essentially true. A relatively high percentage of these children do grow up with emotional problems, and a lower percentage do achieve greater success than would be expected. The causes of their difficulties are indeed mostly environmental in that they are thrust into the mediocre, conventional, conforming society which holds to the principle that the silent majority, which is more pragmatic than conceptual, is usually right. Also, since their IQ (which is basically a statistical relative concept rather than an absolute one) is in the highest fraction of one percent of the population, they find it difficult to communicate with all but a few people.

A comment should be made about the methods used in the story for measuring infant intelligence. The techniques described are based on correlational techniques; they are essentially atheoretical. Although they sound sensible, they are not used today. In general, the measurement of infant intelligence by special tests has not been proven to be particularly valid or reliable. These tests must take measurements before language develops, and since so much of man's intelligence is symbolically based on language, early intelligence measurement becomes hit or miss because the tests are based on nonverbal indicators.

Some other interesting points are made in the story. In discussing telepathic ability, Fast states that it must be released in childhood or it is permanently blocked. This is the "critical period" concept discussed in the introductory chapter notes. In general, the story suggests that whole areas of every human being's mind are blocked in childhood. This is probably true, but asserting it as an absolute may be an overstatement, one which assumes repression—a psychoanalytic (Freudian) position rather than one absolutely agreed on. In addition, stating, as the story does, that a human being is the sum of all his memories is also basically true, but is held more by psychoanalytic theorists, who are past oriented, than by humanists or existentialists, who are future or present oriented.

THE FIRST MEN   *Howard Fast*

By Airmail:

Calcutta, India
Nov. 4th, 1945

Mrs. Jean Arbalaid
Washington, D.C.

My dear sister:

I found it. I saw it with my own eyes, and thereby I am convinced that I have a useful purpose in life—overseas investigator for the anthropological whims of my sister. That, in any case, is better than boredom. I have no desire to return home; I will not go into any further explanations or reasons. I am neurotic, unsettled and adrift. I got my discharge in Karachi, as you know. I am very happy to be an ex-GI and a tourist, but it took me only a few weeks to become bored to distraction. So I was quite pleased to have a mission from you. The mission is completed.

It could have been more exciting. The plain fact of the matter is that the small Associated Press item you sent me was quite accurate in all of its details. The little village of Chunga is in Assam. I got there by plane, narrow gauge train and oxcart—a fairly pleasant trip at this time of the year, with the back of the heat broken; and there I saw the child, who is now fourteen years old.

I am sure you know enough about India to realize that fourteen is very much an adult age for a girl in these parts—the majority of them are married by then. And there is no question about the age. I spoke at length to the mother and father, who identified the child by two very distinctive birthmarks. The identification was substantiated by relatives and other villagers—all of whom remembered the birthmarks. A circumstance not unusual or remarkable in these small villages.

The child was lost as an infant—at eight months, a common story, the parents working in the field, the child set down, and then the child gone. Whether it crawled at that age or not, I can't say; at any rate, it was a healthy, alert and curious infant. They all agree on that point.

How the child came to the wolves is something we will never know. Possibly a bitch who had lost her own cubs carried the infant off. That is the most likely story, isn't it? This is not *lupus*, the European variety, but *pallipes*, its local cousin, nevertheless a respectable animal in size and disposition, and not something to stumble over on a dark night. Eighteen days ago, when the child was found, the villagers had to kill five wolves to take her, and she herself fought like a devil out of hell. She had lived as a wolf for thirteen years.

Will the story of her life among the wolves ever emerge? I don't know. To all effects and purposes, she is a wolf. She cannot stand upright—the curvature of her spine being beyond correction. She runs on all fours and her knuckles are covered with heavy callus. They are trying to teach her to use her hands for grasping and holding, but so far unsuccessfully. Any clothes they dress her in, she tears off, and as yet she has not been able to grasp the meaning of speech, much less talk. The Indian anthropologist, Sumil Gojee, has been working with her for a week now, and he has little hope that any real communication will ever be possible. In our terms and by our measurements, she is a total idiot, an infantile imbecile, and it is likely that she will remain so for the rest of her life.

On the other hand, both Professor Gojee and Dr. Chalmers, a government health service man, who came up from Calcutta to examine the child, agree that there are no physical or hereditary elements to account for the child's mental condition, no malformation of the cranial area and no history of imbecilism in her background. Everyone in the village attests to the normalcy— indeed, alertness and brightness—of the infant; and Professor Gojee makes a point of the alertness and adaptability she must have required to survive for thirteen years among the wolves. The child responds excellently to reflex tests, and neurologically, she appears to be sound. She is strong—beyond the strength of a thirteen-year- old—wiry, quick in her movements, and possesses an uncanny sense of smell and hearing.

Professor Gojee has examined records of eighteen similar cases recorded in India over the past hundred years, and in every case, he says, the recovered child was an idiot in our terms—or a wolf in objective terms. He points out that it would be incorrect to call this child an idiot or an imbecile—any more than we would call a wolf an idiot or an imbecile. The child is a wolf, perhaps a very superior wolf, but a wolf nevertheless.

I am preparing a much fuller report on the whole business. Meanwhile, this letter contains the pertinent facts. As for money—I am very well heeled indeed, with eleven hundred dollars I won in a crap game. Take care of yourself and your brilliant husband and the public health service.

Love and Kisses,
Harry

By cable:
HARRY FELTON
HOTEL EMPIRE
CALCUTTA, INDIA.
NOVEMBER 10, 1945
THIS IS NO WHIM, HARRY, BUT VERY SERIOUS INDEED. YOU DID NOBLY. SIMILAR CASE IN PRETORIA. GENERAL HOSPITAL, DR. FELIX VANOTT. WE HAVE MADE ALL ARRANGEMENTS WITH AIR TRANSPORT.

JEAN ARBALAID

By Airmail:

Pretoria, Union of South Africa
November 15, 1945

Mrs. Jean Arbalaid
Washington, D.C.

My dear sister:

You are evidently a very big wheel, you and your husband, and I wish I knew what your current silly season adds up to. I suppose in due time you'll see fit to tell me. But in any case, your priorities command respect. A full colonel was bumped, and I was promptly whisked to South Africa, a beautiful country of pleasant climate and, I am sure, great promise.

I saw the child, who is still being kept in the General Hospital here, and I spent an evening with Dr. Vanott and a young and reasonably attractive Quaker lady, Miss Gloria Oland, an anthropologist working among the Bantu people for her Doctorate. So, you see, I will be able to provide a certain amount of background material—more as I develop my acquaintance with Miss Oland.

Superficially, this case is remarkably like the incident in Assam. There it was a girl of fourteen; here we have a Bantu boy of eleven. The girl was reared by the wolves; the boy, in this case, was reared by the baboons—and rescued from them by a White Hunter, name

31

of Archway, strong, silent type, right out of Hemingway. Unfortunately, Archway has a nasty temper and doesn't like children, so when the boy understandably bit him, he whipped the child to within an inch of its life. "Tamed him," as he puts it.

At the hospital, however, the child has been receiving the best of care and reasonable if scientific affection. There is no way of tracing him back to his parents, for these Basutoland baboons are great travelers and there is no telling where they picked him up. His age is a medical guess, but reasonable. That he is of Bantu origin, there is no doubt. He is handsome, long-limbed, exceedingly strong, and with no indication of any cranial injury. But like the girl in Assam, he is—in our terms—an idiot and an imbecile.

That is to say, he is a baboon. His vocalization is that of a baboon. He differs from the girl in that he is able to use his hands to hold things and to examine things, and he has a more active curiosity; but that, I am assured by Miss Oland, is the difference between a wolf and a baboon.

He too has a permanent curvature of the spine; he goes on all fours as the baboons do, and the back of his.fingers and hands are heavily callused. After tearing off his clothes the first time, he accepted them, but that too is a baboon trait. In this case, Miss Oland has hope for his learning at least rudimentary speech, but Dr. Vanott doubts that he ever will. Incidentally, I must take note that in those eighteen cases Professor Gojee referred to, there was no evidence of human speech being learned beyond its most basic elements.

So goes my childhood hero, Tarzan of the Apes, and all the noble beasts along with him. But the most terrifying thought is this—what is the substance of man himself, if this can happen to him? The learned folk here have been trying to explain to me that man is a creature of his thought and that his thought is to a very large extent shaped by his environment; and that this thought process—or mentation as they call it—is based on words. Without words, thought becomes a process of pictures, which is on the animal level and rules out all, even the most primitive, abstract concepts. In other words, man cannot become man by himself: he is the result of other men and of the totality of human society and experience.

The man raised by the wolves is a wolf, by the baboons a baboon—and this is implacable, isn't it? My head has been swimming with all sorts of notions, some of them not at all pleasant. My dear sister, what are you and your husband up to? Isn't it time you broke down and told old Harry? Or do you want me to pop off to Tibet? Anything to please you, but preferably something that adds up.

Your ever-loving Harry

By Airmail:

Washington, D.C.
November 27, 1945

Mr. Harry Felton
Pretoria, Union of South Africa

Dear Harry:

You are a noble and sweet brother, and quite sharp too. You are also a dear. Mark and I want you to do a job for us, which will enable you to run here and there across the face of the earth, and be paid for it too. In order to convince you, we must spill out the dark secrets of our work—which we have decided to do, considering you an upright and trustworthy character. But the mail, it would seem, is less trustworthy; and since we are working with the Army, which has a constitutional dedication to *top-secret* and similar nonsense, the information goes to you via diplomatic pouch. As of receiving this, consider yourself employed; your expenses will be paid, within reason, and an additional eight thousand a year for less work than indulgence.

So please stay put at your hotel in Pretoria until the pouch arrives. Not more than ten days. Of course, you will be notified.

Love, affection and respect,
Jean

By diplomatic pouch:

Washington, D.C.
December 5, 1945

Mr. Harry Felton
Pretoria, Union of South Africa

Dear Harry:

Consider this letter the joint effort of Mark and myself. The conclusions are also shared. Also, consider it a very serious document indeed.

You know that for the past twenty years, we have both been deeply concerned with child psychology and child development. There is no need to review our careers or our experience in the Public Health Service. Our work during the war, as part of the Child Reclamation Program, led to an interesting theory, which we decided to pursue. We were given leave by the head of the service to make this our own project, and recently we were granted a substantial amount of army funds to work with.

Now down to the theory, which is not entirely untested, as you know. Briefly—but with two decades of practical work as a background—it is this: Mark and I have come to the conclusion that within the rank and file of Homo Sapiens is the leavening of a new race. Call them man-plus—call them what you will. They are not of recent arrival; they have been cropping up for hundreds, perhaps thousands of years. But they are trapped in and molded by human environment as certainly and implacably as your Assamese girl was trapped among the wolves or your Bantu boy among the baboons.

By the way, your two cases are not the only attested ones we have. By sworn witness, we have records of seven similar cases, one in Russia, two in Canada, two in South America, one in West Africa, and, just to cut us down to size, one in the United States. We also have hearsay and folklore of three hundred and eleven parallel cases over a period of fourteen centuries. We have in fourteenth century Germany, in the folio MS of the monk, Hubercus, five case histories which he claims to have observed. In all of these cases, in the seven cases witnessed by people alive today, and in all but sixteen of the hearsay cases, the result is more or less precisely what you have seen and described yourself: the child reared by the wolf is a wolf.

Our own work adds up to the parallel conclusion: the child reared by a man is a man. If man-plus exists, he is trapped and caged as certainly as any human child reared by animals. Our proposition is that he exists.

Why do we think this super-child exists? Well, there are many reasons, and neither the time nor the space to go into all in detail. But here are two very telling reasons. Firstly, we have case histories of several hundred men and women, who as children had IQs of 150 or above. In spite of their enormous intellectual promise as children, less than 10 per cent have succeeded in their chosen careers. Roughly another 10 per cent have been institutionalized as mental cases beyond recovery. About 14 per cent have had or require therapy in terms of mental health problems. Six per cent have been suicides, 1 per cent in prison, 27 per cent have had one or more divorces, 19 per cent are chronic failures at whatever they attempt—and the rest are undistinguished in any important manner. All of the IQs have dwindled—almost in the sense of a smooth graph line in relation to age.

Since society has never provided the full potential for such a mentality, we are uncertain as to what it might be. But we can guess that against it, they have been reduced to a sort of idiocy—an idiocy that we call normalcy.

The second reason we put forward is this: we know that man uses only a tiny fraction of his brain. What blocks him from the rest of it? Why has nature given him equipment that he cannot put to use? Or has society prevented him from breaking the barriers around his own potential?

There, in brief, are two reasons. Believe me, Harry, there are many more—enough for us to have convinced some very hard-headed and unimaginative government people that we deserve a chance to release *superman*. Of course, history helps—in its own mean manner. It would appear that we are beginning another war—with Russia this time, a cold war, as some have already taken to calling it. And among other things, it will be a war of intelligence—a commodity in rather short supply, as some of our local mental giants have been frank enough to admit. They look upon our man-plus as a secret weapon, little devils who will come up with death rays and superatom bombs when the time is ripe. Well, let them. It is inconceivable to imagine a project like this under benign sponsorship. The important thing is that Mark and I have been placed in full charge of the venture—millions of dollars, top priority—the whole works. But nevertheless, *secret to the ultimate.* I cannot stress this enough.

Now, as to your own job—if you want it. It develops step by step. First step: in Berlin, in 1937, there was a Professor Hans Goldbaum. Half Jewish. The head of the Institute of Child Therapy. He published a small monograph on intelligence testing in children, and he put forward claims—which we are inclined to believe—that he could determine a child's IQ during its first year of life, in its pre-speech period. He presented some impressive tables of estimations and subsequent checked results, but we do not know enough of his method to practice it ourselves. In other words, we need the professor's help.

In 1937, he vanished from Berlin. In 1943, he was reported to be living in Cape Town—the last address we have for him. I enclose the address. Go to Cape Town, Harry darling. (Myself talking, not Mark.) If he has left, follow him and find him. If he is dead, inform us immediately.

Of course you will take the job. We love you and we need your help.

Jean

By Airmail:

Cape Town, South Africa
December 20, 1945

Mrs. Jean Arbalaid
Washington, D.C.

My dear sister:

Of all the hairbrained ideas! If this is our secret weapon, I am prepared to throw in the sponge right now. But a job is a job.

It took me a week to follow the Professor's meandering through Cape Town—only to find out that he took off for London in 1944. Evidently, they needed him there. I am off to London.

Love,
Harry

By diplomatic pouch:

Washington, D.C.
December 26, 1945

Mr. Harry Felton
London, England

Dear Harry:

This is dead serious. By now, you must have found the professor. We believe that despite protestations of your own idiocy, you have enough sense to gauge his method. Sell him this venture. Sell him! We will give him whatever he asks—and we want him to work with us as long as he will.

Briefly, here is what we are up to. We have been allocated a tract of eight thousand acres in northern California. We intend to establish an environment there—under military guard and security. In the beginning, the outside world will be entirely excluded. The environment will be controlled and exclusive.

Within this environment, we intend to bring forty children to maturity—to a maturity that will result in man-plus.

As to the details of this environment—well that can wait. The immediate problem is the children. Out of forty, ten will be found in the United States; the other thirty will be found by the professor and yourself—outside of the United States.

Half are to be boys; we want an even boy-girl balance. They are to be between the ages of six months and nine months, and all are to show indications of an exceedingly high IQ—that is, if the professor's method is any good at all.

We want five racial groupings: Caucasian, Indian, Chinese, Malayan and Bantu. Of course, we are sensible of the vagueness of these groupings, and you have some latitude within them. The six so-called *Caucasian* infants are to be found in European types, and two Mediterranean types. A similar breakdown might be followed in other areas.

Now understand this—no cops and robbers stuff, no OSS, no kidnapping. Unfortunately, the world abounds in war orphans—and in parents poor and desperate enough to sell their children. When you want a child and such a situation arises, buy! Price is no object. I will have no maudlin sentimentality or scruples. These children will be loved and cherished—and if you should acquire any by purchase, you will be giving a child life and hope.

When you find a child, inform us immediately. Air transport will be at your disposal—and we are making all arrangements for wet nurses and other details of child care. We shall also have medical aid at your immediate disposal. On the other hand, we want healthy children—within the general conditions of health within any given area.

Now good luck to you. We are depending on you and we love you. And a merry Christmas.

Jean

By diplomatic pouch:

Copenhagen, Denmark
February 4, 1946

Mrs. Jean Arbalaid
Washington, D.C.

Dear Jean:

I seem to have caught your silly *top-secret* and *classified* disease, and I have been waiting for a free day and a diplomatic pouch to sum up my various adventures. From my "guarded" cables, you know that the professor and I have been doing a Cook's Tour of the baby market. My dear sister, this kind of shopping spree does not sit at all well with me. However, I gave my word, and there you are. I will complete and deliver.

By the way, I suppose I continue to send these along to Washington, even though your "environment," as you call it, has been established. I'll do so until otherwise instructed.

There was no great difficulty in finding the professor. Being in uniform—I have since acquired an excellent British wardrobe—and having all the fancy credentials you were kind enough to supply, I went to the War Office. As they say, every courtesy was shown to Major Harry Felton, but I feel better in civilian clothes. Anyway, the professor had been working with a child reclamation project, living among the ruins of the East End, which is pretty badly shattered. He is an astonishing little man, and I have become quite fond of him. On his part, he is learning to tolerate me.

I took him to dinner—you were the lever that moved him, my dear sister. I had no idea how famous you are in certain circles. He looked at me in awe, simply because we share a mother and father.

Then I said my piece, all of it, no holds barred. I had expected your reputation to crumble into dust there on the spot, but no such thing. Goldbaum listened with his mouth and his ears and every fiber of his being. The only time he interrupted me was to question me on the Assamese girl and the Bantu boy; and very pointed and meticulous questions they were. When I had finished, he simply shook his head—not in disagreement but with sheer excitement and delight. I then asked him what his reaction to all this was.

"I need time," he said. "This is something to digest. But the concept is wonderful—daring and wonderful. Not that the reasoning behind it is so novel. I have thought of this—so many anthropologists have. But to put it into practice, young man—ah, your sister is a wonderful and remarkable woman!"

There you are, my sister. I struck while the iron was hot, and told him then and there that you wanted and needed his help, first to find the children and then to work in the environment.

"The environment," he said; "you understand that is everything, everything. But how can she change the environment? The environment is total, the whole fabric of human society, self-deluded and superstitious and sick and irrational and clinging to legends and fantasies and ghosts. Who can change that?"

So it went. My anthropology is passable at best, but I have read all your books. If my answers were weak in that department, he did manage to draw out of me a more or less complete picture of Mark and yourself. He then said he would think about the whole matter. We made an appointment for the following day, when he would explain his method of intelligence determination in infants.

We met the next day, and he explained his methods. He made a great point of the fact that he did not test but rather determined, within a wide margin for error. Years before, in Germany, he had worked out a list of fifty characteristics which he noted in infants. As these infants matured, they were tested regularly by normal methods—and the results were checked against his original observations. Thereby, he began to draw certain conclusions, which he tested again and again over the next fifteen years. I am enclosing an unpublished article of his which goes into greater detail. Sufficient to say that he convinced me of the validity of his methods. Subsequently, I watched him examine a hundred and four British infants—to come up with our first choice. Jean, this is a remarkable and brilliant man.

On the third day after I had met him, he agreed to join the project. But he said this to me, very gravely, and afterwards I put it down exactly as he said it:

You must tell your sister that I have not come to this decision lightly. We are tampering with human souls—and perhaps even with human destiny. This experiment may fail, but if it succeeds it can be the most important event of our time—even more important and consequential than this war we have just fought. And you must tell her something else. I had a wife and three children, and they were put to death because a nation of men turned into beasts. I watched that, and I could not have lived through it unless I believed, always, that what can turn into a beast can also turn into a man. We are neither. But if we go to

39

create man, we must be humble. We are the tool, not the craftsman, and if we succeed, we will be less than the result of our work.

There is your man, Jean, and as I said, a good deal of a man. Those words are verbatim. He also dwells a great deal on the question of environment, and the wisdom and judgment and love necessary to create this environment. I think it would be helpful if you could send me a few words at least concerning this environment you are establishing.

We have now sent you four infants. Tomorrow, we leave for Rome—and from Rome to Casablanca.

But we will be in Rome at least two weeks, and a communication should reach me there.

More seriously—
And not untroubled,
Harry

By diplomatic pouch:

Via Washington, D.C.
February 11, 1946

Mr. Harry Felton
Rome, Italy

Dear Harry:

Just a few facts here. We are tremendously impressed by your reactions to Professor Goldbaum, and we look forward eagerly to his joining us. Meanwhile, Mark and I have been working night and day on the environment. In the most general terms, this is what we plan.

The entire reservation—all eight thousand acres—will be surrounded by a wire fence and will be under army guard. Within it, we shall establish a home. There will be between thirty and forty teachers—or group parents. We are accepting only married couples who love children and who will dedicate themselves to this venture. That they must have additional qualifications goes without saying.

Within the proposition that somewhere in man's civilized development something went wrong, we are returning to the prehistory form of group marriage. That is not to say that we will cohabit indiscriminately—but the children will be given to understand that parentage is a whole, that we are all their mothers and fathers, not by blood but by love.

We shall teach them the truth, and where we do not know the truth, we shall not teach. There will be no myths, no legends, no lies, no superstitions, no premises and no religions. We shall teach love and cooperation and we shall give love and security in full measure. We shall also teach them the knowledge of mankind.

During the first nine years, we shall command the environment entirely. We shall write the books they read, and shape the history and circumstances they require. Only then will we begin to relate the children to the world as it is.

Does it sound too simple or too presumptuous? It is all we can do, Harry, and I think Professor Goldbaum will understand that full well. It is also more than has ever been done for children before.

So good luck to both of you. Your letters sound as if you are changing, Harry—and we feel a curious process of change within us. When I put down what we are doing, it seems almost too obvious to be meaningful. We are simply taking a group of very gifted children and giving them knowledge and love. Is this enough to break through to that part of man which is unused and unknown? Well, we shall see. Bring us the children, Harry, and we shall see.

With love,
Jean

In the early spring of 1965, Harry Felton arrived in Washington and went directly to the White House. Felton had just turned fifty; he was a tall and pleasant-looking man, rather lean, with graying hair. As President of the Board of Shipways, Inc.—one of the largest import and export houses in America—he commanded a certain amount of deference and respect from Eggerton, who was then Secretary of Defense. In any case, Eggerton, who was nobody's fool, did not make the mistake of trying to intimidate Felton.

Instead, he greeted him pleasantly; and the two of them, with no others present, sat down in a small room in the White House, drank each other's good health, and talked about things.

Eggerton proposed that Felton might know why he had been asked to Washington.

"I can't say that I do know," Felton said.

"You have a remarkable sister."

"I have been aware of that for a long time," Felton smiled.

"You are also very close-mouthed, Mr. Felton," the secretary observed. "So far as we know, not even your immediate family has ever heard of man-plus. That's a commendable trait."

"Possibly and possibly not. It's been a long time."

"Has it? Then you haven't heard from your sister lately?"

"Almost a year," Felton answered.

"It didn't alarm you?"

"Should it? No, it didn't alarm me. My sister and I are very close, but this project of hers is not the sort of thing that allows for social relations. There have been long periods before when I have not heard from her. We are poor letter writers."

"I see," nodded Eggerton.

"I am to conclude that she is the reason for my visit here?"

"Yes."

"She's well?"

"As far as we know," Eggerton said quietly.

"Then what can I do for you?"

"Help us, if you will," Eggerton said, just as quietly. "I am going to tell what has happened, Mr. Felton, and then perhaps you can help us."

"Perhaps," Felton agreed.

"About the project, you know as much as any of us; more, perhaps, since you were in at the inception. So you realize that such a project must be taken very seriously or laughed off entirely. To date, it has cost the government eleven million dollars, and that is not something you laugh off. Now you understand that the unique part of this project was its exclusiveness. That word is used advisedly and specifically. Its success depended upon the creation of a unique and exclusive environment, and in terms of that environment, we agreed not to send any observers into the reservation for a period of fifteen years. Of course, during those fifteen years, there have been many conferences with Mr. and Mrs. Arbalaid and with certain of their associates, including Dr. Goldbaum.

"But out of these conferences, there was no progress report that dealt with anything more than general progress. We were given to understand that the results were rewarding and exciting, but very little more. We honored our part of the agreement, and at the end of the fifteen-year period, we told your sister and her husband that we would have to send in a team of observers. They pleaded for an extension of time—maintaining that it was critical to the success of the entire program—and they pleaded persuasively enough to win a three-year extension. Some months ago, the three-year period was over. Mrs. Arbalaid came to Washington and begged a further extension. When we refused, she agreed that our team could come into the reservation in ten days. Then she returned to California."

Eggerton paused and looked at Felton searchingly.

"And what did you find?" Felton asked.

"You don't know?"

"I'm afraid not."

"Well—" the Secretary said slowly, "I feel like a damn fool when I think of this, and also a little afraid. When I say it, the fool end predominates. We went there and we found nothing."

"Oh?"

"You don't appear too surprised, Mr. Felton?"

"Nothing my sister does has ever surprised me. You mean the reservation was empty—no sign of anything?"

"I don't mean that, Mr. Felton, I wish I did mean that. I wish it was so pleasantly human and down to earth. I wish we thought that your sister and her husband were two clever and unscrupulous swindlers who had taken the government for eleven million. That would warm the cockles of our hearts compared to what we do have. You see, we don't know whether the reservation is empty or not, Mr. Felton, because the reservation is not there."

"What?"

"Precisely. The reservation is not there."

"Come now," Felton smiled. "My sister is a remarkable woman, but she doesn't make off with eight thousand acres of land. It isn't like her."

"I don't find your humor entertaining, Mr. Felton."

"No. No, of course not. I'm sorry. Only when a thing makes no sense at all—how could an eight-thousand-acre stretch of land not be where it was? Doesn't it leave a large hole?"

"If the newspapers get hold of it, they could do even better than that, Mr. Felton."

"Why not explain," Felton said.

"Let me try to—not to explain but to describe. This stretch of land is in the Fulton National Forest, rolling country, some hills, a good stand of redwood—a kidney-shaped area. It was wire-fenced, with army guards at every approach. I went there with our inspection team, General Meyers, two army physicians, Gorman, the psychiatrist, Senator Totenwell of the Armed Services Committee, and Lydia Gentry, the educator. We crossed the country by plane and drove the final sixty miles to the reservation in two government cars. A dirt road leads into it. The guard on this road halted us. The reservation was directly before us. As the guard approached the first car, the reservation disappeared."

"Just like that?" Felton whispered. "No noise—no explosion?"

"No noise, no explosion. One moment, a forest of redwoods in front of us—then a gray area of nothing."

"Nothing? That's just a word. Did you try to go in?"

"Yes—we tried. The best scientists in America have tried. I myself am not a very brave man, Mr. Felton, but I got up enough courage to walk up to this gray edge and touch it. It was very cold and very hard—so cold that it blistered these three fingers."

He held out his hand for Felton to see.

"I became afraid then. I have not stopped being afraid." Felton nodded. "Fear—such fear," Eggerton sighed.

"I need not ask you if you tried this or that?"

"We tried everything, Mr. Felton, even—I am ashamed to say—a very small atomic bomb. We tried the sensible things and the foolish things. We went into panic and out of panic, and we tried everything."

"Yet you've kept it secret?"

"So far, Mr. Felton."

"Airplanes?"

"You see nothing from above. It looks like mist lying in the valley."

"What do your people think it is?"

Eggerton smiled and shook his head. "They don't know. There you are. At first, some of them thought it was some kind of force field. But the mathematics won't work, and of course it's cold. Terribly cold. I am mumbling. I am not a scientist and not a mathematician, but they also mumble, Mr. Felton. I am tired of that kind of thing. That is why I asked you to come to Washington and talk with us. I thought you might know."

"I might," Felton nodded.

For the first time, Eggerton became alive, excited, impatient. He mixed Felton another drink. Then he leaned forward eagerly and waited. Felton took a letter out of his pocket.

"This came from my sister," he said.

"You told me you had no letter from her in almost a year!"

"I've had this almost a year," Felton replied, a note of sadness in his voice. "I haven't opened it. She enclosed this sealed envelope with a short letter, which only said that she was well and quite happy, and that I was to open and read the other letter when it was absolutely necessary to do so. My sister is like that; we think the same way. Now, I suppose it's necessary, don't you?"

The Secretary nodded slowly but said nothing. Felton opened the letter and began to read aloud.

My dear Harry:

June 12, 1964

As I write this, it is twenty-two years since I have seen you or spoken to you. How very long for two people who have such love and regard for each other as we do! And now that you have found it necessary to open this letter and read it, we must face the fact that in all probability we will never see each other again. I hear that you have a wife and three children—all wonderful people. I think it is hardest to know that I will not see them or know them.

Only this saddens me. Otherwise, Mark and I are very happy—and I think you will understand why.

About the barrier—which now exists or you would not have opened the letter—tell them that there is no harm to it and no one will be hurt by it. It cannot be broken into because it is a negative power rather than a positive one, an absence instead of a presence. I will have more to say about it later, but possibly explain it no better. Some of the children could likely put it into intelligible words, but I want this to be my report, not theirs.

Strange that I still call them children and think of them as children—when in all fact we are the children and they are adults. But they still have the quality of children that we know best, the strange innocence and purity that vanishes so quickly in the outside world.

And now I must tell you what came of our experiment—or some of it. Some of it, for how could I ever put down the story of the strangest two decades that men ever lived through? It is all incredible and it is all commonplace. We took a group of wonderful children, and we gave them an abundance of love, security and truth—but I think it was the factor of love that mattered most. During the first year, we weeded out each couple that showed less than a desire to love these children. They were easy to love. And as the years passed, they became our children—in every way. The children who were born to the couples in residence here simply joined the group. No one had *a father or a mother*; we were a living, functioning group in which all men were the fathers of all children and all women the mothers of all children.

No, this was not easy, Harry—among ourselves, the adults, we had to fight and work and examine and turn ourselves inside out again and again, and tear our guts and hearts out, so that we could present an environment that had never been before, a quality of sanity and truth and security that exists nowhere else in all this world.

Now shall I tell you of an American Indian boy, five years old, composing a splendid symphony? Or of the two children, one Bantu, one Italian, one a boy, one a girl, who at the age of six built a machine to measure the speed of light? Will you believe that we, the adults, sat quietly and listened to these six-year-olds explain to us that since the speed of light is a constant everywhere, regardless of the motion of material bodies, the distance between the stars cannot be mentioned in terms of light, since that is not distance on our plane of being? Then believe also that I put it poorly. In all of these matters, I have the sensations of an uneducated immigrant whose child is exposed to all the wonders of school and knowledge. I understand a little, but very little.

If I were to repeat instance after instance, wonder after wonder—at the age of six and seven and eight and nine, would you think of the poor, tortured, nervous creatures whose parents boast that they have an IQ of 160, and in the same breath bemoan the fate that did not give them normal children? Well, ours were and are *normal* children. Perhaps the first normal children this world has seen in a long time. If you heard them laugh or sing only once, you would know that. If you could see how tall and strong they are, how fine of body and movement. They have a quality that I have never seen in children before.

Yes, I suppose, dear Harry, that much about them would shock you. Most of the time, they wear no clothes. Sex has always been a joy and a good thing to them, and they face it and enjoy it as naturally as we eat and drink—more naturally, for we have no gluttons in sex or food, no ulcers of the belly or the soul. They kiss and caress each other and do many other things that the world has specified as shocking, nasty, etc.—but whatever they do, they do with grace and joy. Is all this possible? I tell you that it has been my life for almost twenty years now. I live with boys and girls who are without evil or sickness, who are like pagans or gods—however you would look at it.

But the story of the children and of their day-to-day life is one that will be told properly and in its own time and place. All the indications I have put down here add up only to great gifts and abilities. Mark and I never had any doubts about these results; we knew that if we controlled an environment that was predicated on the future, the children would learn more than any children do on the outside. In their seventh year of life they were dealing easily and naturally with scientific problems normally taught on the college level, or higher, outside. This was to be expected, and we would have been very disappointed if something of this sort had not developed. But it was the unexpected that we hoped for and watched for—the flowering of the mind of man that is blocked in every single human being on the outside.

And it came. Originally, it began with a Chinese child in the fifth year of our work. The second was an American child, then a Burmese. Most strangely, it was not thought of as anything very unusual, nor did we realize what was happening until the seventh year, when there were already five of them.

Mark and I were taking a walk that day—I remember it so well, lovely, cool and clear California day—when we came on a group of children in a meadow. There were about a dozen children there. Five of them sat in a little circle, with a sixth in the center of the circle. Their heads were almost touching. They were full of little giggles, ripples of mirth and satisfaction. The rest of the children sat in a group about ten feet away—watching intently.

As we came to the scene, the children in the second group put their fingers to their lips, indicating that we should be quiet. So we stood and watched without speaking. After we were there about ten minutes, the little girl in the center of the circle of five leaped to her feet, crying ecstatically.

"I heard you! I heard you! I heard you!"

There was a kind of achievement and delight in her voice that we had not heard before, not even from our children. Then all of the children there rushed together to kiss her and embrace her, and they did a sort of dance of play and delight around her. All this we watched with no indication of surprise or even very great curiosity. For even though this was the first time anything like this—beyond our guesses or comprehension—had ever happened, we had worked out our own reaction to it.

When the children rushed to us for our congratulations, we nodded and smiled and agreed that it was all very wonderful. "Now, it's my turn, mother," a Senegalese boy told me. "I can almost do it already. Now there are six to help me, and it will be easier."

"Aren't you proud of us?" another cried.

We agreed that we were very proud, and we skirted the rest of the questions. Then, at our staff meeting that evening, Mark described what had happened.

"I noticed that last week," Mary Hengel, our semantics teacher, nodded. "I watched them, but they didn't see me."

47

"How many were there?" Professor Goldbaum asked intently.

"Three. A fourth in the center—their heads together. I thought it was one of their games and I walked away."

"They make no secret of it," someone observed.

"Yes," I said, "they took it for granted that we knew what they were doing."

"No one spoke," Mark said. "I can vouch for that."

"Yet they were listening," I said. "They giggled and laughed as if some great joke was taking place—or the way children laugh about a game that delights them."

It was Dr. Goldbaum who put his finger on it. He said, very gravely, "Do you know, Jean—you always said that we might open that great area of the mind that is closed and blocked in us. I think that they have opened it. I think they are teaching and learning to listen to thoughts."

There was a silence after that, and then Atwater, one of our psychologists, said uneasily, "I don't think I believe it. I've investigated every test and report on telepathy ever published in this country—the Duke stuff and all the rest of it. We know how tiny and feeble brain waves are—it is fantastic to imagine that they can be a means of communication."

"There is also a statistical factor," Rhoda Lannon, a mathematician, observed. "If this faculty existed even as a potential in mankind, is it conceivable that there would be no recorded instance of it?"

"Maybe it has been recorded," said Fleming, one of our historians. "Can you take all the whippings, burnings and hangings of history and determine which were telepaths?"

"I think I agree with Dr. Goldbaum," Mark said. "The children are becoming telepaths. I am not moved by a historical argument, or by a statistical argument, because our obsession here is environment. There is no record in history of a similar group of unusual children being raised in such an environment. Also, this may be—and probably is—a faculty which must be released in childhood or remain permanently blocked. I believe Dr. Haenigson will bear me out when I say that mental blocks imposed during childhood are not uncommon."

"More than that." Dr. Haeñigson, our chief psychiatrist, nodded. "No child in our society escapes the need to erect some mental block in his mind. Whole areas of every human being's mind are blocked in early childhood. This is an absolute of human society."

Dr. Goldbaum was looking at us strangely. I was going to say something—but I stopped. I waited and Dr. Goldbaum said:

"I wonder whether we have begun to realize what we may have done. What is a human being? He is the sum of his memories, which are locked in his brain, and every moment of experience simply builds up the structure of those memories. We don't know as yet what is the extent or power of the gift these children of ours appear to be developing, but suppose they reach a point where they can share the totality of memory? Is it not simply that among themselves there can be no lies, no deceit, no rationalization, no secrets, no guilts—it is more than that."

Then he looked from face to face, around the whole circle of our staff. We were beginning to comprehend him. I remember my own reactions at that moment, a sense of wonder and discovery and joy and heartbreak too; a feeling so poignant that it brought tears to my eyes.

"You know, I see," Dr. Goldbaum nodded. "Perhaps it would be best for me to speak about it. I am much older than any of you—and I have been through, lived through the worst years of horror and bestiality that mankind ever knew. When I saw what I saw, I asked myself a thousand times: What is the meaning of mankind—if it has any meaning at all, if it is not simply a haphazard accident, an unusual complexity of molecular structure? I know you have all asked yourselves the same thing. Who are we? What are we destined for? What is our purpose? Where is sanity or reason in these bits of struggling, clawing, sick fish? We kill, we torture, we hurt and destroy as no other species does. We ennoble murder and falsehood and hypocrisy and superstition; we destroy our own bodies with drugs and poisonous food; we deceive ourselves as well as others—and we hate and hate and hate.

"Now something has happened. If these children can go into each other's minds completely—then they will have a single memory, which is the memory of all of them. All experience will be common to all of them, all knowledge, all dreams—and they will be immortal. For as one dies, another child is linked to the whole, and another and another. Death will lose all meaning, all of its dark horror. Mankind will begin, here, in this place, to fulfill a part of its intended destiny—to become a single, wonderful unit, a whole—almost in the old words of your poet, John Donne, who sensed what we have all sensed at one time, that no man is an island unto himself. Has any thoughtful man lived without having a sense of that singleness of mankind? I don't think so. We have been living in darkness, in the night, struggling each of us with his own poor brain and then dying with all the memories of a lifetime. It is no wonder that we have achieved so little. The wonder is that we have achieved so much. Yet all that we know, all that we have done will be nothing compared to what these children will know and do and create—"

So the old man spelled it out, Harry—and saw almost all of it from the beginning. That was the beginning. Within the next twelve months, each one of our children was linked to all of the others telepathically. And in the years that followed, every child born in our reservation was shown the way into that linkage by the children. Only we, the adults, were forever barred from joining it. We were of the old, they of the new; their way was closed to us forever— although they could go into our minds, and did. But never could we feel them there or see them there, as they did each other.

I don't know how to tell you of the years that followed, Harry. In our little, guarded reservation, man became what he was always destined to be, but I can explain it only imperfectly. I can hardly comprehend, much less explain, what it means to inhabit forty bodies simultaneously, or what it means to each of the children to have the other personalities within them, a part of them—what it means to live as man and woman always and together. Could the children explain it to us? Hardly, for this is a transformation that must take place, from all we can learn, before puberty—and as it happens, the children accept it as normal and natural—indeed as the most natural thing in the world. We were the unnatural ones—and one thing they never truly comprehended is how we could bear to live in our aloneness, how we could bear to live with the knowledge of death as extinction.

We are happy that this knowledge of us did not come at once. In the beginning, the children could merge their thoughts only when their heads were almost touching. Bit by bit, their command of distance grew—but not until they were in their fifteenth year did they have the power to reach out and probe with their thoughts anywhere on earth. We thank God for this. By then the children were ready for what they found. Earlier, it might have destroyed them.

I must mention that two of our children met accidental death— in the ninth and the eleventh year. But it made no difference to the others, a little regret, but no grief, no sense of great loss, no tears or weeping. Death is totally different to them than to us; a loss of flesh; the personality itself is immortal and lives consciously in the others.

When we spoke of a marked grave or a tombstone, they smiled and said that we could make it if it would give us any comfort. Yet later, when Dr. Goldbaum died, their grief was deep and terrible, for his was the old kind of death.

Outwardly, they remained individuals—each with his or her own set of characteristics, mannerisms, personality. The boys and the girls make love in a normal sexual manner—though all of them share the experience. Can you comprehend that? I cannot—but for them everything is different. Only the unspoiled devotion of mother for helpless child can approximate the love that binds them together—yet here it is also different, deeper even than that.

Before the transformation took place, there was sufficient of children's petulance and anger and annoyance—but after it took place, we never again heard a voice raised in anger or annoyance. As they themselves put it, when there was trouble among them, they washed it out—when there was sickness, they healed it; and after the ninth year, there was no more sickness—even three or four of them, when they merged their minds, could go into a body and cure it.

I use these words and phrases because I have no others, but they don't describe. Even after all these years of living with the children, day and night, I can only vaguely comprehend the manner of their existence. What they are outwardly, I know, free and healthy and happy as no men were before, but what their inner life is remains beyond me.

I spoke to one of them about it once, Arlene, a tall, lovely child whom we found in an orphanage in Idaho. She was fourteen then. We were discussing personality, and I told her that I could not understand how she could live and work as an individual, when she was also a part of so many others, and they were a part of her.

"But I remain myself, Jean. I could not stop being myself."

"But aren't the others also yourself?"

"Yes. But I am also them."

"But who controls your body?"

"I do. Of course."

"But if they should want to control it instead of you?"

"Why?"

"If you did something they disapproved of," I said lamely.

"How could I?" she asked. "Can you do something you disapprove of?"

"I am afraid I can. And do."

"I don't understand. Then why do you do it?"

51

So these discussions always ended. We, the adults, had only words for communication. By their tenth year, the children had developed methods of communication as far beyond words as words are beyond the dumb motions of animals. If one of them watched something, there was no necessity for it to be described; the others could see it through his eyes. Even in sleep, they dreamed together.

I could go on for hours attempting to describe something utterly beyond my understanding, but that would not help, would it, Harry? You will have your own problems, and I must try to make you understand what happened, what had to happen. You see, by the tenth year, the children had learned all we knew, all we had among us as material for teaching. In effect, we were teaching a single mind, a mind composed of the unblocked, unfettered talent of forty superb children; a mind so rational and pure and agile that to them we could only be objects of loving pity.

We have among us Axel Cromwell, whose name you will recognize. He is one of the greatest physicists on earth, and it was he who was mainly responsible for the first atom bomb. After that, he came to us as one would go into a monastery—an act of personal expiation. He and his wife taught the children physics, but by the eighth year, the children were teaching Cromwell. A year later, Cromwell could follow neither their mathematics nor their reasoning; and their symbolism, of course, was out of the structure of their own thoughts.

Let me give you an example. In the far outfield of our baseball diamond, there was a boulder of perhaps ten tons. (I must remark that the athletic skill, the physical reactions of the children, was in its own way almost as extraordinary as their mental powers. They have broken every track and field record in existence—often cutting world records by one third. I have watched them run down our horses. Their movements can be so quick as to make us appear sluggards by comparison. And they love baseball—among other games.)

We had spoken of either blasting the boulder apart or rolling it out of the way with one of our heavy bulldozers, but it was something we had never gotten to. Then, one day, we discovered that the boulder was gone—in its place a pile of thick red dust that the wind was fast leveling. We asked the children what had happened, and they told us that they had reduced the boulder to dust—as if it was no more than kicking a small stone out of one's path. How? Well, they had loosened the molecular structure and it had become dust. They explained, but we could not understand. They tried to explain to Cromwell how their thoughts could do this, but he could no more comprehend it than the rest of us.

I mention one thing. They built an atomic fusion power plant, out of which we derive an unlimited store of power. They built what they call free fields into all our trucks and cars, so that they rise and travel through the air with the same facility they have on the ground. With the power of thought, they can go into atoms, rearrange electrons, build one element out of another—and all this is elementary to them, as if they were doing tricks to amuse us and amaze us.

So you see something of what the children are, and now I shall tell you what you must know.

In the fifteenth year of the children, our entire staff met with them. There were fifty-two of them now, for all the children born to us were taken into their body of singleness—and flourished in their company, I should add, despite their initially lower IQs. A very formal and serious meeting, for in thirty days the team of observers were scheduled to enter the reservations. Michael, who was born in Italy, spoke for them; they needed only one voice.

He began by telling us how much they loved and cherished us, the adults who were once their teachers. "All that we have, all that we are, you have given us," he said. "You are our fathers and mothers and teachers—and we love you beyond our power to say. For years now, we have wondered at your patience and self-giving, for we have gone into your minds and we know what pain and doubt and fear and confusion you all live with. We have also gone into the minds of the soldiers who guard the reservation. More and more, our power to probe grew—until now there is no mind anywhere on earth that we cannot seek out and read.

"From our seventh year, we knew all the details of this experiment, why we were here and what you were attempting—and from then until now, we have pondered over what our future must be. We have also tried to help you, whom we love so much, and perhaps we have been a little help in easing your discontents, in keeping you as healthy as possible, and in easing your troubled nights in that maze of fear and nightmare that you call sleep.

"We did what we could, but all our efforts to join you with us have failed. Unless that area of the mind is opened before puberty, the tissues change, the brain cells lose all potential of development, and it is closed forever. Of all things, this saddens us most—for you have given us the most precious heritage of mankind, and in return we have given you nothing."

"That isn't so," I said. "You have given us more than we gave you."

"Perhaps," Michael nodded. "You are very good and kind people. But now the fifteen years are over, and the team will be here in thirty days—"

I shook my head. "No. They must be stopped."

"And all of you?" Michael asked, looking from one to another of the adults.

Some of us were weeping. Cromwell said:

"We are your teachers and your fathers and mothers, but you must tell us what to do. You know that."

Michael nodded, and then he told us what they had decided. The reservation must be maintained. I was to go to Washington with Mark and Dr. Goldbaum—and somehow get an extension of time. Then new infants would be brought into the reservation by teams of the children, and educated here.

"But why must they be brought here?" Mark asked. "You can reach them wherever they are—go into their minds, make them a part of you?"

"But they can't reach us," Michael said. "Not for a long time. They would be alone—and their minds would be shattered. What would the people of your world outside do to such children? What happened to people in the past who were possessed of devils, who heard voices? Some became saints, but more were burned at the stake."

"Can't you protect them?" someone asked.

"Some day—yes. Now, no—there are not enough of us. First, we must help move children here, hundreds and hundreds more. Then there must be other places like this one. It will take a long time. The world is a large place and there are a great many children. And we must work carefully. You see, people are so filled with fear—and this would be the worst fear of all. They would go mad with fear and all that they would think of is to kill us."

"And our children could not fight back," Dr. Goldbaum said quietly. "They cannot hurt any human being, much less kill one. Cattle, our old dogs and cats, they are one thing—"

(Here Dr. Goldbaum referred to the fact that we no longer slaughtered our cattle in the old way. We had pet dogs and cats, and when they became very old and sick, the children caused them peacefully to go to sleep—from which they never awakened. Then the children asked us if we might do the same with the cattle we butchered for food.)

"—but not people," Dr. Goldbaum went on. "They cannot hurt

people or kill people. We are able to do things that we know are wrong, but that is one power we have that the children lack. They cannot kill and they cannot hurt. Am I right, Michael?"

"Yes—you are right." Michael nodded. "We must do it slowly and patiently—and the world must not know what we are doing until we have taken certain measures. We think we need three years more. Can you get us three years, Jean?"

"I will get it," I said.

"And we need all of you to help us. Of course we will not keep any of you here if you wish to go. But we need you—as we have always needed you. We love you and value you, and we beg you to remain with us. . . ."

Do you wonder that we all remained, Harry—that no one of us could leave our children—or will ever leave them, except when death takes us away? There is not so much more that I must tell now.

We got the three years we needed, and as for the gray barrier that surrounds us, the children tell me that it is a simple device indeed. As nearly as I can understand, they altered the time sequence of the entire reservation. Not much—by less than one ten-thousandth of a second. But the result is that your world outside exists this tiny fraction of a second in the future. The same sun shines on us, the same winds blow, and from inside the barrier, we see your world unaltered. But you cannot see us. When you look at us, the present of our existence has not yet come into being—and instead there is nothing, no space, no heat, no light, only the impenetrable wall of nonexistence.

From inside, we can go outside—from the past into the future. I have done this during the moments when we experimented with the barrier. You feel a shudder, a moment of cold—but no more.

There is also a way in which we return, but understandably, I cannot spell it out.

So there is the situation, Harry. We will never see each other again, but I assure you that Mark and I are happier than we have ever been. Man will change, and he will become what he was intended to be, and he will reach out with love and knowledge to all the universes of the firmament. Isn't that what man has always dreamt of, no war or hatred or hunger or sickness or death? We are fortunate to be alive while this is happening, Harry—we should ask no more.

With all my love,
Jean

Felton finished reading, and then there was a long, long silence while the two men looked at each other. Finally, the Secretary spoke:

"You know we shall have to keep knocking at that barrier—trying to find a way to break through?"

"I know."

"It will be easier, now that your sister has explained it."

"I don't think it will be easier," Felton said tiredly. "I do not think that she has explained it."

"Not to you and me, perhaps. But we'll put the eggheads to work on it. They'll figure it out. They always do."

"Perhaps not this time."

"Oh, yes," the Secretary nodded. "You see, we've got to stop it. We can't have this kind of thing—immoral, godless, and a threat to every human being on earth. The kids were right. We would have to kill them, you know. It's a disease. The only way to stop a disease is to kill the bugs that cause it. The only way. I wish there was another way, but there isn't."

the examination

Felix Gotschalk

One aspect of development which continues to generate lively discussion and controversy is the development of intelligence. One of the oldest issues remains the debate about the relative importance of heredity (genetics) and environment (experience). Raging anew is this debate as it applies to the intelligence of black people. The following story stimulates our thinking on these issues by creating a situation where a typical intelligence tester finds himself trying to measure the intelligence of what he believes to be a young black girl of limited intelligence. Before he is through, the tables are turned, and tester and test-taker reverse their roles. In the process of reading the story we are challenged to reevaluate how we typically measure intelligence. As a bonus we are also challenged to test our own vocabularies. As the test administrator asks his client vocabulary words, we as readers are challenged to think of the answers before they are given.

The setting for the story is the administration of one of the classic and still most popular intelligence tests for children, the Stanford-Binet Intelligence Scale. The Stanford-Binet is constructed as a developmental age scale, with its tasks arranged by age levels. The tester begins at a level below the child's chronological age, and, moving upward, tries to establish a "basal age"—the highest age level at which the child can pass all subtests. Each additional subtest passed is worth a score of two months more, and adding these months to the basal age, the tester establishes the child's "mental age." He divides the mental age by the child's chronological age and then multiplies the quotient by 100 to establish the Intelligence Quotient or IQ.

The part of the test which we witness in "The Examination" is the vocabulary section. As a child's "mental age" increases he is supposed to know words which are increasingly difficult, based on increased rarity of use. In the story, the tester is challenged to explain this principle of measuring intelligence. Is one person more intelligent because he knows more rare words than another person? Or is his ability to solve his life's problems a better criterion? In general, the Binet scale has been criticized for overemphasizing verbal skills in its assessment of intelligence. As a response to this criticism, the Wechsler scales of intelligence, which followed the Binet scale, included a "Performance" section, emphasizing skills of manual dexterity and spatial relations as well as verbal skills.

There is strong evidence that genetics plays an important role in determining intelligence. The correlation between the intelligence of parents and their natural children is about twice as high as for their adopted children. Similarly, the intelligence of identical twins is much more highly correlated than that of fraternal twins, who are genetically different. Most impressively, identical twins brought up in different environments still correlate very highly in intelligence—higher than fraternal twins reared together. Nevertheless, genetics is not the whole story, as identical twins reared in the same environment have the highest correlation of all matched groups.

The importance of genetics in the intelligence of black people has been raised by psychologist Arthur Jensen. Jensen maintains, from statistical analyses of intelligence test data done on various groups, that intelligence is determined about 80 per cent by genetics. Noting that blacks on the average score 5 to 20 IQ points lower than whites on intelligence tests, he suggests that there may be some genetic cause for this discrepancy. Critics of Jensen argue that he has overinterpreted his data based on correlations, which do not establish cause and effect relationships. They account for the difference by citing environmental differences between the races, as well as the white middle class bias of the tests, which does not allow them to measure black intelligence accurately. Jensen counters that remedial programs have not been successful, even though they tried to compensate for environmental deprivation. His critics retort that these programs have changed only part of the black child's environment, since the child still often goes back to slums and poor nutrition. Supporting their view is an interesting study on the effect of the Israeli kibbutz on the IQ of children of African and European Jews. Raised out of the kibbutz in different environments, the children of white European Jews have a mean IQ 20 points higher than the children of darker African Jews. However, when both groups are raised for four years in the same total environment of the kibbutz nursery, their mean IQ scores are exactly alike.

THE EXAMINATION   *Felix C. Gotschalk*

The small black child sat on the white vinyl chair and gave off an aura of coal-stove smoke and lard. Her wool coat was too hot but she kept it on. A waxy sleeper stuck in the corner of her eye and she sniffled productively.

"Do you want a Kleenex?" the examiner asked, an edge of weariness showing through his overt kindness.

"Naw," the girl said softly. The examiner took one of the 1906 Binet forms from a stack atop a cabinet and sat down across the desk from the girl. The form bore 1937 and 1960 restandardization copyright dates.

"Do you feel all right today?" he asked.

"Yeah." The reply was flat.

"Do you have to go to the bathroom?"

"Naw." The examiner pushed the Binet form across the waxed formica surface to the girl.

"The first thing I'd like for you to do is write your name right here." The girl took the pencil, rotated the page 90 degrees starboard, and wrote left-handed, straight down the line, right at her navel. Her pencil grip was crablike, even hemiplegic, but she printed "PAMELA" well enough, adding a very slight stylistic flourish to the final A. The examiner took the form once more and filled in several blanks with a ballpoint pen.

"Let's see," he said, "today is April the seventeenth, 1974, and when is your birthday?"

"I don't know," the girl said faintly.

"Let's see again. Here it is. You were born February the first, 1966. So, you are eight years and two months." The examiner wrote "8-2" in the chronological age blank. "And, you're a girl," he chuckled in a friendly tone, "I'll put that down." He printed "NF" for Negro female.

"Where do you live, Pamela?"

"You know thet wott house ova dair?" The child pointed out the window.

"I think so." The examiner was used to responses like this.

"I live ona dert road."

"What school do you go to now?"

"South Main-Jones."

"And what grade are you in?"

"Thudd."

"Did you go to kindergarten?"

"Ah went to Haidstott."

"What's your daddy's name?"

The dark face brightened at the question. "Ah got me two daddies."

"Yay—good." The examiner fell in easily with the drift of the response.

"Are they good to you?"

"Yeah." The examiner scanned the referral sheet for the name of the child's mother: PATRICIA ANN TUGGERT OWEN RAIKES.

"What kind of work does your daddy do?"

"He break up rocks at the quarry."

"Do you have any special hobbies, or things you like to do a whole lot?"

"Ah locks to watch teevee."

"What shows do you like best?"

The girl looked thoughtful. The examiner had his head down when the child's pupils swam away into pinheads, glowed a fiery white for half a second, then returned to wet black and brown cow-eyes.

"Ah locks Gilgun's eye-lun and the Frintstones," the girl said.

"Do you have to do any work around your house?"

"Ah hev to wash deeshes sometimes."

"Do you get some money to spend sometimes?"

"Yeah."

"What do you like to buy with money?"

"Canny."

The examiner filled in his name on the Binet face-sheet: PAUL MACK GRASSY, ED.D. He looked at his Nivada Grenchen. It read 9:22. Better get on with it, he thought.

"Well, I'm supposed to try you on a few little tests today, to find out something about how much you know, how smart you are. Is school hard for you, or easy?"

"Hodd."

"Well, let's try a few of these test things. Some of them are questions. Talking. Then, there are some pictures and puzzles that are sort of fun." The girl shifted in the chair and took off her coat. The examiner thought the girl's movements to be fluid and smooth and rapid. He began the testing:

"I want to find out how many words you know. Listen, and when I say a word, you tell me what it means. What is an orange?"

"Uh froot," she replied.

"Right. What is an envelope?"

"For a letter." The examiner rummaged in a drawer for a cigar. A sensor pad extended from the child's brow, rotated briefly, and retracted into the wiry black hairs. A few feet away, under a corner of the carpet, a roach suddenly ate its brood and felt its tropisms waver. The examiner looked back at the Binet text.

"The next word is 'straw.' What is a straw?"

"You suck it."

"What is a puddle?"

"A puddle of water."

"And, let's see here, the next word is 'tap.' What does that word mean?"

"You make a little noise."

"Good. A little noise. 'Gown.' What is a gown?"

"A nightgown."

"The next word is 'roar.' What does 'roar' mean?"

"Noise."

"Well, there are lots of kinds of noises. What would you say about 'roar' to tell exactly what it means?"

The child looked steadily at the examiner. "Ain't noise right?"

Grassy glanced at the text and saw the one-word response "noise" was a plus score. "Well, that's good enough. Let's try some more. 'eyelash.' What is that?"

"Hair that protects your eyes," the girl said fairly quickly. Grassy now knew that the child was probably average in mental abilities, having scored successes with vocabulary terms standardized on population samples of eight-year-olds.

"Well, you're pretty good at this. You say school is hard for you?"

"Sometimes."

"Do you try hard?"

"Not all the time."

"Well, the next word is, let's see, 'Mars.' What is Mars, anyway?"

"A planet." The child put a small hand on the desk and some formica molecules sundered deep in their microcosms. No blood vessels were visible in the child's hand.

"'Juggler' is the next word," the examiner said.

"A juggler is a man that juggles balls up and down."

"'Scorch.' What does 'scorch' mean?"

"To burn," Pamela said in a clearing and increasingly perky voice. Aft of her dextral mastoid an auxiliary cardiac pump puckered and hot proline surged across her synapses.

Grassy knew now that the girl had passed vocabulary items designed for random samplings of eleven-year-olds. He began to feel that the girl might be a sleeper, a bright but dull-acting child. He leaned in closer to her and locked in steady eye contact. He started just slightly. The girl's eyes dilated quickly, like an owl's. He looked closer. "The black parts of your eyes are big," he said gently and interestedly. "Do you have good vision and hearing?"

Pam smiled engagingly, with a charming glimmer of shyness, and said yes. Her eyes fell on a wart in the web of Grassy's hand. Her eyeballs ellipsed to 50-power magnification and 100 candlepower. The wart looked like a raised crater stuffed with pointed fleshy buds. She beamed in a micro-laser at the precise azimuth and the wart spores withered and disappeared. Grassy did not see the wart wink out of existence.

"It looks like you're going to be extra smart, Pam," he said. "You know some hard words for a girl your age. Let's try a few harder ones. How about 'lecture'? Have you ever heard that word?"

"A speech," came the reply.

"Right. A speech. Very good. Now, what is 'skill'? Ess, kay, eye, ell, ell?"

"Something you do real well," Pam said, brightening perceptibly.

"Hey, you get better as you go along," Grassy said, with more enthusiasm than he usually expressed. "Do you have any special skills? Things you do well?" The girl's memorytrace engrams flashed in the subvocal input "3-D KINESTHETIC CHESS," but she looked neutrally at Grassy and said no.

"Well. How about this word. It is 'brunette.' Do you know what that is?"

"Black hair like mine." Pam seemed to give off some coy femininity.

"Right," Grassy said. "How about 'muzzle'?"

"What you put on a dog's face."

"How do you know that word?"

"A lady cross our road had to put one on her dawg cawz it wuz meen." The girl had reached a vocabulary level of twelve chronological years, and Grassy was beginning to be impressed and vaguely disquieted.

"'Haste' is the next word, Pam," he said with an edge of expectancy and diffuse concern. "Do you know what that is?"

"Hurry," the girl said, and Grassy sensed a whisker of mockery in her voice. The room temperature had risen to 70.4 and an all but imperceptible hum was flicking at his auditory limens.

"Here's a hard one and it's hard to say. 'Peculiarity.' Anyone ever tell you that word?" Pam's lips parted to reveal serrated teeth. She closed her mouth quickly and gave Grassy a shy and unguarded look. "Yes," she said thoughtfully, "that means rare, or queer." *Alternate synonyms*, Grassy thought. *This little thing is at least superior.*

"Why did your parents want you to come and get tested?" he asked, thumbing through the referral notes.

"I really don't know," Pam said.

Grassy could not find the referral face-sheet. "Now I know I had that sheet. What did I do with it?" He looked up to see the girl looking at him quite intently. The look was instantly familiar. Bela Lugosi had greeted guests at Castle Dracula with the same vague expectancy. Grassy suaved off a nudging anxiety and returned to the Binet forms.

"What was the last word I asked you?"

"'Peculiarity.'"

"Yes, well, let's try 'priceless.' "'Priceless.'"

"'Invaluable.'"

The reply was rapid, and the vocal nuance distantly goading, as if Pam had advance knowledge of the answers and was putting Grassy on. He looked searchingly at her. "My dear girl," he said earnestly, "I am amazed and gratified and puzzled by your knowing that word, and by your giving a synonym. That's the most advanced way of responding to vocabulary tasks. Do you understand what I am saying to you?"

Pam dropped her chin and softly said yes. "I try to read a lot," she said, "and I learn a lot from the trivid and the tape banks."

"Well, let's see how far you can go with the words. The next one is 'regard.' What does 'regard' mean?"

"You look at something."

Amazing, Grassy thought. "How about 'tolerate'?"

"Endure."

"Here's a huge word. 'Disproportionate.'"

"Out of size—out of shape." Grassy realized that his mouth was gaping open and that his Harsh Marsh Maduro had gone out and was smelly. He lit the cigar and clenched it in his teeth. A diffuse wreath of smoke floated toward Pam, and then stopped, inches from her face. The force-field isomorph read the smoke's particulate locus and Pam marveled why humanoids chose to ignite dried leaves and allow the combusted cells' smoke to play among the lungs and the sinus pockets and the olfactory shafts.

Pam had now defined Binet vocabulary words as well as average adults, and an extrapolated IQ on this one parameter would translate to 170 plus. Grassy truly prized bright kids, bright adults, anybody who showed the secret handclasp responses which betokened optimal brain-cell number, configuration, and condition. He was rarely if ever threatened intellectually. Now Pam grew more adult and supra-adult every minute. "Have you ever heard your voice on tape?" he asked her.

"No."

"Youre doing so very well that I'd like to record some of the things you say. Okay?"

"Okay."

He flicked the cassette on and palmed the record slot.

"Here's a short word. 'Lotus.' What's that?"

"A plant. A Chinese plant. And an English racing car."

"How about 'shrewd'?"

"Discerning."

How the goddam mother hell could an eight-year-old humanoid know that word, Grassy thought.

"'Mosaic,'" he said in a fringe-stentorian tone.

"An art form in which pictures or designs are made with stone, glass, or tile. Or"—and here she looked vaguely professorial—"Of, or pertaining to, Moses." The response scored at SUPERIOR ADULT, LOCUS II.

"Nobody ever gets this one," Grassy said. "The word is 'stave.' "

"A curved board in a barrel."

"How in the world did you come to know a rare word like that?" Grassy had a whining shimmer in his tone.

"Definitive corollaries of linguistic gestalten are, of course, a matter of public information." Pam sounded robotlike.

Grassy felt his jowls go flaccid and his eyes begin to blink. He felt strangely introversive. He thumbed the Norelco to rewind, then to stop, then to a replay: a 132-cycle hum spat through the mike speaker, and a wavering overlay of pulsating psychophysical tones contrapunted through the basal pitch. Pam's eyes glowed a soft luminosity and antenna buds appeared at her parietal lobes. "You're an alien." Grassy tried to sound unafraid.

"Affirmative."

"What do you want?"

"I want to continue the evaluation."

"You want to define the rest of the words?"

"Negative. I want to put the remaining words to you as a testee." Pam's silver arm spread across the desk like a chrome piston and took the Binet text.

"First," she began, "is it true that humanoid language sounds evolved from the cries of animals?"

Grassy moved toward the door, but a modstun force-field enveloped him. He felt as if he had walked into a warm gossamer membrane.

"Be seated, please," the girl said. "You are in no danger. No harm will come to you."

Grassy sat down trembling. The girl vectored in a tranquilizing matrix of oxygen dilutants. "Well?" she said, "what is your response to my question?"

"I'm afraid I don't know. I guess I'm weak in the psycholinguistics bit."

"Is it true that what you term 'intelligence' is assessed by psychologists through linguistic exchanges with the evaluees?"

"Yes," Grassy answered, "although verbal expression, or particular verbal facility, is not a firm requirement. We can test mutes."

Pam's tungsten helices whirred in ambergris gelatin. She scanned the remaining Binet word lists. "How was word number twenty-six selected as a linguistic gestalten held to measure intelligence? The word is 'bewail.'"

"The words are weeded out on statistical difficulty curves during the test standardization process. Intelligent people seem to know harder words than unintelligent people. 'Bewail' ranked as one of the tougher words, because the standardization sample showed that a middle locus of superior adults knew the word."

"But, since the term 'superior' is taxonomic and dependent on performance, are you not talking circularly?" Pam asked. Then she passed quickly on: "What does the term mean to you?" she asked Grassy.

Grassy realized that his daily access to test items had not made him as test-wise as he might have thought, and the realization was a kind of double-edged sword. The specificity of his own mental abilities seemed preserved, yet the blind spots he had were being revealed; i.e., access to intelligence tests had not made him any more intelligent. And, he thought, this is somehow goddam good. "'Bewail' means something like being sad," Grassy ventured.

"Deplore. Lament. Bemoan," Pam said quickly. "How about word number twenty-seven. 'Ocher.' Oh-Kerr."

"That's a mythological monster, a kind of troll that lives under bridges," Grassy said, trying to be playful. Pam smiled.

"I can read your ideational dynamics, your subvocal engrams. And I see much dissonance there—cognitive dissonance, one of your colleagues has called it. You think and feel one way, look and act another, and talk yet another. Do you really know what the term 'ocher' means?"

"As far as I know, it's a monster."

"An earthy clay with iron ore in it," Pam said.

"Oh yeah," Grassy said, "now I remember." He dropped his cigar on the rug beside the telephone. As he bent to pick it up, he lifted the receiver from its cradle, knowing that the local operator would come on the line in a few seconds. Pam's ears had sprouted tufts of crystalline cilia, and her eyes rotated to show at least a dozen wetly glowing facets. Her lip line had become more compressed, like a surgical slash on a bloodless cadaver. Her teeth meshed together like ring gears. Grassy wondered if she actually ate, in the sense of placing foliage or flesh or carrion in her mouth and ingesting it in some way.

"What does 'repose' mean to you?" she asked.

"To lie down, crap out, get supine," Grassy replied.

"Rest. Inactivity. Tranquillity. How about 'ambergris'?"

"Hello? Hello." The switchboard operator's voice came on the phone.

"Excuse me," said Grassy, and reached for the phone. He tried to tell the operator to ring the police, but Pam read his thoughts and masked out his laryngeal striations.

Her arm telescoped across the desk and her ball-socketed hand rotated to replace the receiver. "My dear Ducktoor Grassy," she said, "I am totally superordinate in relation to you. Please permit me to complete the questioning. As a scientist, or a quasi, or para-scientist, perhaps you are interested in my motives: they include the assessment of humanoid verbalizations as they differ from their supposed ideational bases. In other words, I know what you are thinking. I want to hear what you *say*. Now take this term 'amber-gris.'"

"It's a puller, put in perfumes."

"True, but definitively diffuse. My data banks read the term as denoting a waxy gray substance excreted by sperm whales. It is actually an excretory lubricant. 'Limpet,'" Pam continued.

Her voice had lowered and softened, so that she sounded like the Lonesome Gal from old radio days. She still hummed softly, like a diapason cipher.

Grassy felt just enough playfulness to nudge against the force-field periodically, but he also felt quiescent and interested in Pam the alien. Grassy gently rotated the waxed tips of his mustache with his thumb and forefinger. "Limpet, limpet. I believe that relates to a quiet pool—a limpid pool, a calm dark pool."

"Shellfish. Mollusks. Conicals." Pam sounded computerized again. "Such a term is communicatively esoteric. Have you truly found that this is a utilitarian word? Do you need to know that the word denotes a genetic group, a taxonomic cluster?"

"Intelligent people often seem to know esoteric things. But, the Esso Terrier per se is defined as a statistical or actuarial norm. In other words, a person who is bright or who tests as being artifactual-ly or psychometrically bright is not that way because he has scavenged for nits or groveled compulsively. He is rather like the TV receiving stations that monitored the 1970 moon landings: powerful, rich, self-actualizing, high in perceptual sensitivity."

"You pretty well imply an hereditary or structurally invariant basis for intelligence," Pam said.

"We have wrangled over that for at least seventy years," Grassy said, half-waving off the questioning nuance of the tone, "and never got it adequately resolved. Historically, aristocrats have claimed an attendant right to high intelligence, while the serfs assumed a yoke of stupidity. There were people who felt that they had no *right* to be bright because they were poor. There now seems to be a measurable hierarchy of intelligence groupings, which is only partially related to socio-economic class."

Pam seemed to listen attentively, her cilia waving like anemone sepals and her eyes now showing a more assuring humanoid warmth. Her charisma index wavered with her persona variations, so that she seemed both child and god, both small and overpowering, both human and suprahuman.

"What does 'frustrate' mean?"

"To feel bugged, miffed, or irritated."

"Foil, baffle, defeat, ineffectuate," Pam clacked out. "'Flaunt.'"

"If you've *got* it, flaunt it," Grassy said in weak camaraderie. "I think it means something like bragging or teasing."

"To make a gaudy, ostentatious, or defiant display," the succinct definition clacked out again. "'Incrustation,'"she continued neutrally.

"Like barnacles all over a ship."

"A hard outer layer or coating." Grassy began to feel stirringly dumb.

"'Retroactive,'" Pam continued.

"Applicable to recent events, like retroactive pay raises," Grassy said.

"Having application to or effect on things prior to its enactment or effectuation." Pam stood up. She was now about six feet tall. "Would you stand, please?" she asked. "I want to get your somatotype parameters and your brain mass relative to total organismic displacement."

Grassy got up awkwardly, his chair rolling off the beaverboard template and onto the red carpet. Pam now looked like the Statue of Liberty. Grassy felt the barely liminal comfort of the forcefield, as if he were dozing before a lingering hardwood fire.

The alien seemed to center herself in front of Grassy, like a surveyor's rod man. "Be quite still, please," she said, increasing the force-field density. A segmented antenna appeared at her waistline and she moved around the desk to Grassy's side. Standing closely ventral-ventral, she embraced him with eight chrome pseudopods. His body was yoked to hers. He closed his eyes. "Do you feel anything when I do this?" she asked, somehow sweetly.

"No," he said, "What is it you are doing?"

"Getting a holographic mold of your body. The pseudopods are vectoring in isomorphic tape measures, so to say. It will take just a few more seconds." Grassy opened his eyes inches from the alien face. It was smooth, like wetly polished marble.

"Your vertical spine and curved horizontal ribs must cause you discomfort," she said. "Do you sometimes move like quadrupeds, to ease the feeling?"

"No. Never."

"Did you evolve from quadrupeds?"

"I don't really know."

"Do you ever regress to quadruped or anthropoid behaviors? For instance, do you groom or preen one another?"

"Occasionally, but such behaviors are considered in questionable taste."

"Do you smell your armpits or axillary vellus areas?"

"Rarely," Grassy replied.

"Are you capable of self-fellation?"

"An anatomic impossibility. But no, I recall one case reported by Kinsey, of a man who utilized this method for several years."

"Are you in any sense cloacal, like serpents?"

"No, but urinary fluids and seminal fluids do share a single distal ducting, so that we are probably more cloacal than we would care to admit."

"Is it true that orgasm is held to be the pinnacle of humanoid experience?"

"I think yes." The pseudopods retracted and Pam spun slowly, like a heavy periscope, and glided off a few feet.

"Would you like to question me any more?" she asked.

Grassy looked sheepish. "I am too sedated to do much good. Do you fear capture by us?"

"No." Pam sat down and her appearance changed wispily. "I can alter my appearance from raw diffusion to lead monoliths. I am impervious to physical harm. You could not capture me. Come, complete the few terms left on the test, and you can ask me anything you wish." They sat in their original positions as testee and tester and exchanged long neutral looks.

"This is ironic, or humbling, or something," Grassy said. "My intelligence, however you wish to define it, plus my educational credentials and professional experience, accord me a statutory sphere of competency, and a certain implied superordinacy in assessing people's behaviors. I naturally bring this reinforced orientation to you, an overtly deprived member of a racial minority group, and you obliterate it as an alien. Now you want me back in the examiner's role. Do you feel sadistic motives?"

"We feel no such motives. We have no need or wish to express aggression. Come, the appointment span will be over soon. Ask me the last few words and I will tell you something about my organismic grouping."

Grassy looked half-heartedly at the Binet text. He felt like he was about to read *The Readers Digest* to a national Mensa group. "Word number forty-three is 'philanthropy.'"

"Love of mankind. Desire to help mankind. Something that helps mankind."

"'Piscatorial.'"

"Of fishes, fishermen, or fishing."

"'Milksop.'" Grassy felt disgusted and somehow ashamed.

"Unmanly man or boy. Mollycoddle, Sissy."

"Do you have sexes among your people?" Grassy put in.

"No. We do not reproduce. We are made of insoluble crystalline matrices, held in quasi-permeable colloid states by reverse parity."

"Parity in the sense of right-handed and left-handed atoms?"

"No." Pam smiled through her little-girl physiognomy. "Two Oriental physicists won one of your prizes years ago by showing experimentally that atoms are not handed."

"Are your crystalline units homogeneous? Are you reductionistic?"

"Your celestial galaxy is a macrocosmic homology of our crystalline structures. We have homogeneity in the sense of spinning spheroids, a space medium or host environment, and inertias born of centrifugal force. Try the toughest Binet words."

"'Harpy.'"

"Mythological bird-woman creatures, perceived as an inverted major detail on Card Nine of the Rorschach plates."

"How did you know that?"

"It is bold in your subvocal engrams."

"'Depredation,'" said Grassy.

"Plundering, laying waste, robbery."

"'Perfunctory.'"

"Done without care or interest or as a routine form."

"'Achromatic.'"

"Colorless."

"Do you have a light spectrum in your perceptual world?" Grassy asked.

"Yes," Pam said, "but we are able to see the bands of coloration all along the angstrom unit abscissa. You humans are really quite limited, what with your range of visible light equal to about one-twentieth of the total actual light. For instance, I can see the alternating current in your stereo system, the radio waves in the atmosphere, as well as gammas and ultraviolets and all the rest. You are really unable to protect yourself from such things as X-rays."

"'Casuistry' is the next word," Grassy continued. He heard the muffled steps and voices of several people outside his door. Pam was fully in the guise of the little girl.

"Some sheriffs deputies are outside," she said. "The switch-board operator got my wavelength when you picked up the phone receiver. These frequencies are enough to make birds wake up screaming and hippopotami burst from the surface of their quiet pools. Listen to me now, don't make a fool of yourself. They will not believe your reporting that I am an alien life form. I can be totally Pamela. So be cool, as you say. *And,* casuistry is a philosophical term denoting the solving of special cases of right and wrong in conduct by. . . ."

A heavily authoritative knocking rang through the cheap beige paint and thin pine wood of the door. "Dr. Grassy? Are you all right?"

Grassy scrambled up from his chair and all but wrenched the plastic knob from the door. Two fatly dumb-looking deputies filled the framing space.

"She's a goddam alien!" Grassy sang out to the men, his arms flailing the air, his eyes white-wide and rolling, "She's got spaghet-tini oozing from her ears and an antenna in her navel! She's got teeth like bank-vault hinges, her eyes glow like coals, and she's got eight chrome-plated goddam fucking arms!"

A small but determined social worker winced, then moved easily between the ballooning hulks of the deputies, and all but sprinted to the small sobbing form of the dull-looking negroid girl.

"Look out!" Grassy trumpeted. "She's pure, raw, crystalline-matrix colloid! She just looks like a lidda durl. Don't touch her, dammit."

He felt fingers big as hotdogs close around his arms and he was held very firmly against a wall. "Man, this fox has really flipped," one of the deputies said, getting a ham-sized hand inside Grassy's Sansabelt. Pam was crying little shudders of fear and being hugged and cooed over by the social worker.

"Idiots!" Grassy grated broken resonance at the gathering group of staff members. "I tell you that girl is an alien being. She is not humanoid. You can find out for yourself, just take her clothes off! She's a labyrinth of data storage tiers! She knew every one of the goddam Binet vocabulary words!" Pam was crying louder and being hugged closer.

"Let's get this dude out of here," the deputy said. "He's blown all his fuses." They hustled Grassy down the hallway.

"'Homunculus'!" he called back to Pam. "Hoe-Mun-Kew-Luss.

Tell them what that means, Pam. 'Sudorific'! 'Sudorific'! 'Parterre'!
Goddamn 'parterre'! No priest-prodding, nun-knocking fair, Pam!
You didn't finish the test!"

Grassy heard Pam's voice close at his ear as he was trundled
into the car: "'Homunculus.' A little man. Dwarf. A model of a
human body used for demonstrating anatomy."

"See?" He sat up intently. "She knew those answers. She's
talking to me now. I tell you she is an alien organism."

"Relax, Doc," the deputy said, "we'll get it all straight."

Grassy jumped slightly as the alien voice returned: "'Sudorific': causing or increasing sweat. 'Parterre': part of a theater beneath
the balcony and behind the parquet."

"See? See?" Grassy said. "She's still talking. She knows about
dwarfs, and sweat, and theaters. These are things most of us don't
know about. Nobody ever gets those words right. You believe me,
don't you?"

"Sure, Doc," one of the men said. The deputies exchanged
tight, knowing smiles as the car drove off.

the playground

Ray Bradbury

We know life piece by piece as we experience it. Principles and concepts may be defined clearly in books, but life itself is not so precise. It keeps shifting—first creating one illusion, then another. Meanings are ambiguous. Opinions differ from person to person, and the view of the same individual may change from time to time.

Ray Bradbury's "The Playground" captures this motion and ambiguity of life. It explores the questions: What is childhood play like? What does the child learn from play? Is childhood the best time or the most hellish time of one's life? When we've finished the story, we have "experienced" the playground. The little tale shimmers with sense impressions: the sight of a hopscotch game or a squabbling heap of children; the sound of bat against ball and yelling boys; the smell of camphor and pink Mercurochrome, dark licorice, and mint. Bradbury is a master in creating a sense of place. But we may not agree about the meaning of what we read. We may argue as to whether Charles Underhill made a wise decision about letting his son go to the playground. Or even about who Tommy Marshall is. Is he real or fantasy? Did Charles merely make him up to get the kind of advice he wanted to hear? Bradbury is always at his best in creating on paper a believable world where the real and the imagined mingle.

The protagonist of the story is Charles Underhill, whose wife has recently died, leaving him with a three-year-old son, Jim. His sister, who is helping him raise his child, insists Jim is now old enough to begin playing with other children on the playground. Charles disagrees.

From the point of view of developmental psychology, the story involves the interplay of two of the eight psychosocial stages of man suggested by Erik Erikson. As Erikson describes them, at each stage there is a problem and conflict which the individual must face and resolve if he is to resolve subsequent problems at later stages. Jim, the child, must face the conflict of his third year of life: Autonomy versus Doubt. The child must explore and manipulate his environment, overcoming his fear in doing so, and establishing confidence, rather than doubting his adequacy. Charles, the man and father, must face the conflict of middle age: Generativity versus Self-absorption. The individual's concern must extend beyond himself—to the next generation, to his family, or to future generations of society in general. Otherwise, he becomes overly concerned with his own physical, material, and emotional well-being.

The story suggests that Jim, the boy, is willing to face the challenge of his conflict, even though he is physically frail and emotionally sensitive. It is Charles who is having a difficult time. He seems to be overreacting with concern for his child. The psychologist must ask why he is doing this. One answer is that he is projecting his own fears about the playground onto his son. Going deeper, is it this playground which is actually so brutal, or does it remind him of the playgrounds of his youth which he feared as a child? Had he repressed his fear then into the depths of his unconscious only to have it loosened now as an adult by the repetition of the conflict, which he is reliving through his son? A learning theorist might suggest that there is "stimulus generalization" for Charles between the playgrounds of his youth and the playground in the story.

In trying to understand Charles, we must also take into consideration the recent death of his wife. Although his sister is helping to care for the child, Charles must feel intensely that now he must be both father and mother to the child. Also, he may unconsciously feel guilt and responsibility for his wife's death, and he may be "displacing" (changing the object of it) onto his son, making sure no injury comes to him.

Finally, we must ask whether Charles makes the correct decision for his son. On the one hand, playground battles might irreparably damage Jim physically, and more important, damage him emotionally, which would interfere with his later development. Since Jim is a sensitive child, he might remain fixated at this stage of development, retarding his ability to deal with later stages. The other side of the argument would state that Jim must take the risks of the playground if he is to learn how to deal with the outside world, both physically and emotionally. As Erikson suggests, this is the time of life when he must establish a sense of adequacy. Avoiding the problem now, rather than attempting to solve it, sets the stage for and models neurotic behavior rather than healthy, adaptive patterns.

THE PLAYGROUND   *Ray Bradbury*

A thousand times before and after his wife's death, Mr. Charles Underhill ignored the Playground on his way to and from his commuter's limited train. He neither liked nor disliked the Playground; he hardly knew it existed.

But only this morning his sister Carol, who had occupied the empty space across the breakfast table from him each day for six months, quietly broached the subject.

"Jim's almost three years old now," she said. "So tomorrow I'm going to start him at the Playground."

"Playground?" said Mr. Underhill.

At his office, he underlined a memorandum with black ink: *Look at Playground.*

That afternoon, the thunder of the train subsiding in his body, Underhill struck up through town on his usual path home, newspaper tucked crisply under his arm to prevent reading himself past the park. So it was, at five-ten in the late day, that he came to the cool iron fence and the open gate of the Playground, and stood for a long, long time, frozen there, gazing in at it all. . . .

At first there seemed absolutely nothing whatever to see. And then as he adjusted his attention outward from his usual interior monologue, the scene before him, a grey, blurred television image, came to a slow focus.

75

Primarily, he was aware of dim voices, faint underwater cries emerging from a series of vague streaks and zigzag lines and shadows. Then, as if someone had kicked the machine, screams jumped at him in full throat, visions leaped clear. Now he saw the children! They were dashing across the Playground meadow, fighting, pummeling, scratching, falling, every wound bleeding or about to bleed or freshly caked over. A dozen cats thrown among sleeping dogs could not have shrieked as loud! With incredible clarity, Mr. Underhill saw the tiniest cuts and scabs on knees and faces.

He weathered the first blast of sound, blinking. His nostrils took over when his eyes and ears retired in panic.

He sniffed the cutting odors of salve, raw adhesive, camphor, and pink Mercurochrome, so strong it lay bitter on his tongue. An iodine wind blew through the steel fence wires which glinted dully in the grey light of the overcast day. The rushing children were hell cut loose in a vast pinball table, a colliding, and banging, and totaling of hits and misses, thrusts and plungings to a grand and as yet unforeseen total of brutalities.

And was he mistaken or was the light within the Playground of a peculiar intensity? Every child seemed to possess four shadows: one dark, and three faint penumbras which made it strategically impossible to tell which way their swift bodies were racing until they bashed their targets. Yes, the oblique, pressing light made the Playground seem deep, far away, and remote from his touching. Or perhaps it was the hard steel wire fence, not unlike those barriers in zoos, beyond which *anything* might happen.

A pen of misery, thought Underhill. Why do children insist on making life horrible for each other? Oh, the continual torture. He heard himself sigh with immense relief. Thank God, childhood was over and done for him. No more pinchings, bruisings, senseless passions, and shattered dreams.

A gust of wind tore the paper from his hand. He ran after it down the Playground steps. Clutching the paper, he retreated hastily. For in that one brief instant, stranded in the Playground's atmosphere, he had felt his hat grow too large, his coat too cumbersome, his belt too loose, his shoes too big; he had left like a small boy playing businessman in his father's clothes; the gate behind him had loomed impossibly tall, while the sky pressed a huge weight of greyness at his eyes, and the scent of iodine, like a tiger's breath exhaled upon him, blew his hair. He tripped and almost fell, running back.

He stood outside the Playground, like someone who has just emerged, in shock, from a terrible cold sea.

"Hello, Charlie!"

He heard the voice and turned to see who had called him. There on top a metal slide, a boy of some nine years was waving. "Hello, Charlie . . . !"

Mr. Charles Underhill raised a hand. But I don't *know* that boy, he thought. And why should he call me by my first name?

The boy was smiling high in the misty air, and now, jostled by other yelling children, rushed shrieking down the slide.

Underhill stood bemused by what he saw. Now the Playground was an immense iron industry whose sole product was pain, sadism, and sorrow. If you watched half an hour there wasn't a face in the entire enclosure that didn't wince, cry, redden with anger, pale with fear, one moment or another. Really! Who said childhood was the best time of life? When in reality it was the most terrible, the most merciless era, the barbaric time when there were no police to protect you, only parents preoccupied with themselves and their taller world. No, if he had his way, he touched the cold fence with one hand, they'd nail a new sign here: TORQUEMADA'S GREEN.

And as for that boy, the one who had called out to him, who was he? There was something familiar there, perhaps in the hidden bones, an echo of some old friend; probably the son of a successfully ulcered father.

So this is the playground where my son will play, thought Mr. Underhill. So this is it.

Hanging his hat in the hall, checking his lean image in the watery mirror, Underhill felt wintry and tired. When his sister appeared, and his son came tapping on mouse-feet, he greeted them with something less than full attention. The boy clambered thinly over him, playing KING OF THE HILL. And the father, fixing his gaze to the end of the cigar he was slowly lighting, finally cleared his throat and said, "I've been thinking about that playground, Carol."

"I'm taking Jim over tomorrow."

"Not really? *That* playground?"

His mind rebelled. The smell and look of the place were still vivid. That writhing world with its atmosphere of cuts and beaten noses, the air as full of pain as a dentist's office, and those horrid

77

tic-tac-toes and frightening hopscotches under his feet as he picked up his newspaper, horrid and frightening for no reason he could see.

"What's wrong with *that* playground?" asked Carol.

"Have you seen it?" He paused in confusion. "Damn it, I mean, the children there. It's a Black Hole."

"All the children are from well-to-do families."

"Well, they shove and push like little Gestapos," said Underhill. "It'd be like sending a boy to a flour-mill to be crushed into meal by a couple of two-ton grinders! Every time I think of Jim playing in that barbaric pit, I freeze."

"You know very well it's the only convenient park for miles around."

"I don't care about that. All I care is I saw a dozen kinds of bats and clubs and air guns. By the end of the first day, Jim would be in splinters. They'd have him barbecued, with an orange in his mouth."

She was beginning to laugh. "How you exaggerate!"

"I'm serious!"

"You can't live Jim's life for him. He has to learn the hard way. He's got to take a little beating and beat others up; boys are like that."

"I don't *like* boys like that."

"It's the happiest time of life."

"Nonsense. I used to look back on childhood with great nostalgia. But now I realize I was a sentimental fool. It was nothing but screaming and running in a nightmare and coming home drenched with terror, from head to foot. If I could possibly save Jim from that, I would."

"That's impractical and, thank God, impossible."

"I won't have him near that place, I tell you. I'll have him grow up a neurotic recluse first."

"Charlie!"

"I will! Those little beasts, you should've seen them. Jim's my son, he is; he's not yours, remember." He felt the boy's thin legs about his shoulders, the boy's delicate fingers rumpling his hair. "I won't have him butchered."

"He'll get it in school. Better to let him take a little shoving about now, when he's three, so he's prepared for it."

"I've thought of that, too." Mr. Underhill held fiercely to his son's ankles which dangled like warm, thin sausages on either lapel. "I might even get a private tutor for him."

"Oh, Charles!"

They did not speak during dinner.

After dinner, he took Jim for a brief walk while his sister was washing the dishes. They strolled past the Playground under the dim street lamps. It was a cooling September night, with the first dry spice of autumn in it. Next week, and the children would be raked in off the fields like so many leaves and set to burning in the schools, using their fire and energy for more constructive purposes. But they would be here after school, ramming about, making projectiles of themselves, crashing and exploding, leaving wakes of misery behind every miniature war.

"Want to go in," said Jim, leaning against the high wire fence, watching the late-playing children beat each other and run.

"No, Jim, you don't want that."

"Play," said Jim, his eyes shinning with fascination, as he saw a large boy kick a small boy and the small boy kick a smaller boy to even things up.

"Play, daddy."

"Come along, Jim, you'll never get in that mess if *I* can help it." Underhill tugged the small arm firmly.

"I want to play." Jim was beginning to blubber now. His eyes were melting out of his face and his face was becoming a wrinkled orange of color.

Some of the children heard the crying and glanced over. Underhill had the terrible sense of watching a den of foxes suddenly startled and looking up from the white, hairy ruin of a dead rabbit. The mean yellow-glass eyes, the conical chins, the sharp white teeth, the dreadful wiry hair, the brambly sweaters, the iron-colored hands covered with a day's battle-stains. Their breath moved out to him, dark licorice and mint and juicy-fruit so sickeningly sweet, so combined as to twist his stomach. And over this the hot mustard smell of someone tolerating an early chest cold; the greasy stink of flesh smeared with hot camphorous salves cooking under a flannel sheath. All these cloying, and somehow depressing, odors of pencils, chalk, grass, and slateboard erasers, real or imagined, summoned old memory in an instant. Popcorn mortared their teeth, and green jelly showed in their sucking, blowing nostrils. God! God!

They saw Jim, and he was new to them. They said not a word, but as Jim cried louder and Underhill, by main force, dragged him like a cement bag along the walk, the children followed with their glowing eyes. Underhill felt like pushing his fist at them and crying, "You little beasts, you won't get *my* son!"

And then, with beautiful irrelevance, the boy at the top of the blue-metal slide, so high he seemed almost in a mist, far away, the boy with the somehow familiar face, called out to him, waving and waving.

"Hello, Charlie . . . !"

Underhill paused and Jim stopped crying.

"See you later, Charlie . . . !"

And the face of the boy way up there on that high and very lonely slide was suddenly like the face of Thomas Marshall, an old business friend who lived just around the block, but whom he hadn't seen in years.

"See you later, Charlie."

Later, later? What did the fool boy mean?

"I know *you*, Charlie!" called the boy. "Hi!"

"What?" gasped Underhill.

"Tomorrow night, Charlie, hey!" And the boy fell off the slide and lay choking for breath, face like a white cheese from the fall, while children jumped him and tumbled over.

Underhill stood undecided for five seconds or more, until Jim thought to cry again and then, with the golden fox eyes upon them, in the first chill of autumn, he dragged Jim all the way home.

The next afternoon Mr. Underhill finished at the office early and took the three o'clock train, arriving out in Green Town at three-twenty-five, in plenty of time to drink in the brisk rays of the autumnal sun. Strange how one day it is suddenly autumn, he thought. One day it is summer and the next, how could you measure or tell it? Something about the temperature or the smell: Or the sediment of age knocked loose from your bones during the night and circulating in your blood and heart, giving you a slight tremble and a chill? A year older, a year dying, was *that* it?

He walked up toward the Playground, planning the future. It seemed you did more planning in autumn than any other season. This had to do with dying, perhaps. You thought of death and you automatically planned. Well, then, there was to be a tutor for Jim, *that* was positive; none of those horrible schools for him. It would pinch the bank account a bit, but Jim would at least grow up a happy boy. They would pick and choose his friends. Any slambang bullies would be thrown out as soon as they so much as touched Jim. And as for this Playground? Completely out of the question!

"Oh hello, Charles."

He looked up suddenly. Before him, at the entrance to the wire enclosure, stood his sister. He noted instantly that she called him Charles, instead of Charlie. Last night's unpleasantness had not quite evaporated. "Carol, what're you doing *here?*"

She flushed guiltily and glanced in through the fence.

"You didn't," he said.

His eyes sought among the scrabbling, running, screaming children. "Do you mean to say . . . ?"

His sister nodded, half amused. "I thought I'd bring him early—"

"Before I got home, so I wouldn't know, is *that* it?"

"That was it."

"Good God, Carol, where *is* he?"

"I just came to see."

"You mean you left him there all afternoon?"

"Just for five minutes while I shopped."

"And you *left* him. Good God!" Underhill seized her wrist. "Well, come on, find him, get him out of there!"

They peered in together past the wire to where a dozen boys charged about, girls slapped each other, and a squabbling heap of children took turns at getting off, making a quick run, and crashing one against another.

"That's where he is, I *know* it!" said Underhill.

Just then, across the field, sobbing and wailing, Jim ran, six boys after him. He fell, got up, ran, fell again, shrieking, and the boys behind shot beans through metal blowers.

"I'll stuff those blowers up their noses!" said Underhill. "Run, Jim! Run!"

Jim made it to the gate. Underhill caught him. It was like catching a rumpled, drenched wad of material. Jim's nose was bleeding, his pants were ripped, he was covered with grime.

"*There's* your playground," said Underhill, on his knees, staring up from his son, holding him, at his sister. "*There* are your sweet, happy innocents, your well-to-do, piddling Fascists. Let me catch this boy there again and there'll be hell to pay. Come on, Jim. All right, you little bastards, get back there!" he shouted.

"We didn't do nothing," said the children.

"What's the world coming to?" Mr. Underhill questioned the universe.

"Hi! Charlie!" said the strange boy, standing to one side. He waved casually and smiled.

"Who's that?" asked Carol.

"How in hell do *I* know?" said Underhill.

"Be seeing you, Charlie. So long," called the boy, fading off.

Mr. Underhill marched his sister and his son home.

"Take your hand off my elbow!" said Carol.

He was trembling; absolutely, continually trembling with rage when he got to bed. He had tried some coffee, but nothing stopped it. He wanted to beat their pulpy little brains out, those gross Cruickshank children; yes, that phrase fit them, those fox-fiend, melancholy Cruickshank children, with all the guile and poison and slyness in their cold faces. In the name of all that was decent, what manner of child was this new generation! A bunch of cutters and hangers and bangers, a drove of bleeding, moronic thumb-screwers, with the sewage of neglect running in their veins? He lay violently jerking his head from one side of his hot pillow to the other, and at last got up and lit a cigarette, but it wasn't enough. He and Carol had had a huge battle when they got home. He had yelled at her and she had yelled back, peacock and peahen shrieking in a wilderness where law and order were insanities laughed at and quite forgotten.

He was ashamed. You didn't fight violence with violence, not if you were a gentleman. You talked very calmly. But Carol didn't give you a chance, damn it! She wanted the boy put in a vise and squashed. She wanted him reamed and punctured and given the laying-on-of-hands. To be beaten from playground to kindergarten, to grammar school, to junior high, to high school. If he was lucky, in high school, the beatings and sadisms would refine themselves, the sea of blood and spittle would drain back down the shore of years and Jim would be left upon the edge of maturity, with God knows what outlook to the future, with a desire, perhaps, to be a wolf among wolves, a dog among dogs, a fiend among fiends. But there was enough of that in the world, already. The very thought of the next ten or fifteen years of torture was enough to make Mr. Underhill cringe; he felt his own flesh impaled with b-b shot, stung, burned, fisted, scrounged, twisted, violated, and bruised. He quivered, like a jellyfish hurled violently into a concrete mixer. Jim would never survive it. Jim was too delicate for this horror.

Underhill walked in the midnight rooms of his house thinking of all this, of himself, of the son, the Playground, the fear; there was no part of it he did not touch and turn over with his mind. How much, he asked himself, how much of this is being alone, how much due to Ann's dying, how much to my need, and how much is the reality of the Playground itself, and the children? How much rational and how much nonsense? He twitched the delicate weights upon the scale and watched the indicator glide and fix and glide again, back and forth, softly, between midnight and dawn, between black and white, between raw sanity and naked insanity. He should not hold so tight, he should let his hands drop away from the boy. And yet—there was no hour that looking into Jim's small face he did not see Ann there, in the eyes, in the mouth, in the turn of the nostrils, in the warm breathing, in the glow of blood moving just under the thin shell of flesh. I have a right, he thought, to be afraid. I have every right. When you have two precious bits of porcelain and one is broken and the other, the last one, remains, where can you find the time to be objective, to be immensely calm, to be anything else but concerned?

No, he thought, walking slowly, in the hall, there seems to be nothing I can do except go on being afraid and being afraid of being afraid.

"You needn't prowl the house all night," his sister called from her bed, as she heard him pass her open door. "You needn't be childish. I'm sorry if I seem dictatorial or cold. But you've got to make up your mind. Jim simply cannot have a private tutor. Ann would have wanted him to go to a regular school. And he's got to go back to that playground tomorrow and keep going back until he's learned to stand on his own two feet and until he's familiar to all the children; then they won't pick on him so much."

Underhill said nothing. He got dressed quietly in the dark and, downstairs, opened the front door. It was about five minutes to midnight as he walked swiftly down the street in the shadows of the tall elms and oaks and maples, trying to outdistance his rage and outrage. He knew Carol was right, of course. This was the world, you lived in it, you accepted it. But that was the very trouble! He had been through the mill already, he knew what it was to be a boy among lions, his own childhood had come rushing back to him in the last few hours, a time of terror and violence, and now he could not bear to think of Jim's going through it all, those long years, especially if you were a delicate child, through no fault of your own, your bones thin, your face pale, what could you expect but to be harried and chased?

He stopped by the Playground, which was still lit by one great overhead lamp. The gate was locked for the night, but that one light remained on until twelve. He wanted to tear the contemptible place down, rip up the steel fences, obliterate the slides, and say to the children, "Go home! Play in your backyards!"

How ingenious, the cold, deep playground. You never knew where anyone lived. The boy who knocked your teeth out, who was

83

he? Nobody knew. Where did he live? Nobody knew. How to find him? Nobody knew. Why, you could come here one day, beat the living tar out of some smaller child, and run on the next day to some *other* playground. They would never find you. From playground to playground, you could take your criminal tricks, with everyone forgetting you, since they never knew you. You could return to this playground a month later, and if the little child whose teeth you knocked out was there and recognized you, you could deny it. "No, I'm not the one. Must be some other kid. This is my first time here! No, not me!" And when his back is turned, knock him over. And run off down nameless streets, a nameless person.

What can I possibly do? thought Underhill. Carol's been more than generous with her time; she's been good for Jim, no doubt of it. A lot of the love she would have put into a marriage has gone to him this year. I can't fight her forever on this, and I can't tell her to leave. Perhaps moving to the country might help. No, no, impossible; the money. But I can't leave Jim here, either.

"Hello, Charlie," said a quiet voice.

Underhill snapped about. Inside the Playground fence, seated in the dirt, making diagrams with one finger in the cool dust, was the solemn nine-year-old boy. He didn't glance up. He said "Hello, Charlie," just sitting there, easily, in that world beyond the hard steel fence.

Underhill said, "How do you know my name?"

"I know it." The boy crossed his legs, comfortably, smiling quietly. "You're having lots of trouble."

"How'd you get in there so late? Who are you?"

"My name's Marshall."

"Of course! Tom Marshall's son, Tommy! I *thought* you looked familiar."

"More familiar than you think." The boy laughed gently.

"How's your father, Tommy?"

"Have you seen him lately?" the boy asked.

"On the street, briefly, two months ago."

"How did he look?"

"What?"

"How did Mr. Marshall *look?*" asked the boy. It seemed strange he refused to say "my father."

"He looked all right. Why?"

"I guess he's happy," said the boy. Mr. Underhill saw the boy's arms and legs and they were covered with scabs and scratches.

"Aren't you going home, Tommy?"

"I sneaked out to see you. I just knew you'd come. You're afraid."

Mr. Underhill didn't know what to say.

"Those little monsters," he said at last.

"Maybe I can help you." The boy made a dust triangle.

It was ridiculous. "How?"

"You'd give anything, wouldn't you, if you could spare Jim all this? You'd trade places with him if you could?"

Mr. Underhill nodded, frozen.

"Well, you come down here tomorrow afternoon at four. Then I can help you."

"How do you mean, help?"

"I can't tell you outright," said the boy. "It has to do with the Playground. Any place where there's lots of evil, that makes power. You can feel it, can't you?"

A kind of warm wind stirred off the bare field under the one high light. Underhill shivered. Yes, even now, at midnight, the Playground seemed evil, for it was used for evil things. "Are all playgrounds like this?"

"Some. Maybe this is the only one like this. Maybe it's just how *you* look at it, Charlie. Things are what you *want* them to be. A lot of people think this is a *swell* playground. They're right, too. It's how you look at it, maybe. What I wanted to say, though, is that Tom Marshall was like you. He worried about Tommy Marshall and the Playground and the kids. too. He wanted to save Tommy the trouble and the hurt, also."

This business of talking about people as if they were remote made Mr. Underhill uncomfortable.

"So we made a bargain," said the boy.

"Who with?"

"With the Playground, I guess, or whoever runs it."

"Who runs it?"

"I've never seen him. There's an office over there under the grandstand. A light burns in it all night. It's a bright, blue light, kind of funny. There's a desk there with no papers in it and an empty chair. The sign says *Manager*, but nobody ever sees the man."

"He must be around."

"That's right," said the boy. "Or I wouldn't be where I am, and someone else wouldn't be where they are."

"You certainly talk grownup."

The boy was pleased. "Do you want to know who I really am? I'm not Tommy Marshall at all. I'm Tom Marshall, the father." He sat there in the dust, not moving, late at night, under the high and faraway light, with the late wind blowing his shirt collar gently under his chin, blowing the cool dust. "I'm Tom Marshall, the father. I know it'll be hard for you to believe. But it *is* true. I was afraid for Tommy. I was the way you are now about Jim. So I made this deal with the Playground. Oh, there are others who did the same, here. If you look close, you'll see them among the other children, by the expression in their eyes."

Underhill blinked. "You'd better run home to bed."

"You want to believe me. You want it to be true. I saw your eyes just then! If you could trade places with Jim, you would. You'd like to save him all that torture, let him be in your place, grownup, the real work over and done."

"Any decent parent sympathizes with his children."

"You, more than most. You feel every bite and kick. Well, you come here tomorrow. You can make a deal, too."

"Trade places?" It was an incredible, an amusing, but an oddly satisfying thought. "What would I have to do?"

"Just make up your mind."

Underhill tried to make his next question sound very casual, a joke, but his mind was in a rage again. "What would I pay?"

"Nothing. You'd just have to play in the Playground."

"All day?"

"And go to school, of course."

"And grow up again?"

"Yes, and grow up again. Be here at four tomorrow afternoon."

"I have to work in the city tomorrow."

"Tomorrow," said the boy.

"You'd better get home to bed, Tommy."

"My name is *Tom* Marshall." The boy sat there.

The Playground lights went out.

Mr. Underhill and his sister did not speak at breakfast. He usually phoned her at noon to chat about this or that, but he did not phone. But at one-thirty, after a bad lunch, he dialed the house number. When Carol answered he hung up. Five minutes later he phoned again.

"Charlie, was that you who called five minutes ago?"

"Yes," he said.

"I thought I heard you breathing before you hung up. What'd you call about, dear?" She was being sensible again.

"Oh, just called."

"It's been a bad two days, hasn't it? You *do* see what I mean, don't you, Charlie? Jim *must* go to the Playground and get a few knocks."

"A few knocks, yes."

He saw the blood and the hungry foxes and the torn rabbits.

"And learn to give and take," she was saying, "and fight if he has to."

"Fight if he has to," he murmured.

"I knew you'd come around."

"Around," he said. "You're right. No way out. He must be sacrificed."

"Oh, Charlie, you *are* odd."

He cleared his throat. "Well, that's settled."

"Yes."

I wonder what it would be like, he thought.

"Everything else okay?" he asked the phone.

He thought of the diagrams in the dust, the boy seated there with the hidden bones in his face.

"Yes," she said.

"I've been thinking," he said.

"Speak up."

"I'll be home at three," he said, slowly, piecing out the words like a man hit in the stomach, gasping for breath. "We'll take a walk, you and Jim and I," he said, eyes shut.

"Wonderful!"

"To the Playground," he said and hung up.

It was really autumn now, the real chill, the real snap; overnight the trees burnt red and snapped free of their leaves, which spiraled about Mr. Underhill's face as he walked up the front steps, and there were Carol and Jim, bundled up against the sharp wind, waiting for him.

"Hello!" they cried to one another, with much embracing and kissing. "There's Jim down here!" "There's Daddy up there!" They laughed and he felt paralyzed and in terror of the late day. It was almost four. He looked at the leaden sky, which might pour down molten silver any moment, a sky of lava and soot and a wet wind blowing out of it. He held his sister's arm very tightly as they walked. "Aren't you friendly, though?" She smiled.

"It's ridiculous, of course," he said, thinking of something else. "What?"

They were at the Playground gate.

"Hello, Charlie. Hi!" Far away, atop the monstrous slide stood the Marshall boy, waving, not smiling now.

"You wait here," said Mr. Underhill to his sister. "I'll be only a moment. I'll just take Jim in."

"All right."

He grasped the small boy's hand. "Here we go, Jim. Stick close to Daddy."

They stepped down the hard concrete steps and stood in the flat dust. Before them, in a magical sequence, stood the diagrams, the gigantic tic-tac-toes, the monstrous hop-scotches, the amazing numerals and triangles and oblongs the children had scrabbled in the incredible dust.

The sky blew a huge wind upon him and he was shivering. He grasped the little boy's hand still tighter and turned to his sister. "Goodbye," he said. For he was believing it. He was in the Playground and believing it, and it was for the best. Nothing too good for Jim. Nothing at all in this outrageous world! And now his sister was laughing back at him, "Charlie, you idiot!"

Then they were running, running across the dirt Playground floor, at the bottom of a stony sea that pressed and blew upon them. Now Jim was crying, "Daddy, Daddy!" and the children racing to meet them, the boy on the slide yelling, the tic-tac-toe and hop-scotches whirling, a sense of bodiless terror gripping him, but he knew what he must do and what must be done and what would happen. Far across the field footballs sailed, baseballs whizzed, bats flew, fists flashed up, and the door of the Manager's office stood open, the desk empty, the seat empty, a lone light burning over it.

Underhill stumbled, shut his eyes and fell, crying out, his body clenched by a hot pain, mouthing strange words, everything in turmoil.

"There you are, Jim," said a voice.

And he was climbing, climbing, eyes closed, climbing metal-ringing ladder rungs, screaming, wailing, his throat raw.

Mr. Underhill opened his eyes.

He was on top of the slide. The gigantic, blue metal slide which seemed ten thousand feet high. Children crushed at his back, children beat him to go on, slide! slide!

And he looked, and there, going off across the field, was a man in a black overcoat. And there, at the gate, was a woman waving and the man standing there with the woman, both of them looking in at him, waving, and their voices calling, "Have a good time! Have a good time, Jim!"

He screamed. He looked at his hands, in a panic of realization. The small hands, the thin hands. He looked at the earth far below. He felt his nose bleeding and there was the Marshall boy next to him. "Hi!" cried the other, and bashed him in the mouth. "Only twelve years here!" cried the other in the uproar.

Twelve years! thought Mr. Underhill, trapped. And time is different to children. A year is like ten years. No, not twelve years of childhood ahead of him, but a century, a century of *this*.

"Slide!"

Behind him the stink of Musterole, Vick's Vaporub, peanuts, chewed hot tar, spearmint gum and blue fountain-pen ink, the smell of kite-twine and glycerin soap, a pumpkin smell of Hallowe'en and a papier-mâché fragrance of skull masks, and the smell of dry scabs, as he was pinched, pummeled, shoved. Fists rose and fell, he saw the fox faces and beyond, at the fence, the man and woman standing there, waving. He shrieked, he covered his face, he felt himself pushed, bleeding, to the rim of nothingness. Headfirst, he careened down the slide, screeching, with ten thousand monsters behind. One thought jumped through his mind a moment before he hit bottom in a nauseous mound of claws.

This is hell, he thought, *this is hell*!

And no one in the hot, milling heap contradicted him.

2

PSYCHOBIOLOGY

Psychobiology is the branch of experimental psychology which studies physical structure, function, and biochemistry as they relate to behavior. Investigators seek answers to questions about how the physical systems of humans and other organisms help determine their behavior. How do physical and psychological survival depend upon each other? How does impairment of physiological, neurological, or genetic structure limit an organism's psychological functioning? How does depriving an individual of his physical needs affect his behavior? In summary, how does the basic physiological nature of the animal determine what it can and cannot do?

While primary interest is on the human organism, research involves the observation of animals on all levels on the evolutionary scale. Animals as simple as flatworms and sponges, as moderately complex as rats, cats, and dogs, and as complicated as apes have been observed. While these animals are sometimes studied in their own right, they are basically employed to help investigate questions relating to human systems, when ethical considerations do not allow experimental procedures to use human subjects. Methods are often technical and quasi-medical. For example, parts of the brains of various organisms have been surgically removed or electrically stimulated in order to observe consequent changes in behavior. Deprivation and other alterations of nutrition have been employed to study effects on vital motivational systems like hunger and thirst. Endocrine extracts, hormones, and other biochemical substances have been systematically varied to analyze subsequent changes in areas like sexual behavior, sleep patterns, and attentiveness.

Man is an animal with an evolutionary history spanning millions of years. The first life forms on our planet were simple, single-celled organisms. Multicellular organisms with specialized cells followed. Evolutionary development has been in the direction of complexity and diversity, with survival of those life forms which were able to adapt to new conditions.

When a man is born, he brings with him a genetic inheritance from the human species. Within this species inheritance, however, are individual variations which are also transmitted genetically from generation to generation. With the monumental breakthrough in the study of genetic transmission recently reported by researchers investigating the roles of DNA and RNA, the field of behavioral genetics has become an increasingly important area of psychobiology. In our modern age, nuclear weapons and "wonder" drugs like thalidomide produce unexpected genetic mutations, and their effects on development and behavior remain a problem to be studied. Moreover, with the promise in the not so distant future of cloning and the selective breeding of eugenics, behavioral genetics will most certainly be an important field of psychology.

As we noted, man receives a species and an individual inheritance which have a part in determining his behavior. But his environment—or nurture—also influences his behavior. Which contribution—nature or nurture—is more influential has been a long-standing controversy. It pervades the field of psychology, from problems of intelligence testing to the causes of schizophrenia.

Within the field of psychobiology, another area of major

interest is the study of brain physiology and its relationship to behavioral function. Although much has been learned, many doors remain to be opened. It is known that the convoluted outer layer of the brain, the *cerebrum*, controls sensory and movement function, and due to its vast associational area, basically it is responsible for man's strong intellectual superiority over lower animals. The *cerebellum*, smaller and located under the cerebrum to the rear, controls balance and coordination; the *medulla*, in the inner stem of the brain on top of the spinal cord, controls vital functions like heartbeat, breathing, and digestion.

Recently the great importance of other parts of the brainstem has been recognized. The *reticular formation*, on the brainstem above the medulla, is now known to play the brain's most vital role in controlling sleep, waking and general arousal, while the *hypothalamus*, a small egg-shaped body just above the reticular formation, has been shown to help determine functions like hunger, thirst, and emotional behavior. Still to be thoroughly understood is the overall effect of the *limbic system*, a series of small bodies also located in the brainstem area.

The nerve cell or *neuron*, the basic material of the brain and the rest of the nervous system, has also been studied at great length. Somewhat resembling a maple leaf, a neuron is comprised of a cell body with antennaelike extensions called *dendrites*, and a long stemlike structure called the *axon*. Each neuron transmits impulses from its dendrite to axon, meeting—although not touching—the next neuron at a synapse, triggering this next neuron to fire by depositing chemicals on its dendrites. Actual nerves consist of thousands of neurons combined like cables. Basically, they serve three functions: (1) transmitting messages to the brain (afferent nerve fibers); (2) transmitting messages within the brain (connectors); and (3) transmitting messages from the brain to the muscles (efferent nerve fibers).

Closely allied to the neurological system in regulating behavior is another system. This system is biochemical in nature and controlled by the endocrine glands. The important role of the pituitary gland in regulating bodily growth is well documented, as is the role of the thyroid in regulating body metabolism, body growth, and intellectual development. Everybody knows what it means to "get our adrenalin flowing," but research has shown how

93

complex and delicate the play and counterplay of adrenal gland secretions actually are. Delicacy might also characterize the role of insulin in regulating the body's sugar consumption, and let us not forget the gonads or sex glands, which have an enormous effect on growth and behavior.

Psychobiology is an area where psychology overlaps and interacts with many areas of biological science: physiology, neurology, embryology, and genetics. The result is a dynamic field, with much research, new discovery, and change.

flowers for algernon

Daniel Keyes

In this famous story we meet an unusual man, Charlie Gordon, and a precocious mouse, Algernon. Author Daniel Keyes employs a technique known as epistolary fiction which was used by Samuel Richardson in 1740 in *Pamela*, usually regarded as the first English novel. We come to know Charlie Gordon and what happens to him through a series of reports he writes. The epistolary technique is a powerful one, giving us a sense of immediacy as we observe Charlie's tragedy. In this science fiction world, as Charlie experiences radical changes in his mental capacity, we can follow the alterations in intelligence levels which he undergoes through the content, sentence patterns, and spelling in his reports.

As psychologists we are interested in both the behavioral consequences of these alterations and Charlie's feelings about what his experience is like. In a broader sense we are interested in the alterations of many areas of Charlie's behavior—physical, mental, and emotional behavior—all illustrating the pervasive and overriding influence the brain has on many aspects of the functioning of a human being.

As the story begins, Charlie, at age 37, has an I.Q. of 68. He works in a factory where, among other jobs, he cleans toilets. His stupidity makes him the brunt of all the office jokes. Miss Kinnian, an instructor at a night school Charlie attends, recommends him—because of his intense desire to learn—as the subject for an experiment a psychologist and a neurosurgeon are conducting. Drs. Strauss and Nemur have, through brain surgery, tripled the intelligence of a mouse named Algernon. When Charlie competes against Algernon in tests, the mouse always wins.

Because Charlie is highly motivated to become intelligent, he agrees to submit to the same surgery that made Algernon brilliant.

95

The operation takes place on March 10, and as Charlie reports in his journal, "The operashun dint hurt." He dreams of the day when, as the doctors have promised, he will be smart enough to beat Algernon in the tests and races.

His progress is dramatic. On April 6 he reports, "I beat Algernon! I dint even know I beat him until Burt the tester told me. Then the second time I lost because I got so excited I fell off the chair before I finished. But after that I beat him eight more times. I must be getting smart to beat a smart mouse like Algernon. But I don't *feel* smarter."

Charlie is exposed to a crash learning course. As his mental capacity increases, on April 21 he reports that his I.Q. will soon be over 200. He learns foreign languages, history, mathematics; he has an insatiable appetite for learning. His awareness of the world around him expands and changes. He begins research on a study: the calculus of intelligence.

As the experiment progresses, Charlie develops a great fondness for Algernon; he and the mouse have shared the same experience. When one day the mouse turns on Charlie and bites his hand as he is being fondled, the wound is symbolic in its foreshadowing of the action which is to follow. Algernon experiences a reversal in the growth of his intelligence. His motivation and eating habits change. As he regresses mentally, his motor activity is impaired. Impairment of glandular activity, loss of coordination, and progressive amnesia follow. When Algernon dies, we learn of the actual brain deterioration: a smoothing out of the brain's convolutions (the more the convolutions, the better and more intelligent the functioning) and a broadening of the brain's fissures, suggesting more difficulty in maintaining connections and, therefore, associations between different areas of the brain which might be separated by fissures.

Charlie is intelligent and perceptive enough to immediately raise the question: Will the same thing happen to me? Will my brain deteriorate? Charlie gives that answer to us in his progress reports for the next three months.

Science fiction is a relatively new fictional form, rooted in the writings of H. G. Wells and Jules Verne in the late nineteenth and early twentieth century and coming to full flower after World War II.

As is true of any new form, there have been many poor science fiction stories written, but, increasingly, very good ones are appearing as science fiction gains maturity. One of the charges made against science fiction is that it is weak in character development, that we never meet rounded, multidimensional characters as we do in mainstream fiction. "Flowers for Algernon" refutes that accusation. With great economy, author Daniel Keyes has created Charlie, one of the most memorable characters in science fiction.

As the story ends, Charlie—a little like St. Francis of Assisi in loving simple living things—requests, "Please if you get a chanse put some flowrs on Algernons grave in the bak yard. . . ."

And he imparts some simple wisdom to us smart folks. Appreciate the good feeling of knowing things and being smart; it's uncomfortable not to understand. Then, Charlie suggests in his simplicity that humility—letting people laugh at you and perhaps being able to laugh at yourself—might serve us all well in being the friendly, pleasant person that he is. At the end one cannot help but love Charlie, and maybe that is what we all really want anyway: to be loved.

FLOWERS FOR ALGERNON   *Daniel Keyes*

progris riport 1—martch 5, 1965

Dr. Strauss says I shud rite down what I think and evrey thing that happins to me from now on. I dont know why but he says its importint so they will see if they will use me. I hope they use me. Miss Kinnian says maybe they can make me smart. I want to be smart. My name is Charlie Gordon. I am 37 years old. I have nuthing more to rite now so I will close for today.

progris riport 2—martch 6

I had a test today. I think I faled it. And I think maybe now they wont use me. What happind is a nice young man was in the room and he had some white cards and ink spillled all over them. He sed Charlie what do yo see on this card. I was very skared even tho I had my rabits foot in my pockit because when I was a kid I always faled tests in school and I spillled ink to.

I told him I saw a inkblot. He said yes and it made me feel good. I thot that was all but when I got up to go he said Charlie we are not thru yet. Then I dont remember so good but he wantid me to say what was in the ink. I dint see nuthing in the ink but he said there was picturs there other pepul saw some picturs. I couldnt see any picturs. I reely tryed. I held the card close up and then far away. Then I said if I had my glases I coud see better I usally only ware my glases in the movies or TV but I said they are in the closit in the hall. I got them. Then I said let me see that card agen I bet Ill find it now.

I tryed hard but I only saw the ink. I told him maybe I need new glases. He rote something down on a paper and I got skared of faling the test. I told him it was a very nice inkblot with littel points all around the edges. He looked very sad so that wasnt it. I said please let me try agen. Ill get it in a few minits becaus Im not so fast sometimes. Im a slow reeder too in Miss Kinnians class for slow adults but I'm trying very hard.

He gave me a chance with another card that had 2 kinds of ink spilled on it red and blue.

He was very nice and talked slow like Miss Kinnian does and he explaned it to me that it was a *raw shok*. He said pepul see things in the ink. I said show me where. He said think. I told him I think a inkblot but that wasn't rite eather. He said what does it remind you—pretend something. I closed my eyes for a long time to pretend. I told him I pretend a fowntan pen with ink leeking all over a table cloth.

I don't think I passed the *raw shok* test

progris riport 3—martch 7

Dr Strauss and Dr Nemur say it dont matter about the inkblots. They said that maybe they will still use me. I said Miss Kinnian never gave me tests like that one only spelling and reading. They said Miss Kinnian told that I was her bestist pupil in the adult nite school becaus I tryed the hardist and I reely wantid to lern. They said how come you went to the adult nite scool all by yourself Charlie. How did you find it. I said I asked pepul and sumbody told me where I shud go to lern to read and spell good. They said why did you want to. I told them becaus all my life I wantid to be smart and not dumb. But its very hard to be smart. They said you know it will probly be tempirery. I said yes. Miss Kinnian told me. I dont care if it herts.

Later I had more crazy tests today. The nice lady who gave it to me told me the name and I asked her how do you spellit so I can rite it my progris riport. THEMATIC APPERCEPTION TEST. I dont know the frist 2 words but I know what *test* means. You got to pass it or you get bad marks. This test lookd easy becaus I could see the picturs. Only this time she dint want me to tell her the picturs. That mixd me up. She said make up storys about the pepul in the picturs.

I told her how can you tell storys about pepul you never met. I said why shud I make up lies. I never tell lies any more becaus I always get caut.

She told me this test and the other one the raw-shok was for getting personality. I laffed so hard. I said how can you get that thing from inkblots and fotos. She got sore and put her picturs away. I don't care. It was sily. I gess I faled that test too.

Later some men in white coats took me to a difernt part of the hospitil and gave me a game to play. It was like a race with a white mouse. They called the mouse Algernon. Algernon was in a box with a lot of twists and turns like all kinds of walls and they gave me a pencil and a paper with lines and lots of boxes. On one side it said START and on the other end it said FINISH. They said it was *amazed* and that Algernon and me had the same *amazed* to do. I dint see how we could have the same *amazed* if Algernon had a box and I had a paper but I dint say nothing. Anyway there wasnt time because the race started.

One of the men had a watch he was trying to hide so I wouldnt see it so I tryed not to look and that made me nervus.

Anyway that test made me feel worser than all the others because they did it over 10 times with different *amazeds* and Algernon won every time. I dint know that mice were so smart. Maybe thats because Algernon is a white mouse. Maybe white mice are smarter than other mice.

progris riport 4—Mar 8

Their going to use me! Im so excited I can hardly write. Dr Nemur and Dr Strauss had a argament about it first. Dr Nemur was in the office when Dr Strauss brot me in. Dr Nemur was worryed about using me but Dr Strauss told him Miss Kinnian rekemmended me the best from all the people who she was teaching. I like Miss Kinnian becaus shes a very smart teacher. And she said Charlie your going to have a second chance. If you volunteer for this experament you mite get smart. They dont know if it will be perminint but theirs a chance. Thats why I said ok even when I was scared because she said it was an operashun. She said dont be scared Charlie you done so much with so little I think you deserv it most of all.

So I got scaird when Dr. Nemur and Dr. Strauss argud about it. Dr. Strauss said I had something that was very good. He said I had a good *motorvation*. I never even knew I had that. I felt proud when he said that not every body with an eye-q of 68 had that thing. I dant know what it is or where I got it but he said Algernon had it too. Algernons *motor-vation* is the cheese they put in his box. But it cant be that because I didn't eat any cheese this week.

Then he told Dr Nemur something I dint understand so while they were talking I wrote down some of the words.

He said Dr. Nemur I know Charlie is not what you had in mind as the first of your new brede of intelek** (couldnt get the word) superman. But most people of his low ment** are host** and uncoop** they are usually dull apath** and hard to reach. He has a good natcher hes intristed and eager to please.

Dr Nemur said remember he will be the first human beeng ever to have his intelijence tripled by surgicle meens.

Dr. Strauss said exakly. Look at how well hes lerned to read and write for his low mentel age its as grate an acheve** as you and I lerning einstines therey of **vity without help. That shows the inteness motor-vation. Its comparat** a tremen** achev** I say we use Charlie.

I dint get all the words but it sounded like Dr Strauss was on my side and like the other one wasnt.

Then Dr Nemur nodded he said all right maybe your right. We will use Charlie. When he said that I got so exited I jumped up and shook his hand for being so good to me. I told him thank you doc you wont be sorry for giving me a second chance. And I mean it like I told him. After the operashun Im gonna try to be smart. Im gonna try awful hard.

progris riport 5—Mar 10

Im skared. Lots of the nurses and the people who gave me the tests came to bring me candy and wish me luck. I hope I have luck. I got my rabits foot and my lucky penny. Only a black cat crossed me when I was comming to the hospitil. Dr Strauss says dont be supersitis Charlie this is science. Anyway Im keeping my rabits foot with me.

I asked Dr Strauss if Ill beat Algernon in the race after the operashun and he said maybe. If the operashun works Ill show that mouse I can be as smart as he is. Maybe smarter. Then Ill be abel to read better and spell the words good and know lots of things and be like other people. I want to be smart like other people. If it works perminint they will make everybody smart all over the wurld.

They dint give me anything to eat this morning. I dont know what that eating has to do with getting smart. Im very hungry and Dr. Nemur took away my box of candy. That Dr Nemur is a grouch. Dr Strauss says I can have it back after the operashun. You cant eat befor a operashun. . . .

progress report 6—Mar 15

The operashun dint hurt. He did it while I was sleeping. They took off the bandijis from my head today so I can make a PROG-RESS REPORT. Dr. Nemur who looked at some of my other ones says I spell PROGRESS wrong and told me how to spell it and REPORT too. I got to try and remember that.

I have a very bad memary for spelling. Dr Strauss says its ok to tell about all the things that happin to me but he says I should tell more about what I feel and what I think. When I told him I dont know how to think he said try. All the time when the bandijis were on my eyes I tryed to think. Nothing happened. I dont know what to think about. Maybe if I ask him he will tell me how I can think now that Im supposed to get smart. What do smart people think about. Fancy things I suppose. I wish I knew some fancy things alredy.

progress report 7—mar 19

Nothing is happining. I had lots of tests and different kinds of races with Algernon. I hate that mouse. He always beats me. Dr. Strauss said I got to play those games. And he said some time I got to take those tests over again. Those inkblots are stupid. And those pictures are stupid too. I like to draw a picture of a man and a woman but I wont make up lies about people.

I got a headache from trying to think so much. I thot Dr Strauss was my frend but he dont help me. He dont tell me what to think or when Ill get smart. Miss Kinnian dint come to see me. I think writing these progress reports are stupid too.

progress report 8—Mar 23

Im going back to work at the factory. They said it was better I shud go back to work but I cant tell anyone what the operashun was for and I have to come to the hospitil for an hour evry night after work. They are gonna pay me mony every month for learning to be smart.

Im glad Im going back to work because I miss my job and all my frends and all the fun we have there.

Dr Strauss says I shud keep writing things down but I dont have to do it every day just when I think of something or something speshul happins. He says dont get discoridged because it takes time and it happins slow. He says it took a long time with Algernon before he got 3 times smarter than he was before. Thats why Algernon beats me all the time because he had that operashun too. That makes me feel better. I coud probly do that *amazed* faster than a reglar mouse. Maybe some day Ill beat him. That would be something. So far Algernon looks smart perminent.

Mar 25 (I dont have to write PROGRESS REPORT on top any more just when I hand it in once a week for Dr Nemur. I just have to put the date on. That saves time)

We had a lot of fun at the factory today. Joe Carp said hey look where Charlie had his operashun what did they do Charlie put some brains in. I was going to tell him but I remembered Dr Strauss said no. Then Frank Reilly said what did you do Charlie forget your key and open your door the hard way. That made me laff. Their really my friends and they like me.

Sometimes somebody will say hey look at Joe or Frank or George he really pulled a Charlie Gordon. I dont know why they say that but they always laff. This morning Amos Borg who is the 4 man at Donnegans used my name when he shouted at Ernie the office boy. Ernie lost a packige. He said Ernie for godsake what are you trying to be a Charlie Gordon. I dont understand why he said that.

Mar 28 Dr Strauss came to my room tonight to see why I dint come in like I was suppose to. I told him I dont like to race with Algernon any more. He said I dont have to for a while but I shud come in. He had a present for me. I thot it was a little television but it wasnt. He said I got to turn it on when I go to sleep. I said your kidding why shud I turn it on when Im going to sleep. Who ever herd of a thing like that. But he said if I want to get smart I got to do what he says. I told him I dint think I was going to get smart and he puts his hand on my sholder and said Charlie you dont know it yet but your getting smarter all the time. You wont notice for a while. I think he was just being nice to make me feel good because I dont look any smarter.

Oh yes I almost forgot. I asked him when I can go back to the class at Miss Kinnians school. He said I wont go their. He said that soon Miss Kinnian will come to the hospitil to start and teach me speshul.

Mar 29   That crazy TV kept up all night. How can I sleep with something yelling crazy things all night in my ears. And the nutty pictures. Wow. I don't know what it says when Im up so how am I going to know when Im sleeping.

Dr Strauss says its ok. He says my brains are lerning when I sleep and that will help me when Miss Kinnian starts my lessons in the hospitl (only I found out it isn't a hospitil its a labatory.) I think its all crazy. If you can get smart when your sleeping why do people go to school. That thing I don't think will work. I use to watch the late show and the late late show on TV all the time and it never made me smart. Maybe you have to sleep while you watch it.

progress report 9—April 3

Dr Strauss showed me how to keep the TV turned low so now I can sleep. I don't hear a thing. And I still dont understand what it says. A few times I play it over in the morning to find out what I lerned when I was sleeping and I don't think so. Miss Kinnian says Maybe its another langwidge. But most times it sound american. It talks faster then even Miss Gold who was my teacher in 6 grade.

I told Dr. Strauss what good is it to get smart in my sleep. I want to be smart when Im awake. He says its the same thing and I have two minds. Theres the *subconscious* and the *conscious* (thats how you spell it). And one dont tell the other one what its doing. They

103

dont even talk to each other. Thats why I dream. And boy have I been having crazy dreams. Wow. Ever since that night TV. The late late late show.

I forgot to ask him if it was only me or if everybody had those two minds.

(I just looked up the word in the dictionary Dr Strauss gave me. The word is *subconscious. adj. Of the nature of mental operations yet not present in consciousness; as, subconscious conflict of desires.)* There's more but I still dont know what it means. This isnt a very good dictionary for dumb people like me.

Anyway the headache is from the party. My friends from the factery Joe Carp and Frank Reilly invited me to go to Muggsys Saloon for some drinks. I don't like to drink but they said we will have lots of fun. I had a good time.

Joe Carp said I shoud show the girls how I mop out the toilet in the factory and he got me a mop. I showed them and everyone laffed when I told that Mr. Donnegan said I was the best janiter he ever had because I like my job and do it good and never miss a day except for my operashun.

I said Miss Kinnian always said Charlie be proud of your job because you do it good.

Everybody laffed and we had a good time and they gave me lots of drinks and Joe said Charlie is a card when hes potted. I dont know what that means but everybody likes me and we have fun. I cant wait to be smart like my best friends Joe Carp and Frank Reilly.

I dont remember how the party was over but I think I went out to buy a newspaper and coffe for Joe and Frank and when I came back there was no one their. I looked for them all over till late. Then I dont remember so good but I think I got sleepy or sick. A nice cop brot me back home Thats what my landlady Mrs Flynn says.

But I got a headache and a big lump on my head. I think maybe I fell but Joe Carp says it was the cop they beat up drunks some times. I don't think so. Miss Kinnian says cops are to help people. Anyway I got a bad headache and Im sick and hurt all over. I dont think Ill drink anymore.

April 6 I beat Algernon! I dint even know I beat him until Burt the tester told me. Then the second time I lost because I got so exited I fell off the chair before I finished. But after that I beat him 8 more times. I must be getting smart to beat a smart mouse like Algernon. But I dont *feel* smarter.

I wanted to race Algernon some more but Burt said thats

enough for one day. They let me hold him for a minit. Hes not so bad. Hes soft like a ball of cotton. He blinks and when he opens his eyes their black and pink on the eges.

I said can I feed him because I felt bad to beat him and I wanted to be nice and make friends. Burt said no Algernon is a very specshul mouse with an operashun like mine, and he was the first of all the animals to stay smart so long. He told me Algernon is so smart that every day he has to solve a test to get his food. Its a thing like a lock on a door that changes every time Algernon goes in to eat so he has to lern something new to get his food. That made me sad because if he couldnt lern he woud be hungry.

I don't think its right to make you pass a test to eat. How woud Dr Nemur like it to have to pass a test every time he wants to eat. I think Ill be friends with Algernon.

April 9   Tonight after work Miss Kinnian was at the laboratory. She looked like she was glad to see me but scared. I told her dont worry Miss Kinnian Im not smart yet and she laffed. She said I have confidence in you Charlie the way you struggled so hard to read and right better than all the others. At werst you will have it for a littel wile and your doing something for science.

We are reading a very hard book. Its called *Robinson Crusoe* about a man who gets merooned on a dessert Iland. Hes smart and figers out all kinds of things so he can have a house and food and hes a good swimmer. Only I feel sorry because hes all alone and has no frends. But I think their must be somebody else on the iland because theres a picture with his funny umbrella looking at footprints. I hope he gets a frend and not be lonly.

April 10   Miss Kinnian teaches me to spell better. She says look at a word and close your eyes and say it over and over until you remember. I have lots of truble with *through* that you say *threw* and *enough* and *tough* that you dont say *enew and tew.* You got to say *enuff* and *tuff.* Thats how I use to write it before I started to get smart. Im confused but Miss Kinnian says theres no reason in spelling.

Apr 14   Finished *Robinson Crusoe.* I want to find out more about what happens to him but Miss Kinnian says thats all there is. *Why.*

Apr 15 Miss Kinnian says Im lerning fast. She read some of the Progress Reports and she looked at me kind of funny. She says Im a fine person and Ill show them all. I asked her why. She said never mind but I shouldnt feel bad if I find out everybody isnt nice like I think. She said for a person who god gave so little to you done more then a lot of people with brains they never even used. I said all my friends are smart people but there good. They like me and they never did anything that wasnt nice. Then she got something in her eye and she had to run out to the ladys room.

Apr 16 Today, I lerned, the *comma*, this is a comma (,) a period, with a tail, Miss Kinnian, says its importent, because, it makes writing, better, she said, somebody, coud lose, a lot of money, if a comma, isnt, in the, right place, I dont have, any money, and I dont see, how a comma, keeps you, from losing it.

Apr 17 I used the comma wrong. Its punctuation. Miss Kinnian told me to look up long words in the dictionary to lern to spell them. I said whats the difference if you can read it anyway. She said its part of your education so now on Ill look up all the words Im not sure how to spell. It takes a long time to write that way but I only have to look up once and after that I get it right.

You got to mix them up, she showed? me" how to mix! them (and now; I can! mix up all kinds" of punctuation, in! my writing? There, are lots! of rules? to lern; but Im gettin'g them in my head.

One thing I like about, Dear Miss Kinnian: (thats the way it goes in a business letter if I ever go into business) is she, always gives me' a reason" when—I ask. She's a gen'ius! I wish I cou'd be smart" like, her;

(Punctuation, is; fun!)

Apr 18 What a dope I am! I didn't even understand what she was talking about. I read the grammar book last night and it explanes the whole thing. Then I saw it was the same way as Miss Kinnian was trying to tell me, but I didn't get it.

Miss Kinnian said that the TV working in my sleep helped out. She and I reached a plateau. Thats a flat hill.

After I figured out how punctuation worked, I read over all my old Progress Reports from the beginning. Boy, did I have crazy spelling and punctuation! I told Miss Kinnian I ought to go over the pages and fix all the mistakes but she said, "No, Charlie, Dr. Nemur wants them just as they are. That's why he let you keep them after they were photostated, to see your own progress. You're coming along fast, Charlie."

That made me feel good. After the lesson I went down and played with Algernon. We don't race any more.

April 20   I feel sick inside. Not sick like for a doctor, but inside my chest it feels empty like getting punched and a heartburn at the same time. I wasn't going to write about it, but I guess I got to, because its important. Today was the first time I ever stayed home from work.

Last night Joe Carp and Frank Reilly invited me to a party. There were lots of girls and some men from the factory. I remembered how sick I got last time I drank too much, so I told Joe I didn't want anything to drink. He gave me a plain coke instead.

We had a lot of fun for a while. Joe said I should dance with Ellen and she would teach me the steps. I fell a few times and I couldn't understand why because no one else was dancing besides Ellen and me. And all the time I was tripping because somebody's foot was always sticking out.

Then when I got up I saw the look on Joe's face and it gave me a funny feeling in my stomack. "He's a scream," one of the girls said. Everybody was laughing.

"Look at him. He's blushing. Charlie is blushing."

"Hey, Ellen, what'd you do to Charlie? I never saw him act like that before."

I didn't know what to do or where to turn. Everyone was looking at me and laughing and I felt naked. I wanted to hide. I ran outside and I threw up. Then I walked home. It's a funny thing I never knew that Joe and Frank and the others liked to have me around all the time to make fun of me.

Now I know what it means when they say "to pull a Charlie Gordon."

I'm ashamed.

progress report 11

April 21   Still didn't go into the factory. I told Mrs. Flynn my landlady to call and tell Mr. Donnegan I was sick. Mrs. Flynn looks at me very funny lately like she's scared.

I think it's a good thing about finding out how everybody laughs at me. I thought about it a lot. It's because I'm so dumb and I don't even know when I'm doing something dumb. People think it's funny when a dumb person can't do things the same way they can.

Anyway, now I know I'm getting smarter every day. I know punctuation and I can spell good. I like to look up all the hard words in the dictionary and I remember them. I'm reading a lot now, and Miss Kinnian says I read very fast. Sometimes I even understand what I'm reading about, and it stays in my mind. There are times when I can close my eyes and think of a page and it all comes back like a picture.

Besides history, geography and arithmetic, Miss Kinnian said I should start to learn foreign languages. Dr. Strauss gave me some more tapes to play while I sleep. I still don't understand how that conscious and unconscious mind works, but Dr. Strauss says not to worry yet. He asked me to promise that when I start learning college subjects next week I wouldn't read any books on psychology—that is, until he gives me permission.

I feel a lot better today, but I guess I'm still a little angry that all the time people were laughing and making fun of me because I wasn't so smart. When I become intelligent like Dr. Strauss says, with three times my I.Q. of 68, then maybe I'll be like everyone else and people will like me.

I'm not sure what an I.Q. is. Dr. Nemur said it was something that measured how intelligent you were—like a scale in the drug-store weighs pounds. But Dr. Strauss had a big argument with him and said an I.Q. didn't weigh intelligence at all. He said an I.Q. showed how much intelligence you could get, like the numbers on the outside of a measuring cup. You still had to fill the cup up with stuff.

Then when I asked Burt, who gives me my intelligence tests and works with Algernon, he said that both of them were wrong (only I had to promise not to tell them he said so). Burt says that the I.Q. measures a lot of different things including some of the things you learned already, and it really isn't any good at all.

So I still don't know what I.Q. is except that mine is going to be over 200 soon. I didn't want to say anything, but I don't see how if they don't know *what* it is, or *where* it is—I don't see how they know *how much* of it you've got.

Dr. Nemur says I have to take a *Rorshach Test* tomorrow. I wonder what *that* is.

April 22 I found out what a Rorshach is. It's the test I took before the operation—the one with the inkblots on the pieces of cardboard.

I was scared to death of those inkblots. I knew the man was going to ask me to find the pictures and I knew I couldn't. I was thinking to myself, if only there was some way of knowing what kind of pictures were hidden there. Maybe there weren't any pictures at all. Maybe it was just a trick to see if I was dumb enough to look for something that wasn't there. Just thinking about that made me sore at him.

"All right, Charlie," he said, "you've seen these cards before, remember?"

"Of course I remember."

The way I said it, he knew I was angry, and he looked surprised. "Yes, of course. Now I want you to look at this. What might this be? What do you see on this card? People see all sorts of things in these inkblots. Tell me what it might be for you—what it makes you think of."

I was shocked. That wasn't what I had expected him to say. "You mean there are no pictures hidden in those inkblots?"

He frowned and took off his glasses. "What?"

"Pictures. Hidden in the inkblots. Last time you told me everyone could see them and you wanted me to find them too."

He explained to me that the last time he had used almost the exact same words he was using now. I didn't believe it, and I still have the suspicion that he misled me at the time just for the fun of it. Unless—I don't know any more—could I have been *that* feeble-minded?

We went through the cards slowly. One looked like a pair of bats tugging at something. Another one looked like two men fencing with swords. I imagined all sorts of things. I guess I got carried away. But I didn't trust him any more, and I kept turning them around, even looking on the back to see if there was anything there I was supposed to catch. While he was making his notes, I peeked out of the corner of my eye to read it. But it was all in code that looked like this:

$$WF + A \qquad DdF - Ad \text{ orig.} \qquad WF - A$$
$$SF + obj$$

The test still doesn't make sense to me. It seems to me that anyone could make up lies about things that they didn't really imagine? Maybe I'll understand it when Dr. Strauss lets me read up on psychology.

April 25 I figured out a new way to line up the machines in the factory, and Mr. Donnegan says it will save him ten thousand dollars a year in labor and increased production. He gave me a $25 bonus.

I wanted to take Joe Carp and Frank Reilly out to lunch to celebrate, but Joe said he had to buy some things for his wife, and Frank said he was meeting his cousin for lunch. I guess it'll take a little time for them to get used to the changes in me. Everybody seems to be frightened of me. When I went over to Amos Borg and tapped him, he jumped up in the air.

People don't talk to me much any more or kid around the way they used to. It makes the job kind of lonely.

April 27 I got up the nerve today to ask Miss Kinnian to have dinner with me tomorrow night to celebrate my bonus.

At first she wasn't sure it was right, but I asked Dr. Strauss and he said it was okay. Dr. Strauss and Dr. Nemur don't seem to be getting along so well. They're arguing all the time. This evening I heard them shouting. Dr. Nemur was saying that it was *his* experiment and *his* research, and Dr. Strauss shouted back that he contributed just as much, because he found me through Miss Kinnian and he performed the operation. Dr. Strauss said that someday thousands of neuro-surgeons might be using his technique all over the world.

Dr. Nemur wanted to publish the results of the experiment at the end of the month. Dr. Strauss wanted to wait a while to be sure. Dr. Strauss said Dr. Nemur was more interested in the Chair of Psychology at Princeton than he was in the experiment. Dr. Nemur said Dr. Strauss was nothing but an opportunist trying to ride to glory on *his* coattails.

When I left afterwards, I found myself trembling. I don't know why for sure, but it was as if I'd seen both men clearly for the first time. I remember hearing Burt say Dr. Nemur had a shrew of a wife who was pushing him all the time to get things published so he could become famous. Burt said that the dream of her life was to have a big shot husband.

April 28 I don't understand why I never noticed how beautiful Miss Kinnian really is. She has brown eyes and feathery brown hair that comes to the top of her neck. She's only thirty-four! I think from the beginning I had the feeling that she was an unreachable genius—and very, very old. Now, every time I see her she grows younger and more lovely.

We had dinner and a long talk. When she said I was coming along so fast I'd be leaving her behind, I laughed.

"It's true, Charlie. You're already a better reader than I am. You can read a whole page at a glance while I can take in only a few lines at a time. And you remember every single thing you read. I'm lucky if I can recall the main thoughts and the general meaning."

"I don't feel intelligent. There are so many things I don't understand."

She took out a cigarette and I lit it for her. "You've got to be a *little* patient. You're accomplishing in days and weeks what it takes normal people to do in a lifetime. That's what makes it so amazing. You're like a giant sponge now, soaking things in. Facts, figures, general knowledge. And soon you'll begin to connect them, too. You'll see how different branches of learning are related. There are many levels, Charlie, like steps on a giant ladder that take you up higher and higher to see more and more of the world around you.

"I can see only a little bit of that, Charlie, and I won't go much higher than I am now, but you'll keep climbing up and up, and see more and more, and each step will open new worlds that you never even knew existed." She frowned. "I hope . . . I just hope to God—"

"What?"

"Never mind, Charles. I just hope I wasn't wrong to advise you to go into this in the first place."

I laughed. "How could that be? It worked, didn't it? Even Algernon is still smart."

We sat there silently for a while and I knew what she was thinking about as she watched me toying with the chain of my rabbit's foot and my keys. I didn't want to think of that possibility any more than elderly people want to think of death. I *knew* that this was only the beginning. I knew what she meant about levels because I'd seen some of them already. The thought of leaving her behind made me sad.

I'm in love with Miss Kinnian.

progress report 12

April 30 I've quit my job with Donnegan's Plastic Box Company. Mr. Donnegan insisted it would be better for all concerned if I left. What did I do to make them hate me so?

The first I knew of it was when Mr. Donnegan showed me the petition. Eight hundred names, everyone in the factory, except Fanny Girden. Scanning the list quickly, I saw at once that hers was the only missing name. All the rest demanded that I be fired.

Joe Carp and Frank Reilly wouldn't talk to me about it. No one else would either, except Fanny. She was one of the few people I'd known who set her mind to something and believed it no matter what the rest of the world proved, said or did—and Fanny did not believe that I should have been fired. She had been against the petition on principle and despite the pressure and threats she'd held out.

"Which don't mean to say," she remarked, "that I don't think there's something mighty strange about you, Charlie. Them changes. I don't know. You used to be a good, dependable, ordinary man—not too bright maybe, but honest. Who knows what you done to yourself to get so smart all of a sudden. Like everybody around here's been saying, Charlie, it's not right."

"But how can you say that, Fanny? What's wrong with a man becoming intelligent and wanting to acquire knowledge and understanding of the world around him?"

She stared down at her work and I turned to leave. Without looking at me, she said: "It was evil when Eve listened to the snake and ate from the tree of knowledge. It was evil when she saw that she was naked. If not for that none of us would ever have to grow old and sick, and die."

Once again, now, I have the feeling of shame burning inside me. This intelligence has driven a wedge between me and all the people I once knew and loved. Before, they laughed at me and despised me for my ignorance and dullness; now, they hate me for my knowledge and understanding. What in God's name do they want of me?

They've driven me out of the factory. Now I'm more alone than ever before. . . .

May 15 Dr. Strauss is very angry at me for not having written any progress reports in two weeks. He's justified because the lab is now paying me a regular salary. I told him I was too busy thinking and reading. When I pointed out that writing was such a slow process that it makes me impatient with my poor handwriting, he suggested I learn to type. It's much easier to write now because I can type seventy-five words a minute. Dr. Strauss continually reminds me of the need to speak and write simply so people will be able to understand me.

I'll try to review all the things that happened to me during the last two weeks. Algernon and I were presented to the *American Psychological Association* sitting in convention with the *World Psychological Association.* We created quite a sensation. Dr. Nemur and Dr. Strauss were proud of us.

I suspect that Dr. Nemur, who is sixty—ten years older than Dr. Strauss—finds it necessary to see tangible results of his work. Undoubtedly the result of pressure by Mrs. Nemur.

Contrary to my earlier impressions of him, I realize that Dr. Nemur is not at all a genius. He has a very good mind, but it struggles under the spectre of self-doubt. He wants people to take him for a genius. Therefore, it is important for him to feel that his work is accepted by the world. I believe that Dr. Nemur was afraid of further delay because he worried that someone else might make a discovery along these lines and take the credit from him.

Dr. Strauss on the other hand might be called a genius, although I feel that his areas of knowledge are too limited. He was educated in the tradition of narrow specialization; the broader aspects of background were neglected far more than necessary—even for a neurosurgeon.

I was shocked to learn that the only ancient languages he could read were Latin, Greek, and Hebrew, and that he knows almost nothing of mathematics beyond the elementary levels of the calculus of variations. When he admitted this to me, I found myself almost annoyed. It was as if he'd hidden this part of himself in order to deceive me, pretending—as do many people I've discovered—to be what he is not. No one I've ever known is what he appears to be on the surface.

Dr. Nemur appears to be uncomfortable around me. Sometimes when I try to talk to him, he just looks at me strangely and turns away. I was angry at first when Dr. Strauss told me I was giving Dr. Nemur an inferiority complex. I thought he was mocking me and I'm oversensitive at being made fun of.

How was I to know that a highly respected psychoexperimentalist like Nemur was unacquainted with Hindustani and Chinese? It's absurd when you consider the work that is being done in India and China today in the very field of his study.

I asked Dr. Strauss how Nemur could refute Rahajamati's attack on his method and results if Nemur couldn't even read them in the first place. That strange look on Dr. Strauss' face can mean only one of two things. Either he doesn't want to tell Nemur what they're saying in India, or else—and this worries me—Dr. Strauss doesn't know either. I must be careful to speak and write clearly and simply so that people won't laugh.

May 18 I am very disturbed. I saw Miss Kinnian last night for the first time in over a week. I tried to avoid all discussions of intellectual concepts and to keep the conversation on a simple, everyday level, but she just stared at me blankly and asked me what I meant about the mathematical variance equivalent in Dorbermann's *Fifth Concerto.*

When I tried to explain she stopped me and laughed. I guess I got angry, but I suspect I'm approaching her on the wrong level. No matter what I try to discuss with her, I am unable to communicate. I must review Vrostadt's equations on *Levels of Semantic Progression.* I find that I don't communicate with people much any more. Thank God for books and music and things I can think about. I am alone in my apartment at Mrs. Flynn's boardinghouse most of the time and seldom speak to anyone.

May 20 I would not have noticed the new dishwasher, a boy of about sixteen, at the corner diner where I take my evening meals if not for the incident of the broken dishes.

They crashed to the floor, shattering and sending bits of white china under the tables. The boy stood there, dazed and frightened, holding the empty tray in his hand. The whistles and catcalls from the customers (the cries of "hey, there go the profits!" . . . *"Mazeltov!"* . . . and "well, *he* didn't work here very long . . ." which invariably seem to follow the breaking of glass or dishware in a public restaurant) all seemed to confuse him.

When the owner came to see what the excitement was about, the boy cowered as if he expected to be struck and threw up his arms as if to ward off the blow.

"All right! All right, you dope," shouted the owner, "don't just stand there! Get the broom and sweep that mess up. A broom . . . a broom, you idiot! It's in the kitchen. Sweep up all the pieces."

The boy saw that he was not going to be punished. His frightened expression disappeared and he smiled and hummed as he came back with the broom to sweep the floor. A few of the rowdier customers kept up the remarks, amusing themselves at his expense.

"Here, sonny, over here there's a nice piece behind you. . . ."

"C'mon, do it again. . . ."

"He's not so dumb. It's easier to break'em than to wash'em. . . ."

As his vacant eyes moved across the crowd of amused onlookers, he slowly mirrored their smiles and finally broke into an uncertain grin at the joke which he obviously did not understand.

I felt sick inside as I looked at his dull, vacuous smile, the wide, bright eyes of a child, uncertain but eager to please. They were laughing at him because he was mentally retarded.

And I had been laughing at him too.

Suddenly, I was furious at myself and all those who were smirking at him. I jumped up and shouted, "Shut up! Leave him alone! It's not his fault he can't understand. He can't help what he is! But for God's sake . . . he's still a human being!"

The room grew silent. I cursed myself for losing control and creating a scene. I tried not to look at the boy as I paid my check and walked out without touching my food. I felt ashamed for both of us.

How strange it is that people of honest feelings and sensibility, who would not take advantage of a man born without arms or legs or eyes—how such people think nothing of abusing a man born with low intelligence. It infuriated me to think that not too long ago, I like this boy, had foolishly played the clown.

And I had almost forgotten.

I'd hidden the picture of the old Charlie Gordon from myself because now that I was intelligent it was something that had to be pushed out of my mind. But today in looking at that boy, for the first time I saw what I had been. *I was just like him!*

Only a short time ago, I learned that people laughed at me. Now I can see that unknowingly I joined with them in laughing at myself. That hurts most of all.

I have often reread my progress reports and seen the illiteracy, the childish naïveté, the mind of low intelligence peering from a dark room, through the keyhole, at the dazzling light outside. I see that even in my dullness I knew that I was inferior, and that other people had something I lacked—something denied me. In my mental blindness, I thought that it was somehow connected with the ability to read and write, and I was sure that if I could get those skills I would automatically have intelligence too.

Even a feeble-minded man wants to be like other men.

A child may not know how to feed itself, or what to eat, yet it knows of hunger.

This then is what I was like, I never knew. Even with my gift of intellectual awareness, I never really knew.

This day was good for me. Seeing the past more clearly, I have decided to use my knowledge and skills to work in the field of increasing human intelligence levels. Who is better equipped for this work? Who else has lived in both worlds? These are my people. Let me use my gift to do something for them.

Tomorrow, I will discuss with Dr. Strauss the manner in which I can work in this area. I may be able to help him work out the problems of widespread use of the technique which was used on me. I have several good ideas of my own.

There is so much that might be done with this technique. If I could be made into a genius, what about thousands of others like myself? What fantastic levels might be achieved by using this technique on normal people? Or *geniuses?*

There are so many doors to open. I am impatient to begin.

progress report 13

May 23 It happened today. Algernon bit me. I visited the lab to see him as I do occasionally, and when I took him out of his cage, he snapped at my hand. I put him back and watched him for a while. He was unusually disturbed and vicious.

May 24 Burt, who is in charge of the experimental animals, tells me that Algernon is changing. He is less co-operative; he refuses to run the maze any more; general motivation has decreased. And he hasn't been eating. Everyone is upset about what this may mean.

May 25 They've been feeding Algernon, who now refuses to work the shifting-lock problem. Everyone identifies me with Algernon. In a way we're both the first of our kind. They're all pretending that Algernon's behavior is not necessarily significant for me. But it's hard to hide the fact that some of the other animals who were used in this experiment are showing strange behavior.

Dr. Strauss and Dr. Nemur have asked me not to come to the lab any more. I know what they're thinking but I can't accept it. I am going ahead with my plans to carry their research forward. With all due respect to both of these fine scientists, I am well aware of their limitations. If there is an answer, I'll have to find it out for myself. Suddenly, time has become very important to me.

May 29 I have been given a lab of my own and permission to go ahead with the research. I'm on to something. Working day and night. I've had a cot moved into the lab. Most of my writing time is spent on the notes which I keep in a separate folder, but from time to time I feel it necessary to put down my moods and my thoughts out of sheer habit.

I find the *calculus of intelligence* to be a fascinating study. Here is the place for the application of all the knowledge I have acquired. In a sense it's the problem I've been concerned with all my life.

May 31 Dr. Strauss thinks I'm working too hard. Dr. Nemur says I'm trying to cram a lifetime of research and thought into a few weeks. I know I should rest, but I'm driven on by something inside that won't let me stop. I've got to find the reason for the sharp regression in Algernon. I've got to know *if* and *when* it will happen to me.

June 4
LETTER TO DR. STRAUSS (*copy*)

Dear Dr. Strauss:

Under separate cover I am sending you a copy of my report entitled, "The Algernon-Gordon Effect: A Study of Structure and Function of Increased Intelligence," which I would like to have you read and have published.

As you see, my experiments are completed. I have included in my report all of my formulae, as well as mathematical analysis in the appendix. Of course, these should be verified.

Because of its importance to both you and Dr. Nemur (and need I say to myself, too?) I have checked and rechecked my results a dozen times in the hope of finding an error. I am sorry to say the results must stand. Yet for the sake of science, I am grateful for the little bit that I here add to the knowledge of the function of the human mind and of the laws governing the artificial increase of human intelligence.

I recall your once saying to me that an experimental *failure* or the *disproving* of a theory was as important to the advancement of learning as a success would be. I know now that this is true. I am sorry, however, that my own contribution to the field must rest upon the ashes of the work of two men I regard so highly.

Yours truly,
Charles Gordon

encl.:rept.

June 5 I must not become emotional. The facts and the results of my experiments are clear, and the more sensational aspects of my own rapid climb cannot obscure the fact that the tripling of intelligence by the surgical technique developed by Drs. Strauss and Nemur must be viewed as having little or no practical applicability (at the present time) to the increase of human intelligence.

As I review the records and data on Algernon, I see that although he is still in his physical infancy, he has regressed mentally. Motor activity is impaired; there is a general reduction of glandular activity; there is an accelerated loss of co-ordination.

There are also strong indications of progressive amnesia.

As will be seen by my report, these and other physical and mental deterioration syndromes can be predicted with statistically significant results by the application of my formula.

The surgical stimulus to which we were both subjected has resulted in an intensification and acceleration of all mental processes. The unforeseen development, which I have taken the liberty of calling the *Algernon-Gordon Effect*, is the logical extension of the entire intelligence speed-up. The hypothesis here proven may be described simply in the following terms: Artificially increased intelligence deteriorates at a rate of time directly proportional to the quantity of the increase.

I feel that this, in itself, is an important discovery.

As long as I am able to write, I will continue to record my thoughts in these progress reports. It is one of my few pleasures. However, by all indications, my own mental deterioration will be very rapid.

I have already begun to notice signs of emotional instability and forgetfulness, the first symptoms of the burnout.

June 10 Deterioration progressing. I have become absentminded. Algernon died two days ago. Dissection shows my predictions were right. His brain had decreased in weight and there was a general smoothing out of cerebral convolutions as well as a deepening and broadening of brain fissures.

I guess the same thing is or will soon be happening to me. Now that it's definite, I don't want it to happen.

I put Algernon's body in a cheese box and buried him in the back yard. I cried.

June 15 Dr. Strauss came to see me again. I wouldn't open the door and I told him to go away. I want to be left to myself. I have become touchy and irritable. I feel the darkness closing in. It's hard to throw off thoughts of suicide. I keep telling myself how important this introspective journal will be.

It's a strange sensation to pick up a book that you've read and enjoyed just a few months ago and discover that you don't remember it. I remembered how great I thought John Milton was, but when I picked up *Paradise Lost* I couldn't understand it at all. I got so angry I threw the book across the room.

I've got to try to hold on to some of it. Some of the things I've learned. Oh, God, please don't take it all away.

June 19 Sometimes, at night, I go out for a walk. Last night I couldn't remember where I lived. A policeman took me home. I have the strange feeling that this has all happened to me before—a long time ago. I keep telling myself I'm the only person in the world who can describe what's happening to me.

June 21 Why can't I remember? I've got to fight. I lie in bed for days and I don't know who or where I am. Then it all comes back to me in a flash. Fugues of amnesia. Symptoms of senility—second childhood. I can watch them coming on. It's so cruelly logical. I learned so much and so fast. Now my mind is deteriorating rapidly. I won't let it happen. I'll fight it. I can't help thinking of the boy in the restaurant, the blank expression, the silly smile, the people laughing at him. No—please—not that again. . . .

June 22 I'm forgetting things that I learned recently. It seems to be following the classic pattern—the last things learned are the first things forgotten. Or is that the pattern? I'd better look it up again. . . .

I reread my paper on the *Algernon-Gordon Effect* and I get the strange feeling that it was written by someone else. There are parts I don't even understand.

Motor activity impaired. I keep tripping over things, and it becomes increasingly difficult to type.

June 23 I've given up using the typewriter completely. My co-ordination is bad. I feel that I'm moving slower and slower. Had a terrible shock today. I picked up a copy of an article I used in my research, Krueger's *Uber Psychische Ganzheit,* to see if it would help me understand what I had done. First I thought there was something wrong with my eyes. Then I realized I could no longer read German. I tested myself in other languages. All gone.

June 30 A week since I dared to write again. It's slipping away like sand through my fingers. Most of the books I have are too hard for me now. I get angry with them because I know that I read and understood them just a few weeks ago.

I keep telling myself I must keep writing these reports so that somebody will know what is happening to me. But it gets harder to form the words and remember spellings. I have to look up even simple words in the dictionary now and it makes me impatient with myself.

Dr. Strauss comes around almost every day, but I told him I wouldn't see or speak to anybody. He feels guilty. They all do. But I don't blame anyone. I knew what might happen. But how it hurts.

July 7 I don't know where the week went. Todays Sunday I know because I can see through my window people going to church. I think I stayed in bed all week but I remember Mrs. Flynn bringing food to me a few times. I keep saying over and over Ive got to do something but then I forget or maybe its just easier not to do what I say Im going to do.

I think of my mother and father a lot these days. I found a picture of them with me taken at a beach. My father has a big ball under his arm and my mother is holding me by the hand. I dont remember them the way they are in the picture. All I remember is my father drunk most of the time and arguing with mom about money.

He never shaved much and he used to scratch my face when he hugged me. My mother said he died but Cousin Miltie said he heard his mom and dad say that my father ran away with another woman. When I asked my mother she slapped my face and said my father was dead. I don't think I ever found out which was true but I don't care much. (He said he was going to take me to see cows on a farm once but he never did. He never kept his promises. . . .)

July 10 My landlady Mrs Flynn is very worried about me. She says the way I lay around all day and dont do anything I remind her of her son before she threw him out of the house. She said she doesnt like loafers. If Im sick its one thing, but if Im a loafer thats another thing and she wont have it. I told her I think Im sick.

I try to read a little bit every day, mostly stories, but sometimes I have to read the same thing over and over again because I dont know what it means. And its hard to write. I know I should look up all the words in the dictionary but its so hard and Im so tired all the time.

Then I got the idea that I would only use the easy words instead of the long hard ones. That saves time. I put flowers on Algernons grave about once a week. Mrs Flynn thinks I'm crazy to put flowers on a mouses grave but I told her that Algernon was special.

July 14 Its sunday again. I dont have anything to do to keep me busy now because my television set is broke and I dont have any money to get it fixed. (I think I lost this months check from the lab. I dont remember)

I get awful headaches and asperin doesnt help me much. Mrs Flynn knows Im really sick and she feels very sorry for me. Shes a wonderful woman whenever someone is sick.

July 22 Mrs Flynn called a strange doctor to see me. She was afraid I was going to die. I told the doctor I wasnt too sick and that I only forget sometimes. He asked me did I have any friends or relatives and I said no I dont have any. I told him I had a friend called Algernon once but he was a mouse and we used to run races together. He looked at me kind of funny like he thought I was crazy.

He smiled when I told him I used to be a genius. He talked to me like I was a baby and he winked at Mrs Flynn. I got mad and chased him out because he was making fun of me the way they all used to.

July 24 I have no more money and Mrs. Flynn says I got to go to work somewhere and pay the rent because I havent paid for over two months. I dont know any work but the job I used to have at Donnegans Plastic Box Company. I dont want to go back there because they all knew me when I was smart and maybe theyll laugh at me. But I dont know what else to do to get money.

July 25 I was looking at some of my old progress reports and its very funny but I cant read what I wrote. I can make out some of the words but they dont make sense.

Miss Kinnian came to the door but I said go away I dont want to see you. She cried and I cried too but I wouldn't let her in because I didn't want her to laugh at me. I told her I didn't like her any more. I told her I didn't want to be smart any more. Thats not true. I still love her and I still want to be smart but I had to say that so shed go away. She gave Mrs Flynn money to pay the rent. I dont want that. I got to get a job.

Please . . . please let me not forget how to read and write. . . .

July 27 Mr Donnegan was very nice when I came back and asked him for my old job of janitor. First he was very suspicious but I told him what happened to me then he looked very sad and put his hand on my shoulder and said Charlie Gordon you got guts.

Everybody looked at me when I came downstairs and started working in the toilet sweeping it out like I used to. I told myself Charlie if they make fun of you dont get sore because you remember their not so smart as you once thot they were. And besides they were once your friends and if they laughed at you that doesnt mean anything because they liked you too.

One of the new men who came to work there after I went away made a nasty crack he said hey Charlie I hear your a very smart fella a real quiz kid. Say something intelligent. I felt bad but Joe Carp came over and grabbed him by the shirt and said leave him alone you lousy cracker or Ill break your neck. I didnt expect Joe to take my part so I guess hes really my friend.

Later Frank Reilly came over and said Charlie if anybody bothers you or trys to take advantage you call me or Joe and we will set em straight. I said thanks Frank and I got choked up so I had to turn around and go into the supply room so he wouldnt see me cry. Its good to have friends.

July 28 I did a dumb thing today I forgot I wasnt in Miss Kinnians class at the adult center any more like I used to be. I went in and sat down in my old seat in the back of the room and she looked at me funny and she said Charles. I dint remember she ever called me that before only Charlie so I said hello Miss Kinnian Im redy for my lesin today only I lost my reader that we was using. She startid to cry and run out of the room and everybody looked at me and I saw they wasnt the same pepul who used to be in my class.

Then all of a sudden I remembered some things about the operashun and me getting smart and I said holy smoke I reely pulled a Charlie Gordon that time. I went away before she come back to the room.

Thats why Im going away from New York for good. I dont want to do nothing like that agen. I dont want Miss Kinnian to feel sorry for me. Evry body feels sorry at the factery and I dont want that eather so Im going someplace where nobody knows that Charlie Gordon was once a genus and now he cant even reed a book or rite good.

Im taking a cuple of books along and even if I cant reed them Ill practise hard and maybe I wont forget every thing I lerned. If I try reel hard maybe Ill be a littel bit smarter than I was before the operashun. I got my rabits foot and my luky penny and maybe they will help me.

If you ever reed this Miss Kinnian dont be sorry for me Im glad I got a second chanse to be smart becaus I lerned a lot of things that I never even new were in this world and Im grateful that I saw it all for a little bit. I dont know why Im dumb agen or what I did wrong maybe its becaus I dint try hard enuff. But if I try and practis very hard maybe Ill get a little smarter and know what all the words are. I remember a littel bit how nice I had a feeling with the blue book that has the torn cover when I red it. Thats why Im gonna keep trying to get smart so I can have that feeling agen. Its a good feeling to know things and be smart. I wish I had it rite now if I did I would sit down and reed all the time. Anyway I bet Im the first dumb person in the world who ever found out something importent for sience. I remember I did something but I dont remember what. So I gess its like I did it for all the dumb pepul like me.

Good-by Miss Kinnian and Dr Strauss and evreybody. And P.S. please tell Dr Nemur not to be such a grouch when pepul laff at him and he would have more frends. Its easy to make frends if you let pepul laff at you. Im going to have lots of frends where I go.
P.P.S. Please if you get a chanse put some flowrs on Algernons grave in the bak yard. . . .

the brain

Norbert Wiener

The story begins: "The brain is a funny organ." It goes on from there to involve brains in various shapes, sizes, and capacities. Along the way the author weaves a tale which somehow combines aspects of *The Godfather* and *One Flew Over the Cuckoo's Nest*. It is also a simple tale of revenge, albeit the method of revenge is relatively subtle and sophisticated. Complex and simple at the same time? This characterizes not only the story, but the brain as well.

The second sentence of the story tells us that ". . . it can be touched and cut with no local sensation at all." In essence, touching and cutting the brain are the ways in which we relate the parts of the brain to behavioral function, the relationship that physiological psychologists are most interested in. Touching in this modern age of electronics is done by electrical stimulation of the brain, or E.S.B. Stimulating either specific excitatory or inhibitory areas can turn on or turn off specific behaviors and reactions. For example, Canadian Dr. Wilder Penfield electrically stimulated specific areas of the cerebral cortex of a number of his patients and produced vivid memories in which they clearly visualized distant relatives or heard orchestras playing familiar tunes. Dr. Jose Delgado electrically stimulated a specific area of the brain of a bull that was about to charge him. Since this area inhibits aggression, the bull stopped dead in its tracks—to the delight of Delgado. As our leading sentence suggests, Penfield's patients reported that they had not felt a thing. No inquiry was made of Delgado's bull.

Cutting specific areas of the brain can also tell us a great deal about their functions. If as a result of lesions in specific areas specific functions are then impaired or impeded, we can conclude that these areas have at least some control over the missing or reduced function. Cutting lesions in the brain is a more permanent process than E.S.B., since neurons—the cells which make up the brain—do not regenerate when destroyed as other cells of the body do. Therefore, as an experimental technique, it is only used on research with animals.

As we learn in the story, one cutting technique that has been used on humans as a psychosurgical procedure is the prefrontal lobotomy. The lobotomy technique involves severing the connection between the thalamus and the frontal lobe of the cortex. The surgery was first developed by the Portuguese neurosurgeon Egas Moniz in 1935. In 1949 he won the Nobel Prize in Medicine for his work in this area. Such surgery has been used to control the emotional component of neurosis and psychosis, and success rates have been reported at about 65 percent. In the story, however, the narrator expresses his reservations about the technique. Some of the reported negative aftereffects are impairment of the sense of responsibility, a flattening of feeling and emotion, and a loss of ambition and imagination. Perhaps most important, the surgical procedure produces irreversible damage to the patient's brain. With the advent of drugs which also accomplish control of emotionality without irreversible brain damage, lobotomies are used rather rarely today.

It is interesting to note that in the story a version of a lobotomy is performed on a habitual criminal. In the 1950s prefrontal lobotomies were reportedly used with "success" on "severe psychopaths," a controversial diagnostic category which is often used to describe habitual offenders. Critics have severely criticized this use of lobotomy. One of the famous—or perhaps infamous—uses of the technique on a habitual troublemaker was the lobotomy performed on McMurphy, the hero of Ken Kesey's *One Flew Over the Cuckoo's Nest*. The success of McMurphy's surgery is much more debatable than that of the operation performed in the following story.

THE BRAIN *Norbert Wiener*

The brain is a funny organ. It controls all the sensations of the body and yet it can be touched and cut with no local sensation at all. One man will die of a slight concussion and another can have a crowbar shot through his head with nothing but a ruined disposition to show for it. Recently it has become fashionable to do all sorts of weird things to the brain with needles and hot wires in order to cure or relieve some of the many forms of depressive insanity. It's an ugly business—I don't like it. Sometimes it cuts out a man's conscience, and pretty nearly every time it does eerie things to his judgment and personal balance.

There was a fellow in Chicago, for instance, a big-shot salesman with an insurance company. The only trouble with him was that he had the blues so bad that they never knew whether he would leave for home via the elevator or the tenth-story window. His company begged him to have a little piece of his prefrontal lobe out, and he consented. After that, Mr. Big-shot became Mr. Bigger-shot. As a matter of fact, he outsold every salesman in the history of the company. As a token of their regard, they made him vice-president. They forgot one thing, however, that a man with a prefrontal lobotomy isn't very good at following the pea under the walnut shell. When he got out of the selling game into higher finance, he went flat and so did the company. No, I shouldn't like to have anyone tamper with my inner wiring diagrams.

This brings me to a case which came to my attention the other day. I belong to a small group of scientists which meets once a month in the private room of a little restaurant. We have a scientific paper to give an excuse for our meeting, but the real reason for it is a miscellaneous interest and an unbridled loquacity on the part of the whole gang. It's no place for the striped pants boys. We rib one another unmercifully; and if you can't take it, the door is always open. I myself am something in between a mathematician and an engineer, but perhaps the bulk of us are medical men. Heaven help the waitresses when the medical boys get talking freely! I won't go so far as to assert that the electric lights go blue, and that the atmosphere smells of sulphur at times, but that is the general idea.

Waterman is in our good graces. He runs a state madhouse some fifty miles away, and looks like the amiable and prosperous

proprietor of a delicatessen shop. He is short, fat, walrus-mous-
tached and completely without vanity. He usually has a lame duck
in tow. This time he came in with a rather tall, sallow man, whose
name I didn't get. I did get the impression that he was a doctor, but
he had some of the curious hesitation in company that I have seen in
prospectors or engineers who have been too long away from normal
civilization, confined in the mountains of Korea or the backwoods of
Borneo. It is a mixture of lost familiarity with civilization and
overdeveloped self-consciousness and self-criticism. Some of those
boys had had to do things that no civilized man can do with
impunity to himself, and they carry around the marks ever after.

I do not know how the conversation got around to frontal
lobotomy. I think one of the engineering guests asked about it as a
possibility for a distant relative who was a mental patient. Everybody present had an opinion about it. A few of them spoke for it, but
most of them—even the brain surgeons—did not want any part of it.

Then we got talking about what a modern automobile accident
can do to a child's brain. The discussion was not exactly dainty,
even as doctors' discussions go. The talk was going hot and heavy;
and I do not think anyone noticed anyone but the fellow he was
talking to. Suddenly there was a little crash. We looked around to
see Waterman's friend cold out on the floor. His forehead was
covered with beads of sweat. Waterman knelt down beside him and
felt his pulse.

"I don't think it's anything serious," he said. "He is a patient of
mine, but very intelligent, and I thought it might cheer him up a bit
to come along. He is suffering from amnesia, and we don't know his
real name. I shouldn't have taken the chance of bringing him here.
Come on, let's carry him out. It won't be necessary to break up the
meeting."

Waterman telephoned to his hospital for an ambulance, while
two or three of our medical contingent got in touch with the
proprietor of the restaurant. He was flustered, but told us to carry the
unconscious man to a couch in a back room. Our patient was
beginning to come to a bit. He was in an obvious state of emotional
excitement and confusion. He kept talking incoherently. Among the
words that came out were "gangster," "little Paul," "Martha," and
"the crash." The words formed sentences, but they were spoken too
low for us to understand them.

Waterman fetched his bag up from the cloakroom. He administered some sedative; a barbiturate, I think. For a while, it quieted
our man; but you never can tell about these sedatives. After a while

the patient opened his eyes. His mutterings became louder and more intelligible. The words were fairly coherent.

Waterman is a good enough doctor to use opportunities when he finds them.

"This is my chance," he said. "He's on a talking jag. Some six weeks ago a cop picked him up in a doorway. The police turned him over to us. He doesn't even remember his name. We know that he has been a doctor, and it isn't hard to see that he has been through some pretty times. Up to now he's been getting back strength, and we haven't wanted to disturb his recovery by questioning him too much. However, since we seem to have got him into a talkative mood, here goes!"

The return of the banished memory was fascinating to watch. Waterman is a smooth worker, and it was a delight to hear him ask questions. The new personality emerged like the face of a drowned man when they bring him to the surface with grappling irons. I haven't kept any record of what I saw; but Waterman was writing steadily in a little black notebook. The following conversation is a transcription of his record.

Q. "What is your name?"

A. "My name is Arthur Cole."

Q. "You are a doctor, aren't you?"

A. "I am."

Q. "What medical school did you go to?"

A. "Central Western Medical, in Chicago. Class of 1926."

Q. "Where did you pass your internship?"

A. "I was surgical intern at the Physicians and Surgeons Charity Hospital in Chicago. You know where the hospital is—down at the South End."

I dimly remembered the Physicians and Surgeons Charity Hospital in Chicago. It was a dingy pile of greasy red brick in that festering hell of dead streets where the South End meets the West End.

Q. "Surgical intern. That's interesting—did you go in for any special branch of surgery?"

A. "Yes, of course, for two years I took pretty much what they gave me, but I always wanted to be a brain surgeon. What was I saying? I'm afraid I am very confused. I had forgotten altogether that I had been a brain surgeon."

Q. "Oh, so you were a brain surgeon. What did you do after your internship?"

A. "I remember a long line of locked corridors and barbed windows. What was it called? It must have been a hospital for the insane. Oh yes, now I recollect. The Mere—Mere—Meredith County Hospital for the insane. That's in Illinois isn't it?"

Q. "I think it is. Do you remember what they called the town?"

A. "Buckminster. No, it wasn't Buckminster. Now, I have it, it was Leominster."

Q. "Yes, that's right, it is at Leominster. How old were you when you went there?"

A. "About thirty."

Q. "Do you remember the year?"

A. "It was in 1931."

Q. "Did you go there alone?"

A. "I went there with my wife. I am married, aren't I? What happened to my wife? She's here, isn't she? Oh, my God! Martha—Martha."

His voice rose to an incoherent scream. Waterman said, "I'm afraid we shall have to try some more sedative. I'm going to make the dose as light as I can. I don't want to lose this opportunity to find out more about him."

The excitement of the patient gradually subsided as the drug took hold. For a few minutes he seemed too dazed to say anything. Then the confusion began to wear off and Waterman recommenced his inquiries.

Q. "You must help us if we are to help you," he said. "Pull yourself together. How long had you been married when you went to Leominster?"

A. "Not two years. Martha was a nurse at the Chicago Charity Hospital. Martha Sorenson was her name. She came from Minnesota, I remember. Her father owned a wheat farm somewhere near the North Dakota line. We went back there to be married."

Q. "Any children?"

A. "Yes, a boy—Paul. Now it all comes back to me."

He sunk his head in his arms and began to weep. He burst into incoherent cries. "Where is Paul? Where is Paul?" It seemed indecent to be the witness of such pain.

Waterman stood by the head of the couch where Cole lay. I had always thought of him as the life of the party—gay, witty and salty. I had never seen Waterman, the doctor. He was quiet and dignified, and his voice was more soothing than any anodyne. He was Aesculapius himself, the God of Healing.

Q. "Calm yourself, Dr. Cole," he said. "We want to help you, but you are the only man who can teach us how to. Tell us something about the County Hospital. Did you live in?"

A. "For a few months. Then we took an old farmhouse about a mile away. Martha thought we could fix it up, but I didn't see how we could ever dig through that mess of trash and dirt. Martha could make even a pigsty livable. Let's see: I remember there was a U. S. highway passing in front of the house."

He sank onto his face, his head between his arms—his shoulders heaved. "The brakes," he said. "I can hear them scream. The crash! The car turned over. Blood on the road—blood on the road! I could see it and I couldn't do a thing."

Waterman motioned to us to be quiet. I felt the shame of witnessing another man's naked suffering. Gradually the sobs subsided. Again Waterman took up the inquisition.

"Now, don't bother yourself to put it all together," he said. "Just let me ask you questions. It will all come out easier that way. Let's see. What sort of a place was this Goodair?"

A. "Oh, just one of those farming towns, set down on the prairie by pure chance. It was a farming town; that is, except for the factory."

Q. "The factory—what was that? What did it make?"

A. "I never could tell. The people in the town—well, you couldn't believe a word they said. You know the gossip in a small place like that."

Q. "What sort of gossip?"

A. "Some people said it was a bootleg headquarters, and others that it was a headquarters for making drugs. Anyhow, I never liked the place."

Q. "Why not?"

A. "It was a low building of crumbling concrete left over from World War I. I took a walk over there one day. I always felt that somebody was watching me, and I didn't dare to go very near. It was surrounded by a tangle of giant pigweed, and ditches half-filled with a scummy green water. There were a lot of dismantled wrecks of old cars there, and some neglected farm machinery. Nobody ever seemed to go there for weeks at a time, but every now and then we saw a big car drive up just about dusk."

Q. "What sort of a car?"

A. "It looked like a fancy limousine, but it drove like a truck—and the man in it—"

Q. "When did you see the man?"

A. "That was when the car was coming down our road at about eighty miles just before—Oh God! I saw my car open up like a wet paper boat and spring across the road. They were in it. My Paul—my Martha—my poor little Paul."

Cole became inarticulate again; he twitched all over. I have only seen the like in an experimental animal on the operating table. Waterman gave him another dose, I don't know whether of sedative or stimulant, and Cole gradually quieted down.

Q. "Tell me about the man in the car."

A. "Tall and fat and well-dressed. A red scar went from the corner of his eye to his mouth."

Q. "Do you remember what they called him?"

A. "Macaluso, I think. But they never spoke of him by his name. The country people didn't talk of him much, but when they did they called him *The Brain.*"

Q. "Was he the man who made the drugs?"

A. "I think so, but a friend of mine told me that he was a big-shot bank robber, too. A slick article, they said. The police had been looking for him a long time, but they hadn't been able to get anything on him which would stick."

Q. "What happened after the accident?"

The patient made as if to answer, but the words would not come through his mouth. The doctor waited silently until Cole seemed to take hold of himself. He spoke bitterly, forcing his words between his teeth.

A. "It broke my wife's back," he said. "From then to the day she died, she never walked one step. My boy had the left side of his skull crushed in against the seat in front. When I saw it, it was flat and utterly without shape. My partner at the hospital was a good man and saved his life. That is, saved him as a blind, deaf, paralyzed, healthy lump of flesh. With the care that he will get in an institution he will probably outlive most well children. You know what that means. Care that you can't get at a state institution and money—money—money. Or else that I would have to live all my life with this horror right in front of me. My God! It can't be real. It isn't real."

Q. "Didn't they ever try to compensate you for the damage? Of course, I don't mean that they could really compensate you, but you must have needed a lot of money to take care of your wife and child."

A. "They tried to compensate me, all right. A few days after the accident, I was approached over the phone by a local lawyer named Peterson. Peterson was regarded as a pretty slick article in the village. He wanted to know some lawyer representing me whom he could get in touch with. I had a friend named Epstein who did some of the hospital's legal business, so I gave Peterson his name. Epstein told me to keep off the telephone, and to stall Peterson until after he had a chance to talk with me."

Q. "What happened then?"

A. "Epstein came over, and I asked him why he was so cagey. He told me that Peterson was hand in glove with Macaluso and did his legal business for him. He also told me something about the Brain's connections and his tie-up with the county authorities. It did not seem possible to do anything against him. While Epstein was talking Peterson came in. He had a dapperly-waxed little moustache, a frock coat, and an eyeglass hung on a black ribbon. I didn't like the sight of him, but I must say that he was polite."

Q. "He made you an offer though, didn't he?"

A. "He didn't let us know who his principal was, and he disclaimed all responsibility. He tendered me a check for $30,000 for full release. His patter was pretty glib, but I couldn't turn down his money. I would have taken it, if Epstein hadn't told him that we couldn't sign the paper for less than $50,000, as the hospital expenses were going to be so severe and long-lasting. Peterson made a show of protest and I had the good sense to keep quiet. Finally Peterson came across with an offer of $50,000, and Epstein advised me to accept it."

Q. "Well, that compensation must have left you in a financially possible position. What happened then?"

A. "There wasn't anything we could do about Paul. He could eat and he was healthy enough in a vegetative way, but he wasn't my child any more. He had to stay in bed, and he was blind, deaf, and paralyzed. There wasn't a trace of intelligence to be seen. We managed to get him taken at one of the few institutions for cases of that sort, but he was scarcely enough of a human being for us to see him except at long intervals."

Q. "What happened to your wife?"

A. "They took care of her at the State General Hospital about twenty miles away. At first she did pretty well, and then I even thought of building a special house for her with ramps and special kitchen equipment. However her kidneys had not been too good for years and that is always the weak point for paraplegics. She went downhill rapidly. In about three months she sank into a uremic coma and never opened her eyes again. She died in the late fall, but mercifully my colleagues in the hospital were good to me, so we could be together as much as possible in the last days. The funeral was at her home in Minnesota. Her father was a grim old Swedish farmer and did not say much, but I could see he was a broken man."

Q. "I don't see that there was anything left to keep you at Leominster. Did you go back?"

A. "Yes, I did. The train from the West came into the station at about ten in the evening. I noticed two rather strange-looking fellows loitering about and they seemed to be waiting for me. One was a big six-foot bruiser with a broken nose. The other was a lean, wizened, sallow man of ordinary height. He wore a tight overcoat, kept his hat well over his eyes and his hands in his pockets. The prize fighter sidled over to me and said in a hoarse, wheezy voice, 'We've got a job for you. The Boss is hurt.' 'The Boss,' said I, 'do I know him?' 'Sure you do,' wheezed the prize fighter. 'Everybody knows him. You know him. They call him the Brain. We was driving down the turnpike at a pretty fair clip (it wasn't more than eighty), when a cow steps into the road. Well, the cow's beef, and the car's junk. It turned over three times. The Brain was thrown up against the windshield and we don't like his looks. We keeps ourselves to ourselves, and we was on private business so we can't take the Brain to a hospital. It's a job down your line. We know you and they tell us you're a guy who can turn out a classy piece of work. We think you're a right guy. If you aren't, it don't matter anyhow. Come along.'

"I said I would have to go back to the hospital to collect my bag. 'Big boy,' said Tight Overcoat, 'be good and do what you're told. Come along.' Then he said to the other fellow, 'Beefy, you talk too much.'

"There wasn't anybody around that I could call and the shops were closed up. I didn't like the looks of the situation, but there was nothing to do but come along. They drove out about a mile and a half to the concrete factory surrounded by lank growths of pigweed and beggar's lice. Somebody yelled out, 'Hey, give us the high sign.'

"Beefy muttered something which seemed to be satisfactory. Then they took me by both arms and hustled me into an office. It was comfortable and even elegant, quite different from what I had expected from the bare boards and broken windows of the rest of the factory. They pushed me into the room and I tripped over the threshold and fell on my face. I got up again and found there were a couple of other men in the room. One of them was Peterson. He helped me to get up. The other fellow was a brisk business executive type in a brown tweed suit. I never did learn his name, but I think he was the Brain's tie-up with big business. Peterson said to me, 'I am sorry that we have got to be somewhat unceremonious with you, but we are not in a position in which we can choose our methods or our manners. We do not wish you any harm, but you must understand that you have got to be discreet. Mr. Macaluso has just had an accident, and it would not be discreet to take him to a hospital. We are depending on you for help, and I promise you that you will be paid well for it."

"'Supposing I say no?'" I looked slowly at their faces and turned cold.

"'In that case, Doctor Cole, we shall have to take measures to protect ourselves. You are an intelligent man, and I am sure you will appreciate the nature of those measures?'

"I hesitated a moment and then made up my mind. 'All right, I'll do it. Where is the patient?' They opened up the door of an inner office, furnished even more luxuriously than the main one. The Brain was sitting on an overstuffed leather chair with his head lolling back over the cushion. His face was covered with an unhealthy deep flush, and the scar stood out even more clearly than I had remembered. His mouth was open. His breath came out stentoriously, and there was a line of dried blood coming from his left nostril, as if a stream had been stenched not more than a minute or two ago. His head was wrapped in a clean towel. 'Mr. Macaluso was engaged in a business trip of a very private nature,' said Brown-tweed. 'His car hit a cow. He was thrown into the wind-shield. It would be highly undesirable for us, and I may say for you, if any news of his condition should leak out.'

"I unwrapped the bandage. Macaluso's eyes were staring forward into emptiness. The pupils were unequal. I started to palpate the forehead. It was out-of-shape like a watermelon kicked by a horse. As I touched the skull, Peterson leaned forward; Brown-tweed looked at his fingernails, and stood up suddenly as the bone grated when I pressed on it. It was a clear case of depressed fracture of the left frontal bone. I took my fingers away and told Brown-tweed that I would have to operate at once, and that I would have to send back for my tools.

"'Don't worry about that,' he said. 'We have already taken steps to secure anything that may be needed.'

"He passed me a doctor's bag with J. McC. in gold letters just under the handle.

"Isn't that Dr. McCall's bag?" I said.

"'It might be,' said the other fellow, 'but that is no concern of yours. How carelessly they do make these car locks.'

"I felt better when I knew I had McCall's bag to work with. His techniques are somewhat different from mine, but anyway I would have a good kit. They were all there—trephine, elevators, electric saw, sodium amytal, novocaine, and alcohol.

"'Can you make it?' said my new friend.

"I can," said I, hoping I could. I felt very calm and very powerful.

"I looked around for a pan to boil water in and some towels and a good flat table to work on. The business man followed my eyes.

"'You can use the desk,' he said. 'The Brain won't worry about a few spots on it. The water is already hot in the lavatory, and we have plenty of towels in the linen room. Cupid there used to work as an attendant in the State Hospital until he cooked a patient. That's all right, Cupid,' he remarked. 'It's quite all right to talk before the Doctor.'

"Evidently somebody had known how to prepare for an operation. There were a couple of pair of clean coveralls to take the place of surgical gowns. I put one on, and Cupid put on the other. We laid him out—comfortably flat on his back.

"I got busy. The atmosphere was easier and I first shaved the whole head and bathed it in alcohol. Then I injected the novocaine. When this had taken hold, I injected a deeper local anaesthetic into the tissues around the crushed frontal sinus. I didn't want to use a general anaesthetic because it was too important to watch the return of the patient to consciousness as the pressure was relieved. Then I cut the flap of scalp and heard the grating of the trephine as it bit itself into the bone.

"I must admit that Cupid was a good surgical nurse. He knew just when to pass me a hemostatic forceps on a gauze pad, and he seemed to appreciate what I was doing. Even under these weird circumstances, I must admit that I felt complimented.

"Perhaps the most unpleasant moment of the operation is when the sawed circle breaks off from the rest of the skull. Then there is the problem of stenching the flow of blood from under the dura, the brain's cellophane wrapping. I could see Macaluso beginning to come to life again and I could hear his softer and more regular breathing. He opened his eyes. They had lost their glassy unequal stare and his lips began to mouth words.

"'Where am I?' he said. 'What has happened?'

"'Take it easy, Brain,' said the businesslike man. 'You've had an accident. You are in good hands. Dr. Cole is taking care of you.'

"'Cole,' he said. 'I had a little business with him a while ago. He's a right guy. Can I speak with him?'

"'Here I am,' I said as calmly as I could. 'What have you to tell me?'

"'I am sorry about that other accident. You took it like a brick. Bygones is bygones. You'll do a good job on me, won't you?'

"I suppose that if he had not flicked me on the raw like this, reminding me of my loss, the whole thing might have come out differently. As it was, I made my mind up. I tried to keep all appearance of emotion suppressed; but I felt white and when I started to reassure the Brain, and tell him that I was giving his case my closest personal consideration and the advantage of my best judgment, Cupid turned around and looked at me in a way that I didn't like.

"'We are not through yet,' I said. 'Now be very quiet, and I will finish the operation and clean up.'

"I knew what I was going to do, and I don't think I have ever been more deft. At any rate, I was going to settle my relations with Mr. Macaluso once and for all.

"Suddenly Cupid called out, 'Say, Doc, what's you doing? That doesn't look Kosher to me.'

"I said to him quietly, 'This is my judgment and I am taking the responsibility.' I felt I had the upper hand.

"The other fellow from the car, the one who pushed a revolver at me through his pocket, turned to Macaluso and said, 'Brain, Cupid is opening his trap again.' The patient was bandaged except for a small area of operation, but he was perfectly conscious. I like to have them that way in brain operations. It's safer, and besides the brain's surface has no feeling.

"'That's all right,' he said. 'Cole is a friend of mine. Don't let Cupid hold up the operation. He talks too much.'

"I had completed the debridement, and still had one particular job to do before replacing the bit of skull removed by the trephine.

"'Look out,' said Cupid. 'He is . . .'

"The man who had had his hands in his pocket hit Cupid over the head with the butt of his revolver. 'Shut your damn trap,' he said. Cupid lay dead to the world on the floor, and a stream of blood began to creep from one ear. I suppose he had a fracture of the base of the skull, but they wouldn't let me attend to him. I don't even know whether he died or not. I had to walk over Cupid's body to get to the washroom to clean up. When I came back Brown-tweed was waiting. 'Here are $50,000,' he said. 'You understand that you are through at Leominster. If we ever find you in this part of the country again, you know just how long you will last. We will furnish you transportation to the coast, and you can set yourself up in business again under another name. Now remember, or else.'

"I didn't say anything. The money didn't mean a damn thing to me. Nothing did. The Brain started mumbling through his bandages, 'Give him $100,000, boys. I feel fine.'

"I told them what to do for him and took the money offered— ninety-nine shiny new thousand dollar bills and one thousand in fifties and hundreds. They gave me a ticket to San Francisco. Beefy drove me through the night to the Chicago airport. He did not leave until I was safe aboard the through plane to San Francisco. Once I was on the plane, I took all the money but a few dollars for my immediate needs and folded it up in the big envelope that I found in the pouch behind the seat in front of me. I addressed it to the County Hospital and gave it to the stewardess to mail. Now I had no debts, no money and no friends in the world. It did not seem real. I could go anywhere, and I had nowhere to go. At last I was in a cold sweat, and felt as if the half of me was dead and in the grave. That's about all I remember. I have dim recollections of tramp jungles, freight yards, and riding the rods. How I ever got into Dr. Waterman's care I don't remember. They told me a policeman picked me up for a drunk in a doorway."

Cole had spoken more and more slowly as his drugs took hold, and the rest that he desperately needed began. He closed his eyes and passed into a quiet sleep.

I asked Waterman, "Do you believe this yarn?"

"I hate to say," said Waterman. "The man has certainly been through hell, but there is nothing in what he says that a good imagination couldn't invent. I don't quite get his remarks about what he did to the Brain before closing up the wound. There is nothing particularly impressive about reducing a depressed fracture. Have you any ideas?"

"I don't know," I said. "He could have killed Macaluso on the spot, but he didn't. I don't quite see what he was getting at."

We heard a distant siren growing louder and in a few minutes the ambulance from the State Hospital drove up. Two agile young attendants came in under the direction of a white-clad intern. They picked Cole up, transferred him to a stretcher, and carried him away.

Waterman was tired and sat with us for a few minutes before driving out to the hospital in his own car. We smoked in silence.

"I think he dropped something," said Waterman. "Isn't that a wallet?" It contained a coin or two and a few mementos belonging to his present hospital period.

"Wait a minute," said Waterman. "I think I know something about these wallets. They have a secret compartment inside. Give it to me." He took it and after a little manipulation, he turned it inside out.

"Yes, I think there is a secret compartment. Let's see what's in it."

It contained nothing but a Chicago newspaper clipping two years old. It said:

BRAIN GANG WIPED OUT
Plutoria Bank Break Flops
One Hundred Grand Loot Recovered

It went on to tell of a bank robbery attempt made by Macaluso and his henchmen. The attempt had failed grossly. The bank officials were more than ready for the robbers and gave a good account of themselves in the exchange of shots. Those of the robbers who survived to make a getaway were caught between their pursuers and a fast freight where they had to cross the tracks. Not one lived to tell the tale. The paper commented on the incident, remarking that the Brain was known as a careful operator who always planned his jobs well, and that this was the first time he had omitted the most ordinary and elementary precautions.

Waterman took a long puff on his pipe and let the smoke escape upward. I was completely puzzled.

"I don't understand," I said. "It just doesn't make sense. What do you suppose really happened?"

"I don't know," he answered, "but I can guess. In the course of the operation Cole had exposed Macaluso's frontal lobe. It would have been a matter of only a few seconds to undercut it and perform what would be the equivalent of a thoroughgoing frontal lobotomy. It would not have driven Macaluso out of his mind, but would have made him thoroughly unfit to carry out any plans requiring judgment and caution."

I puffed my cigar. "It's not a nice story," I said, "but at any rate, it was a thoroughly successful operation."

socrates

John Christopher

Atomic research, culminating in the bomb dropped on the Japanese at Hiroshima in World War II, made the world dramatically aware of the dangers of radiation. It can produce monstrous defects through genetic mutation. Similarly, mutation may also occur from X-ray radiation. "Socrates" is delightful science fantasy, where the results of mutation are pleasant rather than ugly. It is a dog lover's story, for here we meet Socrates, a dog who actually possesses all the superior characteristics every fond dog owner would like to believe his dog has—and more!

Socrates is a dog with such high intelligence that he seems human. Creatures of high intelligence are often torn with inner conflict which—as Shakespeare dramatized in *Hamlet*—may lead to their tragic destruction. Socrates is no exception. His superior sense perceptions and intelligence, the gift of genetic mutation from his mother, are at war with his instincts. He is attracted to the wise Professor, the narrator of the story, because the Professor fulfills the desire for and delight in learning which his intellect needs. But his instincts command loyalty to his master, Jennings, who is a monstrous and unreasonable man. How Socrates copes with conflicting demands forms the plot of the story.

Socrates' mother, Glory, had been exposed to radiation which had altered the DNA structure of her germ cells. Now, she has produced a litter of mutated pups with extraordinary brains and other extraordinary growth potential. These special potentials have combined with the usual maturing schedule for dogs—which is much faster than in the human being—as well as with the usual special capacities of dogs, like their scent tracking and advanced hearing, making Socrates truly a superbeing. The question at the end of the story is whether Socrates' mutation is dominant or recessive. Can Socrates father another super litter like himself?

141

A review of genetic structures makes clear how mutations occur. The chromosomes, in the nucleus of all cells, contain the genetic material. The chromosomes consist mainly of DNA (deoxyribonucleic acid), and they are shaped like twisted ladders. At various locations along this ladder are the genes, which instruct other cells in the body on how to develop by forming copies of the genes made of RNA within these cells. Alterations of DNA structure are called mutations, and they can occur either in cells of the body or in germ cells used in reproduction. If they occur in the body cells, they cause changes in the body of the organism affected—the process believed to be operating in leukemia. However, if the cell affected is the germ cell, then the individual's progeny are affected as well as future generations: a true mutation, a new breed. If the new mutation is dominant, it will overcome and reproduce in the actual bodies of future generations, in the phenotype; but if it is recessive, it will remain dormant in the genotype and not the phenotype, only showing itself if the individual mates with another of its species that also has this trait as a recessive trait.

Socrates' tragedy in the story grows out of the conflict of his high degree of intelligence and reasoning ability (characteristics we associate with humans) and his instincts (a term often used to explain complex behavior in animals). This raises a question hotly argued for centuries: What sets human beings apart from other animals? From the point of view of structure and functioning, chromosome makeup and reproduction, human beings are intimately part of the great family of mammals. But human beings are bipedal; they stand on two legs. They are the only members of their entire subgroup, the primates, that habitually walk on two legs. As far as evolution is concerned, erect posture is usually the point at which the human line begins. Human beings possess many other minor structural differences from their closest primate relatives, such as loss of a thick covering of body hair, permanently distended breasts of the female, and absence of large canine teeth. Human behavior, too, is much more rich, complex, and diverse.

Instinct is defined as an innate, fixed behavior pattern, and the term is used to explain complex behaviors in animals, like returning to spawning grounds, or building characteristic nests for the species—behaviors which seemingly could not have been learned.

In general, American psychologists shy away from using the term *instinct* to explain behavior in higher animals, preferring instead explanations based on learning. But the work of Lorenz (1966) and others has somewhat bolstered the concept of instinct, especially in explaining animal behavior.

The issue of instinct in the story, "Socrates," is whether indeed a dog does have an instinct to follow his master and be loyal to him. Is this true or a myth? An explanation based on learning rather than instinct would propose that a dog will follow the source of its rewards—like food—which become prepotent over the fact that this reward source might also be the source of punishment through whippings, etc.

An interesting alternative explanation might be the process of *imprinting* discovered by Lorenz and others who have studied animals. The process refers to the fact that a young animal will follow another animal that is present during a critical period in its development. At a later time it selects an animal of the same species as a mate. The period for dogs is reported to be at thirteen weeks, after which they apparently cannot be used as pets. For Socrates, who matured rapidly, the critical period may have been a good deal sooner. We learn that he was not being fed by his mother after a week, but instead received his food from his master, Jennings. His critical imprint period probably occurred during the time Jennings was feeding him. Why doesn't Socrates then try to mate with one of Jenning's species, a human female? Well, Socrates was an unusually intelligent dog, wise enough to mate with Tess, the Professor's golden retriever.

As the story ends, we wonder: What traits will the puppies possess? Is the mutation of Socrates dominant or recessive? Will it dominate over the traits transmitted by Tess and produce another super litter? A happy guess would be that the mutation is dominant, since the traits have already been transmitted by the genes of Socrates' mother over her mate—unless her mate had also been affected by radiation, which is possible. In that event, it was the combination of two recessive genes which produced Socrates.

SOCRATES   *John Christopher*

I had closed the lab for the afternoon and was walking down toward the front gate, meaning to take a bus into town, when I heard the squeals from the direction of the caretaker's cottage. I'm fond of animals and hate to hear them in pain, so I walked through the gate into the cottage yard. What I saw horrified me.

Jennings, the caretaker, was holding a young puppy in his hand and beating its head against the stone wall. At his feet were three dead puppies, and as I came through the gate he tossed a fourth among them, and picked up the last squirming remnant of the litter. I called out sharply, "Jennings! What's going on?"

He turned to face me, still holding the puppy in his hand. He is a surly-looking fellow at best, but now he looked thunderous.

"What the hell do you think I'm doing?" he demanded. "Killing off a useless litter—that's what I'm doing."

He held the pup out for me to observe.

"Here," he went on, "have a look at this and you'll see why."

I looked closely. It was the queerest pup I had ever seen. It had a dirty, tan coat and abnormally thick legs. But it was the head that drew attention. It must have been fully four times the size of any ordinary pup of its breed; so big that, although its neck was sturdy, the head seemed to dangle on it like an apple on a stalk.

"It's a queer one, all right," I admitted.

"Queer?" he exclaimed. "It's a monster, that's what it is." He looked at me angrily. "And I know the cause of it. I'm not a fool. There was a bit in the Sunday papers a couple of weeks back about it. It's them electrical X-ray machines you have up at the house. It said in the paper about X-rays being able to influence what's to be born and make monsters of them. And look at this for a litter of pedigree airedales; not one that would make even a respectable mongrel. Thirty quid the price of this litter at the very least."

"It's a pity," I said, "but I'm pretty sure the company won't accept responsibility. You must have let your bitch run loose beyond the inner gate and there's no excuse for that. It's too bad you didn't see that bit in the Sunday paper a few weeks earlier; you might have kept her chained up more. You know you've been warned about going near the plant."

"Yes," he snarled, "I know what chance I've got of getting money out of those crooks. But at least I can get some pleasure out of braining this lot."

He prepared to swing the pup against the wall. It had been quiet while we were talking, but now it gave one low howl and opened large eyes in a way that seemed frantically to suggest that it had been listening to our conversation, and knew its fate was sealed. I grabbed hold of Jennings' arm pretty roughly.

"Hold on," I said. "When did you say those pups were born?"

"This morning," he growled.

I said, "But its eyes are open. And look at the color! Have you ever seen an airedale with blue eyes before?"

He laughed unpleasantly. "Has anybody ever seen an airedale with a head like that before, or a coat like that? It's no more an airedale than I am. It's a cur. And I know how to deal with it."

The pup was whining to itself, as though realizing the futility of making louder noises. I pulled my wallet out.

"I'll give you a quid for it," I said.

He whistled. "You must be mad," he said. "But why should that worry me? It's your money. Taking it now?"

"I can't," I said. "My landlady wouldn't let me. But I'll pay you ten bob a week if you will look after it till I can find it a place. Is it a deal?"

He put his hand out again. "In advance?"

I paid him.

"I'll look after it, guv-nor, even though it goes against the grain. At any rate it'll give Glory something to mother."

At least once a day, sometimes twice, I used to call in to see how the pup was getting along. It was progressing amazingly. At the end of the second week Jennings asked for an increase of 2/6d. in the charge for keeping it, and I had to agree. It had fed from the mother for less than a week, after which it had begun to eat its own food, and with a tremendous appetite.

Jennings scratched his unkempt head when he looked at it. "I don't know. I've never seen a dog like it. Glory didn't give it no lessons in eating or drinking. It just watched her from the corner and one day, when I brought fresh stuff down, it set on it like a wolf. It ain't natural."

Watching the pup eat, I was amazed myself. It seemed to have more capacity for food than its mother, and you could almost see it putting on weight and size. And its cleverness! It was hardly more than a fortnight old when I surprised it carefully pawing the latch of the kennel door open, to get at some food that Jennings had left outside while going out to open the gates. But even at that stage I don't think it was such superficial tricks that impressed me, so much as the way I would catch it watching Jennings and me as we leaned over the kennel fence discussing it. There was such an air of attentiveness about the way it sat, with one ear cocked, a puzzled frown on that broadbrowed, most uncanine face.

Jennings said one day, "Thought of a name for him yet?"

"Yes," I said. "I'm going to call him Socrates."

"Socrates?" repeated Jennings. "Something to do with football?"

I smiled. "There was another great thinker with that name several thousand years ago. A Greek."

"Oh," Jennings said scornfully. "A Greek. . . ."

One Friday evening I brought a friend down to see Socrates—a man who had made a study of dogs. Jennings wasn't in. This didn't surprise me because he habitually got drunk at least one evening a week and Friday was his favorite. I took my friend around to the kennels.

He didn't say anything when he saw the pup, which was now, after three weeks, the size of a large fox terrier. He examined it carefully, as though he were judging a prize winner at Cruft's. Then he put it down and turned to me.

"How old did you say this dog is?" he asked.

I told him.

He shook his head. "If it were anyone but you who told me, I would call him a liar," he said. "Man, I've never seen anything like it. And that head. . . . You say the rest of the litter were the same?"

"The bodies looked identical," I told him. "That's what impressed me. You are liable to get queer freak mutations around these new labs of ours—double-headed rats and that sort of thing—but five the same in one litter! That looked like a true mutation to me."

He said, "Mutations I'm a bit shaky about, but five alike in one litter look like a true breed to me. What a tragedy that fool killed them."

"He killed a goose that might have laid him some very golden eggs," I said. "Quite apart from the scientific importance of it—I should imagine a biologist would go crazy at the thought—a new mutated breed like this would have been worth a packet. Even this one dog might have all sorts of possibilities. Look!"

Socrates had pushed an old tin against the wall of the kennel and was using it in an attempt to scale the fence barring the way to the outer world. His paws scrabbled in vain a few inches from the top.

"Good God!" my friend said. "If it can do that after a month. . . ."

We turned and left the kennels. As we came out I collided with Jennings. He reeled drunkenly past us.

"Come to feed little Shocratesh," he said thickly.

I held his shoulder. "That's all right," I said. "We've seen to them."

When I dropped in the following day, I was surprised to see a huge, roughly painted sign hanging over the kennel door. It read:

"PRIVATE. NO ADMITTANCE."

I tried the door, but it was locked. I looked around. Jennings was watching me.

"Hello, Professor," he said. "Can't you read?"

I said, "Jennings, I've come for the pup. My friend is going to look after him at his kennels."

Jennings grinned. "Sorry," he said, "the dog's not for sale."

"What do you mean?" I exclaimed. "I bought him four weeks ago. And I've been paying you for his keep."

"You got any writing that says that, Professor?" he asked. "You got a bill of sale?"

"Don't be ridiculous, Jennings," I said. "Open the door up."

"You even got any witnesses?" he asked. He came over to me confidentially.

"Look," he said, "you're a fair man. I heard you telling your friend last night that dog's a gold mine. You know I own him by rights. Here, I'm a fair man myself. Here's three pounds five, the money I've had from you in the last four weeks. You know he's my gold mine by rights. You wouldn't try to do a man like me. You know I paid five quid stud fee for that litter."

"It was a bargain," I said. "You were going to throw the pup at the wall—don't forget that. You wouldn't even know the dog was anything out of the ordinary now, except for listening to a private conversation last night." I found my wallet. "Here's ten pounds. That will make good the stud fee and a little extra profit for yourself into the bargain."

He shook his head. "I'm not selling, Professor. And I know my rights in the law. You've got no proof; I've got possession."

I said, "You idiot! What can you do with him? He will have to be examined by scientists, tested, trained. You don't know anything about it."

Jennings spat on the ground. "Scientists!" he exclaimed. "No, I'm not taking him to no scientists. I've got a bit of money saved up. I'm off away from here tomorrow. *I'll* do the training. And you watch the theaters for the big billboards in a few months' time— George Jennings and his Wonder Dog, Socrates! I'll be up at the West End inside a year."

It was only three months later that I saw the name on the bills outside the Empire Theater in Barcaster. There had been no word from Jennings during that time. As he had said he would, he had gone with the dog, vanishing completely. Now he was back, and the bill read as he had told me it would:

GEORGE JENNINGS
AND HIS WONDER DOG,
SOCRATES

I went in and bought a seat in the front row. There were some knockabout comedians fooling together on the stage; and after them a team of rather tired-looking acrobats. Jennings was the third in appearance. He strode on to a fanfare of trumpets, and behind him loped Socrates.

He was bigger and his rough, tan coat was shaggier than ever. His head was more in proportion to his body, too, but it was still huge. He looked nearer to a St. Bernard than any breed I could think of, but he was very little like a St. Bernard. He was just Socrates, with the same blue eyes blazing that had surprised me that after-noon four months before.

Jennings had taught him tricks, all right. As they reached the center of the stage, Socrates staggered up on to his hind legs, waddled to the footlights and saluted the audience. He swung effortlessly from the trapezes the acrobats had left, spelled out words in reply to Jennings' questions, pulling alphabet blocks forward with his teeth. He went through all the repertoire that trick dogs usually follow, capping them with an assurance that made the audience watch in respectful silence. But when he left, walking stiffly off the stage, the ovation was tremendous. They came back half a dozen times for encores, Socrates saluting gravely each time the mob of hysterical humans before him. When they had left for the last time, I walked out, too.

I bribed the doorman to let me know the name of Jennings' hotel. He wasn't staying with the rest of the music-hall people, but by himself in the Grand. I walked over there late in the evening, and had my name sent up. The small, grubby page boy came back in a few minutes.

"Mr. Jennings says you're to go right up," he told me, and added the floor and room number.

I knocked and heard Jennings' voice answer, "Come in!"

He seemed more prosperous than the Jennings I had known, but there was the same shifty look about him. He was sitting in front of the fire wearing an expensive blue-and-gold dressing gown, and as I entered the room he poured himself whisky from a decanter. I noticed that his hand shook slightly.

"Why," he said thickly, "if it isn't the professor! Always a pleasure to see old friends. Have a drink, Professor."

He helped me to whisky.

"Here's to you, Professor," he said, "and to Socrates, the Wonder Dog!"

I said, "Can I see him?"

He grinned. "Any time you like. Socrates!"

A door pushed open and Socrates walked in, magnificent in his bearing and in the broad, intelligent face from which those blue eyes looked out. He advanced to Jennings' chair and dropped into immobility, head couched between powerful paws.

"You seen our show?" Jennings asked.

I nodded.

"Great, isn't it? But it's only the beginning. We're going to show them! Socrates, do the new trick."

Socrates jumped up and left the room, returning a moment later pulling a small wooden go-cart, gripping a rope attached to it in his teeth. I noticed that the cart had a primitive pedal arrangement near the front, fixed to the front wheels. Socrates suddenly leaped into the cart, and moving the pedals with his paws, propelled himself along the room. As he reached the wall, the cart swerved and I noticed that his tail worked a rudderlike arrangement for steering. He went the reverse length of the room and turned again, but this time failed to allow enough clearance. The cart hit the side wall and Socrates toppled off.

Jennings rose to his feet in an instant. He snatched a whip from the wall, and, while Socrates cowered, thrashed him viciously, cursing him all the time for his failure.

I jumped forward and grappled with Jennings. At last I got the whip away from him and he fell back exhausted in the chair and reached for the whisky decanter.

I said angrily, "You madman! Is this how you train the dog?"

He looked up at me over his whisky glass. "Yes," he said, "this is my way of training him! A dog's got to learn respect for his master. He doesn't understand anything but the whip. Socrates!"

He lifted his whip hand, and the dog cowered down.

"I've trained him," he went on. "He's going to be the finest performing dog in the world before I'm through."

I said, "Look, Jennings, I'm not a rich man, but I've got friends who will advance me money. I'll get you a thousand pounds for Socrates."

He sneered. "So you want to cash in on the theaters, too?"

"I promise that if you sell Socrates to me, he will never be used for profit by anyone."

He laughed. "A hell of a lot I care what would happen to him if I sold him. But I'm not selling; not for a penny under £20,000. Why, the dog's a gold mine."

"You are determined about that?" I asked.

He got up again. "I'll get you the advance bills for our next engagement," he said. "Top billing already! Hang on; they're only next door."

He walked out unsteadily. I looked down to where Socrates lay, watching everything in the way that had fascinated me when he was a pup. I called to him softly:

"Socrates."

He pricked up his ears. I felt crazy, but I had to do it. I whispered to him, "Socrates, follow me back as soon as you can get away. Here, take the scent from my coat."

I held my sleeve out to him, and he sniffed it. He wagged his huge, bushy tail slowly. Then Jennings was back with his billheads, and I made my excuses and left.

I walked back—a matter of two or three miles. The more I thought, the more insane did it seem that the dog could have heeded and understood my message. It had been an irrational impulse.

I had found new accommodations in the months since Jennings' disappearance; in a cottage with a friendly old couple. I had brought Tess, my own golden retriever, from home, and they both adored her. She was sitting on the inside window ledge as I walked slowly up the garden path, and her barks brought old Mrs. Dobby to the door to let me in. Tess came bouncing to meet me and her silky paws were flung up toward my chest. I patted and stroked her into quietness and, after washing, settled down to a pleasant tea.

Two or three hours later, the Dobbys having gone to bed, I was sitting reading by the fire when I heard a voice at the door.

I called, "Who's there?"

This time it was a little more distinct, though still garbled, as though by a person with a faulty palate. I heard, "Socrates."

I threw the door open quickly. Socrates stood there, eyes gleaming, tail alert. I looked beyond him into the shadows.

"Who's brought you, old chap?" I asked.

Socrates looked up. His powerful jaws opened. I could see teeth gleaming whitely.

Socrates said, slurring the words, but intelligible, "Me. Can speak."

I brought him in, shelving my incredulity. Sitting in the Dobbys' cosy room in front of a glowing fire, it seemed more fantastic than ever. Half to myself, I said, "I can't believe it."

Socrates had sat down on the rug. "True, though," he said.

I asked, "Does Jennings know?"

Socrates replied, "No. Have told no one else. Would only make into tricks."

"But Jennings knows you can hear and understand things?"

"Yes. Could not hide. Jennings whips until I learn. Easier to learn at once."

His voice, a kind of low, articulate growling, became more readily understandable as I listened to it. After a few minutes it did not seem at all strange that I was sitting by the fire talking to a half-grown but large mongrel dog. He told me how he had practiced human speech by himself, forcing his throat to adapt itself to the complexities, succeeding through a long process of trial and error.

I said, in amazement, "But, Socrates, you are barely four months old!"

His brow wrinkled. "Yes. Strange. Everything goes so fast for me. Big—old. . . ."

"Maturity," I supplied. "Of course there have been 'talking dogs' before, but they were just stunts, no real intelligence. Do you realize what a phenomenon you are, Socrates?"

The vast canine face seemed to smile. "How not realize?" he asked. "All other dogs—such fools. Why that, Professor?"

I told him of his birth. He seemed to grasp the idea of X-ray mutation very easily. I suppose one can always swallow the facts of one's own existence. He remembered very little of that first month of infancy. When I told him of the fate of the rest of his litter, he was saddened.

"Perhaps best not to know that," he said. "Sad to think I might have had brothers and sisters like me. Not to be always a trick dog."

"You don't need to be a trick dog, Socrates," I said. "Look, we'll go away. I've got friends who will help. You need never see Jennings again."

Socrates said, "No. Not possible. Jennings the master. I must go back."

"But he beats you! He may beat you for going out now."

"He will," Socrates said. "But worth it to come see you."

"Look, Socrates," I said. "Jennings isn't your master. No free intelligence should be a slave to another. Your intelligence is much more advanced than Jennings'."

The big head shook. "For men, all right. Dogs different."

"But you aren't even Jennings' dog," I said. I told him the story of Jennings' trickery; how he had sold Socrates to me and then refused to acknowledge the sale. Socrates was not impressed.

"Always Jennings' dog," he said. "Not remember anything else. Must go back. You not dog—not understand."

I said halfheartedly, "We would have a fine time, Socrates. You could learn all sorts of things. And be free, completely free."

But I knew it was no use. Socrates, as he said, was still a dog, even though an intelligent one, and the thousands of years of instinctive slavery to a human master had not been quenched by the light that brought intelligence and reasoning to his brain.

He said, "Will come here to learn. Will get away often."

"And be beaten by Jennings every time you go back?"

Socrates shivered convulsively. "Yes," he said. "Worth it. Worth it to learn things. You teach?"

"I'll teach you anything I can, Socrates," I promised.

"Can mutate more dogs like me?"

I hated to say it. "No, Socrates. You were a fluke, an accident. X-rays make monsters; once in a million, million times, perhaps, something like you happens."

The bushy tail drooped disconsolately. The huge head rested a moment between the paws. Then he stood up, four-legged, an outcast.

"Must go now. Will come again soon."

I let him out and saw him lope away into the night. I turned back into the warm firelit room. I thought of Socrates, running back through the night to Jennings' whip and I knew what anger and despair were.

Socrates came quite frequently after that. He would sit in front of me while I read to him from books. At first he wanted to be taught to read for himself, but the difficulty of turning pages with his clumsy paws discouraged him. I read to him from all the books he wanted.

His appetite was voracious, but lay chiefly along nontechnical lines; naturally enough, in view of the impossibility of his ever being able to do even the simplest manual experiments. Philosophy interested him, and I found my own education improving with Socrates' as he led me deeper and deeper into mazes of idealism, epistemology and sublineation. He enjoyed poetry, too, and composed a few rough poems, which had the merit of a strange nonhuman approach. But he would not let me write them down; now I can remember only a few isolated lines.

His most intense interest was in an unexpected field. I mentioned casually one day some new development in physical research, and his mind fastened on the subject immediately. He told me he could see all sorts of queer things which he knew humans could at the best sense only vaguely. He spent nearly an hour one evening describing to me the movements of a strange spiral-shaped thing that, he said, was spinning around slowly in one corner of my room, now and then increasing and decreasing in size and making sudden jumps. I walked over to the place he indicated and put my hand through vacancy.

"Can hear it, too," Socrates said. "High, sweet noise."

"Some people have unusual senses and report similar things," I told him.

He made me read through every book I could find on paranormal phenomena, in search of explanations of the oddities that surrounded him, but they annoyed him.

"So many fools," he said wearily, when we put down one book that had painstakingly linked up poltergeists with angels. "They did not see. They only wanted to. They thought they did."

The Dobbys were a little curious at my new habit of reading aloud in my room, and once I saw them glancing suspiciously at Socrates when he changed his speech into a growl as they came into the house from the garden. But they accepted his strange appearances and disappearances quite easily, and always made a fuss of him when he happened to turn up during my absence.

We did not always read. At times we would go out into the fields, and he and Tess would disappear in search of rabbits and birds and all the other things that fascinate dogs in the country. I would see them a field away, breasting the wind together. Socrates badly needed such outings. Jennings rarely took him out, and, as Socrates spent all the time he could filch from Jennings' training activities with me, he saw no other dogs and had no other exercise. Tess was very fond of him and sometimes whined when we shut her out from my room, in order to read and talk undisturbed. I asked Socrates about her once.

He said, "Imagine all dogs intelligent; all men fools. You the only intelligent man. You talk to dogs, but you not like pretty women, even though they are fools?"

Then, for months, Socrates disappeared, and I learned that Jennings was touring the north of England, having a sensational success. I saw also the announcement that he was to return to Barcaster for a fortnight early in November. I waited patiently. On the morning before he was due to open, Socrates returned.

He was looking as fit as ever physically, but mentally the tour had been a strain for him. In philosophy he had always inclined to defeatism, but it had been defeat with a sense of glory. He had reveled in Stapledon's works, and drawn interesting comparisons between himself and Stapledon's wonder sheepdog. Now, however, there was a listlessness about him that made his defeatism a drab and unhappy thing. He would not read philosophy, but lay silent while I read poetry to him.

Jennings, I discovered, had steadily increased his bouts of drunkenness. Socrates told me that he had to carry the act by himself now; Jennings was generally too drunk to give even the most elementary instructions on the stage.

And, of course, with the drunkenness came the whippings. There were nasty scars on the dog's back. I treated them as well as I could, but increasingly I hated and dreaded the time when he would say, "Must go now," and I would see him lope off, tail low, to face Jennings' drunken fury.

I remonstrated with him again, begging him to come away with me, but it was beyond reason. The centuries of slavery could not be eradicated. He always went back to Jennings.

Then he came one afternoon. It had been raining for days, and he was wet through. He would not stay in front of the fire to dry. The rain was slackening a little. I took my raincoat, and, with Tess frisking beside us, we set out. We walked on in silence. Even Tess grew subdued.

At last, Socrates said, "Can't go on for long. Whipped me again last night. Felt something burn my mind. Almost tore his throat out. I will do it soon and they will shoot me."

"They won't shoot you," I said. "You come to me. You will be all right. Come now, Socrates. Surely you don't want to go on serving Jennings when you know you may have to kill him?"

He shivered, and the raindrops ran off his shaggy back.

"Talking no good," he said. "I must go back. And if he whips me too much, I must kill him. I will be shot. Best that way."

We had reached the river. I paused on the bridge that spanned it a few inches above the swirling currents of the flood, and looked out. The river was high after the rain, running even more swiftly than it usually did. Less than a quarter of a mile away was the fall, where the water cascaded over the brink into a raging turmoil below. I was looking at it abstractly when I heard Jennings' voice.

He stood at the other end of the bridge. He was raging drunk.

He called, "So there you are! And that's what you've been up to—sneaking off to visit the professor. I thought I might catch you here."

He advanced menacingly up the bridge. "What you need, my lad, is a taste of the whip."

He was brandishing it as he walked. I waited until he had almost reached the place where Socrates was cowering on the boards, waiting for the blow, and then I charged him savagely. He fought for a moment, but I was sober and he was not. I caught one of his legs and twisted. He pulled viciously away, staggered, fell—and disappeared into the violently flowing river.

I saw his face appear a few yards down. He screamed and went under again. I turned to Socrates.

"It's all over," I said. "You are free. Come home, Socrates."

The head appeared again, and screamed more faintly. Socrates stirred. He called to Jennings for the first and last time, "Master!"

Then he was over the bridge and swimming down frantically toward the drowning man. I called after him, but he took no notice. I thought of jumping in myself, but I knew I could not last even to reach him. With Tess at my heels, I raced around the bank to the place where the water roared over the fall.

I saw them just as they reached the fall. Socrates had reached him, and was gripping the coat in his teeth. He tried to make for the bank, but there was no chance. They swept over the edge and into the fury below. I watched for their reappearance for some time, but they did not come up.

They never came up.

I think sometimes of the things Socrates might have done if he had been given the chance. If only for those queer things he saw that we cannot see, his contribution to knowledge would have been tremendous. And when I think that he was less than a year old when he died, the lost possibilities awe and sadden me.

I cannot escape the conclusion that at his full maturity he would have outstripped all the specialists in the strange fields he might have chosen to work in.

There is just one thing that worries me still. His was a true mutation; the identical litter showed that. But was it a dominant one? Could the strength and vigor of his intelligence rise above the ordinary traits of an ordinary dog? It's a point that means a great deal.

Tess is going to have pups.

nine lives

Ursula K. Le Guin

"We're each of us alone, to be sure. What can you do but hold your hand out in the dark?" asks Captain Pugh, the geologist in "Nine Lives." He recognizes that to be human is to be existentially alone. The aloneness and uniqueness of each human require that he actively reach out to other existentially alone individual humans.

But what if you were not a unique individual with nothing else in the universe just like you? What if there were eight other individuals *exactly* like you? What kind of emotional relationships would you develop if you were a member of a nine-clone? This is the question posed in "Nine Lives," by Ursula Le Guin, one of the highly admired writers of science fiction in a field where women are increasingly making their presence felt. In developing the answer to her "what if" query, she creates another planet, Libra, with an environment hostile to human life. Into this isolated setting she places just two sets of characters: Captain Owen Pugh and his technical assistant, Martin; and the nine Chow clones. We watch as—forced to live within the same shelter—they interact.

Ursula Le Guin uses this device to imaginatively explore the possibilities of *cloning*, one of a number of new breakthroughs in knowledge in the field of biology. So major are the developments that it has been termed the biomedical revolution. As biologists gain more understanding of life's basic processes, and particularly its control mechanisms—DNA, for example—the possibility becomes more real that we can begin to manipulate them. In *The Second Genesis* (1969), Albert Rosenfeld proposed that the time is approaching when man can begin to remake and alter his physical structures and means of reproduction.

The process of cloning basically involves isolating a cell from an organism, growing the nucleus of that cell in culture, and developing from it a carbon copy of the organism from which the cell came. A more detailed explanation of cloning is given in "Nine Lives." To date, successful cloning has only been done with frogs, not humans; but it is fascinating to speculate about what the results might be if cloning techniques for humans were perfected.

Questions about clones are many, and some of them are explored in this story. First, who would be cloned? Here copies are made of a genius whose intelligence is at the 99th percentile. But to the suggestion that great men ought to be cloned, geneticist Dr. Theodosius Dobzhansky of Rockefeller University replied: "It can show no lack of respect for the greatness of men like Darwin, Galileo, and Beethoven, to name a few, to say that a world with many millions of Darwins, Galileos, or Beethovens may not be the best possible world." The long-standing argument of whether heredity or environment is more influential in shaping the individual might be answered by cloning. Each clone would have exactly the same genetic makeup. If identical clones were put in different environments, any differences between clones which developed could be attributed only to the environment.

"Nine Lives" points out some interesting advantages and disadvantages of clones. Since they have the same genetic endowment, they have virtually the same brains and bodies and can communicate with each other effectively. This produces a high level of efficiency when they work on technical problems. It also eliminates any difficulties in emotional adjustment since they share similar emotions and can easily empathize with each other. As a result, within their group, the clones are very secure, self-sufficient, and independent. Since they are literally inside each other's brains, their sexual communication is also excellent, adding to their sense of security and independence.

However, we discover that for this group self-sufficiency and security are a double-edged sword, creating disadvantages along with its benefits. It creates a deficiency in the clone members' interpersonal relations with those outside the clone. They do not need outsiders, so they do not know how to communicate with them on a human level. They do not really see others, and because they do not need sympathy, they do not give it.

Having raised the question of what it would be like to be a

member of a clone, Le Guin draws this kind of picture for us in answer. But then she moves her plot to a second developmental stage by raising another question. What if, as a secure member of a clone group, you found yourself in total isolation because a catastrophe had wiped out all the others in the group? How would you cope? It is the answer to this question which forms the climax of "Nine Lives."

NINE LIVES   *Ursula K. Le Guin*

She was alive inside, but dead outside, her face a black and dun net of wrinkles, tumors, cracks. She was bald and blind. The tremors that crossed Libra's face were mere quiverings of corruption: underneath, in the black corridors, the halls beneath the skin, there were crepitations in darkness, ferments, chemical nightmares that went on for centuries. "Oh the damned flatulent planet," Pugh murmured as the dome shook and a boil burst a kilometer to the southwest, spraying silver pus across the sunset. The sun had been setting for the last two days. "I'll be glad to see a human face."

"Thanks," said Martin.

"Yours is human to be sure," said Pugh, "but I've seen it so long I can't see it."

Radvid signals cluttered the communicator which Martin was operating, faded, returned as face and voice. The face filled the screen, the nose of an Assyrian king, the eyes of a samurai, skin bronze, eyes the color of iron: young, magnificent. "Is that what human beings look like?" said Pugh with awe. "I'd forgotten."

"Shut up, Owen, we're on."

"Libra Exploratory Mission Base, come in please, this is *Passerine* launch."

"Libra here. Beam fixed. Come on down, launch."

"Expulsion in seven E-seconds. Hold on." The screen blanked and sparkled.

"Do they all look like that? Martin, you and I are uglier men than I thought."

"Shut up, Owen. . . ."

For twenty-two minutes Martin followed the landing-craft down by signal and then through the cleared dome they saw it, small star in the blood-colored east, sinking. It came down neat and quiet, Libra's thin atmosphere carrying little sound. Pugh and Martin closed the headpieces of their imsuits, zipped out of the dome airlocks, and ran with soaring strides, Nijinsky and Nureyev, toward the boat. Three equipment modules came floating down at four-minute intervals from each other and hundred-meter intervals east of the boat. "Come on out," Martin said on his suit radio, "we're waiting at the door."

"Come on in, the methane's fine," said Pugh.

The hatch opened. The young man they had seen on the screen came out with one athletic twist and leaped down onto the shaky dust and clinkers of Libra. Martin shook his hand, but Pugh was staring at the hatch, from which another young man emerged with the same neat twist and jump, followed by a young woman who emerged with the same neat twist, ornamented by a wriggle, and the jump. They were all tall, with bronze skin, black hair, high-bridged noses, epicanthic fold, the same face. They all had the same face. The fourth was emerging from the hatch with a neat twist and jump. "Martin bach," said Pugh, "we've got a clone."

"Right," said one of them, "we're a ten-clone. John Chow's the name. You're Lieutenant Martin?"

"I'm Owen Pugh."

"Alvaro Guillen Martin," said Martin, formal, bowing slightly. Another girl was out, the same beautiful face; Martin stared at her and his eye rolled like a nervous pony's. Evidently he had never given any thought to cloning, and was suffering technological shock. "Steady," Pugh said in the Argentine dialect, "it's only excess twins." He stood close by Martin's elbow. He was glad himself of the contact.

It is hard to meet a stranger. Even the greatest extrovert meeting even the meekest stranger knows a certain dread, though he may not know he knows it. Will he make a fool of me wreck my image of myself invade me destroy me change me? Will he be different from me? Yes, that he will. There's the terrible thing: the strangeness of the stranger.

After two years on a dead planet, and the last half year isolated as a team of two, oneself and one other, after that it's even harder to meet a stranger, however welcome he may be. You're out of the habit of difference, you've lost the touch; and so the fear revives, the primitive anxiety, the old dread.

The clone, five males and five females, had got done in a couple of minutes what a man might have got done in twenty: greeted Pugh and Martin, had a glance at Libra, unloaded the boat, made ready to go. They went, and the dome filled with them, a hive of golden bees. They hummed and buzzed quietly, filled up all silences, all spaces with a honey-brown swarm of human presence. Martin looked bewilderedly at the long-limbed girls, and they smiled at him, three at once. Their smile was gentler than that of the boys, but no less radiantly self-possessed.

"Self-possessed," Owen Pugh murmured to his friend, "that's it. Think of it, to be oneself ten times over. Nine seconds for every motion, nine ayes on every vote. It would be glorious!" But Martin was asleep. And the John Chows had all gone to sleep at once. The dome was filled with their quiet breathing. They were young, they didn't snore. Martin sighed and snored, his hershey-bar-colored face relaxed in the dim afterglow of Libra's primary, set at last. Pugh had cleared the dome and stars looked in, Sol among them, a great company of lights, a clone of splendors. Pugh slept and dreamed of a one-eyed giant who chased him through the shaking halls of Hell.

From his sleeping-bag Pugh watched the clone's awakening. They all got up within one minute except for one pair, a boy and a girl, who lay snugly tangled and still sleeping in one bag. As Pugh saw this there was a shock like one of Libra's earthquakes inside him, a very deep tremor. He was not aware of this, and in fact thought he was pleased at the sight; there was no other such comfort on this dead hollow world, more power to them who made love. One of the others stepped on the pair. They woke and the girl sat up flushed and sleepy, with bare golden breasts. One of her sisters murmured something to her; she shot a glance at Pugh and disappeared in the sleeping-bag, followed by a giant giggle, from another direction a fierce stare, from still another direction a voice: "Christ, we're used to having a room to ourselves. Hope you don't mind, Captain Pugh."

"It's a pleasure," Pugh said half-truthfully. He had to stand up then, wearing only the shorts he slept in, and he felt like a plucked rooster, all white scrawn and pimples. He had seldom envied Martin's compact brownness so much. The United Kingdom had come through the Great Famines well, losing less than half its population: a record achieved by rigorous food-control. Black-marketeers and hoarders had been executed. Crumbs had been shared. Where in richer lands most had died and a few had thriven, in Britain fewer died and none throve. They all got lean. Their sons were lean, their grandsons lean, small, brittle-boned, easily infected. When civilization became a matter of standing in lines, the British had kept queue, and so had replaced the survival of the fittest with the survival of the fair-minded. Owen Pugh was a scrawny little man. All the same, he was there.

At the moment he wished he wasn't.

At breakfast a John said, "Now if you'll brief us, Captain Pugh—"

"Owen, then."

"Owen, we can work out our schedule. Anything new on the mine since your last report to your Mission? We saw your reports when *Passerine* was orbiting Planet V, where they are now."

Martin did not answer, though the mine was his discovery and project, and Pugh had to do his best. It was hard to talk to them. The same faces, each with the same expression of intelligent interest, all leaned toward him across the table at almost the same angle. They all nodded together.

Over the Exploitation Corps insignia on their tunics each had a nameband, first name John and last name Chow of course, but the middle names different. The men were Aleph, Kaph, Yod, Gimel, and Samedh; the women Sadhe, Daleth, Zayin, Beth, and Resh. Pugh tried to use the names but gave it up at once; he could not even tell sometimes which one had spoken, for the voices were all alike.

Martin buttered and chewed his toast, and finally interrupted: "You're a team. Is that it?"

"Right," said two Johns.

"God, what a team! I hadn't seen the point. How much do you each know what the others are thinking?"

"Not at all, properly speaking," replied one of the girls, Zayin. The others watched her with the proprietary, approving look they had. No ESP, nothing fancy. But we think alike. We have exactly the same equipment. Given the same stimulus, the same problem, we're likely to be coming up with the same reactions and solutions at the same time. Explanations are easy—don't even have to make them, usually. We seldom misunderstand each other. It does facilitate our working as a team."

"Christ yes," said Martin. "Pugh and I have spent seven hours out of ten for six months misunderstanding each other. Like most people. What about emergencies, are you as good at meeting the unexpected problem as a nor . . . an unrelated team?"

"Statistics so far indicate that we are," Zayin answered readily. Clones must be trained, Pugh thought, to meet questions, to reassure and reason. All they said had the slightly bland and stilted quality of answers furnished to the Public. "We can't brainstorm as singletons can, we as a team don't profit from the interplay of varied minds; but we have a compensatory advantage. Clones are drawn from the best human material, individuals of IIQ 99th percentile, Genetic Constitution alpha double A, and so on. We have more to draw on than most individuals do."

"And it's multiplied by a factor of ten. Who is—who was John Chow?"

"A genius surely," Pugh said politely. His interest in cloning was not so new and avid as Martin's.

"Leonardo Complex type," said Yod. "Biomath, also a cellist, and an undersea hunter, and interested in structural engineering problems, and so on. Died before he'd worked out his major theories."

"Then you each represent a different facet of his mind, his talents?"

"No," said Zayin, shaking her head in time with several others. "We share the basic equipment and tendencies, of course, but we're all engineers in Planetary Exploitation. A later clone can be trained to develop other aspects of the basic equipment. It's all training; the genetic substance is identical. We *are* John Chow. But we were differently trained."

Martin look shell-shocked. "How old are you?"

"Twenty-three."

"You say he died young. Had they taken germ cells from him beforehand or something?"

Gimel took over: "He died at twenty-four in an aircar crash. They couldn't save the brain, so they took some intestinal cells and cultured them for cloning. Reproductive cells aren't used for cloning since they have only half the chromosomes. Intestinal cells happen to be easy to despecialize and reprogram for total growth."

"All chips off the old block," Martin said valiantly. "But how can . . . some of you be women . . . ?"

Beth took over: "It's easy to program half the clonal mass back to the female. Just delete the male gene from half the cells and they revert to the basic, that is, the female. It's trickier to go the other way, have to hook in artificial Y chromosomes. So they mostly clone from males, since clones function best bisexually."

Gimel again: "They've worked these matters of technique and function out carefully. The taxpayer wants the best for his money, and of course clones are expensive. With the cell-manipulations, and the incubation in Ngama Placentae, and the maintenance and training of the foster-parent groups, we end up costing about three million apiece."

"For your next generation," Martin said, still struggling, "I suppose you . . . you breed?"

"We females are sterile," said Beth with perfect equanimity: "you remember that the Y chromosome was deleted from our original cell. The male can interbreed with approved singletons, if they want to. But to get John Chow again as often as they want, they just reclone a cell from this clone."

Martin gave up the struggle. He nodded and chewed cold toast. "Well," said one of the Johns, and all changed mood, like a flock of starlings that change course in one wingflick, following a leader so fast that no eye can see which leads. They were ready to go. "How about a look at the mine? Then we'll unload the equipment. Some nice new models in the roboats; you'll want to see them. Right?" Had Pugh or Martin not agreed they might have found it hard to say so. The Johns were polite but unanimous; their decisions carried. Pugh, Commander of Libra Base 2, felt a qualm. Could he boss around this superman-woman-entity-of-ten? and a genius at that? He stuck close to Martin as they suited for outside. Neither said anything.

Four apiece in the three large jetsleds, they slipped off north from the dome, over Libra's dun rugose skin, in starlight.

"Desolate," one said.

It was a boy and girl with Pugh and Martin. Pugh wondered if these were the two that had shared a sleeping bag last night. No doubt they wouldn't mind if he asked them. Sex must be as handy as breathing, to them. Did you two breathe last night?

"Yes," he said, "it is desolate."

"This is our first time Off, except training on Luna." The girl's voice was definitely a bit higher and softer.

"How did you take the big hop?"

"They doped us. I wanted to experience it." That was the boy; he sounded wistful. They seemed to have more personality, only two at a time. Did repetition of the individual negate individuality?

"Don't worry," said Martin, steering the sled, "you can't experience no-time because it isn't there."

"I'd just like to once," one of them said. "So we'd know."

The Mountains of Merioneth showed leprotic in starlight to the east, a plume of freezing gas trailed silvery from a vent-hole to the west, and the sled tilted groundward. The twins braced for the stop at one moment, each with a slight protective gesture to the other. Your skin is my skin, Pugh thought, but literally, no metaphor. What would it be like, then, to have someone as close to you as that? Always to be answered when you spoke, never to be in pain alone. Love your neighbor as you love yourself. . . . That hard old problem was solved. The neighbor was the self: the love was perfect.

And here was Hellmouth, the mine.

Pugh was the Exploratory Mission's ET geologist, and Martin his technician and cartographer; but when in the course of a local survey Martin had discovered the U-mine, Pugh had given him full credit, as well as the onus of prospecting the lode and planning the Exploitation Team's job. These kids had been sent out from Earth years before Martin's reports got there, and had not known what their job would be until they got here. The Exploitation Corps simply sent out teams regularly and blindly as a dandelion sends out its seeds, knowing there would be a job for them on Libra or the next planet out or one they hadn't even heard about yet. The Government wanted uranium too urgently to wait while reports drifted home across the light-years. The stuff was like gold, old-fashioned but essential, worth mining extraterrestrially and shipping interstellar. Worth its weight in people, Pugh thought sourly, watching the tall young men and women go one by one, glimmering in starlight, into the black hole Martin had named Hellmouth.

As they went in their homeostatic forehead-lamps brightened. Twelve nodding gleams ran along the moist, wrinkled walls. Pugh heard Martin's radiation counter peeping twenty to the dozen up ahead. "Here's the drop-off," said Martin's voice in the suit intercom, drowning out the peeping and the dead silence that was around them. "We're in a side-fissure; this is the main vertical vent in front of us." The black void gaped, its far side not visible in the headlamp beams. "Last vulcanism seems to have been a couple of thousand years ago. Nearest fault is twenty-eight kilos east, in the Trench. This region seems to be as safe seismically as anything in the area. The big basalt-flow overhead stabilizes all these substructures, so long as it remains stable itself. Your central lode is thirty-six meters down and runs in a series of five bubble-caverns northeast. It is a lode, a pipe of very high-grade ore. You saw the percentage figures, right? Extraction's going to be no problem. All you've got to do is get the bubbles topside."

"Take off the lid and let'em float up." A chuckle. Voices began to talk, but they were the same voice and the suit radio gave them no location in space. "Open the thing right up. —Safer that way. —But it's a solid basalt roof, how thick, ten meters here? —Three to twenty, the report said. —Blow good ore all over the lot. —Use this access we're in, straighten it a bit and run slider-rails for the robos. —Import burros. —Have we got enough propping material? —What's your estimate of total payload mass, Martin?"

"Say over five million kilos and under eight."

"Transport will be here in ten E-months. —It'll have to go pure. —No, they'll have the mass problem in NAFAL shipping licked by now; remember it's been sixteen years since we left Earth last Tuesday. —Right, they'll send the whole lot back and purify it in Earth orbit. —Shall we go down, Martin?"

"Go on. I've been down."

The first one—Aleph? (Heb., the ox, the leader)—swung onto the ladder and down; the rest followed. Pugh and Martin stood at the chasm's edge. Pugh set his intercom to exchange only with Martin's suit, and noticed Martin doing the same. It was a bit wearing, this listening to one person think aloud in ten voices, or was it one voice speaking the thoughts of ten minds?

"A great gut," Pugh said, looking down into the black pit, its veined and warted walls catching stray gleams of headlamps far below. "A cow's bowel. A bloody great constipated intestine."

Martin's counter peeped like a lost chicken. They stood inside the epileptic planet, breathing oxygen from tanks, wearing suits impermeable to corrosives and harmful radiations, resistant to a two-hundred-degree range of temperatures, tear-proof, and as shock-resistant as possible given the soft vulnerable stuff inside.

"Next hop," Martin said, "I'd like to find a planet that has nothing whatever to exploit."

"You found this."

"Keep me home next time."

Pugh was pleased. He had hoped Martin would want to go on working with him, but neither of them was used to talking much about their feelings, and he had hesitated to ask. "I'll try that," he said.

"I hate this place. I like caves, you know. It's why I came in here. Just spelunking. But this one's a bitch. Mean. You can't ever let down in here. I guess this lot can handle it, though. They know their stuff."

"Wave of the future, whatever," said Pugh.

The wave of the future came swarming up the ladder, swept Martin to the entrance, gabbled at and around him: "Have we got enough material for supports? —If we convert one of the extractorservos to anneal, yes. —Sufficient if we miniblast? —Kaph can calculate stress."

Pugh had switched his intercom back to receive them; he looked at them, so many thoughts jabbering in an eager mind, and at Martin standing silent among them, and at Hellmouth, and the wrinkled plain. "Settled! How does that strike you as a preliminary schedule, Martin?"

"It's your baby," Martin said.

Within five E-days the Johns had all their material and equipment unloaded and operating, and were starting to open up the mine. They worked with total efficiency. Pugh was fascinated and frightened by their effectiveness, their confidence, their independence. He was no use to them at all. A clone, he thought, might indeed be the first truly stable, self-reliant human being. Once adult it would need nobody's help. It would be sufficient to itself physically, sexually, emotionally, intellectually. Whatever he did, any member of it would always receive the support and approval of his peers, his other selves. Nobody else was needed.

Two of the clone stayed in the dome doing calculations and paperwork, with frequent sled-trips to the mine for measurements and tests. They were the mathematicians of the clone, Zayin and Kaph. That is, as Zayin explained, all ten had had thorough mathematical training from age three to twenty-one, but from twenty-one to twenty-three she and Kaph had gone on with math while the others intensified other specialties, geology, mining engineering, electronic engineering, equipment robotics, applied atomics, and so on. "Kaph and I feel," she said, "that we're the element of the clone closest to what John Chow was in his singleton lifetime. But of course he was principally in biomath, and they didn't take us far in that."

"They needed us most in this field," Kaph said, with the patriotic priggishness they sometimes evinced.

Pugh and Martin soon could distinguish this pair from the others, Zayin by gestalt, Kaph only by a discolored left fourth fingernail, got from an ill-aimed hammer at the age of six. No doubt there were many such differences, physical and psychological, among them; nature might be identical, nurture could not be. But the differences were hard to find. And part of the difficulty was that they really never talked to Pugh and Martin. They joked with them, were polite, got along fine. They gave nothing. It was nothing one could complain about; they were very pleasant, they had the standardized American friendliness. "Do you come from Ireland, Owen?"

"Nobody comes from Ireland, Zayin."

"There are lots of Irish-Americans."

"To be sure, but no more Irish. A couple of thousand in all the island, the last I knew. They didn't go in for birth-control, you know, so the food ran out. By the Third Famine there were no Irish left at all but the priesthood, and they were all celibate, or nearly all."

Zayin and Kaph smiled stiffly. They had no experience of either bigotry or irony. "What are you then, ethnically?" Kaph asked, and Pugh replied, "A Welshman."

"Is it Welsh that you and Martin speak together?"

None of your business, Pugh thought, but said, "No, it's his dialect, not mine: Argentinean. A descendant of Spanish."

"You learned it for private communication?"

"Whom had we here to be private from? It's just that sometimes a man likes to speak his native language."

"Ours is English," Kaph said unsympathetically. Why should they have sympathy? That's one of the things you give because you need it back.

"Is Wells quaint?" asked Zayin.

"Wells? Oh, Wales, it's called. Yes. Wales is quaint." Pugh switched on his rock-cutter, which prevented further conversation by a synapse-destroying whine, and while it whined he turned his back and said a profane word in Welsh.

That night he used the Argentine dialect for private communication. "Do they pair off in the same couples, or change every night?"

Martin looked surprised. A prudish expression, unsuited to his features, appeared for a moment. It faded. He too was curious. "I think it's random."

"Don't whisper, man, it sounds dirty. I think they rotate."

"On a schedule?"

"So nobody gets omitted."

Martin gave a vulgar laugh and smothered it. "What about us? Aren't we omitted?"

"That doesn't occur to them."

"What if I proposition one of the girls?"

"She'd tell the others and they'd decide as a group."

"I am not a bull," Martin said, his dark, heavy face heating up. "I will not be judged—"

"Down, down, *machismo*," said Pugh. "Do you mean to proposition one?"

Martin shrugged, sullen. "Let'em have their incest."

"Incest is it, or masturbation?"

"I don't care, if they'd do it out of earshot!"

The clone's early attempts at modesty had soon worn off, unmotivated by any deep defensiveness of self or awareness of others. Pugh and Martin were daily deeper swamped under the intimacies of its constant emotional-sexual-mental interchange: swamped yet excluded.

"Two months to go," Martin said one evening.

"To what?" snapped Pugh. He was edgy lately and Martin's sullenness got on his nerves.

"To relief."

In sixty days the full crew of their Exploratory Mission were due back from their survey of the other planets of the system. Pugh was aware of this.

"Crossing off the days on your calendar?" he jeered.

"Pull yourself together, Owen."

"What do you mean?"

"What I say."

They parted in contempt and resentment.

Pugh came in after a day alone on the Pampas, a vast lava-plain the nearest edge of which was two hours south by jet. He was tired, but refreshed by solitude. They were not supposed to take long trips alone, but lately had often done so. Martin stooped under bright lights, drawing one of his elegant, masterly charts: this one was of the whole face of Libra, the cancerous face. The dome was otherwise empty, seeming dim and large as it had before the clone came. "Where's the golden horde?"

Martin grunted ignorance, crosshatching. He straightened his back to glance around at the sun, which squatted feebly like a great red toad on the eastern plain, and at the clock, which said 18:45. "Some big quakes today," he said, returning to his map. "Feel them down there? Lot of crates were falling around. Take a look at the seismo."

The needle jigged and wavered on the roll. It never stopped dancing here. The roll had recorded five quakes of major intensity back in mid-afternoon; twice the needle had hopped off the roll. The attached computer had been activated to emit a slip reading, "Epicenter 61' N by 4'24" E."

"Not in the Trench this time."

"I thought it felt a bit different from usual. Sharper."

"In Base One I used to lie awake at night feeling the ground jump. Queer how you get used to things."

"Go spla if you didn't. What's for dinner?"

"I thought you'd have cooked it."

"Waiting for the clone."

Feeling put upon, Pugh got out a dozen dinnerboxes, stuck two in the Instobake, pulled them out. "All right, here's dinner."

"Been thinking," Martin said, coming to the table. "What if some clone cloned itself? Illegally. Made a thousand duplicates—ten thousand. Whole army. They could make a tidy power-grab, couldn't they?"

"But how many millions did this lot cost to rear? Artificial placentae and all that. It would be hard to keep secret, unless they had a planet to themselves. . . . Back before the Famines when Earth had national governments, they talked about that: clone your best soldiers, have whole regiments of them. But the food ran out before they could play that game."

They talked amicably, as they used to do.

"Funny," Martin said, chewing. "They left early this morning, didn't they?"

"All but Kaph and Zayin. They thought they'd get the first payload aboveground today. What's up?"

"They weren't back for lunch."

"They won't starve, to be sure."

"They left at seven."

"So they did." Then Pugh saw it. The air-tanks held eight hours' supply.

"Kaph and Zayin carried out spare cans when they left. Or they've got a heap out there."

"They did, but they brought the whole lot in to recharge." Martin stood up, pointing to one of the stacks of stuff that cut the dome into rooms and alleys.

"There's an alarm signal on every imsuit."

"It's not automatic."

Pugh was tired and still hungry. "Sit down and eat, man. That lot can look after themselves."

Martin sat down, but did not eat. "There was a big quake, Owen. The first one. Big enough, it scared me."

After a pause Pugh sighed and said, "All right."

Unenthusiastically, they got out the two-man sled that was always left for them, and headed it north. The long sunrise covered everything in poisonous red jello. The horizontal light and shadow made it hard to see, raised walls of fake iron ahead of them through which they slid, turned the convex plain beyond Hellmouth into a great dimple full of bloody water. Around the tunnel entrance a wilderness of machinery stood, cranes and cables and servos and wheels and diggers and robocarts and sliders and control-huts, all slanting and bulking incoherently in the red light. Martin jumped from the sled, ran into the mine. He came out again, to Pugh. "Oh God, Owen, it's down," he said. Pugh went in and saw, five meters from the entrance, the shiny, moist, black wall that ended the tunnel. Newly exposed to air, it looked organic, like visceral tissue. The tunnel entrance, enlarged by blasting and double-tracked for robocarts, seemed unchanged until he noticed thousands of tiny spiderweb cracks in the walls. The floor was wet with some sluggish fluid.

"They were inside," Martin said.

"They may be still. They surely had extra air-cans—"

"Look, Owen, look at the basalt flow, at the roof; don't you see what the quake did, look at it."

The low hump of land that roofed the caves still had the unreal look of an optical illusion. It had reversed itself, sunk down, leaving a vast dimple or pit. When Pugh walked on it he saw that it too was cracked with many tiny fissures. From some a whitish gas was seeping, so that the sunlight on the surface of the gas-pool was shafted as if by the waters of a dim red lake.

"The mine's not on the fault. There's no fault here!"

Pugh came back to him quickly. "No, there's no fault, Martin. Look, they surely weren't all inside together."

Martin followed him and searched among the wrecked machines dully, then actively. He spotted the airsled. It had come down heading south, and stuck at an angle in a pothole of colloidal dust. It had carried two riders. One was half sunk in the dust, but his suit-meters registered normal functioning; the other hung strapped onto the tilted sled. Her imsuit had burst open on the broken legs, and the body was frozen hard as any rock. That was all they found. As both regulation and custom demanded, they cremated the dead at once with the laser-guns they carried by regulation and had never used before. Pugh, knowing he was going to be sick, wrestled the survivor onto the two-man sled and sent Martin off to the dome with him. Then he vomited, and flushed the waste out of his suit, and finding one four-man sled undamaged followed after Martin, shaking as if the cold of Libra had got through to him.

The survivor was Kaph. He was in deep shock. They found a swelling on the occiput that might mean concussion, but no fracture was visible.

Pugh brought two glasses of food-concentrate and two chasers of aquavit. "Come on," he said. Martin obeyed, drinking off the tonic. They sat down on crates near the cot and sipped the aquavit.

Kaph lay immobile, face like beeswax, hair bright black to the shoulders, lips stiffly parted for faintly gasping breaths.

"It must have been the first shock, the big one," Martin said. "It must have slid the whole structure sideways. Till it fell in on itself. There must be gas layers in the lateral rocks, like those formations in the Thirty-first Quadrant. But there wasn't any sign—" As he spoke the world slid out from under them. Things leaped and clattered, hopped and jigged, shouted Ha! Ha! Ha! "It was like this at fourteen hours," said Reason shakily in Martin's voice; amidst the unfastening and ruin of the world. But Unreason sat up, as the tumult lessened and things ceased dancing, and screamed aloud.

Pugh leaped across his spilled aquavit and held Kaph down. The muscular body failed him off. Martin pinned the shoulders down. Kaph screamed, struggled, choked; his face blackened. "Oxy," Pugh said, and his hand found the right needle in the medical kit as if by homing instinct; while Martin held the mask he struck the needle home to the vagus nerve, restoring Kaph to life.

"Didn't know you knew that stunt," Martin said, breathing hard.

"The Lazarus Jab; my father was a doctor. It doesn't often work," Pugh said. "I want that drink I spilled. Is the quake over? I can't tell."

"Aftershocks. It's not just you shivering."

"Why did he suffocate?"

"I don't know, Owen. Look in the book."

Kaph was breathing normally and his color was restored, only the lips were still darkened. They poured a new shot of courage and sat down by him again with their medical guide. "Nothing about cyanosis or asphyxiation under 'shock' or 'concussion.' He can't have breathed in anything with his suit on. I don't know. We'd get as much good out of *Mother Mog's Home Herbalist.* . . . 'Anal Hemorrhoids,' fy!" Pugh pitched the book to a crate-table. It fell short, because either Pugh or the table was still unsteady.

"Why didn't he signal?"

"Sorry?"

"The eight inside the mine never had time. But he and the girl must have been outside. Maybe she was in the entrance, and got hit by the first slide. He must have been outside, in the control-hut maybe. He ran in, pulled her out, strapped her onto the sled, started for the dome. And all that time never pushed the panic button in his imsuit. Why not?"

"Well, he'd had that whack on his head. I doubt he ever realized the girl was dead. He wasn't in his senses. But if he had been I don't know if he'd have thought to signal us. They looked to one another for help."

Martin's face was like an Indian mask, grooves at the mouth corners, eyes of dull coal. "That's so. What must he have felt, then, when the quake came and he was outside, alone—"

In answer Kaph screamed.

He came up off the cot in the heaving convulsions of one suffocating, knocked Pugh right down with his flailing arm, staggered into a stack of crates and fell to the floor, lips blue, eyes white. Martin dragged him back onto the cot and gave him a whiff of oxygen, then knelt by Pugh, who was just sitting up, and wiped at his cut cheekbone. "Owen, are you all right, are you going to be all right, Owen?"

"I think I am," Pugh said. "Why are you rubbing that on my face?"

It was a short length of computer-tape, now spotted with Pugh's blood. Martin dropped it. "Thought it was a towel. You clipped your cheek on that box there."

"Is he out of it?"

"Seems to be."

They stared down at Kaph lying stiff, his teeth a white line inside dark parted lips.

"Like epilepsy. Brain damage maybe?"

"What about shooting him full of meprobamate?"

Pugh shook his head. "I don't know what's in that shot I already gave him for shock. Don't want to overdose him."

"Maybe he'll sleep it off now."

"I'd like to myself. Between him and the earthquake I can't seem to keep on my feet."

"You got a nasty crack there. Go on, I'll sit up for a while."

Pugh cleaned his cut cheek and pulled off his shirt, then paused.

"Is there anything we ought to have done—have tried to do—"

"They're all dead," Martin said heavily, gently.

Pugh lay down on top of his sleeping-bag, and one instant later was awakened by a hideous, sucking, struggling noise. He staggered up, found the needle, tried three times to jab it in correctly and failed, began to massage over Kaph's heart. "Mouth-to-mouth," he said, and Martin obeyed. Presently Kaph drew a harsh breath, his heartbeat steadied, his rigid muscles began to relax.

"How long did I sleep?"

"Half an hour."

They stood up sweating. The ground shuddered, the fabric of the dome sagged and swayed. Libra was dancing her awful polka again, her Totentanz. The sun, though rising, seemed to have grown larger and redder; gas and dust must have been stirred up in the feeble atmosphere.

"What's wrong with him, Owen?"

"I think he's dying with them."

"Them—But they're dead, I tell you."

"Nine of them. They're all dead, they were crushed or suffocated. They were all him, he is all of them. They died, and now he's dying their deaths one by one."

"Oh pity of God," said Martin.

The next time was much the same. The fifth time was worse, for Kaph fought and raved, trying to speak but getting no words out, as if his mouth were stopped with rocks or clay. After that the attacks grew weaker, but so did he. The eighth seizure came at about four-thirty; Pugh and Martin worked till five-thirty doing all they could to keep life in the body that slid without protest into death. They kept him, but Martin said, "The next will finish him." And it did; but Pugh breathed his own breath into the inert lungs, until he himself passed out.

He woke. The dome was opaqued and no light on. He listened and heard the breathing of two sleeping men. He slept, and nothing woke him till hunger did.

The sun was well up over the dark plains, and the planet had stopped dancing. Kaph lay asleep. Pugh and Martin drank tea and looked at him with proprietary triumph.

When he woke Martin went to him: "How do you feel, old man?" There was no answer. Pugh took Martin's place and looked into the brown, dull eyes that gazed toward but not into his own. Like Martin he quickly turned away. He heated food-concentrate and brought it to Kaph. "Come on, drink."

He could see the muscles in Kaph's throat tighten. "Let me die," the young man said.

"You're not dying."

Kaph spoke with clarity and precision: "I am nine-tenths dead. There is not enough of me left alive."

That precision convinced Pugh, and he fought the conviction. "No," he said, peremptory. "They are dead. The others. Your brothers and sisters. You're not them, you're alive. You are John Chow. Your life is in your own hands."

The young man lay still, looking into a darkness that was not there.

Martin and Pugh took turns taking the Exploitation hauler and a spare set of robos over to Hellmouth to salvage equipment and protect it from Libra's sinister atmosphere, for the value of the stuff was, literally, astronomical. It was slow work for one man at a time, but they were unwilling to leave Kaph by himself. The one left in the dome did paperwork, while Kaph sat or lay and stared into his darkness, and never spoke. The days went by silent.

The radio spat and spoke: the Mission calling from ship. "We'll be down on Libra in five weeks, Owen. Thirty-four E-days nine hours I make it as of now. How's tricks in the old dome?"

"Not good, chief. The Exploit team were killed, all but one of them, in the mine. Earthquake. Six days ago."

The radio crackled and sang starsong. Sixteen seconds lag each way; the ship was out around Planet 11 now. "Killed, all but one? You and Martin were unhurt?"

"We're all right, chief."

Thirty-two seconds.

"*Passerine* left an Exploit team out here with us. I may put them on the Hellmouth project then, instead of the Quadrant Seven project. We'll settle that when we come down. In any case you and Martin will be relieved at Dome Two. Hold tight. Anything else?"

"Nothing else."

Thirty-two seconds.

"Right then. So long, Owen."

Kaph had heard all this, and later on Pugh said to him, "The chief may ask you to stay here with the other Exploit team. You know the ropes here." Knowing the exigencies of Far Out Life, he wanted to warn the young man. Kaph made no answer. Since he had said, "There is not enough of me left alive," he had not spoken a word.

"Owen," Martin said on suit intercom, "he's spla. Insane. Psycho."

"He's doing very well for a man who's died nine times."

"Well? Like a turned-off android is well? The only emotion he has left is hate. Look at his eyes."

"That's not hate, Martin. Listen, it's true that he has, in a sense, been dead. I cannot imagine what he feels. But it's not hatred. He can't even see us. It's too dark."

"Throats have been cut in the dark. He hates us because we're not Aleph and Yod and Zayin."

"Maybe. But I think he's alone. He doesn't see us or hear us, that's the truth. He never had to see anyone else before. He never was alone before. He had himself to see, talk with, live with, nine other selves all his life. He doesn't know how you go it alone. He must learn. Give him time."

Martin shook his heavy head. "Spla," he said. "Just remember when you're alone with him that he could break your neck one-handed."

"He could do that," said Pugh, a short, soft-voiced man with a scarred cheekbone; he smiled. They were just outside the dome airlock, programming one of the servos to repair a damaged hauler. They could see Kaph sitting inside the great half-egg of the dome like a fly in amber.

"Hand me the insert pack there. What makes you think he'll get any better?"

"He has a strong personality, to be sure."

"Strong? Crippled. Nine-tenths dead, as he put it."

"But he's not dead. He's a live man: John Kaph Chow. He had a jolly queer upbringing, but after all every boy has got to break free of his family. He will do it."

"I can't see it."

"Think a bit, Martin bach. What's this cloning for? To repair the human race. We're in a bad way. Look at me. My IIQ and GC are half this John Chow's. Yet they wanted me so badly for the Far Out Service that when I volunteered they took me and fitted me out with an artificial lung and corrected my myopia. Now if there were enough good sound lads about would they be taking one-lunged shortsighted Welshmen?"

"Didn't know you had an artificial lung."

"I do then. Not tin, you know. Human, grown in a tank from a bit of somebody; cloned, if you like. That's how they make replacement-organs, the same general idea as cloning, but bits and pieces instead of whole people. It's my own lung now, whatever. But what I am saying is this, there are too many like me these days, and not enough like John Chow. They're trying to raise the level of the human genetic pool, which is a mucky little puddle since the population crash. So then if a man is cloned, he's a strong and clever man. It's only logic, to be sure."

Martin grunted; the servo began to hum.

Kaph had been eating little; he had trouble swallowing his food, choking on it, so that he would give up trying after a few bites. He had lost eight or ten kilos. After three weeks or so, however, his appetite began to pick up, and one day he began to look through the clone's possessions, the sleeping-bags, kits, papers which Pugh had stacked neatly in a far angle of a packing-crate alley. He sorted, destroyed a heap of papers and oddments, made a small packet of what remained, then relapsed into his walking coma.

Two days later he spoke. Pugh was trying to correct a flutter in the tape-player, and failing; Martin had the jet out, checking their maps of the Pampas. "Hell and damnation!" Pugh said, and Kaph said in a toneless voice, "Do you want me to do that?"

Pugh jumped, controlled himself, and gave the machine to Kaph. The young man took it apart, put it back together, and left it on the table.

"Put on a tape," Pugh said with careful casualness, busy at another table.

Kaph put on the topmost tape, a chorale. He lay down on his cot. The sound of a hundred human voices singing together filled the dome. He lay still, his face blank.

In the next days he took over several routine jobs, unasked. He undertook nothing that wanted initiative, and if asked to do anything he made no response at all.

"He's doing well," Pugh said in the dialect of Argentina.

"He's not. He's turning himself into a machine. Does what he's programmed to do, no reaction to anything else. He's worse off than when he didn't function at all. He's not human any more."

Pugh sighed. "Well, good night," he said in English. "Good night, Kaph."

"Good night," Martin said; Kaph did not.

Next morning at breakfast Kaph reached across Martin's plate for the toast. "Why don't you ask for it," Martin said with the geniality of repressed exasperation. "I can pass it."

"I can reach it," Kaph said in his flat voice.

"Yes, but look. Asking to pass things, saying good night or hello, they're not important, but all the same when somebody says something a person ought to answer. . . ."

The young man looked indifferently in Martin's direction; his eyes still did not seem to see clear through to the person he looked toward. "Why should I answer?"

"Because somebody has said something to you."

"Why?"

Martin shrugged and laughed. Pugh jumped up and turned on the rock-cutter.

Later on he said, "Lay off that, please, Martin."

"Manners are essential in small isolated crews, some kind of manners, whatever you work out together. He's been taught that, everybody in Far Out knows it. Why does he deliberately flout it?"

"Do you tell yourself good night?"

"So?"

"Don't you see Kaph's never known anyone but himself?"

Martin brooded and then broke out, "Then by God this cloning business is all wrong. It won't do. What are a lot of duplicate geniuses going to do for us when they don't even know we exist?"

Pugh nodded. "It might be wiser to separate the clones and bring them up with others. But they make such a grand team this way."

"Do they? I don't know. If this lot had been ten average inefficient ET engineers, would they all have been in the same place at the same time? Would they all have got killed? What if, when the quake came and things started caving in, what if all those kids ran the same way, farther into the mine, maybe, to save the one that was farthest in? Even Kaph was outside and went in. . . . It's hypothetical. But I keep thinking, out of ten ordinary confused guys, more might have got out."

"I don't know. It's true that identical twins tend to die at about the same time, even when they have never seen each other. Identity and death, it is very strange. . . ."

The days went on, the red sun crawled across the dark sky, Kaph did not speak when spoken to, Pugh and Martin snapped at each other more frequently each day. Pugh complained of Martin's snoring. Offended, Martin moved his cot clear across the dome and also ceased speaking to Pugh for some while. Pugh whistled Welsh dirges until Martin complained, and then Pugh stopped speaking for a while.

The day before the Mission ship was due, Martin announced he was going over to Merioneth.

"I thought at least you'd be giving me a hand with the computer to finish the rock-analyses," Pugh said, aggrieved.

"Kaph can do that. I want one more look at the Trench. Have fun," Martin added in dialect, and laughed, and left.

"What is that language?"

"Argentinean. I told you that once, didn't I?"

"I don't know." After a while the young man added. "I have forgotten a lot of things, I think."

"It wasn't important, to be sure," Pugh said gently, realizing all at once how important this conversation was. "Will you give me a hand running the computer, Kaph?"

He nodded.

Pugh had left a lot of loose ends, and the job took them all day. Kaph was a good co-worker, quick and systematic, much more so than Pugh himself. His flat voice, now that he was talking again, got on the nerves; but it didn't matter, there was only this one day left to get through and then the ship would come, the old crew, comrades and friends.

During tea-break Kaph said, "What will happen if the Explorer ship crashes?"

"They'd be killed."

"To you, I mean."

"To us? We'd radio SOS all signals, and live on half rations till the rescue cruiser from Area Three Base came. Four and a half E-years away it is. We have life support here for three men for, let's see, maybe between four and five years. A bit tight, it would be."

"Would they send a cruiser for three men?"

"They would."

Kaph said no more.

"Enough cheerful speculations," Pugh said cheerfully, rising to get back to work. He slipped sideways and the chair avoided his hand; he did a sort of half-pirouette and fetched up hard against the dome-hide. "My goodness," he said, reverting to his native idiom, "what is it?"

"Quake," said Kaph.

The teacups bounced on the table with a plastic cackle, a litter of papers slid off a box, the skin of the dome swelled and sagged. Underfoot there was a huge noise, half sound half shaking, a subsonic boom.

Kaph sat unmoved. An earthquake does not frighten a man who died in an earthquake.

Pugh, white-faced, wiry black hair sticking out, a frightened man, said, "Martin is in the Trench."

"What trench?"

"The big fault line. The epicenter for the local quakes. Look at the seismograph." Pugh struggled with the stuck door of a still-jittering locker.

"Where are you going?"

"After him."

"Martin took the jet. Sleds aren't safe to use during quakes. They go out of control."

"For God's sake, man, shut up."

Kaph stood up, speaking in a flat voice as usual. "It's unnecessary to go out after him now. It's taking an unnecessary risk."

"If his alarm goes off, radio me," Pugh said, shut the headpiece of his suit, and ran to the lock. As he went out Libra picked up her ragged skirts and danced a belly-dance from under his feet clear to the red horizon.

Inside the dome, Kaph saw the sled go up, tremble like a meteor in the dull red daylight, and vanish to the northeast. The hide of the dome quivered; the earth coughed. A vent south of the dome belched up a slow-flowing bile of black gas.

A bell shrilled and a red light flashed on the central control board. The sign under the light read Suit Two and scribbled under that, A.G.M. Kaph did not turn the signal off. He tried to radio Martin, then Pugh, but got no reply from either.

When the aftershocks decreased he went back to work, and finished up Pugh's job. It took him about two hours. Every half hour he tried to contact Suit One, and got no reply, then Suit Two and got no reply. The red light had stopped flashing after an hour.

It was dinnertime. Kaph cooked dinner for one, and ate it. He lay down on his cot.

The aftershocks had ceased except for faint rolling tremors at long intervals. The sun hung in the west, oblate, pale-red, immense. It did not sink visibly. There was no sound at all.

Kaph got up and began to walk about the messy, half-packed-up, overcrowded, empty dome. The silence continued. He went to the player and put on the first tape that came to hand. It was pure music, electronic, without harmonies, without voices. It ended. The silence continued.

Pugh's uniform tunic, one button missing, hung over a stack of rock-samples. Kaph stared at it a while.

The silence continued.

The child's dream: There is no one else alive in the world but me. In all the world.

Low, north of the dome, a meteor flickered.

Kaph's mouth opened as if he were trying to say something, but no sound came. He went hastily to the north wall and peered out into the gelantinous red light.

The little star came in and sank. Two figures blurred the airlock. Kaph stood close beside the lock as they came in. Martin's imsuit was covered with some kind of dust so that he looked raddled and warty like the surface of Libra. Pugh had him by the arm.

"Is he hurt?"

Pugh shucked his suit, helped Martin peel off his. "Shaken up," he said, curt.

"A piece of cliff fell onto the jet," Martin said, sitting down at the table and waving his arms. "Not while I was in it, though. I was parked, see, and poking about that carbon-dust area when I felt things humping. So I went out onto a nice bit of early igneous I'd noticed from above, good footing and out from under the cliffs. Then I saw this bit of the planet fall off onto the flyer, quite a sight it was, and after a while it occurred to me the spare aircans were in the flyer, so I leaned on the panic button. But I didn't get any radio reception, that's always happening here during quakes, so I didn't know if the signal was getting through either. And things went on jumping around and pieces of the cliff coming off. Little rocks flying around, and so dusty you couldn't see a meter ahead. I was really beginning to wonder what I'd do for breathing in the small hours, you know, when I saw old Owen buzzing up the Trench in all that dust and junk like a big ugly bat—"

"Want to eat?" said Pugh.

"Of couse I want to eat. How'd you come through the quake here, Kaph? No damage? It wasn't a big one actually, was it, what's the seismo say? My trouble was I was in the middle of it. Old Epicenter Alvaro. Felt like Richter Fifteen there—total destruction of planet—"

"Sit down," Pugh said. "Eat."

After Martin had eaten a little his spate of talk ran dry. He very soon went off to his cot, still in the remote angle where he had removed it when Pugh complained of his snoring. "Good night, you one-lunged Welshman," he said across the dome.

"Good night."

There was no more out of Martin. Pugh opaqued the dome, turned the lamp down to a yellow glow less than a candle's light, and sat doing nothing, saying nothing, withdrawn.

The silence continued.

"I finished the computations."

Pugh nodded thanks.

"The signal from Martin came through, but I couldn't contact you or him."

Pugh said with effort, "I should not have gone. He had two hours of air left even with only one can. He might have been heading home when I left. This way we were all out of touch with one another. I was scared."

The silence came back, punctuated now by Martin's long, soft snores.

"Do you love Martin?"

Pugh looked up with angry eyes: "Martin is my friend. We've worked together, he's a good man." He stopped. After a while he said, "Yes, I love him. Why did you ask that?"

Kaph said nothing, but he looked at the other man. His face was changed, as if he were glimpsing something he had not seen before; his voice too was changed. "How can you . . . ? How do you . . . ?"

But Pugh could not tell him. "I don't know," he said, "it's practice, partly. I don't know. We're each of us alone, to be sure. What can you do but hold your hand out in the dark?"

Kaph's strange gaze dropped, burned out by its own intensity.

"I'm tired," Pugh said. "That was ugly, looking for him in all that black dust and muck, and mouths opening and shutting in the ground. . . . I'm going to bed. The ship will be transmitting to us by six or so." He stood up and stretched.

"It's a clone," Kaph said. "The other Exploit team they're bringing with them."

"Is it, then?"

"A twelveclone. They came out with us on the *Passerine*."

Kaph sat in the small yellow aura of the lamp seeming to look past it at what he feared: the new clone, the multiple self of which he was not part. A lost piece of a broken set, a fragment, inexpert at solitude, not knowing even how you go about giving love to another individual, now he must face the absolute, closed self-sufficiency of the clone of twelve; that was a lot to ask of the poor fellow, to be sure. Pugh put a hand on his shoulder in passing. "The chief won't ask you to stay here with a clone. You can go home. Or since you're Far Out maybe you'll come on farther out with us. We could use you. No hurry deciding. You'll make out all right."

Pugh's quiet voice trailed off. He stood unbuttoning his coat, stooped a little with fatigue. Kaph looked at him and saw the thing he had never seen before: saw him: Owen Pugh, the other, the stranger who held his hand out in the dark.

"Good night," Pugh mumbled, crawling into his sleeping-bag and half asleep already, so that he did not hear Kaph reply after a pause, repeating, across darkness, benediction.

3

SENSATION PERCEPTION AND AWARENESS

Much of psychology is formulated in terms of stimulus and response. In order for an organism to respond to stimuli, it must first be able to receive them and then be able to process the information received into meaningful material. The organism's senses receive what is going on "out there" in bits and pieces. Instantly the brain attempts to perceive "what it is" in its overall context. Hopefully, based on this complete picture the individual can then decide what to do about it.

In important respects, the complete process involves the two basic components discussed elsewhere: psychobiology and learning. The organism uses its sense organs to receive stimuli and also uses its body's biochemical substances to enhance its awareness and attention. Neurons and neurological circuits transmit incoming messages to the central nervous system, coding the information into patterns of electrical impulses which the brain can utilize. Finally the brain interprets incoming information, combining it into meaningful wholes and storing it so that new material can be added to the old. It learns to match perceptions of new situations with others it has experienced and thereby decides how to respond to them.

Besides psychobiology and learning, the basic sensory processes also involve the organism in processes which are studied in psychophysics and human engineering. Psychophysics becomes important because environmental stimuli are "out there" in the form of physical energy. Light occurs in the form of electromagnetic energy light waves. Sound is actually mechanical energy—pressure changes of air molecules or sound waves. Our experiences of odors and tastes are reactions to chemical energy, while the skin senses of touch, pain, warm, and cold are basically reactions to change in mechanical energy. The two basic psychophysical requirements for each of the sense organs is, first, to receive (be sensitive to) this particular kind of physical energy it must process and, second, to convert the units of energy it receives into electrical energy for use by the nervous system.

The field of human engineering involves questions of equipment and location. For example, the eye has specialized cells called rods and cones which are primarily sensitive to light intensity and color, respectively. The ear is really three ears—the outer, middle, and inner ears—which must receive, amplify, and differentiate between various sounds.

A crucial aspect of all sensory equipment is its built-in limitations or thresholds. The problem of absolute threshold is that each sensory system can pick up only a limited range of the type of environmental energy that it is sensitive to. Differences are present across and within species. A dog can hear the tones of a dog whistle and can track animal scents over long distances. Both capacities are beyond human limits. Differences within species are illustrated by the fact that you may wear glasses while others you know do not. Differences also exist in sensitivity to changes in stimuli. The amount of stimulus change necessary before an individual can notice it is called his difference threshold or his "just-noticeable difference" for the stimulus specified. Location is important for all of the senses. Each organ has to plug into the nervous system and also has to be conveniently located for reception of its specified stimulus. Location is probably most important for the skin senses. Different parts of the body are differentially sensitive to pain, touch, warm, and cold. One of the earliest accomplishments of research in psychophysics was to map the body in this regard.

An integral system of factors mediating our response to incoming stimuli is our level of awareness and the attention we give to the stimuli. The nature of the stimuli itself plays an important part in attracting attention, as any good advertising executive or everyday girl watcher can attest. Novelty plays a part in attracting idle curiosity, but it is especially important in the orienting reaction, the automatic self-preservation reaction to new stimuli engaged in by all species. Research into the orienting reaction has shown that turning attention toward a novel, and possibly threatening stimulus, also includes the lowering of sensory thresholds, increased muscle tone, faster brain waves and heartbeat—in general, a highly increased sensitivity. The organism, however, cannot psychobiologically or physiologically maintain this increase indefinitely, and when the stimulus's novelty is reduced, the organism relaxes its awareness or *habituates* to the stimulus. Ultimately the organism must reduce its awareness to the level of sleep, characterized by altered brain waves and periods of dreaming, where there is inhibition of motor activity accompanied by rapid eye movements (REM).

Once the organism receives patterns of stimuli, it must engage in the process of perception. Its brain must organize what its senses have received and its nervous system has transmitted, making meaningful wholes out of its experiences.

The process of perceptual organization has been the main domain of gestalt psychology. The gestaltists emphasize the wholeness and unity of perceptions, stressing principles like figure-ground (background), similarity, and closure to explain how parts of a perceptual field are grouped and organized into complete pictures. Gestalt principles are the basis for the Rorschach test, where individuals are asked to organize and give meaning to meaningless blots.

Closely allied to gestalt principles are mechanisms used for depth perception and perceptual constancy. Depth perception is important in everyday activity like driving a car and in specialized activity like playing basketball. Light and shadow, linear perspective and the fact that each of our eyes views an object from a slightly different angle (retinal disparity) all give us cues in perceiving depth. As objects like a basketball hoop or a pedestrian move nearer or farther away, we still see them as maintaining relatively constant size, even though the actual stimulus received by the eye's retina varies greatly in size. Similarly we perceive color as constant, even though lighting conditions may vary, and we also perceive shapes as constant when we view them from different angles. These and other perceptual constancies give consistency to our experience, helping us maintain a more comfortable existence within the world around us.

Although the accuracy of perceptions is generally maintained, there are instances where it also breaks down. We have all seen examples of optical illusions which play with our perception and often fool us. We also often see what we believe, rather than vice versa. Psychedelic drugs like LSD can alter and distort perception, as can extreme mental disturbances like schizophrenia. Finally, the validity of extrasensory perception (perceptions which require no sensory stimulation) is under investigation.

through other eyes

R. A. Lafferty

Sensation and perception are two processes which we often take for granted. In the following story Charles Cogsworth thinks that he is an exception. He is a rather clever fellow who likes to invent fascinating machines which have the knack of transcending time and space. This time around, in order to check on his sensory and perceptual processes, he has invented a machine which will allow him to see the world through the eyes of other people. He correctly believes that the mechanics of the invention can be worked out simply enough. However, in his success, he learns that even he has grossly underestimated the complexity and importance of the processes he is tampering with. In seeing through the eyes of others he gains a new and frighteningly clear understanding of them. Moreover, he also gains a new perspective of himself, which does nothing less than change his life.

As Cogsworth explains, the mechanics of tuning into the sensory process involves the sensory cortex of the brain. Stimuli from the environment are received by receptor cells specialized for each sense. These cells change the energy received into neural energy which is then transmitted through the nervous system to the sensory cortex. Each of the senses is projected onto a different area of the cortex, the visual sense onto the occipital lobe, the auditory onto the temporal lobe, and so forth.

As is suggested in the story, there are individual differences among people in their ability to receive sensory information (although this point is probably overemphasized in the story). We each have thresholds below which we do not receive information. For example, we do not hear sounds below our threshold for loudness reception. However, other species, like dogs, with different thresholds, may be able to pick them up. Within the human

187

species there are differences, as the proliferation of eyeglasses, contact lenses, and hearing aids attests.

It is also suggested in the story that women may be more sensitive to sensory stimulation than men, an issue which would contribute to their heightened "intuition." While the existence of this special capacity has never been settled scientifically, we can speculate on various explanations for this sex difference. It could be inherited; i.e. something in women's genes makes them more sensitive to sensory stimulation. On the other hand, the difference could be learned. Perhaps due to reinforcements in the society related to sex roles, women learn to tone up their sensory capacity, while men are conditioned to tone down their sensitivity. Perhaps both phenomena occur simultaneously.

As Cogsworth learns, people not only receive sensory stimulation differently. They also perceive differently. We are all being constantly bombarded by a myriad of separate sensory stimuli. Of course, we do not react to them separately; rather we integrate them so that we see shapes and forms and hear symphonies. Here is where the more objective sensory receptors take a back seat to the more subjective perceptive powers of the human brain. Based on each individual's own experience, he gives his own individual meaning to what he perceives. To Cogsworth's chagrin, he realizes that one man's clouds are another woman's mass of twisted bodies; one man's grass is another woman's clumps of snakes. One man's filthiness is another woman's beauty.

Cogsworth is not prepared for all of the diversity he finds with his new machine. Moreover, he is overwhelmed by how much an individual's perceptions determine his general outlook on life. He realizes that he had never truly understood or appreciated most of his friends and colleagues before seeing through their eyes. He learns that perception is really a joint process of stimuli and perceiver and that, to a great extent, each perceiver actively colors his own world. Ultimately he concludes that these truths apply to him too. By seeing through other eyes and comparing the perceptions of others with his own, he truly understands himself for the first time in his life.

THROUGH OTHER EYES   *R. A. Lafferty*

"I don't think I can stand the dawn of another Great Day," said Smirnov. "It always seems a muggy morning, a rainy afternoon, and a dismal evening. You remember the Recapitulation Correlator?"

"Known popularly as the Time Machine. But, Gregory, that was and is a success. All three of them are in constant use, and they will construct at least one more a decade. They are invaluable."

"Yes. It was a dismal success. It has turned my whole life gray. You remember our trial run, the recapitulation of the Battle of Hastings?"

"It *was* a depressing three years we spent there. But how were we to know it was such a small affair—covering less than five acres of that damnable field and lasting less than twenty minutes? And how were we to know that an error of four years had been made in history even as recent as that? Yes, we scanned many depressing days and many muddy fields in that area before we recreated it."

"And our qualified success at catching the wit of Voltaire at first hand?"

"Gad! That cackle! There can never by anything new in nausea to one who has sickened of that. What a perverted old woman he was!"

"And Nell Guinn?"

"There is no accounting for the taste of a king. What a completely tasteless morsel!"

"And the crowning of Charlemagne?"

"The king of chilblains. If you wanted a fire, you carried it with · you in a basket. That was the coldest Christmas I ever knew. But the mead seemed to warm them; and we were the only ones present who could not touch it or taste it."

"And when we went further back and heard the wonderful words of the divine poetess Sappho."

"Yes, she had just decided that she would have her favorite cat spayed. We listened to her for three days and she talked of nothing else. How fortunate the world is that so few of her words have survived."

"And watching the great Pythagoras at work."

"And the long days he spent on that little surveying problem.

How one longed to hand him a slide rule through the barrier and explain its workings."

"And our eavesdropping on the great lovers Tristram and Isolde."

"And him spending a whole afternoon trying to tune that cursed harp with a penny whistle. And she could talk of nothing but the bear grease she used on her hair, and how it was nothing like the bear grease back home. But she was a cute little lard barrel, quite the cutest we found for several centuries in either direction. One wouldn't be able to get one's arms all the way around her; but I can understand how, to one of that era and region, it would be fun trying."

"Ah yes. Smelled like a cinnamon cookie, didn't she? And you recall Lancelot?"

"Always had a bad back that wouldn't let him ride. And that trick elbow and the old groin wound. He spent more time on the rubbing table than any athlete I ever heard of. If I had a high-priced quarterback who was never ready to play, I'd sure find a way of breaking his contract. No use keeping him on the squad just to read his ten-year-old press clippings. Any farm boy could have pulled him off his nag and stomped him into the dirt."

"I wasn't too happy about Aristotle the day we caught him. That barbarous north-coast Greek of his! Three hours he had them all busy curling his beard. And his discourse of the *Beard in Essential* and the *Beard in Existential*, did you follow that?"

"No, to tell the truth I didn't. I guess it was pretty profound."

They were silent and sad for a while, as are men who have lost much.

"The machine was a success," said Smirnov at last, "and yet the high excitement of it died dismally for us."

"The excitement is in the discovery of the machine," said Cogsworth. "It is never in what the machine discovers."

"And this new one of yours," said Smirnov, "I hardly want to see you put it into operation. I am sure it will be a shattering disappointment to you."

"I am sure of it also. And yet it is greater than the other. I am as excited as a boy."

"You were a boy before, but you will never be again. I should think it would have aged you enough, and I cannot see what fascination this new one will have for you. At least the other recaptured the past. This will permit you to see only the present."

"Yes, but through other eyes."

"One pair of eyes is enough. I do not see any advantage at all except the novelty. I am afraid that this will be only a gadget."

"No. Believe me, Smirnov, it will be more than that. It may not even be the same world when viewed through different eyes. I believe that what we regard as one may actually be several billion different universes, each made only for the eyes of the one who sees it."

The Cerebral Scanner, newly completed by Charles Cogsworth, was not an intricate machine. It was a small but ingenious amplifying device, or battery of amplifiers, designed for the synchronous—perhaps "sympathetic" would be a better word—coupling of two very intricate machines: two human brains. It was an amplifier only. A subliminal coupling, or the possibility of it, was already assumed by the inventor. Less than a score of key aspects needed emphasizing for the whole thing to come to life.

Here the only concern was with the convoluted cortex of the brain itself, that house of consciousness and terminal of the senses, and with the quasi-electrical impulses which are the indicators of its activity. It had been a long-held opinion of Cogsworth that, by the proper amplification of a near score of these impulses in one brain, a transmission could be effected to another so completely that one man might for an instant see with the eyes of another—also see inwardly with that man's eyes, have the same imaginings and daydreams, perceive the same universe as the other perceived. And it would not be the same universe as the seeking man knew.

The Scanner had been completed, as had a compilation of the dossiers of seven different brains: a collection of intricate brain-wave data as to frequency, impulse, flux and field, and Lyall-wave patterns of the seven cerebrums which Cogsworth would try to couple with his own.

The seven were those of Gregory Smirnov, his colleague and counselor in so many things; of Gaetan Balbo, the cosmopolitan and supra-national head of the Institute; of Theodore Grammont, the theoretical mathematician; of E. E. Euler, the many-tentacled executive; of Karl Kleber, the extraordinary psychologist; of Edmond Guillames, the skeptic and bloodless critic; and of Valery Mok, a lady of beauty and charm whom Cogsworth had despaired of ever understanding by ordinary means.

This idea of his—to enter into the mind of another, to peer from behind another's eyes into a world that could not be the same—this idea had been with him all his life. He recalled how it had first come down on him in all its strength when he was quite small.

"It may be that I am the only one who sees the sky black at night and the stars white," he had said to himself, "and everybody else sees the sky white and the stars shining black. And I say the sky is black, and they say the sky is black; but when they say black they mean white."

Or: "I may be the only one who can see the outside of a cow, and everybody else sees it inside out. And I say that it is the outside, and they say that it is the outside; but when they say outside they mean inside."

Or: "It may be that all the boys I see look like girls to everyone else, and all the girls look like boys. And I say 'That is a girl,' and they say 'That is a girl'; only when they say a girl they mean a boy."

And then had come the terrifying thought: "What if I am a girl to everyone except me?"

This did not seem very intelligent to him even when he was small, and yet it became an obsession to him.

"What if to a dog all dogs look like men and all men look like dogs? And what if a dog looks at me and thinks that I am a dog and he is a boy?"

And this was followed once by the shattering afterthought: "And what if the dog is right?

"What if a fish looks up at a bird and a bird looks down at a fish? And the fish thinks that he is the bird and the bird is the fish, and that he is looking down on the bird that is really a fish, and the air is water and the water is air?

"What if, when a bird eats a worm, the worm thinks he is the bird and the bird is the worm? And that his outside is his inside, and that the bird's inside is his outside? And that he has eaten the bird instead of the bird eating him?"

This was illogical. But how does one know that a worm is not illogical? He has much to make him illogical.

And as he grew older Charles Cogsworth came on many signs that the world he saw was not the world that others saw. There came smaller but persistent signs that every person lives in a different world.

It was early in the afternoon, but Charles Cogsworth sat in darkness. Gregory Smirnov had gone for a walk in the country as he said he would. He was the only other one who knew that the experiment was being made. He is the only one who would have agreed to the experiment, though the others had permitted their brain-wave dossiers to be compiled on another pretext.

All beginnings come quietly, and this one was a total success. The sensation of seeing with the eyes of another is new and glorious, though the full recognition of it comes slowly.

"He is a greater man than I," said Cogsworth. "I have often suspected it. He has a placidity which I do not own, though he has not my fever. And he lives in a better world."

It was a better world, greater in scope and more exciting in detail.

"Who would have thought of giving such a color to grass, if it is grass? It is what he calls grass, but it is not what I call grass. I wonder if I should ever be content to see it as I saw it. It is a finer sky than I had known, and more structured hills. The old bones of them stand out for him as they do not for me, and he knows the water in their veins.

"There is a man walking toward him, and he is a grander man than I have ever seen. Yet I have also known the shadow of this man, and his name is Mr. Dottle, both to myself and to Gregory. I had thought that Dottle was a fool, but now I know that in the world of Gregory no man is a fool. I am looking through the inspired and almost divine eyes of a giant, and I am looking at a world that has not yet grown tired."

For what seemed like hours Charles Cogsworth lived in the world of Gregory Smirnov; and he found here, out of all his life, one great expectation that did not fail him.

Then, after he had rested a while, he looked at the world through the wide eyes of Gaetan Balbo.

"I am not sure that he is a greater man than I, but he is a wider man. Nor am I sure that he looks into a greater world. I would not willingly trade for his, as I would for Gregory's. Here I miss the intensity of my own. But it is fascinating, and I will enjoy returning to it again and again. And I know whose eyes these are. I am looking through the eyes of a king."

Later he saw through the eyes of Theodore Grammont, and felt a surge of pity.

"If I am blind compared to Gregory, then this man is blind compared to me. I at least know that the hills are alive; he believes them to be imperfect polyhedrons. He is in the middle of a desert and is not even able to talk to the devils who live there. He has abstracted the world and numbered it, and doesn't even know that the world is a live animal. He has built his own world of great complexity, but he cannot see the color of its flanks. This man has achieved so much only because he was denied so much at the beginning. I understand now that only the finest theory is no more

193

than a fact gnawed on vicariously by one who has no teeth. But I will return to this world too, even though it has no body to it. I have been seeing through the eyes of a blind hermit."

Delightful and exciting as this was, yet it was tiring. Cogsworth rested for a quarter of an hour before he entered the world of E. E. Euler. When he entered it he was filled with admiration.

"An ordinary man could not look into a world like this. It would drive him out of his wits. It is almost like looking through the eyes of the Lord, who numbers all the feathers of the sparrow and every mite that nestles there. It is the interconnection vision of all the details. It appalls. It isn't an easy world even to look at. Great Mother of Ulcers! How does he stand it? Yet I see that he loves every tangled detail, the more tangled the better. This is a world in which I will be able to take only a clinical interest. Somebody must hold these reins, but happily it is not my fate. To tame this hairy old beast we live on is the doom of Euler. I look for a happier doom."

He had been looking through the eyes of a general.

The attempt to see into the world of Karl Kleber was almost total failure. The story is told of the behaviorist who would study the chimpanzee. He put the curious animal in a room alone and locked the door on it; then went to the keyhole to spy; the keyhole was completely occupied by the brown eyeball of the animal spying back at him.

Something of the sort happened here. Though Karl Kleber was unaware of the experiment, yet the seeing was in both directions. Kleber was studying Cogsworth in those moments by some quirk of circumstance. And even when Cogsworth was able to see with the eyes of Kleber, yet it was himself he was seeing.

"I am looking through the eyes of a peeper," he said. "And yet, what am I myself?"

If the world of Gregory Smirnov, first entered, was the grandest, so that of Edmond Guillames, which Cogsworth entered last but one, was in all ways the meanest. It was a world seen from the inside of a bile duct. It was not a pleasant world, just as Edmond was not a pleasant man. But how could one be other than a skeptic if all his life he had seen nothing but a world of rubbery bones and bloodless flesh clothed in crippled colors and obscene forms?

"The mole of another's world would be nobler than a lion in his," said Cogsworth. "Why should one not be a critic who has so much to criticize? Why should one not be an unbeliever when faced with the dilemma that this unsavory world was either made by God or hatched by a cross-eyed ostrich? I have looked through the eyes of a fool into a fools' world."

As Cogsworth rested again he said, "I have seen the world through the eyes of a giant, of a king, of a blind hermit, of a general, of a peeping tom, of a fool. There is nothing left but to see it through the eyes of an angel."

Valery Mok may or may not have been an angel. She was a beautiful woman, and angels, in the older and more authentic iconography, were rather stern men with shaggy pinions.

Valery wore a look of eternal amusement, and was the embodiment of all charm and delight, at least to Charles Cogsworth. He believed her to be of high wit. Yet, if driven into a corner, he would have been unable to recall one witty thing she had ever said. He regarded her as of perfect kindness, and she *was* more or less on the agreeable side. Yet, as Smirnov had put it, she was not ordinarily regarded as extraordinary.

It was only quite lately that Cogsworth was sure that it was love he felt for her rather than bafflement. And, as he had despaired of ever understanding her by regular means, though everyone else understood her easily enough in as much as mattered, he would now use irregular means for his understanding.

He looked at the world through the eyes of Valery Mok, saying, "I will see the world through the eyes of an angel."

A change came over him as he looked, and it was not a pleasant change. He looked through her eyes quite a while—not, perhaps, as long as he had looked through the eyes of Gregory—yet for a long time, unable to tear himself away.

He shuddered and trembled and shrank back into himself.

Then he let it alone, and buried his face in his arms.

"I have looked at the world through the eyes of a pig," he said.

Charles Cogsworth spent six weeks in a sanatorium, which, however, was not called that. He had given the world his second great invention, and its completion had totally exhausted him. As in many such mercurial temperaments, the exaltation of discovery had been followed by an interlude of deep despondency on its completion.

Yet he was of fundamentally sound constitution and he had the best of care. But when he recovered it was not into his old self. He now had a sort of irony and smiling resignation that was new to him. It was as though he had discovered a new and more bitter world for himself in looking into the worlds of others.

Of his old intimates only Gregory Smirnov was still close to him.

"I can guess the trouble, Charles," said Gregory. "I rather

feared this would happen. In fact I advised against her being one of the subjects of the experiment. It is simply that you know very little about women."

"I have read all the prescribed texts, Gregory. I took a six-week seminar under Zamenoff. I am acquainted with almost the entire body of the work of Bopp concerning women. I have spent nearly as many years as you in the world, and I generally go about with my eyes open. I surely understand as much as is understandable about them."

"No. They are not your proper field. I could have predicted what has shocked you. You had not understood that women are so much more sensuous than men. But it would be better if you explained just what it was that shocked you."

"I had thought that Valery was an angel. It is simply that it was a shock to find that she is a pig."

"I doubt if you understand pigs any better than you understand women. I myself, only two days ago, had a pig's-eye view of the world, and that with your own Cerebral Scanner. I have been doing considerable work with it in the several weeks that you have been laid up. There is nothing in the pig's-eye world that would shock even the most fastidious. It is a dreamy world of all-encompassing placidity, almost entirely divorced from passion. It's a gray shadowy world with very little of the unpleasant. I had never before known how wonderful is the feel of simple sunlight and of cool earth. Yet we would soon be bored with it; but the pig is not bored."

"You divert me, Gregory, but you do not touch the point of my shock. Valery is beautiful—or was to me before this. She seemed kind and serene. Always she appeared to contain a mystery that amused her vastly, and which I suspected would be the most wonderful thing in the world once I understood it."

"And her mystery is that she lives in a highly sensuous world and enjoys it with complete awareness? Is that what has shocked you?"

"You do not know the depth of it. It is ghastly. The colors of that world are of unbelievable coarseness, and the shapes reek. The smells are the worst. Do you know how a tree smells to her?"

"What kind of tree?"

"Any tree. I think it was an ordinary elm."

"The Slippery Elm has a pleasant aroma in season. The others, to me, have none."

"No. It was not. Every tree has a strong smell in her world. This was an ordinary elm tree, and it had a violent musky obscene smell that delighted her. It was so strong that it staggered. And to her the grass itself is like clumps of snakes, and the world itself is flesh. Every bush is to her a leering satyr, and she cannot help but brush into them. The rocks are spidery monsters and she loves them. She sees every cloud as a mass of twisting bodies and she is crazy to be in the middle of them. She hugged a lamp post and her heart beat like it would fight its way out of her body.

"She can smell rain at a great distance and in a foul manner, and she wants to be in the middle of it. She worships every engine as a fire monster, and she hears sounds that I thought nobody could ever hear. Do you know what worms sound like inside the earth? They're devilish, and she would writhe and eat dirt with them. She can rest her hand on a guard rail, and it is an obscene act when she does it. There is a filthiness in every color and sound and shape and smell and feel."

"And yet, Charles, she is but a slightly more than average attractive girl, given to musing, and with a love of the world and a closeness to it that most of us have lost. She has a keen awareness of reality and of the grotesqueness that is its main mark. You yourself do not have this deeply; and when you encounter it in its full strength, it shocks you."

"You mean this is normal?"

"There is no normal. There are only differences. When you moved into our several worlds they did not shock you to the same extent, for most of the corners are worn off our worlds. But to move into a pristine universe is more of a difference than you were prepared for."

"I cannot believe that that is all it is."

Charles Cogsworth would not answer the letters of Valery Mok, nor would he see her. Yet her letters were amusing and kind, and carried a trace of worry for him.

"I wonder what I smell like to her?" he asked himself. "Am I like an elm tree, or a worm in the ground? What color am I to her? Is my voice obscene? She says she misses the sound of my voice. It should be possible to undo this. Am I also to her like a column of snakes or a congeries of spiders?"

For he wasn't well yet from what he had seen.

But he did go back to work, and nibbled at the edges of mystery with his fantastic device. He even looked into the worlds of other women. It was as Smirnov has said: they were more sensuous than men but none of them to the shocking degree of Valery.

He saw with the eyes of other men. And of animals: the soft

pleasure of the fox devouring a ground squirrel, the bloody anger of a lamb furious after milk, the crude arrogance of the horse, the intelligent tolerance of the mule, the voraciousness of the cow, the miserliness of the squirrel, the sullen passion of the catfish. Nothing was quite as might have been expected.

He learned the jealousy and hatred that beautiful women hold against the ugly, the untarnished evil of small children, the diabolic possession of adolescents. He even, by accident, saw the world through the fleshless eyes of a poltergeist, and through the eyes of creatures that he could not identify at all. He found nobility in places that almost balanced the pervading baseness.

But mostly he loved to see the world through the eyes of his friend Gregory Smirnov, for there was a grandeur on everything when seen through a giant's eyes.

And one day he saw Valery Mok through the eyes of Smirnov when they met accidentally. Something of his old feeling came back to him, and something that even surpassed his former regard. She was here magnificent, as was everything in that world. And there had to be a common ground between that wonderful world with her in it and the hideous world seen through her own eyes.

"I am wrong somewhere," said Cogsworth. "It is because I do not understand enough. I will go and see her."

But instead she came to see him.

She burst in on him furiously one day.

"You are a stick. You are a stick with no blood in it. You are a pig made out of sticks. You live with dead people, Charles, You make everything dead. You are abominable."

"I a pig, Valery? Possibly. But I never saw a pig made out of sticks."

"Then see yourself. That is what you are."

"Tell me what this is about."

"It is about you. You are a pig made out of sticks, Charles. Gregory Smirnov let me use your machine. I saw the world the way you see it. I saw it with a dead man's eyes. You don't even know that the grass is alive. You think it's only grass."

"I also saw the world with your eyes, Valery."

"Oh, is that what's been bothering you? Well, I hope it livened you up a little. It's a livelier world than yours."

"More pungent, at least."

"Lord, I should hope so. I don't think you even have a nose. I don't think you have any eyes. You can look at a hill and your heart doesn't even skip a beat. You don't even tingle when you walk over a field."

"You see grass like clumps of snakes."

"That's better than not even seeing it alive."

"You see rocks like big spiders."

"That's better than just seeing them like rocks. I love snakes and spiders. You can watch a bird fly by and not even hear the stuff gurgling in its stomach. How can you be so dead? And I always liked you so much. But I didn't know you were dead like that."

"How can one love snakes and spiders?"

"How can one love anything? It's even hard not to love you, even if you don't have any blood in you. By the way, what gave you the idea that blood was that dumb color: Don't you even know that blood is red?"

"I see it red."

"You *don't* see it red. You just call it red. That silly color isn't red. What I call red is red."

And he knew that she was right.

And after all, how can one not love anything? Especially when it becomes beautiful when angry, and when it is so much alive that it tends to shock by its intense awareness those who are partly dead.

Now Charles Cogsworth was a scientific man, and he believed that there are no insoluble problems. He solved this one too; for he had found that Valery was a low-flying bird, and he began to understand what was gurgling inside her.

And he solved it happily.

He is working on a Correlator for his Scanner now. When this is perfected, it will be safe to give the device to the public. You will be able to get the combination in about three years at approximately the price of a medium-sized new car. And if you will wait another year, you may be able to get one of the used ones reasonably.

The Correlator is designed to minimize and condition the initial view of the world seen through other eyes, to soften the shock of understanding others.

Misunderstandings can be agreeable. But there is something shattering about sudden perfect understanding.

and he built a crooked house

Robert A. Heinlein

Perception is a process by which we become acquainted with
the outside world so that it becomes a reliable medium within
which we can function. Robert A. Heinlein, author of *Stranger in a
Strange Land*, and one of science fiction's most prolific and most
admired writers, creates a new world with a new dimension in
"And He Built a Crooked House." Into this little world of four
dimensions he places three characters whose perceptions have
learned to cope with only three dimensions. How will they react in
this new environment where they have had no experience in
perceiving?

They seem to lose their depth perception but gain a kind of
circular vision which enables them to see themselves from the
back. In the house they can see down from enormous heights and
even into the nothingness of deep space. One of the characters
explains, "I think space is folded over through the fourth dimension here and we are looking past the fold." All this sounds like a
pure world of science fiction, but like much science fiction, it
moves toward fact. Since 1940, when this story was written, the
experiences of the astronauts in space demonstrate that earthly
rules of perception are not always applicable everywhere. On earth
up and down remain constant. In space, without gravity, our
perceptions of up and down change. Up becomes the direction of
our head, down the direction of our feet, but the background,
rather than being constant as on earth, shifts.

The general questions about perception relating to the story
are: What happens to our perceptual processes when these usually
reliable principles lose their reliability? How would we react to the
changes which we would experience? We have had one line of
answers from illusions which play on our expectations and then

fool us. In fact, one of the most famous illusions is the distorted room (which most introductory psychology textbooks illustrate) where our expectation for seeing parallel ceiling and floor lines is used to make a man appear to grow enormously as he walks from one side of a room to another. The room has converging floor and ceiling lines instead of parallel lines.

Part of the organization which we became familiar with and learn to depend on are the two dimensions of the vertical and horizontal, and the third dimension of depth. We learn that we can move up and down, sideways, and back and forth. By doing this, we experience distances and build up expectations allowing us to estimate distances. The field of perception in psychology has studied the rules which we all use to give us a relatively constant picture of what is out there and how we fit into it. Basically, we use the whole picture, the whole context of what we perceive to make specific judgments, like the size of objects, their shape, their color. For the perception of depth we use devices like linear perspective, light and shadow, and atmospheric perspective, where objects in the distance are generally seen more dimly than those in the foreground.

Now for a visit to the crooked house, where these perceptions do not apply. In its little, enclosed world, things are different. In fact, in reading the story, you might momentarily get a feeling you're in a space ship, viewing the earth from a new perspective. Like Teal, the architect who built the house, or Mrs. Bailey, his client, you may be either delighted or distressed by a change in the dimensions of your world.

AND HE BUILT A CROOKED HOUSE
Robert A. Heinlein

Americans are considered crazy anywhere in the world.

They will usually concede a basis for the accusation but point to California as the focus of the infection. Californians stoutly maintain that their bad reputation is derived solely from the acts of the inhabitants of Los Angeles County. Angelenos will, when pressed, admit the charge but explain hastily, "It's Hollywood. It's not our fault—we didn't ask for it; Hollywood just grew."

The people in Hollywood don't care; they glory in it. If you are interested, they will drive you up Laurel Canyon "—where we keep the violent cases." The Canyonites—the brown-legged women, the trunks-clad men constantly busy building and rebuilding their slaphappy unfinished houses—regard with faint contempt the dull creatures who live down in the flats, and treasure in their hearts the secret knowledge that they, and only they, know how to live.

Lookout Mountain Avenue is the name of a side canyon which twists up from Laurel Canyon. The other Canyonites don't like to have it mentioned; after all, one must draw the line somewhere!

High up on Lookout Mountain at number 8775, across the street from the Hermit—the original Hermit of Hollywood—lived Quintus Teal, graduate architect.

Even the architecture of southern California is different. Hot dogs are sold from a structure built like and designated "The Pup." Ice cream cones come from a giant stucco ice cream cone, and neon proclaims "Get the Chili Bowl Habit!" from the roofs of buildings which are disputably chili bowls. Gasoline, oil, and free road maps are dispensed beneath the wings of trimotored transport planes, while the certified rest rooms, inspected hourly for your comfort, are located in the cabin of the plane itself. These things may surprise, or amuse, the tourist, but the local residents, who walk bareheaded in the famous California noonday sun, take them as a matter of course.

Quintus Teal regarded the efforts of his colleagues in architecture as fainthearted, fumbling, and timid.

"What is a house?" Teal demanded of his friend, Homer Bailey.

"Well—" Bailey admitted cautiously—"speaking in broad terms, I've always regarded a house as a gadget to keep off the rain."

"Nuts! You're as bad as the rest of them."

"I didn't say the definition was complete—"

"Complete! It isn't even in the right direction. From that point of view we might just as well be squatting in caves. But I don't blame you," Teal went on magnanimously, "You're no worse than the lugs you find practicing architecture. Even the Moderns—all they've done is to abandon the Wedding Cake School in favor of the Service Station School, chucked away the gingerbread and slapped on some chromium, but at heart they are as conservative and traditional as a county courthouse. Neutra! Schindler! What have those bums got? What's Frank Lloyd Wright got that I haven't got?"

"Commissions," his friend answered succinctly.

"Huh? Wha' d'ju say?" Teal stumbled slightly in his flow of words, did a slight double take, and recovered himself. "Commissions. Correct. And why? Because I don't think of a house as an upholstered cave; I think of it as a machine for living, a vital process, a live dynamic thing, changing with the mood of the dweller—not a dead, static, oversized coffin. Why should we be held down by the frozen concepts of our ancestors? Any fool with a little smattering of descriptive geometry can design a house in the ordinary way. Is the static geometry of Euclid the only mathematics? Are we to completely disregard the Picard-Vessiot theory? How about modular systems? To say nothing of the rich suggestions of stereochemistry. Isn't there a place in architecture for transformation, for homomorphology, for actional structures?"

"Blessed if I know," answered Bailey. "You might just as well be talking about the fourth dimension for all it means to me."

"And why not? Why should we limit ourselves to the—Say!" He interrupted himself and stared into distances. "Homer, I think you've really got something. After all, why not? Think of the infinite richness of articulation and relationship in four dimensions. What a house, what a house—" He stood quite still, his pale bulging eyes blinking thoughtfully.

Bailey reached up and shook his arm. "Snap out of it. What the hell are you talking about, four dimensions? Time is the fourth dimension; you can't drive nails into *that*."

Teal shrugged him off. "Sure. Sure. Time is a fourth dimension, but I'm thinking about a fourth spatial dimension, like length, breadth and thickness. For economy of materials and convenience of arrangement you couldn't beat it. To say nothing of the saving of

203

ground space—you could put an eight-room house on the land now occupied by a one-room house. Like a tesseract—"

"What's a tesseract?"

"Didn't you go to school? A tesseract is a hypercube, a square figure with four dimensions to it, like a cube has three, and a square has two. Here, I'll show you." Teal dashed out into the kitchen of his apartment and returned with a box of toothpicks, which he spilled on the table between them, brushing glasses and a nearly empty Holland gin bottle carelessly aside. "I'll need some plasticine. I had some around here last week." He burrowed into a drawer of the littered desk which crowded one corner of his dining room and emerged with a lump of oily sculptor's clay. "Here's some."

"What are you going to do?"

"I'll show you." Teal rapidly pinched off small masses of the clay and rolled them into pea-sized balls. He stuck toothpicks into four of these and hooked them together into a square. "There! That's a square."

"Obviously."

"Another one like it, four more toothpicks, and we make a cube." The toothpicks were now arranged in the framework of a square box, a cube, with the pellets of clay holding the corners together. "Now we make another cube just like the first one, and the two of them will be two sides of the tesseract."

Bailey started to help him roll the little balls of clay for the second cube, but became diverted by the sensuous feel of the docile clay and started working and shaping it with his fingers.

"Look," he said, holding up his effort, a tiny figurine, "Gypsy Rose Lee."

"Looks more like Gargantua; she ought to sue you. Now pay attention. You open up one corner of the first cube, interlock the second cube at one corner, and then close the corner. Then take eight more toothpicks and join the bottom of the first cube to the bottom of the second, on a slant, and the top of the first to the top of the second, the same way." This he did rapidly, while he talked.

"What's that supposed to be?" Bailey demanded suspiciously.

"That's a tesseract, eight cubes forming the sides of a hypercube in four dimensions."

"It looks more like a cat's cradle to me. You've only got two cubes there anyhow. Where are the other six?"

"Use your imagination, man. Consider the top of the first cube in relation to the top of the second; that's cube number three. Then the two bottom squares, then the front faces of each cube, the back faces, the right hand, the left hand—eight cubes." He pointed them out.

"Yeah, I see 'em. But they still aren't cubes; they're watchamacallems—prisms. They are not square, they slant."

"That's just the way you look at it, in perspective. If you drew a picture of a cube on a piece of paper, the side squares would be slaunchwise, wouldn't they? That's perspective. When you look at a four-dimensional figure in three dimensions, naturally it looks crooked. But those are all cubes just the same."

"Maybe they are to you, brother, but they still look crooked to me."

Teal ignored the objections and went on. "Now consider this as the framework of an eight-room house; there's one room on the ground floor—that's for service, utilities, and garage. There are six rooms opening off it on the next floor, living room, dining room, bath, bedrooms, and so forth. And up at the top, completely enclosed and with windows on four sides, is your study. There! How do you like it?"

"Seems to me you have the bathtub hanging out of the living-room ceiling. Those rooms are interlaced like an octopus."

"Only in perspective, only in perspective. Here, I'll do it another way so you can see it." This time Teal made a cube of toothpicks, then made a second of halves of toothpicks, and set it exactly in the center of the first by attaching the corners of the small cube to the large cube by short lengths of toothpick. "Now—the big cube is your ground floor, the little cube inside is your study on the top floor. The six cubes joining them are the living rooms. See?"

Bailey studied the figure, then shook his head. "I still don't see but two cubes, a big one and a little one. Those other six things, they look like pyramids this time instead of prisms, but they still aren't cubes."

"Certainly, certainly, you are seeing them in different perspective. Can't you see that?"

"Well, maybe. But that room on the inside, there. It's completely surrounded by the thingamajigs. I thought you said it had windows on four sides."

"It has—it just looks like it was surrounded. That's the grand feature about a tesseract house, complete outside exposure for every room, yet every wall serves two rooms and an eight-room house requires only a one-room foundation. It's revolutionary."

"That's putting it mildly. You're crazy, Bud; you can't build a house like that. That inside room is on the inside, and there she stays."

Teal looked at his friend in controlled exasperation. "It's guys like you that keep architecture in its infancy. How many square sides has a cube?"

"Six."

"How many of them are inside?"

"Why, none of 'em. They're all on the outside."

"All right. Now listen—a tesseract has eight cubical sides, *all on the outside.* Now watch me. I'm going to open up this tesseract like you can open up a cubical pasteboard box, until it's flat. That way you'll be able to see all eight of the cubes." Working very rapidly he constructed four cubes, piling one on top of the other in an unsteady tower. He then built out four more cubes from the four exposed faces of the second cube in the pile. The structure swayed a little under the loose coupling of the clay pellets, but it stood, eight cubes in an inverted cross, a double cross, as the four additional cubes stuck out in four directions. "Do you see it now? It rests on the ground-floor room, the next six cubes are the living rooms, and there is your study, up at the top."

Bailey regarded it with more approval than he had the other figures. "At least I can understand it. You say that is a tesseract, too?"

"That is a tesseract unfolded in three dimensions. To put it back together you tuck the top cube onto the bottom cube, fold those side cubes in till they meet the top cube and there you are. You do all this folding through a fourth dimension of course; you don't distort any of the cubes, or fold them into each other."

Bailey studied the wobbly framework further. "Look here," he said at last, "why don't you forget about folding this thing up through a fourth dimension—you can't anyway—and build a house like this?"

"What do you mean, I can't? It's a simple mathematical problem—"

"Take it easy, son. It may be simple in mathematics, but you could never get your plans approved for construction. There isn't any fourth dimension; forget it. But this kind of a house—it might have some advantages."

Checked, Teal studied the model. "Hm-m-m—maybe you've got something. We could have the same number of rooms, and we'd save the same amount of ground space. Yes, and we would set that middle cross-shaped floor northeast, southwest, and so forth, so that every room would get sunlight all day long. That central axis lends itself nicely to central heating. We'll put the dining room on the northeast and the kitchen on the southeast, with big view windows in every room. OK, Homer, I'll do it! Where do you want it built?"

"Wait a minute! Wait a minute! I didn't say you were going to build it for me!"

"Of course I am. Who else? Your wife wants a new house; this is it."

"But Mrs. Bailey wants a Georgian house—"

"Just an idea she had. Women don't know what they want!"

"Mrs. Bailey does."

"Just some idea an out-of-date architect has put in her head. She drives a 1941 car, doesn't she? She wears the very latest styles—why should she live in an eighteenth-century house? This house will be even later than a 1941 model; it's years in the future. She'll be the talk of the town."

"Well—I'll have to talk to her."

"Nothing of the sort. We'll surprise her with it. Have another drink."

"Anyhow, we can't do anything about it now. Mrs. Bailey and I are driving up to Bakersfield tomorrow. The company's bringing in a couple of wells tomorrow."

"Nonsense. That's just the opportunity we want. It will be a surprise for her when you get back. You can just write me a check right now, and your worries are over."

"I oughtn't to do anything like this without consulting her. She won't like it."

"Say, who wears the pants in your family anyhow?"

The check was signed about halfway down the second bottle.

Things are done fast in southern California. Ordinary houses there are usually built in a month's time. Under Teal's impassioned heckling the tesseract house climbed dizzily skyward in days rather than weeks, and its cross-shaped second story came jutting out at the four corners of the world. He had some trouble at first with the inspectors over these four projecting rooms but by using strong girders and folding money he had been able to convince them of the soundness of his engineering.

By arrangement, Teal drove up in front of the Bailey residence the morning after their return to town. He improvised on his two-tone horn. Bailey stuck his head out the front door. "Why don't you use the bell?"

"Too slow," answered Teal cheerfully. "I'm a man of action. Is

Mrs. Bailey ready? Ah, there you are, Mrs. Bailey! Welcome home, welcome home. Jump in, we've got a surprise for you!"

"You know Teal, my dear," Bailey put in uncomfortably.

Mrs. Bailey sniffed. "I know him. We'll go in our own car, Homer."

"Certainly, my dear."

"Good idea," Teal agreed; "'s got more power than mine; we'll get there faster. I'll drive, I know the way." He took the keys from Bailey, slid into the driver's seat, and had the engine started before Mrs. Bailey could rally her forces.

"Never have to worry about my driving," he assured Mrs. Bailey, turning his head as he did so, while he shot the powerful car down the avenue and swung onto Sunset Boulevard; "it's a matter of power and control, a dynamic process, just my meat—I've never had a serious accident."

"You won't have but one," she said bitingly. "Will you *please* keep you eyes on the traffic?"

He attempted to explain to her that a traffic situation was a matter, not of eyesight, but intuitive integration of courses, speeds, and probabilities, but Bailey cut him short. "Where is the house, Quintus?"

"House?" asked Mrs. Bailey suspiciously. "What's this about a house, Homer? Have you been up to something without telling me?"

Teal cut in with his best diplomatic manner. "It certainly is a house, Mrs. Bailey. And what a house! It's a surprise for you from a devoted husband. Just wait till you see it—"

"I shall," she agreed grimly. "What style is it?"

"This house sets a new style. It's later than television, newer than next week. It must be seen to be appreciated. By the way," he went on rapidly, heading off any retort, "did you folks feel the earthquake last night?"

"Earthquake? What earthquake? Homer, was there an earthquake?"

"Just a little one," Teal continued, "about two A.M. If I hadn't been awake, I wouldn't have noticed it."

Mrs. Bailey shuddered. "Oh, this awful country! Do you hear that, Homer? We might have been killed in our beds and never have known it. Why did I ever let you persuade me to leave Iowa?"

"But, my dear," he protested hopelessly, "you wanted to come out to California; you didn't like Des Moines."

"We needn't go into that," she said firmly. "You are a man; you should anticipate such things. Earthquakes!"

"That's one thing you needn't fear in your new home, Mrs. Bailey," Teal told her. "It's absolutely earthquake-proof; every part is in perfect dynamic balance with every other part."

"Well, I hope so. Where is this house?"

"Just around this bend. There's the sign now." A large arrow sign, of the sort favored by real-estate promoters, proclaimed in letters that were large and bright even for southern California:

THE HOUSE OF THE FUTURE!!!
Colossal—Amazing—Revolutionary
SEE HOW YOUR GRANDCHILDREN WILL LIVE!
Q. Teal, Architect

"Of course that will be taken down," he added hastily, noting her expression, "as soon as you take possession." He slued around the corner and brought the car to a squealing halt in front of the House of the Future. "*Voilà!*" He watched their faces for response.

Bailey stared unbelievingly, Mrs. Bailey in open dislike. They saw a simple cubical mass, possessing doors and windows, but no other architectural features, save that it was decorated in intricate mathematical designs. "Teal," Bailey asked slowly, "what have you been up to?"

Teal turned from their faces to the house. Gone was the crazy tower with its jutting second-story rooms. No trace remained of the seven rooms above ground floor level. Nothing remained but the single room that rested on the foundations. "Great jumping cats!" he yelled. "I've been robbed!"

He broke into a run.

But it did him no good. Front or back, the story was the same: the other seven rooms had disappeared, vanished completely. Bailey caught up with him and took his arm.

"Explain yourself. What is this about being robbed? How come you built anything like this—it's not according to agreement."

"But I didn't. I built just what we had planned to build, an eight-room house in the form of a developed tesseract. I've been sabotaged; that's what it is! Jealousy! The other architects in town didn't dare let me finish this job; they knew they'd be washed up if I did."

"When were you last here?"

"Yesterday afternoon."

"Everything all right then?"

"Yes. The gardeners were just finishing up."

Bailey glanced around at the faultlessly manicured landscaping. "I don't see how seven rooms could have been dismantled and carted away from here in a single night without wrecking this garden."

Teal looked around, too. "It doesn't look it. I don't understand it."

Mrs. Bailey joined them. "Well? Well? Am I to be left to amuse myself? We might as well look it over as long as we are here, though I'm warning you, Homer, I'm not going to like it."

"We might as well," agreed Teal, and drew a key from his pocket with which he let them in the front door. "We may pick up some clues."

The entrance hall was in perfect order, the sliding screens that separated it from the garage space were back, permitting them to see the entire compartment. "This looks all right," observed Bailey. "Let's go up on the roof and try to figure out what happened. Where's the staircase? Have they stolen that, too?"

"Oh, no," Teal denied, "look—" He pressed a button below the light switch; a panel in the ceiling fell away and a light, graceful flight of stairs swung noiselessly down. Its strength members were the frosty silver of duralumin, its treads and risers transparent plastic. Teal wriggled like a boy who has successfully performed a card trick, while Mrs. Bailey thawed perceptibly.

"Pretty slick," Bailey admitted. "However it doesn't seem to go any place—"

"Oh, that—" Teal followed his gaze. "The cover lifts up as you approach the top. Open stair wells are anachronisms. Come on." As predicted, the lid of the staircase got out of their way as they climbed the flight and permitted them to debark at the top, but not, as they had expected, on the roof of the single room. They found themselves standing in the middle one of the five rooms which constituted the second floor of the original structure.

For the first time on record Teal had nothing to say. Bailey echoed him, chewing on his cigar. Everything was in perfect order. Before them, through open doorway and translucent partition, lay the kitchen, a chef's dream of up-to-the-minute engineering, Monel metal, continuous counter space, concealed lighting, functional arrangement. On the left the formal, yet gracious and hospitable, dining room awaited guests, its furniture in parade-ground alignment.

Teal knew before he turned his head that the drawing room and lounge would be found in equally substantial and impossible existence.

"Well, I must admit this *is* charming," Mrs. Bailey approved, "and the kitchen is just *too* quaint for words—though I would never have guessed from the exterior that this house had so much room upstairs. Of course *some* changes will have to be made. That secretary now—if we moved it over *here* and put the settle over *there—*"

"Stow it, Matilda," Bailey cut in brusquely. "What d'yuh make of it, Teal?"

"Why, Homer Bailey! The very id—"

"Stow it," he said. "Well, Teal?"

The architect shuffled his rambling body. "I'm afraid to say. Let's go on up."

"How?"

"Like this." He touched another button; a mate, in deeper colors, to the fairy bridge that had let them up from below offered them access to the next floor. They climbed it, Mrs. Bailey expostulating in the rear, and found themselves in the master bedroom. Its shades were drawn, as had been those on the level below, but the mellow lighting came on automatically. Teal at once activated the switch which controlled still another flight of stairs, and they hurried up into the topfloor study.

"Look, Teal," suggested Bailey when he had caught his breath, "can we get to the roof above this room? Then we could look around."

"Sure, it's an observatory platform." They climbed a fourth flight of stairs, but when the cover at the top lifted to let them reach the level above, they found themselves, not on the roof, but *standing in the ground-floor room where they had entered the house.*

Mr. Bailey turned a sickly gray. "Angels in heaven," he cried, "this place is haunted. We're getting out of here." Grabbing his wife he threw open the front door and plunged out.

Teal was much too preoccupied to bother with their departure. There was an answer to all this, an answer that he did not believe. But he was forced to break off considering it because of hoarse shouts from somewhere above him. He lowered the staircase and rushed upstairs. Bailey was in the central room leaning over Mrs. Bailey, who had fainted. Teal took in the situation, went to the bar built into the lounge, and poured three fingers of brandy, which he returned with and handed to Bailey. "Here—this'll fix her up."

Bailey drank it.

"That was for Mrs. Bailey," said Teal.

"Don't quibble," snapped Bailey. "Get her another." Teal took the precaution of taking one himself before returning with a dose earmarked for his client's wife. He found her just opening her eyes.

"Here, Mrs. Bailey," he soothed, "this will make you feel better."

"I never touch spirits," she protested, and gulped it.

"Now tell me what happened," suggested Teal. "I thought you two had left."

"But we did—we walked out the front door and found ourselves up here, in the lounge."

"The hell you say! Hm-m-m—wait a minute." Teal went into the lounge. There he found that the big view window at the end of the room was open. He peered cautiously through it. He stared, not out at the California countryside, but into the ground-floor room—or a reasonable facsimile thereof. He said nothing, but went back to the stairwell, which he had left open, and looked down it. The ground-floor room was still in place. Somehow, it managed to be in two different places at once, on different levels.

He came back into the central room and seated himself opposite Bailey in a deep, low chair, and sighted him past his upthrust bony knees. "Homer," he said impressively, "do you know what has happened?"

"No, I don't—but if I don't find out pretty soon, something is going to happen and pretty drastic, too!"

"Homer, this is a vindication of my theories. This house is a real tesseract."

"What's he talking about, Homer?"

"Wait, Matilda—now Teal, that's ridiculous. You've pulled some hanky-panky here and I won't have it—scaring Mrs. Bailey half to death, and making me nervous. All I want is to get out of here, with no more of your trapdoors and silly practical jokes."

"Speak for yourself, Homer," Mrs. Bailey interrupted, "I was *not* frightened; I was just shook all over queer for a moment. It's my heart; all of my people are delicate and highstrung. Now about this tessy thing—explain yourself, Mr. Teal. Speak up."

He told her as well as he could in the face of numerous interruptions the theory back of the house. "Now as I see it, Mrs. Bailey," he concluded, "this house, while perfectly stable in three dimensions, was not stable in four dimensions. I had built a house in the shape of an unfolded tesseract; something happened to it, some jar or side thrust, and it collapsed into its normal shape—it folded up." He snapped his fingers suddenly. "I've got it! The earthquake!"

"Earthquake?"

"Yes, yes, the little shake we had last night. From a four-dimensional standpoint this house was like a plane balanced on edge. One little push and it fell over, collapsing along its natural joints into a stable four-dimensional figure."

"I thought you boasted about how safe this house was."

"It is safe—three-dimensionally."

"I don't call a house safe," commented Bailey edgily, "that collapses at the first little trembler."

"But look around you, man!" Teal protested. "Nothing has been disturbed, not a piece of glassware cracked. Rotation through a fourth dimension can't affect a three-dimensional figure any more than you can shake letters off a printed page. If you had been sleeping in here last night, you would never have awakened."

"That's just what I'm afraid of. Incidentally, has your great genius figured out any way for us to get out of this booby trap?"

"Huh? Oh, yes, you and Mrs. Bailey started to leave and landed back up here, didn't you? But I'm sure there is no real difficulty— we came in, we can go out. I'll try it." He was up and hurrying downstairs before he had finished talking. He flung open the front door, stepped through, and found himself staring at his companions, down the length of the second-floor lounge. "Well, there does seem to be some slight problem," he admitted blandly. "A mere technicality, though—we can always go out a window." He jerked aside the long drapes that covered the deep French windows set in one side wall of the lounge. He stopped suddenly.

"Hm-m-m," he said, "this is interesting—very."

"What is?" asked Bailey, joining him.

"This." The window stared directly into the dining room instead of looking outdoors. Bailey stepped back to the corner where the lounge and the dining room joined the central room at ninety degrees.

"But that can't be," he protested, "that window is maybe fifteen, twenty feet from the dining room."

"Not in a tesseract," corrected Teal. "Watch." He opened the window and stepped through, talking back over his shoulder as he did so.

From the point of view of the Baileys he simply disappeared.

But not from his own viewpoint. It took him some seconds to catch his breath. Then he cautiously disentangled himself from the rosebush to which he had become almost irrevocably wedded, making a mental note the while never again to order landscaping which involved plants with thorns, and looked around him.

He was outside the house. The massive bulk of the ground-floor room thrust up beside him. Apparently he had fallen off the roof.

He dashed around the corner of the house, flung open the front door and hurried up the stairs. "Homer!" he called out, "Mrs. Bailey! I've found a way out!"

Bailey looked annoyed rather than pleased to see him. "What happened to you?"

"I fell out. I've been outside the house. You can do it just as easily—just step through those French windows. Mind the rosebush, though—we may have to build another stairway."

"How did you get back in?"

"Through the front door."

"Then we shall leave the same way. Come, my dear." Bailey set his hat firmly on his head and marched down the stairs, his wife on his arm.

Teal met them in the lounge. "I could have told you that wouldn't work," he announced. "Now here's what we have to do: As I see it, in a four-dimensional figure a three-dimensional man has two choices every time he crosses a line of juncture, like a wall or a threshold. Ordinarily he will make a ninety-degree turn through the fourth dimension, only he doesn't feel it with his three dimensions. Look." He stepped through the very window that he had fallen out of a moment before. Stepped through and arrived in the dining room, where he stood, still talking.

"I watched where I was going and arrived where I intended to." He stepped back into the lounge. "The time before I didn't watch and I moved on through normal space and fell out of the house. It must be a matter of subconscious orientation."

"I'd hate to depend on subconscious orientation when I step out for the morning paper."

"You won't have to; it'll become automatic. Now to get out of the house this time—Mrs. Bailey, if you will stand here with your back to the window, and jump backward, I'm pretty sure you will land in the garden."

Mrs. Bailey's face expressed her opinion of Teal and his ideas. "Homer Bailey," she said shrilly, "are you going to stand there and let him suggest such—"

"But Mrs. Bailey," Teal attempted to explain, "we can tie a rope on you and lower you down eas—"

"Forget it, Teal," Bailey cut him off brusquely. "We'll have to find a better way than that. Neither Mrs. Bailey nor I are fitted for jumping."

Teal was temporarily nonplused; there ensued a short silence. Bailey broke it with, "Did you hear that, Teal?"

"Hear what?"

"Someone talking off in the distance. D'you s'pose there could be someone else in the house, playing tricks on us, maybe?"

"Oh, not a chance. I've got the only key."

"But I'm sure of it," Mrs. Bailey confirmed. "I've heard them ever since we came in. Voices. Homer, I can't stand much more of this. Do something."

"Now, now, Mrs. Bailey," Teal soothed, "don't get upset. There can't be anyone else in the house, but I'll explore and make sure. Homer, you stay here with Mrs. Bailey and keep an eye on the rooms on this floor." He passed from the lounge into the ground-floor room and from there to the kitchen and on into the bedroom. This led him back to the lounge by a straight-line route, that is to say, by going straight ahead on the entire trip he returned to the place from which he started.

"Nobody around," he reported. "I opened all of the doors and windows as I went—all except this one." He stepped to the window opposite the one through which he had recently fallen and thrust back the drapes.

He saw a man with his back toward him, four rooms away. Teal snatched open the French window and dived through it, shouting, "There he goes now! Stop, thief!"

The figure evidently heard him; it fled precipitately. Teal pursued, his gangling limbs stirred to unanimous activity, through drawing room, kitchen, dining room, lounge—room after room, yet in spite of Teal's best efforts he could not seem to cut down the four-room lead that the interloper had started with.

He saw the pursued jump awkwardly but actively over the low sill of a French window and in so doing knock off his hat. When he came to the point where his quarry had lost his headgear, he stooped and picked it up, glad of an excuse to stop and catch his breath. He was back in the lounge.

"I guess he got away from me," he admitted. "Anyhow, here's his hat. Maybe we can identify him."

Bailey took the hat, looked at it, then snorted and slapped it on Teal's head. It fitted perfectly. Teal looked puzzled, took the hat off, and examined it. On the sweat band were the initials "Q.T." It was his own.

Slowly comprehension filtered through Teal's features. He

went back to the French window and gazed down the series of rooms through which he had pursued the mysterious stranger. They saw him wave his arms semaphore fashion. "What are you doing?" asked Bailey.

"Come see." The two joined him and followed his stare with their own. Four rooms away they saw the backs of three figures, two male and one female. The taller, thinner of the men was waving his arms in a silly fashion.

Mrs. Bailey screamed and fainted again.

Some minutes later, when Mrs. Bailey had been resuscitated and somewhat composed, Bailey and Teal took stock. "Teal," said Bailey, "I won't waste any time blaming you; recriminations are useless and I'm sure you didn't plan for this to happen, but I suppose you realize we are in a pretty serious predicament. How are we going to get out of here? It looks now as if we would stay until we starve; every room leads into another room."

"Oh, it's not that bad. I got out once, you know."

"Yes, but you can't repeat it—you tried."

"Anyhow we haven't tried all the rooms. There's still the study."

"Oh, yes, the study. We went through there when we first came in, and didn't stop. Is it your idea that we might get out through its windows?"

"Don't get your hopes up. Mathematically, it ought to look into the four side rooms on this floor. Still we never opened the blinds; maybe we ought to look."

"'Twon't do any harm anyhow. Dear, I think you had best just stay here and rest—"

"Be left alone in this horrible place? I should say not!" Mrs. Bailey was up off the couch where she had been recuperating even as she spoke.

They went upstairs. "This is the inside room, isn't it, Teal?" Bailey inquired as they passed through the master bedroom and climbed up on toward the study. "I mean it was the little cube in your diagram that was in the middle of the big cube, and completely surrounded."

"That's right," agreed Teal. "Well, let's have a look. I figure this window ought to give into the kitchen." He grasped the cords of Venetian blinds and pulled them.

It did not. Waves of vertigo shook them. Involuntarily they fell to the floor and grasped helplessly at the pattern on the rug to keep from falling. "Close it! Close it!" moaned Bailey.

Mastering in part a primitive atavistic fear, Teal worked his way back to the window and managed to release the screen. The window had looked *down* instead of *out*, down from a terrifying height.

Mrs. Bailey had fainted again.

Teal went back after more brandy while Bailey chafed her wrists. When she had recovered, Teal went cautiously to the window and raised the screen a crack. Bracing his knees, he studied the scene. He turned to Bailey. "Come look at this, Homer. See if you recognize it."

"You stay away from there, Homer Bailey!"

"Now, Matilda, I'll be careful." Bailey joined him and peered out.

"See up there? That's the Chrysler Building, sure as shooting. And there's the East River, and Brooklyn." They gazed straight down the sheer face of an enormously tall building. More than a thousand feet away a toy city, very much alive, was spread out before them. "As near as I can figure it out, we are looking down the side of the Empire State Building from a point just above its tower."

"What is it? A mirage?"

"I don't think so—it's too perfect. I think space is folded over through the fourth dimension here and we are looking past the fold."

"You mean we aren't really seeing it?"

"No, we're seeing it all right. I don't know what would happen if we climbed out this window, but I for one don't want to try. But what a view! Oh, boy, what a view! Let's try the other windows."

They approached the next window more cautiously, and it was well that they did, for it was even more disconcerting, more reason-shaking, than the one looking down the gasping height of the skyscraper. It was a simple seascape, open ocean and blue sky—but the ocean was where the sky should have been, and contrariwise. This time they were somewhat braced for it, but they both felt seasickness about to overcome them at the sight of waves rolling overhead; they lowered the blind quickly without giving Mrs. Bailey a chance to be disturbed by it.

Teal looked at the third window. "Game to try it, Homer?"

"Hrrumph—well, we won't be satisfied if we don't. Take it easy." Teal lifted the blind a few inches. He saw nothing, and raised it a little more—still nothing. Slowly he raised it until the window was fully exposed. They gazed out at—nothing.

217

Nothing, nothing at all. What color is nothing? Don't be silly! What shape is it? Shape is an attribute of *something*. It had neither depth nor form. It had not even blackness. It was *nothing*.

Bailey chewed at his cigar. "Teal, what do you make of that?"

Teal's insouciance was shaken for the first time. "I don't know, Homer, I don't rightly know—but I think that window ought to be walled up." He stared at the lowered blind for a moment. "I think maybe we looked at a place where space *isn't*. We looked around a fourth-dimensional corner and there wasn't anything there." He rubbed his eyes. "I've got a headache."

They waited for a while before tackling the fourth window. Like an unopened letter, it might *not* contain bad news. The doubt left hope. Finally the suspense stretched too thin and Bailey pulled the cord himself, in the face of his wife's protests.

It was not so bad. A landscape stretched away from them, right side up, and on such a level that the study appeared to be a ground-floor room. But it was distinctly unfriendly.

A hot, hot sun beat down from lemon-colored sky. The flat ground seemed burned a sterile, bleached brown and incapable of supporting life. Life there was strange stunted trees that lifted knotted, twisted arms to the sky. Little clumps of spiky leaves grew on the outer extremities of these misshapen growths.

"Heavenly day," breathed Bailey, "where is that?"

Teal shook his head, his eyes troubled. "It beats me."

"It doesn't look like anything on Earth. It looks more like another planet—Mars, maybe."

"I wouldn't know. But, do you know, Homer, it might be worse than that, worse than another planet, I mean."

"Huh? What's that you say?"

"It might be clear out of our space entirely. I'm not sure that that is our sun at all. It seems too bright."

Mrs. Bailey had somewhat timidly joined them and now gazed out at the outre scene. "Homer," she said in a subdued voice, "those hideous trees—they frighten me."

He patted her hand.

Teal fumbled with the window catch.

"What are you doing?" Bailey demanded.

"I thought if I stuck my head out the window I might be able to look around and tell a bit more."

"Well—all right," Bailey grudged, "but be careful."

"I will." He opened the window a crack and sniffed. "The air is all right, at least." He threw it open wide.

His attention was diverted before he could carry out his plan. An uneasy tremor, like the first intimation of nausea, shivered the entire building for a long second, and was gone.

"Earthquake!" They all said it at once. Mrs. Bailey flung her arms around her husband's neck.

Teal gulped and recovered himself, saying, "It's all right, Mrs. Bailey. This house is perfectly safe. You know you can expect settling tremors after a shock like last night." He had just settled his features into an expression of reassurance when the second shock came. This one was no mild shimmy but the real seasick roll.

In every Californian, native-born or grafted, there is a deep-rooted primitive reflex. An earthquake fills him with soul-shaking claustrophobia which impels him blindly to *get outdoors!* Model Boy Scouts will push aged grandmothers aside to obey it. It is a matter of record that Teal and Bailey landed on top of Mrs. Bailey. Therefore, she must have jumped through the window first. The order of precedence cannot be attributed to chivalry; it must be assumed that she was in readier position to spring.

They pulled themselves together, collected their wits a little, and rubbed sand from their eyes. Their first sensation was relief at feeling the solid sand of the desert land under them. Then Bailey noticed something that brought them to their feet and checked Mrs. Bailey from bursting into the speech that she had ready.

"Where's the house?"

It was gone. There was no sign of it at all. They stood in the center of flat desolation, the landscape they had seen from the window. But aside from the tortured, twisted tree there was nothing to be seen but the yellow sky and the luminary overhead, whose furnacelike glare was already almost insufferable.

Bailey looked slowly around, then turned to the architect. "Well, Teal?" His voice was ominous.

Teal shrugged helplessly. "I wish I knew. I wish I could even be sure that we were on Earth."

"Well, we can't stand here. It's sure death if we do. Which direction?"

"Any, I guess, Let's keep a bearing on the sun."

They had trudged on for an undetermined distance when Mrs. Bailey demanded a rest. They stopped. Teal said in an aside to Bailey, "Any ideas?"

"No . . . no, none. Say, do you hear anything?"

Teal listened. "Maybe—unless it's my imagination."

"Sounds like an automobile. Say, it *is* an automobile!"

They came to the highway in less than another hundred yards. The automobile, when it arrived, proved to be an elderly, puffing light truck, driven by a rancher. He crunched to a stop at their hail. "We're stranded. Can you help us out?"

"Sure. Pile in."

"Where are you headed?"

"Los Angeles."

"Los Angeles? Say, where is this place?"

"Well, you're right in the middle of the Joshua-Tree National Forest."

The return was as dispiriting as the Retreat from Moscow. Mr. and Mrs. Bailey sat up in front with the driver while Teal bumped along in the body of the truck, and tried to protect his head from the sun. Bailey subsidized the friendly rancher to detour to the tesseract house, not because they wanted to see it again, but in order to pick up their car.

At last the rancher turned the corner that brought them back to where they had started. But the house was no longer there.

There was not even the ground-floor room. It had vanished. The Baileys, interested in spite of themselves, poked around the foundations with Teal.

"Got any answers for this one, Teal?" asked Bailey.

"It must be that on that last shock it simply fell through into another section of space. I can see now that I should have anchored it at the foundations."

"That's not all you should have done."

"Well, I don't see that there is anything to get downhearted about. The house was insured, and we've learned an amazing lot. There are possibilities, man, possibilities! Why, right now I've got a great new revolutionary idea for a house—"

Teal ducked in time. He was always a man of action.

the subliminal man

J. G. Ballard

"The Subliminal Man" selects an aspect of our contemporary society and magnifies it to extreme proportions so that we can take a good look at it. Two aspects of the story are particularly interesting: subliminal advertising and thresholds in sensory systems. "The Subliminal Man" portrays a future society where the population—constantly bombarded by advertising—has only one interest, that of consuming. Except for one rebel—Hathaway. Like Henry Thoreau, he believes there are times when you should refuse to conform, times when you should become a majority of one. The appearance of huge, mysterious signs along the highway is for him a warning that the time has come to act.

Subliminal advertising is a minor issue in the study of sensation and perception, but it does have an interesting history. In the 1950s it was tried in movie theaters to get people to buy drinks and popcorn, but its effects were marginal or at least uncertain. The public clamored in indignation when it heard about subliminal advertising. The ethical considerations coupled with the uncertainty of the results apparently led to its abandonment.

However, the psychological principles upon which it is based are essentially sound. For our sensory systems, such as vision, there are absolute thresholds in such parameters as duration of presentation of the stimulus. Stimuli presented for durations less than the absolute thresholds cannot be recognized consciously and absorbed; those presented longer than threshold can be absorbed and recognized. To complicate matters, however, research evidence by Lazarus and McCleary[1] suggests a grey, narrow area between these conditions in which we can absorb

1. Richard S. Lazarus and Robert A. McCleary, "Autonomic Discrimination with Awareness: A Study of Subception," *Psychological Review* 58 (1951): 113–22.

221

(perceive) stimuli but not recognize them. This phenomenon has been called *subception*—perception below the level of awareness. Subliminal advertising would present stimuli at this level of duration to get messages through the sensory and perceptual systems, hoping to influence individuals to do certain things without their being aware of the influence.

An issue of more concern in psychology is the level of sensory stimulation in our mass society today. Is this continuous external bombardment of stimuli from advertising signs and sounds, from the mass media, from mass traffic, interfering with and reducing our abilities to think clearly? Is the constant advertising bombardment telling us what to buy and what to want seriously interfering with our ability to decide for ourselves what it is we *truly* want? Do advertisers manipulate our insecurities at unconscious levels so that we are obsessed with deodorants, sex appeal toothpastes, and big cars? If the answers are yes, then, as the story suggests, the issues involved are nothing less than the insidious erosion and usurpation of our freedom to control our own minds.

The story dramatizes the problem by portraying a typical consuming couple—Dr. Franklin and his wife, Judith. The rebellious Hathaway tries to make Dr. Franklin aware of what is happening to him, but as the story ends, we wonder what has happened to Dr. Franklin's will. Has the overall level of bombardment of stimuli lulled his will to fight back?

The story also provides interesting examples of principles for attracting attention.[2] Some of them are:

(1) *Change or contrast:* This is seen in the change in stimuli in the spot commercials which hold and actually condition the attention of Judith Franklin. She is conditioned on a variable interval schedule of reinforcement, never knowing when her viewing will be rewarded by the secret numbers. Contrast is used to get Dr. Franklin's attention on the road by having the background for the road signs, the highways, and the standardized make of car not distract attention, thereby putting the strange new signs in increased contrast to the road.

(2) *Size:* All other things being equal, something large attracts

2. F. Ruch and P. Zimbardo, *Psychology and Life*, 8th ed. (Glenview, Ill.: Scott, Foresman, 1971), pp. 267–68.

more attention than something small. The bigness of the signs in the story makes use of this factor.

(3) *Intensity:* Stimuli of high intensity are better than low. Bright colors are better than pastels, as is illustrated by the red "airport" lights on the new signs, as well as the brightness of the signs already there.

(4) *Repetition of stimuli:* Weak stimuli frequently repeated can be more effective than one strong stimuli. This is the major principle in the subliminal technique: the weak stimulus, although barely picked up, is repeated over and over again. Repetition is a double-edged sword, however, because constant repetition can result in sensory adaptation and eventual loss of attention.

(5) *Personal need and interest:* The same stimuli will be more effective to those who are interested in it or need it. Franklin's wife feels she needs a fourth TV set; Franklin at first does not. The shows on TV attract his wife because of her interest; they do not attract him.

(6) *Individuation:* People maintain their attention to things that are relevant to them individually, such as their names. The signs in the supermarket foyers listing the names of the best consumers use this principle.

In general, all these factors work together as a system, rather than separately. The story illustrates the overall impact of all these factors as an overpowering campaign to get people to consume. What about an individual like Hathaway who resents this kind of manipulation? How can he survive? How can he fight back?

THE SUBLIMINAL MAN   *J. G. Ballard*

"The signs, Doctor! Have you seen the signs?"

Frowning with annoyance, Dr. Franklin quickened his pace and hurried down the hospital steps towards the line of parked cars. Over his shoulder he caught a glimpse of a man in ragged sandals and lime-stained jeans waving to him from the far side of the drive, then break into a run when he saw Franklin try to evade him.

"Dr. Franklin! The signs!"

Head down, Franklin swerved around an elderly couple approaching the out-patient department. His car was over a hundred yards away. Too tired to start running himself, he waited for the young man to catch him.

"All right, Hathaway, what is it this time?" he snapped irritably. "I'm getting sick of you hanging around here all day."

Hathaway lurched to a halt in front of him, uncut black hair like an awning over his eyes. He brushed it back with a claw-like hand and turned on a wild smile, obviously glad to see Franklin and oblivious of the latter's hostility.

"I've been trying to reach you at night, Doctor, but your wife always puts the phone down on me," he explained without a hint of rancor, as if well-used to this kind of snub. "And I didn't want to look for you inside the Clinic." They were standing by a privet hedge that shielded them from the lower windows of the main administrative block, but Franklin's regular rendezvous with Hathaway and his strange messianic cries had already been the subject of amused comment.

Franklin began to say: "I appreciate that—" but Hathaway brushed this aside. "Forget it, Doctor, there are more important things happening now. They've started to build the first big signs! Over a hundred feet high, on the traffic islands just outside town. They'll soon have all the approach roads covered. When they do, we might as well stop thinking."

"Your trouble is that you're thinking too much," Franklin told him. "You've been rambling about these signs for weeks now. Tell me, have you actually seen one signaling?"

Hathaway tore a handful of leaves from the hedge, exasperated by this irrelevancy. "Of course I haven't, that's the whole point,

Doctor." He dropped his voice as a group of nurses walked past, watching him uneasily out of the corners of their eyes. "The construction gangs were out again last night, laying huge power cables. You'll see them on the way home. Everything's nearly ready now."

"They're traffic signs," Franklin explained patiently. "The flyover has just been completed. Hathaway, for God's sake relax. Try to think of Dora and the child."

"I *am* thinking of them!" Hathaway's voice rose to a controlled scream. "Those cables were 40,000-volt lines, Doctor, with terrific switch-gear. The trucks were loaded with enormous metal scaffolds. Tomorrow they'll start lifting them up all over the city, they'll block off half the sky! What do you think Dora will be like after six months of that? We've got to stop them, Doctor, they're trying to transistor-ize our brains!"

Embarrassed by Hathaway's high-pitched shouting, Franklin had momentarily lost his sense of direction and helplessly searched the sea of cars for his own. "Hathaway, I can't waste any more time talking to you. Believe me, you need skilled help, these obsessions are beginning to master you."

Hathaway started to protest, and Franklin raised his right hand firmly. "Listen. For the last time, if you can show me one of these new signs, and prove that it's transmitting subliminal commands, I'll go to the police with you. But you haven't got a shred of evidence, and you know it. Subliminal advertising was banned thirty years ago, and the laws have never been repealed. Anyway, the technique was unsatisfactory, any success it had was marginal. Your idea of a huge conspiracy with all these thousands of giant signs everywhere is preposterous."

"All right, Doctor." Hathaway leaned against the bonnet of one of the cars. His moods seemed to switch abruptly from one level to the next. He watched Franklin amiable. "What's the matter—lost your car?"

"All your damned shouting has confused me." Franklin pulled out his ignition key and read the number off the tag: "NYN 299-566-367-21—can you see it?"

Hathaway leaned around lazily, one sandal up on the bonnet, surveying the square of a thousand or so cars facing them. "Difficult, isn't it, when they're all identical, even the same color? Thirty years ago there were about ten different makes, each in a dozen colors."

Franklin spotted his car, began to walk towards it. "Sixty years ago there were a hundred makes. What of it? The economies of standardization are obviously bought at a price."

Hathaway drummed his palm lightly on the roofs. "But these cars aren't all that cheap, Doctor. In fact, comparing them on an average income basis with those of thirty years ago they're about forty percent more expensive. With only one make being produced you'd expect a substantial reduction in price, not an increase."

"Maybe," Franklin said, opening his door. "But mechanically the cars of today are far more sophisticated. They're lighter, more durable, safer to drive."

Hathaway shook his head skeptically. "They *bore* me. The same model, same styling, same color, year after year. It's a sort of communism." He rubbed a greasy finger over the windshield. "This is a new one again, isn't it, Doctor? Where's the old one—you only had it for three months?"

"I traded it in," Franklin told him, starting the engine. "If you ever had any money you'd realize that it's the most economical way of owning a car. You don't keep driving the same one until it falls apart. It's the same with everything else—television sets, washing machines, refrigerators. But you aren't faced with the problem—you haven't got any."

Hathaway ignored the gibe, and leaned his elbow on Franklin's window. "Not a bad idea, either, Doctor. It gives me time to think. I'm not working a twelve-hour day to pay for a lot of things I'm too busy to use before they're obsolete."

He waved as Franklin reversed the car out of its line, then shouted into the wake of exhaust: "Drive with your eyes closed, Doctor!"

On the way home Franklin kept carefully to the slowest of the four-speed lanes. As usual after his discussions with Hathaway he felt vaguely depressed. He realized that unconsciously he envied Hathaway's footloose existence. Despite the grimy cold-water apartment in the shadow and roar of the flyover, despite his nagging wife and their sick child, and the endless altercations with the landlord and the supermarket credit manager, Hathaway still retained his freedom intact. Spared any responsibilities, he could resist the smallest encroachment upon him by the rest of society, if only by generating obsessive fantasies, such as his latest one about subliminal advertising.

The ability to react to stimuli, even irrationally, was a valid criterion of freedom. By contrast, what freedom Franklin possessed was peripheral, sharply demarked by the manifold responsibilities in the center of his life—the three mortages on his home, the mandatory rounds of cocktail and TV parties, the private consultancy occupying most of Saturday which paid the installments on the multitude of household gadgets, clothes, and past holidays. About the only time he had to himself was driving to and from work.

But at least the roads were magnificent. Whatever other criticisms might be leveled at the present society, it certainly knew how to build roads. Eight, ten, and twelve-lane expressways interlaced across the continent, plunging from overhead causeways into the giant car parks in the center of the cities, or dividing into the great suburban arteries with their multiacre parking aprons around the marketing centers. Together the roadways and car parks covered more than a third of the country's entire area, and in the neighborhood of the cities the proportion was higher. The old cities were surrounded by the vast, dazzling abstract sculptures of the cloverleaves and flyovers, but even so the congestion was unremitting.

The ten-mile journey to his home in fact covered over twenty-five miles and took him twice as long as it had done before the construction of the expressway, the additional miles contained within the three giant clover-leaves. New cities were springing from the motels, cafes, and car marts around the highways. At the slightest hint of an intersection a shanty town of shacks and filling stations sprawled away among the forest of electric signs and route indicators, many of them substantial cities.

All around him cars bulleted along, streaming towards the suburbs. Relaxed by the smooth motion of the car, Franklin edged outward into the next speed-lane. As he accelerated from 40 to 50 m.p.h., a strident ear-jarring noise drummed out from his tires, shaking the chassis of the car. Ostensibly an aid to lane discipline, the surface of the road was covered with a mesh of small rubber studs, spaced progressively further apart in each of the lanes so that the tire hum resonated exactly on 40, 50, 60, and 70 m.p.h. Driving at an intermediate speed for more than a few seconds became physiologically painful, and soon resulted in damage to the car and tires.

When the studs wore out they were replaced by slightly different patterns, matching those of the latest tires, so that regular tire changes were necessary, increasing the safety and efficiency of the expressway. It also increased the revenues of the car and tire manufacturers, for most cars over six months old soon fell to pieces,

227

under the steady battering, but this was regarded as a desirable end, the greater turnover reducing the unit price and making necessary more frequent model changes, as well as ridding the roads of dangerous vehicles.

A quarter of a mile ahead, at the approach to the first of the clover-leaves, the traffic stream was showing, huge police signs signaling "Lanes Closed Ahead" and "Drop Speed by 10 m.p.h." Franklin tried to return to the previous lane, but the cars were jammed bumper to bumper. As the chassis began to shudder and vibrate, jarring his spine, he clamped his teeth and tried to restrain himself from sounding the horn. Other drivers were less self-controlled, and everywhere engines were plunging and snarling, horns blaring. Road taxes were now so high, up to 30 percent of income (by contrast, income taxes were a bare 2 percent) that any delay on the expressways called for an immediate government inquiry, and the major departments of state were concerned with the administration of the road systems.

Nearer the clover-leaf the lanes had been closed to allow a gang of construction workers to erect a massive metal sign on one of the traffic islands. The palisaded area swarmed with engineers and surveyors and Franklin assumed that this was the sign Hathaway had seen unloaded the previous night. His apartment was in one of the gimcrack buildings in the settlement that straggled away around a nearby flyover, a low-rent area inhabited by service station personnel, waitresses, and other migrant labor.

The sign was enormous, at least 100 feet high, fitted with heavy concave grilles similar to radar bowls. Rooted in a series of concrete caissons, it reared high into the air above the approach roads, visible for miles. Franklin craned up at the grilles, tracing the power cables from the transformers up into the intricate mesh of metal coils that covered their surface. A line of red aircraft-warning beacons was already alight along the top strut, and Franklin assumed that the sign was part of the ground approach system of the city airport ten miles to the east.

Three minutes later, as he accelerated down the two-mile link of straight highway to the next clover-leaf, he saw the second of the giant signs looming up into the sky before him.

Changing down into the 40 m.p.h. lane, Franklin uneasily watched the great bulk of the second sign recede in his rearview mirror. Although there were no graphic symbols among the wire coils covering the grilles, Hathaway's warnings still sounded in his ears. Without knowing why, he felt sure that the signs were not part of the airport approach system. Neither of them was in line with the principal airlanes. To justify the expense of siting them in the center of the expressway—the second sign required elaborate angled buttresses to support it on the narrow island—obviously meant that their role related in some way to the traffic streams.

Two hundred yards away was a roadside automart, and Franklin abruptly remembered that he needed some cigarettes. Swinging the car down the entrance ramp, he joined the queue slowly passing the self-service dispenser at the far end of the rank. The automart was packed with cars, each of the five purchasing ranks lined with tired-looking men hunched over their wheels.

Inserting his coins (paper money was no longer in circulation, unmanageable by the automats) he took a carton from the dispenser. This was the only brand of cigarettes available—in fact there was only one brand of everything—though giant economy packs were an alternative. Moving off, he opened the dashboard locker.

Inside, still sealed in their wrappers, were three other cartons.

A strong fish-like smell pervaded the house when he reached home, steaming out from the oven in the kitchen. Sniffing it uneagerly, Franklin took off his coat and hat, and found his wife crouched over the TV set in the lounge. An announcer was dictating a stream of numbers, and Judith scribbled them down on a pad, occasionally cursing under her breath. "What a muddle!" she snapped finally. "He was talking so quickly I took only a few things down."

"Probably deliberate," Franklin commented. "New panel game?"

Judith kissed him on the cheek, discreetly hiding the ashtray loaded with cigarette butts and chocolate wrappings. "Hullo, darling, sorry not to have a drink ready for you. They've started this series of Spot Bargains. They give you a selection of things on which you get a ninety percent trade-in discount at the local stores, if you're in the right area and have the right serial numbers. It's all terribly complicated."

"Sounds good, though. What have you got?"

Judith peered at her checklist. "Well, as far as I can see the only thing is the infra-red barbecue spit. But we have to be there before eight o'clock tonight. It's seven-thirty already."

"Then that's out. I'm tired, angel, I need something to eat." When Judith started to protest he added firmly: "Look, I don't want

229

a new infra-red barbecue spit, we've only had this one for two months. Damn it, it's not even a different model."

"But, darling, don't you see, it makes it cheaper if you keep buying new ones. We'll have to trade ours in at the end of the year anyway, we signed the contract, and this way we save at least twenty dollars. These Spot Bargains aren't just a gimmick, you know. I've been glued to that set all day." A note of irritation had crept into her voice, but Franklin sat his ground, doggedly ignoring the clock.

"Right, we lose twenty dollars. It's worth it." Before she could remonstrate he said: "Judith, please, you probably took the wrong number down anyway." As she shrugged and went over to the bar he called: "Make it a stiff one. I see we have health foods on the menu."

"They're good for you, darling. You know you can't live on ordinary foods all the time. They don't contain any proteins or vitamins. You're always saying we ought to be like people in the old days and eat nothing but health foods."

"I would, but they smell so awful." Franklin lay back, nose in the glass of whiskey, gazing at the darkened skyline outside.

A quarter of a mile away, gleaming out above the roof of the neighborhood supermarket, were the five red beacon lights. Now and then, as the headlamps of the Spot Bargainers swung up across the face of the building, he could see the square massive bulk of the giant sign clearly silhouetted against the evening sky.

"Judith!" He went into the kitchen and took her over to the window. "That sign, just behind the supermarket. When did they put it up?"

"I don't know." Judith peered at him curiously. "Why are you so worried, Robert? Isn't it something to do with the airport?"

Franklin stared thoughtfully at the dark hull of the sign. "So everyone probably thinks."

Carefully he poured his whiskey into the sink.

After parking his car on the supermarket apron at seven o'clock the next morning, Franklin carefully emptied his pockets and stacked the coins in the dashboard locker. The supermarket was already busy with early morning shoppers and the line of thirty turnstiles clicked and slammed. Since the introduction of the "24-hour spending day" the shopping complex was never closed. The bulk of the shoppers were discount buyers, housewives contracted to make huge volume purchases of food, clothing, and appliances against substantial overall price cuts, and forced to drive around all day from supermarket to supermarket, frantically trying to keep pace with their purchase schedules and grappling with the added incentives inserted to keep the schemes alive.

Many of the women had teamed up, and as Franklin walked over to the entrance a pack of them charged towards their cars, stuffing their pay slips into their bags and gesticulating at each other. A moment later their cars roared off in a convoy to the next marketing zone.

A large neon sign over the entrance listed the latest discount—a mere 5 percent—calculated on the volume of turnover. The highest discounts, sometimes up to 25 percent, were earned in the housing estates where junior white-collar workers lived. There, spending had a strong social incentive, and the desire to be the highest spender in the neighborhood was given moral reinforcement by the system of listing all the names and their accumulating cash totals on a huge electric sign in the supermarket foyers. The higher the spender, the greater his contribution to the discounts enjoyed by others. The lowest spenders were regarded as social criminals, free-riding on the backs of others.

Luckily this sytem had yet to be adopted in Franklin's neighborhood. Not because the professional men and their wives were able to exercise more discretion, but because their higher incomes allowed them to contract into more expensive discount schemes operated by the big department stores in the city.

Ten yards from the entrance Franklin paused, looking up at the high metal sign mounted in an enclosure at the edge of the car park. Unlike the other signs and hoardings that proliferated everywhere, no attempt had been made to decorate it, or disguise the gaunt bare rectangle of riveted steel mesh. Power lines wound down its sides, and the concrete surface of the car park was crossed by a long scar where a cable had been sunk.

Franklin strolled along, then fifty feet from the sign stopped and turned, realizing that he would be late for the hospital and needed a new carton of cigarettes. A dim but powerful humming emanated from the transformers below the sign, fading as he retraced his steps to the supermarket.

Going over to the automats in the foyer, he felt for his change, then whistled sharply when he remembered why he had deliberately emptied his pockets.

"The cunning thing!" he said, loud enough for two shoppers to stare at him. Reluctant to look directly at the sign, he watched its reflection in one of the glass doorpanes, so that any subliminal message would be reversed.

Almost certainly he had received two distinct signals—"Keep Away" and "Buy Cigarettes." The people who normally parked their cars along the perimeter of the apron were avoiding the area under the enclosure, the cars describing a loose semicircle fifty feet around it.

He turned to the janitor sweeping out the foyer. "What's that sign for?"

The man leaned on his broom, gazing dully at the sign. "Dunno," he said, "must be something to do with the airport." He had an almost fresh cigarette in his mouth, but his right hand reached unconsciously to his hip pocket and pulled out a pack. He drummed the second cigarette absently on his thumbnail as Franklin walked away.

Everyone entering the supermarket was buying cigarettes.

Cruising quietly along the 40 m.p.h. lane, Franklin began to take a closer interest in the landscape around him. Usually he was either too tired or too preoccupied to do more than think about his driving, but now he examined the expressway methodically, scanning the roadside cafes for any smaller versions of the new signs. A host of neon displays covered the doorways and windows, but most of them seemed innocuous, and he turned his attention to the larger billboards erected along the open stretches of the expressway. Many of these were as high as four-story houses, elaborate three-dimensional devices in which giant glossy-skinned housewives with electric eyes and teeth jerked and postured around their ideal kitchens, neon flashes exploding from their smiles.

The areas on either side of the expressway were wasteland, continuous junkyards filled with cars and trucks, washing machines and refrigerators, all perfectly workable but jettisoned by the economic pressure of the succeeding waves of discount models. Their intact chrome hardly tarnished, the mounds of metal shells and cabinets glittered in the sunlight. Nearer the city the billboards were sufficiently close together to hide them, but now and then, as he slowed to approach one of the flyovers, Franklin caught a glimpse of the huge pyramids of metal, gleaming silently like the refuse ground of some forgotten El Dorado.

That evening Hathaway was waiting for him as he came down the hospital steps. Franklin waved him across the court, then led the way quickly to his car.

"What's the matter, Doctor?" Hathaway asked as Franklin wound up the windows and glanced around the lines of parked cars. "Is someone after you?"

Franklin laughed somberly. "I don't know. I hope not, but if what you say is right, I suppose there is."

Hathaway leaned back with a chuckle, propping one knee up on the dashboard. "So you've seen something, Doctor, after all."

"Well, I'm not sure yet, but there's just a chance you may be right. This morning at the Fairlawne supermarket. . . ." He broke off, uneasily remembering the huge blank sign and the abrupt way in which he had turned back to the supermarket as he approached it, then described his encounter.

Hathaway nodded slowly. "I've seen the sign there. It's big, but not as big as some that are going up. They're building them everywhere now. All over the city. What are you going to do, Doctor?"

Franklin gripped the wheel tightly. Hathaway's thinly veiled amusement irritated him. "Nothing, of course. Damn it, it may be just autosuggestion, you've probably got me imagining—"

Hathaway sat up with a jerk, his face mottled and savage. "Don't be absurd, Doctor! If you can't believe your own senses what chance have you left? They're invading your brain; if you don't defend yourself they'll take it over completely! We've got to act now, before we're all paralyzed."

Wearily Franklin raised one hand to restrain him. "Just a minute. Assuming that these signs *are* going up everywhere, what would be their object? Apart from wasting the enormous amount of capital invested in all the other millions of signs and billboards, the amounts of discretionary spending power still available must be infinitesimal. Some of the present mortgage and discount schemes reach half a century ahead, so there can't be much slack left to take up. A big trade war would be disastrous."

"Quite right, Doctor," Hathaway rejoined evenly, "but you're forgetting one thing. What would supply that extra spending power? A big increase in production. Already they've started to raise the working day from twelve hours to fourteen. In some of the appliance plants around the city Sunday working is being introduced as a norm. Can you visualize it, Doctor—a seven-day week, everyone with at least three jobs."

Franklin shook his head. "People won't stand for it."

"They will. Within the last twenty-five years the gross national product has risen by 50 percent, but so have the average hours worked. Ultimately we'll all be working and spending twenty-four hours a day, seven days a week. No one will dare refuse. Think what a slump would mean—millions of lay-offs, people with time on their hands and nothing to spend it on. Real leisure, not just time spent buying things." He seized Franklin by the shoulder. "Well, Doctor, are you going to join me?"

Franklin freed himself. Half a mile away, partly hidden by the four-story bulk of the Pathology Department, was the upper half of one of the giant signs, workmen still crawling across its girders. The airlines over the city had deliberately been routed away from the hospital, and the sign obviously had no connection with approaching aircraft.

"Isn't there a prohibition on subliminal living? How can the unions accept it?"

"The fear of a slump. You know the new economic dogmas. Unless output rises by a steady inflationary 5 percent the economy is stagnating. Ten years ago increased efficiency alone would raise output, but the advantages there are minimal now and only one thing is left. More work. Increased consumption and subliminal advertising will provide the spur."

"What are you planning to do?"

"I can't tell you, Doctor, unless you accept equal responsibility for it."

"Sounds rather Quixotic," Franklin commented. "Tilting at windmills. You won't be able to chop those things down with an axe."

"I won't try." Hathaway suddenly gave up and opened the door. "Don't wait too long to make up your mind, Doctor. By then it may not be yours to make up." With a wave he was gone.

On the way home Franklin's skepticism returned. The idea of the conspiracy was preposterous, and the economic arguments were too plausible. As usual, though, there had been a hook in the soft bait Hathaway dangled before him—Sunday working. His own consultancy had been extended into Sunday morning with his appointment as visiting factory doctor to one of the automobile plants that had started Sunday shifts. But instead of resenting this incursion into his already meager hours of leisure, he had been glad. For one frightening reason—he needed the extra income.

Looking out over the lines of scurrying cars, he noticed that at least a dozen of the great signs had been erected along the expressway. As Hathaway had said, more were going up everywhere, rearing over the supermarkets in the housing developments like rusty metal sails.

Judith was in the kitchen when he reached home, watching the TV program on the hand-set over the cooker. Franklin climbed past a big cardboard carton, its seals still unbroken, which blocked the doorway, and kissed her on the cheek as she scribbled numbers down on her pad. The pleasant odor of pot-roast chicken—or, rather, a gelatine dummy of a chicken fully flavored and free of any toxic or nutritional properties—mollified his irritation at finding her still playing the Spot Bargains.

He tapped the carton with his foot. "What's this?"

"No idea, darling, something's always coming these days, I can't keep up with it all." She peered through the glass door at the chicken—an economy twelve-pounder, the size of a turkey, with stylized legs and wings and an enormous breast, most of which would be discarded at the end of the meal (there were no dogs or cats these days, the crumbs from the rich man's table saw to that) and then glanced at him pointedly.

"You look rather worried, Robert. Bad day?"

Franklin murmured noncommittally. The hours spent trying to detect false clues in the faces of the Spot Bargain announcers had sharpened Judith's perceptions, and he felt a pang of sympathy for the legion of husbands similarly outmatched.

"Have you been talking to that crazy beatnik again?"

"Hathaway? As a matter of fact I have. He's not all that crazy." He stepped backwards into the carton, almost spilling his drink. "Well, what is this thing? As I'll be working for the next fifty Sundays to pay for it I'd like to find out."

He searched the sides, finally located the label. "*A TV set?* Judith, do we need another one? We've already got three. Lounge, dining room, and the hand-set. What's the fourth for?"

"The guest room, dear, don't get so excited. We can't leave a hand-set in the guest room, it's rude. I'm trying to economize, but four TV sets is the bare minimum. All the magazines say so."

"*And* three radios?" Franklin stared irritably at the carton. "If we do invite a guest here how much time is he going to spend alone in his room watching television? Judith, we've got to call a halt. It's not as if these things were free, or even cheap. Anyway, television is a total waste of time. There's only one program. It's ridiculous to have four sets."

"Robert, there are *four* channels."

"But only the commercials are different." Before Judith could reply the telephone rang. Franklin lifted the kitchen receiver, listened to the gabble of noise that poured from it. At first he wondered whether this was some off-beat prestige commercial, then realized it was Hathaway in a manic swing.

"Hathaway!" he shouted back. "Relax, man! What's the matter now?"

"—Doctor, you'll have to believe me this time. I tell you I got on to one of the islands with a stroboscope, they've got hundreds of high-speed shutters blasting away like machine-guns straight into people's faces and they can't see a thing, it's fantastic! The next big campaign's going to be cars and TV sets, they're trying to swing a two-month model change—can you imagine it, Doctor, a new car every two months? God Almighty, it's just—"

Franklin waited impatiently as the five-second commercial break cut in (all telephone calls were free, the length of the commercial extending with range—for long-distance calls the ratio of commercial to conversation was as high as 10:1, the participants desperately trying to get a word in edgeways between the interminable interruptions), but just before it ended he abruptly put the telephone down, then removed the receiver from the cradle.

Judith came over and took his arm. "Robert, what's the matter? You look terribly strained."

Franklin picked up his drink and walked through into the lounge. "It's just Hathaway. As you say, I'm getting a little too involved with him. He's starting to prey on my mind."

He looked at the dark outline of the sign over the supermarket, its red warning lights glowing in the night sky. Blank and nameless, like an area forever closed off in an insane mind, what frightened him was its total anonymity.

"Yet I'm not sure," he muttered. "So much of what Hathaway says makes sense. These subliminal techniques are the sort of last-ditch attempt you'd expect from an overcapitalized industrial system."

He waited for Judith to reply, then looked up at her. She stood in the center of the carpet, hands folded limply, her sharp, intelligent face curiously dull and blunted. He followed her gaze out over the rooftops, then with an effort turned his head and quickly switched on the TV set.

"Come on," he said grimly. "Let's watch television. God, we're going to need that fourth set."

A week later Franklin began to compile his inventory. He saw nothing more of Hathaway; as he left the hospital in the evening the familiar scruffy figure was absent. When the first of the explosions sounded dimly around the city and he read of the attempts to sabotage the giant signs he automatically assumed that Hathaway was responsible, but later he heard on a newscast that the detonations had been set off by construction workers excavating foundations.

More of the signs appeared over the rooftops, isolated on the palisaded islands near the suburban shopping centers. Already there were over thirty on the ten-mile route from the hospital, standing shoulder to shoulder over the speeding cars like giant dominoes. Franklin had given up his attempt to avoid looking at them, but the slim possibility that the explosions might be Hathaway's counterattack kept his suspicions alive.

He began his inventory after hearing the newscast, discovered that in the previous fortnight he and Judith had traded in their

Car (previous model 2 months old)
2 TV sets (4 months)
Power mower (7 months)
Electric cooker (5 months)
Hair dryer (4 months)
Refrigerator (3 months)
2 radios (7 months)
Record player (5 months)
Cocktail bar (8 months)

Half these purchases had been made by himself, but exactly when he could never recall realizing at the time. The car, for example, he had left in the garage near the hospital to be greased: that evening he had signed for the new model as he sat at its wheel, accepting the salesman's assurance that the depreciation on the two-month trade-in was virtually less than the cost of the grease-job. Ten minutes later, as he sped along the expressway, he suddenly realized that he had bought a new car. Similarly, the TV sets had been replaced by identical models after developing the same irritating interference pattern (curiously, the new sets also displayed the pattern, but as the salesman assured them, this promptly vanished two days later).

Not once had he actually decided of his own volition that he wanted something and then gone out to a store and bought it!

237

He carried the inventory around with him, adding to it as necessary, quietly and without protest analyzing these new sales techniques, wondering whether total capitulation might be the only way of defeating them. As long as he kept up even a token resistance, the inflationary growth curve would show a controlled annual 10 percent climb. With that resistance removed, however, it would begin to rocket upwards out of control. . . .

Then, driving home from the hospital two months later, he saw one of the signs for the first time.

He was in the 40 m.p.h. lane, unable to keep up with the flood of new cars, had just passed the second of the three clover-leaves when the traffic half a mile away began to slow down. Hundreds of cars had driven up onto the grass verge, and a large crowd was gathering around one of the signs. Two small black figures were climbing up the metal face, and a series of huge grid-like patterns of light flashed on and off, illuminating the evening air. The patterns were random and broken, as if the sign was being tested for the first time.

Relieved that Hathaway's suspicions had been completely groundless, Franklin turned off onto the soft shoulder, then walked forward through the spectators as the lights blinked and stuttered in their faces. Below, behind the steel palisades around the island, was a large group of police and engineers, craning up at the men scaling the sign a hundred feet over their heads.

Suddenly Franklin stopped, the sense of relief fading instantly. With a jolt he saw that several of the police on the ground were armed with shotguns, and that the two policemen climbing the sign carried submachine guns slung over their shoulders. They were converging on a third figure, crouched by a switchbox on the penultimate tier, a ragged bearded man in a grimy shirt, a bare knee poking through his jeans.

Hathaway!

Franklin hurried towards the island, the sign hissing and spluttering, fuses blowing by the dozen.

Then the flicker of lights cleared and steadied, blazing out continuously, and together the crowd looked up at the decks of brilliant letters. The phrases, and every combination of them possible, were entirely familiar, and Franklin knew that he had been reading them unconsciously in his mind for weeks as he passed up and down the expressway.

BUY NOW BUY NOW BUY NOW BUY NOW BUY NOW NEW CAR
NOW NEW CAR NOW NEW CAR NOW YES YES YES YES YES
YES YES YES YES YES YES

Sirens blaring, two patrol cars swung up onto the verge through
the crowd and plunged across the damp grass. Police spilled from
its doors, batons in their hands, and quickly began to force back the
crowd. Franklin held his ground as they approached, started to say:
"Officer, I know the man—" but the policeman punched him in the
chest with the flat of his hand. Winded, he stumbled back among the
cars, leaned helplessly against a fender as the police began to break
the windshields, the hapless drivers protesting angrily, those further
back rushing for their vehicles.

The noise fell away abruptly when one of the submachine guns
fired a brief roaring burst, then rose in a massive gasp of horror as
Hathaway, arms outstretched, let out a cry of triumph and pain, and
jumped.

"But, Robert, what does it really matter?" Judith asked as
Franklin sat inertly in the lounge the next morning. "I know it's
tragic for his wife and daughter, but Hathaway was in the grip of an
obsession. If he hated advertising signs so much why didn't he
dynamite those we *can* see, instead of worrying so much about those
we can't?"

Franklin stared at the TV screen, hoping the program would
distract him.

"Hathaway was *right*," he said simply.

"Was he? Advertising is here to stay. We've no real freedom of
choice, anyway. We can't spend more than we can afford, the
finance companies soon clamp down."

"You accept that?" Franklin went over to the window. A quarter
of a mile away, in the center of the estate, another of the signs was
being erected. It was due east from them, and in the early morning
light the shadows of its rectangular superstructure fell across the
garden, reaching almost to the steps of the French windows at his
feet. As a concession to the neighborhood, and perhaps to allay any
suspicions while it was being erected by an appeal to petty snob-
bery, the lower sections had been encased in mock-Tudor paneling.

Franklin stared at it numbly, counting the half-dozen police
lounging by their patrol cars as the construction gang unloaded

239

prefabricated grilles from a couple of trucks. Then he looked at the sign by the supermarket, trying to repress his memories of Hathaway and the pathetic attempts the man had made to convince Franklin and gain his help.

He was still standing there an hour later when Judith came in, putting on her hat and coat, ready to visit the supermarket.

Franklin followed her to the door. "I'll drive you down there, Judith," he said in a flat dead voice. "I have to see about booking a new car. The next models are coming out at the end of the month. With luck we'll get one of the early deliveries."

They walked out into the trim drive, the shadows of the great signs swinging across the quiet neighborhood as the day progressed, sweeping over the heads of the people on their way to the supermarket like the dark blades of enormous scythes.

such stuff

John Brunner

"Such Stuff" is a study of dreams which begins in scientific fact and ends in poetic fantasy. For fact, the experiment described in the story draws heavily on material from William C. Dement, a psychologist whose research in dreams gained prominence around 1960. For fantasy, the ending of the story moves beyond possible worlds to a fascinating and chilling conclusion. The story takes its title from a line in William Shakespeare's last play, *The Tempest*. Prospero, the philosophical magician, notes: "We are such stuff as dreams are made on, and our little life is rounded with a sleep." The world of sleep and dreams is a mysterious realm which has always fascinated man, and Shakespeare explores the subject again and again in his plays.

Today, deep interest in the phenomenon of sleep continues. Psychologists Eugene Aserinsky and Nathaniel Kleitman discovered that when dreaming occurs, there are rapid movements of the eyes (REM), although the body remains relatively stationary. Brain wave patterns during this state of sleep, which occurs four or five times a night (indicating that we dream that many times during a normal night's sleep), resemble brain waves of an active, alert, waking person. But it appears that a mechanism in the brain which operates during REM sleep inhibits motor activity by blocking nerve impulses traveling to the muscles. The body "goes limp" during REM sleep. This device protects the sleeper from action during his dreams.

Dement's research demonstrates that dreaming serves a purpose: people cannot maintain psychological equilibrium without it. Dement's subjects did essentially the same experiment that is the crux of our story. Subjects, who were studied for only five nights, were awakened when they began to dream in their REM periods.

Thus they were deprived of dreaming, as opposed to control subjects who were also awakened, but only in non–REM periods. First, it was found that subjects awakened at the beginning of REM started more REM periods each successive night of deprivation. When they were then finally allowed to dream, their dreaming increased by 60 percent. Dement also found that the daytime behavior of his subjects deprived of dreams changed drastically, with increases in tension, anxiety, irritability, inability to concentrate, memory lapses, and food intake. REM–deprived cats who were allowed to go longer periods without dreaming became hyperaggressive, hypersexual, and ate their food in half the usual time.

In "Such Stuff" John Brunner creates a grotesque conflict between the sleeping and the waking. Dr. Wills watches with fascinated horror while subject, Starling, dreamlessly sleeps—for six months. And without apparent adverse effects. Can he be the one exception, the one person who does not react like everyone else? Is he the one negative case who can disprove the theory that dreaming is necessary?

Dr. Wills is filled with moral anguish, complaining to his superior, Dr. Daventry, who has designed the experiment: "All our other cases suggest that serious mental disturbances result from interference with the dreaming process. Even the most resistant of our other volunteers broke down after less than two weeks. We've prevented Starling from dreaming every night for five months now, and even if there are no signs of harm yet it's probable that we *are* harming him."

While the experiment has no apparent negative effect on Starling, it does on Dr. Wills. In creating the ending of the story, perhaps author Brunner borrowed again from Shakespeare's *Tempest*. Ferdinand, the romantic hero of that play, has been washed ashore on an island as the result of a tempest at sea, where his father and shipmates were apparently drowned. Ferdinand, not himself because of the anguish of his loss, explains, "My spirits, as in a dream, are all bound up." In a like way, in our short story, the anguished spirits of Dr. Wills become all bound up—in a strange fashion—with the dreams of Starling.

SUCH STUFF   *John Brunner*

With the leads of the electroencephalograph stringing out from his skull like webs spun by a drunken spider, the soft adhesive pads laid on his eyes like pennies, Starling resembled a corpse which time had festooned with its musty garlands. But a vampire-corpse, plump and rosy in its state of not-quite-death. The room was as still as any mausoleum, but it smelt of floor polish, not dust; his coffin was a hospital bed and his shroud a fluffless cotton blanket.

Except for the little yellow pilot lights in the electronic equipment beside the bed, which could just be seen through the ventilation holes in the casing, the room was in darkness. But when Wills opened the door from the corridor the shaft of light which came over his shoulder enabled him to see Starling clearly.

He would rather not have seen him at all—laid out thus, lacking candles only because he was not dead. That could be remedied, given the proper tools: a sharpened stake, a silver bullet, crossroads at which to conduct the burial—

Wills checked himself, his face prickly with new sweat. It had hit him again! The insane idea kept recurring, like reflex, like pupils expanding under belladonna, for all he could do to drive it down. Starling lay like a corpse because he had grown used to not pulling loose the leads taped to his head—*that's all! That's all! That's all!*

He used the words like a club to beat his mind into submission. Starling had slept like this for months. He lay on one side, in a typical sleeper's attitude, but because of the leads he barely moved enough in the course of a night to disturb the bedclothes. He breathed naturally. Everything was normal.

Except that he had done it for months, which was incredible and impossible and not in the least natural.

Shaking from head to foot, Wills began to step back through the door. As he did so, it happened again—now it was happening dozens of times a night. A dream began.

The electroencephalograph recorded a change in brain activity. The pads on Starling's eyes sensed eye movements and signaled them. A relay closed. A faint but shrill buzzer sounded.

Starling grunted, stirred, moved economically as though to dislodge a fly that had settled on him. The buzzer stopped. Starling had been woken; the thread of his dream was snapped.

And he was asleep again.

Wills visualized him waking fully and realizing he was not alone in the room. Cat-silent, he crept back into the corridor and closed the door, his heart thundering as though he had had a narrow escape from disaster.

Why? In daytime he could talk normally with Starling, run tests on him as impersonally as on anyone else. Yet at night—

He slapped down visions of Starling by day, Starling corpselike in his bed at night, and moved down the long corridor with his teeth set to save them from chattering. He paused at other doors, pressing his ear to them or glancing inside for a moment. Some of those doors led to private infernos which ought to have jarred on his own normality with shocking violence, as they always used to. But none affected him like Starling's passiveness—not even the moaning prayers of the woman in Room 11, who was being hounded to death by imaginary demons.

Conclusion: his normality had gone.

That thought also recurred in spite of attempts to blank it out. In the long corridor which framed his aching mind like a microwave guide tube, Wills faced it. And found no grounds for rejecting it. They were in the wards; he in the corridor. So what? Starling was in a ward, and he was not a patient. He was sane, free to leave whenever he wished. In remaining here he was simply being co-operative.

And telling him to go away would solve nothing at all.

His rounds were over. He went back toward the office like a man resolutely marching toward inevitable doom. Lambert—the duty nurse—was snoring on the couch in the corner; it was against regulations for the duty nurse to sleep, but Wills had had more than he could bear of the man's conversation about drink and women and what he was missing tonight on television and had told him to lie down.

He prodded Lambert to make him close his mouth and sat down at the desk, drawing the night report toward him. On the printed lines of the form his hand crawled with its shadow limping behind, leaving a trail of words contorted like the path of a crazy snail.

5 a.m. All quiet except Room 11. Patient there normal.

Then he saw what he had written. Angrily, he slashed a line through the last word, another and another till it was illegible, and substituted "much as usual." Normal!

I am in the asylum of myself.

He tilted the lamp on the desk so it shone on his face and turned to look at himself in the wall mirror provided for the use of female duty nurses. He was a little haggard after the night without sleep, but nothing else was visibly wrong with him. Much as usual, like the patient in Room 11.

And yet Starling was sleeping the night away without dreams, undead.

Wills started, fancying that something black and threadlike had brushed his shoulder. A picture came to him of Starling reaching out from his bed with the tentacle leads of the e.e.g., as if he were emitting them from spinnerets, and weaving the hospital together into a net of his own, trapping Wills in the middle like a fly.

He pictured himself being drained of his juices, like a fly.

Suddenly Lambert was sitting up on the couch, his eyes flicking open like the shutters of a house being aired for a new day. He said, "What's the matter, doc? You're as white as a flaming sheet!"

There was no black threadlike thing on his shoulder. Wills said with an effort, "Nothing. Just tired, I think."

He thought of sleeping, and wondered what he would dream.

The day was bright and warm. He was never good at sleeping in the daytime; when he woke for the fourth or fifth time, unrested, he gave up. It was Daventry's day for coming here, he remembered. Maybe he should go and talk to him.

He dressed and went out of doors, his eyes dark-ringed. In the garden a number of the less ill patients were working listlessly. Daventry and the matron moved among them, complimenting them on their flowers, their thorough weeding, the lack of aphis and blackfly. Daventry had no interest in gardening except insofar as it was useful for therapy. The patients, no matter how twisted their minds were, recognized this, but Daventry apparently didn't know they knew. Wills might have laughed, but he felt laughter was receding from him. Unused faculties, like unused limbs, atrophy.

Daventry saw him approach. The bird eyes behind his glasses flicked poultry-wise over him, and a word passed from the thin-lipped mouth to the matron, who nodded and moved away. The sharp face was lit by a smile; brisk legs began to carry him over the tiny lawn, which was not mown by the patients because mowers were too dangerous.

"Ah, Harry!" in Daventry's optimistic voice. "I want a word with you. Shall we go to the office?" He took Wills's arm as he turned, companionably; Wills, who found the habit intolerable, broke the grip before it closed.

He said, "As it happens, I want a word with you, too."

The edginess of his tone sawed into Daventry's composure. The bird eyes scanned his face, the head tipped a little on one side. The list of Daventry's mannerisms was a long one, but he knew the reasons for all of them and often explained them.

"Hah!" he said, "I can guess what this will be about!"

They passed into the building and walked side by side with their footsteps beating irregularly like two palpitating hearts. In the passageway Daventry spoke again.

"I presume there's been no change in Starling, or you'd have left a note for me—you were on night duty last night, weren't you? I didn't see him today, unfortunately; I was at a conference and didn't get here till lunchtime."

Wills looked straight ahead, to the looming door of Daventry's office. He said, "No—no change. But that's what I wanted to talk about. I don't think we should go on."

"Ah!" said Daventry. It was automatic. It meant something altogether different, like "I'm astonished"—but professionally Daventry disavowed astonishment. The office accepted them, and they sat down to the idiot noise of a bluebottle hammering its head on the window.

"Why not?" Daventry said abruptly.

Wills had not yet composed his answer. He could hardly speak of the undead Starling with pads on his eyes like pennies, of the black tentacles reaching out through the hospital night, of the formulated but suppressed notion that he must be treated with sharp stakes and silver bullets, and soon. He was forced to throw up improvization like an emergency earthwork, knowing it could be breached at a dozen points.

"Well—all our other cases suggest that serious mental disturbance results from interference with the dreaming process. Even the most resistant of our other volunteers broke down after less than two weeks. We've prevented Starling from dreaming every night for five months now, and even if there are no signs of harm yet it's probable that we *are* harming him."

Daventry had lit a cigarette while Wills talked. Now he waved it in front of him, as though to ward off Wills's arguments with an adequate barrier—a wisp of smoke.

"Good gracious, Harry!" he said affably. "What damage are we doing? Did you detect any signs of it last time you ran Starling through the tests?"

"No—that was last week and he's due for another run

tomorrow—no, what I'm saying is that everything points to dreaming being essential. We may not have a test in the battery which shows the effect of depriving Starling of his dreams, but the effect must be there."

Daventry gave a neutral nod. He said. "Have you asked Starling's own opinion on this?"

Again, concede defeat from honesty: "Yes. He said he's perfectly happy to go on. He said he feels fine."

"Where is he at the moment?"

"Today's Tuesday. He goes to see his sister in the town on Tuesday afternoons. I could check if you like, but—"

Daventry shrugged. "Don't bother, I have good news for you, you see. In my view, six months is quite long enough to establish Starling's tolerance of dream deprivation. What's next of interest is the nature of his dreams when he's allowed to resume. So three weeks from now I propose to end the experiment and find out."

"He'll probably wake himself up reflexively," Wills said.

Daventry was prepared to take the words with utmost seriousness. He said. "What makes you think that?"

Wills had meant it as a bitter joke; when he reconsidered, he found reason after all. He said, "The way he's stood the treatment when no one else could. Like everyone else we tested, his dreaming frequency went up in the first few days; then it peaked at about thirty-four times a night, and dropped back to its current level of about twenty-six, which has remained constant for about four months now. Why? His mind seems to be malleable, and I can't believe that. People need dreams; a man who can manage without them is as unlikely as one who can do without food or water."

"So we thought," Daventry said briskly. Wills could see the conference papers being compiled in his mind, the reports for the *Journal of Psychology* and the four pages in *Scientific American,* with photographs. And so on. "So we thought. Until we happened across Starling, and he just proved we were wrong."

"I—" began Wills. Daventry took no notice and went on.

"Dement's work at Mount Sinai wasn't utterly definitive, you know. Clinging to first findings is a false attitude. We're now compelled to drop the idea that dreaming is indispensable, because Starling has gone without dreams for months and so far as we can tell—or, I grant that: so far and no further—he hasn't suffered under the experience."

He knocked ash into a bowl on his desk. "Well, that was my news for you, Harry: that we finish the Starling series at the six-month mark. Then we'll see if he goes back to normal dreaming. There was nothing unusual about his dreaming before he volunteered; it will be most interesting. . . ."

It was cold comfort, but it did give him a sort of deadline to work to. It also rid him of part of the horror he had suffered from having to face the presence in his mind of the vampire-corpse like a threat looming down the whole length of his future life-path. It actually heartened him till the time came to retest Starling.

He sat waiting in his office for half an hour beforehand, because everything was otherwise quiet and because before he came up for psychological examination Starling always underwent a physical examination by another member of the staff. Not that the physicals ever turned anything up. But the psychologicals hadn't either. It was all in Wills's mind. Or in Starling's. But if it was in Starling's, he himself didn't know.

He knew the Starling file almost by heart now—thick, much thumbed, annotated by himself and by Daventry. Nonetheless, he turned back to the beginning of it, to the time five months and a week ago when Starling was just one volunteer among six men and six women engaged in a follow-up to check on Dement's findings of 1960 with superior equipment.

There were transcripts of dreams with Freudian commentary, in their limited way extraordinarily revealing, but not giving a hint of the most astonishing secret—that Starling could get by without them.

> I am in a railway station. People are going to work and coming home at the same time. A tall man approaches and asks for my ticket. I try to explain that I haven't bought one yet. He grows angry and calls a policeman, but the policeman is my grandfather. I cannot understand what he says.

> I am talking to one of my schoolteachers, Mr. Bullen. I am very rich and I have come to visit my old school. I am very happy. I invite Mr. Bullen to ride in my car, which is big and new. When he gets in the door handle comes off in his hand. The door won't lock. I cannot start the engine. The car is old and covered with rust. Mr. Bullen is very angry but I do not care very much.

> I am in a restaurant. The menu is in French and I order something I don't know. When it comes I can't eat it. I call the manager to make a complaint and he arrives in a sailor's uniform. The restaurant is on a boat and rocks so that I feel ill. The manager says he will put me in irons. People in the restaurant laugh at me. I break the plates on which

the food is served, but they make no noise and no one notices. So I eat the food after all.

That last one was exactly what you would expect from Starling, Wills thought. He ate the food after all, and liked it.

These were records extracted from the control period—the week during which his dreams and those of the other volunteers were being noted for comparison with later ones, after the experiment had terminated. In all the other eleven cases that was from three days to thirteen days later. But in Starling's—!

The dreams fitted Starling admirably. Miserable, small-minded, he had gone through life being frustrated, and hence the dreams went wrong for him, sometimes through the intervention of figures of authority from childhood, such as his hated grandfather and the schoolteacher. It seemed that he never fought back; he ate the food after all.

No wonder he was content to go on cooperating in Daventry's experiment, Wills thought bleakly. With free board and lodging, no outside problems involved, he was probably in paradise.

Or a kind of gratifying hell.

He turned up the dreams of the other volunteers—the ones who had been driven to quit after a few nights. The records of their control week showed without exception indications of sexual tension, dramatized resolutions of problems, positive attacks on personal difficulties. Only Starling provided continual evidence of total surrender.

Not that he was outwardly inadequate. Considering the frustration he had endured first from his parents, then from his tyrannical grandfather and his teachers, he had adjusted well. He was mild-mannered and rather shy, and he lived with his sister and her husband, but he held down a fairly good job, and he had a small, constant circle of acquaintances mainly met through his sister's husband, on whom he made no great impression but who all "quite liked" him.

Quite was a word central to Starling's life. Hardly any absolutes. Yet—his dreams to the contrary—he could never have surrendered altogether. He's made the best of things.

The volunteers were a mixed bag: seven students, a teacher on sabbatical leave, an out-of-work actor, a struggling writer, a beatnik who didn't care, and Starling. They were subjected to the process developed by Dement at New York's Mount Sinai Hospital, as improved and automatized by Daventry—the process still being applied to Starling even now, which woke him with a buzzer whenever the signs indicating dreaming occurred. In the eleven other cases, the effect found was the same as what Dement established: interrupting the subjects' dreaming made them nervous, irritable, victims of uncontrolled nervous tension. The toughest quit after thirteen days.

Except for Starling, that was to say.

It wasn't having their sleep disturbed that upset them; that could be proved by waking them between, instead of during, dreams. It was not being *allowed* to dream that caused trouble.

In general, people seemed to spend about an hour a night dreaming, in four or five "installments." That indicated that dreaming served a purpose: what? Dissipation of antisocial tensions? A grooming of the ego as repressed desires were satisfied? That was too glib an answer. But without Starling to cock a snook in their faces, the experimenters would have accepted a similar generalization and left the matter there till the distant day when the science of mind was better equipped to weigh and measure the impalpable stuff of dreams.

Only Starling *had* cropped up. At first he reacted predictably. The frequency of his dreaming shot up from five times a night to twenty, thirty and beyond, as the buzzer aborted each embryo dream, whirling into nothing his abominable grandfather, his tyrannical teachers—

Was there a clue there? Wills had wondered that before. Was it possible that, whereas other people *needed* to dream, Starling hated it? Were his dreams so miserable that to go without them was a liberation to him?

The idea was attractive because it was straightforward, but it didn't hold water. In the light of previous experiments, it was about equivalent to saying that a man could be liberated from the need to excrete by denying him food and water.

But there was no detectable effect on Starling! He had not lost weight, nor grown more irritable; he talked lucidly, he responded within predictable limits to IQ tests and Rorschach tests and every other test Wills could find.

It was purely unnatural.

Wills checked himself. Facing his own reaction squarely, he saw it for what it must be—an instinctive but irrational fear, like the fear of the stranger who comes over the hill with a different accent and different table manners. Starling was human; *ergo*, his reactions were natural; *ergo*, either the other experiments had agreed by coincidence and dreaming wasn't indispensable, or Starling's reactions were the same as everyone's and were just being held down until they blew like a boiler straining past its tested pressure.

There were only three more weeks to go, of course.

The habitual shy knock came to the door. Wills grunted for Starling to come in, and wondered as he looked at him how the sight of him passive in bed could inspire him to thoughts of garlic, sharpened stakes and burial at crossroads.

The fault must be in his own mind, not in Starling's.

The tests were exactly as usual. That wrecked Wills's tentative idea about Starling welcoming the absence of his dreams. If indeed he was liberated from a burden, that should show up in a trend toward a stronger, more assured personality. The microscopic trend he actually detected could be assigned to the fact that for several months Starling had been in this totally undemanding and restful environment.

No help there.

He shoved aside the pile of test papers. "Mr. Starling," he said, "what made you volunteer for these experiments in the first place? I must have asked you before, but I've forgotten."

It was all on the file, but he wanted to check.

"Why, I don't really know, doctor," Starling's mild voice said. Starling's cowlike eyes rested on his face. "I think my sister knew someone who had volunteered, and my brother-in-law is a blood donor and kept saying that everyone should do something to benefit society, and while I didn't like the idea of being bled, because I've never liked injections and things like that, this idea seemed all right, so I said I'd do it. Then, of course, when Dr. Daventry said I was unusual and would I go on with it, I said I hadn't suffered by it and I didn't see why I shouldn't, if it was in the cause of science—"

The voice droned on, adding nothing new. Starling was very little interested in new things. He had never asked Wills the purpose of any test he submitted to; probably he had never asked his own doctor what was on a prescription form filled out for him, being content to regard the medical abbreviations as a kind of talisman. Perhaps he was so used to being snubbed or choked off if he showed too much interest that he felt he was incapable of understanding the pattern of which Wills and the hospital formed part.

He *was* malleable. It was the galling voice of his brother-in-law, sounding off about his uselessness, which pushed him into this. Watching him, Wills realized that the decision to offer himself for the experiment was probably the biggest he had ever taken, compa-

251

rable in the life of anyone else with a decision to marry, or to go into a monastery. And yet that was wrong, too. Starling didn't make decisions on such a level. Things like that would merely happen to him.

Impulsively, Wills said, "And how about when the experiment is over, Mr. Starling? I suppose it can't go on forever."

Placid, the voice shaped inevitable words. "Well, you know, doctor, I hadn't given that very much thought."

No, it wasn't a liberation to him to be freed of his dreaming. It was nothing to him. Nothing was anything to him. Starling was undead. Starling was neuter in a human scale of values. Starling was the malleable thing that filled the hole available for it, the thing without will of its own which made the best of what there was and did nothing more.

Wills wished he could punish the mind that gave him such thoughts, and asked their source to go from him. But though his physical presence went, his nonexistent existence stayed, and burned and loomed and was impassive and cocked snooks in every hole and corner of Wills's chaotic brain.

Those last three weeks were the worst of all. The silver bullet and the sharpened stake, the crossroads for the burial—Wills chained the images down in his mind, but he ached from the strain of hanging on to the chains. *Horror, horror, horror,* sang an eldritch voice somewhere deep and dark within him. *Not natural,* said another in a professionally judicious tone. He fought the voices and thought of other things.

Daventry said—and was correct according to the principles of the experiment, of course—that so as to have a true control for comparison they must simply disconnect the buzzer attached to the e.e.g. when the time came, and not tell Starling what they had done, and see what happened. He would be free to finish his dreams again. Perhaps they would be more vivid, and he would remember more clearly after such a long interruption. He would—

But Wills listened with only half an ear. They hadn't predicted Starling's reaction when they deprived him of dreams; why should they be able to predict what would happen when he received them back? A chill premonition iced solid in his mind, but he did not mention it to Daventry. What it amounted to was this: whatever Starling's response was, it would be the wrong one.

He told Daventry of his partial breaking of the news that the experiment was to end, and his chief frowned.

"That's a pity, Harry," he said. "Even Starling might put two and two together when he realizes six months have gone by. Never mind. We'll let it run for another few days, shall we? Let him think that he was wrong about the deadline."

He looked at the calendar. "Give him three extra days," he said. "Cut it on the fourth. How's that?"

By coincidence—or not?—Wills's turn for night duty came up again on that day; it came up once in eight days, and the last few times had been absolutely unbearable. He wondered if Daventry had selected the date deliberately. Maybe. What difference did it make?

He said, "Will you be there to see what happens?"

Daventry's face set in a reflex mask of regret. "Unfortunately, no—I'm attending a congress in Italy that week. But I have absolute confidence in you, Harry, you know that. By the way, I'm doing up a paper on Starling for *Journ. Psych.*"—mannerisms, as always: he made it into the single word "jurnsike"—"and I think you should appear as co-author."

Cerberus duly sopped, Daventry went on his way.

That night the duty nurse was Green, a small clever man who knew judo. In a way that was a relief; Wills usually didn't mind Green's company, and had even learned some judo holds from him, useful for restraining but not harming violent patients. Tonight, though. . . .

They spoke desultorily together for the first half-hour of the shift, but Wills sometimes lost track of the conversation because his mind's eye was distracted by a picture of what was going on in that room along the corridor where Starling held embalmed court among shadows and pilot lights. No one breached his privacy now as he went to bed; he did everything for himself, attached the leads, planted the penny-pads on his eyes, switched on the equipment. There was some risk of his discovering that the buzzer was disconnected, but it had always been set to sound only after thirty minutes or more of typical simple sleep-readings.

Starling, though he never did anything to tire himself out, always went to sleep quickly. Another proof of his malleable mind, Wills thought sourly. To get into bed suggested going to sleep, and he slept.

Usually, it was three-quarters of an hour before the first attempted dream would burgeon in his round skull. For six months and a couple of days the buzzer had smashed the first and all that followed; the sleeper had adjusted his position without much disturbing the bedding, and—

But not tonight.

After forty minutes Wills got up, dry-lipped. "I'll be in Starling's room if you want me," he said. "We've turned off his buzzer, and he's due to start dreaming again—normally." The word sounded unconvincing.

Green nodded, picking up a magazine from the table. "On to something pretty unusual there, aren't we, doc?" he said.

"God only knows," Wills said, and went out.

His heart was pumping so loudly he felt it might waken the sleepers around him; his footsteps sounded like colossal hammer blows and his blood roared in his ears. He had to fight a dizzy, tumbling sensation which made the still lines of the corridor—floor-with-wall a pair of lines, wall-with-ceiling another pair—twist like a four-strand plait, like the bit of a hand drill or a stick of candy turned mysteriously and topologically outside-in. Swaying as though drunk, he came to Starling's door and watched his hand go to the handle.

I refuse the responsibility. I'll refuse to co-author the paper on him. It's Daventry's fault.

Nevertheless he acquiesced in opening the door, as he had acquiesced all along in the experiment.

He was intellectually aware that he entered soundlessly, but he imagined himself going like an elephant on broken glass. Everything was as usual, except, of course, the buzzer.

He drew a rubber-shod chair to a position from which he could watch the paper tapes being paid out by the e.e.g., and sat down. As yet there were only typical early sleep rhythms—Starling had not yet started his first dream of the night. If he waited till that dream arrived, and saw that all was going well, perhaps it would lay the phantoms in his mind.

He put his hand in the pocket of his jacket and closed it around a clove of garlic.

Startled, he drew the garlic out and stared at it. He had no memory of putting it there. But the last time he was on night duty and haunted by the undead appearance of Starling as he slept, he had spent most of the silent hours drawing batwing figures, stabbing their hearts with the point of his pencil, sketching crossroads around them, throwing the paper away with the hole pierced in the center of the sheet.

Oh, God! It was going to be such a relief to be free of this obsession!

But at least providing himself with a clove of garlic was a harmless symptom. He dropped it back in his pocket. He noticed two things at the same time directly afterward. The first was the alteration in the line on the e.e.g. tapes which indicated the beginning of a dream. The second was that he had a very sharp pencil in his pocket, as well as the clove of garlic—

No, not a pencil. He took it out and saw that it was a piece of rough wood, about eight inches long, pointed at one end. That was all he needed. That, and something to drive it home with. He fumbled in all his pockets. He was carrying a rubber hammer for testing reflexes. Of course, that wouldn't do, but anyway. . . .

Chance had opened a gap in Starling's pajama jacket. He poised the stake carefully over his heart and swung the hammer.

As though the flesh were soft as cheese, the stake sank home. Blood welled up around it like a spring in mud, trickled over Starling's chest, began to stain the bed. Starling himself did not awaken, but simply went more limp—naturally, for he was undead and not asleep. Sweating, Wills let the rubber hammer fall and wondered at what he had done. Relief filled him as the unceasing stream of blood filled the bed.

The door behind him was ajar. Through it he heard the cat-light footfalls of Green, and his voice saying urgently, "It's Room 11, doc! I think she's—"

And then Green saw what had been done to Starling.

His eyes wide with amazement, he turned to stare at Wills. His mouth worked, but for a while his expression conveyed more than the unshaped words he uttered.

"*Doc!*" Green said finally, and that was all.

Wills ignored him. He looked down at the undead, seeing the blood as though it were luminous paint in the dim-lit room—on his hands, his coat, the floor, the bed, flooding out now in a river, pouring from the pens that waggled the traces of a dream on the paper tapes, making his feet squelch stickily in his wet shoes.

"You've wrecked the experiment," Daventry said coldly as he came in. "After I'd been generous enough to offer you co-authorship of my paper in *Journ. Psych.*, too! How could you?"

Hot shame flooded into Wills's mind. He would never be able to face Daventry again.

"We must call a policeman," Daventry said with authority.

255

"Fortunately, he always said he thought he ought to be a blood donor."

He took up from the floor a gigantic syringe, like a hypodermic for a titan, and after dipping the needle into the river of blood hauled on the plunger. The red level rose inside the glass.

And *click*.

Through a crack in Wills's benighted skull a fact dropped. Daventry was in Italy. Therefore he couldn't be here. Therefore he wasn't. Therefore—

Wills felt his eyes creak open like old heavy doors on hinges stiff with rust, and found that he was looking down at Starling in the bed. The pens tracing the activity of his brain had reverted to a typical sleep-rhythm. There was no stake. There was no blood.

Weak with relief, Wills shuddered at remembered horror. He leaned back in his chair, struggling to understand.

He had told himself that whatever Starling's reaction to being given back his dreams might be, it would be the wrong one. Well, here it was. He couldn't have predicted it. But he could explain it now—more or less. Though the mechanics of it would have to wait a while.

If he was right about Starling, a lifetime of frustration and making the best of things had sapped his power of action to the point at which he never even considered tackling an obstacle. He would just meekly try and find a way around it. If there wasn't one—well, there wasn't, and he left it at that.

Having his dreams stopped was an obstacle. The eleven other volunteers, more aggressive, had developed symptoms which expressed their resentment in manifold ways: irritability, rage, insulting behavior. But not Starling. To Starling it was unthinkable to express resentment.

Patiently, accustomed to disappointment because that was the constant feature of his life, he had sought a way around the obstacle. And he had found it. He had learned how to dream with someone else's mind instead of his own.

Of course, until tonight the buzzer had broken off every dream he attempted, and he had endured that like everything else. But tonight there was no buzzer, and he had dreamed *in* and *with* Wills. The driving of the stake, the blood, the intrusion of Green, the appearance of Daventry, were part of a dream to which Wills contributed some images and Starling contributed the rest, such as the policeman who didn't have time to arrive, and the giant hypodermic. He feared injections.

Wills made up his mind. Daventry wouldn't believe him—not unless he experienced the phenomenon himself—but that was a problem for tomorrow. Right now he had had enough, and more than enough. He was going to reconnect the buzzer and get the hell out of here.

He tried to lift his arm toward the boxes of equipment on the bedside table, and was puzzled to find it heavy and sluggish. Invisible weights seemed to hang on his wrist. Even when, sweating, he managed to force his hand toward the buzzer, his fingers felt like sausages and would not grip the delicate wire he had to attach to the terminal.

He had fought for what seemed like an eternity, and was crying with frustration, when he finally understood.

The typical pattern of all Starling's dreams centered on failure to achieve what he attempted; he expected his greatest efforts to be disappointed. Hence Wills, his mind somehow linked to Starling's and his consciousness seeming to Starling to be a dream, would never be able to reconnect that buzzer.

Wills let his hands fall limp on his dangling arms. He looked at Starling, naked fear rising in his throat. How much dreaming could a man do in a single night when he had been deprived for six mortal months?

In his pocket was a sharp wooden stake and a hammer. He was going to put an end to Starling's dreaming once and for all.

He was still in the chair, weeping without tears, tied by invisible chains, when Starling awoke puzzled in the morning and found him.

4

LEARNING AND COGNITION

Learning is defined as any relatively permanent change in behavior which occurs as a result of experience or practice. It is a key process in human behavior; in order to survive and function effectively, the individual must be able to learn how environmental events are related to each other and how his actions are related to the environment.

In the introduction to Chapter 2 on psychobiology, the controversy over the relative importance of heredity and environment was cited. As genetics and consequent biological development are the hereditary determinants, so the major determinants for the environmental influence are the learning processes of the individual. Historically, American psychology has always put heavy emphasis on learning, staying in tune with the strong American belief that one's family background is less important for success than one's will to work hard and learn. Ever since John B. Watson, mentor of American psychology, brashly stated that he could train anyone—regardless of background—to be a "doctor, lawyer, beggar, or thief," psychologists in this country have endeavored to understand the learning process.

It is a complex process which can be studied on many levels, from the simple and automatic principles of conditioning to the complex and creative methods of thinking and problem solving. Research into conditioning processes has emphasized observation and training of relatively simple organisms like rats and pigeons, assuming that principles discovered in this way will also apply to humans. Emphasis shifts to study of humans as researchers try to establish principles of the verbal areas of learning, remembering, and forgetting. The cognitive functioning of the human brain, with its abilities of language, thought, and organization, dominates the study of concept formation and problem solving.

Classical conditioning is one type of learning process, and its importance and principles were first demonstrated by the Russian, Ivan Pavlov. He showed in his famous experiments how dogs could be conditioned to automatically salivate when subjected to stimuli like a bell or a light, after these stimuli had continuously been associated with a stimulus like meat powder, to which a dog naturally salivates. Pavlov also demonstrated that in order to sustain the conditioned response of the dog (salivation to the light or bell), it was necessary to reinforce the process by periodically providing an additional taste of meat. The Russian's major contribution, however, was to demonstrate that with substitution of one stimulus for another, dogs could automatically learn (be conditioned) to associate new stimuli with old responses.

Operant conditioning, described by B. F. Skinner, is another approach to the learning process which has received a great amount of attention. Skinner has demonstrated how behavior can be shaped to specifications by immediately rewarding correct responses. Skinner's methods deemphasize stimulus conditions and virtually ignore the role of punishment. Nevertheless, they have successfully been used to train animals like pigeons to learn complex behavior like playing Ping-Pong. More recently, his methods have been extensively applied for behavior modification in humans. In general, they have been most successful in controlled environments, like schizophrenia wards, where patients are given tokens for correct behaviors. Skinner would ultimately want society at large to be remodeled so that there would be clearer and more direct ways of rewarding constructive behavior instead of the present situation, which he feels emphasizes the punishment of disapproved behavior.

Verbal learning research has centered around the study of memory and the principles by which learning efficiency can be maximized. Ever since Ebbinghaus invented the "nonsense syllable," researchers have been arranging them in long serial lists or in pairs, attempting to clarify various effects which promote or interfere with retention. Recent research has also suggested that there may be two basic memory processes, long term and short term. In addition, researchers have been seeking answers to practical problems of learning. Research into transfer of learning would suggest that learning Latin does not particularly improve learning of other subjects. Studies of massed versus spaced learning have suggested that for the same amount of study, time-spaced studying with rest periods is generally more productive than cramming. Furthermore, research into learning sets has suggested that there are principles of learning how to learn, like picking up important cues in learning situations, which good technicians of learning learn to use.

As the demands on man become more complex, he must use his cognitive capacities, powers which virtually separate him from other animals. Man's brain gives him unique powers of language and symbolization which enable him to form abstract concepts, solve complex problems, and think creatively. Man also has unique powers to use his experience in order to anticipate and to visualize complex situations, forming "cognitive maps" of these situations. When solving problems, he has the ability to reorganize his perceptions and cognitions, allowing him to gain new insights and solutions to his problems. Finally, only man has the freedom, self-consciousness, and independence to be truly creative. Although man shares many conditioning principles with Pavlov's dogs and Skinner's pigeons, his creativity truly puts him in a class by himself.

learning theory

James McConnell

"Learning Theory," written by psychologist James McConnell, is a story about conditioning and the Skinner box. He is well known in the field of learning for his experiments on earthworms. (Later, in the story notes for "The Man Who Devoured Books," these experiments are briefly summarized.) As we read McConnell's delightful story, we can readily understand how he has earned a reputation for his sense of humor. The story is built on comic reversal. The narrator is a professor of psychology who mysteriously finds himself in an odd situation; rather than observing a Skinner box, he is *in* one! He wryly comments that perhaps he is dead and the box may be hell; if so, it is proper punishment for his previous crimes of confining animals in the box. Throughout the story there are references to guilt or ethical considerations about the way animals in Skinner boxes are treated.

As the story progresses, it is interesting to watch the methodology of the narrator at work. He discovers himself in an incomprehensible situation and immediately formalizes the problems to be solved. Where am I? Why am I here? Who is He (the captor)? Next, with close observation he begins to collect data. We recognize the principles of conditioning underlying the routine he describes in his box. First, he talks about his feeding schedule, or more technicially, the "schedule of reinforcement" with which he is being conditioned. He says he is fed every twelve hours, indicating a "fixed interval schedule" (every twelve hours without any variation). However, he also reports that he must vary the number of responses (bar presses) each time to get his food, indicating that he is also on a "variable ratio schedule." His habit of pressing feverishly when he thinks that the twelve hours are coming due—with little or no pressing in between—suggests the "scalloped" learning curve typical of the "fixed interval schedule." Actually, he is on a complex schedule involving both interval and ratio.

Later, he must learn to traverse a maze, suggesting a higher order learning task he must master. Still later, when put into the jumping stand, he is put into a combined "avoidance learning" and "escape learning" apparatus and procedure. He must avoid the water and escape the shock on the floor. Also involved is apparently a discrimination pattern, where he must learn which door is correct according to a preplanned pattern. Then he gets involved in the issue of secondary reinforcement.

By this time he has formulated a solid hypothesis about where he is and who is holding him captive. The next question: How do I escape? His solution to that problem is ingenious.

References in the story to issues or names of significance in the learning field are accurate. Hull, Spence, and Tolman are famous learning theorists. When the narrator says of his captor, "Good God! . . . He is a *psychologist!* . . . [they] worry about behavior first, physiology second," he refers to the experimental psychologist's feverish concentration on behavior.

At the end of the story, McConnell raises some very important issues which are so touchy that they tend to be avoided by most learning theorists. He suggests that theories are born of the equipment one uses; that this equipment limits the kind of behavior the theories have to account for. This is certainly a provocative issue, perhaps challenging Skinner and others as to the generality of their findings and approaches. Moreover, McConnell further suggests that if animals do not behave according to the theory (the way they are *supposed* to), they are labeled as "abnormal" and usually destroyed. Again, this seems to be a challenge—or at least a needle—to the learning establishment.

LEARNING THEORY　　*James McConnell*

I am writing this because I presume He wants me to. Otherwise He would not have left paper and pencil handy for me to use. And I put the word "He" in capitals because it seems the only thing to do. If I am dead and in hell, then this is only proper. However, if I am merely a captive somewhere, then surely a little flattery won't hurt matters.

As I sit here in this small room and think about it, I am impressed most of all by the suddenness of the whole thing. At one moment I was out walking in the woods near my suburban home. The next thing I knew, here I was in a small, featureless room, naked as a jaybird, with only my powers of rationalization to stand between me and insanity. When the "change" was made (whatever the change was), I was not conscious of so much as a momentary flicker between walking in the woods and being here in this room. Whoever is responsible for all of this is to be complimented—either He has developed an instantaneous anesthetic or He has solved the problem of instantaneous transportation of matter. I would prefer to think it the former, for the latter leads to too much anxiety.

As I recall, I was immersed in the problem of how to teach my class in beginning psychology some of the more abstruse points of Learning Theory when the transition came. How far away life at the University seems at the moment: I must be forgiven if now I am much more concerned about where I am and how to get out of here than about how freshmen can be cajoled into understanding Hull or Tolman.

Problem #1: Where am I? For an answer, I can only describe this room. It is about twenty feet square, some twelve feet high, with no windows, but with what might be a door in the middle of one of the walls. Everything is of a uniform gray color, and the walls and ceiling emit a fairly pleasant achromatic light. The walls themselves are of some hard material which might be metal since it feels slightly cool to the touch. The floor is of a softer, rubbery material, that yields a little when I walk on it. Also, it has a rather "tingly" feel to it, suggesting that it may be in constant vibration. It is somewhat warmer than the walls, which is all to the good since it appears I must sleep on the floor.

The only furniture in the room consists of what might be a table

---

and what passes for a chair. They are not quite that, but they can be made to serve this purpose. On the table I found the paper and the pencil. No, let me correct myself. What I call paper is good deal rougher and thicker than I am used to, and what I call a pencil is nothing more than a thin round stick of graphite which I have sharpened by rubbing one end of it on the table.

And that is the sum of my surroundings. I wish I knew what He has done with my clothes. The suit was an old one, but I am worried about the walking boots. I was very fond of those boots—they were quite expensive and I would hate to lose them.

The problem still remains to be answered, however, as to just where in the hell I am—if not in hell itself!

Problem #2 is a knottier one—Why am I here? Were I subject to paranoid tendencies, I would doubtless come to the conclusion that my enemies had kidnapped me. Or perhaps that the Russians had taken such an interest in my research that they had spirited me away to some Siberian hideout and would soon appear to demand either cooperation or death. Sadly enough, I am too reality oriented. My research was highly interesting to me, and perhaps to a few other psychologists who like to dabble in esoteric problems of animal learning, but it was scarcely startling enough to warrant such attention as kidnapping.

So I am left as baffled as before. Where am I, and why? And who is He?

I have decided to forego all attempts at keeping this diary according to "days" or "hours." Such units of time have no meaning in my present circumstances, for the light remains constant all the time I am awake. The human organism is not possessed of as neat an internal clock as some of the lower species. Far too many studies have shown that a human being who is isolated from all external stimulation soon loses his sense of time. So I will merely indicate breaks in the narrative and hope that He will understand that if He wasn't bright enough to leave me with my wristwatch, He couldn't expect me to keep an accurate record.

Nothing much has happened. I have slept, been fed and watered, and have emptied my bladder and bowels. The food was waiting on the table when I awoke last time. I must say that He has little of the gourmet in Him. Protein balls are not my idea of a feast royal. However, they will serve to keep body and soul together (presuming, of course, that they *are* together at the moment). But I must object to my source of liquid refreshment. The meal made me very thirsty, and I was in the process of cursing Him and everybody else when I noticed a small nipple which had appeared in the wall while I was asleep. At first I thought that perhaps Freud was right after all, and that my libido had taken over control of my imagery. Experimentation convinced me, however, that the thing was real, and that it is my present source of water. If one sucks on the thing, it delivers a slightly cool and somewhat sweetish flow of liquid. But really, it's a most undignified procedure. It's bad enough to have to sit around all day in my birthday suit. But for a full professor to have to stand on his tiptoes and suck on an artificial nipple in order to obtain water is asking a little too much. I'd complain to the Management if only I knew to whom to complain!

Following eating and drinking, the call to nature became a little too strong to ignore. Now, I was adequately toilet-trained with indoor plumbing, and the absence of same is most annoying. However, there was nothing much to do but choose a corner of the room and make the best of a none too pleasant situation. (As a side-thought, I wonder if the choosing of a corner was in any way instinctive?) However, the upshot of the whole thing was my learning what is probably the purpose of the vibration of the floor. For the excreted material disappeared through the floor not too many minutes later. The process was a gradual one. Now I will be faced with all kinds of uncomfortable thoughts concerning what might possibly happen to me if I slept too long.

Perhaps this is to be expected, but I find myself becoming a little paranoid after all. In attempting to solve my Problem #2, why I am here, I have begun to wonder if perhaps some of my colleagues at the University are not using me as a subject in some kind of experiment. It would be just like McCleary to dream up some fantastic kind of "human-in-isolation" experiment and use me as a pilot observer. You would think that he'd have asked my permission first. However, perhaps it's important that the subject not know what's happening to him. If so, I have one happy thought to console me. If McCleary *is* responsible for this, he'll have to take over the teaching of my classes for the time being. And how he hates teaching Learning Theory to freshmen.

You know, this place seems dreadfully quiet to me.

Suddenly I have solved two of my problems. I know both where I am and who He is. And I bless the day that I got interested in the perception of motion.

I should say to begin with that the air in this room seems to have more than the usual concentration of dust particles. This didn't seem particularly noteworthy until I noticed that most of them seemed to pile up along the floor against one wall in particular. For a while I was sure that this was due to the ventilation system—perhaps there was an outgoing airduct there where this particular wall was joined to the floor. However, when I went over and put my hand to the floor there, I could feel no breeze whatsoever. Yet even as I held my hand along the dividing line between the wall and the floor, dust motes covered my hand with a thin coating. I tried this same experiment everywhere else in the room to no avail. This was the only spot where the phenomenon occurred, and it occurred along the entire length of this one wall.

But if ventilation was not responsible for the phenomenon, what was? All at once there popped into my mind some calculations I had made when the rocket boys had first proposed a manned satellite station. Engineers are notoriously naive when it comes to the performance of a human being in most situations, and I remembered that the problem of the perception of the satellite's rotation seemingly had been ignored by the slip-stick crowd. They had planned to rotate the doughnut-shaped satellite in order to substitute centrifugal force for the force of gravity. Thus the outer shell of the doughnut would appear to be "down" to anyone inside the thing. Apparently they had not realized that man is at least as sensitive to angular rotation as he is to variations in the pull of gravity. As I figured the problem then, if a man aboard the doughnut moved his head as much as three or four feet outwards from the center of the doughnut, he would have become fairly dizzy! Rather annoying it would have been, too, to have been hit by a wave of nausea every time one sat down in a chair. Also, as I pondered the problem, it became apparent that dust particles and the like would probably show a tendency to move in a direction opposite to the direction of the rotation, and hence pile up against any wall or such that impeded their flight.

Using the behavior of the dust particles as a clue, I then climbed atop the table and leapt off. Sure enough, my head felt like a mule had kicked it by the time I landed on the floor. My hypothesis was confirmed.

So I am aboard a spaceship.

The thought is incredible, but in a strange way comforting. At least now I can postpone worrying about heaven and hell—and somehow I find the idea of being in a spaceship much more to the liking of a confirmed agnostic. I suppose I owe McCleary an apology—I should have known he would never have put himself in a position where he would have to teach freshmen all about learning.

And, of course, I know who "He" is. Or rather, I know who He *isn't*, which is something else again. Surely, though, I can no longer think of Him as being human. Whether I should be consoled at this or not, I have no way of telling.

I still have no notion of *why* I am here, however, nor why this alien chose to pick me of all people to pay a visit to His spaceship. What possible use could I be? Surely if He were interested in making contact with the human race, He would have spirited away a politician. After all, that's what politicians are for! Since there has been no effort made to communicate with me, however, I must reluctantly give up any cherished hopes that His purpose is that of making contact with *genus homo*.

Or perhaps He's a galactic scientist of some kind, a biologist of sorts, out gathering specimens. Now, that's a particularly nasty thought. What if He turned out to be a physiologist, interested in cutting me open eventually, to see what makes me tick? Will my innards be smeared over a glass slide for scores of youthful Hims to peer at under a microscope? Brrrr! I don't mind giving my life to Science, but I'd rather do it a little at a time.

If you don't mind, I think I'll go do a little repressing for a while.

Good God! I should have known it! Destiny will play her little tricks, and all jokes have their cosmic angles. He is a *psychologist!* Had I given it due consideration, I would have realized that whenever you come across a new species, you worry about behavior first, physiology second. So I have received the ultimate insult—or the ultimate compliment. I don't know which. I have become a specimen for an alien psychologist!

This thought first occurred to me when I awoke after my latest sleep (which was filled, I must admit, with most frightening dreams). It was immediately obvious that something about the room had changed. Almost at once I noticed that one of the walls now had a lever of some kind protruding from it, and to one side of the lever, a small hole in the wall with a container beneath the hole. I wandered over to the lever, inspected it a few moments, then accidentally depressed the thing. At once there came a loud clicking noise, and a protein ball popped out of the hole and fell into the container.

For just a moment a frown crossed my brow. This seemed somehow so strangely familiar. Then, all at once, I burst into wild laughter. The room had been changed into a gigantic Skinner Box! For years I had been studying animal learning by putting white rats in a Skinner Box and following the changes in the rats' behavior. The rats had to learn to press the lever in order to get a pellet of food, which was delivered to them through just such an apparatus as is now affixed to the wall of my cell. And now, after all of these years, and after all of the learning studies I had done, to find myself trapped like a rat in a Skinner Box! Perhaps this was hell after all, I told myself, and the Lord High Executioner's admonition to "let the punishment fit the crime" was being followed.

Frankly, this sudden turn of events has left me more than a little shaken.

I seem to be performing according to theory. It didn't take me long to discover that pressing the lever would give me food some of the time, while at other times all I got was the click and no protein ball. It appears that approximately every twelve hours the thing delivers me a random number of protein balls—the number has varied from five to fifteen so far. I never know ahead of time how many pellets—I mean protein balls—the apparatus will deliver, and it spews them out intermittently. Sometimes I have to press the lever a dozen times or so before it will give me anything, while at other times it gives me one ball for each press. Since I don't have a watch on me, I am never quite sure when the twelve hours have passed, so I stomp over to the lever and press it every few minutes when I think it's getting close to time to be fed. Just like my rats always did. And since the pellets are small and I never get enough of them, occasionally I find myself banging away on the lever with all the compulsion of a stupid animal. But I missed the feeding time once and almost starved to death (so it seemed) before the lever delivered food the next time. About the only consolation to my wounded pride is that at this rate of starvation, I'll lose my bay window in short order.

At least He doesn't seem to be fattening me up for the kill. Or maybe he just likes lean meat!

I have been promoted. Apparently He in His infinite alien wisdom has declared that I'm intelligent enough to handle the

Skinner-type apparatus, so I've been promoted to solving a maze. Can you picture the irony of the situation? All of the classic Learning Theory methodology is practically being thrown in my face. If only I could communicate with Him! I don't mind being subjected to tests nearly as much as I mind being underestimated. Why, I can solve puzzles hundreds of times more complex than what He's throwing at me. But how can I tell Him?

As it turns out, the maze is much like our standard T-mazes, and is not too difficult to learn. It's a rather long one, true, with some 23 choice points along the way. I spent the better part of half an hour wandering through the thing the first time I found myself in it. Surprisingly enough, I didn't realize the first time out what I was in, so I made no conscious attempt to memorize the correct turns. It wasn't until I reached the final turn and found food waiting for me that I recognized what I was expected to do. The next time through the maze my performance was a good deal better, and I was able to turn in a perfect performance in not too long a time. However, it does not do my ego any good to realize that my own white rats could have learned the maze a little sooner than I did.

My "home cage," so to speak, still has the Skinner apparatus in it, but the lever delivers food only occasionally now. I still give it a whirl now and again, but since I'm getting a fairly good supply of food at the end of the maze each time, I don't pay the lever much attention.

Now that I am very sure of what is happening to me, quite naturally my thoughts have turned to how I can get out of this situation. Mazes I can solve without too much difficulty, but how to escape apparently is beyond my intellectual capacity. But then, come to think of it, there was precious little chance for my own experimental animals to get out of my clutches. And assuming that I am unable to escape, what then? After He has finished putting me through as many paces as He wishes, where do we go from there? Will He treat me as I treated most of my non-human subjects—that is, will I get tossed into a jar containing chloroform? "Following the experiment, the animals were sacrificed," as we so euphemistically report in the scientific literature. This doesn't appeal to me much, as you can imagine. Or maybe if I seem particularly bright to Him, He may use me for breeding purposes, to establish a colony of His own. Now, that might have possibilities. . . .

Oh, damn Freud anyhow!

And damn Him too! I had just gotten the maze well learned

when He upped and changed things on me. I stumbled about like a bat in the sunlight for quite some time before I finally got to the goal box. I'm afraid my performance was pretty poor. What He did was just to reverse the whole maze so that it was it a mirror image of what it used to be. Took me only two trials to discover the solution. Let Him figure that one out if He's so smart!

My performance on the maze reversal must have pleased Him, because now He's added a new complication. And again I suppose I could have predicted the next step if I had been thinking along the right direction. I woke up a few hours ago to find myself in a totally different room. There was nothing whatsoever in the room, but opposite me were two doors in the wall—one door a pure white, the other jet black. Between me and the doors was a deep pit, filled with water. I didn't like the looks of the situation, for it occurred to me right away that He had devised a kind of jumping stand for me. I had to choose which of the doors was open and led to food. The other door would be locked. If I jumped at the wrong door, and found it locked, I'd fall in the water. I needed a bath, that was for sure, but I didn't relish getting it in this fashion.

While I stood there watching, I got the shock of my life. I meant it quite literally. The bastard had thought of everything. When I used to run rats on jumping stands, to overcome their reluctance to jump, I used to shock them. He's following exactly the same pattern. The floor in this room is wired but good. I howled and jumped about and showed all the usual anxiety behavior. It took me less than two seconds to come to my senses and make a flying leap at the white door, however.

You know something? That water is ice-cold!

I have now, by my own calculations, solved no fewer than 87 different problems on the jumping stand, and I'm getting sick and tired of it. Once I got angry and just pointed at the correct door—and got shocked for not going ahead and jumping. I shouted bloody murder, cursing Him at the top of my voice, telling Him if He didn't like my performance, He could damn' well lump it. All He did, of course, was to increase the shock.

Frankly, I don't know how much longer I can put up with this. It's not that the work is difficult. If He were giving me half a chance to show my capabilities, I wouldn't mind it. I suppose I've contemplated a thousand different means of escaping, but none of them is worth mentioning. But if I don't get out of here soon, I shall go stark raving mad!

For almost an hour after it happened, I sat in this room and just wept. I realize that it is not the style in our culture for a grown man to weep, but there are times when cultural taboos must be forgotten. Again, had I thought much about the sort of experiments He must have had in mind, I most probably could have predicted the next step. Even so, I most likely would have repressed the knowledge.

One of the standard problems which any learning psychologist is interested in is this one—will an animal learn something if you fail to reward him for his performance? There are many theorists, such as Hull and Spence, who believe that reward (or "reinforcement," as they call it) is absolutely necessary for learning to occur. This is mere stuff and nonsense, as anyone with a grain of sense knows, but nonetheless the "reinforcement" theory has been dominant in the field for years now. We fought a hard battle with Spence and Hull, and actually had them with their backs to the wall at one point, when suddenly they came up with the concept of "secondary reinforcement." That is, anything associated with a reward takes on the ability to act as a reward itself. For example, the mere sight of food would become a reward in and of itself—almost as much a reward, in fact, as is the eating of the food. The *sight* of food, indeed! But nonetheless, it saved their theories for the moment.

For the past five years now, I have been trying to design an experiment that would show beyond a shadow of a doubt that the *sight* of a reward was not sufficient for learning to take place. And now look at what has happened to me!

I'm sure that He must lean toward Hull and Spence in His theorizing, for earlier today, when I found myself in the jumping stand room, instead of being rewarded with my usual protein balls when I made the correct jump, I—I'm sorry, but it is difficult to write about even now. For when I made the correct jump and the door opened and I started towards the food trough, I found it had been replaced with a photograph. A calendar photograph. You know the one. Her name, I think, is Monroe.

I sat on the floor and cried. For five whole years I have been attacking the validity of the secondary reinforcement theory, and now I find myself giving Him evidence that the theory is correct! For I cannot help "learning" which of the doors is the correct one to jump through. I refuse to stand on the apparatus and have the life shocked out of me, and I refuse to pick the wrong door all the time and get an icy bath time after time. It isn't fair! For He will doubtless put it all down to the fact that the mere *sight* of the photograph is functioning as a reward, and that I am learning the problems merely to be able to see Miss What's-her-name in her bare skin!

I can just see Him now, sitting somewhere else in this space-ship, gathering in all the data I am giving Him, plotting all kinds of learning curves, chortling to Himself because I am confirming all of His pet theories. I just wish. . . .

Almost an hour has gone by since I wrote the above section. It seems longer than that, but surely it's been only an hour. And I have spent the time deep in thought. For I have discovered a way out of this place, I think. The question is, dare I do it?

I was in the midst of writing that paragraph about His sitting and chortling and confirming His theories, when it suddenly struck me that theories are born of the equipment that one uses. This has probably been true throughout the history of all science, but perhaps most true of all in psychology. If Skinner had never invented his blasted box, if the maze and the jumping stand had not been developed, we probably would have entirely different theories of learning today than we now have. For if nothing else, the type of equipment that one uses drastically reduces the type of behavior that one's subjects can show, and one's theories have to account only for the type of behavior that appears in the laboratories.

It follows from this also that any two cultures that devise the same sort of experimental procedures will come up with almost identical theories.

Keeping all of this in mind, it's not hard for me to believe that He is an iron-clad reinforcement theorist, for He uses all of the various paraphernalia that they use, and uses it in exactly the same way.

My means of escape is, therefore, obvious. He expects from me confirmation of all His pet theories. Well, he won't get it any more! I know all of His theories backwards and forwards, and this means I know how to give Him results that will tear His theories right smack in half!

I can almost predict the results. What does any learning theorist

273

do with an animal that won't behave properly, that refuses to give the results that are predicted? One gets rid of the beast, quite naturally. For one wishes to use only healthy, normal animals in one's work, and any animal that gives "unusual" results is removed from the study but quickly. After all, if it doesn't perform as expected, it must be sick, abnormal, or aberrant in one way or another. . . .

There is no guarantee, of course, what method He will employ to dispose of my now annoying presence. Will He "sacrifice" me? Or will He just return me to the "permanent colony"? I cannot say. I know only that I will be free from what is now an intolerable situation.

Just wait until He looks at His results from now on!

FROM: Experimenter-in-Chief, Interstellar Labship PSYCH-145

TO: Director, Bureau of Science

Thlan, my friend, this will be an informal missive. I will send the official report along later, but I wanted to give you my subjective impressions first.

The work with the newly discovered species is, for the moment, at a standstill. Things went exceedingly well at first. We picked what seemed to be a normal, healthy animal and smattered it into our standard test apparatus. I may have told you that this new species seemed quite identical to our usual laboratory animals, so we included a couple of the "toys" that our home animals seem so fond of—thin pieces of material made from woodpulp and a tiny stick of graphite. Imagine our surprise, and our pleasure, when this new specimen made exactly the same use of the materials as have all of our home colony specimens. Could it be that there are certain innate behavior patterns to be found throughout the universe in the lower species?

Well, I merely pose the question. The answer is of little importance to a Learning Theorist. Your friend Verpk keeps insisting that the use of these "toys" may have some deeper meaning to it, and that perhaps we should investigate further. At his insistence, then, I include with this informal missive the materials used by our first subject. In my opinion, Verpk is guilty of gross anthropomorphism, and I wish to have nothing further to do with the question. However, this behavior did give us hope that our newly discovered colony would yield subjects whose performance would be exactly in accordance with standard theory.

And, in truth, this is exactly what seemed to be the case. The animal solved the Bfian Box problem in short order, yielding as beautiful data as I have ever seen. We then shifted it to maze, maze-reversal, and jumping stand problems, and the results could not have confirmed our theories better had we rigged the data. However, when we switched the animal to secondary reinforcement problems, it seemed to undergo a strange sort of change. No longer was its performance up to par. In fact, at times it seemed to go quite berserk. For part of the experiment, it would perform superbly. But then, just as it seemed to be solving whatever problem we set it to, its behavior would subtly change into patterns that obviously could not come from a normal specimen. It got worse and worse, until its behavior departed radically from that which our theories predicted. Naturally, we knew then that something had happened to the animal, for our theories are based upon thousands of experiments with similar subjects, and hence our theories must be right. But our theories hold only for normal subjects, and for normal species, so it soon became apparent to us that we had stumbled upon some abnormal type of animal.

Upon due consideration, we returned the subject to its home colony. However, we also voted almost unanimously to request from you permission to take steps to destroy the complete colony. It is obviously of little scientific use to us, and stands as a potential danger that we must take adequate steps against. Since all colonies are under your protection, we therefore request permission to destroy it.

I must report, by the way, that Verpk's vote was the only one which was cast against this procedure. He has some silly notion that one should study behavior as one finds it. Frankly, I cannot understand why you have seen fit to saddle me with him on this expedition, but perhaps you have your reasons.

Verpk's vote notwithstanding, however, the rest of us are of the considered opinion that this whole new colony must be destroyed, and quickly. For it is obviously diseased or some such—as reference to our theories has proven. And should it by some chance come in contact with our other colonies, and infect our other animals with whatever disease or aberration it has, we would never be able to predict their behavior again. I need not carry the argument further, I think.

275

May we have your permission to destroy the colony as soon as possible, then, so that we may search out yet other colonies and test our theories against other healthy animals? For it is only in this fashion that science progresses.

Respectfully yours,
Iowyy   END

susie's reality

Bob Stickgold

What is reality? How do we learn about its "ins and outs"? How do we use our understanding of it to function in the "real world"? These philosophical and psychologically technological questions are explored in the story you are about to read. The story's primary learner is Susie, one of a group of monkeys serving as a subject in a psychology experiment. The primary experimenter is Steve Spencer, a graduate student in psychology who is doing his doctoral thesis. Steve and his colleagues, Chuck and Sue, devise an experimental procedure which aims to investigate whether Susie and her monkey friends can be taught the rules of different "realities" as a basis for their functional existence. Susie learns to function very well in her "reality," thank you, and in the process shocks the foundations of Steve's supposedly secure conceptions in answer to the first question posed above.

There have been many learning theories and approaches which have attempted to blueprint how we learn. The operant conditioning approach of B. F. Skinner is discussed and drama-tized in the story "Learning Theory." The more cognitive learning theory of Edward Tolman would appear to be helpful in explaining how Susie learns about her "reality." Tolman believed that through experience we learn to hold *expectancies* about the world we live in, be it a learning maze, a cage, or the outside environment. Animals and human beings both construct *cognitive maps* of what to expect in their worlds—where their goals are and how probable their behaviors will be in leading to achievement of their goals. They are continually seeking confirmation of how accurate their preconceived maps of their environments are, eventually building up a repertoire of behaviors which correspond to accurate maps, discarding (extinguishing) behaviors which don't correspond.

277

A similar learning approach which emphasizes expectancies of strictly human subjects in social situations is Julian B. Rotter's social learning theory. Rotter's basic equation for human goal-seeking behavior suggests that behavior potential is a function of how rewarding the goal is and how high the expectancy is that the particular behavior will attain the goal. For example, your potential for studying behavior will be low if good grades are not rewarding to you, or if you believe (expect) that studying will not lead to good grades even if they are rewarding to you. At the end of our story, both Steve and his girl friend Sue are seeking the same highly needed (rewarding) goal in reference to Susie. Sue believes strongly (has a high expectancy) that covering her eyes will attain that goal, while Steve does not. Consequently, she tries the behavior, while Steve tries other behaviors which he believes will attain the goal.

As in many of our stories, there are references in "Susie's Reality" to issues and research in other areas of psychology. Piaget's stages of cognitive development are discussed in the chapter Developmental Processes, as is Harlow's research on surrogate mothers. General issues are discussed in Sensation, Perception and Awareness, while the burning issue of differing conceptions of reality and their relation to insanity is discussed in the story, "The Yellow Pill," which appears in the book's final chapter.

SUSIE'S REALITY   *Bob Stickgold*

Steve Spencer tried to hide all of his six-two frame behind the lichen-covered rock and comprehend the magnitude of the slide which had somehow failed to kill him. A huge slab of granite had cleaved his protective boulder in half seconds earlier and he was not yet convinced that a hard shove wouldn't turn that life-saving stone into a joint executioner and gravemarker. His body ached from fatigue. He hadn't moved a muscle in an hour and a half and his hair was tickling his nose. It was at times like this that he promised to have his shoulder-length blond hair chopped to a crewcut.

These old mountains will never be the same, he thought. *But unless my aim improves, neither will the rest of the world. . . .*

He stared dumbly at the carbine by his side and tried to justify murdering poor, scared Susie. It would make a pretty lousy ending for his doctoral thesis.

When the doctoral research committee approved his proposal Steve was jubilant. His lean frame arranged itself randomly over the old stuffed chair that adorned his living room. Chuck Dorin, his roommate and co-worker, tried to ignore him. Chuck's upcoming psychology test would definitely keep Chuck from being in a good mood for the next twenty-four hours.

"You know," commented Steve, "this just might set a departmental record for the laziest doctoral project ever to pass the research committee. All I have to do is take toys away from them when they're not looking. It's just that simple, stealing from babies."

Chuck's broad shoulders, topped by a tangle of curly black hair that looked as if it might or might not be hiding a head, gave no sign that he might be listening.

"You know?" taunted Steve.

Chuck turned his large frame and caromed a box of tissues off Steve's left shoulder. "Get off it," he grumbled. "You're about as cynical as a pair of newlyweds. I've never seen you so excited about anything—"

When he thought about it Steve doubted that newlyweds got nearly this excited.

The whole project had come up more or less by accident and, in the end, Steve had to give Sue Malor credit for giving him the idea in the first place. They had gone out for pizza after an unusually bad movie and Steve had tried to explain to her the development of the "object concept" in infants.

"It was way back in the nineteen-twenties that Piaget first introduced the 'object concept' into his studies of the development of intelligence in infants," he began. Sue's lithe figure sat back in the chair, a straw tenuously running from her lips to a coke.

"According to Piagetian theory a newborn infant has no idea that the objects he sees are real. To him they are merely parts of a picture, with no reality of their own. But as the infant gets older he starts to experience the objects in other ways. He learns that what can be seen can also be felt and sometimes heard or smelled. In time, he realizes that these properties go together. But the object still is real only in his perception. If the object is covered—or hidden—the infant shows no sign that he is aware that it still exists." Steve was building steam, his long, bony arms gesturing as he spoke.

"By six months he starts to understand that the objects have independent existences. If you put a watch—or toy—under a pillow and then show him where it is he will learn to look for it there. Even so, if you then put it under—say—his blanket, he's still likely to look for it under the pillow. It isn't until the infant is eighteen months old that he finally realizes that objects have truly independent existences—that they are not present merely by virtue of his perception of them. So the child only slowly evolves the concept of the inherent reality of objects—and only through constantly recurring reinforcements in his everyday life." By now Steve's comments were only vaguely aimed at Sue.

She pushed a strand of long black hair from her eye and absently tucked it behind her ear. "No one has convinced me that some things really exist." She was still foul-tempered from a chemistry class where she had just been told that sometimes electrons were waves and sometimes they were particles. "All you scientists ever do is make up stupid theories and then cram everything into them. Time is relative, momentum is quantized, matter is waves, and light is particles. Good thing those infants decide that objects are real. They would look pretty dumb trying to fit them into any other theory." She blew through the straw into Steve's face. "Not that an illustrious graduate student couldn't get the data to fit, but I just thought it might be kind of tricky for a two-year-old." She attempted a horrible face and then settled for sticking out her tongue at him. Steve's face was blank. His eyes were focused on infinity. "Are you all right, Steve?" she asked. "Do you feel sick?" He had consumed quite a large pizza.

"No, no," cried Steve. "What you just said—what did you mean?" Sue could feel the eyes of everyone in the restaurant turn toward her idiotic Steve. She had no idea what he was talking about, but the symptoms were clear. "It's a great idea!" he continued.

Another brainstorm had struck him in the head, she decided, and in the next instant he would be lecturing her wildly, scribbling on napkins and demanding instant comprehension from her. In a couple of days, after he had calmed down, he would explain it again more simply and she would finally find out what it was all about. But she hated these restaurant scenes.

"No sarcasm, please," he said. "You've brought up a fantastic question. What if the child developed a different object concept? What if he decided that when an object disappeared from sight it no longer existed? Don't you see? We can test it in the lab. With monkeys. Use trapdoors, stuff like that. We can convince an infant monkey that objects have no independent reality. It's a beautiful project. Can they learn that an object isn't real? And what will happen if we change things and let them find out that the objects *are* real? It's beautiful! Absolutely beautiful!" His voice trailed off as he began scribbling notes on one napkin after another. She was surprised. For once she had understood what he was talking about the first time through.

Later that night, Steve went through it again, explaining this time to Chuck. "The basic question, then, is: If the experiences of the infant indicate that objects exist only as extensions of its own perceptions, what sorts of conclusions will it draw? Is the development of the concept that objects are real—with independent existences—automatic? Or is it something infants learn through experience."

Chuck asked, "Why limit yourself to whether objects can exist independently? Why not explore all types of 'realities' the infant can be convinced of? What if some objects could never be touched? You could use holograms. And monkeys for infants. That way you could take something like, say, fruit—which we know monkeys like—and present it only as an image. Rig up some gadget to spray the smell in with the image. What would the monkeys do with that?"

Steve was catching on. "Fantastic. We could let them play with a pocket watch and after a while just introduce the sound, and see how the monkeys respond to that—"

The sky was turning a pale blue when they finally gave up and went to bed. They had worked out an even dozen key experiments and both men were exhausted. Steve rose in time to keep a lunch date with Sue.

"I'm going to write up what we were talking about yesterday," he said before they had even found a table. "Chuck and I tossed it around all night and I'm sure I can get it approved as my Ph.D.

project. That'll mean I'll get all the materials and money that I need, plus the time to work on it." Sue was delighted. Something in the back of her head told her that she would be rooting for the monkeys and not for Steve, but it did seem that for once she might be able to keep track of what he was doing.

"You know," she suggested, "it'll be sort of tricky if the monkeys accept whatever reality they are shown."

"How so?" asked Steve.

She realized that was the result he really wanted and saw no problems in accepting it.

"Well, then you'll say that the monkeys were taught that something was real that wasn't—and they accepted it, right?"

"Yeh." Steve seemed to know that he was being set up, but to have no idea just where she was heading.

"Then how will you know that you don't have your realities backward?"

She waited, but he simply stared as if he had already considered the question and its implications long before she asked it. She decided she would have to wait and see.

By the end of the week a heavily documented research proposal was in the hands of the chairman of the doctoral project committee. Ten days later Steve defended the proposal before the committee and it was approved.

It took him and Chuck another week to build the first experimental cage and they unveiled it for Sue with paternal pride. "Every part of the floor is a trapdoor," explained Steve. "We can remove any object from any section of the cage instantly." The contraption stood in one corner of the laboratory, across from the door. It was large—six feet square and four feet high. The floor was a grid of six-inch square tiles. A vast number of wires ran to a series of controls in front of the cage.

"Or put things in," added Chuck. "One of the stages of infant learning is the discovery that when an object disappears from sight one may expect it to show up again—perhaps randomly or in a specific place, but not necessarily where it went out of sight. So we've rigged up some loading platforms that will shoot objects up into the cage so that they just seem to materialize."

"Remember, Sue?" Steve asked. "We were talking that night about a watch placed under the pillow and then moved in earlier experiments with infants? Well, we're going to do something just like that. Whenever our pocket watch 'disappears' through a trap-door, we'll simultaneously sneak another one exactly like it into a predetermined location."

"Behind the surrogate mother," Chuck explained.

"The what?" asked Sue.

"She's not going to like this," Steve cautioned Chuck. He would have preferred not to have the point come up.

"Isn't someone going to explain this little tidbit to me?"

"Okay, it's simple." Steve's tone was defensive. "We can only have one monkey in a cage—otherwise we can't control the experiment. But each cage will contain a surrogate mother—a phony made of wire and cloth, with nipples attached to bottles for feeding the experiment's subject."

"The poor things will go crazy without real mothers to give them affection."

"They won't," countered Chuck. "In previous experiments caged monkeys definitely have not gone crazy. But ours won't even lack affection. Steve and I will be handling them and giving them love as part of the deal. They've got to be able to trust us completely for us to get the right readings."

"If it'll make you feel better," Steve suggested to Sue, "you can pitch in—feed them by bottle whenever you want. It'll be all to the good."

"What are all these other gadgets for?" she asked. She definitely did not like the use of the surrogate mothers and now she was becoming suspicious and worried.

"These were the most fun," Chuck told her, pointing. "They're tiny nozzles—these tubes are attached to aerosol dispensers, so that we can add various smells to the cage without showing the objects the scents belong to."

Steve pointed out a number of buttons located at various points around the cage, each with a single wire running from it. "And these are minispeakers, so that we can do the same thing with sounds—like suggest a rattle or a tom-tom. They're grounded to the cage, so we need only a single thin wire running to each speaker."

Sue looked at a huge piece of equipment sitting on a cart next to the cage. "And this, I suppose, is to dissect their brains with when you're done with them?"

Chuck laughed. "It's a laser. We're using it to produce holograms, three-dimensional images of an object that isn't really there. We can project the image of, say, an orange into the cage. We can use aerosol spray to add the smell to go with the image. Every once in a while the monkey will be able to see and smell an orange, but he'll never be able to grab it."

Sue was impressed. She couldn't imagine how the monkeys might react. Steve told her not to try.

"We're not supposed to assume or try to predict; the purpose of the experiment is to find out what will happen under the test conditions. All we can do now is wait. The shop says it can have the other five cages for us in two weeks. Then we'll be ready to start."

"I'm not so sure I appreciate having one named after me," Sue whispered. She watched the infant monkey named Susie as it fed itself from the surrogate mother. "I don't care what you say, it just isn't natural for that poor thing to have to nurse from a mother made of cloth and wire." Steve was edgy. He didn't care for the isolation of the monkeys any more than Sue did, but it had to be done. The big question was how the monkeys were going to respond to their "realities." Sue seemed to read his mind. "And what you're going to convince those poor creatures is real is going to drive them insane. I'm certain it will."

"Why?" argued Steve. "Do dogs go crazy when they're confronted with radios and television sets? And what about elevators? They go into this little room. Thirty seconds later they leave by the same door and they're in an entirely different place. They don't even seem to notice it."

"But that's different," Sue insisted. "Dogs basically know that objects exist. Radio and television are just things that won't work for them. They probably throw them out the way you throw out what you can't use."

"You don't know that's how they react," protested Steve.

"But neither do you," she persisted. "But with these monkeys you're going to switch things around, so that what used to be real will start disappearing and what used to be untouchable will become solid. What's that going to do to the poor things?"

"Just one poor thing," said Steve. "Just Susie."

"Thanks," Sue growled.

The addition of this new series of experiments was the last change that had been made in the plans for the project—and Steve and Chuck agreed it was the most important. One of the monkeys would find, after twelve months, that objects changed from one "reality class" to another. "Reality classes" referred to the apparent characteristics of a set of items—the classifications had been worked out while they had waited for the cages to be finished. The whole program had finally shaped up into a comprehensive whole. In all, six monkeys would be used—three experimental and three control. The control monkeys would merely live in the special cages, dubbed "reality cages" by Sue. No objects would disappear or reappear, no smells, sounds, or images would be presented out of normal context. These three would be raised in the generally accepted "real" world. Only the three experimental monkeys would be subjected to altered realities—one for six months, one for twelve months, and one for eighteen. After their time was up they would be transferred into other cages, where they would experience standard realities. Steve and Chuck planned to watch carefully the reactions and adaptations of the monkeys to this change.

"Only Susie will have objects changing from one class to another," explained Steve. "For the first six months each of the three experimental animals will be given twelve objects to play with and each will have a different reality or, as we put it, each will belong to a different 'reality class.' Thus, one class will be represented by the orange. It will always be seen and smelled, but the monkeys will never be able to touch it. Another, represented by the watch, will always disappear when out of the monkey's vision, but will reappear immediately in a certain place, behind the surrogate mother. Another class, including a rattle, will disappear, but reappear at a random time and a random place. Bananas will sometimes be real and sometimes only images with smells. And so on. Only the twelve objects will be used. For Fred, who'll spend six months in the reality cages, this will be all that he goes through."

"Go on," said Sue. Steve had never explained the final layout before and Sue was convinced the reason was that he didn't think she would like it. "Paul goes for twelve months and Susie for eighteen. What happens to them?"

"Calm down," Steve said. "I can't explain it to you if you're already convinced that it's going to be something awful. Believe me, it won't be." Sue relented. Her scowl disappeared. "Okay," Steve said. "After the first six months Paul and Susie will be given new objects. Each will be manipulated to fit into one of the twelve reality classes identified by the original twelve objects. Once introduced, each new object will always appear in the same reality class and no contradictions will be made. The question is will the animals learn to categorize objects according to their class? We're hoping that maybe the monkeys will be able to classify the objects after a very short encounter with them. This would tend to show that they actually are aware of the different realities and have accepted them."

"And Susie?" asked Sue. "What special treats does she get for her last six months?"

"Precisely what you suggested," interjected Chuck. He had come in minutes earlier and had been listening quietly. "We're going to take objects that Susie is familiar with, that have always acted in the same way, and switch them into another reality class. The doll, which had always behaved as a real doll, will become just an image. The orange, which she had never been able to grasp, will become a real object. And when the watch is hidden from her, it won't reappear behind the surrogate mother. It'll just stay right where it was put—and I really don't know what you're so upset about." He was mad now—and worried that she might convince Steve to modify the experiments in some way.

"It's just so unnatural," she complained.

"So is wearing clothes—and so is driving a car," he snapped and stomped out of the room.

"It's not just that, Steve." She was still unsettled by the whole affair. "The more I think about it, the less I like what Susie is going to have to go through."

"Well, you won't be the first person ever to empathize with an ape."

"I don't feel just empathy," Sue told him. "What Chuck said is true. Man lives in a completely unnatural world. Look, ever since man became a technological creature scientists have been arguing with the rest of us that what we think is true isn't. So when Armstrong landed on the moon reporters found that something like a quarter of the people they interviewed didn't believe that he was really on the moon. They thought it was all a colossal put-on."

Steve started rolling long strands of hair around a pencil. Since he had let his hair grow he had picked up several of Sue's nervous habits. "So what are you getting at? You think they're as dumb as Susie? Or dumber?"

"No, but they're just as lucky." She groped for words. "Don't you see? Science has destroyed modern man's confidence in reality. He doesn't know whether to believe his senses or not and no attempt is made to clarify the contradiction. That's why I get so mad when some big dome gets up in front of the class and tells me that matter is just waves and not really solid at all. If you were shown an object disappearing and reappearing across the room, you would say, 'Wow, teleportation!' There is no alteration of reality that you wouldn't accept. Sure, in some ways that's a good thing. But this is what I meant when I said I wasn't so sure that objects did exist. Those people who insisted that Armstrong was on a movie set would never have any trouble with disappearing objects. To them it would be a gimmick. For you and me—anything we believe we make our senses accept. Some day we're going to have to confront all of this—and I don't see anyone trying to get ready—"

"I'm sorry," said Steve. "I really don't understand what you're getting at."

"You probably never will," she answered.

Steve slowly raised a hand to wipe his forehead. *Damn her,* he thought. *She's right down there, somewhere.* He had been stupid to fire at that great a distance and it had never dawned on him that a police carbine would fire any differently from the old twenty-two he had grown up with. All he had managed to do was scare Susie enough to convince her to retaliate and she showed no inclination to reveal her position now. He had radioed for more men and had been promised a squad of army sharpshooters, but the men refused to approach within line of sight and the squad had been dropped off two miles down the valley. If they didn't spot her by sunset they wouldn't have a chance, and Coleman had radioed in that the Pentagon had decided to level the whole area if they didn't get her. Susie had sealed her own fate. There was no way out. And he had taught her—was that fair? Yes, he, the ultimate buffoon, had taught her to do it. He was tired and worn out. Nothing made sense. Leveling ten square miles of Rockies to kill a single monkey made more sense than most of the day's events. *A lazy doctoral thesis,* he had called it. How was he going to write this one up?

Steve had somewhat hopefully labeled the occasion a celebration, but a break in the tedium might have been more accurate. The experiment was six months old today and he, Sue, and Chuck had ordered pizza and champagne to celebrate the end of Phase One. Tomorrow two of the monkeys would come out of their reality cages, and Paul and Susie would be introduced to their first new objects. Despite all this, a half-year of boring repetition had drained Steve of his enthusiasm.

"Those damn monkeys accept anything," he complained. "There is absolutely no difference between the experimental animals and the controls. Except in what they take for reality. Whenever the watch disappears they look behind Mama for it. When the rattle disappears they don't expect it back. When the banana turns out to be only an image they ignore it. They're completely predictable—so where's the fun? I'd like to hit one of those beasts on the head with an orange!" It had been five months since any of the experimental animals had shown any interest at all in the sight and smell of an orange.

"For Pete's sake, Steve, how can you complain?" argued Sue. "The experiment so far is a success. Your results have been perfectly clear—and better than you had any right to expect."

"Not to mention," Chuck added, "three publications in six months. I know a lot of people who would give their right arms to be bored like that."

"I'm not complaining about the results," Steve said. "You're both absolutely right—there's no doubt that the monkeys accept whatever reality they're given. They've learned and accepted all twelve reality classes without a flinch. What has me climbing walls is that, beyond the obvious, there hasn't been a single event worth getting excited about."

"Well, that's what this celebration is all about," Sue added cheerily. "Tomorrow you're sure to get some interesting results. Fred comes out of the reality cage and you can hit him with that orange. And I bet Paul and Susie will be happy to see their first new toys in six months."

Steve relaxed. "Okay. I admit I am expecting a little change tomorrow. But somehow I'm convinced that they'll make it as dull as possible." He drank a glass of champagne without pausing. "And you—" He pointed a finger accusingly at Sue. "You have every right to be cheerful. As long as those little brats go on without any shocks or confusion your little conscience feels just fine. I'm almost convinced that anything that would cheer me up would turn you sour."

Sue looked suddenly thoughtful. But, "Wait till tomorrow—" was all she said.

"At this point," he muttered, "I'll take whatever I can get."

The next morning all three were at the lab by eight-thirty. A certain air of confidence was also present. Steve gave each of the monkeys a nut, as he did every morning, then turned to his fellow humans. "Where would you suggest we start?"

"Let's transfer Fred out of the reality cage and give him an orange," urged Sue.

Steve opened Fred's cage and called to Fred. The monkey

scampered to him and leaped into Steve's arms. "Okay, boy, you're in for a little fun." Steve transferred him to another cage across the room. Sue had already placed an orange near the door of the cage. Fred looked at the orange and wandered away.

"He's sure it isn't real," whispered Chuck. "It might take a while."

"We'll wait," Steve decided. "He's got nothing else in the cage to play with, so it shouldn't take too long."

Within five minutes Fred had returned to the orange. He sat and looked at it, then tried to pass his hand through the image. The orange was sent rolling across the cage. Fred froze, his eyes fixed on the orange. He looked at his hand and back at the orange. He circled in the cage nervously for a few minutes, then returned to the fruit. He batted it lightly. It rolled. He hit it again, harder, and finally sent it flying across the cage. He jumped about, screaming in excitement. Finally he pounced on the fruit, held it firmly in his hands. He turned it over and over, put it down, picked it up and went through the whole procedure again. He was convinced. The orange was real.

In minutes he had devoured it.

Steve was delighted. From her purse Sue produced a bottle of wine.

"I think we need another celebration," she proclaimed. "A toast to crazy monkeys." All three gathered around the bottle.

After a semblance of order had returned to the scene, Chuck said, "I want to give Paul or Susie a new toy."

"Something that will disappear and then reappear behind Mama," suggested Sue. For the past six months, the watch had always reappeared behind Mama after disappearing.

"Let's give Paul a bell," Steve said. He pulled one down from a shelf and walked over to Paul's cage. "Paul, I've got a toy for you." Steve rang the bell, then opened the door and set it down in the cage.

Paul took it tentatively, but dropped it when it rang. He picked it up again and it rang again. He dropped it. After going through the same routine a half dozen times he was running around the cage ringing the bell loudly.

"Let's hide it now," said Chuck. He retrieved the bell from Paul. "Here it goes, Paul," Chuck announced and hid it under a large inverted bowl. The bowl was routinely used to make objects "disappear." Steve dropped the bell through the trapdoor beneath the bowl and raised another one into the cage behind Mama. Paul contemplated the bowl. Chuck righted the bowl, showing the empty space. Paul sat a minute, then went slowly over to Mama. Seeing the bell, he let out a shout, picked it up and ran about the cage, ringing it merrily.

"He looked behind Mama first." Sue was delighted. "He looked behind Mama!" Quickly they put the bell under the bowl again. This time Paul didn't even pause, but headed straight for Mama.

"He was damn sure of himself that time," Sue said. "There was no question. He knew the reality class and put the bell right into it."

"Another resounding success," announced Chuck.

Steve grinned. "Another paper."

Everything was going better than they had expected. They tried another orange with Fred. He attacked and devoured it immediately. They gave a bell to Susie and her reactions were identical to Paul's.

"Let's try Susie's trick with it," suggested Chuck. Susie's trick had been worked out jointly by Steve and Susie. For the effective operation of the trapdoors the monkeys had to be looking elsewhere or the object had to be covered to prevent the animal's seeing the mechanism in operation. Susie, unlike both Fred and Paul, had figured this out. After a while she had started to cover her eyes in order to make things disappear. Steve had quickly sensed that this was Susie's intent and had whisked away the watch when she covered her eyes. When she uncovered them and didn't see the watch she headed straight for Mama. Over the next two or three days she and Steve had perfected the trick. Now the bell was put over an exposed trapdoor, in plain sight of Susie. But instead of covering her eyes she grabbed it and started to play with it. Steve retrieved it and tried again. On the fourth try Susie cooperated. She sat about two feet from the bell and covered her eyes. Steve dropped it through a trapdoor and transferred it behind Mama. Susie uncovered her eyes, glanced toward where it had been and headed for Mama.

"Enough," Chuck said. "I can't take any more of this." Sue and Steve agreed and the three left for the day. All three were hung over the next morning.

Once again things fell into a monotonous routine. In a month's time Fred was indistinguishable from his control. Anything he saw he assumed was real. There was nothing left to do with him. Paul and Susie delighted in the occasional new toys they received, but they would classify each object as soon as enough time and events had passed to define which reality class it was in. The tedium returned and the next five months crept past unbearably slowly. Only the question of how Susie would react to an object's changing from one reality to another kept Steve's interest alive. Still, the celebration after one year was considerably gayer than the six-month festivities.

> The sun was slowly creeping toward the mountain peaks and now the lichen-covered boulder cast a dark shadow over Steve. For the first time in two hours he dared to shift his position. Coleman reported that the sharpshooters had taken cover in the brush that surrounded the bottom edge of the scree field, but could catch no sight of Susie. If no one could hit Susie by sunset a helicopter would ferry out all personnel and the bombers would move in. The valley had already been evacuated and Steve had heard a low-flying plane broadcasting warnings to any campers or hikers who might still be in the area. Susie was unable to move without giving away her position, but she could easily sit and wait until dark. Steve broke into a cold sweat as his mind touched on the idea of Susie's bringing about a premature sunset. That way lay madness, he thought, and drove the concept from his mind. If he had any guts he'd take his chances with Susie in the hopes that if Susie got him one of the sharpshooters would get her. God only knew what she could do if she set her mind to it. But he just sat and prayed for the tiny movement that would give away her position.
> *Susie, you have to die anyhow. Let me do it—I started it. . . .*
> If only he had stopped his experiments at twelve months.

"Tomorrow we start Phase Three," Steve announced, "and once again our *ennui* will give way to a succession of astonishing events." He wasn't really drunk, but wine plus the excitement had made him a bit lightheaded.

"I do worry about Susie, though," said Sue. "She seems so much brighter than the others and I'm afraid that the shift may really mess her up."

"Oh, get off it, Sue. I thought you were the one who wasn't so sure that objects existed in the first place. And Susie definitely doesn't believe they do. She should be able to cope well with the change. You'll see. Tomorrow morning we'll put the watch under Susie's bowl and it'll just stay there. Want to bet on what happens?"

"I don't know," she muttered. "I just hope that nothing goes wrong." She finished her wine and the three left.

Monday belonged to Susie. Steve showed no signs of being

tense. He was the scientist now and he was careful to make sure that Susie would get no cue from him of the changes to come. He proceeded through the morning ritual, giving Susie a nut from the jar on the counter. She snatched it from his hand and ran over to Mama. Jumping up and down, she dropped it behind Mama—in a small pile of about a dozen nuts.

The smile disappeared from Steve's face. "What the hell?" He whirled to face Sue. "Is this your idea of an apology to Susie—to give her extra nuts?" Sue's face showed incomprehension. "We went over procedure several times—there were to be no changes in today's routine except for the actual shifting of objects from one reality class to another. So you go and give her a dozen nuts the very morning of the switch!"

"I did not. I couldn't have. Chuck got here before me. He'll tell you I didn't."

"I don't see how she could have, Steve. Someone must have come in before any of us—or else last night."

Steve was in a fury. "Well, if this is someone's idea of a joke it's a pretty poor one." All three stood around, troubled and disappointed.

"Look," said Chuck. "We obviously can't change Susie's schedule today." She was sitting in the far corner of her cage, shivering with fright at Steve's violent outburst. "Let's transfer Paul out of the reality cage today and we can switch Susie's schedule to Wednesday. Two days isn't really going to matter and in a month you'll hardly remember what happened."

"Okay," muttered Steve. "But first I put up a big NO GODDAM FEEDING THE MONKEYS sign. And remind me to make sure that those nuts get moved from Susie's cage. They're right behind Mama, over the loading platform. Whoever put the nuts there had a real sense of humor."

Everything went smoothly until Steve returned from lunch the next afternoon. He was getting over his anger and had again become excited about Susie's switch, set for the next morning. As he wandered past Susie's cage he saw a fresh pile of nuts behind Mama.

He dragged Chuck out of the lab and into the hall.

"Have you been here all afternoon?" he asked. "Since I left for lunch?" The anger in his voice was obvious.

"Essentially. Why?"

"What do you mean, 'essentially'?"

"I mean yes, except that I went downstairs for a coke around twelve-thirty. What's going on around here?"

"Did you give Susie any nuts?" Steve snarled through clenched teeth.

"Of course not."

Steve was in a rage. "There's a new stack of nuts on the trapdoor behind Mama. And if I find the funnyman who's pulling this, I'll kill him! Tonight those nuts go home with me and I'll bring two in every day." He turned to leave. "I'll be back later. If I try to work in this mood I'll drive Susie up a wall. But I'm still changing her over tomorrow morning."

When he came back that afternoon he still couldn't concentrate constructively. People didn't mess up other people's experiments for a joke. Had he somehow managed to offend someone enough to have called down this kind of vengance on himself?

"Steve," Chuck called. "Pay attention to what you're doing."

Steve returned to his senses and realized that Suzie had been covering her eyes, trying to make the rattle disappear. As she repeated the gesture he dropped the toy through the trapdoor.

"Why don't you call it a day?" Chuck suggested. "It would be a real shame if you messed up badly enough for us to have to postpone the transfer again."

Steve nodded. He was tired and discouraged. He trudged out of the lab and took an elevator to the lobby. He was almost out of the building when he realized that he had forgotten the nuts.

In a foul humor he rode back upstairs and slammed into the lab. Chuck was closing the door to Susie's cage.

"You must really be out of it, Steve," chided Chuck. "You left the rattle in Susie's cage. If I hadn't heard her playing with it she would have had it with her all night." The rule that non-real toys should not stay in the cages when the animals were alone was strict.

"How could I have?" insisted Steve. "I dropped it out just before I left."

"Well, no one else has been here since you left, Steve. I'd try to get some extra sleep tonight if I were you. A sleeping pill couldn't hurt any. You're starting to look bad." Steve grunted in irritation and headed for the door. "Don't forget the nuts!" called Chuck. Steve snatched the jar from the bench and stomped out.

Steve was up at six-thirty the next morning. His night had been filled with nightmares featuring Susie and nuts and watches and rattles, appearing and disappearing. He finally awoke in a cold sweat after he himself had disappeared from his last dream. He was tired and groggy and wanted nothing more than to abandon the whole project. Only the realization that in twelve hours the switch would be completed kept him going. Then he could look forward to another six months of luxurious boredom.

He joined Sue for breakfast at eight. She was alert and excited by the day's plans. But she was visibly shaken by Steve's apparent condition. He told her about the nuts and rattle, and his dreams of the night before. A grin crept across her face.

"I'm sorry, Steve—it's just that we've come full circle." She couldn't wipe the smile off her face. "You got this whole scheme from me when I doubted the reality of certain interpretations of matter and phenomena—and I'm almost convinced now you're not so sure yourself that things are what they seem—or as they sometimes are represented to be."

"That's stupid," he growled.

"Come on," she said, rising. "Let's get down to the lab. We wouldn't want Chuck to start without us, would we?"

She showed him a huge pout and Steve had to smile despite himself.

Chuck was waiting when they reached the lab and he was eager to get started. Steve gave Susie her nut and chatted inanely with her for a couple of minutes. Then he gave Susie the watch to play with. As always, Susie accepted it readily. She danced around the cage, pausing now and then to listen to its ticking. After a few minutes Steve wrestled it away from her and slipped it under the bowl. This time it would stay there. In more than a thousand trials during the past year Susie had always seen it disappear and reappear behind Mama. This time it would not.

As always, Susie ran to the surrogate Mama and reached for the watch. It wasn't there. Susie froze. She sat motionless for exactly thirty seconds and then started screaming wildly. Steve showed Susie the watch under the bowl and then covered it again. She stared at the bowl for long seconds and then slowly lifted her hands to cover her eyes.

"She's trying to make it disappear," whispered Sue. "She wants it to disappear. Oh, God—she will go mad this time."

Susie uncovered her eyes, walked cautiously to Mama, and peered behind the dummy parent. Immediately she started chattering happily. She reached behind Mama. In an instant she had the watch in her hand.

For a long time Steve, Sue, and Chuck simply stared at Susie and the watch. No one said a word. No one moved. What was there to say? Without breaking the silence Steve examined the cage. The trapdoors were all wired properly. The releases were in position. The loading platforms were all empty and the receptacle beneath the bowl was empty. He opened the door to the cage and lifted the bowl. There was nothing there. Three blank faces stared at the bowl.

Steve turned to the others. "Have I gone crazy? Did either of you see it? It disappeared. Didn't it?" His voice verged on hysteria.

Sue nodded. "Yes—and then it reappeared behind Mama. We all saw it."

"No!" shouted Chuck. "Someone's pulling some sort of a stunt." He didn't sound at all confident of his explanation. "What's the matter with us? It's obviously some sort of a joke. Look out." He pushed past Steve and examined the wires operating the trapdoors and loading platforms. "Everything seems okay," he muttered, but then disconnected the trapdoors and loading platforms. "This reality bit is going to all of our heads." He retrieved the watch from Susie and placed it under the bowl. "Now let's see this work!"

He felt foolish. Whoever had rigged this gag would never let them forget their reactions. All three were in position to look behind Mama as Susie covered her eyes. Instantly the watch appeared behind Mama.

"This is insane." Steve jammed his hands deep into his pockets. "This just isn't real." He paced back and forth, trying to regain his self-control. "There is a nice rational explanation for all of this. And we're going to find it."

Without saying a word Sue retrieved the watch from Susie. The others stared as she placed the watch on top of the inverted bowl, in plain sight. Susie immediately raised her hands and covered her eyes. A split second later the watch vanished, only to reappear simultaneously behind Mama.

"Oh, my God," whispered Chuck. "Steve—the nuts. They appeared behind the surrogate mother. Just like the watch."

Steve stared straight ahead. "Yes." His voice was controlled. "And I know I didn't leave the rattle in there last night."

Sue turned to Steve. "Susie did it, didn't she? She made her reality work."

Steve started to laugh. "Well, I guess it isn't morning yet. This has got to be just another one of those nightmares I was having last night."

Sue said, "Let's break." She turned to Chuck. "Let's go somewhere else—do something else. I don't want to stay here any longer. Not just now."

"No," said Chuck. "I want to try a couple of things first. Give me the orange." Sue looked at him blankly. "I want to see if it's real to Susie." Susie had never experienced a real orange. Only a hologram and a smell. He took the orange and put it in Susie's cage by the door. All three gazed in silence.

At first Susie simply ignored it. She had seen the holograms many times and had no reason to suspect that this was any different. After a few minutes Steve reached in and gave the orange a shove. He took the watch from the cage and closed the door. Susie studied the orange intently. She had never seen a hologram roll, so this was definitely a novelty. She approached the orange, sat a foot away from it, considering what to do. Finally she reached out an arm and swatted at it. Her hand went right through the orange.

"Let's get out of here," Chuck urged.

"I thought you wanted to test two things," Sue said. She stared at the cage in a trance.

"Forget it," said Chuck. "Right now I want to test a pitcher of beer." The three headed for the door. The watch was still clutched in Steve's right hand. As he followed the others out he pulled the door shut behind him. As it closed he felt the watch vanish from his hand. He hurried away.

They were waiting for him at the elevators. "You can stay here if you want," he said, without slowing down. "I'm taking the stairs." The others followed him.

Their conversation was restricted to the weather as they drank their first pitcher of beer. They were halfway through the second when Chuck violated the unspoken taboo. His face was tense.

"I think I believe it," he said, and suddenly the clamp that had been holding all three silent was released. "It doesn't make any sense and it can't be and it's crazy—but I believe it. Something in the back of my brain keeps saying 'She did it, so what?' And I have no answer."

"I know," said Steve. "The same thoughts have been going through my head. 'Why not?' my head keeps asking. And I don't know why not. I never really could believe in relativity either. I mean that Sue here could take off in a starship, eat lunch, take a shower, land, get off—and I'd be eighty years old. But I accept it anyhow, because I've been told it's true. Well, this is just the opposite. All my training, all my intellect says, 'You're hallucinating, dreaming, undergoing mass hypnosis—' Things like that. But this time something keeps asking, 'Why not?' And I can't answer."

"You know," Sue suggested, "in a way we have gone crazy. I mean I don't think we have, but if what we saw did actually happen—then maybe all those other people who have been locked up for being crazy aren't—at least some of them. I mean, there's one reality that's accepted—and if you perceive or believe in any other you're crazy. And it doesn't matter whether you saw it because you were on drugs or because it really is like that. You're just as crazy in the eyes of the world." She looked from Steve to Chuck and then down at her empty glass. "It's easier," she whispered. "It's easier if you don't try to fight the question of your sanity. Either we are crazy—or we don't know what the word means any more." She had nothing more to say.

"Okay," argued Chuck, "maybe we are crazy—and maybe Susie did all those things we saw her do. I'm not sure which. But if she did do what we saw her do—how could she? I mean, a lot of people have watched a lot of monkeys do a lot of things and I've never heard of this before. If we did see what we think we saw there still has to be a logical explanation for it. It's not going to bring everything crumbling down around us—any more than when people found out that energy could be changed to matter. Forty years ago no one would have believed it possible—but when the transformation proved out it didn't destroy the rest of our structures. We just had to modify them a bit."

"There's no comparison," objected Steve. "If some physicist had given a completely incomprehensible lecture and then showed us a machine that could do what Susie did—we'd have no trouble accepting it. Even if we couldn't understand the explanation, the knowledge that an explanation existed would be all that we'd need. The problem is that we have no explanation for what we just saw. It contradicts everything we've been taught and everything our senses have told us. We can't fit it in anywhere. When you stop to think about it, an aborigine would have more trouble dealing with New York City than we have had with this." Some of the shock was slipping from Steve's mind. He was slowly constructing a web of support for his wounded reality.

"But why did it happen now?" insisted Chuck. "Why us?"

"That's easy," answered Sue. A picture had slowly been forming in her mind, too, but she was afraid of Steve's reaction to it. He wasn't going to like it. "We taught her. Steve, you always said that you would never go into an experiment unwilling to accept any particular results, but that's exactly what you've done.

"What have we been doing for the past year? We asked the question, 'What happens when you teach a monkey from infancy that reality is different from what we know it to be? What happens if you convince the monkey that some objects are insubstantial and others can arbitrarily disappear?' Well, we asked the question and we've gotten our answer. The reality they are taught becomes their reality. I don't mean that they believe what is false—I mean that what is true for them is different from what is true for us. We've all been taught one reality, so we all believe it and it is real for us. Our experiment has never been done before."

"That's not actually correct," Chuck put in. "In ancient times people believed in witches, miracles, stuff like that—and there appeared to be a lot to support their convictions. Whenever quack cures and stories about witches and miracles are discredited, the so-called mysteries seem to stop happening. We have assumed that they never did happen but we don't really know that. We just figured that what we found to be true after we got there was true before. But when you stop to think about it, that sure leaves a lot of unexplained stories. We've just never had anything else to do with the data—so we chucked it out."

"But it still doesn't work," argued Steve. "What about our reality? Maybe Susie expected the watch to disappear and the orange to be insubstantial—but I'll be damned if we did. We expected them both to be just what they always have been for us. How come her reality worked and ours didn't? There were three of us, you know."

"That's not fair," replied Sue. "We don't really have that firm a grip on any particular reality. We've all accepted relativity and the wave theory of matter. Steve, you said minutes ago that if some scientist said a fact was reasonable you'd have no trouble accepting it. Well, you'd have a hell of a time convincing Susie. People give up their realities too easily.

"The three of us are already accepting what happened. We've got no faith in our realities. But Susie's never lost her faith—so hers was just that much stronger. I don't think we ever had much chance against her. That's why crazy people get locked up. The whole purpose of therapy is to convince the person that his or her reality is not real. You know that what I'm saying is almost exactly what a shrink would say. He'd just insist that the reality that the crazy person saw didn't exist. That's the only difference."

"Now that's what I call a minor difference," Steve muttered. 'So what do we do—write it up and submit it? That minor difference might just be major enough to get us all locked up for a good long while. We may be convinced—but there are a few billion people out there who would not."

"I'm not sure," Sue protested. "I think you'll find a lot more support than you could imagine."

"Well, I still want to know where we go from here." Steve felt better, but the thought of trying to convince someone else of what he, Sue, and Chuck thought they had seen happen brought back all of his fears and doubts.

"Convince other people," said Chuck. "Professor Coleman's head of psychology. Let's talk to him. But first we'd better show him."

"Yes—don't tell him what's going to happen," warned Sue. "I think he's more sure of his reality than all of us and Susie put together. If he knows what we're expecting, I'm not sure that he couldn't stop her."

"Besides," said Chuck. "I'd feel better if someone else saw it, too."

"Three more nervous, secretive people I've never seen." Coleman was both irritated and interested. "But it's clear that you're going to be insistent, so let's see what this is all about." Steve had practically dragged the short, stocky Coleman from his office, much to the astonishment of his staff. When they reached the lab they found the door ajar and Susie's cage empty. A neat stretch of bars was missing.

Coleman pushed past Steve to examine the cage.

"Strange," he muttered. "Metal doesn't look like it's been cut. There are no marks at all. How was it done?" He turned to Steve. "I gather this isn't what you intended to show me?"

All three started talking at once. In a matter of minutes Coleman was seriously considering calling for three straitjackets.

Steve took over.

"So you see, Dr. Coleman, Susie must have made the bars disappear, too," he finished. "I know this is going to be hard to—"

The blare of a fire alarm interrupted him.

"There's no test scheduled for today," muttered Coleman. He grabbed a phone and called his office. "They don't know anything about it," he reported. "Let's go."

They took the stairs to the first floor and headed for the front door. As they passed a corridor, they saw a crowd gathered at its end. Someone saw Professor Coleman and hailed him.

Dr. Lewis Pearson, a younger member of the psychology department faculty, waved from the edge of the crowd and was obviously quite upset. Coleman started down the hall at a jog.

Steve, Sue, and Chuck followed him. The crowd parted to let them through.

They found themselves staring at the outer wall of the building. Or, rather, out through the wall. A circle three feet in diameter and some six inches above the floor had been cut out of the wall. It was a perfectly clean hole and it looked disturbingly familiar to the four.

Pearson was speaking hurriedly to Coleman: ". . . and it appears that that's why she pulled the alarm. She's completely incoherent, but she sticks to her story. She says the monkey just covered its eyes and the hole appeared."

"I've called the hospital for an ambulance, but we still have this crazy hole to deal with. Look at it. The edges are clean. How could anyone make a hole like this and not be noticed?" Pearson looked at Coleman for an answer.

"Where's the girl?" asked Coleman. "I think I'd better talk to her."

"She's in your office—the secretaries are taking care of her."

Coleman wordlessly took off for his office, Steve, Sue, and Chuck still a part of his entourage.

"You know she's telling the truth, Coleman, don't you?" Steve said. "We've got to get Susie back. God only knows what she may do if she gets scared."

"When I need your advice I'll ask for it." Coleman spoke over his shoulder as he strode. "If you want to handle the fire department and the police and whatever else—they're yours. But as regards this poor woman, I'm at least temporarily in charge."

Steve walked with him in silence.

They found the girl sitting between two comforting secretaries in Coleman's office. Tears were streaming down her cheeks, and she looked scared.

"I swear I saw it," she said. "I'm not crazy. A monkey just made the hole appear."

Coleman sent the other women away. "We know," he said quietly. "The monkey escaped from one of our labs and we're looking for her. Do you know which way she went after she got out?"

Coleman sounded and looked as if he only half believed his own words.

"Don't play games with me," the girl whispered. "I saw it, I really did—"

Sue came forward and put an arm around the girl.

"Dr. Coleman's not playing games," she said. "He's just having a hard time believing what's happened. So am I. You're not crazy. Not at all. Really."

The girl started to whimper quietly.

"Come on," said Coleman. "We can leave her with my staff. We've got to find that damn monkey of yours."

The fire trucks arrived. Coleman spoke to the fire chief and asked to use the car radio.

"Put me in touch with Chief Heninger." Coleman was contacting the police chief. "Chief Heninger? This is Dr. Coleman, I'm head of the psychology department at the university. I'm afraid we're going to need your help."

"What seems to be the problem?"

Coleman hesitated. This would have to be phrased carefully. "I can't explain all the details, I'm afraid. The project is classified. Government security. We've been conducting some very important experiments with a group of monkeys and one of them has escaped. We need your help to find her and get her back."

"Have you tried the humane society, Dr. Coleman? They're animal exp—"

"You don't understand," Coleman snapped. "Look, Heninger, this monkey is dangerous. It may be more dangerous at this moment than any other living creature. I can't begin to tell you the damage it could cause if it's not caught. This is an emergency and a big one. Get the humane society, too, but we need every man you've got." Coleman paused for a second. "I'll take full responsibility if there's any problem about your committing so many men to it, but we need literally everything you've got. This monkey could wipe out the whole city!"

Quiet static hummed over the radio and Heninger's breathing could be heard in the background.

"What do you mean dangerous?" he finally asked. "This monkey got some kind of disease? Or does—"

Steve grabbed the microphone from Coleman and signaled to the others to be quiet. He began talking in a deep voice, hoping he remembered lines from an amateur theatrical he had appeared in during his undergraduate days. This was a dangerous gambit, he

301

knew, but it was necessary. "Heninger? Just shut up a second. This is Major Pomeroy, Army—CIA liaison from this district." Some of it was coming back to him, but he was also improvising nicely. His confidence grew. "I'm slapping a complete security blanket on this affair right now. That's official. I don't want you talking to any reporters or anyone else about this. You just tell them you're looking for a missing monkey. Don't say a word more. Understand?"

Heninger sounded impressed. "Yes, Major. I understand."

"Good. Are these lines secured?"

"Secured, sir?" Heninger was not at all sure of what was going on.

"Secured. Are they scrambled? Or can just anyone with a radio pick this up?" Steve was beginning to enjoy reliving the old role—these last lines were straight out of that long-ago play.

"No, sir, they're not. We're not set up for anything like that."

Steve turned to Coleman and spoke for Heninger's benefit. "Well, Professor, give him any instructions you can, but remember that the lines are not secured." He handed the microphone back to Coleman and sank back into his seat. He found himself at once exhilarated and scared, but evidently the ploy had worked.

He listed to Coleman.

"Just put every man you have on it. We've got to get her back, and fast." Coleman paused. "And listen, Chief, it's a really strange monkey. When you catch her, tell your men to tie her hands behind her back." He spoke slowly. "And if it looks as if she were going to cover her eyes, shoot her—fast. And shoot to kill."

He looked away from Steve. The decision had been his to make and he had made it.

Silence fell at the other end of the line before Heninger asked, "Is that all, Dr. Coleman?"

"Yes, that's all I can think of now." Coleman sounded exhausted and Steve realized the man had been made to act forcefully out of character. "I'll keep in touch. If you'd tell us the location of any sightings of her, I'd appreciate it."

"Very good, sir. I'll send out the alert right away."

Ten minutes later the call came through on the fire chief's radio. "We've just received a call about a monkey spotted at Morheim and Blake. Car Seventeen is almost there and on its way. We'll keep you informed."

"Right," Steve answered for Coleman. "We're also on our way."

They took off for the area. It would take several minutes to get there.

They weren't halfway there when Heninger called back. He was clearly upset. "Coleman, what the hell kind of monkey is that?"

"What seems to be the problem, Heninger?" asked Steve.

"How the hell should I know? Nelson in Car Seventeen just called in and he's completely incoherent. Keeps saying something about his partner having disappeared while trying to catch that monkey. I'm trying to find out where he went to, but Nelson keeps saying that he just disappeared. He sounded crazy, Coleman, and I want to know what's going on."

Steve took the mike. "Heninger, this is Pomeroy. I thought I told you that this could not be discussed on unsecured lines. You're just going to have to believe that what you're doing is right. We're approaching Morheim and Blake now. Have there been any more sightings?"

"No," reported Heninger glumly. "But my men are fanning out. If the monkey keeps going in the direction she was first heading, she'll be getting into the mountains pretty soon."

The fire chief's car reached Morheim and Blake as Nelson was being taken into another prowl car by fellow cops. As they drove off he looked completely stunned.

"It looks like Susie's taken her first casualty," commented Chuck.

No one answered.

"Coleman, are you there?" It was Heninger.

"I'm here. What do you want?"

"We've lost contact with Car Twelve. We're having all our men on the lookout for it, so that means you, too. Can that monkey. . . . Hold it." A pause came while Heninger talked to someone else. "Coleman, they've found our car at Gasser and Blake." Steve gestured and the fire chief's car turned and headed down Blake. It was five blocks to Gasser. Heninger reported intermittently. "It's sitting in the middle of the street . . . the men inside aren't moving . . . they look like they're frozen in place. I'm getting this from Car Eight, they're sending a man over to Car Twelve. Can't you tell me anything about what we're up against?" There was a pleading tone in Heninger's voice. But they had reached Gasser, and Steve got out of the car, followed by Chuck.

Chuck realized what had happened before anyone. "The holograms," he whispered.

The policeman had just reached Car Twelve. "Wait!" called

Steve, but he was too late. The man had reached for the handle of the car door and had fallen right through the door, through both of the car's occupants and the floor of the car to land heavily on the street below. He started to get up, saw himself merged with the driver and fainted. His partner, who had watched the whole affair from Car Eight, started babbling hysterically into his radio.

Steve reached into the fire chief's car for the mike and called Heninger.

"Listen, Heninger," he said, "I'm afraid things are getting out of hand. I want to change plans—"

"You're damn right they're out of hand!" shouted Heninger. "I just got a call from Coleman's office that Parker, the man from Car Seventeen who disappeared, showed up in one of Coleman's monkey cages. He's stark raving mad. What in God's name is going on? That's five miles from where he disappeared—"

"Heninger, shut up and listen," Steve barked. "Pull your men back a bit. I don't want them to try to capture the monkey. Just follow it at a distance and keep us informed of its whereabouts. We'll try to take it ourselves."

"That's fine with me," retorted Heninger. "It's definitely heading for the mountains."

"Heninger, we're going to want a megaphone and portable two-way radio when we catch up with her," Steve said. He paused for a moment. "And a rifle."

The fire chief's car caught up with Susie in a clearing just outside the city limits. She was heading for the mountains. Four police cars sat at the edge of the field, some two hundred yards from Susie. They had gotten a vague, illogical story about the Car Twelve affair and wanted nothing to do with the monkey. The police gave Steve the megaphone, radio, and a carbine. He had little idea of exactly what he was going to do, but the responsibility was now his. Coleman was a fine administrator, but Susie was Steve's project and would remain so until this issue was settled.

One way or the other, he thought. He took off at a jog after Susie.

"Steve, wait for me," called Sue, running up to him. "I'm coming, too."

Steve said, "You're not coming. First of all, I'd have to worry about you, too. Then—two people are much more likely to panic

Susie. Finally—you'll slow me down. I have no idea how fast she's going to be moving."

He started off again before she could argue and Chuck led her back to the car.

For an hour or so Steve simply followed Susie at a distance. She was aware of his presence, but did nothing about it. She moved slowly, being unsure of the world. Until today her whole life had been spent in a cage and now she had much to cope with.

It would not make the situation any easier, Steve realized, if he startled her now. She would be upset until she began to get accustomed to the vaster world. He had tried twice to call her by megaphone. Each time Susie had only responded by speeding up her pace. He followed her into the mountains for another hour and tried the megaphone again.

"Susie, come here, Susie. It's me, Steve, I've got some nuts for you." They were on the scree field now and Susie's size and agility were giving her greater and greater advantage over Steve. He was losing ground fast.

It was then that he had decided he would have to shoot. He pretended that he would be shooting to wound, but he was far from an expert marksman and she was a good hundred and fifty feet away. The carbine turned out to be more powerful than he had expected and his shot hit the boulders twenty feet above and beyond her. Susie got the message fast. She spun around, screaming angrily, looking for Steve. But he was behind a large lichen-covered boulder, out of her sight. The next thing he knew the mountainside was coming down on top of him.

He was truly frightened now, for the first time in his memory. He had never really considered that his life was at stake in this venture. Losing now would make an even worse ending for his thesis than what had already happened.

It was getting dark and neither Steve nor any of the sharpshooters had seen so much as a hint of Susie. The sun was sinking rapidly. In another fifteen minutes it would be behind the mountains and the helicopter would be coming in to evacuate the area.

The radio came alive with Sue's voice. "Steve, don't do anything until I get there. They're flying me in now. I can stop Susie. The whole situation has changed." Her voice was strained. "I'll be there in five minutes. Tell those army people to hold their fire while I try."

The connection was broken and Steve could already hear the approaching helicopter. He relayed her message to the other hunters just as the aircraft appeared over the ridge. In another minute it was hovering ten feet off the ground and Sue scampered down a rope ladder. The helicopter was gone in an instant, climbing at full thrust.

Steve pointed to the general area where he knew Susie had to be. "Be careful," he whispered.

Sue started slowly toward the hidden monkey.

"Susie, Susie—it's all right, Susie. Come on out, Susie—it's me." She held her hands out in front of her. "I've got some nuts for you." There was a slight movement about fifty feet down the scree field to her right. Sue came to within ten feet of where Susie was hidden. She stopped. "Good Susie, everything's going to be all right, Susie. Here are some nuts." She threw the nuts just to one side of Susie's hiding place. After a moment Susie appeared. Cautiously, she took a nut and ate it. Her nervousness seemed to abate when she saw no one else and she started into the rest of the nuts, keeping one eye on Sue.

Slowly Sue raised her hands from her sides up to her lips. "Goodbye, Susie. Maybe we'll meet again," she whispered and slowly covered her eyes.

Susie was gone.

rat in the skull

Rog Phillips

In the following story with the menacing title, we come face to face with an explosive experiment which probably has never been attempted and never will be done. The experiment delves into some questions which psychologists are very much interested in, as well as some philosophical questions about the soul which most psychologists leave to their colleagues in philosophy and religion. One might even say that the story attempts to answer the question, "When is a rat not a rat?" It is a gripping yarn dramatizing how an experimenter can create and perform an experiment which so intensely involves him that the rest of his life must take a back seat to it. It would be difficult to find a real-life experimenter who would make the degree of sacrifice to his experiment that Dr. MacNare makes. Nevertheless, his fundamental dedication to the pursuit of knowledge in psychology through the experimental method is shared by many psychologists.

The story appears in this section on learning and cognition because it raises and illustrates some interesting and important ideas and concepts in both areas. In the area of learning it illustrates the importance of "feedback," a concept whose practical applications are among the most important in all of psychology. In the area of cognition, it raises the controversial issue of the relationship between thinking and language, as well as the issue of whether animals can use language. Finally, the story raises important ethical issues relating to experimentation with rats and other animals. Was Dr. MacNare's use of his rat ethical? Should the experiment have been carried out?

Dr. MacNare calls his experiment "An Experimental Approach to the Psychological Phenomena of Verification." Further into the story he explains: "Animals—man included—can only do by observing the results. When you move a finger . . . your eyes and sense of touch bring you the information that your finger moved." MacNare calls this process "verification," but the more commonly used term is "feedback." Information fed back visually or by sound is called "external feedback," while that fed back by the sense of touch, as well as from processes within the body is called "internal feedback." Feedback is used by the individual to control his behavior by allowing him to verify what he is doing—should he continue along the same course or should he try something new.

MacNare uses this principle in an unusual way which makes his experiment fascinating. He is going to manipulate the feedback to his rat, making it different from the feedback normally received. When the rat moves one of its feet, instead of giving it visual feedback associated with regular movement, he will give it the auditory feedback normally associated by humans with making sounds. By moving its foot the rat will thus produce artificial human sounds, and hopefully it will learn to associate different foot movements with different sounds. By learning to control vocal production of the sounds of human speech called phonemes, the rat will first learn to speak like a human and then learn to think like a human. This is an ambitious experimental scheme even for science fiction.

The most exciting use of feedback in the real world is biofeedback. Biofeedback, using electronic apparatus, amplifies feedback of internal biological processes. With increased feedback, people have learned to control processes they never could before. People with high blood pressure have learned to reduce it, people with heart problems have learned to alter their heartbeat, and people with migraine headaches have learned to control them. Through the power of feedback, biological processes once thought to be involuntary are now under voluntary control.

The story brings together two important cognitive processes: language and thinking. Human beings use words to symbolize and think about the world around them. Words used as concepts label and relate objects or phenomena which have common characteristics. MacNare believes that with the power to produce words his rat will also acquire the power to conceptualize and reason. His critics contend that even with the power to artificially produce words, the rat does not have the neural brain capacity to conceptualize and reason. Present research supports these critics when considering lower animals like the rat, but they can no longer say that *only* human beings can use language. Two chimpanzees, Washoe and Sarah, have been taught to use human language, although not vocally. Washoe was taught to use sign language like that used by the deaf, while Sarah was taught to manipulate symbols made of colored plastic forms. Both chimps are able to combine their words into sentences, although only simple ones.

The relationship between thought and language is a complex and controversial question. Some experts like Whorf say that the structure of language determines patterns of thinking. Thus a German will think different patterns than a Frenchman because the structure of their languages pushes their thoughts in different directions. Others like Piaget believe that children cannot use words in certain conceptual ways until they develop the thinking capacity to do so. For Skinner both thought and language basically still are behavior, and thus follow behavioral principles. They are best understood and analyzed by looking at how they operate on the environment.

Finally, the story raises issues about the ethics of experimentation. MacNare cannot do his experiment at the university because the college president and trustees believe that it is unethical. Specifically, they feel that MacNare's treatment of the rat and his manipulation of the rat's feedback mechanisms will so alter the rat's experience that the rat will no longer function and thus no longer really be a rat. There is a moral, almost religious, concern that MacNare is upsetting the natural order of things. Although his particular experiment involves an extreme procedure, in general, experimental animals do not live natural lives, and for all intents and purposes they have developed into new and different breeds than their brothers living free. Concern for the treatment of animals as well as people in experiments remains a difficult ethical issue, and each case must be considered on an individual basis. In all cases, the researcher must weigh the potential harm to subjects against the probability of benefit for the society from the additional knowledge that his experiment might uncover. Many experiments can never and will never be done because of these ethical considerations. The experiment in this story just might be one of them.

RAT IN THE SKULL   *Rog Phillips*

Dr. Joseph MacNare was not the sort of person one would expect him to be in the light of what happened. Indeed, it is safe to say that until the summer of 1955 he was more "normal," better adjusted, than the average college professor. And we have every reason to believe that he remained so, in spite of having stepped out of his chosen field.

At the age of thirty-four, he had to his credit a college textbook on advanced calculus, an introductory physics, and seventy-two papers that had appeared in various journals, copies of which were in neat order in a special section of the bookcase in his office at the university, and duplicate copies of which were in equally neat order in his office at home. None of these were in the field of psychology, the field in which he was shortly to become famous—or infamous. But anyone who studies the published writings of Dr. MacNare must inevitably conclude that he was a competent, responsible scientist, and a firm believer in institutional research, research by teams, rather than in private research and go-it-alone secrecy, the course he eventually followed.

In fact, there is every reason to believe he followed this course with the greatest of reluctance, aware of its pitfalls, and that he took every precaution that was humanly possible.

Certainly, on that day in late August, 1955, at the little cabin on the Russian River, a hundred miles upstate from the university, when Dr. MacNare completed his paper on *"An Experimental Approach to the Psychological Phenomena of Verification,"* he had no slightest thought of "going it alone."

It was mid-afternoon. His wife, Alice, was dozing on the small dock that stretched out into the water, her slim figure tanned a smooth brown that was just a shade lighter than her hair. Their eight-year-old son, Paul, was fifty yards upstream playing with some other boys, their shouts the only sound except for the whisper of rushing water and the sound of wind in the trees.

Dr. MacNare, in swim trunks, his lean muscular body hardly tanned at all, emerged from the cabin and came out on the dock.

"Wake up, Alice," he said, nudging her with his foot. "You have a husband again."

"Rat in the Skull" by Rog Phillips, published in *If: Words of Science Fiction.* Copyright © 1958 by Quinn Publishing Co., Inc. Reprinted by permission of the author and the author's agent, Forrest J. Ackerman.

"Well, it's about time," Alice said, turning over on her back and looking up at him, smiling in answer to his happy grin.

He stepped over her and went out on the diving board, leaping up and down on it, higher and higher each time, in smooth coordination, then went into a one and a half gainer, his body cutting into the water with a minimum of splash.

His head broke the surface. He looked up at his wife, and laughed in the sheer pleasure of being alive. A few swift strokes brought him to the foot of the ladder. He climbed, dripping water, to the dock, then sat down by his wife.

"Yep, it's done," he said. "How many days of our vacation left? Two? That's time enough for me to get a little tan. Might as well make the most of it. I'm going to be working harder this winter than I ever did in my life."

"But I thought you said your paper was done!"

"It is. But that's only the beginning. Instead of sending it in for publication, I'm going to submit it to the directors, with a request for facilities and personnel to conduct a line of research based on pages twenty-seven to thirty-two of the paper."

"And you think they'll grant your request?"

"There's no question about it," Dr. MacNare said, smiling confidently. "It's the most important line of research ever opened up to experimental psychology. They'll be forced to grant my request. It will put the university on the map!"

Alice laughed, and sat up and kissed him.

"Maybe they won't agree with you," she said. "Is it all right for me to read the paper?"

"I wish you would," he said. "Where's that son of mine? Upstream?" He leaped to his feet and went to the diving board again.

"Better walk along the bank, Joe. The stream is too swift."

"Nonsense!" Dr. MacNare said.

He made a long shallow dive, then began swimming in a powerful crawl that took him upstream slowly. Alice stood on the dock watching him until he was lost to sight around the bend, then went into the cabin. The completed paper lay beside the typewriter.

Alice had her doubts. "I'm not so sure the board will approve of this," she said. Dr. MacNare, somewhat exasperated, said, "What makes you think that? Pavlov experimented with his dog, physiological experiments with rats, rabbits, and other animals go on all the time. There's nothing cruel about it."

"Just the same . . ." Alice said. So Dr. MacNare cautiously resisted the impulse to talk about his paper with his fellow professors and his most intelligent students. Instead, he merely turned his paper in to the board at the earliest opportunity and kept silent, waiting for their decision.

He hadn't long to wait. On the last Friday of September he received a note requesting his presence in the board room at three o'clock on Monday. He rushed home after his last class and told Alice about it.

"Let's hope their decision is favorable," she said.

"It has to be," Dr. MacNare answered with conviction.

He spent the week-end making plans. "They'll probably assign me a machinist and a couple of electronics experts from the hill," he told Alice. "I can use graduate students for work with the animals. I hope they give me Dr. Munitz from Psych as a consultant, because I like him much better than Veerhof. By early spring we should have things rolling."

Monday at three o'clock on the dot, Dr. MacNare knocked on the door of the board room, and entered. He was not unfamiliar with it, nor with the faces around the massive walnut conference table. Always before he had known what to expect—a brief commendation for the revisions in his textbook on calculus for its fifth printing, a nice speech from the president about his good work as a prelude to a salary raise—quiet, expected things. Nothing unanticipated had ever happened here.

Now, as he entered, he sensed a difference. All eyes were fixed on him, but not with admiration or friendliness. They were fixed more in the manner of a restaurateur watching the approach of a cockroach along the surface of the counter.

Suddenly the room seemed hot and stuffy. The confidence in Dr. MacNare's expression evaporated. He glanced back toward the door as though wishing to escape.

"So it's *you!*" the president said, setting the tone of what followed.

"This is *yours?*" the president added, picking up the neatly typed manuscript, glancing at it, and dropping it back on the table as though it were something unclean.

Dr. MacNare nodded, and cleared his throat anxiously to say yes, but didn't get the chance.

"We—all of us—are amazed and shocked," the president said. "Of course, we understand that psychology is not your field, and you probably were thinking only from the mathematical viewpoint. We are agreed on that. What you propose, though . . ." He shook his head slowly. "It's not only out of the question, but I'm afraid I'm going to have to request that you forget the whole thing—put this paper where no one can see it, preferably destroy it. I'm sorry, Dr. MacNare, but the university simply cannot afford to be associated with such a thing even remotely. I'll put it bluntly because I feel strongly about it, as do the other members of the Board. *If this paper is published or in any way comes to light, we will be forced to request your resignation from the faculty.*"

"But why?" Dr. MacNare asked in complete bewilderment.

"Why?" another board member exploded, slapping the table. "It's the most inhuman thing I ever heard of, strapping a newborn animal onto some kind of frame and tying its legs to control levers, with the intention of never letting it free. The most fiendish and inhuman torture imaginable! If you didn't have such an outstanding record I would be for demanding your resignation at once."

"But that's not true!" Dr. MacNare said. "It's not torture! Not in any way! Didn't you read the paper? Didn't you understand that—"

"I read it," the man said. "We all read it. Every word."

"Then you should have understood—" Dr. MacNare said.

"We read it," the man repeated, "and we discussed some aspects of it with Dr. Veerhof without bringing your paper into it, nor your name."

"Oh," Dr. MacNare said. "Veerhof . . ."

"He says experiments, very careful experiments, have already been conducted along the lines of getting an animal to understand a symbol system and it can't be done. The nerve paths aren't there. Your line of research, besides being inhumanly cruel, would accomplish nothing."

"Oh," Dr. MacNare said, his eyes flashing. "So you know all about the results of an experiment in an untried field without performing the experiments!"

"According to Dr. Veerhof that field is not untried but rather well explored," the board members said. "Giving an animal the means to make vocal sounds would not enable it to form a symbol system."

"I disagree," Dr. MacNare said, seething. "My studies indicate clearly—"

"I think," the president said with a firmness that demanded the floor, "our position has been made very clear, Dr. MacNare. The matter is now closed. Permanently. I hope you will have the good sense, if I may use such a strong term, to forget the whole thing. For

the good of your career and your very nice wife and son. That is all."
He held the manuscript toward Dr. MacNare.

"I can't understand their attitude!" Dr. MacNare said to Alice
when he told her about it.

"Possibly I can understand it a little better than you, Joe," Alice
said thoughtfully. "I had a little of what I think they feel when I
first read your paper. A—a prejudice against the idea of it, is as
closely as I can describe it. Like it would be violating the order of
nature, giving an animal a soul, in a way."

"Then you feel as they do?" Dr. MacNare said.

"I didn't say that, Joe." Alice put her arms around her husband
and kissed him fiercely. "Maybe I feel just the opposite, that if there
is some way to give an animal a soul, we should do it."

Dr. MacNare chuckled. "It wouldn't be quite that cosmic. An
animal can't be given something it doesn't have already. All that can
be done is to give it the means to fully capitalize on what it has.
Animals—man included—can only do by observing the results.
When you move a finger, what you really do is send a neural impulse
out from the brain along one particular nerve or one particular set of
nerves, but you can never learn that, nor just what it is you do. All
that you can know is that when you do a definite *something* your
eyes and sense of touch bring you the information that your finger
moved. But if that finger were attached to a voice element that made
the sound *ah*, and you could never see your finger, all you could ever
know is that when you did that particular *something* you made a
certain vocal sound. Changing the resultant effect of mental commands to include things normally impossible to you may expand the
potential of your mind, but it won't give you a soul if you don't have
one to begin with."

"You're using Veerhof's arguments on me," Alice said. "And I
think we're arguing from separate definitions of a soul. I'm afraid of
it, Joe. It would be a tragedy, I think, to give some animal—a rat,
maybe—the soul of a poet, and then have it discover that it is only a
rat."

"Oh," Dr. MacNare said. "*That* kind of soul. No, I'm not that
optimistic about the results. I think we'd be lucky to get any results
at all, a limited vocabulary that the animal would use meaningfully.
But I do think we'd get that."

"It would take a lot of time and patience."

"And we'd have to keep the whole thing secret from everyone,"
Dr. MacNare said. "We couldn't even let Paul have an inkling of it,

314

because he might say something to one of his playmates, and it would get back to some member of the board. How could we keep it secret from Paul?"

"Paul knows he's not allowed in your study," Alice said. "We could keep everything there—and keep the door locked."

"Then it's settled?"

"Wasn't it, from the very beginning?" Alice put her arms around her husband and her cheek against his ear to hide her worried expression. "I love you, Joe. I'll help you in any way I can. And if we haven't enough in the savings account, there's always what Mother left me."

"I hope we won't have to use any of it, sweetheart," he said.

The following day Dr. MacNare was an hour and a half late coming home from the campus. He had been, he announced casually, to a pet store.

"We'll have to hurry," said Alice. "Paul will be home any minute."

She helped him carry the packages from the car to the study. Together they moved things around to make room for the gleaming new cages with their white rats and hamsters and guinea pigs. When it was done they stood arm in arm viewing their new possessions.

To Alice MacNare, just the presence of the animals in her husband's study brought the research project into reality. As the days passed that romantic feeling became fact.

"We're going to have to do together," Joe MacNare told her at the end of the first week, "what a team of a dozen specialists in separate fields should be doing. Our first job, before we can do anything else, is to study the natural movements of each species and translate them into patterns of robot directives."

"Robot directives?"

"I visualize it this way," Dr. MacNare said. "The animal will be strapped comfortably in a frame so that its body can't move but its legs can. Its legs will be attached to four separate, free-moving levers which make a different electrical contact for every position. Each electrical contact, or control switch, will cause the robot body to do one specific thing, such as move a leg, utter some particular sound through its voice box, or move just one finger. Can you visualize that, Alice?"

Alice nodded.

"Okay. Now, one leg has to be used for nothing but voice sounds. That leaves three legs for control of the movements of the robot body. In body movement there will be simultaneous movements and sequences. A simple sequence can be controlled by one leg. All movements of the robot will have to be reduced to not more than three concurrent sequences of movement of the animal's legs. Our problem, then, is to make the unlearned and the most natural movements of the legs of the animal control the robot body's movements in a functional manner."

Endless hours were consumed in this initial study and mapping. Alice worked at it while her husband was at the university and Paul was at school. Dr. MacNare rushed home each day to go over what she had done and continue the work himself.

He grew more and more grudging of the time his classes took. In December he finally wrote to the three technical journals that had been expecting papers from him for publication during the year that he would be too busy to do them.

By January the initial phase of research was well enough along so that Dr. MacNare could begin planning the robot. For this he set up a workshop in the garage.

In early February he finished what he called the "test frame." After Paul had gone to bed, Dr. MacNare brought the test frame into the study from the garage. To Alice it looked very much like the insides of a radio.

She watched while he placed a husky-looking male white rat in the body harness fastened to the framework of aluminum and tied its legs to small metal rods.

Nothing happened except that the rat kept trying to get free, and the small metal rods tied to its feet kept moving in pivot sockets.

"Now!" Dr. MacNare said excitedly, flicking a small toggle switch on the side of the assembly.

Immediately a succession of vocal sounds erupted from the speaker. They followed one another, making no sensible word.

"*He's* doing that," Dr. MacNare said triumphantly.

"If we left him in that, do you think he'd eventually associate his movements with the sounds?"

"It's possible. But that would be more on the order of what we do when we drive a car. To some extent a car becomes an extension of the body, but you're always aware that your hands are on the steering wheel, your foot on the gas pedal or brake. You extend your awareness consciously. You interpret a slight tremble in the steering wheel as a shimmy in the front wheels. You're oriented primarily to your body and only secondarily to the car as an extension of you."

Alice closed her eyes for a moment, "Mm hm," she said.

"And that's the best we could get, using a rat that knows already it's a rat."

Alice stared at the struggling rat, her eyes round with comprehension, while the loudspeaker in the test frame said, "Ag–pr–ds–raf–os–dg . . ."

Dr. MacNare shut off the sound and began freeing the rat.

"By starting with a newborn animal and never letting it know what it is," he said, "we can get a complete extension of the animal into the machine, in its orientation. So complete that if you took it out of the machine after it grew up, it would have no more idea of what had happened than—than your brain if it were taken out of your head and put on a table!"

"Now I'm getting that *feeling* again, Joe," Alice said, laughing nervously. "When you said that about my brain I thought, 'Or my soul?'"

Dr. McNare put the rat back in its cage.

"There might be a valid analogy there," he said slowly. "If we have a soul that survives after death, what is it like? It probably interprets its surroundings in terms of its former orientation in the body."

"That's a little of what I mean," Alice said. "I can't help it, Joe. Sometimes I feel so sorry for whatever baby animal you'll eventually use, that I want to cry. I feel so sorry for it, because *we will never dare let it know what it really is!*"

"That's true. Which brings up another line of research that should be the work of one expert on the team I ought to have for this. As it is, I'll turn it over to you to do while I build the robot."

"What's that?"

"Opiates," Dr. MacNare said. "What we want is an opiate that can be used on a small animal every few days, so that we can take it out of the robot, bathe it, and put it back again without its knowing about it. There probably is no ideal drug. We'll have to test the more promising ones."

Later that night, as they lay beside each other in the silence and darkness of their bedroom, Dr. MacNare sighed deeply.

"So many problems," he said. "I sometimes wonder if we can solve them all. *See* them all . . ."

To Alice MacNare, later, that night in early February marked the end of the first phase of research—the point where two alternative futures hung in the balance, and either could have been taken. That night she might have said, there in the darkness, "Let's drop it," and her husband might have agreed.

She thought of saying it. She even opened her mouth to say it. But her husband's soft snores suddenly broke the silence of the night. The moment of return had passed.

Month followed month. To Alice it was a period of rushing from kitchen to hypodermic injections to vacuum cleaner to hypodermic injections, her key to the study in constant use.

Paul, nine years old now, took to spring baseball and developed an indifference to TV, much to the relief of both his parents.

In the garage workshop Dr. MacNare made parts for the robot, and kept a couple of innocent projects going which he worked on when his son Paul evinced his periodic curiosity about what was going on.

Spring became summer. For six weeks Paul went to Scout camp, and during those six weeks Dr. MacNare reorganized the entire research project in line with what it would be in the fall. A decision was made to use only white rats from then on. The rest of the animals were sold to a pet store, and a system for automatically feeding, watering, and keeping the cages clean was installed in preparation for a much needed two weeks' vacation at the cabin.

When the time came to go, they had to tear themselves away from their work by an effort of will—aided by the realization that they could get little done with Paul underfoot.

September came all too soon. By mid-September both Dr. MacNare and his wife felt they were on the home stretch. Parts of the robot were going together and being tested, the female white rats were being bred at the rate of one a week so that when the robot was completed there would be a supply of newborn rats on hand.

October came, and passed. The robot was finished, but there were minor defects in it that had to be corrected.

"Adam," Dr. MacNare said one day, "will have to wear this robot all his life. It has to be just right."

And with each litter of baby rats Alice said, "I wonder which one is Adam."

They talked of Adam often now, speculating on what he would be like. It was almost, they decided, as though Adam were their second child.

And finally, on November 2, 1956, everything was ready. Adam would be born in the next litter, due in about three days.

The amount of work that had gone into preparation for the great moment is beyond conception. Four file cabinet drawers were filled with notes. By actual measurement seventeen feet of shelf space was filled with books on the thousand and one subjects that had to be mastered. The robot itself was a masterpiece of engineering that would have done credit to the research staff of a watch manufacturer. The vernier adjustments alone, used to compensate daily for the rat's growth, had eight patentable features.

And the skills that had had to be acquired! Alice, who had never before had a hypodermic syringe in her hand, could now inject a precisely measured amount of opiate into the tiny body of a baby rat with calm confidence in her skill.

After such monumental preparation, the great moment itself was anticlimactic. While the mother of Adam was still preoccupied with the birth of the remainder of the brood, Adam, a pink helpless thing about the size of a little finger, was picked up and transfered to the head of the robot.

His tiny feet, which he would never know existed, were fastened with gentle care to the four control rods. His tiny head was thrust into a helmet attached to a pivot-mounted optical system, ending in the lenses that served the robot for eyes. And finally a transparent plastic cover contoured to the shape of the back of a human head was fastened in place. Through it his feeble attempts at movement could be easily observed.

Thus, Dr. MacNare's Adam was born into his body, and the time of the completion of his birth was one-thirty in the afternoon on the fifth day of November, 1956.

In the ensuing half hour all the cages of rats were removed from the study, the floor was scrubbed, and deodorizers were sprayed, so that no slightest trace of Adam's lowly origins remained. When this was done, Dr. MacNare loaded the cages into his car and drove them to a pet store that had agreed to take them.

When he returned, he joined Alice in the study, and at five minutes before four, with Alice hovering anxiously beside him, he opened the cover on Adam's chest and turned on the master switch that gave Adam complete dominion over his robot body.

Adam was beautiful—and monstrous. Made of metal from the neck down, but shaped to be covered by padding and skin in human semblance. From the neck up the job was done. The face was human, masculine, handsome, much like that of a clothing store dummy except for its mobility of expression, and the incongruity of the rest of the body.

The voice-control lever and contacts had been designed so that the ability to produce most sounds would have to be discovered by Adam as he gained control of his natural right front leg. Now the only sounds being uttered were *oh, ah, mm,* and *ll,* in random order. Similarly, the only movements of his arms and legs were feeble, like those of a human baby. The tremendous strength in his limbs was something he would be unable to tap fully until he had learned conscious coordination.

After a while Adam became silent and without movement. Alarmed, Dr. MacNare opened the instrument panel in the abdomen. The instruments showed that Adam's pulse and respiration were normal. He had fallen asleep.

Dr. MacNare and his wife stole softly from the study, and locked the door.

After a few days, with the care and feeding of Adam all that remained of the giant research project, the pace of the days shifted to that of long-range patience.

"It's just like having a baby," Alice said.

"You know something?" Dr. MacNare asked. "I've had to resist passing out cigars. I hate to say it, but I'm prouder of Adam than I was of Paul when he was born."

"So am I, Joe," Alice said quietly. "But I'm getting a little of that scared feeling back again."

"In what way?"

"He watches me. Oh, I know it's natural for him to, but I do wish you had made the eyes so that his own didn't show as little dark dots in the center of the iris."

"It couldn't be helped," Dr. MacNare said. "He has to be able to see, and I had to set up the system of mirrors so that the two axes of vision would be three inches apart as they are in the average human pair of eyes."

"Oh, I know," said Alice. "Probably it's just something I've seized on. But when he watches me, I find myself holding my breath in fear that he can read in my expression the secret we have to keep from him, that he is a rat."

"Forget it, Alice. That's outside his experience and beyond his comprehension."

"I know," Alice sighed. "When he begins to show some of the signs of intelligence a baby has, I'll be able to think of him as a human being."

"Sure, darling," Dr. MacNare said.

"Do you think he ever will?"

"That," Dr. MacNare said, "is the big question. I think he will.

I think so now even more than I did at the start. Aside from eating and sleeping, he has no avenue of expression except his robot body, and *no source of reward except that of making sense—human sense.*"

The days passed, and became weeks, then months. During the daytime when her husband was at the university and her son was at school, Alice would spend most of her hours with Adam, forcing herself to smile at him and talk to him as she had to Paul when he was a baby. But when she watched his motions through the transparent back of his head, his leg motions remained those of attempted walking and attempted running.

Then, one day when Adam was four months old, things changed—as abruptly as the turning on of a light.

The unrewarding walking and running movements of Adam's little legs ceased. It was evening, and both Dr. MacNare and his wife were there.

For a few seconds there was no sound or movement from the robot body. Then, quite deliberately, Adam said, "Ah."

"Ah," Dr. MacNare echoed. "Mm. Mm, ah. Ma-ma."

"Mm," Adam said.

The silence in the study became absolute. The seconds stretched into eternities. Then—"

"Mm, ah," Adam said. "Mm, ah."

Alice began crying with happiness.

"Mm, ah," Adam said. "Mm, ah. Ma-ma. Mamamamama."

Then, as though the effort had been too much for Adam, he went to sleep.

Having achieved the impossible, Adam seemed to lose interest in it. For two days he uttered nothing more than an occasional involuntary syllable.

"I would call that as much of an achievement as speech itself," Dr. MacNare said to his wife. "His right front leg has asserted its independence. If each of his other three legs can do as well, he can control the robot body."

It became obvious that Adam was trying. Though the movements of his body remained non-purposive, the pauses in those movements became more and more pregnant with what was obviously mental effort.

During that period there was of course room for argument and speculation about it, and even a certain amount of humor. Had

Adam's right front leg, at the moment of achieving meaningful speech, suffered a nervous breakdown? What would a psychiatrist have to say about a white rat that had a nervous breakdown in its right front leg?

"The worst part about it," Dr. MacNare said to his wife, "is that if he fails to make it he'll have to be killed. He can't have permanent frustration forced onto him, and, by now, returning him to his natural state would be even worse."

"And he has such a stout little heart," Alice said. "Sometimes when he looks at me I'm sure he knows what is happening and he wants me to know he's trying."

When they went to bed that night they were more discouraged than they had ever been.

Eventually they slept. When the alarm went off, Alice slipped into her robe and went into the study first, as she always did.

A moment later she was back in the bedroom, shaking her husband's shoulder.

"Joe!" She whispered. "Wake up! Come into the study!"

He leaped out of bed and rushed past her. She caught up with him and pulled him to a stop.

"Take it easy, Joe," she said. "Don't alarm him."

"Oh." Dr. MacNare relaxed. "I thought something had happened."

"Something has!"

They stopped in the doorway of the study. Dr. MacNare sucked in his breath sharply, but remained silent.

Adam seemed oblivious of their presence. He was too interested in something else.

He was interested in his hands. He was holding his hands up where he could see them, and he was moving them independently, clenching and unclenching the metal fingers with slow deliberation.

Suddenly the movement stopped. He had become aware of them. Then, impossibly, unbelievably, he spoke.

"Ma ma," Adam said. Then, "Pa pa."

"Adam!" Alice sobbed, rushing across the study to him and sinking down beside him. Her arms went around his metal body. "Oh, Adam," she cried happily.

It was the beginning. The data of that beginning is not known. Alice MacNare believes it was early in May, but more probably it was in April. There was no time to keep notes. In fact, there was no longer a research project nor any thought of one. Instead, there was

Adam, the person. At least, to Alice he became that, completely. Perhaps, also, to Dr. MacNare.

Dr. MacNare quite often stood behind Adam where he could watch the rat body through the transparent skull case while Alice engaged Adam's attention. Alice did the same, at times, but she finally refused to do so any more. The sight of Adam the rat, his body held in a net attached to the frame, his head covered by the helmet, his four legs moving independently of one another with little semblance of walking or running motion nor even of coordination, but with swift darting motions and pauses pregnant with meaning, brought back to Alice the old feeling of vague fear, and a tremendous surge of pity for Adam that made her want to cry.

Slowly, subtly, Adam's rat body became to Alice a pure brain, and his four legs four nerve ganglia. A brain covered with short white fur; and when she took him out of his harness under opiate to bathe him, she bathed him as gently and carefully as any brain surgeon sponging a cortical surface.

Once started, Adam's mental development progressed rapidly. Dr. MacNare began making notes again on June 2, 1957, just ten days before the end, and it is to these notes that we go for an insight into Adam's mind.

On June 4th Dr. MacNare wrote, "I am of the opinion that Adam will never develop beyond the level of a moron, in the scale of human standards. He would probably make a good factory worker or chauffeur, in a year or two. But he is consciously aware of himself as Adam, he thinks in words and simple sentences with an accurate understanding of their meaning, and he is able to do new things from spoken instructions. There is no question, therefore, but that he has an integrated mind, entirely human in every respect."

On June 7th Dr. MacNare wrote, "Something is developing which I hesitate to put down on paper—for a variety of reasons. Creating Adam was a scientific experiment, nothing more than that. Both the premises on which the project was based have been proven: that the principle of verification is the main factor in learned response, and that, given the proper conditions, some animals are capable of abstract symbol systems and therefore of thinking with words to form meaningful concepts.

"Nothing more was contemplated in the experiment. I stress this because—Adam is becoming deeply religious—and before any mistaken conclusions are drawn from this I will explain what caused this development. It was an oversight of a type that is bound to happen in any complex project.

"Alice's experimental data on the effects of opiates, and especially the data on increasing the dose to offset growing tolerance, were based on observation of the subject alone, without any knowledge of the mental aspects of increased tolerance—which would of course be impossible except with human subjects.

"Unknown to us, Adam has been becoming partly conscious during his bath. Just conscious enough to be vaguely aware of certain sensations, and to remember them afterward. Few, if any, of these half remembered sensations are such that he can fit them into the pattern of his waking reality.

"The one that has had the most pronounced influence on him is, to quote him, 'Feel clean inside. Feel good.' Quite obviously this sensation is caused by his bath.

"With it is a distinct feeling of disembodiment, of being—and these are his own words—'outside my body'! This, of course, is an accurate realization, because to him the robot is his body, and he knows nothing of the existence of his actual, living, rat body.

"In addition to these two effects, there is a third one. A feeling of walking, and sometimes of floating, of stumbling over things he can't see, of talking, of being talked to by disembodied voices.

"The explanation of this is also obvious. When he is being bathed his legs are moved about. Any movement of a leg is to him either a spoken sound or a movement of some part of his robot body. Any movement of his right front leg, for example, tells his mind that he is making a sound. But, since his leg is not connected to the sound system of his robot body, his ears bring no physical verification of the sound. The mental anticipation of that verification then becomes a disembodied voice to him.

"The end result of all this is that Adam is becoming convinced that there is a hidden side of things (which there is), and that it is supernatural (which it is, *in the framework of his orientation*).

"What we are going to have to do is make sure he is completely unconscious before taking him out and bathing him. His mental health is far more important than exploring the interesting avenues opened up by this unforeseen development.

"I do intend, however, to make one simple test, while he is fully awake, before dropping this avenue of investigation."

Dr. MacNare does not state in his notes what this test was to be; but his wife says that it probably refers to the time when he pinched Adam's tail and Adam complained of a sudden, violent headache. This transference is the one well known to doctors. Unoriented pain in the human body manifests itself as a "headache," when the source of the pain is actually the stomach, or the liver, or any one of a hundred spots in the body.

The last notes made by Dr. MacNare were those of June 11, 1957, and are unimportant except for the date. We return, therefore, to actual events, so far as they can be reconstructed.

We have said little or nothing about Dr. MacNare's life at the university after embarking on the research project, nor of the social life of the MacNares. As conspirators, they had kept up their social life to avoid any possibility of the board getting curious about any radical change in Dr. MacNare's habits; but as time went on both Dr. MacNare and his wife became so engrossed in their project that only with the greatest reluctance did they go anywhere.

The annual faculty party at Professor Long's on June 12th was something they could not evade. Not to have gone would have been almost tantamount to a resignation from the university.

"Besides," Alice had said when they discussed the matter in May, "isn't it about time to do a little hinting that you have something up your sleeve?"

"I don't know, Alice," Dr. MacNare had said. Then a smile quirked his lips and he said, "I wouldn't mind telling off Veerhof. I've never gotten over his deciding something was impossible without enough data to pass judgment." He frowned. "We are going to have to let the world know about Adam pretty soon, aren't we? That's something I haven't thought about. But not yet. Next fall will be time enough."

Don't forget, Joe," Alice said at dinner. "Tonight's the party at Professor Long's."

"How can I forget with you reminding me?" Dr. MacNare said, winking at his son.

"And you, Paul," Alice said. "I don't want you leaving the house. You understand? You can watch TV, and I want you in bed by nine thirty."

"Ah, Mom!" Paul protested. "Nine thirty?" He suppressed a grin. He had a party of his own planned.

"And you can wipe the dishes for me. We have to be at Professor Long's by eight o'clock."

"I'll help you," Dr. MacNare said.

"No, you have to get ready. Besides, don't you have to look up something for one of the faculty?"

"I'd forgotten," said Dr. MacNare. "Thanks for reminding me."

After dinner he went directly to the study. Adam was sitting on the floor playing with his wooden blocks. They were alphabet blocks, but he didn't know that yet. The summer project was going to be teaching him the alphabet. Already, though, he preferred placing them in straight rows rather than stacking them up.

At seven o'clock Alice rapped on the door to the study.

"Time to get dressed, Joe," she called.

"You'll be all right while we're gone, Adam?" Dr. MacNare said.

"I be all right, papa," Adam said. "I sleep."

"That's good," Dr. MacNare said. "I'll turn out the light."

At the door he waited until Adam had sat down in the chair he always slept on, and settled himself. Then he pushed the switch just to the right of the door and went out.

"Hurry, dear," Alice called.

"I'm hurrying," Dr. MacNare protested—and, for the first time, he forgot to lock the study door.

The bathroom was next to the study, the wall between them soundproofed by a ceiling-high bookshelf in the study filled with thousands of books. On the other side was the master bedroom, with a closet with sliding panels that opened both on the bedroom and the bathroom. These sliding panels were partly open, so that Dr. MacNare and Alice could talk.

"Did you lock the study door?"

"Of course," Dr. MacNare said. "But I'll check before we leave."

"How is Adam taking being alone tonight?" Alice called.

"Okay," Dr. MacNare said. "Damn!"

"What's the matter, Joe?"

"I forgot to get razor blades."

The conversation died down.

Alice MacNare finished dressing.

"Aren't you ready yet, Joe?" she called. "It's almost a quarter to eight."

"Be right with you. I nicked myself shaving with an old blade. The bleeding's almost stopped now."

Alice went into the living room. Paul had turned on the TV and was sprawled out on the rug.

"You be sure and stay home, and be in bed by nine thirty, Paul," she said. "Promise?"

"Ah, Mom," he protested. "Well, all right."

Dr. MacNare came into the room, still working on his tie. A moment later they went out the front door. They had been gone less than five minutes when there was a knock. Paul jumped to his feet and opened the door.

"Hi, Fred, Tony, Bill," he said.

The boys, all nine years old, sprawled on the rug and watched television. It became eight o'clock, eight thirty, and finally five minutes to nine. The commercial began.

"Where's your bathroom?" Tony asked.

"In there," Paul said, pointing vaguely at the doorway to the hall.

Tony got up off the floor and went into the hall. He saw several doors, all looking much alike. He picked one and opened it. It was dark inside. He felt along the wall for a light switch and found it. Light flooded the room. He stared at what he saw for perhaps ten seconds, then turned and ran down the hall to the living room.

"Say, Paul!" he said. "You never said anything about having a real honest to gosh robot!"

"What are you talking about?" Paul said.

"In that room in there!" Tony said. "Come on. I'll show you!"

The TV program forgotten, Paul, Fred, and Bill crowded after him. A moment later they stood in the doorway to the study, staring in awe at the strange figure of metal that sat motionless in a chair across the room.

Adam, it seems certain, was asleep, and had not been wakened by this intrusion nor the turning on of the light.

"Gee!" Paul said. "It belongs to Dad. We'd better get out of here."

"Naw," Tony said with a feeling of proprietorship at having been the original discoverer. "Let's take a look. He'll never know about it."

They crossed the room slowly, until they were close up to the robot figure, marveling at it, moving around it.

"Say!" Bill whispered, pointing. "What's that in there? It looks like a white rat with its head stuck into that kind of helmet thing."

They stared at it a moment.

"Maybe it's dead. Let's see."

"How you going to find out?"

"See those hinges on the cover?" Tony said importantly. "Watch." With cautious skill he opened the transparent back half of the dome, and reached in, wrapping his fingers around the white rat.

He was unable to get it loose, but he succeeded in pulling its head free of the helmet.

At the same time Adam awoke.

"Ouch!" Tony cried, jerking his hand away. "He bit me!"

"He's alive all right," Bill said. "Look at him glare!" He prodded the body of the rat and pulled his hand away quickly as the rat lunged.

"Gee, look at its eyes," Paul said nervously. "They're getting bloodshot."

"Dirty old rat!" Tony said vindictively, jabbing at the rat with his finger and evading the snapping teeth.

"Get its head back in there!" Paul said desperately. "I don't want papa to find out we were in here!" He reached in, driven by desperation, pressing the rat's head between his fingers and forcing it back into the tight fitting helmet.

Immediately screaming sounds erupted from the lips of the robot. (It was determined by later examination that only when the rat's body was completely where it should be were the circuits operable.)

"Let's get out of here!" Tony shouted, and dived for the door, thereby saving his life.

"Yeah! Let's get out of here!" Fred shouted as the robot figure rose to its feet. Terror enabled him to escape.

Bill and Paul delayed an instant too long. Metal fingers seized them. Bill's arm snapped halfway between shoulder and elbow. He screamed with pain and struggled to free himself.

Paul was unable to scream. Metal fingers gripped his shoulder, with a metal thumb thrust deeply against his larynx, paralyzing his vocal cords.

Fred and Tony had run into the front room. There they waited, ready to start running again. They could hear Bill's screams. They could hear a male voice jabbering nonsense, and finally repeating over and over again, "Oh my, oh my, oh my," in a tone all the more horrible because it portrayed no emotion whatever.

Then there was silence.

The silence lasted several minutes. Then Fred began to sniffle, rubbing his knuckles in his eyes. "I wanta go home," he whimpered.

"Me too."

They took each other's hand and tiptoed to the front door, watching the open doorway to the hall. When they reached the front door Tony opened it, and when it was open they ran, not stopping to close the door behind them.

There isn't much more to tell. It is known that Tony and Fred arrived at their respective homes, saying nothing of what had happened. Only later did they come forward and admit their share in the night's events.

Joe and Alice MacNare arrived home from the party at Professor Long's at twelve thirty, finding the front door wide open, the lights on in the living room, and the television on.

Sensing that something was wrong, Alice hurried to her son's room and discovered he wasn't there. While she was doing that, Joe shut the front door and turned off the television.

Alice returned to the living room, eyes round with alarm, and said, "Paul's not in his room!"

"Adam!" Joe croaked, and rushed into the hallway, with Alice following more slowly.

She reached the open door of the study in time to see the robot figure pounce on Joe and fasten its metal fingers about his throat, crushing vertebrae and flesh alike.

Oblivious to her own danger, she rushed to rescue her already dead husband, but the metal fingers were inflexible. Belatedly she abandoned the attempt and ran into the hallway to the phone.

When the police arrived, they found her slumped against the wall in the hallway. She pointed toward the open doorway of the study, without speaking.

The police rushed into the study. At once there came the sounds of shots. Dozens of them, it seemed. Later both policemen admitted that they lost their heads and fired until their guns were empty.

But it was not yet the end of Adam.

It would perhaps be impossible to conceive the full horror of his last hours, but we can at least make a guess. Asleep when the boys entered the study, he awakened to a world he had never before perceived except very vaguely and under the soporific veil of opiate.

But it was a world vastly different even than that. There is no way of knowing what he saw—probably blurred ghostly figures, monstrous beyond the ability of his mind to grasp, for his eyes were adjusted only to the series of prisms and lenses that enabled him to see and coordinate the images brought to him through the eyes of the robot.

He saw these impossible figures, he felt pain and torture that were not of the flesh as he knew it, but of the spirit; agony beyond agony administered by what he could only believe were fiends from some nether hell.

And then, abruptly, as ten-year-old Paul shoved his head back into the helmet, the world he had come to believe was reality returned. It was as though he had returned to the body from some awful pit of hell, with the soul sickness still with him.

Before him he saw four humanlike figures of reality, but beings unlike the only two he had ever seen. Smaller, seeming to be a part of the unbelievable nightmare he had been in. Two of them fled, two were within his grasp.

Perhaps he didn't know what he was doing when he killed Paul and Bill. It's doubtful if he had the ability to think at all then, only to tremble and struggle in his pitiful little rat body, with the automatic mechanisms of the robot acting from those frantic motions.

But it is known that there were three hours between the deaths of the two boys and the entry of Dr. MacNare at twelve thirty, and during those three hours he would have had a chance to recover, and to think, and to partially rationalize the nightmare he had experienced in realms outside what to him was the world of reality.

Adam must certainly have been calm enough, rational enough, to recognize Dr. MacNare when he entered the study at twelve thirty.

Then why did Adam deliberately kill Joe by breaking his neck? Was it because, in that three hours, he had put together the evidence of his senses and come to the realization that he was not a man but a rat?

It's not likely. It is much more likely that Adam came to some aberrated conclusion dictated by the superstitious feelings that had grown so strongly into his strange and unique existence, that dictated he must kill Joseph.

For it would have been impossible for him to have realized that he was only a rat. You see, Joseph MacNare had taken great care that Adam never, in all his life, should see *another* rat.

There remains only the end of Adam to relate.

Physically it can be only anticlimactic. With his metal body out of commission from a dozen or so shots, two of which destroyed the robot extensions of his eyes, he remained helpless until the coroner carefully removed him.

To the coroner he was just a white rat, and a strangely helpless one, unable to walk or stand as rats are supposed to. Also a strangely vicious one, with red little beads of eyes and lips drawn back from sharp teeth the same as some rabid wild animal.

The coroner had no way of knowing that somewhere in that small, menacing form there was a noble but lost mentality that knew itself as Adam, and held thoughts of a strange and wonderful realm of peace and splendor beyond the grasp of the normal physical senses.

330

The coroner could not know that the erratic motions of that small left front foot, if connected to the proper mechanisms, would have been audible as, perhaps, a prayer, a desperate plea to whatever lay in the Great Beyond to come down and rescue its humble creature.

"Vicious little bastard," the coroner said nervously to the homicide men gathered around Dr. MacNare's desk.

"Let me take care of it," said one of the detectives.

"No," the coroner answered. "I'll do it."

Quickly, so as not to be bitten, he picked Adam up by the tip of the tail and slammed him forcefully against the top of the desk.

the man who devoured books

John Sladek

This is a lighthearted little story, which will probably produce more laughter than learning. Perhaps, though, a good supply of the first enhances the latter. "The Man Who Devoured Books" draws on a favorite theme of science fiction writers—the visit to Earth of creatures from outer space. In early science fiction, these creatures were categorized as "bug-eyed monsters" (BEMS) and usually portrayed as bringing a hideous threat to mankind. Since World War II, the view of creatures from outer space has softened in science fiction, and often, as in this story, they are presented as benign creatures more beneficent in their behavior than humans. The killing of six million Jews in Nazi concentration camps and the napalm bombings and atrocities in the Vietnamese war have made us much more self-critical. We suspect now that perhaps it is we—not creatures from outer space—who behave monstrously.

In the future world of "The Man Who Devoured Books," the Earth has been taken over by the Guzz, creatures of humanitarian concern whose only disagreeable feature is their appearance. It is so disagreeable that "so as not to spook the natives, they wore human forms of plastic." The plot of the story grows out of what happens when Claude Mabry, dishwasher at Stan's Chili Bowl, encounters a Guzz salesman offering him knowledge.

As background for the story, we need to review the Lamarckian view of genetics, which holds that acquired characteristics can be inherited. Jean Lamarck (1744–1829) was a French naturalist. The fourth law of his evolutionary theory states that all that has been acquired or changed in individuals during their life is passed on to their progeny through inheritance. The theory had wide influence in the nineteenth century, although it is not generally accepted by biologists and psychologists today.

The interest of psychologists in this theory was excited again in the late fifties and early sixties because of experiments done with planaria (flatworms). In this fascinating work, planaria were conditioned to contract upon presentation of a light (after the light had been associated with an electric shock). Planaria can regenerate if they are cut into parts, the parts eventually forming full new planaria. The researchers expected that the regenerated worms formed from the brain part of the previously conditioned worms would retain the conditioning, and they wondered about the new worms formed from tail (nonbrain) parts. They found also that these worms retained their conditioning (tested by seeing how many trials it took to get them to contract to the light; both groups of regenerated worms learned this faster than control worms). The researchers theorized that RNA from the originally conditioned worms had been dispersed throughout their bodies as well as their brains, and this was how regenerated worms from their tails retained the change brought on by the original conditioning. They next theorized that if conditioned worms produce special RNA throughout their bodies, the bodies could be ground up and fed to other worms. These other worms would absorb the RNA and also show faster conditioning than control worms, who would be fed the ground up bodies of nonconditioned worms. This was done, and the results supported the theory.

This research in the late fifties and early sixties excited many psychologists in part because the findings seemed to support the Lamarckian view of genetics—that worms who learned something apparently could pass that learning on to other worms, perhaps through inheritance of the previous generation's RNA transmitted through DNA in the germ cells.

The bubble of excitement burst, however, in the late sixties when it was shown through strictly controlled experiments that indeed the new worms could benefit from absorbing the RNA from previously conditioned worms, but it was shown that it wasn't the previous learning of the ground up worms that was important in their producing beneficial RNA. It was simply the stimulation they received that produced the better RNA; light stimulation without conditioning and electric shock stimulation without conditioning would do the trick as well.

One current introductory psychology text notes the excitement caused by the planaria experiments at the time, both in scientific circles and among students on college campuses. The problem of what to do with old psychology professors was finally solved. Grind them up and feed them to the introductory psychology students!

"The Man Who Devoured Books" is a product of the interest aroused by the planaria experiments.

THE MAN WHO DEVOURED BOOKS   *John Sladek*

"We can give you knowledge," said the salesman-thing.

Claude Mabry looked all around his room: mildewed wallpaper, broken linoleum, dirty long underwear slung over a chair that had a weak leg, the clock face that had been cracked and repaired so many times with scotch tape that he could hardly see it said 3:20.

"I'm smart enough for me," he said. "There's such a thing as being too smart for your own good."

"That's right," said the salesman-thing, "and there's such a thing as being so smart you have to wash dishes down at Stan's Chili Bowl to earn enough to live—here."

Claude could not reply. The whole thing reminded him of the Bible: a snake or whatever it was dressed up like a man, offering "knowledge"—it just didn't make sense.

"Look, I don't mean to be unpleasant," said the salesman. "But we Guzz are a hell of a lot more powerful and a hell of a lot smarter than your species. If we'd wanted to, we could have vaporized your whole planet—but it's not our way. So when somebody comes offering to make you smart, don't knock it."

Claude wanted to rip off that grinning, false mansuit and see what the Guzz looked like. He half-rose, then sank back again and looked at the floor.

"If you're so good, why do you want to do anything for me?"

"I don't want to do anything for you. I voted to turn Earth into a bird refuge. But we have a democratic form of government and the majority wanted to make your kind fit citizens to share the universe with us."

"All right, how do I know you can make me smart?"

The salesman opened his briefcase and took out a handful of bright brochures. "Don't take my word for it that we can make you one of the smartest men on Earth," he said. "Don't take it from me that being smart is worthwhile. Millions are trying our plan. Thousands have tried it already. Have a look."

He handed Claude a folder showing full-color pictures of quiet scholars, white-coated scientists, dignified judges and beaming businessmen. Their testimonials were capped with red headlines:

COULDN'T READ OWN NAME—
NOW COMMANDS 20 LANGUAGES!

FAMOUS ECONOMIST
"HATED ARITHMETIC"

"DUMB OX"
TO BRILLIANT THEOLOGIAN—IN 7
MONTHS!

"But—what would I study?"

"Everything." The salesman produced another slick booklet and began turning the pages, showing Claude pictures of happy housewives and hairy-handed laborers reading heavy volumes, farmers peering through microscopes and grannies using slide rules. "We call our system the Interface Way. Every person we accept must study at least two subjects intensively. If the subjects are unrelated, all the better. We mix mathematics with literature, we throw theoretical physics at a medical specialist, we give the mathematician theology."

"What would I get?"

"If we accepted you, you'd be tested. Then we'd know."

"What do you mean, if?" Claude felt he had just been offered a million dollars, but at the word "if" it had shrunk to about a nickle.

The stranger, sensing his anxiety, spoke soothingly. "Don't worry too much about that. We won't be testing your I.Q. or previous knowledge. In fact, the less of either, the better. We want

335

people who haven't had a chance, people who feel useless because the sleeping genius within them has never been awakened. What do you say?"

"I don't know. What would it cost me?"

"All the money in the world couldn't buy you a better education, pal. But all it costs is your signature."

"Well—oh, hell, why not?"

"Why not?" echoed the salesman, handing him a pen. Claude signed a few forms in various colors and the salesman gave him a copy of each.

"Claude," he said, "you've just made your first intelligent decision."

The Guzz had pretty well taken over Earth, in every way. Guzz-developed gadgets were in every home. Clergymen thanked the Lord from their pulpits that the Guzz were not warlike or vicious but a truly democratic—ah—people. The government made daily announcements of new Guzz gifts to humanity.

They quietly disarmed the nuclear powers, they made efficient clean-air and sewage-disposal systems for our cities, they introduced new food sources and birth-control plans in Asia. Hardly a government bureau in the world had not been approached by the Guzz with a suggestion or a gift—and these aliens used no stronger forces than tact and kindly persuasion.

The only disagreeable thing about them was the way they looked—both at home and in Earth-drag.

On their own planet (or so it was said, for no one had yet visited them) the Guzz were disagreeably vermiform. Here, so as not to spook the natives, they wore human forms of plastic. Their movements in these were natural enough, but they all looked alike. As far as most people, including Claude, were concerned, the Guzz were just so many talking store-window dummies.

The first box that arrived was a table-top computer equipped with keyboard, microphone, speaker, and visual display screen. That night when he returned from Stan's Chili Bowl, Claude lay awake looking at all that gleaming, complicated junk and wondering if he might have made a mistake in even hoping. . . .

Next day three packages arrived. The first contained books and a sheaf of documents: a certification that Claude Mabry was eligible for this correspondence course, more copies of the various forms he'd signed—and a booklet entitled: *Welcome, Future Genius!*

> The government of Guzz and your own government wish to take this opportunity to welcome you . . . conditions and bylaws. . . . You may not always see the reasons for instructions given you in this course, but they are necessary to ensure efficient use of your time.

> The enclosed books are for Lesson One. The books required for each lesson will be provided with the lesson. At various points in the program you will be asked to study them thoroughly.

Claude glanced at the titles of the books: *The Interpretation of Dreams,* Sigmund Freud; *Verbal Behavior,* B. F. Skinner; *Towards Information Retrieval,* Fairthorne; were only a few.

The dream book looked interesting but inside, like all the others, it was full of long-winded sentences that didn't mean anything.

The second package contained a tape cassette titled: *Program for Lesson One* and simple instructions for loading it into the teaching computer.

As soon as Claude could do so, he switched on the machine. He might have expected it to give him a problem, to register the fact that it was turned on, or at least to ask his name, but it did none of these things.

Instead, it politely requested him to eat a sandwich.

Claude scratched his head. The Guzz had to be joking. He could imagine them watching him right now, laughing at his stupidity. So this was the big learning course! So this. . . .

He remembered the third package and tore it open. Inside was a cellophane-wrapped sandwich. Though Claude turned it over and over, he could see only one difference between this and any other cellophane-wrapped sandwich: Inside the wrapper was a plain printed name slip. But instead of "ham and cheese" or "peanut butter and grape jelly" it simply read: Eat me.

The bread was a little stale but he enjoyed the salami or para-salami inside.

An hour later he correctly answered a request to explain how and why dreams were subject to syntactical rules. The answer was obvious.

Two hours later he had read Ayer's *The Problem of Knowledge,* read it at skimming speed because it was already perfectly familiar to him.

A lesson or two later Claude had gone through about fifty difficult books without any trouble. He progressed rapidly through the programs, though it did not seem like progress at all: he simply knew what he was doing. Using Fourier analysis to solve problems in electronics seemed something he had always known, just as he had always realized the gross truth of Newtonian mechanics and the finer truth of quantum mechanics, the position of Hubert van Eyck in Flemish painting, the syllogistic properties of an Andrew Marvell poem, the flaws in the historical theories of Spengler and Toynbee—or for that matter, how to prepare *sauce ozéne* with seven ingredients. Scraps of learning, areas of learning, even whole complex structures of learning were suddenly his.

Having learned, he worked. By the fourth lesson Claude had gone through Godel's proof of the necessary incompleteness of mathematical theorems and picked holes in Lucas's application of this to mechanical devices. He had also put forth an aesthetic theory understandable by perhaps ten men, refutable by no more than one. He had nearly destroyed mathematical economics, and devised a tentative translating machine. He was hardly aware that these things had not been done before, nor was he really aware of the transition from his job at the Chili Bowl to a research fellowship at a prominent university.

The transition came about from his publication of various monographs in journals, the names of which he knew only from footnotes in the books he was skimming. Some of the monographs came back. He had sent them to wrong addresses, or to journals long out of print.

Others, like his "Queueing Theory Applied to Neural Activity" and "On Poetic Diction," became classics. Men with tweedy manners but sharp suits and clean attaché cases came to see him. They sat in the steamy, oily kitchen of Stan's Chili Bowl and talked with him about quasar explanations, new codes of international law, and logic mechanisms. True, many prodigies were springing up now that the Guzz offered their massive home study program. But for the time being, genius was still something universities fought over. And so, almost without knowing it (he was thinking of other things),

Claude Mabry gave Stan his notice, packed his T-shirts and blue jeans and entrained for Attica University.

He remembered only isolated facts about this trip; sending a change-of-address card to the Guzz; losing his ticket; not bringing enough paper (and so alighting from the train at Attica, where University officials were waiting to greet him, his hands so full of slips of toilet paper on which were penciled notes toward a theory of history that he could not accept the handshakes of these venerables). Without comment he settled into his new life and went on working.

From time to time he wondered what was in the sandwich that came with each lesson. A wonder drug that unlocked hidden knowledge that lay "sleeping" within him? An intelligence accelerator? Whatever it was, it was essential to the process. The only time he'd tried studying without it, Claude had floundered among symbols that *almost* made sense.

He wondered, too, about the Guzz. The little he learned about their planet and culture (in the final lesson) whetted his appetite for more. He longed to know everything about them, almost to become one of them: They alone would understand what he was doing. It was becoming clear that his colleagues at the university considered him some kind of freak—he would not wear a suit, he could not converse about departmental politics, and he was inhumanly intelligent.

Claude ordered all the information on the Guzz he could get. This proved to be a slim volume by a second-rate anthropologist who had interviewed a few of the aliens. Claude skimmed it and began a treatise of his own.

"Despite the advanced 'democracy' of the Guzz," he wrote, "they reatin a few oddly 'primitive,' even sacramental habits."

There was a knock at the door. The standard face of a Guzz looked around the frame, saw that he was alone and walked its standard body into the office. Without saying anything, it came over and struck him on the forehead. Twitching, Claude slipped to the floor. The visitor busied itself with a set of plastic bags.

The fallen man was muttering. Bending lower, the man-shape heard: ". . . planaria worms? DNA or . . . ?"

"Right you are!" boomed the Guzz. "Yes, we *are* analogous to your planarian worms—so, of course, are you—and we can transmit behavior genetically."

He fished a long knife from one bag and tested its blade against a false thumb. "Of course our genes need help. Obviously our—I

339

mean to include your—children do not learn much from their parents' genes. But these same genes, properly assimilated—"

"I knew it!" Claude croaked, getting up on one elbow. The blow had stunned him, but still the machinery of his mind ground on. With an ecstatic expression he said, "The old taboos against eating the king, eating the old man, the sage, the father, yes?"

"Check." With a hearty chuckle the visitor kneeled by Claude's side and felt for the carotid artery. "Those ridiculous taboos have kept your species back hundreds of thousands of years. We're just now making up the lost time for you."

"The sandwich meat—"

"Housewives, mechanics, professional people—all the people in that brochure you saw. Just think of it!" He waved the knife oratorically, and the plastic face turned up, as if gazing at a vista. "One genius provides three thousand sandwiches, each capable of providing—with no wastage—part of the education for one more genius! Thus learning will transform your whole species—you will become as gods!"

The Guzz returned his attention to the matter at hand. He poised the knife.

"Superman," murmured the genius. "On white or rye."

5

SOCIAL PROCESSES

The study of social processes affecting behavior gives special emphasis to the fact that neither humans nor animals live in isolation. Individuals of all species live with and must relate to others of their species, and this process is organized in what are called societies. When individuals get together, they can do so in pairs, in small groups like panels, in larger groups like classes, and in still larger groups like crowds. They can organize by geography into communities, by common interests into women's liberation groups, and by profession into construction workers and psychologists. They can share common attributes like Mensa (high intelligence) groups, or groups of the retarded; and they can share common heritages, like racial, ethnic, or religious groups. Perhaps the most important factor that interests those who study these relationships is the reciprocal influence created between the individual and the group he belongs and relates to. Both the individual and the group change because they relate to each other.

Unfortunately, throughout history members of all species,

especially human beings, have learned that one of the most efficient ways to influence the behavior of others is through aggression. As has recently been publicized, threats of violent aggression can effectively be used to convince individuals to comply with requests to behave in specified ways—making somebody an offer he cannot refuse. Less romantic but equally effective, muggers in various social situations can influence individuals they meet to part with money and valuables, a behavior in which these victims would not ordinarily engage. In the social psychological laboratory, important research by Milgram has demonstrated how people can be pressured to obey the requests of authority figures to severely aggress against others, an experimental repetition of what may have been similar occurrences in the "field" in Nazi Germany and at My Lai. Moreover, Berkowitz has experimentally demonstrated how learned aggressive cues like guns simply being present in social situations can promote aggression, evidence suggesting the folly of having guns so easily available in this country.

Research into the nature of aggression has revolved around issues nothing short of asking basic questions about the nature of man. Freud strongly believed that man has broad and basic aggressive instincts which he must learn to use and control in order for society to survive. Lorenz similarly stresses the aggressive instincts of all animals, emphasizing their necessity for self-preservation. Others have emphasized the role that society and social learning plays in developing man into an aggressive animal. Dollard and Miller have focused on the integral relationship between frustration and aggression, while Bandura and Walters have demonstrated the important role of aggressive models, like parents and cowboys, which children imitate in the social learning of aggression.

The role of mass communications, in teaching aggression especially in the televising of football games, is still a controversial issue. One side suggests that watching football provides the viewer with an opportunity for catharsis, allowing him to dissipate his aggressive energy by identifying with his favorite team as it "blitzes" and "bombs" its rivals into submission. The other side insists that these activities model and legitimize similar activity in the fan's life, thus promoting aggression.

The interrelationship between the individual and his society has been clearly demonstrated in the insights social psychologists have gained about social motives that influence behavior. McClelland and his colleagues have tried to show how individuals with a strong need for achievement can push their society to important levels of progress. They have conversely suggested that societies strongly influenced by the Protestant work ethic can develop child-rearing patterns which encourage independent efforts to achieve and succeed. Other researchers have demonstrated that people in developing societies have been reared to value the friendship and social approval of their neighbors more than independence and achievement. These people would not "really rather own a Buick" if the car would embarrass their neighbors who could not afford one.

Festinger and his colleagues (among others) have suggested that individuals are strongly motivated to maintain consistency in their beliefs and actions, often to the point of resisting common sense. Festinger specifically has suggested that inconsistency generates *cognitive dissonance,* an unpleasant kind of feeling within the individual which he strives to reduce. The principle of dissonance reduction has been used in attempts to explain how smokers continue to smoke by reducing in their minds the importance of warnings by health officials. Similarly, it has been suggested that the escalation of the Vietnam War continued because government officials did not want to invoke new policies which would have been inconsistent with their original policies. In general, perhaps Festinger's most sobering discovery may be that both individuals and governments would rather be consistent than smart!

In another important area, Asch provided clear but surprising evidence of how some individuals can conform to group decisions even though these decisions are foolish. In order to go along with the rest of the members of groups who were actually working for Asch, individuals tested agreed approximately one-third of the time that obviously shorter lines were longer than the ones appearing alongside them. Asch suggested that if the pressure to go along with a small group could be so powerful in the laboratory, where his subjects had to make unimportant decisions, the pressure to conform to society must be even more powerful. The

343

society prescribes norms for behavior which cut across almost all aspects of life. Goffman has suggested that we all play roles in social situations, almost as if we were actors playing parts in a script. The same person "acts" differently in a classroom than he does in a bar or at home.

In all fairness, it must be said that conformity has both positive and negative aspects. On the positive side, an individual needs to be like other people to be secure in the knowledge that he knows how to act in different situations. Doing as others do also gives us a sense of belonging and acceptance. The negative aspects occur if one must give up too much of his individuality in order to conform. If this occurs, and the individual chooses nonconformity, the result may be alienation: feelings of isolation and loneliness. If the individual drops out of society, the society may lose the benefit of his potential contributions. Again, the basic reciprocity of social processes is demonstrated. The individual and society both influence and need each other.

all the last wars at once

Geo. Alec Effinger

Black humor is the stance of some of our best contemporary writers today—Kurt Vonnegut, for example, in *Slaughterhouse-Five*. It presents in an apparently humorous fashion a situation which—viewed rationally—would be untenable because it is so full of gruesome horror. Our laughter, we know as we read, is sick. It is tragic, not comic, that humans should behave this way. But the device gives us a means of talking about an otherwise almost unspeakable situation. "All the Last Wars at Once" uses black humor to treat a future America where—for thirty days—every group in the country goes to war to eradicate those it considers hostile. The situation is "a thirty-day suspension of all rational codes of conduct."

From a social psychological point of view, individuals relate to other individuals not only as individuals but also as members of identifiable groups. This knowledge not only gives us information about other people but helps us orient ourselves toward them with at least some idea of what to expect from them. The negative aspect of this process is that when we rely too heavily on this process, giving too much weight to stereotypic conceptions of what people in certain groups are supposed to be like, we rob each member of the group of his individuality. Moreover, often we go one step further in our stereotypic conceptions of groups. Our prejudgments of them are often negative. Even before we meet individuals of a certain group, our expectations about them are negative: we engage in prejudice.

Prejudice has long been a lively issue of investigation in social psychology, and there are many interesting aspects of it which have been analyzed. Perhaps one of the first steps in the process of prejudiced thinking is the separation of "us" and "them." This immediately implies that "they" are different from "us," but also that "we" are *better* than "they" are.

Much of the research into *cognitive dissonance* has important relevance here. The theory of cognitive dissonance suggests that we do not like it when the cognitions (ideas, beliefs, opinions) we carry around with us are inconsistent (dissonant) with each other. When dissonance is present, we try to reduce it by changing our cognitions to bring them more in line with others we hold. (We rationalize.) Also, when our beliefs are dissonant with actions we take, we change our beliefs, since actions once taken are permanent and cannot be changed. (We justify our actions.)

One of the strongest cognitions which we carry with us is that "we are good," and since we do not want to change this cognition, we change other cognitions in order to make them *consonant* (the opposite of dissonant in the jargon of the theory) with it. If we are good, then those who are different from us must be bad. If they are bad, this justifies our hating them, and also justifies our taking aggressive action toward them. Unfortunately, the process more often than not proceeds in reverse. Often we take action first because it is the thing to do or because we are forced to do so (soldiers drafted to fight an "enemy") or perhaps for no real reason at all except that we are frustrated and we must take it out on somebody. Often we are told whom to hate by those around us, usually a weak outgroup (a scapegoat group). Once we decide to hate them for irrational reasons, we start looking for reasons to justify our action (besides liking to feel that we are good, we also like to think of ourselves as rational). Thus, our thinking becomes polarized; we emphasize and become sensitive to their bad points, doing the opposite with their good points.

"All the Last Wars at Once" illustrates the many different group identifications in society and unfortunately, as a result, the many ways in which we can engage in "we" and "they" thinking. The first basis is race and then there is sex, the two bases which are easiest to determine because by and large they are visual. The list continues; discrimination is made on the basis of religion, age, and occupation.

The process of rationalizing irrational hatred is best illustrated in the case of the laborers who decide to go to war with the artists. The real, irrational cause of their hatred of artists is that artists, perhaps as a group, are more sensitive and gentle than they and, therefore, pose a threat to the laborers' masculinity. The artists epitomize attributes which the laborers cannot accept in themselves, those of being effeminate. The laborers project their own fears and frustrations over these "weaknesses" by transferring them to the artists, emphasizing them, and polarizing their own thinking by calling the artists "queers." The real issue of masculinity is too explosive and irrational for the laborers to come to terms with, however, and they rationalize their hatred for the artists in terms of producers versus parasites.

At the story's end, the author tries to explain prejudice and hatred in terms of frustration with unacceptable internal weaknesses, which we project onto others, displacing the real object of our aggressions, ourselves. This is certainly an important and psychologically valid explanation of prejudice, although research has also shown how other factors come into play.

Finally, other social psychologically significant issues are present in the story. They are, first, the issue of cooperation versus competition in our society, perhaps suggesting the war as a consequence of America's overemphasis on the latter. Next, the role of the mass media in playing up and dramatizing social issues in our society perhaps plays a part in setting one group against another. Third is the breakdown of trust in communication between governmental authority and its people, certainly an important issue since Watergate.

ALL THE LAST WARS AT ONCE   *Geo. Alec Effinger*

We interrupt this p—
—upt this program to—
—terrupt our regularly scheduled programming to bring you

this bulletin pieced together from the archives of the General Motors Corporation.

"Good afternoon. This is Bob Dunne, NBC News in New Haven, Connecticut. We're standing here in the lobby of the Hotel Taft in New Haven, where the first international race war has just been declared. In just a few seconds, the two men responsible will be coming out of that elevator. (Can you hear me?)

"—elevator. Those of you in the western time zones are probably already—"

The elevator doors opened. Two men emerged, smiling and holding their hands above their heads in victorious, self-congratulatory boxers' handshakes. They were immediately mobbed by newsmen. One of the two men was exceptionally tall, and black as midnight in Nairobi. The other was short, fat, white, and very nervous. The black man was smiling broadly, the white man was smiling and wiping perspiration from his face with a large red handkerchief.

"—C News. The Negro has been identified as the representative of the people of color of all nations. He is, according to the mimeographed flyer distributed scant minutes ago, Mary McLeod Bethune Washington, of Washington, Georgia. The other man with him is identified as Robert Randall La Cygne, of La Cygne, Kansas, evidently the delegate of the Caucasian peoples. When, and by whom, this series of negotiations was called is not yet clear.

"At any rate, the two men, only yesterday sunk in the sticky obscurity of American life, have concluded some sort of bargaining that threatens to engulf the entire world in violent reaction. The actual content of that agreement is still open to specu—"

"—or at any later date."

A close-up on Washington, who was reading from a small black notebook.

"We have thus reached, and passed, that critical moment. This fact has been known and ignored by all men, on both sides of the color line, for nearly a generation. Henceforth, this situation is to be, at least, honest, if bloodier. Bob and I join in wishing you all the best of luck, and may God bless."

"Mr. Washington?"

"Does this necessarily mean—"

"—iated Press here, Mr. Washing—"

"Yes? You, with the hat."

"Yes, sir. Vincent Reynolds, UPI. Mr. Washington, are we to

understand that this agreement has some validity? You are aware that we haven't seen any sort of credentials—"

Washington grinned. "Thank you. I'm glad you brought that up. Credentials? Just you wait a few minutes, and listen outside. Ain't no stoppin' when them rifles start poppin'!"

"Mr. Washington?"

"Yes?"

"Is this to be an all-out, permanent division of peoples?"

"All-out, yes. Permanent, no. Bob and I have decided on a sort of statute of limitations. You go out and get what you can for thirty days. At the end of the month, we'll see what and who's left."

"You can guarantee that there will be no continuation of hostilities at the end of the thirty days?"

"Why, sure! We're all growed up, now, ain't we? Sure, why, you can trust *us*!"

"Then this is a war of racial eradication?"

"Not at all," said Bob La Cygne, who had remained silent, behind Washington's broad seersucker back. "Not at all what I would call a war of eradication. 'Eradicate' is an ugly term. 'Expunge' is the word we arrived at, isn't it, Mary Beth?"

"I do believe it is, Bob."

Washington studied his notebook for a few seconds, ignoring the shouting newsmen around him. No attempt was made by the uniformed guards to stop the pushing and shoving, which had grown somewhat aggravated. Then he smiled brightly, turning to La Cygne. They clasped hands and waved to the flashing bulbs of the photographers.

"No more questions, boys. You'll figure it all out soon enough; that's enough for now." The two men turned and went back into the waiting elevator.

(Tock tockatock tocka tock tock) "And now, the Six O'Clock Report (tocka tock tocka tocka), with (tockatock) Gil Monahan."

(Tocka tocka tock tock tocka)

"Good evening. The only story in the news tonight is the recently declared official hostilities between members of all non-Caucasian races and the white people of the world. Within minutes of the original announcement, open warfare broke out in nearly every multiracially populated area in the U.S. and abroad. At this moment the entire globe is in turmoil; the scene everywhere flickers between bloody combat in the streets and peaceful lulls marked by looting and destruction of private property.

349

"What has happened, in effect, is a thirty-day suspension of all rational codes of conduct. The army and National Guard are themselves paralyzed due to their own internal conflicts. A state of martial law has been declared by almost all governments, but, to our knowledge, nowhere has it been effectively enforced.

"There seems to be absolutely no cooperation between members of the opposite sides, on any level. Even those who most sympathized with the problems of the other are engaged in, using Mary McLeod Bethune Washington's terms, 'getting their own.' Interracial organizations, social groups, and even marriages are splintering against the color barrier.

"We have some reports now from neighboring states that may be of importance to our viewers, concerning the conditions in these areas at the present time. A state of emergency has been declared for the following municipalities in New Jersey: Absecon, Adelphia, Allendale, Allenhurst, Allentown, Allenwood, Alloway, Alpha. . . . Well, as my eye travels over this list of some eight or nine hundred towns I notice that only a few *aren't* listed, notably Convent Station and Peapack. You can pretty well assume that things are bad *all* over. That goes for the New York, Pennsylvania, and Connecticut regions as well.

"We have some footage that was shot in Newark about ten minutes after the New Haven declaration. It's pretty tense out there now. The expert analysts in the news media are astounded that the intense polarization and outbreaks of rioting occurred so quickly. Let's take a look at those films now.

"Apparently there's some diffi—

"I don't know, what can . . . experiencing ourselves some of this interference with . . . refusal to even. . . .

"—rifying. They're running around out there like maniacs, shooting and—

"—flames and the smoke is—you can see the clouds against the sky, between the buildings like waves of—"

It was a pink mimeographed factsheet. Frowning, he stuffed it into his pocket. "Factsheet," eh? It had been several days since Stevie had heard a fact that he could trust.

Nobody was saying *anything* worth listening to. The factsheets had begun the second day with the expected clutter of charges and accusations, but soon everyone realized that this wasn't going to be that kind of war. Nobody gave a good goddamn *what* happened to anyone else. On the third day the few angry allegations that were made were answered with "our own sources do not indicate that, in fact, any such incident actually occurred" or with a curt "T.S., baby!" or, finally, no reply at all. Now the factsheets just bragged, or warned, or threatened.

Stevie was hitchhiking, which was a dangerous thing to do, but no more dangerous than sitting in an apartment waiting for the blazing torches. He felt that if he were going to be a target, a moving target offered the better odds.

He carried a pistol and a rifle that he had liberated from Abercrombie & Fitch. The hot morning sun gleamed on the zippers and studs of his black leathers. He stood by the side of the parkway, smiling grimly to himself as he waited for a ride. Every car that came around the curve was a challenge, one that he was more than willing to accept. There wasn't much traffic lately, and for that Stevie was sorry. He was really getting to dig this.

A car approached, a late model black Imperial with its head-lights burning. He set himself, ready to dodge into the ditch on the side of the road. Stevie stared through the windshield as the car came nearer. He let out his breath suddenly: it was a white chick. It looked like she had liberated the car; maybe she was looking for someone to team up with. Even if she was a dog, it would beat hitching.

The Imperial passed him, slowed, and stopped on the road's shoulder. The chick slid over on the seat, rolling down the window on the passenger's side and shouting to him.

"Hurry up, you idiot. I don't want to sit here much longer."

He ran to the car, pulling open the door to get in. She slammed it shut again, and Stevie stood there confused.

"What the hell—"

"Shut up," she snapped, handing him another pink factsheet. "Read this. And hurry it up."

He read the factsheet. His throat went dry and he began to feel a buzz in his head. At the top of the page was the familiar, fisted Women's Lib symbol. In regulation incendiary rhetoric below it, a few paragraphs explained that it had been decided by the uppermost echelon to strike now for freedom. During the period of severe disorientation, women the world over were taking the opportunity to beat down the revisionist male supremist pigs. Not just the oppressed racial minorities can express their militancy, it said. The female popular liberation front knew no color boundaries. Who did they think they were kidding? Stevie thought.

"You're gonna get plugged by some black bitch, you know that?" he said. He looked up at her. She had a gun pointed at him, aimed at his chest. The buzz in his head grew louder.

"You wanna put that sheet back on the pile? We don't have enough to go around," she said.

"Look," said Stevie, starting to move toward the car. The girl raised the pistol in a warning. He dove to the ground, parallel to the car, and rolled up against the right front wheel. The girl panicked, opening the door to shoot him before he could get away. Stevie fired twice before she sighted him, and she fell to the grassy shoulder. He didn't check to see if she were dead or merely wounded; he took her pistol and got in the car.

"My fellow Americans." The voice of the President was strained and tired, but he still managed his famous promiseless smile. The picture of the Chief Executive was the first to disturb the televisions' colored confetti snow for nearly two weeks.

"We meet tonight to discuss the intolerable situation in which our nation finds itself. With me this evening"—the President indicated an elderly, well-dressed Negro gentleman seated at a desk to the left of the President's—"I have invited the Rev. Dr. Roosevelt Wilson, who will speak to you from his own conscience. Rev. Wilson is known to many of you as an honest man, a community leader, and a voice of collaboration in these times of mistrust and fiscal insecurity."

Across the nation, men in dark turtlenecks ran down searing channels of flame, liberated television sets in their gentle grasp, running so that they might see this special telecast. Across the nation men and women of all persuasions looked at Wilson and muttered, "Well, isn't he the clean old nigger!"

Rev. Wilson spoke, his voice urgent and slow with emotion. "We must do everything that our leaders tell us. We cannot take the law into our own hands. We must listen to the promptings of reason and calm, and find that equitable solution that I'm sure we all desire."

The TV broadcast had been a major accomplishment. Its organization had been a tribute to the cooperation of many dissatisfied men who would rather have been out liberating lawn furniture. But the message of these two paternal figures of authority was more important.

"Thank you, Dr. Wilson," said the President. He stood, smiling into the camera, and walked to a large map that had been set up to his right. He took a pointer in one hand.

"This," he said, "is our beleaguered nation. Each green dot represents a community where the violence that plagues us has gone beyond containable limits." The map was nearly solid green, the first time the USA had been in that condition since the early seventeenth century. "I have asked for assistance from the armed forces of Canada, Mexico and Great Britain, but although I mailed the requests nearly two weeks ago I have yet to receive a reply. I can only assume that we are on our own.

"Therefore, I will make one statement concerning official government policy. As you know, this state of affairs will technically come to an end in about fifteen days. At that time, the government will prosecute *severely* anyone connected with any further disruptions of Federal activities. This is not merely an empty threat; it con—"

A young black man ran before the camera, turning to shout an incoherent slogan. Rev. Wilson saw the pistol in the boy's hand and stood, his face contorted with fear and envy. "The business of America *is* business!" he screamed, and then dropped back into his seat as the black militant shot. The President clutched his chest and cried, "We *must* not . . . lose . . ." and fell to the floor.

The cameras seemed to swing at random, as men rushed about confusedly. From somewhere a white man appeared, perhaps one of the technicians, with his own pistol. He hurried to the desk shouting, "For anarchy!" and shot Dr. Wilson point-blank. The white assassin turned, and the black assassin fired at him. The two killers began a cautious but noisy gun battle in the studio. Here most viewers turned off their sets. "In very poor taste," they thought.

The sign outside: SECOND NATIONAL BANK OF OUR LORD, THE ENGINEER. UNIVERSAL CHURCH OF GOD OR SOME SORT OF COSMIC EMBODIMENT OF GOOD.

Above the entrance to the church fluttered a hastily made banner. The masculine symbol had been crudely painted on a white sheet; the white flag indicated that the worshippers were white males and that blacks and women were "welcome" at their own risk. The population was now split into four mutually antagonistic

353

segments. The separate groups began to realize that there was some point in keeping their members together in little cadres. The streets and apartment buildings were death traps.

Inside the church the men were silent in prayer. They were led by an elderly deacon, whose inexperience and confusion were no greater nor less than any in the congregation.

"Merciful God," he prayed, "in whatever Form the various members of our flock picture Your Corporal Entity or Insubstantial Spirit, we ask that You guide us in this time of direst peril.

"Brother lifts sword against brother, and brother against sister. Husband and wife are torn asunder against Your holiest ordainments. Protect us, and show us our proper response. Perhaps it is true that vengeance is solely Yours; but speak to us, then, concerning Limited Cautionary Retaliation, and other alternatives. We would see a sign, for truly we are lost in the mires of day-to-day living."

The deacon continued his prayer, but soon there began a series of poundings on the door. The deacon stopped for just a second, looking up nervously, his hand straying to his sidearm. When nothing further happened he finished the prayer and the members of the congregation added, if they chose, their amens.

At the end of the service the men rose to leave. They stood at the door, in no hurry to abandon the sanctuary of the church. At last the deacon led them out. It was immediately noticed that a yellow factsheet had been nailed to the outside of the door. The Roman Catholics of the neighborhood had decided to end the centuries-long schism. Why not now, when everybody else was settling their differences? A Final Solution.

A bullet split wood from the door frame. The men standing on the stoop jumped back inside. A voice called from the street, "You damn commie atheist Protestants! We're gonna wipe you out and send your lousy heretic souls straight to Hell!" More gunfire. The stained glass windows of the church shattered, and there were cries from inside.

"They got one of the elders!"

"It's those crummy Catholics. We should have got them when we had the chance. Damn it, now they got us holed up in here."

The next day a blue factsheet was circulated by the Jewish community explaining that they had finally gotten tired of having their gabardine spat on, and that everybody'd just have to watch out. Around the world the remaining clusters of people fractured again, on the basis of creed.

It was getting so you didn't know *whom* you could trust.

Stevie was heading back toward the city when the car went. It made a few preliminary noises, shaking and rattling slower, and then it stopped. For all he knew it might simply have been out of gas. There were eight days left in the prescribed thirty, and he needed a ride.

He took the rifle and the two pistols from the Imperial and stood by the side of the road. It was a lot more dangerous to hitch now than it had been before, for the simple reason that the odds were that anyone who happened by would probably be on the other side of *one* of the many ideological fences. He was still confident, though, that he would be safely picked up, or be able to wrest a car away from its owner.

There was very little traffic. Several times Stevie had to jump for cover as a hostile driver sped by him, shooting wildly from behind the wheel. At last an old Chevy stopped for him, driven by a heavy white man whom Stevie judged to be in his late fifties.

"Come on, get in," said the man.

Stevie climbed into the car, grunting his thanks and settling warily back against the seat.

"Where you going?" asked the man.

"New York."

"Um. You, uh, you a Christian?"

"Hey," said Stevie, "right now we ain't got any troubles at all. We can just drive until we get where we're going. We only have eight days, right? So if we leave off the questions, eight days from now *both* of us'll be happy."

"All right. That's a good point, I guess, but it defeats the whole purpose. I mean, it doesn't seem to enter into the spirit of things."

"Yeah, well, the spirit's getting a little tired."

They rode in silence, taking turns with the driving. Stevie noticed that the old man kept staring at the rifle and two pistols. Stevie searched the car as best he could with his eyes, and it looked to him as though the old man was unarmed himself. Stevie didn't say anything.

"You seen a factsheet lately?" asked the man.

"No," said Stevie. "Haven't seen one in days. I got tired of the whole thing. *Now* who's at it?"

The old man looked at him quickly, then turned back to the road. "Nobody. Nothing new." Stevie glanced at the man now, studying his face curiously. Nothing new.

355

After a while the man asked him for some bullets.

"I didn't think that you had a gun," said Stevie.

"Yeah. I got a .38 in the glove compartment. I keep it there, well, I'm less likely to use it."

"A .38? Well, these shells wouldn't do you any good, anyhow. Besides, I don't really want to give them up yet."

The man looked at him again. He licked his lips, appearing to make some decision. He took his eyes off the road for a moment and lunged across the seat in a dive for one of the loaded pistols. Stevie slammed the edge of his hand into the older man's throat. The man choked and collapsed on the seat. Stevie switched off the engine and steered the car to the side of the road, where he opened the door and dumped the still body.

Before he started the car again, Stevie opened the glove compartment. There was an unloaded revolver and a crumpled fact-sheet. Stevie tossed the gun to the ground by the old man. He smoothed out the wrinkled paper. The youth of the world, it proclaimed, had declared war on everyone over the age of thirty years.

"How you coming with that factsheet?"

The thin man in the green workshirt stopped typing and looked up. "I don't know. It's hard making out your crummy handwriting. Maybe another fifteen minutes. Are they getting restless out there?"

The man in the jacket gulped down some of his lukewarm coffee. "Yeah. I was going to make an announcement, but what the hell. Let 'em wait. They had their vote, they know what's coming. Just finish that factsheet. I want to get it run off and put up before them goddamn Artists beat us to it."

"Look, Larry, them queers'll never think of it in the first place. Calm down."

The man in the workshirt typed in silence for a while. Larry walked around the cold meeting hall, pushing chairs back in place and chewing his cigar nervously. When the stencil was finished, the man in the workshirt pulled it out of the typewriter and handed it to Larry. "All right," he said, "there it is. Maybe you better go read it to them first. They been waiting out there for a couple of hours now."

"Yeah, I guess so," said Larry. He zipped up his green jacket and waited for the man in the workshirt to get his coat. He turned off the lights and locked the door to the hall. Outside was a huge crowd of men, all white and all well into middle age. They cheered when

Larry and the other man came out. Larry held up his hands for quiet.

"All right, listen up," he said. "We got our factsheet here. Before we go and have it run off, I'm going to let you hear it. It says just like what we voted for, so you all should be pretty satisfied."

He read the factsheet, stopping every now and then to wait through the applause and cheers of the men. He looked out at the crowd. They're all brawny veteran-types, he thought. That's what we are: we're Veterans. We been through it all. We're the ones who know what's going on. We're the Producers.

The factsheet explained, in simple language unlike the bitter diatribes of other groups, that the laborers—the Producers—of the world had gotten fed up with doing all the work while a large portion of the population—the goddamn queer Artists—did nothing but eat up all the fruits of honest nine to five work. Artists contributed nothing, and wasted large amounts of our precious resources. It was simple logic to see that the food, clothing, shelter, money and recreational facilities that were diverted from the Producers' use were as good as thrown into the garbage. The Producers worked harder and harder, and got back less and less. Well then, what could you expect to happen? Everything was bound to get worse for everybody.

The men cheered. It was about time that they got rid of the parasites. No one complained when you burned off a leech. And no one could complain when you snuffed out the leechlike elements of normal, organized, Productive society.

Larry finished reading the sheet and asked for questions and comments. Several men started talking, but Larry ignored them and went on speaking himself.

"Now, this doesn't mean," he said, "that we gotta get everybody that doesn't work regular hours like we do. You see that some of the people are hard to tell whether they're Producers like us, or just lousy addict Artists. Like the people that make TV. We can use them. But we have to be careful, because there's a lot of Artists around who are trying to make us think that they're really Producers. Just remember: if you can use it, it's not Art."

The crowd cheered again, and then it began to break up. Some of the men stood around arguing. One of the small groups of Producers that was slowly walking to the parking lot was deeply involved in debating the boundaries separating Artists and Producers.

"I mean, where are we going to stop?" said one. "I don't like the was this divisioning is going. Pretty soon there won't be any groups left to belong to. We'll all be locked up in our homes, afraid to see anybody at all."

"It's not doing us any good," agreed another. "If you go out and get what you want, I mean, take something from a store or something, why, everybody knows you got it when you bring it home. Then *you're* the target. I got less now than when this all started."

A third man watched the first two grimly. He pulled out a factsheet of his own from the pocket of his jacket. "That's commie talk," he said. "You're missing the point of the whole thing. Let me ask you a question. Are you right- or left-handed?"

The first man looked up from the factsheet, puzzled. "I don't see that it makes any difference. I mean, I'm basically left-handed, but I write with my right hand."

The third man stared angrily, in disbelief.

Bang.

YANG and YIN: Male and female. Hot and cold. Mass and energy. Smooth and crunchy. Odd and even. Sun and moon. Silence and noise. Space and time. Slave and master. Fast and slow. Large and small. Land and sea. Good and evil. On and off. Black and white. Strong and weak. Regular and filter king. Young and old. Light and shade. Fire and ice. Sickness and health. Hard and soft. Life and death.

If there *is* a plot, shouldn't you know about it?

One more hour.

Millions of people hid in their holes, waiting out the last minutes of the wars. Hardly anyone was out on the streets yet. No one shouted their drunken celebrations that little bit ahead of schedule. In the night darkness Stevie could still hear the ragged crackings of guns in the distance. Some suckers getting it only an hour from homefree.

The time passed. Warily, people came out into the fresher air, still hiding themselves in shadows, not used yet to walking in the open. Guns of the enthusiasts popped; they would never get a chance like this again, and there were only fifteen minutes left. Forty-second Street chromium knives found their lodgings in unprotected Gotham throats and shoulders.

Times Square was still empty when Stevie arrived. Decomposing corpses sprawled in front of the record and porno shops. A few shadowy forms moved across the streets, far away down the side-walk.

The big ball was poised. Stevie watched it, bored, with murder-ers cringing around him. The huge lighted New Year's globe was ready to drop, waiting only for midnight and for the kissing New Year's VJ-Day crowds. There was Stevie, who didn't care, and the looters, disappointed in the smoked-out, gunfire black, looted stores.

It said it right up there: 11:55. Five more minutes. Stevie pushed himself back into a doorway, knowing that it would be humiliating to get it with only five minutes left. From the vague screams around him he knew that some were still finding it.

People were running by now. The square was filling up. 11:58 and the ball was *just* hanging there: the sudden well of people drew rapid rifle fire, but the crowd still grew. There was the beginning of a murmur, just the hint of the war-is-over madness. Stevie sent himself into the stream, giving himself up to the release and relief.

11:59. . . . The ball seemed . . . to tip . . . and *fell!* 12:00! The chant grew stronger, the New York chant, the smugness returned in all its sordid might. "We're Number One! We're Number One!" The cold breezes drove the shouting through the unlit streets, carrying it on top of the burnt and fecal smells. It would be a long time before what was left would be made livable, but We're Number One! There were still sporadic shots, but these were the usual New York Town killers, doing the undeclared and time-honored violence that goes unnoticed.

We're Number One!

Stevie found himself screaming in spite of himself. He was standing next to a tall, sweating black. Stevie grinned; the black grinned. Stevie stuck out his hand. "Shake!" he said. "We're Number One!"

"We're Number One!" said the black. "I mean, it's *us!* We gotta settle all this down, but, I mean, what's left is *ours!* No more fighting!"

Stevie looked at him, realizing for the first time the meaning of their situation. "Right you are," he said with a catch in his voice. "Right you are, Brother."

"Excuse me."

Stevie and the black turned to see a strangely dressed woman. The costume completely hid any clue to the person's identity, but the voice was very definitely feminine. The woman wore a long, loose robe decorated fancifully with flowers and butterflies. Artifi-cial gems had been stuck on, and the whole thing trimmed with cheap, dimestore "gold-and-silver" piping. The woman's head was entirely hidden by a large, bowl-shaped woven helmet, and from within it her voice echoed excitedly.

"Excuse me," she said. "Now that the preliminary skirmishes are over, don't you think we should get on with it?"

"With what?" asked the black.

"The Last War, the final one. The war against ourselves. It's senseless to keep avoiding it, now."

"What do you mean?" asked Stevie.

The woman touched Stevie's chest. "There. Your guilt. Your frustration. You don't really feel any better, do you? I mean, women don't really hate men; they hate their own weaknesses. People don't really hate other people for their religion or race. It's just that seeing someone different from you makes you feel a little insecure in your own belief. What you hate is your own doubt, and you project the hatred onto the other man."

"She's right!" said the black. "You know, I wouldn't mind it half so much if they'd hate me because of *me*; but nobody ever took the trouble."

"That's what's so frustrating," she said. "If anyone's ever going to hate the *real* you, you know who it'll have to be."

"You're from that Kindness Cult, aren't you?" the black said softly.

"*Shinsetsu*," she said. "Yes."

"You want us to meditate or something?" asked Stevie. The woman dug into a large basket that she carried on her arm. She handed each of them a plump cellophane package filled with a colorless fluid.

"No," said the black as he took his package. "Kerosene."

Stevie held his bag of kerosene uncertainly, and looked around the square. There were others dressed in the *Shinsetsu* manner, and they were all talking to groups that had formed around them.

"Declare war on myself?" Stevie said doubtfully. "Do I have to publish a factsheet first?" No one answered him. People nearby were moving closer so they could hear the *Shinsetsu* woman. She continued to hand out packages as she spoke.

Stevie slipped away, trying to get crosstown, out of the congested square. When he reached a side street he looked back: already the crowd was dotted with scores of little fires, like scattered piles of burning leaves in the backyards of his childhood.

adjustment

Ward Moore

"Adjustment" is a story of conformity. First, it gives us a good portrait of the conformist—his likes and dislikes, his quirks and anxieties. Second, it suggests that conceptions of normality and abnormality are strongly related to the acts of conforming to middle-class standards and ideas of reality. Third, it suggests that the conformist and nonconformist are not as unlike as most people and they themselves might think. To accomplish this, the story creates Squith, the conformist, and confronts him with Wais, the nonconformist.

First, we are given our picture of the conformist. We see that he believes in cleanliness and decency, and has a sense of pride in these values. He believes in common sense, is reliable, has good manners, and is a very stable individual. He is not very creative apparently, but full of typically middle American values. He is antiintellectual and believes strongly in physical fitness. He is a man who always needs to be occupied. He talks a good game about a moderate accumulation of wealth. He likes television, shies away from controversial ideas, and is exasperated by indefiniteness. This suggests a low tolerance for ambiguity, often related to the conventional person.

As the story continues, we get a fuller picture of our conformist. He likes things short, tight, and secure rather than the loose, abandoned style of the handmaidens he acquires. This is also related to his taste in books; he prefers the hard facts rather than the looseness of fiction. As we would guess, he likes art which he can understand. When he comes to live with Wais, the nonconformist whose values and tastes are almost totally opposite, something is bound to change. It does, but not in the conventional way!

The second issue the story raises is the social conformity approach to abnormality. At the beginning, Squith—representing the attitude of the average person—is quick to brand Wais as insane. Later on, when he gets to know Wais, he sees him merely as being "out of step," not mad. He begins to see a certain logic to Wais's thinking, based on Wais's experience of reality. Finally, even Squith gets annoyed at the doctor's narrow view of reality with its implication that anyone who does not view reality in the same way is insane.

Third, the story raises the question of whether the conformist and the nonconformist are not very much alike; whether, in fact, they can learn from each other. Both extremes are perhaps in their own way out of step with reality. The conformist is out of step with the reality of his own feelings and desires. In order to completely "adjust" to society, he must deny some of his own wishes and impulses. In this way he becomes uptight, so that he does not put himself in what he is afraid will be a morally compromising position. He represses these threatening desires and impulses, but they do not go away. This is evidenced by his quickness to condemn these same impulses in others like hippies, exaggerating their immorality and thus justifying to himself why he does not engage in their acts. Often the crux of desires that are repressed is sexual, and we see at the end of the story some of these latent desires coming out in Squith. For example, he expresses his intention of keeping all of his handmaidens rather than the conventional loyalty to just one. He rationalizes, of course, that he must not hurt the others.

Wais, too, apparently learns that the extreme nonconformist, in dropping out, may also be out of step with the truth of the real world, as well as with the challenge of facing that truth. Perhaps he, too, has a certain desire for order and stability, which he represses and fights against because he fears his own loss of freedom. In both cases, the extremes of conformity and noncon-formity suggest underlying desires for the opposite condition which are fought off to reduce arousal of anxiety. This is the defense mechanism called *reaction formation*.

ADJUSTMENT   *Ward Moore*

Dr. Gayler's explanations were superfluous; I understood fully. I've looked through enough books with case histories (Charles X, 24, pronounced hyperthyroid, had recurrent dreams of driving Mary Y down a narrow dirt road in a bathtub) to know that the identities of patients are deliberately obscured. Anyway, curiosity—beyond the normal desire for useful information—isn't a vice of mine. In fact I rather pride myself on not having vices. I'm not the kind who boasts of smoking two packs a day or getting drunk Saturday nights, gambling, or having affairs. I try to lead a clean, decent life, and I'm not ashamed of having been a Boy Scout or a member of the Epworth League.

"You're the nearest we have found to a completely adjusted individual," he said.

I wished he would come to the point. I don't find psychiatrists' offices fascinating; quite the contrary. The advanced paintings on the walls gave me astigmatism. The readable magazines like *Life* and the *National Geographic* were out of date; the unreadable ones, *Accent, Partisan Review, Could,* I thought better left unread. I wasn't bored; no sensible person allows himself to get that way. But if I had, Dr. Gayler and his office would have brought it on.

"You went through high school with an average grade of B; you graduated from D—twenty-fifth in a class of fifty. You were immediately hired by the—"

"Fifth National Bank of Republic City. Where I still work."

"You live with your widowed mother, F—S—," he filled in. "For whom you bought a new washing machine from Sears—"

"Shouldn't that be S—R—?" Perhaps I don't guffaw at stupid jokes, but I have a sense of humor.

"Possibly," conceded Dr. Gayler. "And other household conveniences, on which you owe a balance of—"

"I've never been a day behind on my payments."

"I'm sure of that. Believe me, I'm not playing back facts you already know just to—"

"Then why are you? I don't want to be rude, Doctor, and I can't pretend my time is valuable to anyone but myself—"

"There's a year's salary for two weeks of your time in this for you, Mr. Squith. Two weeks in pleasant, if dull, surroundings, with room, board and laundry thrown in."

"I'm in no position to take two weeks off from the bank."

He smiled and leaned back, "My patient has a close relative who owns a bit of stock in the Fifth National. There'll be no trouble about a vacation with pay."

"Do you mind explaining just what it is you want of me?"

"Not at all, Mr Squith. My patient is a young man of your own age—"

"Twenty-six." I knew he knew I was born in 1934, but I said it anyway.

"Exactly. Unfortunately he lacks your stability. He is, in fact, slightly, ah, disturbed,"

"Insane," I said bluntly. There's no use beating around the bush. Call a spade a spade.

"Not at all. Of course the term has been outmoded for a long time: even so, my patient is not psychotic in the way I think you mean. He has to some extent lost contact with reality—"

"Thinks he's Napoleon?"

Dr. Gayler smiled again. "An infrequent delusion; personally I've never come across it. No, his divorce from reality is more subtle. He knows who he is and in what century he's living. However, he has not been able to accept the disagreeable aspects of life. As you and I do. So he has withdrawn into a world of his own devising—"

"You mean he has hallucinations?"

When I refused his proffered cigarette he lit one himself. "Let's not bother with words that mean different things at different times. Let's just say he has withdrawn."

"All right," I agreed. "I still don't see where I come in."

"I could use several different techniques to help him adjust. Hypnosis. Extended psychoanalysis. Drugs. All timetaking, none entirely satisfactory. However, there is a new method with good results reported. You might call it facsimile-therapy, if you wanted to be facetious."

I didn't want to be facetious. "Being around someone normal will make him normal too?"

He blew smoke through his nostrils before snubbing out the cigarette. "If it were that simple, all sorts of problems would have stopped existing long ago. It would do my patient little good just to observe a man who has no trouble accepting reality—a balanced person like yourself—to listen and talk, on no matter how intimate a basis. He must be convinced of the happiness of an adjusted man.

He must see into the sound mind, to understand how it can accept what his own has rejected. To put it on—metaphorically—to impose it over his own, as one puts a cast on a broken leg to hold the bones and muscles in the proper place while it heals."

I wasn't too pleased at having my mind compared to a plaster cast. Not that I regard myself as a Thinker with a capital T. Intellectuals with round shoulders and spindly legs are just as unwholesome as the opposite. A sound mind in a sound body is my motto.

Still, Dr. Gayler had a point, no matter how clumsily made. Anyone afraid to face the rough and tumble of everyday life must be soft, not to say weak; reinforcement from a man of character was bound to help. I could imagine easily enough what his patient must be like: too much money, and not enough to occupy his time. Dissipated surely, incapable of simple enjoyments; slack-jawed and shifty-eyed.

I was both right and wrong, as I discovered after I talked with Mr. McIlforth—our Cashier and my immediate superior—and decided to accept Dr. Gayler's proposition. I'm afraid I wasn't entirely truthful to my Mother when I explained I was going away on business for two weeks, but then I wasn't entirely untruthful either. At any rate, I packed my bag and arrived at the sanitarium before dinnertime. Dr. Gayler shook hands, a formality I thought rather superfluous, and introduced me to Robert Wais.

Shifty-eyed he was not, but I'm afraid dissipated was accurate. As soon as we were alone (did I say the arrangement called for sharing the same quarters?) he asked, "What about a drink, kid? I'm parched."

I don't like being called kid, and I never take anything but a glass of beer on a warm evening or a toast to auld lang syne on New Year's Eve. "Surely there's some rule in this place against—"

"Not a one." He brought out a bottle and got a tumbler from the bathroom. "That is, not for me, and I guess what goes for me goes for you too. Sky's the limit; drink hearty. Sorry I haven't got anything better than this"—he held up the bottle and I read the famous label which is advertised by testimonials from important people who would have been better advised to avoid alcohol, but of whose taste in liquor there can be no doubt—"but you just can't get decent stuff on this side."

"This side of what?" I asked.

He stared at me over the rim of his glass. "Don't hand me a line. I'm here because I made a deal with my family and that head-shrinker, not because they have me fooled. They kept pestering me till they wore me down and I said I'd give this guff a try if they'd leave me alone afterward."

He was far gone, clearly. "I don't care for any, but don't let me stop you."

"Ease your mind." He tossed the whiskey down, shuddering, and refilled the glass. "So you're to be my model? Two weeks, and I'll be like you?"

Since the poor fellow was not right in his mind, I refused to take offense. "I don't think—"I began, when he came over and clutched my elbow with his free hand.

"Kid," he said, "give it to me straight. What do you really think of the Dodgers this year?"

It wasn't a question I would have expected. "I don't follow baseball closely—football's my game. But aren't the Braves and the Giants—"

"Yah!" he snorted, turning away. I didn't anticipate my two weeks here would be fun; I expected, in fact, to earn what I was being paid; but the close company of a boor was even more objectionable than that of a lunatic. I always say it costs very little to be polite, whether you mean it or not.

He whirled around. "Typical of this side," he commented bitterly. "Brooklyn in fifth place. Fifth place—the second division! Satchel Paige retired and Walter Johnson forgotten. Lavagetto coaching in the bush leagues. Robinson selling Chock Full O' Nuts. Lies, lies! They spend all their time making them up. Do you know what?" He came closer, and whispered. "They even say Matisse is dead and Picasso hasn't given up painting for sculpture!"

For the first time it occurred to me—as it should have sooner— that he might become violent. And the room, more like that of a hotel than a hospital, had no bell to summon attendants, only a phone, and Wais was not far enough gone for me to scream through it for help. Yet his wild talk made me nervous. Brooklyn was in fifth place; Paige, Johnson, Lavagetto and Robinson were forgotten except by nostalgic sportswriters. Matisse . . . Matisse. . . . A paint- er; I was sure I'd read an obituary, and while I didn't go in for grotesque painting, I was pretty sure Picasso hadn't taken up sculpture.

I was relieved when they wheeled in a dumbwaiter with our dinner. There was service for three; Dr. Gayler joined us. Now that we were in his hands his manner was less authoritative than placatory, as though he were wheedling us into liking him and making the experiment succeed. He chatted amiably, addressing us by our given names, which might have been confusing except that he called Wais "Robert" and me "Bob." He talked to me of utility bonds, about which he seemed reasonably well-informed, until Wais showed signs of restlessness, whereupon he turned to him to discuss the music of Schoenberg.

Though this was clearly more to Wais's taste, he was restless, and it wasn't long before he threw himself back in his chair and said petulantly, "Let's get on with it, Doc. Give us the needle or put us in a trance, hand out the pills, or start the free association spinning."

Dr. Gayler looked pained. "Sorry you got the idea drugs or hypnosis was to be used. All I want you to do is relax and permit the empathic currents to flow between you. Let yourself look into Bob's mind."

Wais grunted. "X-rays or telepathy?"

"Call it osmosis if you like," said Gayler genially. "Just don't resist the process."

Wais picked up a book—poetry from the slimness of it—and throwing himself down on the couch, began reading.

Happily his discourtesy wasn't always so open. Or perhaps its scope depended on his moods, for the next day he acted very differently. "One day gone," he announced jovially; "only thirteen to go. Like being marooned on a desert island except we know when the rescue ship's coming. When I was a boy I thought it would be the ideal life, didn't you?"

"I was always too busy for daydreaming," I confessed. "I had a stamp collection, an erector set, model airplanes. And there were scouts and games and shows. And when I went to high school I began selling magazine subscriptions and doing odd jobs. I was never what they used to call an introvert."

I was prepared for some sarcastic remark; instead he began asking personal questions, not rudely, but with genuine interest. His attention overcame my initial reticence; I soon found myself telling him about Mother, and the bank, and how Mr. McIlforth once said I had a natural flair for trust deeds. I'm afraid I went very close to the edge of good taste in mentioning Alice and our tentative agreement, contingent on so many factors that it was unlikely we would be able to marry for years.

He shuddered. "How can you stand it? Doing the same things, day after day?"

"They aren't the same things," I explained. "Each day is different, especially in the bank. It's not like a factory, where you repeat the identical operation over and over. It's a job full of new and rich experience. Every aspect of human nature is revealed to the man in the bank: hopes, ambitions, troubles, catastrophes; thrift, honesty, astuteness, courage. . . .''

"You find all this in the complacent people who come in clutching their bankbooks and deposits. In the anxious, fawning seekers of loans?"

"Yes, because everyone comes to the bank. Plumbers and housewives, executives and clerks. Depositors and borrowers aren't a class apart: they're Everyman."

He shook his head. "You too can discover romance." He pondered for a moment. "And planning to spend the rest of your life with one woman."

"It's customary," I remarked with some irony.

"All is custom, as Herodotus said. If you were a Muslim it would be four."

"I think not. Debauchery is debauchery in any time or place. Just because something is legal or customary doesn't make it right."

"Ha! Where's your celebrated adjustment now?"

We didn't understand each other, as you can see. We had little in common. Yet in spite of his eccentricities we got along fairly well. I could hardly approve of his habits or extremely controversial ideas, but apart from them I found him likeable in a way. I even tolerated his irrational aversion to television—there was supposed to be a set in our quarters, but he peremptorily ordered it out—and his distracting habit of listening to snippets of baseball broadcasts, always turning them off angrily when the behavior of the Brooklyn team or the decision of an umpire displeased him.

"Absurd!" he would rage.

"Well, there isn't much you can do about it."

He gave me a scornful look. "That's what you think." And he would leave the room abruptly.

I couldn't imagine where he went, for though the sanitarium resembled a good hotel, it provided no social recreation, no place where one guest could meet others. There was neither a communal dining room, a moving picture hall, nor other facilities for the gregarious. And he volunteered no information until the first week had passed. It was a particularly disastrous game for the Dodgers, who seemed to have done everything possible to deserve their alternate nickname except put in pinch hitters for their heaviest batters. Wais gave a disgusted click of the switch. "Deal or no deal, I'm going to listen where I can get a decent broadcast of a decent game."

I puzzled over that one. If he couldn't get what he wanted there it was hard to imagine where he could. The radio he'd substituted for the thirty-inch TV was one of those custom jobs that do everything but the laundry. It had AM, FM, shortwave and all possible bands; if there were Martian or Venerian broadcasts I'm sure it would have brought them in. And he had never mentioned any interest in cricket, lacrosse, jai-alai, or the esoteric sports of the Mysterious East. The more I thought of it, the less sense it made.

It was no use to tell myself I couldn't expect a mentally unbalanced individual to make sense. Because I had come, perhaps grudgingly, to learn that Robert Wais, for all his odd poses and eccentricities, usually made sense of a sort. It might not be Mr. McIlforth's or Dr. Gayler's, but within his own frame of reference it was coherent and logical. I didn't particularly like him, nor was I sympathetic toward his moods, whims and notions. But in the peculiar atmosphere of close contact I had seen enough of him and talked with him sufficiently to come a long way from my snap judgment in Dr. Gayler's office that he was insane. Rude, brusque, moody, opinionated, out of step with everybody—certainly. But mad? I doubted it more all the time.

Yet the implications of his childish exclamations and exits were tantalizing. Where did he go? What did he do when he got there? Then, as though to aggravate my interest still further, on the ninth day of Dr. Gayler's "experiment"—I use quotes around the word simply because, so far as I could see, there was nothing more to it than just throwing us together—he muttered, "I'm fed up with this stuff; I'm in the mood for Fred Allen, or even Groucho Marx."

I can pick up a gag as quickly as the next man. "I wouldn't mind a half hour of Bob Hope myself," I said. "Unfortunately for us, Allen passed away, Hope's retired, and Marx isn't on the air Mondays."

"You do believe all the lies they tell you on this side, don't you? Maybe it makes you happy or something. Would I be happy to recapture that lost innocence and give up everything that makes life interesting?" He didn't wait for me to answer the rhetorical question.

A week earlier I would have shrugged it off as pure nonsense, but I had come to see a certain consistency in Wais's speech and actions. Perhaps he had tapes or records of some of the old comedians. Though, if he did, why not play them on the machine in the room? His reference to "lies on this side" could be dismissed readily enough; still. . . .

Next afternoon he complained of a bad headache. I wasn't

surprised: he had been drinking the night before; no matter what he said about the hair of the dog, common sense told me more of the same wouldn't help. "Better take a rest," I suggested.

"Rest is all I get. I must have been out of my mind to come here. Anyway, I want to hear the Dodger-Red Sox game today."

It took me a moment to orient myself. "You mean the Dodger-Giant game. You had it on this morning, don't you remember? You shut it off in a huff when the Brooklyn pitcher was knocked out of the box. I got it back on after you left, and for your information, the Bums lost, nine to one."

He waved his arm. "Oh, that. I'm not going to listen to any more of those phony broadcasts."

Did he think—"Anyway, how could you hear a Brooklyn-Red Sox game? It isn't spring: no exhibition games. And they aren't in the same league, if you remember."

"I remember," he said. "There's nothing wrong with my memory."

"Well, then—" I began.

"Look: conversation makes me dizzy. Be a good fellow and run up and listen to the game. Tell me how it comes out."

"Run up where?"

He closed his eyes. "You'll find it."

My first impulse was to ignore him and retire with a copy of *Time* or *Coronet*. Naturally I was irritated. Cryptic remarks have much the same annoying effect as experimental poetry. Logic furnishes no key with which to puzzle them out. "It" could only refer to an electronic device but (leaving aside the question of why he would have installed it elsewhere) the bland assumption that I would find it "up there" (on the next floor, on the roof, in the sky?) was exasperating in its indefiniteness. Perhaps it was sheer annoyance that sent me forth; certainly I had no expectation of finding anything.

"Up" implied use of a stairway; beyond this, reason offered little help. Feeling somewhat foolish, and keeping an eye open for Dr. Gayler or one of the residents or nurses—trusting a plausible explanation of my presence would pop into my head—I mounted the broad flight of steps which narrowed arbitrarily to a landing. I stared down a long hall at close-set, indistinguishable doors. On impulse I walked to the third on the right and turned the knob.

I cannot say the room I entered was dark. Neither was it light. Silly as it sounds, the only words I could think of to describe it were the biblical ones: "*without form, and void.*" There was one exception to the amorphousness, the vagueness of the room. There was a single focal point of clarity and distinctness at the opposite end, chest-high: a cabinet with dials and speakers, but no knobs.

"... *now we come to the top of the Brooklyn batting order; Gil Hodges in the box, Snider on deck. Last of the seventh here at New Ebbets Field in this crucial game of the 1960 World Series. One out, Reese on first. Ruth winds up with his eye on the runner. The throw to first—not in time. Back on the mound; the pitch—low and inside: ball one. ...*"

A cumbersome joke; what for? The 1960 World Series wouldn't be played for more than three months, and the present standings of both Brooklyn and Boston ruled them out—except mathematically—as possible contestants. This imaginary broadcast, with the background sound effects of the crowd, must have been made by Wais for his amusement. Not for mine, certainly.

"... *Reese takes a big lead off first. Here comes the pitch—foul! The count is—*" The machine gave a click like a hiccup. "*This is not a record or a transcription of any kind; this is the actual voice of Red Barber, brought to you by the Gillette Safety Company. Men! Look sharp. ...*"

A silly business, though adding the last statement to the counterfeit was ingenious. And it was a pleasant fancy to introduce the old greats—all retired now, of course, except manager Reese—into the Brooklyn lineup; a touch of imagination to ignore the conversion of Ruth to an outfielder.

So this was where Wais spent his time. A strange place; one most people wouldn't care for. Yet I could understand how it served as a refuge, a relief from the routine of the sanitarium and the limited imagination of Dr. Gayler. Not very comfortable, perhaps, with nothing to sit on—

Something nudged the calves of my legs. Startled, I turned. One of those wrought-iron and canvas moderne things was just behind me. How I had failed to see it before was a mystery. I sat down somewhat gingerly. If this was all there was, there was no use complaining.

I was still bothered by the unsubstantiality of the room. Surely there ought to be windows? I sniffed automatically: the air was fresh and temperate. Evidently a ventilating system of some kind was introducing, controlling and purifying the air, doing away with the necessity for windows. However, this didn't account for the absence of light, or of walls—

"... *Ruth, head down, walks in from the mound. Glover Cleveland Alexander marches jauntily from the bullpen to see if he can. ...*"

But there was light, I now noticed, a concealed, diffused light, without glare or the yellow or blue quality of any artificial light I knew. As for walls, there were—no, there *was* a wall. A single wall, for the room, a large, in fact an enormous one, was circular in shape. I didn't care for it, though I know such a form is, at least theoretically, more economical and efficient. The wall gave it a solidity I welcomed; there is nothing more confusing than a room which seems to stretch out into endless space. There was a ceiling too, I realized, but as I looked up at it I felt my face reddening. I'm not excessively squeamish, but what I saw painted there, the nymphs and satyrs, gods and goddesses, shepherds and shepherdesses, was so frankly erotic and lascivious that I quickly looked down from the signature, "*J. Fragonard, pinxit,*" to the floor, which I now perceived was covered by a tapestry carpet repeating the same indecent themes.

There was no question the room represented Wais's sensual and decadent tastes. Pictures, hung on flat projections from the round wall, were the kind any kindergarten child—but no; any child of any age would have more restraint.

Except for the space occupied by the radio and an extensive bar stocked with bottles of varying sizes and shapes, brands I never saw on billboards or the backs of magazines, the rest of the wall was taken up by books, no two uniform. One would think that in collecting a large library space would be given to sets of standard authors in good-looking bindings, but there were none.

"*. . . Crack! Did you hear it? Campanella connected with that one! Hodges is coming in to score; Snider's rounding third; Robinson's already passed second. . . .*"

I walked over to the bookcases. *Sophia Scarlett,* by Stevenson; *The Real Life of Rumbold Raysting,* by Dickens; *Left at Home,* by Ring Lardner; Douglas Freeman's *Calhoun*—books assuredly never sponsored by any book club. Where had he gotten such curiosities? Why bring them to the sanitarium?

A door, not the one by which I had entered, opened. Through it came a ravishing young woman—I speak impersonally, as a matter of esthetics—clothed in a veil hiding nothing whatever. Her full, wide mouth smiled in a manner at once timid and inviting.

"Lord!" she exclaimed; "my heart beats again, now that you are here once more. Your lovesick slave is overwhelmed with joy and gratitude for your return." To my embarrassment, she threw herself to the carpet at my feet, twining her arms around my ankles.

I recovered my balance, if not my assurance. "There must be

some mistake, Miss. I'm afraid I haven't the pleasure of knowing you—"

"Oh, my lord, my beloved, my master," she wailed, without releasing her grip or raising her face, "What have I done to displease you? What is my fault that I no longer find favor in your sight? Oh beat me, hurt me—but do not deny me."

"Please, Miss," I mumbled; "there's a misunderstanding somewhere. Believe me, I—Come now, get up. You must be uncomfortable like that. There are always drafts on the floor. Let me introduce myself: I'm Robert—"

"Of course you are Robert, my life. Could you think your miserable Ariadne had forgotten you? Even though you act so strange and cold? Oh, master, take me back again—"

"... *And so that packs up another World Series for the World Champion Brooklyn Club. There will be joy in Flatbush, Bushwick, Greenpoint and even Canarsie tonight....*"

I felt this was intrusive at the moment. "How do you turn that thing off?" I asked. "Or at least get it on to something else?"

"Aren't you happy the Dodgers won, my king?"

"I don't give a da—excuse me, I mean I don't care one way or the other. It's all a rib. You, too; I suppose you work in a nightclub. Though I didn't think they wore this sort of thing even there."

Her cry was pure distress, which she didn't corrupt with tears. "I'll take it off, master; I'll wear nothing that offends you." And she began to do so.

"No, no," I objected quickly. "Keep it on. You might get chilled. Haven't you got anything a little more—ah—opaque to put on top of it?"

"Anything my liege fancies," she answered. "A sarong?"

"I was thinking of something more in the way of a dress, or a—you know—housecoat, or ... or. ..."

The radio (or whatever it was) [blared], "*This is a recording of the Mozart Forty-fourth Piano Concerto, K723; the Boston Symphony Orchestra, conducted by Arthur Nikisch; the solo part by Hans von Bülow.*"

"A housecoat!" cried Ariadne. "Truly I have become hideous in your eyes. And what of your other slaves and concubines?"

"My—Good heavens! Are there more of you?"

"You are joking, lord. The thought of Phyllis, Daphne, Chloe, Iphigenia and Leda brightens your eyes."

Six concubines! Bluebeard, no less. "You better send them away," I said.

She looked up at me, utter shock on her lovely face. "You would condemn them to death?"

"What? You mean they'd die away from here?"

"They—or I—would die away from you, light of our world. Naturally."

Being accountable for the lives of six young women—at least I assumed they must be young—was a new and frightening responsibility. For the first time since I entered the circular room I was tempted to turn back. But if I did, Wais would continue to tempt these creatures into a life of depravity. The least I could do was counteract his influence. "Where are they?"

"Why, awaiting your pleasure, master. Will you sport with us in the pool?"

"Certainly not!" Bathing suits would be more respectable than what Ariadne was wearing, but by now I was ready to believe they might be considered superfluous around here. "Pool?" On the third floor of a sanatarium?"

"I don't know why you speak and act so strangely, lord; but since it is your will it is mine also. And if I have become repulsive, the others may still gladden you."

What was the use of trying to explain to the poor girl that I was no fiend, but a normal and—at least informally—an engaged man? I followed her through the doorway into another and even bigger room, round like the first, except for two moon-shaped bits out of its sides to accommodate other circular rooms. It too was indirectly lit and air-conditioned; most of its area was taken up by a turquoise pool formed like a figure 8.

I hesitate to mention this for fear of being misunderstood, but it was a different set of figures which held my eye. As I had uneasily anticipated, the other five had less on than Ariadne. A great deal less. They were unqualifiedly naked.

What startled me more than their unclad state was their diversity. Ariadne's eyes were the color of the pool; her hair was like rust in the sun; her body—as I couldn't help observing—had the delicate luster of old parchment, except that it was warm and glowing. Leda—I soon learned their names as they clung to me, entreating me to favor them with my smile—was deep, dark brown, the tint and texture of a bronze iris in the shade. Chloe was Chinese; perfectly formed, exquisite, vivacious. There was no doubt about Iphigenia's being a Eurasian, with the delicate complexion and faultless features of the Malay predominating. Blonde Daphne belied the vacuity the word so often implies; black-haired, dark-eyed Phyllis—languid, magnificent—was frightening.

They clustered about me, laughing, teasing, cajoling. Phyllis knelt to untie my shoes, hiding them in a deluge of rippling hair. Leda struggled with my jacket; Chloe removed my tie and unbuttoned my shirt; Iphigenia and Daphne busied themselves also. Their attention was only too clear; they expected me to join them in the water—without swimming trunks.

"Ladies, wait!" I gasped. "I—I don't care for this sort of thing. Honestly."

Their beautiful faces fell. "Lord," pleaded Daphne, "are you tired of us?"

No one could have been cruel enough to answer yes. Besides, it would have been inaccurate; how could I be tired of them when we had just met? "No, no—certainly not. I'm just not in the mood for swimming at the moment."

Leda kissed my ear and whispered something in it which made me jump. Hesitantly Ariadne made a still more scandalous suggestion; I'm sure she could not have realized its outrageousness; Chloe clapped her hands: "I know—you would like a drink."

"If you mean alcohol," I said, retying my tie, "I would not. However, if there is some Coca-Cola round here. . . ."

They surveyed each other with questioning dismay. Iphigenia repeated, "Co-ca-co-la?"

"A harmless and refreshing beverage." I shook my head at their ignorance. "I see there isn't. Never mind; it's all right."

"Our king must have whatever he wishes," exclaimed Ariadne.

"Please don't bother," I said, discomposed at their eagerness to serve me.

"Master, we exist only to do your bidding," insisted Leda. "If we cannot satisfy your wants, we have no purpose."

"Here is your co-ca-co-la, liege," murmured Chloe, casting down her eyes after giving me what I can only describe as a shattering look.

And to be sure, there was the familiar pinch-waisted bottle on a tray in her hands. I drank it gratefully, though it was warm, not wishing to hurt them with criticism; almost immediately Phyllis appeared with another bottle, obviously refrigerated, accompanied by a glass half-full of ice cubes.

They were so overjoyed at this success in catering to my inclination that they became quite unrestrained. I regret to say they tried to drag me into the next room, a glimpse of which I caught through the opened door. It too was round. Mirror-walled and -ceilinged, it gave back an infinite number of images of a circular bed, heaped high with pillows in the center. I could not allow myself to speculate on their designs.

"Ladies," I said firmly, "if we are to be friends, and continue to enjoy these accommodations together—or more accurately, at the same time—we must come to an understanding. I'm sure, in your natural innocence, you don't realize how this scene would look to an outsider. Evil to him who evil thinks, of course, but why give even the appearance of evil?"

"But there is no one to see," Leda pointed out.

"All the more reason for discretion," I said. "If we did what was right only while people were watching, what would the world come to?"

Phyllis' eyes filled with tears; her regal head drooped. "What have we done wrong, lord? Tell us, so we may avoid offending you."

She looked so pitiful that I began to reach out with a brotherly pat of reassurance. But the sudden light in her eyes was so far from being sisterly that I was able to recollect her lack of attire in time, and draw back before touching the bare shoulder. "You haven't done anything wrong. Nothing at all. Simply as a matter of—ah—decorum, I think we ought to make some changes around here."

Daphne said, "Your wish is our law."

This was a trifle undemocratic but not entirely disagreeable. After all, they were lucky to have someone like myself, instead of an unstable character who would take advantage of them. "Let's begin then, by putting on suitable clothing; the common cold is a menace. And I do think you'll be more comfortable in bathing suits when you use the pool. And we can be perfectly friendly without excessive physical contact. Really, that's all. Oh—except possibly it might be better (this is just a suggestion) if you did up your hair, or perhaps cut it short. It seems so—mmm—*abandoned,* hanging down loose like that."

Ariadne, whom I somehow hadn't missed, suddenly reappeared. The transformation left me breathless. She had not accepted my advice about a housecoat; instead she wore slacks and a sweater, both tight. Her hair was piled up, with a few curls spilling down over one ear and cheek. And she carried the delicious odor of good perfume instead of the distracting natural scents which had been perceptible earlier. "Does this content my liege?" she asked modestly.

I tried to be entirely objective. "It's a great improvement. Perhaps, though, if you were to wear a girdle and bra. . . ."

"Master," repeated Daphne tragically, "your wish is our law."

I retreated to the first room, leaving them to their privacy. There was a big moral problem involved. I could take care of the comparatively simple matter of seeing that we did nothing disgraceful, but their evident passion for me was something else again. It hardly seemed fair to torment them with my constant presence when nothing could come of it, yet Ariadne had said that to banish them would be to destroy them. It was a dilemma. If only there were not six of them. *Six . . . !*

Shaking my head, I absently pulled a book from the shelves, *Novel Three,* by Henry Roth, and let the pages run under my thumb. I really haven't time to read many books, and what I have can't be wasted on fiction. I understand writers are paid by the word, so it's only natural for them to turn out as many as possible; for the busy man, practical publishers hire specialists to reduce them to compact form. I put *Novel Three* back on the shelf, and picked up the thin volume next to it. It was *Gibbon's Decline and Fall of the Roman Empire,* condensed by Somerset Maugham, a neat hundred pages of large type. I promised myself I would certainly dip into it someday.

Phyllis entered, rather subdued. I was delighted to see she had not only cut her hair and put on clothes, but had taken my hint about foundation garments. Generously proportioned women like Phyllis particularly need such restraints. "You look very nice," I complimented

I'm afraid I spoke with more enthusiasm than I intended, or else she misinterpreted my tone. I was forced to explain that what she took for granted as the inevitable consequence of my polite remark was both licentious and illicit. I had to insist my preference for clothes was not a matter of their putting them on for me to take off.

Paradoxically, I felt like a brute. She finally dried her eyes and murmured, "Master, may we serve you food?"

I was relieved by the change of subject. "Food? Good idea. What have you got?"

"Anything you fancy, lord. Ortolans drowned in brandy; nightingales' tongues with truffles stewed in port; breast of pheasant in aspic; brook trout a la—"

"What about a nice thick steak? And french fries?"

"Yes, lord," she assented dutifully.

It seemed hardly a minute before they all came in with the

sizzling porterhouse on a smoking platter. They set it down on a table I hadn't noticed earlier, which, I'm glad to say, was a sensible piece of furniture resting on solid legs, not a mobile captured in flight and domesticated. Iphigenia, her finely molded nostrils dilating over the savory aroma, cut the steak into bite-size bits before I could protest I wasn't a child. Leda took them up and put them in my mouth. Chloe did the same service with the french fries, the golden brown of the potatoes blending with the paler gold of her fingers; Ariadne wiped my lips with a delicately fragrant napkin. I felt slightly ridiculous at first, but the food was good—very tender, not highly seasoned, well salted—and the attention was not unpleasant. After all, there isn't anything wrong in being fed by a group of charming girls. Especially since they were now all decently attired.

I unobtrusively let my belt out a notch. Good nourishing food never hurt anyone, but it would be wise to exercise regularly. One of the things this place needed was a rowing machine or similar apparatus, so I could take daily workouts. Another, unquestionably, was a TV screen in addition to the oddly made radio. Come to think of it, there was one right above it, after all.

"Well, ladies," I said jovially, "I think we owe ourselves some recreation. Let's have fun."

They beamed on me, and some of their former enthusiasm returned. Daphne blew me a kiss.

"No, no. You misunderstand me. I mean entertainment. A show or a prizefight, or something like that."

The TV screen lit up; the muscular voice of Milton Cross announced the presentation of *Il Re Lear,* second in a cycle of Verdi works which would include *Fedra, Tartuffe,* and others. There was an overture which I thought rather noisy and then a group of people disguised in thoroughly undeceptive costumes began to sing. I'm not one of those who sneer at either art or opera, but there's a time and place for everything. "This isn't what I call amusement," I grumbled.

There was a great flutter of agitation among the girls. I had a passing wonder whether Alice would ever take so deep and unselfish an interest in making me contented.

The TV screen went into a nervous tizzy of wavy lines. "I'd rather see a good football game," I said, quite aware of the absurdity of the whim, since it was the baseball season.

The screen straightened out as though whacked swiftly.

"*—fect football weather; crisp and clear. Notre Dame will*

defend the west goal. Captain George Gipp's having a last word with Coaches Rockne and Leahy now. Ready for the kickoff; backfield for Paul Brown's All-Stars: Otto Graham at quarter; Jim Thorpe and Red Grange at the halfback spots; Bronko Nagurski at full. It's a long end-over-end boot that bounces on the five, taken by Grange, the Galloping Ghost, behind his own goal line. . . ."

This was the real thing: rough, hard, vital. I settled down comfortably—the functional oddity had given way to a nice, homey, upholstered batwing—and enjoyed myself. Ariadne and Leda leaned over the top of the chair, Daphne and Iphigenia perched on the arms, Chloe and Phyllis sat at my feet. It was all very cosy.

". . . the five, picks up his interference, crosses the ten, the fifteen, helped by a beautiful block from Nagurski, on the seventeen, sidesteps a man on the twenty, the twenty-five, and still moving at the thirty, he might go all the way. . . ."

After the game I taught them gin rummy—Chloe proved particularly adept and was almost as good as I—and we had a gay evening. Perhaps the only drag on my mood was the architecture and furnishings of that circular room, with its nasty ceiling and carpet and all those useless books, all so unsuitable to the sensible, harmless game.

Most annoying was that the place could have been so attractive if it hadn't been designed to flaunt its differences, its eccentricities, its abnormalities. I sketched out in my mind a plan for far less radical living quarters. I'm no architect, but anyone who has observed gracious homes or compact dwellings can combine the best points of what he has seen without plunging into wild, untested experiments just to prove his taste is more advanced than the accepted standard.

I had barely mentally remodeled to my satisfaction when I saw that the oversized room was actually divided up into a convenient apartment with honest corners showing their uncompromising right angles. The girls were enchanted by the improvement (as they had every reason to be) and followed me, giggling and admiring, on a quick tour of inspection. The bedroom was cheerful and neat, certainly not voluptuous; a three-quarter bed, a chest of drawers with Mother's picture on it, a TV screen where the wall and ceiling met, a magazine rack stocked with *Nation's Business, Kiplinger's,* and other useful periodicals, a bright flower print to cheer things up, and a few other homelike odds and ends.

There was a bathroom with a shower, an efficient-looking kitchen which I didn't anticipate using often since the girls' feelings might be hurt if I didn't allow them to provide the meals, and a snug living room with an overstuffed set and a contour chair; bridge and table lamps scattered around instead of concealed fixtures. On top of the TV, now reduced to manageable proportions, a clever combination light and planter was both ornamental and useful as the soft glow fell on the splayed leaves of a well-tended ficus. The floor was carpeted wall-to-wall with flowered broadloom and the ceiling was relievingly bare. There were no distorted Picassos or Modiglianis on the stippled walls, but a group of understandable paintings by Norman Rockwell and N. C. Wyeth. It was the sort of atmosphere where a man could stretch out and forget his cares.

There was also a lock on the door leading to the girls' quarters. A little to my surprise, they did not struggle very hard when I asked them to go, and snapped the latch after them. Oh, Phyllis pouted, Leda tried to hold on to my hands, and Daphne pretended she had lost one of her high-heeled shoes, but in the end I secured my privacy without too much difficulty. In fact, it was so easy I was struck with sudden suspicion. Sure enough, when I switched on the bedroom light, there was Ariadne with the covers pulled up over her head, making believe to be sound asleep.

Her attachment to me was understandable, but she is too nice a girl to go in for that sort of thing. I'm not immune to impulse myself, but my self-respect, particularly in the presence of Mother's picture, helped me not to do anything either of us would be sorry for later. After alternately explaining and coaxing, I finally convinced her that I didn't find her repulsive or ugly or any of the things she concluded must account for my self-control.

After she was gone I sank down into the contour chair. One thing I had to admit: it was convenient to control the TV from across the room, without fiddling with knobs. I got a very unusual program of whirling, changing pastel colors accompanied by soothing music. I thought of making myself a cup of coffee, but I didn't want to be overstimulated and kept awake.

I went to the wall-safe and glanced in at the piles of stock and bond certificates, the bundles of greenbacks, and the bags of coin. Perhaps it was childish of me to take out a canvas sack and let the freshly minted pieces run through my fingers, but it was pleasant. Not at all like handling other people's money in the bank. I was aroused from my revery by an authoritative knock on the door.

Aroused, not startled nor disturbed. It was not the girls' door, but the one leading to the sanitarium. The door was permanently closed where I was concerned. "Bob! Bob Squith! Come out." It was Dr. Gayler's voice.

"No, thanks," I answered lightly. "I'm quite satisfied."

Vehemence replaced urgency. "Bob! You don't belong there. This is an unfortunate, unforeseen development. You can't be happy there; you're too well adjusted to the real world."

Real world? Philosophers have been arguing over the nature of reality for centuries, yet he had undertaken to settle the question. The man was an idiot. What could be more real than the chair in which I was lying back, or the heavy sack in my lap? "Thanks, Doctor. I'm all right."

"Listen," he importuned, "can you hear me?"

"Of course I can hear you. There's nothing wrong with my faculties."

"Certainly there isn't. You were just upset by the strain of close association with Wais. And evidently the transference worked both ways, something quite unexpected. Incidentally, he is adjusting beautifully."

"Glad to hear it," I yawned. "Maybe Mr. McIlforth will give him my old job at the bank."

"Come out now," he begged. "The longer you stay the harder it will be to reach you."

I remember Wais's vexation at being tormented by their nagging. Apparently it was going to be better for me. "That's fine," I said.

"This experience has been hard on you," he went on. "Naturally psychiatric attention will be free. And I'll see to it you get a bonus. A good bonus."

"What do I want with a bonus?" I asked, flipping a gold double-eagle into the air and catching it skillfully. "I never had it so good."

After a long time he went away. I suppose he will come back, but it doesn't matter; I have more stamina than most people. I returned the coins to the safe and got ready for bed. Perhaps—if I can get in touch with Alice and she releases me from our understanding—I shall marry Ariadne. Except that I worry over making the other girls miserable. Especially Phyllis. And Daphne. Maybe things are better the way they are, in fact.

Let well enough alone, I always say.

seventh victim

Robert Sheckley

Does man need violence? If man does have a need for violence, could a society be organized to effectively deal with this need? Could war be eliminated by such a method? In "Seventh Victim," Robert Sheckley's answer is yes, man's nature is aggressive. Then he creates an alternative world with a chilling system for coping with aggressive drives: legalized, selective killing.

The approach to aggression taken in the story is basically Freudian. Freud suggested that aggression is built into or "instinctual" in man; that it is an outgrowth of man's Death Instinct. However, instead of actually killing ourselves because we have this instinct to return to an inorganic state, we externalize this drive, destroying and injuring environmental objects, like other people. Crucial to the story is Freud's "hydraulic" approach to the instinct; it builds up pressure like gas if it is kept in and not acted out. It *must* come out in one way or another. Society, prior to the time in which the story takes place—with its indirect, inauthentic outlets for this aggression—was not doing enough to sublimate or channel the drive to constructive ends. As a result, big group wars were fought when the pressure built up to levels where it could not be controlled.

The approach of the story suggests further that the old system created problems because there was not enough catharsis in the indirect sublimated activity. The society had to provide stronger individual catharsis for those who needed it, to allow these people to periodically get aggression out of their systems. In general, this hydraulic, instinctual approach to aggression is accepted by followers of Freud, but basically rejected by others. While there is some evidence to support the approach coming out of animal studies, like those of Lorenz, other evidence supports the importance of other factors in aggression, such as frustration, learning, and imitation of aggressive models. The "wise and practical men" of the story suggest these aggressive traits are admirable and necessary for survival. Without them the race would retrogress. This is the survival of the fittest view of man and civilization, again supported by some and rejected by others.

As the story opens, Stanton Frelaine, an advertising executive, is ready to claim his seventh victim. Janet Patzig has been assigned to be this victim, and she plays the role well—too well. She manipulates two of Frelaine's motives: catharsis and guilt. She makes it too easy for him to kill her, depriving him of his catharsis. More subtly, however, she manipulates his feelings of guilt about killing her, especially using the fact that she is a woman. Aggression is traditionally viewed in general (also from the Freudian point of view) as masculine. Women are not supposed to be built biologically for aggression, and strength is the domain of the man. Frelaine (like Freud in the opinion of some) is basically a male chauvinist, but more important, he has apparently been brought up to feel guilty about aggressing toward women. Janet uses this very well, appearing the poor, defenseless, depressed, Mona Lisa kind of character. She manipulates him so that first he is conflicted—aggression versus guilt, or Id versus Superego—and then castrates him by generating love feelings in him, so that he has difficulty in acting.

The other important social psychological aspect of the story is the kind of society which has been legitimized by law. Clothing is manufactured with the qualities we look for in the products we buy, but these qualities have been twisted to accommodate the kill. There is safety, privacy, flexibility, variety, personal protection (don't be half safe), and style. Rules of etiquette have been developed: "No one was supposed to know a Victim's name except his Hunter." Recognition and honor societies, like the Tens Club, have emerged. We also see that killing has become the major raison d'être for Frelaine. When he is on a hunt he is alive again, his life has meaning. In general, the society has made all the participants in the hunt cold-blooded killers first and human beings second.

SEVENTH VICTIM   *Robert Sheckley*

Stanton Frelaine sat at his desk, trying to look as busy as an executive should at nine-thirty in the morning. It was impossible. He couldn't concentrate on the advertisement he had written the previous night, couldn't think about business. All he could do was wait until the mail came.

He had been waiting for his notification for two weeks now. The government was behind schedule, as usual.

The glass door of his office was marked *Morger and Frelaine, Clothiers.* It opened, and E. J. Morger walked in, limping slightly from his old gunshot wound. His shoulders were bent; but at the age of 73 he wasn't worrying too much about his posture.

"Well, Stan?" Morger asked. "What about that ad?"

Frelaine had joined Morger 16 years ago, when he was 27. Together they had built Protec-Clothes into a million-dollar concern.

"I suppose you can run it," Frelaine said, handing the slip of paper to Morger. If only the mail would come earlier, he thought.

"'Do you own a Protec-Suit?'" Morger read aloud, holding the paper close to his eyes. "'The finest tailoring in the world has gone into Morger and Frelaine's Protec-Suit, to make it the leader in men's fashions.'"

Morger cleared his throat and glanced at Frelaine. He smiled and read on.

"'Protec-Suit is the safest as well as the smartest. Every Protec-Suit comes with special built-in gun pocket, guaranteed not to bulge. No one will know you are carrying a gun—except you. The gun pocket is exceptionally easy to get at, permitting fast, unhindered draw. Choice of hip or breast pocket.' Very nice." Morger commented.

Frelaine nodded morosely.

"'The Protec-Suit Special has the fling-out gun pocket, the greatest modern advance in personal protection. A touch of the concealed button throws the gun into your hand, cocked, safeties off. Why not drop into the Protec-Store nearest you? Why not *be safe?*'"

"That's fine," Morger said. "That's a very nice, dignified ad."

He thought for a moment, fingering his white mustache. "Shouldn't you mention that Protec-Suits come in a variety of styles, single and double-breasted, one and two button rolls, deep and shallow flares?"

"Right. I forgot."

Frelaine took back the sheet and jotted a note on the edge of it. Then he stood up, smoothing his jacket over his prominent stomach. Frelaine was 43, a little overweight, a little bald on top. He was an amiable-looking man with cold eyes.

"Relax," Morger said. "It'll come in today's mail."

Frelaine forced himself to smile. He felt like pacing the floor, but instead sat on the edge of the desk.

"You'd think it was my first kill," he said, with a deprecating smile.

"I know how it is," Morger said. "Before I hung up my gun, I couldn't sleep for a month, waiting for a notification. I know."

The two men waited. Just as the silence was becoming unbearable, the door opened. A clerk walked in and deposited the mail on Frelaine's desk.

Frelaine swung around and gathered up the letters. He thumbed through them rapidly and found what he had been waiting for—the long white envelope from ECB, with the official government seal on it.

"That's it!" Frelaine said, and broke into a grin. "That's the baby!"

"Fine." Morger eyed the envelope with interest, but didn't ask Frelaine to open it. It would be a breach of etiquette, as well as a violation in the eyes of the law. No one was supposed to know a Victim's name except his Hunter. "Have a good hunt."

"I expect to," Frelaine replied confidently. His desk was in order—had been for a week. He picked up his briefcase.

"A good kill will do you a world of good," Morger said, putting his hand lightly on Frelaine's padded shoulder. "You've been keyed up."

"I know." Frelaine grinned again and shook Morger's hand.

"Wish I was a kid again," Morger said, glancing down at his crippled leg with wryly humorous eyes. "Makes me want to pick up a gun again."

The old man had been quite a Hunter in his day. Ten successful hunts had qualified him for the exclusive Tens Club. And, of course, for each hunt Morger had had to act as Victim, so he had 20 kills to his credit.

"I sure hope my Victim isn't anyone like you," Frelaine said, half in jest.

"Don't worry about it. What number will this be?"

"The seventh."

"Lucky seven. Go to it," Morger said. "We'll get you into the Tens yet."

Frelaine waved his hand and started out the door.

"Just don't get careless," warned Morger. "All it takes is a single slip and I'll need a new partner. If you don't mind, I like the one I've got now."

"I'll be careful," Frelaine promised.

Instead of taking a bus, Frelaine walked to his apartment. He wanted time to cool off. There was no sense in acting like a kid on his first kill.

As he walked, Frelaine kept his eyes strictly to the front. Staring at anyone was practically asking for a bullet, if the man happened to be serving as Victim. Some Victims shot if you just glanced at them. Nervous fellows. Frelaine prudently looked above the heads of the people he passed.

Ahead of him was a huge billboard, offering J. F. O'Donovan's services to the public.

"Victims!" the sign proclaimed in huge red letters. "Why take chances? Use an O'Donovan accredited Spotter. Let us locate your assigned killer. Pay after you get him!"

The sign reminded Frelaine. He would call Morrow as soon as he reached his apartment.

He crossed the street, quickening his stride. He could hardly wait to get home now, to open the envelope and discover who his victim was. Would he be clever or stupid? Rich, like Frelaine's fourth Victim, or poor, like the first and second? Would he have an organized Spotter service, or try to go it on his own?

The excitement of the chase was wonderful, coursing through his veins, quickening his heartbeat. From a block or so away, he heard gunfire. Two quick shots, and then a final one.

Somebody got his man, Frelaine thought. Good for him.

It was a superb feeling, he told himself. He was *alive* again.

At his one-room apartment the first thing Frelaine did was call Ed Morrow, his spotter. The man worked as a garage attendant between calls.

"Hello, Ed? Frelaine."

"Oh, hi, Mr. Frelaine." He could see the man's thin, grease-stained face, grinning flat-lipped at the telephone.

"I'm going out on one, Ed."

"Good luck, Mr. Frelaine," Ed Morrow said. "I suppose you'll want me to stand by?"

"That's right. I don't expect to be gone more than a week or two. I'll probably get my notification of Victim Status within three months of the kill."

"I'll be standing by. Good hunting, Mr. Frelaine."

"Thanks. So long." He hung up. It was a wise safety measure to reserve a first-class spotter. After his kill, it would be Frelaine's turn as Victim. Then, once again, Ed Morrow would be his life insurance.

And what a marvelous spotter Morrow was! Uneducated— stupid, really. But what an eye for people! Morrow was a natural. His pale eyes could tell an out-of-towner at a glance. He was diabolically clever at rigging an ambush. An indispensable man.

Frelaine took out the envelope, chuckling to himself, remembering some of the tricks Morrow had turned for the Hunters. Still smiling, he glanced at the data inside the envelope.

Janet-Marie Patzig.

His Victim was a female!

Frelaine stood up and paced for a few moments. Then he read the letter again. Janet-Marie Patzig. No mistake. A girl. Three photographs were enclosed, her address, and the usual descriptive data.

Frelaine frowned. He had never killed a female.

He hesitated for a moment, then picked up the telephone and dialed.

"Emotional Catharsis Bureau, Information Section," a man's voice answered.

"Say, look," Frelaine said. "I just got my notification and I pulled a girl. Is that in order?" He gave the clerk the girl's name.

"It's all in order, sir," the clerk replied after a minute of checking micro-files. "The girl registered with the board under her own free will. The law says she has the same rights and privileges as a man."

"Could you tell me how many kills she has?"

"I'm sorry, sir. The only information you're allowed is the Victim's legal status and the descriptive data you have received."

"I see." Frelaine paused. "Could I draw another?"

"You can refuse the hunt, of course. That is your legal right. But you will not be allowed another Victim until you have served. Do you wish to refuse?"

"Oh, no," Frelaine said hastily. "I was just wondering. Thank you."

He hung up and sat down in his largest armchair, loosening his belt. This required some thought. Damn women, he grumbled to himself, always trying to horn in on a man's game. Why can't they stay home?

But they were free citizens, he reminded himself. Still, it just didn't seem *feminine*.

He knew that, historically speaking, the Emotional Catharsis Board had been established for men and men only. The board had been formed at the end of the fourth world war—or sixth, as some historians counted it.

At that time there had been a driving need for permanent, lasting peace. The reason was practical, as were the men who engineered it.

Simply—annihilation was just around the corner.

In the world wars, weapons increased in magnitude, efficiency, and exterminating power. Soldiers became accustomed to them, less and less reluctant to use them.

But the saturation point had been reached. Another war would truly be the war to end all wars. There would be no one left to start another.

So this peace *had* to last for all time, but the men who engineered it were practical. They recognized the tensions and dislocations still present, the cauldrons in which wars are brewed. They asked themselves why peace had never lasted in the past.

"Because men like to fight," was their answer.

"Oh, no!" screamed the idealists.

But the men who engineered the peace were forced to postulate, regretfully, the presence of a need for violence in a large percentage of mankind.

Men aren't angels. They aren't fiends, either. They are just very human beings, with a high degree of combativeness.

With the scientific knowledge and the power they had at that moment, the practical men could have gone a long way toward breeding this trait out of the race. Many thought this was the answer.

The practical men didn't. They recognized the validity of competition, love of battle, strength in the face of overwhelming odds. These, they felt, were admirable traits for a race, and insurance toward its perpetuity. Without them, the race would be bound to retrogress.

The tendency toward violence, they found, was inextricably linked with ingenuity, flexibility, drive.

The problem, then: To arrange a peace that would last after they were gone. To stop the race from destroying itself, without removing the responsible traits.

The way to do this, they decided, was to rechannel Man's violence.

Provide him with an outlet, an expression.

The first big step was the legalization of gladiatorial events, complete with blood and thunder. But more was needed. Sublimations worked only up to a point. Then people demanded the real thing.

There is no substitute for murder.

So murder was legalized, on a strictly individual basis, and only for those who wanted it. The governments were directed to create Emotional Catharsis Boards.

After a period of experimentation, uniform rules were adopted.

Anyone who wanted to murder could sign up at the ECB. Giving certain data and assurances, he would be granted a Victim.

Anyone who signed up to murder, under the government rules, had to take his turn a few months later as Victim—if he survived.

That, in essence, was the setup. The individual could commit as many murders as he wanted. But between each, he had to be a Victim. If he successfully killed his Hunter, he could stop, or sign up for another murder.

At the end of ten years, an estimated third of the world's civilized population had applied for at least one murder. The number slid to a fourth, and stayed there.

Philosophers shook their heads, but the practical men were satisfied. War was where it belonged—in the hands of the individual.

Of course, there were ramifications to the game, and elaborations. Once its existence had been accepted it became big business. There were services for Victim and Hunter alike.

The Emotional Catharsis Board picked the Victims' names at random. A Hunter was allowed six months in which to make his kill. This had to be done by his own ingenuity, unaided. He was given the name of his Victim, address and description, and allowed to use a standard caliber pistol. He could wear no armor of any sort.

The Victim was notified a week before the Hunter. He was told only that he was a Victim. He did not know the name of his Hunter. He was allowed his choice of armor, however. He could hire spotters. A spotter couldn't kill; only Victim and Hunter could do that. But he could detect a stranger in town, or ferret out a nervous gunman.

The Victim could arrange any kind of ambush in his power to kill the Hunter.

There were stiff penalties for killing or wounding the wrong man, for no other murder was allowed. Grudge killings and gain killings were punishable by death.

The beauty of the system was that the people who wanted to kill could do so. Those who didn't—the bulk of the population—didn't have to.

At least, there weren't any more big wars. Not even the imminence of one.

Just hundreds of thousands of small ones.

Frelaine didn't especially like the idea of killing a woman; but she *had* signed up. It wasn't his fault. And he wasn't going to lose out on his seventh hunt.

He spent the rest of the morning memorizing the data on his Victim, then filed the letter.

Janet Patzig lived in New York. That was good. He enjoyed hunting in a big city, and he had always wanted to see New York. Her age wasn't given, but to judge from her photographs, she was in her early twenties.

Frelaine phoned for jet reservations to New York, then took a shower. He dressed with care in a new Protec-Suit Special made for the occasion. From his collection he selected a gun, cleaned and oiled it, and fitted it into the fling-out pocket of the suit. Then he packed his suitcase.

A pulse of excitement was pounding in his veins. Strange, he thought, how each killing was a new excitement. It was something you just didn't tire of, the way you did of French pastry or women or drinking or anything else. It was always new and different.

Finally, he looked over his books to see which he would take.

His library contained all the good books on the subject. He wouldn't need any of his Victim books, like L. Fred Tracy's *Tactics for the Victim*, with its insistence on a rigidly controlled environment, or Dr. Frisch's *Don't Think Like a Victim!*

He would be very interested in those in a few months, when he was a Victim again. Now he wanted hunting books.

Tactics for Hunting Humans was the standard and definitive work, but he had it almost memorized. *Development of the Ambush* was not adapted to his present needs.

He chose *Hunting in Cities*, by Mitwell and Clark, *Spotting the Spotter*, by Algreen, and *The Victim's Ingroup*, by the same author.

Everything was in order. He left a note for the milkman, locked his apartment and took a cab to the airport.

In New York, he checked into a hotel in the midtown area, not too far from his Victim's address. The clerks were smiling and attentive, which bothered Frelaine. He didn't like to be recognized so easily as an out-of-town killer.

The first thing he saw in his room was a pamphlet on his bedtable. *How to Get the Most out of your Emotional Catharsis*, it was called, with the compliments of the management. Frelaine smiled and thumbed through it.

Since it was his first visit to New York, Frelaine spent the afternoon just walking the streets in his Victim's neighborhood. After that, he wandered through a few stores.

Martinson and Black was a fascinating place. He went through their Hunter-Hunted room. There were lightweight bulletproof vests for Victims, and Richard Arlington hats, with bulletproof crowns.

On one side was a large display of a new .38 caliber side arm.

"Use the Malvern Strait-shot!" the ad proclaimed. "ECB-approved. Carries a load of 12 shots. Tested deviation less than .001 inch per 1,000 feet. Don't miss your Victim! Don't risk your life without the best! Be safe with Malvern!"

Frelaine smiled. The ad was good, and the small black weapon looked ultimately efficient. But he was satisfied with the one he had.

There was a special sale on trick canes, with concealed four-shot magazine, promising safety and concealment. As a young man, Frelaine had gone in heavily for novelties. But now he knew that the old-fashioned ways were usually the best.

Outside the store, four men from the Department of Sanitation were carting away a freshly killed corpse. Frelaine regretted missing the kill.

He ate dinner in a good restaurant and went to bed early.

Tomorrow he had a lot to do.

The next day, with the face of his Victim before him, Frelaine walked through her neighborhood. He didn't look closely at anyone. Instead, he moved rapidly, as though he were really going somewhere, the way an old Hunter should walk.

He passed several bars and dropped into one for a drink. Then he went on, down a side street off Lexington Avenue.

There was a pleasant sidewalk cafe there. Frelaine walked past it.

And there she was! He could never mistake the face. It was Janet Patzig, seated at a table, staring into a drink. She didn't look up as he passed.

Frelaine walked to the end of the block. He turned the corner and stopped, hands trembling.

Was the girl crazy, exposing herself in the open? Did she think she had a charmed life?

He hailed a taxi and had the man drive around the block. Sure enough, she was just sitting there. Frelaine took a careful look.

She seemed younger than her pictures, but he couldn't be sure. He would guess her to be not much over twenty. Her dark hair was parted in the middle and combed above her ears, giving her a nunlike appearance. Her expression, as far as Frelaine could tell, was one of resigned sadness.

Wasn't she even going to make an attempt to defend herself?

Frelaine paid the driver and hurried to a drugstore. Finding a vacant telephone booth, he called ECB.

"Are you sure that a Victim named Janet-Marie Patzig has been notified?"

"Hold on, sir." Frelaine tapped on the door while the clerk looked up the information. "Yes, sir. We have her personal confirmation. Is there anything wrong, sir?"

"No," Frelaine said. "Just wanted to check."

After all, it was no one's business if the girl didn't want to defend herself.

He was still entitled to kill her.

It was his turn.

He postponed it for that day, however, and went to a movie. After dinner, he returned to his room and read the ECB pamphlet. Then he lay on his bed and glared at the ceiling.

All he had to do was pump a bullet into her. Just ride by in a cab and kill her.

She was being a very bad sport about it, he decided resentfully, and went to sleep.

The next afternoon, Frelaine walked by the cafe again. The girl was back, sitting at the same table. Frelaine caught a cab.

"Drive around the block very slowly," he told the driver.

"Sure," the driver said, grinning with sardonic wisdom.

From the cab, Frelaine watched for spotters. As far as he could tell, the girl had none. Both her hands were in sight upon the table.

An easy, stationary target.

Frelaine touched the button of his double-breasted jacket. A fold flew open and the gun was in his hand. He broke it open and checked the cartridges, then closed it with a snap.

"Slowly, now," he told the driver.

The taxi crawled by the cafe. Frelaine took careful aim, centering the girl in his sights. His finger tightened on the trigger.

"Damn it!" he said.

A waiter had passed by the girl. He didn't want to chance winging someone else.

"Around the block again," he told the driver.

The man gave him another grin and hunched down in his seat. Frelaine wondered if the driver would feel so happy if he knew that Frelaine was gunning for a woman.

This time there was no waiter around. The girl was lighting a cigarette, her mournful face intent on her lighter. Frelaine centered her in his sights, squarely above the eyes, and held his breath.

Then he shook his head and put the gun back in his pocket. The idiotic girl was robbing him of the full benefit of his catharsis.

He paid the driver and started to walk.

It's too easy, he told himself. He was used to a real chase. Most of the other six kills had been quite difficult. The Victims had tried every dodge. One had hired at least a dozen spotters. But Frelaine had gotten to them all by altering his tactics to meet the situation.

Once he dressed as a milkman, another time as a bill collector. The sixth Victim he had had to chase through the Sierra Nevadas. The man had clipped him, too. But Frelaine had done better than that.

How could he be proud of this one? What would the Tens Club say?

That brought Frelaine up with a start. He wanted to get into the club. Even if he passed up this girl, he would have to defend himself against a Hunter. Surviving that, he would still be four hunts away from membership. At that rate, he might never get in.

He began to pass the cafe again, then, on impulse, stopped abruptly.

"Hello," he said.

Janet Patzig looked at him out of sad blue eyes, but said nothing.

"Say look," he said, sitting down. "If I'm being fresh, just tell me and I'll go. I'm an out-of-towner. Here on a convention. And I'd just like someone feminine to talk to. If you'd rather I didn't—"

"I don't care," Janet Patzig said tonelessly.

"A brandy," Frelaine told the waiter. Janet Patzig's glass was still half full.

Frelaine looked at the girl and he could feel his heart throbbing against his ribs. This was more like it—having a drink with your Victim!

"My name's Stanton Frelaine," he said, knowing it didn't matter.

"Janet."

"Janet what?"

"Janet Patzig."

"Nice to know you," Frelaine said, in a perfectly natural voice. "Are you doing anything tonight, Janet?"

"I'm probably being killed tonight," she said quietly.

Frelaine looked at her carefully. Did she realize who he was? For all he knew, she had a gun leveled at him under the table.

He kept his hand close to the fling-out button.

"Are you a Victim?" he asked.

"You guessed it," she said sardonically. "If I were you, I'd stay out of the way. No sense getting hit by mistake."

Frelaine couldn't understand the girl's calm. Was she a suicide? Perhaps she just didn't care. Perhaps she wanted to die.

"Haven't you got any spotters?" he asked, with the right expression of amazement.

"No." She looked at him, full in the face, and Frelaine saw something he hadn't noticed before.

She was very lovely.

"I am a bad, bad girl," she said lightly. "I got the idea I'd like to commit a murder, so I signed for ECB. Then—I couldn't do it."

Frelaine shook his head, sympathizing with her.

"But I'm still in, of course. Even if I didn't shoot, I still have to be a Victim."

"But why don't you hire some spotters?" he asked.

"I couldn't kill anyone," she said. "I just couldn't. I don't even have a gun."

"You've got a lot of courage," Frelaine said, "coming out in the open this way." Secretly, he was amazed at her stupidity.

"What can I do?" she asked listlessly. "You can't hide from a Hunter. Not a real one. And I don't have enough money to make a real disappearance."

"Since it's in your own defense, I should think—" Frelaine began, but she interrupted.

"No. I've made up my mind on that. This whole thing is wrong, the whole system. When I had my Victim in the sights—when I saw how easily I could—I could—"

She pulled herself together quickly.

"Oh, let's forget it," she said, and smiled.

Frelaine found her smile dazzling.

After that, they talked of other things. Frelaine told her of his business, and she told him about New York. She was 22, an unsuccessful actress.

They had supper together. When she accepted Frelaine's invitation to go to the Gladiatorials, he felt absurdly elated.

He called a cab—he seemed to be spending his entire time in New York in cabs—and opened the door for her. She started in. Frelaine hesitated. He could have pumped a shot into her at that moment. It would have been very easy.

But he held his hand. Just for the moment, he told himself.

The Gladiatorials were about the same as those held anywhere else, except that the talent was a little better. There were the usual historical events, swordsmen and netmen, duels with saber and foil.

Most of these, naturally, were fought to the death.

Then bull fighting, lion fighting, and rhino fighting, followed by the more modern events. Fights from behind barricades with bow and arrow. Dueling on a high wire.

The evening passed pleasantly.

Frelaine escorted the girl home, the palms of his hands sticky with sweat. He had never found a woman he liked better. And yet she was his legitimate kill.

He didn't know what he was going to do.

She invited him in and they sat together on the couch. The girl lighted a cigarette for herself with a large lighter, then settled back.

"Are you leaving soon?" she asked him.

"I suppose so," Frelaine said. "The convention is only lasting another day."

She was silent for a moment. "I'll be sorry to see you go. Send roses to my funeral."

They were quiet for a while. Then Janet went to fix him a drink. Frelaine eyed her retreating back. Now was the time. He placed his hand near the button.

But the moment had passed for him, irrevocably. He wasn't going to kill her. You don't kill the girl you love.

The realization that he loved her was shocking. He'd come to kill, not to find a wife.

She came back with the drink and sat down opposite him, staring at emptiness.

"Janet," he said. "I love you."

She sat, just looking at him. There were tears in her eyes.

"You can't," she protested. "I'm a Victim. I won't live long enough to—"

"You won't be killed. I'm your Hunter."

She stared at him a moment, then laughed uncertainly.

"Are you going to kill me?" she asked.

"Don't be ridiculous," he said. "I'm going to marry you."

Suddenly she was in his arms.

"Oh, Lord!" she gasped. "The waiting—I've been so frightened—"

"It's all over," he told her. "Think what a story it'll make for our kids. How I came to murder you and left marrying you."

She kissed him, then sat back and lighted another cigarette.

"Let's start packing," Frelaine said. "I want—"

"Wait," Janet interrupted. "You haven't asked if I love you."

"What?"

She was still smiling, and the cigarette lighter was pointed at him. In the bottom of it was a black hole. A hole just large enough for a .38 caliber bullet.

"Don't kid around," he objected, getting to his feet.

"I'm not being funny, darling," she said.

In a fraction of a second, Frelaine had time to wonder how he could ever have thought she was not much over twenty. Looking at her now—*really* looking at her—he knew she couldn't be much less than thirty. Every minute of her strained, tense existence showed on her face.

"I don't love you, Stanton," she said very softly, the cigarette lighter poised.

Frelaine struggled for breath. One part of him was able to realize detachedly what a marvelous actress she really was. She must have known all along.

Frelaine pushed the button, and the gun was in his hand, cocked and ready.

The blow that struck him in the chest knocked him over a coffee table. The gun fell out of his hand. Gasping, half-conscious, he watched her take careful aim for the *coup de grace*.

"Now I can join the Tens," he heard her say elatedly as she squeezed the trigger.

love, incorporated

Robert Sheckley

"Love, Incorporated" presents love, neatly packaged and ready for sale. It uses a favorite device of the science fiction writer when he wishes to make some kind of social criticism. He creates an alien protagonist who visits Earth, and we see our society freshly through his unacculturated eyes. Often the social critic exaggerates what he is commenting on—like putting a specimen under a microscope—so that we can study it more easily in this magnified form. Using these devices, Robert Sheckley looks at love, aggression, and commercialism in America. His protagonist is Alfred Simon, a young farmer from the agricultural planet of Kazanga IV. His is a practical, hardworking society. Feeling something is missing from his life, he reads poetry and dreams of passion, the moon, and dark sea beaches. Finally he sets out for Earth, where, he has heard, romantic love can be found.

One might ask whether romantic love can be studied by social psychology, and the answer would appear to be yes. Interpersonal attraction has been studied for years in the field (the study of liking), but only recently has romantic love been studied. In 1970, Zick Rubin reported results of his systematic study, in which he was able to construct a scale of measurement. According to the scale, romantic love includes three major components:

(1) Affiliative and dependent need: Feeling miserable without one's partner.

(2) Predisposition to help: Wanting to help cheer up the partner.

(3) Exclusiveness and absorption: Being totally absorbed in the other person.

Rubin's findings indicate that loving and liking one's date is more highly correlated among males than females; however, the females showed a higher correlation between loving their date and their estimate that they would marry. Another finding was that the more people were in love with each other, the more time they spent looking into each other's eyes.

To study love, we first have to ask some basic questions: What is love? If defined, can it be produced by science? Love might be learned through conditioning techniques as well as through the stimulation of certain brain centers. Neither of these techniques is beyond the realm of possibility, since animal experiments in both areas have suggested they are very powerful techniques. While they probably would not be used to train humans to love as in this story, advocates would probably argue that it could be done, if ethical considerations would allow it. It seems safe to assume that techniques that could condition or stimulate love feelings and behaviors might also be able to wipe them out, as happens in "Love, Incorporated."

The story suggests many things about love. In this future world, love is not essential for a society. It is impractical, too expensive, and unsettling. However, although one can survive without it, life becomes sterile and austere, and at the very least, less worth living than when it is there. The story further suggests that when love is in short supply, people will pay a high price for it. In other words, love is an extravagance, like war and lust, and only a washed-out planet like Earth can afford not to deny it to its people. After all, what else do they have?

Sheckley defines love as a feeling, "the self-same feeling that poets and writers have raved about for thousands of years." He goes on to describe other components: "deep and abiding affection, unrestrained passion, complete faithfulness, an almost mystic affection for your defects as well as your virtues, a pitiful desire to please, and . . . that uncontrollable first spark, that blinding moment of love at first sight!"

Love, the story suggests, is a delightful interlude, a relaxation, good for what ails you—physically, psychologically, and intellectually. It is *not* lasting, it is not exclusive, and it does not depend on natural selection. (Computer dating may have already discovered that.) Also, we find that love and marriage do *not* go together like a horse and carriage. However, Tate, the salesman of love in the story, claims these missing attributes are not necessary; missing them does not "invalidate your own experience." Is that our answer? Love is something we can experience at any one given time, and the rest are extras which we should not expect if we don't want to be frustrated, as Alfred Simon finds at the story's end. "Love, Incorporated" makes many interesting assertions about the nature of romantic love which can serve as a starting point for discussion in exploring the subject.

Could love really be packaged, promoted, and sold as it is in the story? The packaging techniques as well as the promotion seem to involve using those things that have been associated with love. If we have been conditioned to love on cues associated with it, then it could be packaged and promoted. Advertisers today try to sell products by associating them with sex. Presumably it could be done to sell both sex and love. Would it sell? We all know that buying and selling are governed by the natural laws of supply and demand, do we not?

LOVE, INCORPORATED   *Robert Sheckley*

Alfred Simon was born on Kazanga IV, a small agricultural planet near Bootes, and there he drove a combine through the wheat fields, and in the long, hushed evenings listened to the recorded love songs of Earth.

Life was pleasant enough on Kazanga, and the girls were buxom, jolly, frank and acquiescent, good companions for a hike through the hills or a swim in the brook, staunch mates for life. But romantic—never! There was good fun to be had on Kazanga, in a cheerful open manner. But there was no more than fun.

Simon felt that something was missing in this bland existence. One day he discovered what it was.

A vendor came to Kazanga in a battered spaceship loaded with books. He was gaunt, white-haired, and a little mad. A celebration was held for him, for novelty was appreciated on the outer worlds.

The vendor told them all the latest gossip; of the price war between Detroit II and III, and how fishing fared on Alana, and what the president's wife on Moracia wore, and how oddly the men of Doran V talked. And at last someone said, "Tell us of Earth."

"Ah!" said the vendor, raising his eyebrows. "You want to hear of the mother planet? Well, friends, there's no place like old Earth, no place at all. On Earth, friends, everything is possible, and nothing is denied."

"Nothing!" Simon asked.

"They've got a law against denial," the vendor explained, grinning. "No one has ever been known to break it. Earth is *different*, friends. You folks specialize in farming? Well, Earth specializes in impracticalities such as madness, beauty, war, intoxication, purity, horror, and the like, and people come from light-years away to sample these wares."

"And love?" a woman asked.

"Why girl," the vendor said gently, "Earth is the only place in the galaxy that still has love! Detroit II and III tried it and found it too expensive, you know, and Alana decided it was unsettling, and there was no time to import it on Moracia or Doran V. But, as I said, Earth specializes in the impractical, and makes it pay."

"Pay?" a bulky farmer asked.

"Of course! Earth is old, her minerals are gone and her fields are barren. Her colonies are independent now, and filled with sober folk such as yourselves, who want value for their goods. So what else can old Earth deal in, except the nonessentials that make life worth living?"

"Were you in love on Earth?" Simon asked.

"That I was," the vendor answered, with a certain grimness. "I was in love, and now I travel. Friends, these books. . . ."

For an exorbitant price, Simon bought an ancient poetry book, and reading, dreamed of passion beneath the lunatic moon, of dawn glimmering whitely upon lovers' parched lips, of locked bodies on a dark seabeach, desperate with love and deafened by the booming surf.

And only on Earth was this possible! For, as the vendor told, Earth's scattered children were too hard at work wrestling a living from alien soil. The wheat and corn grew on Kazanga, and the factories increased on Detroit II and III. The fisheries of Alana were the talk of the Southern star belt, and there were dangerous beasts on Moracia, and a whole wilderness to be won on Doran V. And this was well, and exactly as it should be.

But the new worlds were austere, carefully planned, sterile in their perfections. Something had been lost in the dead reaches of space, and only Earth knew love.

Therefore, Simon worked and saved and dreamed. And in his twenty-ninth year he sold his farm, packed all his clean shirts into a serviceable handbag, put on his best suit and a pair of stout walking shoes, and boarded the Kazanga-Metropole Flyer.

At last he came to Earth, where dreams *must* come true, for there is a law against their failure.

He passed quickly through Customs at Spaceport New York, and was shuttled underground to Times Square. There he emerged blinking into daylight, tightly clutching his handbag, for he had been warned about pickpockets, cutpurses, and other denizens of the city.

Breathless with wonder, he looked around.

The first thing that struck him was the endless array of theatrees, with attractions in two dimensions, three or four, depending upon your preference. And what attractions!

To the right of him a beetling marquee proclaimed: LUST ON VENUS! A DOCUMENTARY ACCOUNT OF SEX PRACTICES AMONG THE INHABITANTS OF THE GREEN HELL! SHOCKING! REVEALING!

He wanted to go in. But across the street was a war film. The billboard shouted, THE SUN BUSTERS! DEDICATED TO THE DAREDEVILS OF THE SPACE MARINES! And further down was a picture called TARZAN BATTLES THE SATURNIAN GHOULS!

Tarzan, he recalled from his reading, was an ancient ethnic hero of Earth.

It was all wonderful, but there was so much more! He saw little open shops where one could buy food of all worlds, and especially such native Terran dishes as pizza, hot dogs, spaghetti and knishes. And there were stores which sold surplus clothing from the Terran spacefleets, and other stores which sold nothing but beverages.

Simon didn't know what to do first. Then he heard a staccato burst of gunfire behind him, and whirled.

It was only a shooting gallery, a long, narrow, brightly painted place with a waist-high counter. The manager, a swarthy fat man with a mole on his chin, sat on a high stool and smiled at Simon.

"Try your luck?"

Simon walked over and saw that, instead of the usual targets, there were four scantily dressed women at the end of the gallery, seated upon bullet-scored chairs. They had tiny bull's eyes painted on their foreheads and above each breast.

"But do you fire real bullets?" Simon asked.

"Of course!" the manager said. "There's a law against false advertising on Earth. Real bullets and real gals! Step up and knock one off!"

One of the women called out, "Come on, sport! Bet you miss me!"

Another screamed, "He couldn't hit the broad side of a space-ship!"

"Sure he can!" another shouted. "Come on, sport!"

Simon rubbed his forehead and tried not to act surprised. After all, this was Earth, where anything was allowed as long as it was commercially feasible.

He asked, "Are there galleries where you shoot men, too?"

"Of course," the manager said. "But you ain't no pervert, are you?"

"Certainly not!"

"You an outworlder?"

"Yes. How did you know?"

"The suit. Always tell by the suit." The fat man closed his eyes and chanted, "Step up, step up and kill a woman. Get rid of a load of repressions! Squeeze the trigger and feel the old anger ooze out of you! Better than a massage! Better than getting drunk! Step up, step up and kill a woman!"

Simon asked one of the girls, "Do you stay dead when they kill you?"

"Don't be stupid," the girl said.

"But the shock—"

She shrugged her shoulders. "I could do worse."

Simon was about to ask how she could do worse, when the manager leaned over the counter, speaking confidentially.

"Look, buddy. Look what I got here."

Simon glanced over the counter and saw a compact submachine gun.

"For a ridiculously low price," the manager said, "I'll let you use the tommy. You can spray the whole place, shoot down the fixtures, rip up the walls. This drives a .45 slug, buddy, and it kicks like a mule. You really know you're firing when you fire the tommy."

"I am not interested," Simon said sternly.

"I've got a grenade or two," the manager said. "Fragmentation, of course. You could really—"

"No!"

"For a price," the manager said, "you can shoot *me*, too, if that's how your tastes run, although I wouldn't have guessed it. What do you say?"

"No! Never! This is horrible!"

The manager looked at him blankly. "Not in the mood now? OK. I'm open twenty-four hours a day. See you later, sport."

"Never!" Simon said, walking away.

"Be expecting you, lover!" one of the women called after him.

Simon went to a refreshment stand and ordered a small glass of cola-cola. He found that his hands were shaking. With an effort he steadied them, and sipped his drink. He reminded himself that he must not judge Earth by his own standards. If people on Earth enjoyed killing people, and the victims didn't mind being killed, why should anyone object?

Or should they?

He was pondering this when a voice at his elbow said, "Hey, bub."

Simon turned and saw a wizened, furtive-faced little man in an oversize raincoat standing beside him.

"Out-of-towner?" the little man asked.

"I am," Simon said. "How did you know?"

"The shoes. I always look at the shoes. How do you like our little planet?"

"It's—confusing," Simon said carefully. "I mean I didn't expect—well—"

"Of course," the little man said. "You're an idealist. One look at your honest face tells me that, my friend. You've come to Earth for a definite purpose. Am I right?"

Simon nodded. The little man said, "I know your purpose, my friend. You're looking for a war that will make the world safe for something, and you've come to the right place. We have six major wars running at all times, and there's never any waiting for an important position in any of them."

"Sorry, but—"

"Right at this moment," the little man said impressively, "the downtrodden workers of Peru are engaged in a desperate struggle against a corrupt and decadent monarchy. One more man could swing the contest! *You*, my friend, could be that man! *You* could guarantee the socialist victory!"

Observing the expression on Simon's face, the little man said quickly, "But there's a lot to be said for an enlightened aristocracy. The wise old kind of Peru (a philosopher-king in the deepest Platonic sense of the word) sorely needs your help. His tiny corps of scientists, humanitarians, Swiss guards, knights of the realm and royal peasants is sorely pressed by the foreign-inspired socialist conspiracy. A single man, now—"

."I'm not interested," Simon said.

"In China, the Anarchists—"

"No."

"Perhaps you'd prefer the Communists in Wales? Or the Capitalists in Japan? Or if your affinities lie with a splinter group such as Feminists, Prohibitionists, Free Silverists, or the like, we could probably arrange—"

"I don't want a war," Simon said.

"Who could blame you?" the little man said, nodding rapidly. "War is hell. In that case, you've come to Earth for love."

"How did you know?" Simon asked.

The little man smiled modestly. "Love and war," he said, "are Earth's two staple commodities. We've been turning them both out in bumper crops since the beginning of time."

"Is love very difficult to find?" Simon asked.

"Walk uptown two blocks," the little man said briskly. "Can't miss it. Tell 'em Joe sent you."

"But that's impossible! You can't just walk out and—"

"What do you know about love?" Joe asked.

"Nothing."

"Well, we're experts on it."

"I know what the books say," Simon said. "Passion beneath the lunatic moon—"

"Sure, and bodies on a dark seabeach desperate with love and deafened by the booming surf."

"You've read the book?"

"It's the standard advertising brochure. I must be going. Two blocks uptown. Can't miss it."

And with a pleasant nod, Joe moved into the crowd.

Simon finished his cola-cola and walked slowly up Broadway, his brow knotted in thought, but determined not to form any premature judgments.

When he reached 44th Street he saw a tremendous neon sign flashing brightly. It said, LOVE, INC.

Smaller neon letters read, *Open 24 Hours a Day!*

Beneath that it read, *Up One Flight.*

Simon frowned, for a terrible suspicion had just crossed his mind. Still, he climbed the stairs and entered a small, tastefully furnished reception room. From there he was sent down a long corridor to a numbered room.

Within the room was a handsome gray-haired man who rose from behind an impressive desk and shook his hand, saying, "Well! How are things on Kazanga?"

"How did you know I was from Kazanga?"

"That shirt. I always look at the shirt. I'm Mr. Tate, and I'm here to serve you to the best of my ability. You are—"

"Simon, Alfred Simon."

"Please be seated, Mr. Simon. Cigarette? Drink? You won't regret coming to us, sir. We're the oldest love-dispensing firm in the business, and much larger than our closest competitor, Passion Unlimited. Moreover, our fees are far more reasonable, and bring you an improved product. Might I ask how you heard of us? Did you see our full page ad in the *Times?* Or—"

"Joe sent me," Simon said.

"Ah, he's an active one," Mr. Tate said, shaking his head playfully. "Well, sir, there's no reason to delay. You've come a long way for love, and love you shall have." He reached for a button on his desk, but Simon stopped him.

Simon said, "I don't want to be rude or anything, but. . . ."

"Yes?" Mr. Tate said, with an encouraging smile.

"I don't understand this," Simon blurted out, flushing deeply, beads of perspiration standing out on his forehead. "I think I'm in the wrong place. I didn't come all the way to Earth just for . . . I mean, you can't really sell *love*, can you? Not *love*! I mean, then it isn't really *love*, is it?"

"But of course!" Mr. Tate said, half rising from his chair in astonishment. "That's the whole point! Anyone can buy sex. Good lord, it's the cheapest thing in the universe, next to human life. But *love* is rare, *love* is special, *love* is found only on Earth. Have you read our brochure?"

"Bodies on a dark seabeach?" Simon asked.

"Yes, that one. I wrote it. Gives something of the feeling, doesn't it? You can't get that feeling from just *anyone*, Mr. Simon. You can get that feeling only from someone who loves you."

Simon said dubiously, "It's not genuine love though, is it?"

"Of course it is! If we were selling simulated love, we'd label it as such. The advertising laws on Earth are strict, I can assure you. Anything can be sold, but it must be labelled properly. That's ethics, Mr. Simon!"

Tate caught his breath, and continued in a calmer tone. "No sir, make no mistake. Our product is not a substitute. It is the exact self-same feeling that poets and writers have raved about for thousands of years. Through the wonders of modern science we can bring this feeling to you at your convenience, attractively packaged, completely disposable, and for a ridiculously low price."

Simon said, "I pictured something more—spontaneous."

"Spontaneity has its charm." Mr. Tate agreed. "Our research labs are working on it. Believe me, there's nothing science can't produce, as long as there's a market for it."

"I don't like any of this," Simon said, getting to his feet. "I think I'll just go see a movie."

"Wait!" Mr. Tate cried. "You think we're trying to put something over on you. You think we'll introduce you to a girl who will *act* as though she loved you, but who in reality will not. Is that it?"

"I guess so," Simon said.

"But it just isn't so! It would be too costly for one thing. For another, the wear and tear on the girl would be tremendous. And it would be psychologically unsound for her to attempt living a lie of such depth and scope."

"Then how do you do it?"

"By utilizing our understanding of science and the human mind."

To Simon this sounded like double-talk. He moved toward the door.

"Tell me something," Mr. Tate said. "You're a bright looking young fellow. Don't you think you could tell real love from a counterfeit item?"

"Certainly."

"There's your safeguard! *You* must be satisfied, or don't pay us a cent."

"I'll think about it," Simon said.

"Why delay? Leading psychologists say that *real* love is a fortifier and a restorer of sanity, a balm for damaged egos, a restorer of hormone balance, and an improver of the complexion. The love we supply you has everything: deep and abiding affection, unrstrained passion, complete faithfulness, an almost mystic affection for your defects as well as your virtues, a pitiful desire to please, *and*, as a plus that only Love, Inc. can supply: that uncontrollable first spark, that blinding moment of love at first sight!"

Mr. Tate pressed a button. Simon frowned undecisively. The door opened, a girl stepped in, and Simon stopped thinking.

She was tall and slender, and her hair was brown with a sheen of red. Simon could have told you nothing about her face, except that it brought tears to his eyes. And if you asked him about her figure, he might have killed you.

"Miss Penny Bright," said Tate, "meet Mr. Alfred Simon."

The girl tried to speak but no words came, and Simon was equally dumb-struck. He looked at her and *knew*. Nothing else mattered. To the depths of his heart he knew that he was truly and completely loved.

They left at once, hand in hand, and were taken by jet to a small white cottage in a pine grove, overlooking the sea, and there they talked and laughed and loved, and later Simon saw his beloved wrapped in the sunset flame like a goddess of fire. And in blue twilight she looked at him with eyes enormous and dark, her known body mysterious again. The moon came up, bright and lunatic, changing flesh to shadow, and she wept and beat his chest with her small fists, and Simon wept too, although he did not know why. And at last dawn came, faint and disturbed, glimmering upon their parched lips and locked bodies, and nearby the booming surf deafened, inflamed, and maddened them.

At noon they were back in the offices of Love, Inc. Penny clutched his hand for a moment, then disappeared through an inner door.

"Was it real love?" Mr. Tate asked.

"Yes!"

"And was everything satisfactory?"

"Yes! It was love, it was the real thing! But why did she insist on returning?"

"Posthypnotic command," Mr. Tate said.

"What?"

"What did you expect? Everyone wants love, but few wish to pay for it. Here is your bill, sir."

Simon paid, fuming. "This wasn't necessary," he said. "Of

407

course I would pay you for bringing us together. Where is she now? What have you done with her?"

"Please," Mr. Tate said soothingly. "Try to calm yourself."

"I don't want to be calm!" Simon shouted. "I want Penny!"

"That will be impossible," Mr. Tate said, with the barest hint of frost in his voice. "Kindly stop making a spectacle of yourself."

"Are you trying to get more money out of me?" Simon shrieked. "All right, I'll pay. How much do I have to pay to get her out of your clutches?" And Simon yanked out his wallet and slammed it on the desk.

Mr. Tate poked the wallet with a stiffened forefinger. "Put that back in your pocket," he said. "We are an old and respectable firm. If you raise your voice again, I shall be forced to have you ejected."

Simon calmed himself with an effort, put the wallet back in his pocket and sat down. He took a deep breath and said, very quietly, "I'm sorry."

"That's better," Mr. Tate said. "I will not be shouted at. However, if you are reasonable, I can be reasonable too. Now, what's the trouble?"

"The trouble?" Simon's voice started to lift. He controlled it and said, "She loves me."

"Of course."

"Then how can you separate us?"

"What has the one thing got to do with the other?" Mr. Tate asked. "Love is a delightful interlude, a relaxation, good for the intellect, for the ego, for the hormone balance, and for the skin tone. But one would hardly wish to *continue* loving, would one?"

"I would," Simon said. "This love was special, unique—"

"They all are," Mr. Tate said. "But as you know, they are all produced in the same way."

"What?"

"Surely you know something about the mechanics of love production?"

"No," Simon said. "I thought it was—natural."

Mr. Tate shook his head. "We gave up natural selection centuries ago, shortly after the Mechanical Revolution. It was too slow, and commercially unfeasible. Why bother with it, when we can produce any feeling at will by conditioning and proper stimulation of certain brain centers? The result? Penny, completely in love with you! Your own bias, which we calculated, in favor of her particular somatotype, made it complete. We always throw in the dark sea-beach, the lunatic moon, the pallid dawn—"

408

"Then she could have been made to love anyone," Simon said slowly.

"Could have been *brought* to love anyone," Mr. Tate corrected.

"Oh, lord, how did she get into this horrible work?" Simon asked.

"She came in and signed a contract in the usual way," Tate said. "It pays very well. And at the termination of the lease, we return her original personality—untouched! But why do you call the work horrible? There's nothing reprehensible about love."

"It wasn't love!" Simon cried.

"But it was! The genuine article! Unbiased scientific firms have made qualitative tests of it, in comparison with the natural thing. In every case, *our* love tested out to more depth, passion, fervor and scope."

Simon shut his eyes tightly, opened them and said, "Listen to me. I don't care about your scientific tests. I love her, she loves me, that's all that counts. Let me speak to her! I want to marry her!"

Mr. Tate wrinkled his nose in distaste. "Come, come, man! You wouldn't want to *marry* a girl like that! But if it's marriage you're after, we deal in that, too. I can arrange an idyllic and nearly spontaneous lovematch for you with a guaranteed government-inspected virgin—"

"No! I love Penny! At least let me speak to her!"

"That will be quite impossible," Mr. Tate said.

"Why?"

Mr. Tate pushed a button on his desk. "Why do you think? We've wiped out the previous indoctrination. Penny is now in love with someone else."

And then Simon understood. He realized that even now Penny was looking at another man with that passion he had known, feeling for another man that complete and bottomless love that unbiased scientific firms had shown to be so much greater than the old-fashioned, commercially unfeasible natural selection, and that upon that same dark seabeach mentioned in the advertising brochure—

He lunged for Tate's throat. Two attendants, who had entered the office a few moments earlier, caught him and led him to the door.

"Remember!" Tate called. "This in no way invalidates your own experience."

Hellishly enough, Simon knew that what Tate said was true.

And then he found himself on the street.

At first, all he desired was to escape from Earth, where the commercial impracticalities were more than a normal man could afford. He walked very quickly, and his Penny walked beside him, her face glorified with love for him, and him, and him, and you, and you.

And of course he came to the shooting gallery.

"Try your luck?" the manager asked.

"Set 'em up," said Alfred Simon.

6

PERSONALITY

The psychology of personality more than other branches of psychology views the person as a whole, integrated system. It attempts to analyze how the system is organized and how it functions. It aims to answer the basic question (in the vernacular of today): How does the individual put it all together? How do individuals integrate both the biological and social processes as part of one system? How important are learning and perception? Where do developmental processes come in, or on the other hand, what about the present and the future?

These questions are, of course, broad and complex, and consequently theories of personality have also been broad and complex. They have drawn criticism from some quarters of psychology for being too speculative and loosely constructed— criticisms probably well taken. However, more than compensating for these weaknesses is the richness of understanding people that these theories demonstrate. For the layman and casual student who wants to understand himself, they have provided ideas which have been both stimulating and helpful. Much of the language of these theories has trickled down to everyday language: for example, terms like "the unconscious," "inferiority complex," or "introvert and extrovert." To the professional, they have provided concepts for both research and psychotherapy.

The first pioneer and most influential personality theorist was, and still is, Sigmund Freud. At the turn of the century Freud, a Viennese neurologist, found that many of the so-called medical problems his patients were complaining about were really psychological problems, often with a sexual basis. This situation set the master's brilliant mind on a quest for answers that would last for over forty years, still incomplete and being modified until the day he died. The result was Freud's theory of personality, "Psychoanalytic Theory," which laid the groundwork for others to follow, and is still probably the richest, most complex, and most provocative personality theory of all.

Freud conceptualized the adult personality by dividing it into three components: the Id, Ego, and Superego. The Id is the component containing the individual's instinctual nature, the sexual and aggressive instincts. The sexual instincts were broadly viewed as life-promoting drives, including love and creativity, powered by energy which Freud called Libido. Aggressive instincts concentrate on death and destruction, destroying rather than promoting life. Both instincts were viewed as seeking immediate satisfaction (the Pleasure Principle), with little concern for the constraints of reality. The need to consider reality generated the development of the Ego, modifying the Id's demands by tempering them with the Reality Principle. Finally, the third component of personality, the Superego, develops when the individual incorporates the moral rules of society taught to him by his parents. For the healthy personality, the personality is controlled by a strong Ego, which steers a satisfactory path between the often conflicting demands of the other two components.

Freud also divided the personality in another important way: the Conscious and the Unconscious. Using the analogy of an iceberg, he saw the Conscious as the upper tip which is visible, with the much larger Unconscious below the surface. The Unconscious contained the residue of childhood memories, drives, and wishes, buried there during childhood by repression, but not completely forgotten. Freud believed that although the individual tried to maintain conscious, rational control of his behavior, he was often controlled by the residues of childhood located in the Unconscious, causing him to be irrational rather than rational.

Another personality theorist using the Unconscious as a basic concept was Carl Jung. Jung, however, expanded and changed the concept to include two levels of the Unconscious: the Personal Unconscious and the Collective Unconscious. The former roughly corresponded to Freud's conception, but the latter included not only personal memories, but also the collected memories of the history of the human race. Jung believed that each and every individual carried archetype (primitive) images in his mind inherited from the ancient ancestors of the modern human race. He suggested that these common images were the reason that people in different cultures, both modern and primitive, share similar myths and dreams. A less controversial idea of Jung was his conception of introversion and extroversion as basic personality modes. In general, Jung broke away from the basic orientations of his teacher Freud, deemphasizing Freud's focus on sex, giving more credence to mystical explanations, and stressing the unity of personality with his concept of the Self.

Alfred Adler, another primary student of Freud's, also broke away from his mentor. Like Jung, Adler used the conception of self to emphasize the basic unity of personality, stressing the fact that each individual develops his own Style of Life, binding his personality and making him a unique human being. Each individual uses his will to move from an initial state of weakness and inferiority to one of power and superiority. The healthy individual does so unselfishly with social interest, consciously self-actualizing, and hopefully reaching the final goal he has been striving for throughout his life.

Although Adler's theory was not as complex or well defined as those of either Freud or Jung, much of his basic approach has been incorporated into the work of the current humanistic school of personality. Modern theorists like Carl Rogers, Gordon Allport, and Abraham Maslow have all used individuality and the conscious striving toward self-actualization as the core of their theories. Likewise, modern existential psychologists like Rollo May emphasize the necessity for each individual to consciously search for his true inner self or identity, to establish his own style of life or, as the existentialists put it, his "being in the world." The existentialists differ from those technically classified as humanistic theorists in their emphasis on existential anxiety. They stress the fact that each of us harbors the anxiety-provoking knowledge that we could die at any moment, knowledge that only human beings have in the entire animal kingdom. Existentially, then, we must make every act count and ultimately give our lives meaning and our existence true essence—a difficult and challenging task.

While the humanists and existentialists have stressed the differences between human beings and the rest of the animal kingdom, learning theorists like Dollard and Miller, and B. F. Skinner, have attempted to describe the human personality by using conditioning terms, emanating, in general, from basic research using laboratory animals. Dollard and Miller have reworked many of Freud's concepts into the language of stimulus and response learning, showing, for example, how Freud's concept of unconscious association could be viewed in light of classical conditioning. Skinner has attempted to generalize his principles of operant conditioning to the external environment, stressing how society shapes human behavior with its built-in reinforcement schedules. In short, both approaches have demonstrated how laboratory learning principles can be applied to social learning in the outside world.

As we have seen, there are many theories with different ideas about personality. Each presents hypotheses suggesting various relationships between personality attributes, as well as between attributes and behavior. How can we tell if Freud's ideas about aggression are more useful than those of Skinner? To resolve this problem we must be able to measure aggression. We must be able to separate someone high in aggression from someone less aggressive if we are to establish if, for example, aggression is related to frustration. Thus personality scales in various forms have been constructed, some measuring many attributes at once, others measuring one at a time; some emphasizing the role of behavior, others emphasizing perception. All try to measure relatively enduring characteristics of the individual.

Personality measurement serves three major purposes. As described above, it serves personality research, which aims to provide empirical evidence in support of the conceptions of various personality theories. Personality measurement also serves selection processes enabling us to choose individuals who possess the attributes which would make them most successful in particular avenues of endeavor. With good personality screening, we can have happier more productive people in lines of work they are best suited for. Thirdly, personality measurement serves an important clinical purpose. By measuring and establishing the strength of certain characteristics of an individual with problems, the clinician can better understand and help that individual. Clinical interviews and projective techniques like the Rorschach Test are among the measurement processes often used for this purpose. With reliability (consistency) and validity (accuracy), instruments of personality measurement can serve the study and applications of the field of personality enormously.

mother

Philip Jose Farmer

This is the story of a mother-son relationship—of Eddie Fetts, who has not resolved his Oedipus complex, as Freud would see it. The story is complex and richly symbolic. Probably the concepts of Otto Rank, one of Freud's disciples, are most meaningful in exploring the symbolism of the story. Rank's major break with Freud was Rank's emphasis on the birth trauma as the basis for emotional development. He insisted that birth is so traumatic and painful for all of us that it leaves us with the overriding wish to return to the pleasant, nurturant, secure, and complete world of the womb. According to the theory, the wish to return is repressed; and its strength and power as an underlying dynamic force in determining behavior separates neurotics from healthy individuals. The neurotic feels thrust out involuntarily into the world, suffering strong separation anxiety, and fear of death. Unconsciously he wants to return, but this is not without conflict, because getting back into the womb involves going through the painful birth trauma in reverse—again going through the female genitals.

This is Rank's interpretation of the Oedipal conflict. If the individual does not resolve the conflict by changing the object of his return to another female, symbolically by having intercourse with her in adulthood, repressing the painful aspects, and maximizing the pleasure, he will remain passive, dependent, and neurotic. On one hand, he still wants and needs his mother's womb, and on the other hand, he hates his mother because she becomes an object of frustration since he obviously cannot reenter her womb. This individual will not be able to grow and mature into a healthy, independent individual who willfully separates himself from his mother to go on to establish a meaningful identity of his own. In times of stress, the neurotic will regress to the former succorant relationship with his mother, which he sees as safe and secure.

Enter our hero, Eddie Fetts, with the author setting the stage for the ultimate regression to the womb in the first sentence of the story: "Look, mother. The clock is running backwards." In actuality, Eddie has a headstart in beginning his regression odyssey because his psychological growth has been arrested and fixated. He is basically still an oral personality: he sings; he passively drinks, sucking on a nipple; he sleeps on his mother's breast. This existence has not been entered into by Eddie without paying a heavy price, however, for he is psychologically powerless and apathetic, and apparently sexually impotent, as is suggested by his abortive marriage. Consequently, he is prone to periods of depression; and he has a drinking problem, relying on Old Red Star rye. All this is symbolized by the heavy albatross hanging around the neck of the ancient mariner—an operatic character with whom Eddie identifies.

Eddie's actual mother, Dr. Paula Fetts, is a very interesting character in her own right because in essence, she is both mother and father to Eddie. She is a super-scientist as well as a super-smothering mother. In her Oedipal relationship with Eddie she is the super-castrator (usually seen as the father in the traditional conception) in addition to being sexual object with her super-womb. Overall, the mother-son relationship in the story is symbiotic, rather than simply parasitic. His mother needs Eddie in the relationship to maintain her ego-boosting self-image as a mother as much as Eddie needs her. Thus, she does all she can to maintain her relationship with Eddie as it is. This is often the situation with smothering mothers in the real world, and why family therapy is used in these cases, instead of treating only the child.

When Eddie and Dr. Fetts crash on the planet Baudelaire, he is captured by a strange immobile creature which he names Mother Polyphema. Symbolically she is the womb. Her concept of masculinity and femininity is interesting. From her point of view, anything that is mobile is a male. For her, then, Eddie's mother is male, while, of course, from his point of view, Dr. Fetts is female biologically. In a sense, Eddie uses the traditional structural basis for determining sex, while Mother Polyphema and her society use function—women's lib in outer space!

The function of Mother Polyphema is strictly female and

417

motherly. She is created by the author in a wayout image of the universal earth mother, suggested to be a universal symbol by Carl Jung. She is all encompassing, all giving and creating of life, all protecting—a living womb.

The social structure of the Mother's society is also worth mentioning. In this society, status allows one to communicate and gossip first, as a sign of deference. In some ways, it is reminiscent of a meeting of a board of directors. The Mother's reaction to a mobile female, Dr. Fetts, is also significant in that she first denies its possibility. This is the primitive defense mechanism of "denial" in which we blot out of our consciousness that which we cannot accept. She also uses her power to destroy Eddie's mother, in part because she is probably jealous of a rival, but also because it is typical to destroy something or someone you do not understand.

Eddie's reaction to his mother's death is psychologically significant in his conflicted reaction. First he giggles, then he wails. Perhaps his first reaction was joy and relief. He was free of her at last, and some of his anger and aggression toward her was satisfied. Then, guilt and anxiety set in—guilt over his feelings and his failure to try to save her, and then the old separation anxiety that he had been abandoned.

The ending of the story is quite powerful psychologically. At first Eddie passively accepts his womb with Mother Polyphema, who gives all and asks little. Without the threat of castration, the Oedipal sexual wish, long repressed, starts pushing itself out; but he is still too guilty to initiate the act, for the Mother reminds him of his real mother and he must not do it with his mother even though he'd love to. We can assume there might have been the same problem with his wife, leading to his impotence. He is still conflicted, goes at it half-heartedly, and drops his penis-symbol scalpel—impotent again.

Luckily, the Mother has no such conflict with her sex object and convinces him to go at it or die. With no real choice, he is free of conflict, and all the combined sexual desire and aggression stored within him which he had for his own mother since he was a child comes out at once. He feels fine, and the symbolic albatross falls off his neck.

Now the Mother has the conflict, for she has not destroyed her mate after intercourse, as has been her custom, and she feels a new emotion toward him—love. Eddie's regression seems to be complete. His Oedipal wish has come true, and he has truly returned to the womb, finally assuming the fetal position.

MOTHER   *Philip Jose Farmer*

"Look, mother. The clock is running backwards."
Eddie Fetts pointed to the hands on the pilot room dial.
Dr. Paula Fetts said, "The crash must have reversed it."
"How could it do that?"
"I can't tell you. I don't know everything, son."
"Oh!"
"Well, don't look at me so disappointedly. I'm a pathologist, not an electronician."
"Don't be so cross, mother. I can't stand it. Not now."
He walked out of the pilot room. Anxiously, she followed him. The burial of the crew and her fellow scientists had been very trying for him. Spilled blood had always made him dizzy and sick; he could scarcely control his hands enough to help her stack the scattered bones and entrails.

He had wanted to put the corpses in the nuclear furnace, but she had forbidden that. The Geigers amidships were ticking loudly, warning that there was invisible death in the stern.

The meteor that struck the moment the ship came out of Translation into normal space had probably wrecked the engine-room. So she had understood from the incoherent high-pitched phrases of a colleague before he fled to the pilot room. She had hurried to find Eddie. She feared his cabin door would still be locked, as he had been making a tape of the aria, "Heavy Hangs the Albatross" from Gianelli's *Ancient Mariner.*

Fortunately, the emergency system had automatically thrown out the locking circuits. Entering, she had called out his name in fear he'd been hurt. He was lying half-unconscious on the floor, but it was not the accident that had thrown him there. The reason lay in the corner, released from his lax hand; a quart free-fall thermos, ribber-nippled. From Eddie's open mouth charged a breath of rye that not even Nodor pills had been able to conceal.

Sharply she had commanded him to get up and onto the bed. Her voice, the first he had ever heard, pierced through the phalanx of Old Red Star. He struggled up, and she, though smaller, had thrown every ounce of her weight into getting him up and onto the bed.

There she had lain down with him and strapped them both in. She understood that the lifeboat had been wrecked also, and that it was up to the captain to bring the yacht down safely to the surface of this charted but unexplored planet, Baudelaire. Everybody else had gone to sit behind the captain, strapped in crashchairs, unable to help except with their silent backing.

Moral support had not been enough. The ship had come in on a shallow slant. Too fast. The wounded motors had not been able to hold her up. The prow had taken the brunt of the punishment. So had those seated in the nose.

Dr. Fetts had held her son's head on her bosom and prayed out loud to her God. Eddie had snored and muttered. Then there was a sound like the clashing of the gates of doom—a tremendous bong as if the ship were a clapper in a gargantuan bell tolling the most frightening message human ears may hear—a blinding blast of light—and darkness and silence.

A few moments later Eddie began crying out in a childish voice, "Don't leave me to die, mother! Come back! Come back!"

Mother was unconscious by his side, but he did not know that. He wept for a while, then he lapsed back into his rye-fogged stupor—if he had ever been out of it—and slept. Again, darkness and silence.

It was the second day since the crash, if "day" could describe that twilight state on Baudelaire. Dr. Fetts followed her son wherever he went. She knew he was very sensitive and easily upset. All his life she had known it and had tried to get between him and anything that would cause trouble. She had succeeded, she thought, fairly well until three months ago when Eddie had eloped.

The girl was Polina Fameux, the ash-blonde long-legged actress whose tridi image, taped, had been shipped to frontier stars where a small acting talent meant little and a large and shapely bosom much. Since Eddie was a well-known Metro tenor, the marriage made a big splash whose ripples ran around the civilized Galaxy.

Dr. Fetts had felt very bad about the elopement, but she had, she hoped, hidden her grief very well beneath a smiling mask. She didn't regret having to give him up; after all, he was a full-grown man, no longer her little boy. But, really, aside from the seasons at the Metro and his tours, he had not been parted from her since he was eight.

That was when she went on a honeymoon with her second husband. And then she and Eddie had not been separated long, for Eddie had gotten very sick, and she'd had to hurry back and take care of him, as he had insisted she was the only one who could make him well.

Moreover, you couldn't count his days at the opera as a total loss, for he vised her every noon and they had a long talk—no matter how high the vise bills ran.

The ripples caused by her son's marriage were scarcely a week old before they were followed by even bigger ones. They bore the news of the separation of Eddie and his wife. A fortnight later, Polina applied for divorce on grounds of incompatibility. Eddie was handed the papers in his mother's apartment. He had come back to her the day he and Polina had agreed they "couldn't make a go of it," or, as he phrased it to his mother, "couldn't get together."

Dr. Fetts was, of course, very curious about the reason for their parting, but, as she explained to her friends, she "respected" his silence. What she didn't say was that she had told herself the time would come when he would tell her all.

Eddie's "nervous breakdown" started shortly afterward. He had been very irritable, moody, and depressed, but he got worse the day a so-called friend told Eddie that whenever Polina heard his name mentioned, she laughed loud and long. The friend added that Polina had promised to tell someday the true story of their brief merger.

That night his mother had to call in a doctor.

In the days that followed, she thought of giving up her position as research pathologist at De Kruif and taking all her time to help him "get back on his feet." It was a sign of the struggle going on in her mind that she had not been able to decide within a week's time. Ordinarily given to swift consideration and resolution of a problem, she could not agree to surrender her beloved quest into tissue regeneration.

Just as she was on the verge of doing what was for her the incredible and the shameful, tossing a coin, she had been vised by her superior. He told her she had been chosen to go with a group of biologists on a research cruise to ten preselected planetary systems.

Joyfully, she had thrown away the papers that would turn Eddie over to a sanatorium. And, since he was quite famous, she had used her influence to get the government to allow him to go along. Ostensibly, he was to make a survey of the development of opera on planets colonized by Terrans. That the yacht was not visiting any colonized globes seemed to have been missed by the bureaus concerned. But it was not the first time in the history of a government that its left hand knew not what its right was doing.

Actually, he was to be "rebuilt" by his mother, who thought herself much more capable of curing him than any of the prevalent A, F, J, R, S, K, or H therapies. True, some of her friends reported amazing results with some of the symbol-chasing techniques. On the other hand, two of her close companions had tried them all and had gotten no benefits from any of them. She was his mother; she could do more for him than any of those "alphabatties"; he was flesh of her flesh, blood of her blood. Besides, he wasn't so sick. He just got awfully blue sometimes and made theatrical but insincere threats of suicide or else just sat and stared into space. But she could handle him.

So now it was that she followed him from the backward-running clock to his room. And saw him step inside, look for a second, and then turn to her with a twisted face.

"Neddie is ruined, mother. Absolutely ruined."

She glanced at the piano. It had torn loose from the wall-racks at the moment of impact and smashed itself against the opposite wall. To Eddie it wasn't just a piano; it was Neddie. He had a pet name for everything he contacted for more than a brief time. It was as if he hopped from one appellation to the next, like an ancient sailor who felt lost unless he was close to the familiar and designated points of the shoreline. Otherwise, Eddie seemed to be drifting helplessly in a chaotic ocean, one that was anonymous and amorphous.

Or, analogy more typical of him, he was like the night-clubber who feels submerged, drowning, unless he hops from table to table, going from one well-known group of faces to the next, avoiding the featureless and unnamed dummies at the strangers' tables.

He did not cry over Neddie. She wished he would. He had been so apathetic during the voyage. Nothing, not even the unparalleled splendor of the naked stars nor the inexpressible alienness of strange planets had seemed to lift him very long. If he would only weep or laugh loudly or display some sign that he was reacting violently to what was happening. She would even have welcomed his striking her in anger or calling her "bad" names.

But no, not even during the gathering of the mangled corpses, when he looked for a while as if he were going to vomit, would he give way to his body's demand for expression. She understood that if he were to throw up, he would be much better for it, would have gotten rid of much of the psychic disturbance along with the physical.

He would not. He had kept on raking flesh and bones into the large plastic bags and kept a fixed look of resentment and sullenness.

She hoped now that the loss of his piano would bring tears and shaking shoulders. Then she could take him in her arms and give him sympathy. He would be her little boy again, afraid of the dark, afraid of the dog killed by a car, seeking her arms for the sure safety, the sure love.

"Never mind, baby," she said. "When we're rescued, we'll get you a new one."

"When—!"

He lifted his eyebrows and sat down on the bed's edge.

"What do we do now?"

She became very brisk and efficient.

"The ultrad automatically started working the moment the meteor struck. If it's survived the crash, it's still sending SOS's. If not, then there's nothing we can do about it. Neither of us knows how to repair it.

"However, it's possible that in the last five years since this planet was located, other expeditions may have landed here. Not from Earth but from some of the colonies. Or from nonhuman globes. Who knows? It's worth taking a chance. Let's see."

A single glance was enough to wreck their hopes. The ultrad had been twisted and broken until it was no longer recognizable as

423

the machine that sent swifter-than-light waves through the no-ether.

Dr. Fetts said with false cheeriness, "Well, that's that! So what? It makes things too easy. Let's go into the storeroom and see what we can see."

Eddie shrugged and followed her. There she insisted that each take a panrad. If they had to separate for any reason, they could always communicate and also, using the DF's—the built-in direction finders—locate each other. Having used them before, they knew the instrument's capabilities and how essential they were on scouting or camping trips.

The panrads were lightweight cylinders about two feet high and eight inches in diameter. Crampacked, they held the mechanisms of two dozen different utilities. Their batteries lasted a year without charging, they were practically indestructible and worked under almost any conditions.

Keeping away from the side of the ship that had the huge hole in it, they took the panrads outside. The long wave bands were searched by Eddie while his mother moved the dial that ranged up and down the shortwaves. Neither really expected to hear anything, but to search was better than doing nothing.

Finding the modulated wave-frequencies empty of any significant noises, he switched to the continuous waves. He was startled by a dot-dashing.

"Hey, mom! Something in the 1000 kilocycles! Unmodulated!"

"Naturally, son," she said with some exasperation in the midst of her elation. "What would you expect from a radio-telegraphic signal?"

She found the band on her own cylinder. He looked blankly at her. "I know nothing about radio, but that's not Morse."

"What? You must be mistaken!"

"I—I don't think so."

"Is it or isn't it? Good God, son, can't you be certain of *anything!*"

She turned the amplifier up. As both of them had learned Galacto-Morse through sleeplearn techniques, she checked him at once.

"You're right. What do you make of it?"

His quick ear sorted out the pulses.

"No simple dot and dash. Four different time-lengths."

He listened some more.

"They've got a certain rhythm, all right. I can make out definite groupings. Ah! That's the sixth time I've caught that particular one. And there's another. And another."

Dr. Fetts shook her ash-blond head. She could make out nothing but a series of zzt-zzt-zzt's.

Eddie glanced at the DF needle.

"Coming from NE by E. Should we try to locate?"

"Naturally," she replied. "But we'd better eat first. We don't know how far away it is, or what we'll find there. While I fix a hot meal, you get our field trip stuff ready."

"O.K.," he said with more enthusiasm than he had shown for a long time.

When he came back he ate everything in the large dish his mother had prepared on the unwrecked galley stove.

"You always did make the best stew," he said.

"Thank you. I'm glad you're eating again, son. I am surprised. I thought you'd be sick about all this."

He waved vaguely but energetically.

"The challenge of the unknown. I have a sort of feeling this is going to turn out much better than we thought. Much better."

She came close and sniffed his breath. It was clean, innocent even of stew. That meant he'd taken Nodor, which probably meant he'd been sampling some hidden rye. Otherwise, how explain his reckless disregard of the possible dangers? It wasn't like him.

She said nothing, for she knew that if he tried to hide a bottle in his clothes or field sack while they were tracking down the radio signals, she would soon find it. And take it away. He wouldn't even protest, merely let her lift it from his limp hand while his lips swelled with resentment.

They set out. Both wore knapsacks and carried the panrads. He carried a gun over his shoulder, and she had snapped onto her sack her small black bag of medical and lab supplies.

High noon of late autumn was topped by a weak red sun that barely managed to make itself seen through the eternal double layer of clouds. Its companion, an even smaller blob of lilac, was setting on the northwestern horizon. They walked in a sort of bright twilight, the best that Baudelaire ever achieved. Yet, despite the lack of light, the air was warm. It was a phenomenon common to certain

425

planets behind the Horsehead Nebula, one being investigated but as yet unexplained.

The country was hilly, with many deep ravines. Here and there were prominences high enough and steep-sided enough to be called embryo mountains. Considering the roughness of the land, however, there was a surprising amount of vegetation. Pale green, red, and yellow bushes, vines, and little trees clung to every bit of ground, horizontal or vertical. All had comparatively broad leaves that turned with the sun to catch the light.

From time to time, as the two Terrans strode noisily through the forest, small multicolored insect-like and mammal-like creatures scuttled from hiding place to hiding place. Eddie decided to carry his gun in the crook of his arm. Then, after they were forced to scramble up and down ravines and hills and fight their way through thickets that became unexpectedly tangled, he put it back over his shoulder, where it hung from a strap.

Despite their exertions, they did not tire quickly. They weighed about twenty pounds less than they would have on Earth and, though the air was thinner, it was richer in oxygen.

Dr. Fetts kept up with Eddie. Thirty years the senior of the twenty-three-year-old, she passed even at close inspection for his older sister. Longevity pills took care of that. However, he treated her with all the courtesy and chivalry that one gave one's mother and helped her up the steep inclines, even though the climbs did not appreciably cause her deep chest to demand more air.

They paused once by a creek bank to get their bearings.

"The signals have stopped," he said.

"Obviously," she replied.

At that moment the radar-detector built into the panrad began to ping. Both of them automatically looked upward.

"There's no ship in the air."

"It can't be coming from either of those hills," she pointed out. "There's nothing but a boulder on top of each one. Tremendous rocks."

"Nevertheless, it's coming from there, I think. Oh! Oh! Did you see what I saw? Looked like a tall stalk of some kind being pulled down behind that big rock."

She peered through the dim light. "I think you were imagining things, son. I saw nothing."

Then, even as the pinging kept up, the zzting started again. But after a burst of noise, both stopped.

"Let's go up and see what we shall see," she said.

"Something screwy," he commented. She did not answer.

They forded the creek and began the ascent. Halfway up, they stopped to sniff in puzzlement at a gust of some heavy odor coming downhill.

"Smells like a cageful of monkeys," he said.

"In heat," she added. If his was the keener ears, hers was the sharper nose.

They went on up. The RD began sounding its tiny hysterical gonging. Nonplused, Eddie stopped. The DF indicated the radar pulses were not coming from the top of the hill they were climbing, as formerly, but from the other hill across the valley. Abruptly, the panrad fell silent.

"What do we do now?"

"Finish what we started. This hill. Then we go to the other one."

He shrugged and then hastened after her tall slim body in its long-legged coveralls. She was hot on the scent, literally, and nothing could stop her. Just before she reached the bungalow-sized boulder topping the hill, he caught up with her. She had stopped to gaze intently at the DF needle, which swung wildly before it stopped at neutral. The monkey-cage odor was very strong.

"Do you suppose it could be some sort of radio-generating mineral?" she asked, disappointedly.

"No, those groupings were semantic. And that smell. . . ."

"Then, what—?"

He didn't know whether to feel pleased or not that she had so obviously and suddenly thrust the burden of responsibility and action on him. Both pride and a curious shrinking affected him. But he did feel exhilarated. Almost, he thought, he felt as if he were on the verge of discovering what he had been looking for for a long time. What the object of his search had been, he could not say. But he was excited and not very much afraid.

He unslung his weapon, a two-barreled combination shotgun and rifle. The panrad was still quiet.

"Maybe the boulder is camouflage for a spy outfit," he said. He sounded silly, even to himself.

Behind him, his mother gasped and screamed. He whirled and raised his gun, but there was nothing to shoot. She was pointing at the hilltop across the valley, shaking, and saying something incoherent.

He could make out a long slim antenna seemingly projecting from the monstrous boulder crouched there. At the same time, two thoughts struggled for first place in his mind: one, that it was more than a coincidence that both hills had almost identical stone structures on their brows, and, two, that the antenna must have been recently stuck out, for he was sure he had not seen it the last time he looked.

He never got to tell her his conclusions, for something thin and flexible and irresistible seized him from behind. Lifted into the air, he was borne backwards. He dropped the gun and tried to grab the bands or tentacles around him and tear them off with his bare hands. No use.

He caught one last glimpse of his mother running off down the hillside. Then a curtain snapped down, and he was in total darkness.

Eddie sensed himself, still suspended, twirled around. He could not know for sure, of course, but he thought he was facing in exactly the opposite direction. Simultaneously, the tentacles binding his legs and arms were released. Only his waist was still gripped. It was pressed so tightly that he cried out with pain.

Then, boot-toes bumping on some resilient substance, he was carried forward. Halted, facing he knew not what horrible monster, he was suddenly assailed—not by a sharp beak or tooth or knife or some other cutting or mangling instrument—but by a dense cloud of that same monkey perfume.

In other circumstances, he might have vomited. Now his stomach was not given the time to consider whether it should clean house or not. The tentacle lifted him higher and thrust him against something soft and yielding—something fleshlike and womanly— almost breastlike in texture and smoothness and warmth and in its hint of gentle curving.

He put his hands and feet out to brace himself, for he thought for a moment he was going to sink in and be covered up— enfolded—ingested. The idea of a gargantuan amoeba-thing hiding within a hollow rock—or a rocklike shell—made him writhe and yell and shove at the protoplasmic substance.

But nothing of the kind happened. He was not plunged into a smothering and slimy jelly that would strip him of his skin and then his flesh and then dissolve his bones. He was merely shoved repeatedly against the soft swelling. Each time, he pushed or kicked or struck at it. After a dozen of these seemingly purposeless acts, he was held away, as if whatever was doing it was puzzled by his behavior.

He had quit screaming. The only sounds were his harsh breathing and the zzzts and pings from the panrad. Even as he became aware of them, the zzzts changed tempo and settled into a recognizable pattern of bursts—three units that crackled out again and again.

"Who are you? Who are you?"

Of course, it could just as easily have been, "What are you?" or "What the hell!" or "Nov smoz ka pop?"

Or nothing—semantically speaking.

But he didn't think the latter. And when he was gently lowered to the floor, and the tentacle went off to only-God-knew-where in the dark, he was sure that the creature was communicating—or trying to—with him.

It was this thought that kept him from screaming and running around in the lightless and fetid chamber, brainlessly seeking an outlet. He mastered his panic and snapped open a little shutter in the panrad's side and thrust in his right-hand index finger. There he poised it above the key and in a moment, when the thing paused in transmitting, he sent back, as best he could, the pulses he had received. It was not necessary for him to turn on the light and spin the dial that would put him on the 1000 kc. band. The instrument would automatically key that frequency in with the one he had just received.

The oddest part of the whole procedure was that his whole body was trembling almost uncontrollably—one part excepted. That was his index finger, his one unit that seemed to him to have a definite function in this otherwise meaningless situation. It was the section of him that was helping him to survive—the only part that knew how—at that moment. Even his brain seemed to have no connection with his finger. That digit was himself, and the rest just happened to be linked to it.

When he paused, the transmitter began again. This time the units were unrecognizable. There was a certain rhythm to them, but he could not know what they meant. Meanwhile, the RD was pinging. Something somewhere in the dark hole had a beam held tightly on him.

He pressed a button on the panrad's top, and the built-in flashlight illuminated the area just in front of him. He saw a wall of reddish-gray rubbery substance. On the wall was a roughly circular, light gray swelling about four feet in diameter. Around it, giving it a

Medusa appearance, were coiled twelve very long, very thin tentacles.

Though he was afraid that if he turned his back to them the tentacles would seize him once more, his curiosity forced him to wheel about and examine his surroundings with the bright beam. He was in an egg-shaped chamber about thirty feet long, twelve wide, and eight-to-ten high in the middle. It was formed of a reddish-gray material, smooth except for irregular intervals of blue or red pipes. Veins and arteries?

A door-sized portion of the wall had a vertical slit running down it. Tentacles fringed it. He guessed it was a sort of iris and that it had opened to drag him inside. Starfish-shaped groupings of tentacles were scattered on the walls or hung from the ceiling. On the wall opposite the iris was a long and flexible stalk with a cartilaginous ruff around its free end. When Eddie moved, it moved, its blind point following him as a radar antenna tracks the thing it is locating. That was what it was. And unless he was wrong, the stalk was also a C. W. transmitter-receiver.

He shot the light around. When it reached the end farthest from him, he gasped. Ten creatures were huddled together facing him! About the size of half-grown pigs, they looked like nothing so much as unshelled snails; they were eyeless, and the stalk growing from the forehead of each was a tiny duplicate of that on the wall. They didn't look dangerous. Their open mouths were little and toothless, and their rate of locomotion must be slow, for they moved like snails, on a large pedestal of flesh—a foot-muscle.

Nevertheless, if he were to fall asleep they could overcome him by force of numbers, and those mouths might drip an acid to digest him, or they might carry a concealed poisonous sting.

His speculations were interrupted violently. He was seized, lifted, and passed on to another group of tentacles. He was carried beyond the antenna-stalk and toward the snail-beings. Just before he reached them, he was halted, facing the wall. An iris, hitherto invisible, opened. His light shone into it, but he could see nothing but convolutions of flesh.

His panrad gave off a new pattern of dit-dot-deet-dats. The iris widened until it was large enough to admit his body, if he were shoved in head first. Or feet first. It didn't matter. The convolutions straightened out and became a tunnel. Or a throat. From thousands of little pits emerged thousands of tiny, razor sharp teeth. They flashed out and sank back in, and before they had disappeared thousands of other wicked little spears darted out and past the receding fangs.

Meat-grinder.

Beyond the murderous array, at the end of the throat, was a huge pouch of water. Steam came from it, and with it an odor like that of his mother's stew. Dark bits, presumably meat, and pieces of vegetables floated on the seething surface.

Then the iris closed, and he was turned around to face the slugs. Gently, but unmistakably, a tentacle spanked his buttocks. And the panrad zzzted a warning.

Eddie was not stupid. He knew now that the ten creatures were not dangerous unless he molested them. In which case he had just seen where he would go if he did not behave.

Again he was lifted and carried along the wall until he was shoved against the light gray spot. The monkey-cage odor, which had died out, became strong again. Eddie identified its source with a very small hole which appeared in the wall.

When he did not respond—he had no idea yet how he was supposed to act—the tentacles dropped him so unexpectedly that he fell on his back. Unhurt by the yielding flesh, he rose.

What was the next step? Exploration of his resources. Itemization: The panrad. A sleeping-bag which he wouldn't need as long as the present too-warm temperature kept up. A bottle of Old Red Star capsules. A free-fall thermos with attached nipple. A box of A-2-Z rations. A Foldstove. Cartridges for his double-barrel, now lying outside the creature's boulderish shell. A roll of toilet paper. Toothbrush. Paste. Soap. Towel. Pills: Nodor, hormone, vitamin, longevity, reflex, and sleeping. And a thread-thin wire, a hundred feet long when uncoiled, that held prisoner in its molecular structure a hundred symphonies, eighty operas, a thousand different types of musical pieces, and two thousand great books ranging from Sophocles and Dostoevski to the latest bestseller. It could be played inside the panrad.

He inserted it, pushed a button, and spoke, "Eddie Fett's recording of Puccini's *Che gelida manina,* please."

And while he listened approvingly to his own magnificent voice, he zipped open a can he had found in the bottom of the sack. His mother had put into it the stew left over from their last meal in the ship.

Not knowing what was happening, yet for some reason sure he was for the present safe, he munched meat and vegetables with a contented jaw. Transition from abhorrence to appetite sometimes came easily for Eddie.

He cleaned out the can and finished with some crackers and a chocolate bar. Rationing was out. As long as the food lasted, he would eat well. Then, if nothing turned up, he would. . . . But then, he reassured himself as he licked his fingers, his mother, who was free, would find some way to get him out of his trouble.

She always had.

The panrad, silent for a while, began signaling. Eddie spotlighted the antenna and saw it was pointing at the snail-beings, which he had, in accordance with his custom, dubbed familiarly. Sluggos, he called them.

The Sluggos crept toward the wall and stopped close to it. Their mouths, placed on the tops of their heads, gaped like so many hungry young birds. The iris opened, and two lips formed into a spout. Out of it streamed steaming-hot water and chunks of meat and vegetables. Stew! Stew that fell exactly into each waiting mouth.

That was how Eddie learned the second phase of Mother Polyphema's language. The first message had been, "What are you?" This was, "Come and get it!"

He experimented. He tapped out a repetition of what he'd last heard. As one, the Sluggos—except the one then being fed—turned to him and crept a few feet before halting, puzzled.

Inasmuch as Eddie was broadcasting, the Sluggos must have had some sort of built-in DF. Otherwise they wouldn't have been able to distinguish between his pulses and their Mother's.

Immediately after, a tentacle smote Eddie across the shoulders and knocked him down. The panrad zzzted its third intelligible message: "Don't ever do that!"

And then a fourth, to which the ten young obeyed by wheeling and resuming their former positions.

"This way, children."

Yes, they were the offspring, living, eating, sleeping, playing, and learning to communicate in the womb of their mother—the Mother. They were the mobile brood of this vast immobile entity that had scooped up Eddie as a frog scoops up a fly. This Mother. She who had once been just such a Sluggo until she had grown hog-size and had been pushed out of her Mother's womb. And who, rolled into a tight ball, had free-wheeled down her natal hill, straightened out at the bottom, inched her way up the next hill, rolled down, and so on. Until she found the empty shell of an adult who had died. Or, if she wanted to be a first-class citizen in her society and not a prestigeless *occupée*, she found the bare top of a tall hill—or any eminence that commanded a big sweep of territory—and there squatted.

And there she put out many thread-thin tendrils into the soil and into the cracks in the rocks, tendrils that drew sustenance from the fat of her body and grew and extended downwards and ramified into other tendrils. Deep underground the rootlets worked their instinctive chemistry; searched for and found the water, the calcium, the iron, the copper, the nitrogen, the carbons, fondled earthworms and grubs and larvae, teasing them for the secrets of their fats and proteins; broke down the wanted substance into shadowy colloidal particles; sucked them up the thready pipes of the tendrils and back to the pale and slimming body crouching on a flat space atop a ridge, a hill, a peak.

There, using the blueprints stored in the molecules of the cerebellum, her body took the building blocks of elements and fashioned them into a very thin shell of the most available material, a shield large enough so she could expand to fit it while her natural enemies—the keen and hungry predators that prowled twilighted Baudelaire—nosed and clawed it in vain.

Then, her evergrowing bulk cramped, she would resorb the hard covering. And if no sharp tooth found her during that process of a few days, she would cast another and a larger. And so on through a dozen or more.

Until she had become the monstrous and much reformed body of an adult and virgin female. Outside would be the stuff that so much resembled a boulder, that was, actually, rock: either granite, diorite, marble, basalt, or maybe just plain limestone. Or sometimes iron, glass, or cellulose.

Within was the centrally located brain, probably as large as a man's. Surrounding it, the tons of organs: the nervous system, the mighty heart, or hearts, the four stomachs, the microwave and long-wave generators, the kidneys, bowels, tracheae, scent and taste organs, the perfume factory which made odors to attract animals and birds close enough to be seized, and the huge womb. And the antennae—the small one inside for teaching and scanning the young, and a long and powerful stalk on the outside, projecting from the shelltop, retractable if danger came.

The next step was from virgin to Mother, lower case to upper-case as designated in her pulse-language by a longer pause before a word. Not until she was deflowered could she take a high place in her society. Immodest, unblushing, she herself made the advances, the proposals, and the surrender.

After which, she ate her mate.

The clock in the panrad told Eddie he was in his thirtieth day of imprisonment when he found out that little bit of information. He was shocked, not because it offended his ethics, but because he himself had been intended to be the mate. And the dinner.

His finger tapped, "Tell me, Mother, what you mean."

He had not wondered before how a species that lacked males could reproduce. Now he found that, to the Mothers, all creatures except themselves were male. Mothers were immobile and female. Mobiles were male. Eddie had been mobile. He was, therefore, a male.

He had approached this particular Mother during the mating season, that is, midway through raising a litter of young. She had scanned him as he came along the creekbanks at the valley bottom. When he was at the foot of the hill, she had detected his odor. It was new to her. The closest she could come to it in her memorybanks was that of a beast similar to him. From her description, he guessed it to be an ape. So she had released from her repertoire its rut stench. When he seemingly fell into the trap, she had caught him.

He was supposed to attack the conception-spot, that light gray swelling on the wall. After he had ripped and torn it enough to begin the mysterious workings of pregnancy, he would have been popped into her stomach-iris.

Fortunately, he had lacked the sharp beak, the fang, the claw. And she had received her own signals back from the panrad.

Eddie did not understand why it was necessary to use a mobile for mating. A Mother was intelligent enough to pick up a sharp stone and mangle the spot herself.

He was given to understand that conception would not start unless it was accompanied by a certain titillation of the nerves—a frenzy and its satisfaction. Why this emotional state was needed, Mother did not know.

Eddie tried to explain about such things as genes and chromosomes and why they had to be present in highly-developed species.

Mother did not understand.

Eddie wondered if the number of slashes and rips in the spot corresponded to the number of young. Or if there were a large number of potentialities in the heredity-ribbons spread out under the conception-skin. And if the haphazard irritation and consequent stimulation of the genes paralleled the chance combining of genes in human male-female mating. Thus resulting in offspring with traits that were combinations of their parents.

Or did the inevitable devouring of the mobile after the act indicate more than an emotional and nutritional reflex? Did it hint that the mobile caught up scattered gene-nodes, like hard seeds, along with the torn skin, in its claws and tusks, that these genes survived the boiling in the stew-stomach, and were later passed out in the feces? Where animals and birds picked them up in beak, tooth, or foot, and then, seized by other Mothers in this oblique rape, transmitted the heredity-carrying agents to the conception-spots while attacking them, the nodules being scraped off and implanted in the skin and blood of the swelling even as others were harvested? Later, the mobiles were eaten, digested, and ejected in the obscure but ingenious and never-ending cycle? Thus ensuring the continual, if haphazard, recombining of genes, chances for variations in offspring, opportunities for mutations, and so on?

Mother pulsed that she was nonpulsed.

Eddie gave up. He'd never know. After all, did it matter?

He decided not, and rose from his prone position to request water. She pursed up her iris and spouted a tepid quartful into his thermos. He dropped in a pill, swished it around till it dissolved, and drank a reasonable facsimile of Old Red Star. He preferred the harsh and powerful rye, though he could have afforded the smoothest. Quick results were what he wanted. Taste didn't matter, as he disliked all liquor tastes. Thus he drank what the Skid Row bums drank and shuddered even as they did, renaming it Old Rotten Tar and cursing the fate that had brought them so low they had to gag such stuff down.

The rye glowed in his belly and spread quickly through his limbs and up to his head, chilled only by the increasing scarcity of the capsules. When he ran out—then what? It was at times like this that he most missed his mother.

Thinking about her brought a few large tears. He snuffled and drank some more and when the biggest of the Sluggos nudged him for a back-scratching, he gave it instead a shot of Old Red Star. A slug for Sluggo. Idly, he wondered what effect a taste for rye would have on the future of the race when these virgins became Mothers.

At that moment he was shaken by what seemed a life-saving idea. These creatures could suck up the required elements from the earth and with them duplicate quite complex molecular structures.

Provided, of course, they had a sample of the desired substance to brood over in some cryptic organ.

Well, what is easier to do than give her one of the cherished capsules? One could become any number. Those, plus the abundance of water pumped up through hollow underground tendrils from the nearby creek, would give enough to make a master-distiller green!

He smacked his lips and was about to key her his request when what she was transmitting penetrated his mind.

Rather cattily, she remarked that her neighbor across the valley was putting on airs because she, too, held prisoner a communicating mobile.

The Mothers had a society as hierarchical as table-protocol in Washington or peck-order in a barnyard. Prestige was what counted, and prestige was determined by the broadcasting power, the height of the eminence on which the Mother sat, which governed the extent of her radar-territory, and the abundance and novelty and wittiness of her gossip. The creature that had snapped Eddie up was a queen. She had precedence over thirty-odd of her kind; they all had to let her broadcast first, and none dared start pulsing until she quit. Then, the next in order began, and so on down the line. Any of them could be interrupted at any time by Number One, and if any of the lower echelon had something interesting to transmit, she could break in on the one then speaking and get permission from the queen to tell her tale.

Eddie knew this, but he could not listen in directly to the hilltop-gabble. The thick, pseudo-granite shell barred him from that and made him dependent upon her womb-stalk for relayed information.

Now and then Mother opened the door and allowed her young to crawl out. There they practiced beaming and broadcasting at the Sluggos of the Mother across the valley. Occasionally that Mother deigned herself to pulse the young, and Eddie's keeper reciprocated to her offspring.

Turnabout.

The first time the children had inched through the exit-iris, Eddie had tried. Ulysses-like, to pass himself off as one of them and crawl out in the midst of the flock. Eyeless, but no Polyphemus, Mother had picked him out with her tentacles and hauled him back in.

It was following that incident that he had named her Polyphema.

He knew she had increased her own already powerful prestige tremendously by possession of that unique thing—a transmitting mobile. So much had her importance grown that the Mothers on the fringes of her area passed on the news to others. Before he had learned her language, the entire continent was hooked up. Polyphema had become a veritable gossip columnist; tens of thousands of hillcrouchers listened in eagerly to her accounts of her dealings with the walking paradox: a semantic male.

That had been fine. Then, very recently, the Mother across the valley had captured a similar creature. And in one bound she had become Number Two in the area and would, at the slightest weakness on Polyphema's part, wrest the top position away.

Eddie became wildly excited at the news. He had often day-dreamed about his mother and wondered what she was doing. Curiously enough, he ended many of his fantasies with lip-mutterings, reproaching her almost audibly for having left him and for making no try to rescue him. When he became aware of his attitude, he was ashamed. Nevertheless, the sense of desertion colored his thoughts.

Now that he knew she was alive and had been caught, probably while trying to get him out, he rose from the lethargy that had lately been making him doze the clock around. He asked Polyphema if she would open the entrance so he could talk directly with the other captive. She said yes. Eager to listen in on a conversation between two mobiles, she was very co-operative. There would be a mountain of gossip in what they would have to say. The only thing that dented her joy was that the other Mother would also have access.

Then, remembering she was still Number One and would broadcast the details first, she trembled so with pride and ecstasy that Eddie felt the floor shaking.

Iris open, he walked through it and looked across the valley. The hillsides were still green, red, and yellow, as the plants on Baudelaire did not lose their leaves during winter. But a few white patches showed that winter had begun. Eddie shivered from the bite of cold air on his naked skin. Long ago he had taken off his clothes. The womb-warmth had made garments too uncomfortable; moreover, Eddie, being human, had had to get rid of waste products. And Polyphema, being a Mother, had had perodically to flush out the dirt with warm water from one of her stomachs. Every time the trachea-vents exploded streams that swept the undesirable elements out through her door-iris, Eddie had become soaked. When he abandoned dress, his clothes had gone floating out. Only by sitting on his pack did he keep it from a like fate.

Afterward, he and the Sluggos had been dried off by warm air pumped through the same vents and originating from the mighty battery of lungs. Eddie was comfortable enough—he'd always liked showers—but the loss of his garments had been one more thing that kept him from escaping. He would soon freeze to death outside unless he found the yacht quickly. And he wasn't sure he remembered the path back.

So now, when he stepped outside, he retreated a pace or two and let the warm air from Polyphema flow like a cloak from his shoulders.

Then he peered across the half-mile that separated him from his mother, but he could not see her. The twilight state and the dark of the unlit interior of her captor hid her.

He tapped in Morse, "Switch to the talkie, same frequency." Paula Fetts did so. She began asking him frantically if he were all right.

He replied he was fine.

"Have you missed me terribly, son?"

"Oh, very much."

Even as he said this he wondered vaguely why his voice sounded so hollow. Despair at never again being able to see her, probably.

"I've almost gone crazy, Eddie. When you were caught I ran away as fast as I could. I had no idea what horrible monster it was that was attacking us. And then, halfway down the hill, I fell and broke my leg. . . ."

"Oh, no, mother!"

"Yes. But I managed to crawl back to the ship. And there, after I'd set it myself, I gave myself B.K. shots. Only, my system didn't react like it's supposed to. There are people that way, you know, and the healing took twice as long.

"But when I was able to walk, I got a gun and a box of dynamite. I was going to blow up what I thought was a kind of rock-fortress, an outpost for some kind of exit. I'd no idea of the true nature of these beasts. First, though, I decided to reconnoiter. I was going to spy on the boulder from across the valley. But I was trapped by this thing.

"Listen, son. Before I'm cut off, let me tell you not to give up hope. I'll be out of here before long and over to rescue you."

"How?"

"If you remember, my lab kit holds a number of carcinogens for field work. Well, you know that sometimes a Mother's conception-spot when it is torn up during mating, instead of begetting young, goes into cancer—the opposite of pregnancy. I've injected a carcinogen into the spot and a beautiful carcinoma has developed. She'll be dead in a few days."

"Mom! You'll be buried in that rotting mass!"

"No. This creature has told me that when one of her species dies, a reflex opens the labia. That's to permit their young—if any—to escape. Listen, I'll—"

A tentacle coiled about him and pulled him back through the iris, which shut.

When he switched back to C.W., he heard, "Why didn't you communicate? What were you doing? Tell me! Tell me!"

Eddie told her. There was a silence that could only be interpreted as astonishment. After Mother had recovered her wits, she said, "From now on, you will talk to the other male through me."

Obviously, she envied and hated his ability to change wavebands, and, perhaps, had a struggle to accept the idea.

"Please," he persisted, not knowing how dangerous were the waters he was wading in, "please let me talk to my mother di—"

For the first time, he heard her stutter.

"Wha-wha-what? Your Mo-Mo-Mother?"

"Yes. Of course."

The floor heaved violently beneath his feet. He cried out and braced himself to keep from falling and then flashed on the light. The walls were pulsating like shaken jelly, and the vascular columns had turned from red and blue to gray. The entrance-iris sagged open, like a lax mouth, and the air cooled. He could feel the drop in temperature in her flesh with the soles of his feet.

It was some time before he caught on.

Polyphema was in a state of shock.

What might have happened had she stayed in it, he never knew. She might have died and thus forced him out into the winter before his mother could escape. If so, and he couldn't find the ship, he would die. Huddled in the warmest corner of the egg-shaped chamber, Eddie contemplated that idea and shivered to a degree for which the outside air couldn't account.

However, Polyphema had her own method of recovery. It consisted of spewing out the contents of her stew-stomach, which had doubtless become filled with the poisons draining out of her system from the blow. Her ejection of the stuff was the physical manifestation of the psychical catharsis. So furious was the flood that her foster son was almost swept out in the hot tide, but she, reacting instinctively, had coiled tentacles about him and the Sluggos. Then she followed the first upchucking by emptying her other three water-pouches, the second hot and the third lukewarm and the fourth, just filled, cold.

Eddie yelped as the icy water doused him.

Polyphema's irises closed again. The floor and walls gradually quit quaking; the temperature rose; and her veins and arteries regained their red and blue. She was well again. Or so she seemed.

But when, after waiting twenty-four hours, he cautiously approached the subject, he found she not only would not talk about it, she refused to acknowledge the existence of the other mobile.

Eddie, giving up hope of conversation, thought for quite a while. The only conclusion he could come to, and he was sure he'd grasped enough of her psychology to make it valid, was that the concept of a mobile female was utterly unacceptable.

Her world was split into two: mobile and her kind, the immobile. Mobile meant food and mating. Mobile meant—male. The Mothers were—female.

How the mobiles reproduced had probably never entered the hillcrouchers' minds. Their science and philosophy were on the instinctive body-level. Whether they had some notion of spontaneous generation or amoeba-like fission being responsible for the continued population of mobiles, or they'd just taken for granted they "growed," like Topsy, Eddie never found out. To them, they were female and the rest of the protoplasmic cosmos was male.

That was that. Any other idea was more than foul and obscene and blasphemous. It was—unthinkable.

Polyphema had received a deep trauma from his words. And though she seemed to have recovered, somewhere in those tons of unimaginably complicated flesh a bruise was buried. Like a hidden flower, dark purple, it bloomed, and the shadow it cast was one that cut off a certain memory, a certain tract, from the light of consciousness. That bruise-stained shadow covered that time and event which the Mother, for reasons unfathomable to the human being, found necessary to mark KEEP OFF.

Thus, though Eddie did not word it, he understood in the cells of his body, he felt and knew, as if his bones were prophesying and his brain did not hear, what came to pass.

Sixty-six hours later by the panrad clock, Polyphema's entrance-lips opened. Her tentacles darted out. They came back in, carrying his helpless and struggling mother.

Eddie, roused out of a doze, horrified, paralyzed, saw her toss her lab kit at him and heard an inarticulate cry from her. And saw her plunged, headforemost, into the stomach-iris.

Polyphema had taken the one sure way of burying the evidence.

Eddie lay face down, nose mashed against the warm and faintly throbbing flesh of the floor. Now and then his hands clutched spasmodically as if he were reaching for something that someone kept putting just within his reach and then moving away.

How long he was there he didn't know, for he never again looked at the clock.

Finally, in the darkness, he sat up and giggled inanely, "Mother always did make good stew."

That set him off. He leaned back on his hands and threw his head back and howled like a wolf under a full moon.

Polyphema, of course, was dead-deaf, but she could radar his posture, and her keen nostrils deduced from his body-scent that he was in terrible fear and anguish.

A tentacle glided out and gently enfolded him.

"What is the matter?" zzted the panrad.

He stuck his finger in the keyhole.

"I have lost my mother!"

"?"

"She's gone away, and she'll never come back."

"I don't understand. *Here I am.*"

Eddie quit weeping and cocked his head as if he were listening to some inner voice. He snuffled a few times and wiped away the tears, slowly disengaged the tentacle, patted it, walked over to his pack in a corner, and took out the bottle of Old Red Star capsules. One he popped into the thermos; the other he gave to her with the request she duplicate it, if possible. Then he stretched out on his side, propped on one elbow like a Roman in his sensualities, sucked the rye through the nipple, and listened to a medley of Beethoven, Moussorgsky, Verdi, Strauss, Porter, Feinstein, and Waxworth.

So the time—if there were such a thing there—flowed around Eddie. When he was tired of music or plays or books, he listened in on the area hookup. Hungry, he rose and walked—or often just crawled—to the stew-iris. Cans of rations lay in his pack; he had planned to eat those until he was sure that—what was it he was forbidden to eat? Poison? Something had been devoured by Polyphema and the Sluggos. But sometime during the music-rye orgy, he had forgotten. He now ate quite hungrily and with thought for nothing but the satisfaction of his wants.

Sometimes the door-iris opened, and Billy Greengrocer hopped in Billy looked like a cross between a cricket and a kangaroo. He was the size of a collie, and he bore in a marsupialian pouch vegetables and fruit and nuts. These he extracted with shiny green, chitinous claws and gave to Mother in return for meals of stew. Happy symbiote, he chirruped merrily while his many-faceted eyes, revolving independently of each other, looked one at the Sluggos and the other at Eddie.

Eddie, on impulse, abandoned the 1000 kc. band and roved the frequencies until he found that both Polyphema and Billy were emitting a 108 wave. That, apparently, was their natural signal. When Billy had his groceries to deliver, he broadcast. Polyphema, in turn, when she needed them, sent back to him. There was nothing intelligent on Billy's part; it was just his instinct to transmit. And the Mother was, aside from the "semantic" frequency, limited to that one band. But it worked out fine.

Everything was fine. What more could a man want? Free food, unlimited liquor, soft bed, air-conditioning, showerbaths, music, intellectual works (on the tape), interesting conversation (much of it was about him), privacy, and security.

If he had not already named her, he would have called her Mother Gratis.

Nor were creature comforts all. She had given him the answers to all his questions, all. . . .

Except one.

That was never expressed vocally by him. Indeed, he would have been incapable of doing so. He was probably unaware that he had such a question.

But Polyphema voiced it one day when she asked him to do her a favor.

Eddie reacted as if outraged.

"One does not—! One does not—!"

He choked, and then he thought, how ridiculous! She is not—

And looked puzzled, and said, "But she is."

He rose and opened the lab kit. While he was looking for a scalpel, he came across the carcinogens. He threw them through the half-opened labia far out and down the hillside.

Then he turned and, scalpel in hand, leaped at the light gray swelling on the wall. And stopped, staring at it, while the instrument fell from his hand. And picked it up and stabbed feebly and did not even scratch the skin. And again let it drop.

"What is it? What is it?" crackled the panrad hanging from his wrist.

Suddenly, a heavy cloud of human odor—mansweat—was puffed in his face from a nearby vent.

"? ? ? ?"

And he stood, bent in a half-crouch, seemingly paralyzed. Until tentacles seized him in fury and dragged him toward the stomach-iris, yawning man-sized.

Eddie screamed and and writhed and plunged his finger in the panrad and tapped, "All right! All right!"

And once back before the spot, he lunged with a sudden and wild joy; he slashed savagely; he yelled. "Take that! And that, P . . . " and the rest was lost in a mindless shout.

He did not stop cutting, and he might have gone on and on until he had quite excised the spot had not Polyphema interfered by dragging him towards her stomach-iris again. For ten seconds he hung there, helpless and sobbing with a mixture of fear and glory.

Polyphema's reflexes had almost overcome her brain. Fortunately, a cold spark of reason lit up a corner of the vast, dark, and hot chapel of her frenzy.

The convulsions leading to the steaming, meat-laden pouch closed and the foldings of flesh rearranged themselves. Eddie was suddenly hosed with warm water from what he called the "sanitation" stomach. The iris closed. He was put down. The scalpel was put back in the bag.

For a long time Mother seemed to be shaken by the thought of what she might have done to Eddie. She did not trust herself to transmit until her nerves were settled. When they were, she did not refer to his narrow escape. Nor did he.

He was happy. He felt as if a spring, tight-coiled against his bowels since he and his wife had parted, was now, for some reason, released. The dull vague pain of loss and discontent, the slight fever and cramp in his entrails, and the apathy that sometimes afflicted him were gone. He felt fine.

Meanwhile, something akin to deep affection had been lighted, like a tiny candle under the drafty and overtowering roof of a cathedral. Mother's shell housed more than Eddie; it now curved over an emotion new to her kind. This was evident by the next event that filled him with terror.

For the wounds in the spot healed and the swelling increased into a large bag. Then the bag burst and ten mouse-sized Sluggos struck the floor. The impact had the same effect as a doctor spanking a newborn baby's bottom; they drew in their first breath with shock and pain; their uncontrolled and feeble pulses filled the ether with shapeless SOS's.

When Eddie was not talking with Polyphema or listening in or drinking or sleeping or eating or bathing or running off the tape, he played with the Sluggos. He was, in a sense, their father. Indeed, as they grew to hog-size, it was hard for their female parent to distinguish him from her young. As he seldom walked any more, and was often to be found on hands and knees in their midst, she could not scan him too well. Moreover, something in the heavywet air or in the diet had caused every hair on his body to drop off. He grew very fat. Generally speaking, he was one with the pale, soft, round, and bald offspring. A family likeness.

There was one difference. When the time came for the virgins to be expelled, Eddie crept to one end, whimpering, and stayed there until he was sure Mother was not going to thrust him out into the cold, hard, and hungry world.

That final crisis over, he came back to the center of the floor. The panic in his breast had died out, but his nerves were still quivering. He filled his thermos and then listened for a while to his own tenor singing the "Sea Things" aria from his favorite opera, Gianelli's *Ancient Mariner*. Suddenly, he burst out and accompanied himself, finding himself thrilled as never before by the concluding words.

> *And from my neck so free*
> *The Albatross fell off, and sank*
> *Like lead into the sea.*

Afterwards, voice silent but heart singing, he switched off the wire and cut in on Polyphema's broadcast.

Mother was having trouble. She could not precisely describe to the continent-wide hook-up this new and almost inexpressible emotion she felt about the mobile. It was a concept her language was not prepared for. Nor was she helped any by the gallons of Old Red Star in her bloodstream.

Eddie sucked at the plastic nipple and nodded sympathetically and drowsily at her search for words. Presently, the thermos rolled out of his hand.

He slept on his side, curled in a ball, knees on his chest and arms crossed, neck bent forward. Like the pilot room chronometer whose hands reversed after the crash, the clock of his body was ticking backwards, ticking backwards. . . .

In the darkness, in the moistness, safe and warm, well fed, much loved.

dreaming is a private thing

Isaac Asimov

In "Dreaming Is A Private Thing" Isaac Asimov speculates about a new form of entertainment, the "dreamies." Theoretically, they will be like the movies, but much better. As the title suggests, they will contact the individual on a much more private, inner level. As in the movies and all other forms of art, there will be devotees and detractors of "dreamies" as well as people who will have a special talent to create them. These last will be known as "dreamers," and they will provide many a pleasurable experience for others.

Like all other creators of art, the serious "dreamer" will try to communicate his deepest thoughts and innermost feelings to his audience. He will portray his personal views of the present, as well as his visions of the future. In doing so, he will rely on his past experience, and like other creators, his creations will also reveal his own unique personality. Compared to the others, however, his medium will provide a more direct line to the inner core of his personality, since many psychologists believe that one of the most revealing and insightful ways to understand the personality of an individual is to understand his dreams—a very complex and difficult task.

The first psychologist to emphasize dream analysis was Sigmund Freud in his *Interpretation of Dreams* (1900). Freud believed that dreams were wish fulfillments coming originally from the individual's unconscious. The actual or "manifest" dreams that we are all familiar with do not show these wish fulfillments, or the "latent" dream, directly, but rather disguise and distort them in order to protect us from knowing our real childhood wishes, which we find difficult to accept as we grow up. Freud felt that the majority of dreams of adults deal with sexual material and erotic wishes. Thus in the story there are references to Freudian symbols, meaning-disguised elements in dreams representing sexual material. There are phallic (penis) symbols, as well as vaginal symbols, e.g., "narrow crevasses between mountain peaks." Contrary to popular belief, Freud tried to make it clear, however, that not all symbols in dreams are sexual. For example, he felt that in dreams, human forms were regularly represented by houses. He stated: "The assertion that all dreams require a sexual interpretation, against which critics rage so incessantly, occurs nowhere in my *Interpretation of Dreams.* It is not to be found in any of the numerous editions of this book, and is an obvious contradiction to other views expressed in it."

One of Freud's critics was Carl Jung. Jung agreed with Freud that dream analysis was one of the best means to analyze the unconscious and thus the personality. However, his interpretation of dream material did not emphasize wish fulfillment and sexual symbols. He found rather that individual dreams contained symbols and themes from ancient mythology and religion. He therefore postulated a layer of the unconscious, deeper than Freud's conception, which Jung called the "collective" or "transpersonal" unconscious. This layer contained universal rather than simple personal themes, and Jung believed that analyzing the meaning of dreams on this level added to his ability to understand his patients' personalities.

In our story, there is repeated mention of the "overtones" of dreams. The word "overtones" is a musical term, referring to the *complexity* of tones, which adds to their richness and determines why one instrument sounds different from another. In the context of the story, overtones also denotes the complexity of the dreams often produced by good "dreamers." These dreams present themes which have associations and meanings stemming from all levels of consciousness, as suggested by Freud and Jung. In addition, the dreams engage as many of the senses as possible. As Weill says in the story, when a good "dreamer" dreams about a steak, he not only sees it, but also smells it, tastes it, feels it, "and a hundred other things all at once."

One might ask if a particular kind of personality is more likely to be a good "dreamer" than another. In the projected picture of our story, it is difficult to say directly. However, there is some information on the topic which supports William Sheldon's "body type" approach to personality. Simply stated, Sheldon has related three major body types of individuals to three major personality types. There is the round, chubby individual (the endomorph), who tends to have an emotional personality; there is the square muscular type (the mesomorph), who leans toward action; and then there is the thin, angular type (the ectomorph), who tends to do a lot of thinking and cerebral activity. In our story, good "dreamers" are described as "thinkers," and thus we would expect them to correspond to our last body type. What do we find? Our potential dreamer is described as being of "average height but underweight . . . a narrow chin, a pale skin, and a troubled look."

A final comment should be made about the complaint made by our super "dreamer" that he wanted to stop dreaming and start living. Dreaming or fantasizing can be detrimental if done to excess, like almost anything else. Recent evidence suggests, however, that there are many positive aspects of fantasy and most of us would do well to increase our use of this activity. Fantasy can be beneficial in three major areas: planning, rehearsing, and creating. It can help in planning our futures if we can visualize ourselves in prospective new roles and activities, giving us some advanced knowledge about how we might feel doing them. We can also rehearse in our fantasies our future activities. Evidence suggests that this type of rehearsal can improve our actual performance. Finally, fantasy has always played an important role in creativity. Imagining new combinations of things or new ways of doing things is an essential activity preceding the actual creation. Perhaps we can all be more creative if we take more time to dream the impossible dream.

DREAMING IS A PRIVATE THING   *Isaac Asimov*

Jesse Weill looked up from his desk. His old spare body, his sharp high-bridge nose, deep-set shadowy eyes, and amazing shock of white hair had trademarked his appearance during the years that Dreams, Inc., had become world-famous.

He said, "Is the boy here already, Joe?"

Joe Dooley was short and heavyset. A cigar caressed his moist lower lip. He took it away for a moment and nodded. "His folks are with him. They're all scared."

"You're sure this is not a false alarm, Joe? I haven't got much time." He looked at his watch. "Government business at two."

"This is a sure thing, Mr. Weill." Dooley's face was a study in earnestness. His jowls quivered with persuasive intensity. "Like I told you, I picked him up playing some kind of basketball game in the schoolyard. You should've seen the kid. He stunk. When he had his hands on the ball, his own team had to take it away, and fast, but just the same he had all the stance of a star player. Know what I mean? To me it was a giveaway."

"Did you talk to him?"

"Well, sure. I stopped him at lunch. You know me." Dooley gestured expansively with his cigar and caught the severed ash with his other hand. "'Kid,' I said—"

"And he's dream material?"

"I said, 'Kid, I just came from Africa and—'"

"All right." Weill held up the palm of his hand. "Your word I'll always take. How you do it I don't know, but when you say a boy is a potential dreamer, I'll gamble. Bring him in."

The youngster came in between his parents. Dooley pushed chairs forward, and Weill rose to shake hands. He smiled at the youngster in a way that turned the wrinkles of his face into benevolent creases.

"You're Tommy Slutsky?"

Tommy nodded wordlessly. He was about ten and a little small for that. His dark hair was plastered down unconvincingly, and his face was unrealistically clean.

Weill said, "You're a good boy?"

The boy's mother smiled at once and patted Tommy's head

449

maternally (a gesture which did not soften the anxious expression on the youngster's face). She said, "He's always a very good boy."

Weill let this dubious statement pass. "Tell me, Tommy," he said, and held out a lollipop which was first hesitantly considered, then accepted. "Do you ever listen to dreamies?"

"Sometimes," said Tommy in an uncertain treble. Mr. Slutsky cleared his throat. He was broad-shouldered and thick-fingered, the type of laboring man that, every once in a while, to the confusion of eugenics, sired a dreamer. "We rented one or two for the boy. Real old ones."

Weill nodded. He said, "Did you like them, Tommy?"

"They were sort of silly."

"You think up better ones for yourself, do you?"

The grin that spread over the ten-year-old features had the effect of taking away some of the unreality of the slicked hair and washed face.

Weill went on, gently, "Would you like to make up a dream for me?"

Tommy was instantly embarrassed. "I guess not."

"It won't be hard, It's very easy. . . . Joe."

Dooley moved a screen out of the way and rolled forward a dream-recorder.

The youngster looked owlishly at it.

Weill lifted the helmet and brought it close to the boy. "Do you know what this is?"

Tommy shrank away. "No."

"It's a thinker. That's what we call it because people think into it. You put it on your head and think anything you want."

"Then what happens?"

"Nothing at all. It feels nice."

"No," said Tommy, "I guess I'd rather not."

His mother bent hurriedly toward him. "It won't hurt, Tommy. You do what the man says." There was an unmistakable edge to her voice.

Tommy stiffened and looked as though he might cry,.but he didn't. Weill put the thinker on him.

He did it gently and slowly and let it remain there for some thirty seconds before speaking again, to let the boy assure himself it would do no harm, to let him get used to the insinuating touch of the fibrils against the sutures of his skull (penetrating the skin so finely as to be almost insensible), and finally to let him get used to the faint hum of the alternating field vortices.

Then he said, "Now would you think for us?"

"About what?" Only the boy's nose and mouth showed.

"About anything you want. What's the best thing you would like to do when school is out?"

The boy thought a moment and said, with rising inflection, "Go on a stratojet?"

"Why not? Sure thing. You go on a jet. It's taking off right now." He gestured lightly to Dooley, who threw the freezer into circuit.

Weill kept the boy only five minutes and then let him and his mother be escorted from the office by Dooley. Tommy looked bewildered but undamaged by the ordeal.

Weill said to the father, "Now, Mr. Slutsky, if your boy does well on this test, we'll be glad to pay you five hundred dollars each year until he finishes high school. In that time all we'll ask is that he spend an hour a week some afternoon at our special school."

"Do I have to sign a paper?" Slutsky's voice was a bit hoarse.

"Certainly. This is business, Mr. Slutsky."

"Well, I don't know. Dreamers are hard to come by, I hear."

"They are. They are. But your son, Mr. Slutsky, is not a dreamer yet. He might never be. Five hundred dollars a year is a gamble for us. It's not a gamble for you. When he's finished high school, it may turn out he's not a dreamer, yet you've lost nothing. You've gained maybe four thousand dollars altogether. If he *is* a dreamer, he'll make a nice living and you certainly haven't lost then."

"He'll need special training, won't he?"

"Oh, yes, most intensive. But we don't have to worry about that till after he's finished high school. Then, after two years with us, he'll be developed. Rely on me, Mr. Slutsky."

"Will you guarantee that special training?"

Weill, who had been shoving a paper across the desk at Slutsky and punching a pen wrong-side-to at him, put the pen down and chuckled. "Guarantee? No. How can we when we don't know for sure yet if he's a real talent? Still, the five hundred a year will stay yours."

Slutsky pondered and shook his head. "I tell you straight out, Mr. Weill—after your man arranged to have us come here, I called Luster-Think. They said they'll guarantee training."

Weill sighed. "Mr. Slutsky, I don't like to talk against a competitor. If they say they'll guarantee training, they'll do as they say, but they can't make a boy a dreamer if he hasn't got it in him, training or not. If they take a plain boy without the proper talent and put him through a development course, they'll ruin him. A dreamer he won't be, that I guarantee you. And a normal human being he won't be, either. Don't take the chance of doing it to your son.

"Now Dreams, Inc., will be perfectly honest with you. If he can be a dreamer, we'll make him one. If not, we'll give him back to you without having tampered with him and say, 'Let him learn a trade.' He'll be better and healthier that way. I tell you, Mr. Slutsky—I have sons and daughters and grandchildren so I know what I say—I would not allow a child of mine to be pushed into dreaming if he's not ready for it. Not for a million dollars."

Slutsky wiped his mouth with the back of his hand and reached for the pen. "What does this say?"

"This is just an option We pay you a hundred dollars in cash right now. No strings attached. We'll study the boy's reverie. If we feel it's worth following up, we'll call you in again and make the five-hundred-dollars-a-year deal. Leave yourself in my hands, Mr. Slutsky, and don't worry. You won't be sorry."

Slutsky signed.

Weill passed the document through the file slot and handed an envelope to Slutsky.

Five minutes later, alone in the office, he placed the unfreezer over his own head and absorbed the boy's reverie intently. It was a typically childish daydream. First Person was at the controls of the plane, which looked like a compound of illustrations out of the filmed thrillers that still circulated among those who lacked the time, desire, or money for dream-cylinders.

When he removed the unfreezer, he found Dooley looking at him.

"Well, Mr. Weill, what do you think?" said Dooley with an eager and proprietary air.

"Could be, Joe. Could be. He has the overtones, and for a ten-year-old boy without a scrap of training it's hopeful. When the plane went through a cloud, there was a distinct sensation of pillows. Also the smell of clean sheets, which was an amusing touch. We can go with him a ways, Joe."

"Good." Joe beamed happily at Weill's approval.

"But I tell you, Joe, what we really need is to catch them still sooner. And why not? Someday, Joe, every child will be tested at birth. A difference in the brain there positively must be, and it should be found. Then we could separate the dreamers at the very beginning."

"Hell, Mr. Weill," said Dooley, looking hurt. "What would happen to my job then?"

Weill laughed. "No cause to worry yet, Joe. It won't happen in our lifetimes. In mine, certainly not. We'll be depending on good talent scouts like you for many years. You just watch the play-grounds and the streets"—Weill's gnarled hand dropped to Dooley's shoulder with a gentle approving pressure—"and find us a few more Hillarys and Janows, and Luster-Think won't ever catch us. . . . Now get out. I want lunch, and then I'll be ready for my two o'clock appointment. The government, Joe, the government." And he winked portentously.

Jesse Weill's two o'clock appointment was with a young man, apple-cheeked, spectacled, sandy-haired, and glowing with the intensity of a man with a mission. He presented his credentials across Weill's desk and revealed himself to be John J. Byrne, an agent of the Department of Arts and Sciences.

"Good afternoon, Mr. Byrne," said Weill. "In what way can I be of service?"

"Are we private here?" asked the agent. He had an unexpected baritone.

"Quite private."

"Then, if you don't mind, I'll ask you to absorb this." Byrne produced a small and battered cylinder and held it out between thumb and forefinger.

Weill took it, hefted it, turned it this way and that, and said with a denture-revealing smile, "Not the produce of Dreams, Inc., Mr. Byrne."

"I didn't think it was," said the agent. "I'd still like you to absorb it. I'd set the automatic cutoff for about a minute, though."

"That's all that can be endured?" Weill pulled the receiver to his desk and placed the cylinder in the unfreeze compartment. He removed it, polished either end of the cylinder with his handker-chief, and tried again. "It doesn't make good contact," he said "An amateurish job."

He placed the cushioned unfreeze helmet over his skull and adjusted the temple contacts, then set the automatic cutoff. He leaned back and clasped his hands over his chest and began absorbing.

His fingers grew rigid and clutched at his jacket. After the cutoff had brought absorption to an end, he removed the unfreezer and looked faintly angry. "A raw piece," he said. "It's lucky I'm an old man so that such things no longer bother me."

Byrne said stiffly, "It's not the worst we've found. And the fad is increasing."

453

Weill shrugged. "Pornographic dreamies. It's a logical development, I suppose."

The government man said, "Logical or not, it represents a deadly danger for the moral fiber of the nation."

"The moral fiber," said Weill, "can take a lot of beating. Erotica of one form or another has been circulated all through history."

"Not like this, sir. A direct mind-to-mind stimulation is much more effective than smoking-room stories or filthy pictures. Those must be filtered through the senses and lose some of their effect in that way."

Weill could scarcely argue that point. He said, "What would you have me do?"

"Can you suggest a possible source for this cylinder?"

"Mr. Byrne, I'm not a policeman."

"No, no, I'm not asking you to do our work for us. The Department is quite capable of conducting its own investigations. Can you help us, I mean, from your own specialized knowledge? You say your company did not put out that filth. Who did?"

"No reputable dream-distributor. I'm sure of that. It's too cheaply made."

"That could have been done on purpose."

"And no professional dreamer originated it."

"Are you sure, Mr. Weill? Couldn't dreamers do this sort of thing for some small illegitimate concern for money—or for fun?"

"They could, but not this particular one. No overtones. It's two-dimensional. Of course, a thing like this doesn't need overtones."

"What do you mean—overtones?"

Weill laughed gently. "You are not a dreamie fan?"

Byrne tried not to look virtuous and did not entirely succeed. "I prefer music."

"Well, that's all right, too," said Weill tolerantly, "but it makes it a little harder to explain overtones. Even people who absorb dreamies might not be able to explain if you asked them. Still, they'd know a dreamie was no good if the overtones were missing, even if they couldn't tell you why. Look, when an experienced dreamer goes into reverie, he doesn't think a story like in the old-fashioned television or bookfilms. It's a series of little visions. Each one has several meanings. If you studied them carefully, you'd find maybe five or six. While absorbing them in the ordinary way, you would never notice, but careful study shows it. Believe me, my psychological staff puts in long hours on just that point. All the overtones, the different meanings, blend together into a mass of guided emotion. Without them, everything would be flat, tasteless.

"Now, this morning I tested a young boy. A ten-year-old with possibilities. A cloud to him isn't just a cloud; it's a pillow, too. Having the sensations of both, it was more than either. Of course, the boy's very primitive. But when he's through with his schooling, he'll be trained and disciplined. He'll be subjected to all sorts of sensations. He'll store up experience. He'll study and analyze classic dreamies of the past. He'll learn how to control and direct his thoughts, though, mind you. I have always said that when a good dreamer improvises—"

Weill halted abruptly, then proceeded in less impassioned tones, "I shouldn't get excited. All I'm trying to bring out now is that every professional dreamer has his own type of overtones which he can't mask. To an expert it's like signing his name on the dreamie. And I, Mr. Byrne, know all the signatures. Now that piece of dirt you brought me has no overtones at all. It was done by an ordinary person. A little talent, maybe, but like you and me, he can't think."

Bryne reddened a trifle. "Not everyone can't think, Mr. Weill, even if they don't make dreamies."

"Oh, tush," said Weill wagged his hand in the air. "Don't be angry with what an old man says, I don't mean *think* as in *reason*. I mean *think* as in *dream*. We all can dream after a fashion, just like we all can run. But can you and I run a mile in under four minutes? You and I can talk, but are we Daniel Websters? Now when I think of a steak, I think of the word. Maybe I have a quick picture of a brown steak on a platter. Maybe you have a better pictorialization of it, and you can see the crisp fat and the onions and the baked potato. I don't know. But a *dreamer* . . . he sees it and smells it and tastes it and everything about it, with the charcoal and the satisfied feeling in the stor ach and the way the knife cuts through it, and a hundred other things all at once. Very sensual. Very sensual. You and I can't do it."

"Well, then," said Byrne, "no professional dreamer has done this. That's something, anyway." He put the cylinder in his inner jacket pocket. "I hope we'll have your full cooperation in squelching this sort of thing."

"Positively, Mr. Byrne. With a whole heart."

"I hope so." Byrne spoke with a consciousness of power. "It's not up to me, Mr. Weill, to say what will be done and what won't be done, but this sort of thing"—he tapped the cylinder he had brought—"will make it awfully tempting to impose a really strict censorship on dreamies."

He rose. "Good day, Mr. Weill."

"Good day, Mr. Byrne. I'll hope always for the best."

Francis Belanger burst into Jesse Weill's office in his usual steaming tizzy, his reddish hair disordered and his face aglow with worry and a mild perspiration. He was brought up sharply by the sight of Weill's head cradled in the crook of his elbow and bent on the desk until only the glimmer of white hair was visible.

Belanger swallowed. "Boss?"

Weill's head lifted. "It's you, Frank?"

"What's the matter, boss? Are you sick?"

"I'm old enough to be sick, but I'm on my feet. Staggering, but on my feet. A government man was here."

"What did he want?"

"He threatens censorship. He brought a sample of what's going around. Cheap dreamies for bottle parties."

"God damn!" said Belanger feelingly.

"The only trouble is that morality makes for good campaign fodder. They'll be hitting out everywhere. And to tell the truth, we're vulnerable, Frank."

"*We* are? Our stuff is clean. We play up adventure and romance."

Weill thrust out his lower lip and wrinkled his forehead.

"Between us, Frank, we don't have to make believe. Clean? It depends on how you look at it. It's not for publication, maybe, but you know and I know that every dreamie has its Freudian connotations. You can't deny it."

"Sure, if you *look* for it. If you're a psychiatrist—"

"If you're an ordinary person, too. The ordinary observer doesn't know it's there, and maybe he couldn't tell a phallic symbol from a mother image even if you pointed them out. Still, his subconscious knows. And it's the connotations that make many a dreamie click."

"All right, what's the government going to do? Clean up the subconscious?"

"It's a problem. I don't know what they're going to do. What we have on our side, and what I'm mainly depending on, is the fact that the public loves its dreamies, and won't give them up. . . .

Meanwhile, what did you come in for? You want to see me about something, I suppose?"

Belanger tossed an object onto Weill's desk and shoved his shirttail deeper into his trousers.

Weill broke open the glistening plastic cover and took out the enclosed cylinder. At one end was engraved in a too-fancy script in pastel blue: *Along the Himalayan Trail*. It bore the mark of Luster-Think.

"The Competitor's Product." Weill said it with capitals, and his lips twitched. "It hasn't been published yet. Where did you get it, Frank?"

"Never mind. I just want you to absorb it."

Weill sighed. "Today everyone wants me to absorb dreams. Frank, it's not dirty?"

Belanger said testily, "It has your Freudian symbols. Narrow crevasses between the mountain peaks. I hope that won't bother you."

"I'm an old man. It stopped bothering me years ago, but that other thing was so poorly done it hurt. . . . All right, let's see what you've got here."

Again the recorder. Again the unfreezer over his skull and at the temples. This time Weill rested back in his chair for fifteen minutes or more, while Francis Belanger went hurriedly through two cigarettes.

When Weill removed the headpiece and blinked dream out of his eyes, Belanger said, "Well, what's your reaction, boss?"

Weill corrugated his forehead. "It's not for me. It was repetitious. With competition like this, Dreams, Inc., doesn't have to worry yet."

"That's your mistake, boss. Luster-Think's going to win with stuff like this. We've got to do something."

"Now, Frank—"

"No, you listen. This is the coming thing."

"*This?*" Weill stared with half-humorous dubiety at the cylinder. "It's amateurish. It's repetitious. Its overtones are very unsubtle. The snow had a distinct lemon sherbet taste. Who tastes lemon sherbet in snow these days, Frank? In the old days, yes. Twenty years ago, maybe. When Lyman Harrison first made his Snow Symphonies for sale down South, it was a big thing. Sherbet and candy-striped mountaintops and sliding down chocolate-covered cliffs. It's slapstick, Frank. These days it doesn't go."

"Because," said Belanger, "you're not up with the times, boss. I've got to talk to you straight. When you started the dreamie business, when you bought up the basic patents and began putting them out, dreamies were luxury stuff. The market was small and individual. You could afford to turn out specialized dreamies and sell them to people at high prices."

"I know," said Weill, "and we've kept that up. But also we've opened a rental business for the masses."

"Yes, we have, and it's not enough. Our dreamies have subtlety, yes. They can be used over and over again. The tenth time you're still finding new things, still getting new enjoyment. But how many people are connoisseurs? And another thing. Our stuff is strongly individualized. They're First Person."

"Well?"

"Well, Luster-Think is opening dream-palaces. They've opened one with three hundred booths in Nashville. You walk in, take your seat, put on your unfreezer, and get your dream. Everyone in the audience gets the same one."

"I've heard of it, Frank, and it's been done before. It didn't work the first time, and it won't work now. You want to know why it won't work? Because in the first place, dreaming is a private thing. Do you like your neighbor to know what you're dreaming? In the second place, in a dream palace the dreams have to start on schedule, don't they? So the dreamer has to dream not when he wants to but when some palace manager says he should. Finally, a dream one person likes, another person doesn't like. In those three hundred booths, I guarantee you, a hundred and fifty people are dissatisfied. And if they're dissatisfied, they won't come back."

Slowly Belanger rolled up his sleeves and opened his collar. "Boss," he said, "you're talking through your hat. What's the use of proving they won't work? They *are* working. The word came through today that Luster-Think is breaking ground for a thousand-booth palace in St. Louis. People can get used to public dreaming if everyone else in the same room is having the same dream. And they can adjust themselves to having it at a given time, as long as it's cheap and convenient.

"Damn it, boss, it's a social affair. A boy and a girl go to a dream-palace and absorb some cheap romantic thing with stereotyped overtones and commonplace situations, but still they come out with stars sprinkling their hair. They've had the same dream together. They've gone through identical sloppy emotions. They're *in tune*, boss. You bet they go back to the dream-palace, and all their friends go, too."

"And if they don't like the dream?"

"That's the point. That's the nub of the whole thing. They're bound to like it. If you prepare Hillary specials with wheels within wheels within wheels, with surprise twists on the third-level undertones, with clever shifts of significance and all the other things we're so proud of, why, naturally, it won't appeal to everyone. Specialized dreamies are for specialized tastes. But Luster-Think is turning out simple jobs in Third Person so both sexes can be hit at once. Like what you've just absorbed. Simple, repetitious, commonplace. They're aiming at the lowest common denominator. No one will love it, maybe, but no one will hate it."

Weill sat silent for a long time, and Belanger watched him. Then Weill said. "Frank, I started on quality, and I'm staying there. Maybe, you're right. Maybe dream-palaces are the coming thing. If so, we'll open them, but we'll use good stuff. Maybe Luster-Think underestimates ordinary people. Let's go slowly and not panic. I have based all my policies on the theory that there's always a market for quality. Sometimes, my boy, it would surprise you how big a market."

"Boss—"

The sounding of the intercom interrupted Belanger.

"What is it, Ruth?" said Weill.

The voice of his secretary said. "It's Mr. Hillary, sir. He wants to see you right away. He says it's important."

"Hillary?" Weill's voice registered shock. Then, "Wait five minutes, Ruth, then send him in."

Weill turned to Belanger. "Today, Frank, is definitely not one of my good days. A dreamer should be at home with his thinker. And Hillary's our best dreamer, so he especially should be at home. What do you suppose is wrong with him?"

Belanger, still brooding over Luster-Think and dream-palaces, said shortly, "Call him in and find out."

"In one minute. Tell me, how was his last dream? I haven't absorbed the one that came in last week."

Belanger came down to earth. He wrinkled his nose. "Not so good."

"Why not?"

"It was ragged. Too jumpy. I don't mind sharp transitions for the liveliness, you know, but there's got to be some connection, even if only on a deep level."

"Is it a total loss?"

"No Hillary dream is a *total* loss. It took a lot of editing, though. We cut it down quite a bit and spliced in some old pieces he'd sent us now and then. You know, detached scenes. It's still not Grade A, but it will pass."

"You told him about this, Frank?"

"Think I'm crazy, boss? Think I'm going to say a harsh word to a dreamer?"

And at that point the door opened and Weills' comely young secretary smiled Sherman Hillary into the office.

Sherman Hillary, at the age of thirty-one, could have been recognized as a dreamer by anyone. His eyes, though unspectacled, had nevertheless the misty look of one who either needs glasses or who rarely focuses on anything mundane. He was of average height but underweight, with black hair that needed cutting, a narrow chin, a pale skin, and a troubled look.

He muttered, "Hello, Mr. Weill," and half-nodded in hangdog fashion in the direction of Belanger.

Weill said heartily, "Sherman, my boy, you look fine. What's the matter? A dream is cooking only so-so at home? You're worried about it? Sit down, sit down."

The dreamer did, sitting at the edge of the chair and holding his thighs stiffly together as though to be ready for instant obedience to a possible order to stand up once more.

He said, "I've come to tell you, Mr. Weill, I'm quitting."

"Quitting?"

"I don't want to dream any more, Mr. Weill."

Weill's old face looked older now than at any other time during the day. "Why, Sherman?"

The dreamer's lips twisted. He blurted out, "Because I'm not *living*, Mr. Weill. Everything passes me by. It wasn't so bad at first. It was even relaxing. I'd dream evenings, weekends when I felt like it, or any other time. And when I didn't feel like it, I wouldn't. But now, Mr. Weill, I'm an old pro. You tell me I'm one of the best in the business and the industry looks to me to think up new subleties and new changes on the old reliables like the flying reveries and the worm-turning skits."

Weill said. "And is anyone better than you, Sherman? Your little sequence on leading an orchestra is selling steadily after ten years."

"All right, Mr. Weill, I've done my part. It's gotten so I don't go out any more. I neglect my wife. My little girl doesn't know me. Last week we went to a dinner party—Sarah made me—and I don't remember a bit of it. Sarah says I was sitting on the couch all evening just staring at nothing and humming. She said everyone kept looking at me. She cried all night. I'm tired of things like that, Mr. Weill. I want to be a normal person and live in this world. I promised her I'd quit, and I will, so it's good-bye, Mr. Weill." Hillary stood up and held out his hand awkwardly.

Weill waved it gently away. "If you want to quit, Sherman, it's all right. But do an old man a favor and let me explain something to you."

"I'm not going to change my mind," said Hillary.

"I'm not going to try to make you. I just want to explain something. I'm an old man, and even before you were born I was in this business, so I like to talk about it. Humor me, Sherman? Please?"

Hillary sat down. His teeth clamped down on his lower lip, and he stared sullenly at his fingernails.

Weill said, "Do you know what a dreamer is, Sherman? Do you know what he means to ordinary people? Do you know what it is to be like me, like Frank Belanger, like your wife Sarah? To have crippled minds that can't imagine, that can't build up thoughts? People like myself, ordinary people, would like to escape just once in a while this life of ours. We can't. We need help.

"In olden times it was books, plays, movies, radio, television. They gave us make-believe, but that wasn't important. What *was* important was that for a little while our own imaginations were stimulated. We could think of handsome lovers and beautiful princesses. We could be attractive, witty, strong, capable— everything we weren't.

"But always the passing of the dream from dreamer to absorber was not perfect. It had to be translated into words in one way or another. The best dreamer in the world might not be able to get any of it into words. And the best writer in the world could put only the smallest part of his dream into words. You understand?

"But now, with dream-recording, any man can dream. You, Sherman, and a handful of men like you supply those dreams directly and exactly. It's straight from your head into ours, full strength. You dream for a hundred million people every time you dream. You dream a hundred million dreams at once. This is a great thing, my boy. You give all those people a glimpse of something they could not have by themselves."

Hillary mumbled, "I've done my share." He rose desperately to his feet. "I'm through. I don't care what you say. And if you want to sue me for breaking our contract, go ahead and sue. I don't care."

Weill stood up, too. "Would I sue you? . . . Ruth"—he spoke into the intercom—"bring in our copy of Mr. Hillary's contract."

He waited. So did Hillary and Belanger. Weill smiled faintly, and his yellowed fingers drummed softly on his desk.

His secretary brought in the contract. Weill took it, showed its face to Hillary, and said, "Sherman, my boy, unless you *want* to be with me, it's not right you should stay."

Then before Belanger could make more than the beginning of a horrified gesture to stop him, he tore the contract into four pieces and tossed them down the waste-chute. "That's all."

Hillary's hand shot out to seize Weill's. "Thanks, Mr. Weill," he said earnestly, his voice husky. "You've always treated me very well, and I'm grateful. I'm sorry it had to be like this."

"It's all right, my boy. It's all right."

Half in tears, still muttering thanks, Sherman Hillary left.

"For the love of Pete, boss, why did you let him go?" demanded Belanger. "Don't you see the game? He'll be going straight to Luster-Think. They've bought him off."

Weill raised his hand. "You're wrong. You're quite wrong. I know the boy, and this would not be his style. Besides," he added dryly, "Ruth is a good secretary, and she knows what to bring me when I ask for a dreamer's contract. The real contract is still in the safe, believe me.

"Meanwhile, a fine day I've had. I had to argue with a father to give me a chance at new talent, with a government man to avoid censorship, with you to keep from adopting fatal policies, and now with my best dreamer to keep him from leaving. The father I probably won out over. The government man and you, I don't know. Maybe yes, maybe no. But about Sherman Hillary, at least, there is no question. The dreamer will be back."

"How do you know?"

Weill smiled at Belanger and crinkled his cheeks into a network of fine lines. "Frank, my boy, you know how to edit dreamies so you think you know all the tools and machines of the trade. But let me tell you something. The most important tool in the dreamie business is the dreamer himself. He is the one you have to understand most of all, and I understand them.

"Listen. When I was a youngster—there were no dreamies

then—I knew a fellow who wrote television scripts. He would complain to me bitterly that when someone met him for the first time and found out who he was, they would say: 'Where do you get those crazy ideas?'

"They honestly didn't know. To them it was an impossibility to even think of one of them. So what could my friend say? He used to talk to me about it and tell me: 'Could I say, "I don't know"? When I go to bed, I can't sleep for ideas dancing in my head. When I shave, I cut myself; when I talk, I lose track of what I'm saying; when I drive, I take my life in my hands. And always because ideas, situations, dialogues are spinning and twisting in my mind. I can't tell you where I get my ideas. Can you tell me, maybe, your trick of *not* getting ideas, so I, too, can have a little peace?'

"You see, Frank, how it is. *You* can stop work here any time. So can I. This is our job, not our life. But not Sherman Hillary. Wherever he goes, whatever he does, he'll dream. While he lives, he must think; while he thinks, he must dream. We don't hold him prisoner; our contract isn't an iron wall for him. His own skull is his prisoner. He'll be back. What can he do?"

Belanger shrugged. "If what you say is right, I'm sort of sorry for the guy."

Weill nodded sadly. "I'm sorry for all of them. Through the years I've found out one thing. It's their business: making people happy. Other people."

alter ego

Hugo Correa

"Alter Ego" is interesting in its application to Self-Theory and its relationship to existential psychology. An important aspect of Self-Theory is its observation that the human being has the power to psychologically step outside himself and reflect back onto himself, assessing who he is. It further suggests that we carry around with us this self-concept, although perhaps we are not always aware of it. It is necessary that we achieve this concept so we know who we are and what we can do. There is a certain duality of self to the concept, sometimes referred to as "self as object." In this story, the alter ego personifies this ability, and the process is carried on physically as well as psychologically.

The existential psychologists go one step further by suggesting that we must take stock of ourselves—search for ourselves—in order to find our true identities. In the story, the protagonist Antonio does not do this through his alter ego until it is too late. Salvatore Maddi would suggest that Antonio is suffering from an "existential neurosis." He has been playing the social role of the salesman and has been serving his biological needs through materialistic pursuits, but he has lost track of what he really wants to do. Consequently, his life has become empty and meaningless. He cannot commit himself fully to anything or anyone and has become alienated and cynical. He has become a cold, mechanical "museum piece," without the courage to choose the life he really wants to live. There is only one choice of integrity left for him, one last gasp of free will, and that is suicide. Can he, through his new mechanical device, the alter ego, find the courage to perform this final act?

ALTER EGO   *Hugo Correa*

"Here is your Alter Ego, sir. Kindly sign the receipt."

Antonio opened the box and stepped back in amazement. There he was, arms close to the body, completely naked and motionless. If the upright position were not unnatural in a sleeper, he would have attempted to wake the android, so true to life did the color of the skin look, the little wrinkles beginning to show around the eyes, the thin lips, the high forehead. The straight hair was carefully combed, like that of its human counterpart.

He took up the control box and, following the instructions, put the android in motion. It walked slowly and naturally, with none of the grotesque movements so typical of automatons in the past. It was just as though it actually possessed bones, muscles, nerves and the organs of a living being. Antonio made it go through the elementary motions—sit, dress, light a cigarette, scratch its ear. "If android-owners wish to enjoy them," said the instructions manual, "they must first study their own selves very carefully, at least as to their mimicry, gestures, gait, etc."

Antonio, expert now at handling his double, put on the introjection helmet. For a moment his eyes blinked in the dark. But once the ocular switch was turned on he recovered the use of his eyes. The living room looked as if he were seeing it from another angle. What was it? Simply that he was beginning to see through the android's eyes. Alter Ego was standing in the middle of the room facing the door, blinking naturally. The instruments moved the synthetic eyelids simultaneously with Antonio's. The man pressed a button and the double turned. He could see himself sitting in the chair, his head hidden in the helmet, the controls on his knee. Once the audio channel was working there was no doubt that he was now in the middle of the room; he could hear the street noises and those he made when shifting his position in the armchair. And smell. How to breathe through Alter Ego. The odorophones gave him the sensation of air breathed elsewhere. He tried the voice of his duplicate self; as soon as Alter Ego opened his mouth, Antonio heard himself speaking from the middle of the room.

"How are you, Antonio? You've been born again. Don't you feel like a fish in a bowl when they've just changed the water?"

Antonio listened to his own voice with complacency. He had Alter Ego walk about the room, took him to the window and, leaning out, watched the bright city under a burning sky sprinkled with helicopters. Everything looked more beautiful than when he used his own eyes; the sky was bluer and more luminous, the skyscrapers showed gayer and brighter colors. Yes, Alter Ego was showing him the true face of things. The sensations that he received through his double made him feel suddenly at peace with humankind. In his imagination the emotions of youth revived, the memories that time had slowly erased leaving behind faint images willingly or unwittingly forgotten. But now he felt overcome by a strange courage and a desire for remembrance. He could look over his past life serenely, recall youthful thoughts, aspirations, the way he had little by little given up what he loved most in order to make a position for himself.

"Remember when you wanted to be an actor and play The Emperor Jones? How you went about for weeks with your mind on his soliloquies? How you made love to Valentina, the girl who attended dramatic school with you and encouraged you because she believed in you?"

Alter Ego spoke with a clear, resonant voice, his gestures those of a man used to the stage. He lit a cigarette, inhaled deeply, then let out a thin wisp of smoke. He stopped in front of a picture of Antonio at his desk, a satisfied smile on his face, photographs, notices, billboards all round him.

"There's nothing wrong with selling toothpaste, particularly when it's a good product and properly manufactured. After all, it even has a social function; it ensures white teeth and a pleasant breath. Did you ever think of Jones's lines to Smithers as related to your own activities: 'Ain't a man's talkin' big what makes him big—long as he makes folks believe it?' You managed that as a salesman. Trouble was you never believed the big things that the great salesman Antonio said."

Alter Ego inhaled deeply, and through the bluish cloud surveyed the man in the chair whose face was hidden by the helmet. Wonders of electronics! The papillophones gave him the taste and slight heat of the smoke.

"Smoking by remote control—what a boon for today's practical men who are anxious to do all things without committing themselves too much! You get the same enjoyment that the smoker does while you run none of the risks. It is the hedonistic principle fulfilled."

Alter Ego opened an antique cupboard and turned to Antonio with an indefinable smile.

"A museum piece, as so many men are. Aren't most men today just museum pieces after all? To begin with, they are unable to fulfill their own aspirations. They all stop halfway. You're no exception; you wanted to be an actor, and you ended up selling toothpaste because there was more money in it. You gave up Valentina because she was humble, had no ambition. You had friends, true ones, people with whom you could talk about any number of useless things. Useless? Your new acquaintances only understand the language of finance. 'Is there money in that?' they ask you when you innocently attempt to get them out of their easy chairs, showing them your inner world where your aspirations are beginning to rust, fatally, resignedly, like metal corroded by oxide. You did learn to talk like them, though. Not any better! There are no levels in that world."

Alter Ego finished smoking, put out the cigarette with a theatrical gesture and faced Antonio, pointing at him accusingly.

"And now, will your mechanical double do what you don't dare do with your own hands?"

The android stood motionless, looking at the silent helmet. A dense silence floated in the room. The glass eyes glowed. Slowly, Alter Ego turned to the open cupboard. His face hardened. He took out a pistol, examined it critically and advanced toward the man with a curious solemnity, as though walking through a temple while a ceremony is being held.

"Man is the supreme inventor. He made these weapons to kill men, and doubles to pass judgment on himself."

After the briefest pause he added, drily:

"The cycle is closed," and carefully aimed at the figure in the chair.

the man in the rorschach shirt

Ray Bradbury

One of the most famous personality tests is the Rorschach Test, named after its creator, Hermann Rorschach. This is the test in which individuals are asked to examine inkblots and tell a psychologist what they see and where they see it. Their answers can tell a trained tester a great deal about their personalities. Our story goes one step further. It introduces us to a Rorschach shirt, as well as its inventor, Immanuel Brokaw, an intriging and fascinating personality in his own right. As the "Man in the Rorschach Shirt" he stimulates and puzzles us. Where did he come from, and why does he do his Rorschach shirt thing? As we look at his shirt, could it be that he is seeing right through us?

The Rorschach Test is only one of many different approaches to personality assessment, each intended to give the administrator important information about the client. The Rorschach is probably the most widely used example of the assessment technique called the "projective" test. This type of test gives the individual ambiguous, indefinite, or incomplete stimuli, allowing him a great deal of opportunity to stamp his own impressions and meaning into his responses. He projects his own personality onto these stimuli, much as a movie projector projects a visual story onto a blank screen.

In the particular case of the Rorschach Test, the ambiguous stimuli were originally blots of ink put on pieces of paper which were then folded. Some have different colored ink, although the majority are plain black. Testers are interested in the content of what people see in these basically meaningless blots, as well as how the perceptions of their clients are organized. The test comes out of the gestalt tradition in psychology which emphasizes the role of perception in the study of personality. A highly competent

468

tester and a freely responding client can produce a wealth of information which can then be used to help the client better understand himself. Likewise, the colored stimuli on Brokaw's shirt can produce a wealth of information about the respondent. As Brokaw explains, some of the responses to his shirt can generate conversation that can last all day. Here again, the respondent can often gain a great deal of self-understanding, while Brokaw thoroughly enjoys himself.

Other projective techniques regularly used in personality assessment are the Thematic Apperception Test (T.A.T.) and sentence completion techniques. The T.A.T. presents more concrete stimuli, in the form of drawings and photographs, than the Rorschach. Here, the subjects are asked to compose stories relating to the stimuli. Subjects use their own experiences to compose the stories, and thus, as for the Rorschach Test, they project their own personalities into their responses. Sentence completion techniques typically present to the subject beginnings of sentences which he completes using his own material, again revealing information about his personality.

There are many other procedures and techniques used to measure personality attributes. In personality inventories the individual is asked to agree or disagree with many different statements about himself. The pattern of his answers is then analyzed in light of specific traits or qualities. The Minnesota Multiphasic Personality Inventory (M.M.P.I.) and the Edwards Personal Preference Scale (E.P.P.S.) are typical examples of this type of test. Techniques like adjective checklists, where subjects check off adjectives which correspond to how they feel, direct observation of behavior, and physiological measurements are also used. Last, but certainly not least, are the many structured and unstructured interview procedures, where a great deal of information can be learned simply by asking the client directly.

Brokaw, the man in the Rorschach shirt, is certainly an interesting personality in his own right. He had been a highly successful psychiatrist when one day he decided to give it all up and do something different. In the story he tells us why. Different personality theories might suggest important and varying reasons for his behavior. Erik Erikson might suggest that Brokaw had an "identity crisis," where he lost confidence in himself to the point where he had serious doubts that he could keep his personality together. Erikson emphasizes the age of adolescence as the intense period when an identity crisis is most likely to occur. Brokaw states that even though he was sixty at the time of his crisis, he felt like he was fifteen, "... a self-crucified bundle of doubt, horror and absolute imperfection."

Existential personality theorists might suggest that Brokaw's life had lost its meaning. With Erikson they might surmise that he had to change his life in order to search for and fulfill his sense of authenticity and integrity. Victor Frankl, a modern existential psychologist, suggests that there is meaning for an individual who suffers while making a sacrifice. If an individual knows why he makes an important sacrifice, he can gain important insights about his personality.

In another interesting statement, Brokaw admits that he had reached the point where he could not face reality, and he had to say "Reality is not all! I refuse this knowledge." Freud and others believed that man did not and could not know the truth about himself and the world around him. Ironically, Freud suggested that one of the ways we defend ourselves against the reality of our shortcomings is to see them in other people, a process which he called "projection." If the name rings a bell, it should. It is the same term and in many ways the same process operating as when one takes the Rorschach Test.

THE MAN IN THE RORSCHACH SHIRT   *Ray Bradbury*

Brokaw.
What a name!
Listen to it bark, growl, yip; hear the bold proclamation of:
Immanuel Brokaw!

A fine name for the greatest psychiatrist who ever tread the waters of existence without capsizing.

Toss a pepper-ground Freud casebook in the air and all students sneezed:

Brokaw!

Whatever happened to him?

One day, like a high-class vaudeville act, he vanished.

With the spotlight out, his miracles seemed in danger of reversal. Psychotic rabbits threatened to leap back into hats. Smokes were sucked back into loud-powder gun muzzles. We all waited.

Silence for ten years. And more silence.

Brokaw was lost, as if he had thrown himself with shouts of laughter into mid-Altantic. For what? To plumb for Moby Dick? To psychoanalyze that colorless fiend and see what he really had against mad Ahab?

Who knows?

I last saw him running for a twilight plane, his wife and six Pomeranian dogs yapping far behind him on the dusky field.

"Good-bye forever!"

His happy cry seemed a joke. But I found men flaking his goldleaf name from his office door next day, as his great fat-women couches were hustled out into the raw weather toward some Third Avenue auction.

So the giant who had been Gandhi-Moses-Christ-Buddha-Freud all layered in one incredible Armenian dessert had dropped through a hole in the clouds. To die? To live in secret?

Ten years later I rode on a California bus along the lovely shores of Newport.

The bus stopped. A man in his 70s bounced on, jingling silver into the coin box like manna. I glanced up from the rear of the bus and gasped.

"Brokaw! By the saints!"

And with or without sanctification, there he stood. Reared up like God manifest, bearded, benevolent, pontifical, erudite, merry, accepting, forgiving, messianic, tutorial, forever, and eternal. . . .

Immanuel Brokaw.

But not in a dark suit, no.

Instead, as if they were vestments of some proud new church, he wore:

Bermuda shorts. Black leather Mexican sandals. A Los Angeles Dodgers' baseball cap. French sunglasses. And. . . .

The shirt! Ah, God! The shirt!

A wild thing, all lush creeper and live flytrap undergrowth, all pop-op dilation and contraction, full-flowered and crammed at every interstice and crosshatch with mythological beasts and symbols!

Open at the neck, this vast shirt hung wind-whipped like a thousand flags from a parade of united but neurotic nations.

But now Dr. Brokaw tilted his baseball cap, lifted his French sunglasses to survey the bus seats. Striding slowly down the aisle, he wheeled, he paused, he whispered, now to this man, this woman, that child.

I was about to cry out when I heard him say:

"Well, what do you make of it?"

A small boy, stunned by the circus-poster effect of the old man's attire, blinked. The old man nudged:

"My *shirt*, boy! What do you *see*!?"

"Horses! Dancing horses!"

"Bravo!" The doctor beamed, patted him and strode on. "And *you*, sir?"

A young man, quite taken with the forthrightness of this invader from some summer world, said:

"Why . . . clouds, of course."

"Cumulus or nimbus?"

"Er . . . not storm clouds, no, no. Fleecy, sheep clouds."

"Well done!"

The psychiatrist plunged on.

"*Mademoiselle?*"

"Surfers!" A teenage girl stared. "There're the waves, big ones. Surfboards. Super!"

And so it went, on down the length of the bus, and as the great man progressed, a few scraps and titters of laughter sprang up, then, grown infectious, turned to roars of hilarity. By now a dozen passengers had heard the first responses and so fell in with the game. This woman saw skyscrapers! The doctor winked. That man saw crossword puzzles. The doctor shook his hand. This child found zebras all optical illusion on an African wild. The doctor slapped the animals and made them jump! This old woman saw vague Adams and misty Eves being driven from half-seen Gardens. The doctor scooched in on the seat with her awhile; they talked in fierce whispered elations; then up he jumped and forged on. Had the old woman seen an Eviction? This young one saw the Couple invited back in!

Dogs, lightnings, cats, cars, mushroom clouds, man-eating tiger lilies!

Each person, each response brought greater outcries. We found ourselves all laughing together. This fine old man was a happening of nature, a caprice, God's rambunctious will, sewing all our separateness up in one.

Elephants! Elevators! Alarums! Dooms!

Each answer seemed funnier than the previous, and no one shouted louder his great torrents of laughter than this grand, tall and marvelous physician who asked for, got, and cured us of our hair balls on the spot. Whales. Grass meadows. Lost cities. Beauteous women. He paused. He wheeled. He flapped his wildly colored shirt. He towered before me.

"Sir, what do *you* find?"

"Why, Dr. Brokaw, of course!"

The old man's laughter stopped as if he were shot. He seized my shoulders as if to wrench me into focus.

"Simon Wincelaus, is that *you!*"

"Me, me!" I laughed. "Good grief, Doctor, I thought you were dead years ago. What's this you're up to?"

"Up to?" He squeezed and shook my hands. Then he snorted a great self-forgiving laugh as he gazed down along the acreage of ridiculous shirting. "Up to? Retired. Swiftly gone." His peppermint breath warmed my face. "And now best known hereabouts as . . . listen! . . . the Man in the Rorschach Shirt."

"In the what?" I cried.

"Rorschach Shirt."

Light as a carnival gas balloon, he touched into the seat beside me.

We rode along by the blue sea under a bright summer sky.

The doctor gazed ahead, as if reading my thoughts in a vast skywriting among the clouds.

"Why, you ask, why? I see your face, startled, at the airport years ago. My Going Away Forever day. My plane should have been named the *Happy Titanic*. On it I sank forever into the traceless sky. Yet here I am in the absolute flesh, yes? Not drunk, nor mad, nor riven by age and retirement's boredom. Where, what, how come?"

"Yes," I said, "why *did* you retire, with everything pitched for you? Skill, reputation, money. Not a breath of——"

"Scandal? None! Why, then? Because this old camel had not one but two humps broken by two straws. Two amazing straws. Hump number one—"

The bus hummed softly on the road.

His voice rose and fell with the hum.

"You know my photographic memory? Blessed, cursed, with

total recall. Anything said, seen, done, touched, heard can be snapped back to focus by me, forty, fifty, sixty years later. All, all of it, trapped in here."

He stroked his temples lightly.

"Hundreds of psychiatric cases, delivered through my door, year on year. And never once did I check my notes on any of those sessions. I found, early on, I need only play back what I had heard inside my head. Sound tapes were kept as a double check, but never listened to. There you have the stage set for the whole shocking business.

"One day in my sixtieth year a woman patient spoke a single word. I asked her to repeat it. Why? Suddenly I had felt my semicircular canals shift as if some valves had opened upon cool fresh air at a subterranean level.

"'Best,'" she said.

"'I thought you said "beast,"'" I said.

"'Oh, no, Doctor, "best."'"

"One word. One pebble dropped off the edge. And then—the avalanche. For, distinctly, I had heard her claim, 'He loved the beast in me,' which is one kettle of sexual fish, eh? When in reality she had said, 'He loved the best in me,' which is quite another pan of cold cod, you must agree.

"That night I could not sleep. My ears felt strangely clear, as if I had just gotten over a thirty-year cold. I suspected myself, my past, my senses; so at three in the deadfall morning I motored to my office and found the worst:

"The recalled conversations of hundreds of cases in my mind were not the same as those recorded on my tapes or typed out in my secretaries' notes!"

"You mean . . . ?"

"I mean when I heard beast, it was truly best. Dumb was really numb. Ox was cocks, and vice versa. I heard bed. Someone had said head. Sleep was creep. Lay was day. Paws was really pause. Rump was merely jump. Fiend was only leaned. Sex was hex, or mix or, God knows, perplex! Yes—mess. No—slow. Binge—hinge. Wrong—long. Side—hide. Name a name, I'd heard it wrong. Ten million dozen misheard nouns! I panicked through my files! Great Jumping Josie!

"All those people! Holy Moses, Brokaw, I cried, all these years down from the Mount, the Word of God like a flea in your ear. And now, late in the day, you think to consult your lightning-scribbled stones. And find your laws, your tablets, *different*!

"Moses fled his offices that night. I ran in the dark, unraveling my despair. I trained to Far Rockaway, perhaps because of its lamenting name.

"I walked by a tumult of waves only equaled by the tumult in my breast. How, I cried, can you have been half-deaf for a lifetime and not known it? And known it only now when, through some fluke, the sense, the gift, returned, how, how?!

"My only answer was a great stroke of thunder wave upon the sands.

"So much for straw number one that broke hump number one of this odd-shaped human camel."

The bus moved along the golden shore road, through a gentle breeze.

"Straw number two?" I asked quietly at last.

Dr. Brokaw held his French sunglasses up so sunlight struck fish glitters all about the cavern of the bus.

"Sight. Vision. Texture. Detail. Aren't they miraculous? Awful in the sense of meaning true awe? What is sight, vision, insight? Do we really want to see the world?"

"Oh, yes," I cried promptly.

"A young man's unthinking answer. No, my dear boy, we do not. At twenty, yes, we think we wish to see, know, be all. So thought I once. But I have had weak eyes most of my life, spent half my days being fitted out with new specs by oculists, see? Well, came the dawn of the corneal lens! At last, I decided, I will fit myself with those bright little teardrop miracles, those invisible disks! Coincidence? Psychosomatic cause and effect? For that same week I got my contact lenses was the week my hearing cleared up! There must be some physicomental connection, but don't hazard me into an informed guess.

"All I know is I had my little crystal corneal lenses ground and installed upon my weak baby-blue eyes and—*voila*!

"There was the world!

"*There* were people!

"And there, God save us, were the multitudinous pores upon the people.

"Simon," he added, grieving gently, eyes shut for a moment behind his dark glasses, "have you ever thought, did you know, that people are for the most part pores?"

"Pores?" I said.

"Pores! A million, ten billion . . . pores. Everywhere and on everyone. People crowding buses, theaters, telephone booths, all pore and little substance. Small pores on tiny women. Big pores on monster men. Pores as numerous as that foul dust which slides pell-mell down churchnave sunbeams late afternoons. Pores. I stared at fine ladies' complexions, not their eyes, mouths or earlobes. Shouldn't a man watch a woman's skeleton hinge and unhinge itself within that sweet pincushion flesh? Yes! But no, I saw only cheese-grater, kitchen-sieve skins. All beauty turned sour grotesque. Swiveling my gaze was like swiveling the two-hundred-inch Palomar telescope in my damned skull. Everywhere I looked I saw the meteor-bombarded moon, in dread super-close-up!

"Myself? God, shaving mornings was exquisite torture. I could not pluck my eyes from my lost battle-pitted face. Damnation, Immanuel Brokaw, I soughed, you are the Grand Canyon at high noon!

"In sum, my contact lenses had made me fifteen years old again. That is, a self-crucified bundle of doubt, horror and absolute imperfection. The worst age in all one's life had returned to haunt me with its pimpled, bumpy ghost.

"I lay, a sleepless wreck. Ah, second adolescence, take pity, I cried. How could I have been so blind so many years? Blind, yes, and knew it, and always said it was of no importance. So I groped about the world as a lustful myope, nearsightedly missing the holes, rips, tears, and bumps on others as well as myself. Now, reality had run me down in the street. And the reality was pores.

"I went to bed for several days. Then I sat up in bed and proclaimed, wide-eyed: Reality is not all! I refuse this knowledge. I legislate against pores! I accept instead those truths we intuit, or make up, to live by.

"I traded in my eyeballs.

"That is, I handed my corneal contact lenses to a sadist nephew who thrives on garbages, lumpy people, hairy things.

"I clapped back on my old undercorrected specs. I strolled through a world of returned and gentle mists. I saw enough but not too much. I found half-discerned ghost peoples I could love again. I saw the 'me' in the morning glass I could once more bed with, admire, and take as chum. I began to laugh each day with new happiness. Softly. Then, very loud.

"What a joke, Simon, life is.

"From vanity we buy lenses that see all and so lose everything!

"And by giving up some small bit-piece of so-called wisdom, reality, truth, we gain back an entirety of life! Who does not know this? Writers do! Intuited novels are far more 'true' than all your scribbled data-fact reportage in the history of the world!

"But at last I had to face the great twin fractures lying athwart my conscience. My eyes. My ears. Holy cow, I said softly. The thousand folk who trod my offices and creaked my couches and looked for echoes in my Delphic cave, preposterous! I had seen none of them, nor heard any clear!

"Who was that Miss Harbottle?

"What of old Dinsmuir?

"What the real color, look, size of Miss Grimes?

"Did Mrs. Scrapwight really resemble and speak like an Egyptian papyrus mummy fallen out of a rug at my desk?

"I could not even guess. Two thousand days of fogs surrounded my lost children, mere voices calling, fading, gone.

"My God, I had wandered the marketplace with an invisible sign, BLIND AND DEAF, and people had rushed to fill my beggar's cup with coins and run off cured. Cured! Isn't *that* miraculous strange? Cured by an old ricket with one arm gone, as't were, and one leg missing. What? What did I say right to them out of hearing wrong? Who indeed were those people? I will never know.

"And then I thought, There are a hundred psychiatrists about town who see and hear more clearly than I. But whose patients walk naked into high seas or leap off playground slides at midnight or truss women up and smoke cigars over them.

"So I had to face the irreducible fact of a successful career.

"The lame do *not* lead the lame, my reason cried, the blind and halt do not cure the halt; the blind! But a voice from the far balcony of my soul replied with immense irony, Beeswax and Bull Durham! You, Immanuel Brokaw, are a porcelain genius, which means cracked but brilliant! Your occluded eyes see, your corked ears hear. Your fractured sensibilities cure at some level below consciousness! Bravo!

"But, no, I could not live with my perfect imperfections. I could not understand nor tolerate this smug secret thing which, through screens and obfuscations, played meadow doctor to the world and cured field beasts.

"I had several choices, then. Put my corneal lenses back in? Buy ear radios to help my rapidly improving sense of sound? And then? Find I had lost touch with my best and hidden mind that had grown comfortably accustomed to thirty years of bad vision and lousy hearing? Chaos both for curer and cured.

"Stay blind and deaf and work? It seemed a dreadful fraud, though my record was laundry-fresh, pressed white and clean.

"So I retired.

"Packed my bags and ran off into golden oblivion to let the incredible wax collect in my most terrible strange ears. . . ."

We rode in the bus along the shore in the warm afternoon. A few clouds moved over the sun. Shadows misted on the sands and the people strewn under the colored umbrellas.

I cleared my throat.

"Will you ever return to practice again, Doctor?"

"I practice now."

"But you just said—"

"Oh, not officially, and not with an office or fees, no, never that again." The doctor laughed quietly. "I am sore-beset by the mystery, anyway. That is, of how I cured all those people with a laying on of hands even though my arms were chopped off at the elbows. Still, now, I do keep my 'hand' in."

"How?"

"This shirt of mine. You saw. You heard."

"Coming down the aisle?"

"Exactly. The colors. The patterns. One thing to that man, another to the girl, a third to the boy. Zebras, goats, lightnings, Egyptian amulets. What, what, what? I ask. And answer, answer, answer. The Man in the Rorschach Shirt.

"I have a dozen such shirts at home.

"All colors, all different pattern mixes. One was designed for me by Jackson Pollock before he died. I wear each shirt for a day, or a week if the going, the answers, are thick, fast, full of excitement, and reward. Then off with the old and on with the new. Ten billion glances, ten billion startled responds!

"Might I not market these Rorschach shirts to your psychoanalyst on vacation? Test your friends? Shock your neighbors? Titillate your wife? No, no. This is my own special, private, most dear fun. No one must share it. Me and my shirts, the sun, the bus, and a thousand afternoons ahead. The beach waits. And on it, my people!

"So I walk the shores of this summer world. There is no winter here, amazing, yes, no winter of discontent it would almost seem, and death a rumor beyond the dunes. I walk along in my own time and way and come on people and let the wind flap my great sailcloth shirt now veering north, south, or south by west and watch their eyes pop, glide, leer, squint, wonder. And when a certain person says a certain word about my ink-slashed cotton colors, I give pause. I chat. I walk with them awhile. We peer into the great glass of the sea. I sidewise peer into their soul. Sometimes we stroll for hours, a longish session with the weather. Usually it takes but that one day and, not knowing with whom they walked, scot-free, they are discharged, all unwitting patients. They walk on down the dusky shore toward a fairer, brighter eve. Behind their backs, the deaf-blind man waves them bon voyage and trots home, there to devour happy suppers, brisk with fine work done.

"Or sometimes I meet some half slumberer on the sand whose troubles cannot all be fetched out to die in the raw light of one day. Then, as by accident, we collide a week later and walk by the tidal churn, doing what has always been done; we have our traveling confessional. For long before pent-up priests and whispers and repentances, friends walked, talked, listened, and in the listening-talk cured each other's sour despairs. Good friends trade hair balls all the time, give gifts of mutual dismays and so are rid of them.

"Trash collects on lawns and in minds. With bright shirt and nailtipped trash stick I set out each dawn to . . . clean up the beaches. So many, oh, so many bodies lying out there in the light. So many minds lost in the dark. I try to walk among them all, without . . . stumbling. . . ."

The wind blew in the bus window cool and fresh, making a sea of ripples through the thoughtful old man's patterned shirt.

The bus stopped.

Dr. Brokaw suddenly saw where he was and leaped up. "Wait!"

Everyone on the bus turned as if to watch the exit of a star performer. Everyone smiled.

Dr. Brokaw pumped my hand and ran. At the far-front end of the bus he turned, amazed at his own forgetfulness, lifted his dark glasses and squinted at me with his weak baby-blue eyes.

"You—" he said.

Already, to him, I was a mist, a pointillist dream somewhere out beyond the rim of vision.

"You . . ." he called into that fabulous cloud of existence that surrounded and pressed him warm and close, "you never *told* me. What? *What*?!"

He stood tall to display that incredible Rorschach shirt, which fluttered and swarmed with ever-changing line and color.

7

ABNORMAL PROCESS
AND THERAPY

Maintaining the equilibrium of the human personality is a complex and delicate task. The task often becomes so difficult that parts or all of personality may break down. The many ways in which these breakdowns occur has become the subject matter of what is commonly called abnormal psychology or psychopathology. Hopefully, when breakdowns do occur, psychology and psychiatry have the knowledge and methods to help remedy the situation by rebuilding the damaged personality, giving it a stronger and more secure foundation with which to attempt to face the stresses and strains of everyday living. This difficult task is the domain of psychotherapy, and there have been many different approaches formulated to accomplish its often elusive goals.

Before discussing the various types of mental and emotional disorders, it must be noted that two commonly used basic terms in the field, "abnormal behavior" and "mental illness," have recently been challenged for being more destructive and misleading than constructive and useful. The concept of abnormality and normality has drawn criticism because it implies that there is a uniform, "right" way to live and solve one's personal problems. Critics suggest that ideas about normality are really social concepts which vary from place to place and embody conventional values specifically of the middle class. They further suggest that we should ask whether behaviors are individually adaptive for the person, rather than trying to determine whether they are "normal" or "abnormal."

The term "mental illness" is also questioned as to whether emotional problems can be categorized as an illness. Critics suggest that illness implies an internal malfunction as the primary cause of difficulties, like a chemical imbalance or a vitamin deficiency. Although chemical imbalances often accompany emotional problems, it is questionable whether they are the causes of these problems. Critics further suggest that these problems are more accurately described as "problems in living" involving an interaction between the individual and society, rather than primarily internal problems. They also find fault with the process of labeling an individual as "having" a mental illness, like schizophrenia, and they have shown that simply calling someone a "schizophrenic" encourages others to treat him and expect him to act as if he is one, often promoting this kind of behavior. Moreover, such identification might help create a destructive self-concept for the individual, from which he begins to believe that he is indeed incapable of more adaptive behavior. Labeling him schizophrenic thus becomes a "self-fulfilling prophecy," promoting and creating more schizophrenic behavior, rather than reducing its occurrence.

Mental and emotional problems are most generally classified as being either neurotic or psychotic. Neurotic problems involve only part of the individual's personality, specific areas in which he may have serious, anxiety-provoking conflicts. These conflicts are so painful and threatening that the individual is forced to avoid them or to continually "shove them under the rug" through repression. Consequently, they remain in various forms rather than effectively being resolved, continuing to make life miserable for the individual. Major variations of neurotic behavior include anxiety reactions, in which the individual is periodically overwhelmed by emormous levels of anxiety; phobic reactions, in which the individual becomes deathly afraid of specific situations like heights or enclosed places; and obsessive-compulsive reactions in which the individual adopts rigid behavior patterns, seemingly driven to repetitiously dwell on certain thoughts, often of death and destruction, and repeat certain behaviors which serve to symbolically protect him from breaking down. The neurotic does not substantially lose contact with reality but rather is doomed to painfully fighting his problems within the confines of reality.

Psychotic disorders are divided into two major classes: schizophrenia and the affective psychoses. Both classes represent rather extreme disorder, including broad and general breakdown of the personality and severe and pervasive withdrawal from reality. It might be said that while the neurotic continues his painful fight for survival within reality, the psychotic has virtually "lost the fight" to stay within these confines. Schizophrenia, rather than a simple malady involving a "split personality," is really a highly complex disorder. Research indicates that the schizophrenic experiences an initial difficulty in focusing his attention on the important parts of his environment. He is literally bombarded with stimuli from all sides at once, overwhelmed and unable to cope with the reality he experiences. His thought processes, desperately trying to assimilate and interpret these experiences, suffer greatly, often uncontrollably going off on wild tangents which appear to be irrelevant to those around him. Individuals can become paranoid, often hearing voices accusing them of various transgressions or directing them to behave in strange ways. Investigators into schizophrenia have suggested that various sources, like genetic defects, poor family relationships, chemical imbalances, and poor communication patterns may all play a role in causing the disorder.

While schizophrenia seems to center on thought processes, the affective psychoses center on emotional behaviors. The classic syndrome, manic-depressive psychosis, focuses on extremes of positive and negative emotion. In the manic phase the individual is overly happy, ebullient, and optimistic. The individual can achieve almost anything—just ask him and he will tell you about it for hours. After a while, it becomes evident that the individual has greatly lost touch with reality and that his ebullience and optimism are really an extreme coverup for deeper, underlying feelings of extreme pessimism and depression. Chances are that the individual will revert to extreme depression sooner or later, when his energy level drops. Often the severely depressed person will continue in this down stage without becoming manic, showing extremely retarded rates of activity and extremely negative emotions and attitudes.

Other psychopathological disorders have also drawn the attention of researchers and clinicians in the field. Among these are disorders definitely traceable to organic malfunctions of the central nervous system. Historically, the major breakthrough in this area occurred when researchers discovered that the mental disorder, general paresis, was caused by the destruction of brain tissue by the spirochetes of syphilis. Other mental disorders and malfunctions including mental retardation have been traced to chemical malfunctions, vitamin deficiencies, endocrine disturbances, and abnormal brain development. Of special interest are the psychoses of old age, caused by brain cell deterioration or hardening of the arteries.

Childhood disorders like infantile autism and childhood schizophrenia also have places of importance. In the former, the child seems to withdraw from the outside world at infancy, consequently cutting off vital social and intellectual development. The latter disorder is characterized by a highly dependent relationship between mother and child, leaving the child unable to adequately develop independence and self-assurance. Another area of great interest is the realm of psychosomatic disorder, whereby physical disorders have been linked to psychological causal patterns. Finally, there are numerous psychosocial disorders. Among these are drug and alcohol addiction, sexual deviations, psychopathic disorders, and the syndromes of alienation—people who physically and emotionally drop out of society.

When an individual finds himself in the midst of virtually any of these disorders, he usually needs help. Hopefully therapy can provide this help, with specific approaches being particularly effective for specific kinds of disorders. Psychotic disorders are most often treated with biological methods of therapy. Drugs like Stelazine and Thorazine have been used to stabilize schizophrenics, while antidepressant drugs are used with severely depressed patients. When immediate treatment is needed, severe depressives also receive electroshock therapy.

Verbal methods of psychotherapy are most effective with neurotics. Freudian psychoanalytic therapy, which involves the uncovering of complex unconscious motivations for neurotic behaviors, is indicated for severely neurotic patients who must delve into the depths of their childhood to gain insight into their problems. Roger's client-centered therapy appears to be more appropriate for milder disturbances in which there is a temporary blockage of growth and self-actualization. Here the therapeutic atmosphere with a warm, accepting counselor can allow the client to become better in touch with himself, hopefully setting him back on the right track.

Behavior therapy has been used successfully to treat a number of different behavior disorders. Wolpe's method of systematic desensitization, whereby patients are trained to relax under conditions which previously made them extremely anxious, has been successful in treating phobias and other disorders. Behavior modification techniques, based on principles of Skinner's operant conditioning, are being used successfully in training retardates and autistic children. Token economies, where patients are rewarded with money-like tokens for engaging in specific behaviors, have had great success in schizophrenia wards. Finally, behavior modification techniques using biofeedback show great promise in the treatment of psychosomatic disorders. Research indicates that individuals can learn to control "automatic" functions like heart rate, blood pressure, and stomach acid secretions, thereby counterconditioning reactions which have been relatively resistant to more traditional methods of psychotherapy.

and now the news

Theodore Sturgeon

In "And Now the News" we watch a man named MacLyle as he progresses from a basically well-functioning individual with a quirk to a psychotic individual. This progression reflects the enlightened approach to psychopathology or abnormal behavior taken by Karl Menninger and others, who suggest there is a continuum for behavior from well-functioning to psychotic. The continuum is one of degree of certain behaviors, rather than in qualitatively different behavior; that is, we all behave in pretty much the same ways, except that some persons engage in certain behaviors to the extent that it throws their whole personality out of kilter. They move out of step with reality to the point where they cannot function in it and must withdraw, creating a psychotic world of their own which supports, explains, justifies, and maintains their behavior and their experience.

MacLyle starts out within the normal range, but with the kind of personality which would predispose him more than someone else with a different personality to certain psychological disturbances. He is basically a reliable, efficient, middle-class individual with regular habits. His only oddity is a compulsive need to listen to news reports. Sturgeon takes great pains to tell us that he is not a "crotchety character with fixed habits and a neurotic neatness" (Freud's anal character), but there are indications that in his regularity he leans in this direction. (Sturgeon throughout the story is against labeling people, but perhaps we can say with confidence that MacLyle has certain neurotic leanings.) The seed for neurosis is there, however. He has had a traumatic experience in the past in which his reliability broke down or at least in which he could not handle a situation. His best friend had suffered from gangrene following an accident while they were skiing together. The friend had broken his leg, and MacLyle went for help. Returning, he could not find the friend. It took three days to discover where he had slipped down the mountain and fallen into a crevasse. By then it was too late to save his leg. The experience left MacLyle with a sense of helplessness and probably a great deal of guilt. He states further that he has always believed in Donne's idea that "any man's death diminishes me, because I am involved in mankind."

All of this combines to make him an obsessive-compulsive neurotic. (Obsessive refers to an idea which one cannot get out of one's head, and compulsive refers to the behavior one uses to deal with the idea and the feeling state behind it.) With MacLyle, the obsessive idea was some combination of the Donne statement and the fact that he was unable to do anything about the deaths of mankind. His strong, repressed feelings, stemming out of the incident on the mountain, are probably a combination of anger, guilt, and anxiety—anger at the world for his friend's suffering and anger at himself for his compliance with the process of suffering on the mountain. He wants to punish himself for his part (the feeling of guilt) and he wants to punish others who also comply with the process by hurting their fellowman. He projects his own guilt feelings onto others, oversensitively blaming them for their behavior, while worrying that he will lose control of his impulses (neurotic anxiety) and actually commit violent crimes against others.

His obsessive-compulsive behavior creates a structured world which supports and controls his psychological problem. By punishing himself in an attempt to cleanse and reduce his guilt, he protects himself from losing control. MacLyle's solution is to symbolically repeat the suffering of his friend by reexperiencing it in listening to news reports of the suffering of others and going through the throes of mourning for each one. In this he tries to undo what happened on the mountain (which, of course, he cannot). The listening act also punishes him. This process repeated over and over acts as a drainage system for his guilt and anger, keeping it under control and beneath the surface, thus protecting him from his impulse to kill others for their transgressions, and himself from self-annihilation.

In taking the tubes out of the radios to prevent his hearing the news, his wife inadvertently destroys the protective structure of his world. As it crumbles, so does his ability to control his feelings and impulses, and thus to effectively live in the real world. Unconsciously, he realizes that he must protect himself and others by withdrawing from the real world. He goes through a short temporary manic phase, in which he energetically settles his estate and provides for himself and his family. The threatening real world is bearing down, and his systems start breaking down. First, the perceptual system goes—he cannot read—and he feels depersonalization, different from the person he was. He becomes frightened, and enters a state of panic. He loses his ability to talk and understand the speech of others; he is entirely encased in his own experience, his own world. He has become schizophrenic, regressed, but at peace.

For himself and society, this is his best alternative. He is at peace and does not bother others. Unfortunately, the *fairly intelligent* psychiatrist cannot see this. (Sturgeon really rakes the poor doctor over the coals.) He mechanically carries his treatment out, assuming, due to his training, that he must bring MacLyle back to society, help him adjust to it and deal with it on its own terms. The doctor plugs in his treatment. He diagnoses, categorizing MacLyle's surface symptoms, robbing him of his individuality. (Sturgeon is commenting here on psychiatry's arbitrary compulsion to categorize and classify people as units rather than as individuals.)

In effect, the doctor then plugs in the next aspect of his treatment without fully understanding the ramifications of his actions. He mechanically uses what he has been taught and what has worked in the past, at least in controlling patients: drugs or chemotherapy. The antipsychotic drugs (chlorpromazine and reserpine) do their thing, and MacLyle is brought back to reality. Often these drugs are enough to allow the patient to adjust to society as long as he continues to take them. (Their use is questioned by psychologists more than by psychiatrists, the former saying that they are used too much as chemical straitjackets.) In this case, the drugs do not work. MacLyle's adjustment to the real world is a violent one, the doctor having eliminated MacLyle's only other alternative, passive but peaceful withdrawal.

AND NOW THE NEWS *Theodore Sturgeon*

The man's name was MacLyle, which by looking at him you can tell wasn't his real name, but let's say this is fiction, shall we? MacLyle had a good job in—well—a soap concern. He worked hard and made good money and got married to a girl called Esther. He bought a house in the suburbs and after it was paid for he rented it to some people and bought a home a little father out and a second car and a freezer and a power mower and a book on landscaping, and settled down to the worthy task of giving his kids all the things he never had.

He had habits and he had hobbies, like everybody else and (like everybody else) his were a little different from anybody's. The one that annoyed his wife the most, until she got used to it, was the news habit, or maybe hobby. MacLyle read a morning paper on the 8:14 and an evening paper on the 6:10, and the local paper his suburb used for its lost dogs and auction sales took up forty after-dinner minutes. And when he read a paper he read it, he didn't mess with it. He read Page 1 first and Page 2 next, and so on all the way through. He didn't care too much for books but he respected them in a mystical sort of way, and he used to say a newspaper was a kind of book, and so would raise particular hell if a section was missing or in upside down, or if the pages were out of line. He also heard the news on the radio. There were three stations in town with hourly broadcasts, one on the hour, and he was usually able to catch them all. During these five-minute periods he would look you right in the eye while you talked to him and you'd swear he was listening to you, but he wasn't. This was a particular trial to his wife, but only for five years or so. Then she stopped trying to be heard while the radio talked about floods and murders and scandal and suicide. Five more years, and she went back to talking right through the broadcasts, but by the time people are married ten years, things like that don't matter; they talk in code anyway, and nine-tenths of their speech can be picked up anytime like ticker tape. He also caught the 7:30 news on Channel 2 and the 7:45 news on Channel 4 on television.

Now it might be imagined from all that that MacLyle was a crotchety character with fixed habits and a neurotic neatness, but this was far from the case. MacLyle was basically a reasonable guy

489

who loved his wife and children and liked his work and pretty much enjoyed being alive. He laughed easily and talked well and paid his bills. He justified his preoccupation with the news in a number of ways. He would quote Donne: "... *any man's death diminishes me, because I am involved in mankind....*" which is pretty solid stuff and hard to argue down. He would point out that he made his trains and his trains made him punctual, but that because of them he saw the same faces at the same time day after endless day, before, during, and after he rode those trains, so that his immediate world was pretty circumscribed, and only a constant awareness of what was happening all over the earth kept him conscious of the fact that he lived in a bigger place than a thin straight universe with his house at one end, his office at the other, and a railway track in between.

It's hard to say just when MacLyle started to go to pieces, or even why, though it obviously had something to do with all that news he exposed himself to. He began to react, very slightly at first; that is, you could tell he was listening. He'd *shh!* you, and if you tried to finish what you were saying he'd run and stick his head in the speaker grille. His wife and kids learned to shut up when the news came on, five minutes before the hour until five after (with MacLyle's switching stations) and every hour on the half-hour, and from 7:30 to 8 for the TV, and during the forty minutes it took him to read the local paper. He was not so obvious about it when he read his paper, because all he did was freeze over the pages like a catatonic, gripping the top corners until the sheets shivered, knotting his jaw and breathing from his nostrils with a strangled whistle.

Naturally all this was a weight on his wife Esther, who tried her best to reason with him. At first he answered her, saying mildly that a man has to keep in touch, you know; but very quickly he stopped responding altogether, giving her the treatment a practiced suburbanite gets so expert in, as when someone mentions a lawn mower just too damn early on Sunday morning. You don't say yes and you don't say no, you don't even grunt, and you don't move your head or even your eyebrows. After a while your interlocutor goes away. Pretty soon you don't hear these ill-timed annoyances any more than you appear to.

It needs to be said again here that MacLyle was, outside his peculiarity, a friendly and easygoing character. He liked people and invited them and visited them, and he was one of those adults who can really listen to a first-grade child's interminable adventures and really care. He never forgot things like the slow leak in the spare tire or antifreeze or anniversaries, and he always got the storm windows up in time, but he didn't rub anyone's nose in his reliability. The first thing in his whole life he didn't take as a matter of course was this news thing that started so small and grew so quickly.

So after a few weeks of it his wife took the bull by the horns and spent the afternoon hamstringing every receiver in the house. There were three radios and two TV sets, and she didn't understand the first thing about them, but she had a good head and she went to work with a will and the can-opening limb of a pocket knife. From each receiver she removed one tube, and one at a time, so as not to get them mixed up, she carried them into the kitchen and meticulously banged their bases against the edge of the sink, being careful to crack no glass and bend no pins, until she could see the guts of the tube rolling around loose inside. Then she replaced them and got the back panels on the sets again.

MacLyle came home and put the car away and kissed her and turned on the living-room radio and then went to hang up his hat. When he returned the radio should have been warmed up but it wasn't. He twisted the knobs a while and bumped it and rocked it back and forth a little, grunting, and then noticed the time. He began to feel a little frantic, and raced back to the kitchen and turned on the little ivory radio on the shelf. It warmed up quickly and cheerfully and gave him a clear sixty-cycle hum, but that was all. He behaved badly from then on, roaring out the information that the sets didn't work, either of them, as if that wasn't pretty evident by that time, and flew upstairs to the boys' room, waking them explosively. He turned on their radio and got another sixty-cycle note, this time with a shattering microphonic when he rapped the case, which he did four times, whereupon the set went dead altogether.

Esther had planned the thing up to this point, but no further, which was the way her mind worked. She figured she could handle it, but she figured wrong. MacLyle came downstairs like a pallbearer, and he was silent and shaken until 7:30, time for the news on TV. The living-room set wouldn't peep, so up he went to the boys' room again, waking them just as they were nodding off again, and this time the little guy started to cry. MacLyle didn't care. When he found out there was no picture on the set, he almost started to cry too, but then he heard the sound come in. A TV set has an awful lot of tubes in it and Esther didn't know audio from video. MacLyle sat down in front of the dark screen and listened to the news. *"Everything seemed to be under control in the riot-ridden border country in*

491

India," said the TV set. Crowd noises and a background of Beethoven's "Turkish March." *"And then—"* Cut music. Crowd noise up: gabble-wurra and a scream. Announcer over: *"Six hours later, this was the scene."* Dead silence, going on so long that MacLyle reached out and thumped the TV set with the heel of his hand. Then, slow swell, Ketelbey's "In a Monastery Garden." *"On a more cheerful note, here are the six finalists in the Miss Continuum contest."* Background music, "Blue Room," interminably, interrupted only once, when the announcer said through a childish chuckle *". . . and she meant it!"* MacLyle pounded himself on the temples. The little guy continued to sob. Esther stood at the foot of the stairs wringing her hands. It went on for thirty minutes like this. All MacLyle said when he came downstairs was that he wanted the paper—that would be the local one. So Esther faced the great unknown and told him frankly she hadn't ordered it and wouldn't again, which of course led to a full and righteous confession of her activities of the afternoon.

Only a woman married better than fourteen years can know a man well enough to handle him so badly. She was aware that she was wrong but that was quite overridden by the fact that she was logical. It would not be logical to continue her patience, so patience was at an end. That which offendeth thee, cast it out, yea, even thine eye and thy right hand. She realized too late that the news was so inextricable part of her husband that in casting it out she cast him out too. And out he went, while whitely she listened to the rumble of the garage door, the car door speaking its sharp syllables, clear as *Exit* in a playscript; the keen of a starter, the mourn of a motor. She said she was glad and went in the kitchen and tipped the useless ivory radio off the shelf and retired, weeping.

And yet, because true life offers few clean cuts, she saw him once more. At seven minutes to three in the morning she became aware of faint music from somewhere; unaccountably it frightened her, and she tiptoed about the house looking for it. It wasn't in the house, so she pulled on MacLyle's trench coat and crept down the steps into the garage. And there, just outside in the driveway, where steel beams couldn't interfere with radio reception, the car stood where it had been all along, and MacLyle was in the driver's seat dozing over the wheel. The music came from the car radio. She drew the coat tighter around her and went to the car and opened the door and spoke his name. At just that moment the radio said *". . . and now the news"* and MacLyle sat bolt upright and *shh'd* furiously. She fell back and stood a moment in a strange transition from unconditional surrender to total defeat. Then he shut the car door and bent forward, his hand on the volume control, and she went back into the house.

After the news report was over and he had recovered himself from the stab wounds of a juvenile delinquent, the grinding agonies of a derailed train, the terrors of the near-crash of a C-119, and the fascination of a cabinet officer, charter member of the We Don't Trust Nobody Club, saying in exactly these words that there's a little bit of good in the worst of us and a little bit of bad in the best of us, all of which he felt keenly, he started the car (by rolling it down the drive because the battery was almost dead) and drove as slowly as possible into town.

At an all-night garage he had the car washed and greased while he waited, after which the automat was open and he sat in it for three hours drinking coffee, holding his jaw set until his back teeth ached, and making occasional, almost inaudible noises in the back of his throat. At nine he pulled himself together. He spent the entire day with his astonished attorney, going through all his assets, selling, converting, establishing, until when he was finished he had a modest packet of cash and his wife would have an adequate income until the children went to college, at which time the house would be sold, the tenants in the older house evicted, and Esther would be free to move to the smaller home with the price of the larger one added to the basic capital. The lawyer might have entertained fears for MacLyle except for the fact that he was jovial and loquacious throughout, behaving like a happy man—a rare form of insanity, but acceptable. It was hard work but they did it in a day, after which MacLyle wrung the lawyer's hand and thanked him profusely and checked into a hotel.

When he awoke the following morning he sprang out of bed, feeling years younger, opened the door, scooped up the morning paper and glanced at the headlines.

He couldn't read them.

He grunted in surprise, closed the door gently, and sat on the bed with the paper in his lap. His hand moved restlessly on it, smoothing and smoothing until the palms were shadowed and the type hazed. The shouting symbols marched across the page like a parade of strangers in some unrecognized lodge uniform, origins unknown, destination unknown, and the occasion for marching only to be guessed at. He traced the letters with his little finger, he measured the length of a word between his index finger and thumb and lifted them up to hold them before his wondering eyes.

493

Suddenly he got up and crossed to the desk, where signs and placards and printed notes were trapped like a butterfly collection under glass—the breakfast menu, something about valet service, something about checking out. He remembered them all and had an idea of their significance—but he couldn't read them. In the drawer was stationery, with a picture of the building and no other buildings around it, which just wasn't so, and an inscription which might have been in Cyrillic for all he knew. Telegram blanks, a bus schedule, a blotter, all bearing hieroglyphs and runes, as far as he was concerned. A phone book full of strangers' names in strange symbols.

He requested of himself that he recite the alphabet. "A," he said clearly, and "Eh?" because it didn't sound right and he couldn't imagine what would. He made a small foolish grin and shook his head slightly and rapidly, but grin or no, he felt frightened. He felt glad, or relieved—most happy anyway, but still a little frightened.

He called the desk and told them to get his bill ready, and dressed and went downstairs. He gave the doorman his parking check and waited while they brought the car round. He got in and turned the radio on and started to drive west.

He drove for some days, in a state of perpetual cold and (for all that) happy fright—roller-coaster fright, horror-movie fright—remembering the significance of a stop sign without being able to read the word STOP across it, taking caution from the shape of a railroad-crossing notice. Restaurants look like restaurants, gas stations like gas stations; if Washington's picture denotes a dollar and Lincoln's five, one doesn't need to read them. MacLyle made out just fine. He drove until he was well into one of those square states with all the mountains and cruised until he recognized the section where, years before he was married, he had spent a hunting vacation. Avoiding the lodge he had used, he took back roads until, sure enough, he came to that deserted cabin in which he had sheltered one night, standing yet, rotting a bit but only around the edges. He wandered in and out of it for a long time, memorizing details because he could not make a list, and then got back into his car and drove to the nearest town, not very near and not very much of a town. At the general store he bought shingles and flour and nails and paint—all sorts of paint, in little cans, as well as big containers of house paint—and canned goods and tools. He ordered a knock-down windmill and a generator, eighty pounds of modeling clay, two loaf pans and a mixing bowl, and a war-surplus jungle hammock. He paid cash and promised to be back in two weeks for the things the store didn't stock, and wired (because it could be done over the phone) his lawyer to arrange for the predetermined eighty dollars a month, which was all he cared to take for himself from his assets. Before he left he stood in wonder before a monstrous piece of musical plumbing called an ophicleide which stood, dusty and majestic, in a corner. (While it might be easier on the reader to make this a French horn or a sousaphone—which would answer narrative purposes quite as well—we're done telling lies here. MacLyle's real name is concealed, his home town cloaked, and his occupation disguised, and dammit it really was a twelve-keyed, 1824, fifty-inch, obsolete brass ophicleide.) The storekeeper explained how his greatgrandfather had brought it over from the old country and nobody had played it for two generations except an itinerant tuba player who had turned pale green on the first three notes and put it down as if it was full of percussion caps. MacLyle asked how it sounded and the man told him, terrible. Two weeks later MacLyle was back to pick up the rest of his stuff, nodding and smiling and saying not a word. He still couldn't read, and now he couldn't speak. Even more, he had lost the power to understand speech. He had paid for the purchases with a hundred-dollar bill and a wistful expression, and then another hundred-dollar bill, and the storekeeper, thinking he had turned deaf and dumb, cheated him roundly but at the same time felt so sorry for him that he gave him the ophicleide. MacLyle loaded up his car happily and left. And that's the first part of the story about MacLyle's being in a bad way.

MacLyle's wife Esther found herself in a peculiar position. Friends and neighbors offhandedly asked her questions to which she did not know the answers, and the only person who had any information at all—MacLyle's attorney—was under bond not to tell her anything. She had not, in the full and legal sense, been deserted, since she and the children were provided for. She missed MacLyle, but in a specialized way; she missed the old reliable MacLyle, and he had, in effect, left her long before that perplexing night when he had driven away. She wanted the old MacLyle back again, not this untrolleyed stranger with the grim and spastic preoccupation with the news. Of the many unpleasant facets of this stranger's personality, one glowed brightest, and that was that he was the sort of man who would walk out the way he did and stay away as long as he had. Ergo, he was that undesirable person just as long as he stayed away, and tracking him down would, if it returned him against his will, return to her only a person who was not the person she missed.

Yet she was dissatisfied with herself, for all that she was the injured party and had wounds less painful than the pangs of conscience. She had always prided herself on being a good wife, and had done many things in the past which were counter to her reason and her desires purely because they were consistent with being a good wife. So as time went on she gravitated away from the "what shall I do?" area into the "what ought a good wife to do?" spectrum, and after a great deal of careful thought, went to see a psychiatrist.

He was a fairly intelligent psychiatrist, which is to say he caught on to the obvious a little faster than most people. For example, he became aware in only four minutes of conversation that MacLyle's wife Esther had not come to him on her own behalf, and further, decided to hear her out completely before resolving to treat her. When she had quite finished and he had dug out enough corroborative detail to get the picture, he went into a long silence and cogitated. He matched the broad pattern of MacLyle's case with his reading and his experience, recognized the challenge, the clinical worth of the case, the probable value of the heirloom diamond pendant worn by his visitor. He placed his fingertips together, lowered his fine young head, gazed through his eyebrows at MacLyle's wife Esther, and took up the gauntlet. At the prospects of getting her husband back safe and sane, she thanked him quietly and left the office with mixed emotions. The fairly intelligent psychiatrist drew a deep breath and began making arrangements with another head-shrinker to take over his other patients, both of them, while he was away, because he figured to be away quite a while.

It was appallingly easy for him to trace MacLyle. He did not go near the lawyer. The solid foundation of all skip tracers and Bureaus of Missings Persons, in their *modus operandi*, is the piece of applied psychology which dictates that a man might change his name and his address, but he will seldom—can seldom—change the things he does, particularly the things he does to amuse himself. The ski addict doesn't skip to Florida, though he might make Banff instead of an habitual Mount Tremblant. A philatelist is not likely to mount butterflies. Hence when the psychiatrist found, among MacLyle's papers, some snapshots and brochures, dating from college days, of the towering Rockies, of bears feeding by the roadside, and especially of season after season's souvenirs of a particular resort to which he had never brought his wife and which he had not visited since he married her, it was worth a feeler, which went out in the form of a request to that state's police for information on a man of such-and-such a description driving so-and-so with out-of-state plates, plus a request that the man not be detained nor warned, but only that he, the fairly intelligent psychiatrist, be notified. He threw out other lines, too, but this is the one that hooked the fish. It was a matter of weeks before a state patrol car happened by MacLyle's favorite general store: after that it was a matter of minutes before the information was in the hands of the psychiatrist. He said nothing to MacLyle's wife Esther except good-by for a while, and this bill is payable now, and then took off, bearing with him a bag of tricks.

He rented a car at the airport nearest MacLyle's hideout and drove a long, thirsty, climbing way until he came to the general store. There he interviewed the proprietor, learning some eighteen hundred items about how bad business could get, how hot it was, how much rain hadn't fallen and how much was needed, the tragedy of being blamed for high markups when anyone with the brains God gave a goose ought to know it cost plenty to ship things out here, especially in the small quantities necessitated by business being so bad and all; and betwixt and between, he learned eight or ten items about MacLyle—the exact location of his cabin, the fact that he seemed to have turned into a deaf-mute who was also unable to read, and that he must be crazy because who but a crazy man would want eighty-four different half-pint cans of house paint or, for that matter, live out here when he didn't have to?

The psychiatrist got loose after a while and drove off, and the country got higher and dustier and more lost every mile, until he began to pray that nothing would go wrong with the car, and sure enough, ten minutes later something had. Any car that made a noise like the one he began to hear was strictly a shot-rod, and he pulled over to the side to worry about it. He turned off the motor and the noise went right on, and he began to realize that the sound was not in the car or even near it, but came from somewhere uphill. There was a mile and a half more of the hill to go, and he drove it in increasing amazement, because that sound got louder and more impossible all the time. It was sort of like music, but like no music currently heard on this or any other planet. It was a solo voice, brass, with muscles. The upper notes, of which there seemed to be about two octaves, were wild and unmusical, the middle was rough, but the low tones were like the speech of these mountains themselves, big up to the sky, hot, and more natural than anything ought to be, basic as a bear's fang. Yet all the notes were perfect—their intervals were perfect—this awful noise was tuned like an electronic organ.

497

The psychiatrist had a good ear, though for a while he wondered how long he'd have any ears at all, and he realized all these things about the sound, as well as the fact that it was rendering one of the more primitive fingering studies from Czerny, Book One, the droning little horror that goes: *do mi fa sol la sol fa mi, re fa sol la ti la sol fa, mi sol la* . . . etcetera, inchworming up the scale and then descending hand over hand.

He saw blue sky almost under his front tires and wrenched the wheel hard over, and found himself in the grassy yard of a madeover prospector's cabin, but that he didn't notice right away because sitting in front of it was what he described to himself, startled as he was out of his professional detachment, as the craziest-looking man he had ever seen.

He was sitting under a parched, wind-warped Englemann spruce. He was barefoot up to the armpits. He wore the top half of a skivvy shirt and a hat the shape of one of those conical Boy Scout tents when one of the Boy Scouts has left the pole home. And he was playing, or anyway practicing, the ophicleide, and on his shoulders was a little moss of spruce needles, a small shower of which descended from the tree every time he hit on or under the low $B_\flat$. Only a mouse trapped inside a tuba during band practice can know precisely what it's like to stand that close to an operating ophicleide.

It was MacLyle all right, looming well fed and filled out. When he saw the psychiatrist's car he went right on playing, but, catching the psychiatrist's eye, he winked, smiled with the small corner of lip which showed from behind the large cup of the mouthpiece, and twiddled three fingers of his right hand, all he could manage of a wave without stopping. And he didn't stop either until he had scaled the particular octave he was working on and let himself down the other side. Then he put the ophicleide down carefully and let it lean against the spruce tree, and got up. The psychiatrist had become aware, as the last stupendous notes rolled away down the mountain, of his extreme isolation with this offbeat patient, of the unconcealed health and vigor of the man, and of the presence of the precipice over which he had almost driven his car a moment before, and had rolled up his window and buttoned the door lock and was feeling grateful for them. But the warm good humor and genuine welcome on MacLyle's sunburned face drove away fright and even caution, and almost before he knew what he was doing the psychiatrist had the door open and was stooping up out of the car, thinking, merry is a disused word but that's what he is, by God, a merry man. He called

498

him by name but either MacLyle did not hear him or didn't care; he just put out a big warm hand and the psychiatrist took it. He could feel hard flat calluses in MacLyle's hand, and the controlled strength an elephant uses to lift a bespangled child in its trunk; he smiled at the image, because after all MacLyle was not a particularly large man, there was just that feeling about him. And once the smile found itself there it wouldn't go away.

He told MacLyle that he was a writer trying to soak up some of this magnificent country and had just been driving wherever the turn of the road led him, and here he was; but before he was half through he became conscious of MacLyle's eyes, which were in some indescribable way very much on him but not at all on anything he said; it was precisely as if he had stood there and hummed a tune. MacLyle seemed to be willing to listen to the sound until it was finished, and even to enjoy it, but that enjoyment was going to be all he got out of it. The psychiatrist finished anyway and MacLyle waited a moment as if to see if there would be any more, and when there wasn't he gave out more of that luminous smile and cocked his head toward the cabin. MacLyle led the way, with his visitor bringing up the rear with some platitudes about nice place you got here. As they entered, he suddenly barked at that unresponsive back, "Can't you hear me?" and MacLyle, without turning, only waved him on.

They walked into such a clutter and clabber of colors that the psychiatrist stopped dead, blinking. One wall had been removed and replaced with glass panes; it overlooked the precipice and put the little building afloat on haze. All the walls were hung with plain white chenille bedspreads, and the floor was white, and there seemed to be much more light indoors here than outside. Opposite the large window was an oversized easel made of peeled poles, notched and lashed together with baling wire, and on it was a huge canvas, most nonobjective, in the purest and most uncomprising colors. Part of it was unquestionably this room, or at least its air of colored confusion here and all infinity yonder. The ophicleide was in the picture, painstakingly reproduced, looking like the hopper of some giant infernal machine, and in the foregound, some flowers; but the central figure repulsed him—more, it repulsed everything which surrounded it. It did not look exactly like anything familiar and, in a disturbed way, he was happy about that.

Stacked on the floor on each side of the easel were other paintings, some daubs, some full of ruled lines and overlapping

499

planes, but all in this achingly pure color. He realized what was being done with the dozens of colors of house paint in little cans which had so intrigued the storekeeper.

In odd places around the room were clay sculptures, most mounted on pedestals made of sections of tree trunks large enough to stand firmly on their sawed ends. Some of the pedestals were peeled, some painted, and in some the bark texture or the bulges or clefts in the wood had been carried right up into the model, and in others clay had been knived or pressed into the bark all the way down to the floor. Some of the clay was painted, some not, some ought to have been. There were free forms and gollywogs, a marsupial woman and a guitar with legs, and some, but not an overweening number, of the symbolisms which preoccupy even fairly intelligent psychiatrists. Nowhere was there any furniture per se. There were shelves at all levels and of varying lengths, bearing nail kegs, bolts of cloth, canned goods, tools and cooking utensils. There was a sort of table but it was mostly a workbench, with a vise at one end and at the other, half finished, a crude but exceedingly ingenious foot-powered potter's wheel.

He wondered where MacLyle slept, so he asked him, and again MacLyle reacted as if the words were not words, but a series of pleasant sounds, cocking his head and waiting to see if there would be any more. So the psychiatrist resorted to sign language, making a pillow of his two hands, laying his head on it, closing his eyes. He opened them to see MacLyle nodding eagerly, then going to the white-draped wall. From behind the chenille he brought a hammock, one end of which was fastened to the wall. The other end he carried to the big window and hung on a hook screwed to a heavy stud between the panes. To lie in that hammock would be to swing between heaven and earth like Mahomet's tomb, with all that sky and scenery virtually surrounding the sleeper. His admiration for this idea ceased as MacLyle began making urgent indications for him to get into the hammock. He backed off warily, expostulating, trying to convey to MacLyle that he only wondered, he just wanted to know: no, *no*, he wasn't tired, dammit; but MacLyle became so insistent that he picked the psychiatrist up like a child sulking at bedtime and carried him to the hammock. Any impulse to kick or quarrel was quenched by the nature of this and all other hammocks to be intolerant of shifting burdens, and by the proximity of the large window, which he now saw was built leaning outward, enabling one to look out of the hammock straight down a minimum of four hundred and eighty feet. So all right, he concluded, if you say so. I'm sleepy.

So for the next two hours he lay in the hammock watching MacLyle putter about the place, thinking more or less professional thoughts.

He doesn't or can't speak (he diagnosed): aphasia, motor. He doesn't or can't understand speech: aphasia, sensory. He won't or can't read and write: alexia. And what else?

He looked at all that art—if it *was* art, and any that was, was art by accident—and the gadgetry: the chuntering windmill outside, the sash-weight door closer. He let his eyes follow a length of clothesline dangling unobtrusively down the leaning center post to which his hammock was fastened, and the pulley and fittings from which it hung, and its extension clear across the ceiling to the back wall, and understood finally that it would, when pulled, open two long, narrow horizontal hatches for through ventilation. A small door behind the chenille led to what he correctly surmised was a primitive powder room, built to overhang the precipice, the most perfect no-plumbing solution for that convenience he had ever seen.

He watched MacLyle putter. That was the only word for it, and his actions were the best example of puttering he had ever seen. MacLyle lifted, shifted, and put things down, backed off to judge, returned to lay an approving hand on the thing he had moved. Net effect, nothing tangible—yet one could not say there was no effect, because of the intense satisfaction the man radiated. For minutes he would stand, head cocked, smiling slightly, regarding the half-finished potter's wheel, then explode into activity, sawing, planing, drilling. He would add the finished piece to the cranks and connecting rods already completed, pat it as if it were an obedient child, and walk away, leaving the rest of the job for some other time. With a wood-rasp he carefully removed the nose from one of his dried clay figures, and meticulously put on a new one. Always there was this absorption in his own products and processes, and the air of total reward in everything. And there was time, there seemed to be time enough for everything, and always would be.

Here is a man, thought the fairly intelligent psychiatrist, in retreat, but in a retreat the like of which my science has not yet described. For observe: he has reacted toward the primitive in terms of supplying himself with his needs with his own hands and by his own ingenuity, and yet there is nothing primitive in those needs themselves. He works constantly to achieve the comforts which his history has conditioned him to in the past—electric lights, cross-ventilation, trouble-free waste disposal. He exhibits a profound humility in the low rates he pays himself for his labor: he is building a potter's wheel apparently in order to make his own cooking vessels, and since wood is cheap and clay free, his vessel can only cost him less than engine-turned aluminum by a very low evaluation of his own efforts.

His skills are less than his energy (mused the psychiatrist). His carpentry, like his painting and sculpture, shows considerable intelligence, but only moderate training; he can construct but not beautify, draw but not draft, and reach the artistically pleasing only by not erasing the random shake, the accidental cut; so that real creation in his work is, like any random effect, rare and unpredictable. Therefore, his reward is in the area of satisfaction—about as wide a generalization as one can make.

What satisfaction? Not in possessions themselves, for this man could have bought better for less. Not in excellence in itself, for he obviously could be satisfied with less than perfection. Freedom, perhaps, from routine, from dominations of work? Hardly, because for all that complexity of this cluttered cottage, it had its order and its system; the presence of an alarm clock conveyed a good deal in this area. He wasn't dominated by regularity—he used it. And his satisfaction? Why, it must lie in this closed circle, himself to himself, and in the very fact of non-communication!

Retreat . . . retreat. Retreat to savagery and you don't engineer your cross-ventilation or adjust a five hundred-foot gravity flush for your john. Retreat into infancy and you don't design and build a potter's wheel. Retreat from people and you don't greet a stranger like. . . .

Wait.

Maybe a stranger who had something to communicate, or some way of communication, wouldn't be so welcome. An unsettling thought, that. Running the risk of doing something MacLyle didn't like would be, possibly, a little more unselfish than the challenge warranted.

MacLyle began to cook.

Watching him, the psychiatrist reflected suddenly that this withdrawn and wordless individual was a happy one, in his own matrix; further, he had fulfilled all his obligations and responsibilities and was bothering no one.

It was intolerable.

It was intolerable because it was a violation of the prime

directive of psychiatry—at least, of that school of psychiatry which he professed, and he was not going to confuse himself by considerations of other, less-tried theories—*It is the function of psychiatry to adjust the aberrant to society, and to restore or increase his usefulness to it.* To yield, to rationalize this man's behavior as balance, would be to fly in the face of science itself; for this particular psychiatry finds it most successful approaches in the scientific method, and it is unprofitable to debate whether or not it is or is not a science. To its practitioner it is, and that's that; it has to be. Operationally speaking, what has been found true, even statistically, must be Truth, and all other things, even Possible, kept the hell out of the toolbox. No known Truth allowed a social entity to secede this way, and, for one, this fairly intelligent psychiatrist was not going to give this—this *suicide* his blessing.

He must, then, find a way to communicate with MacLyle, and when he had found it, he must communicate to him the error of his ways. Without getting thrown over the cliff.

He became aware that MacLyle was looking at him, twinkling. He smiled back before he knew what he was doing, and obeyed MacLyle's beckoning gesture. He eased himself out of the hammock and went to the workbench, where a steaming stew was set out in earthenware bowls. The bowls stood on large plates and were surrounded by a band of carefully sliced tomatoes. He tasted them. They were obviously vine-ripened and had been speckled with a dark green paste which, after studious attention to its aftertaste, he identified as fresh basil mashed with fresh garlic and salt. The effect was symphonic.

He followed suit when MacLyle picked up his own bowl and they went outside and squatted under the old Englemann spruce to eat. It was a quiet and pleasant occasion, and during it the psychiatrist had plenty of opportunity to size up his man and plan his campaign. He was quite sure now how to proceed, and all he needed was opportunity, which presented itself when MacLyle rose, stretched, smiled, and went indoors. The psychiatrist followed him to the door and saw him crawl into the hammock and fall almost instantly asleep.

The psychiatrist went to his car and got out his bag of tricks. And so it was late in the afternoon, when MacLyle emerged stretching and yawning from his nap, he found his visitor under the spruce tree, hefting the ophicleide and twiddling its keys in a perplexed and investigatory fashion. MacLyle strode over to him and lifted the ophicleide away with a pleasant I'll-show-you smile, got the monstrous contraption into position, and ran his tongue around the inside of the mouthpiece, large as a demitasse. He had barely time to pucker up his lips at the strange taste there before his irises rolled up completely out of sight and he collapsed like a grounded parachute. The psychiatrist was able only to snatch away the ophicleide in time to keep the mouthpiece from knocking out MacLyle's front teeth.

He set the ophicleide carefully against the tree and straightened MacLyle's limbs. He concentrated for a moment on the pulse, and turned the head to one side so saliva would not drain down the flaccid throat, and then went back to his bag of tricks. He came back and knelt, and MacLyle did not even twitch at the bite of the hypodermics: a careful blend of the non-soporific tranquilizers Frenquel, Chlorpromazine and Reserpine, and a judicious dose of Scopolamine, a hypnotic.

The psychiatrist got water and carefully sponged out the man's mouth, not caring to wait out another collapse the next time he swallowed. Then there was nothing to do but wait, and plan.

Exactly on schedule, according to the psychiatrist's wrist watch, MacLyle groaned and coughed weakly. The psychiatrist immediately and in a firm quiet voice told him not to move. Also not to think. He stayed out of the immediate range of MacLyle's unfocused eyes and explained that MacLyle must trust him, because he was there to help, and not to worry about feeling mixed-up or disoriented. "You don't know where you are or how you got here," he informed MacLyle. He also told MacLyle, who was past forty, that he was thirty-seven years old, but he knew what he was doing.

MacLyle just lay there obediently and thought these things over and waited for more information. He didn't know where he was or how he had gotten here. He did know that he must trust this voice, the owner of which was here to help him; that he was thirty-seven years old; and his name. In these things he lay and marinated. The drugs kept him conscious, docile, submissive and without guile. The psychiatrist observed and exulted: oh, you azacyclonol, he chanted silently to himself, you pretty piperidyl, handsome hydrochloride, subtle Serpasil. . . . Confidently he left MacLyle and went into the cabin where, after due search, he found some decent clothes and some socks and shoes and brought them out and wrapped the supine patient in them. He helped MacLyle across the clearing and into his car, humming as he did so, for there is none so happy as an expert faced with excellence in his specialty. MacLyle sank back into the cushions and gave one wondering glance at the cabin and at the blare of late light from the bell of the ophicleide; but the psychiatrist told him firmly that these things had nothing to do with him, nothing at all, and MacLyle smiled relievedly and fell to watching the scenery go by, passive as a Pekingese. As they passed the general store MacLyle stirred, but said nothing about it. Instead he asked the psychiatrist if the Ardsmere station was open yet, whereupon the psychiatrist could barely answer him for the impulse to purr like a cat: the Ardsmere station, two stops before MacLyle's suburban town, had burned down and been rebuilt almost six years ago; so now he knew for sure that MacLyle was living in a time preceding his difficulties—a time during which, of course, MacLyle had been able to talk. He crooned his appreciation for Chlorpromazine (which had helped MacLyle be tranquil) and he made up a silent song, o doll o' mine, Scopolamine, which had made him so very suggestible. But all of this the psychiatrist kept to himself, and answered gravely that yes, they had the Ardsmere station operating again. And did he have anything else on his mind?

MacLyle considered this carefully, but since all the immediate questions were answered—unswervingly, he *knew* he was safe in the hands of this man, whoever he was; he knew (he thought) his correct age and that he was expected to feel disoriented; he was also under a command not to think—he placidly shook his head and went back to watching the road unroll under their wheels. "Fallen Rock Zone," he murmured as they passed a sign. The psychiatrist drove happily down the mountain and across the flats, back to the city where he had hired the car. He left it at the railroad station ("Rail Crossing Road," murmured MacLyle) and made reservations for a compartment on the train, aircraft being too open and public for his purposes and far too fast for the hourly rate he suddenly decided to apply.

They had time for a silent and companionable dinner before train time, and then at last they were aboard, solid ground beneath, a destination ahead, and the track joints applauding.

The psychiatrist turned off all but one reading lamp and leaned forward. MacLyle's eyes dilated readily to the dimmer light, and the psychiatrist leaned back comfortably and asked him how he felt. He felt fine and said so. The psychiatrist asked him how old he was and MacLyle told him, thirty-seven, but he sounded doubtful.

Knowing that the Scopolamine was wearing off but the other drugs, the tranquilizers, would hang on for a bit, the psychiatrist drew a deep breath and removed the suggestion; he told MacLyle the truth about his age, and brought him up to the here and now.

MacLyle just looked puzzled for a few minutes and then his features settled into an expression that can only be described as not unhappy. "Porter," was all he said, gazing at the push button on the partition with its little metal sign, and announced that he could read now.

The psychiatrist nodded sagely and offered no comment, being quite willing to let a patient stew in his own juice as long as he produced essence.

MacLyle abruptly demanded to know why he had lost the powers of speech and reading. The psychiatrist raised his eyebrows a little and his shoulders a good deal and smiled one of those "You-tell-me" smiles, and then got up and suggested they sleep on it. He got the porter in to fix the beds and as an afterthought told the man to come back with the evening papers. Nothing can orient a cultural expatriate better than the evening papers. The man did. MacLyle paid no attention to this, one way or the other. He just climbed into the psychiatrist's spare pajamas thoughtfully and they went to bed.

The psychiatrist didn't know if MacLyle had awakened him on purpose or whether the train's slowing down for a watering stop had done it, or both; anyway he awoke about three in the morning to find MacLyle standing beside his bunk looking at him fixedly. He closed his eyes and screwed them tight and opened them again, and MacLyle was still there, and now he noticed that MacLyle's reading lamp was lit and the papers were scattered all over the floor. MacLyle said "You're some kind of a doctor," in a flat voice.

The psychiatrist admitted it.

MacLyle said, "Well, this ought to make some sense to you. I was skiing out here years ago when I was a college kid. Accident, fellow I was with broke his leg. Compound. Made him comfortable as I could and went for help. Came back, he'd slid down the mountain, thrashing around, I guess. Crevasse, down in the bottom; took two days to find him, three days to get him out. Frostbite. Gangrene."

The psychiatrist tried to look as if he was following this.

MacLyle said, "The one thing I always remember, him pulling back the bandages all the time to look at his leg. Knew it was gone, couldn't keep himself from watching the stuff spread around and upward. Didn't like to; *had* to. Tried to stop him, finally had to help him or he'd hurt himself. Every ten, fifteen minutes all the way down to the lodge, fifteen hours, looking under the bandages."

The psychiatrist tried to think of something to say and couldn't, so he looked wise and waited.

MacLyle said, "That Donne, that John Donne I used to spout, I always believed that."

The psychiatrist began to misquote the thing about send not to ask for whom the bell. . . .

"Yeah, that, but especially *'any man's death diminishes me, because I am involved in mankind.'* I believed that," MacLyle repeated. "I believed more than that. Not only death. Damn foolishness diminishes me because I am involved. People all the time pushing people around diminishes me. Everybody hungry for a fast buck diminishes me." He picked up a sheet of newspaper and let it slip away; it flapped off to the corner of the compartment like a huge grave-moth. "I was getting diminished to death and I had to watch it happening to me like that kid with the gangrene, so that's why." The train, crawling now, lurched suddenly and yielded. MacLyle's eyes flickered to the window, where neon beer signs and a traffic light were reluctantly being framed. MacLyle leaned close to the psychiatrist. "I just had to get un-involved with mankind before I got diminished altogether, everything mankind did was my fault. So I did and now here I am involved again." MacLyle abruptly went to the door. "And for that, thanks."

From a dusty throat the psychiatrist asked him what he was going to do.

"Do?" asked MacLyle cheerfully. "Why, I'm going out there and diminish mankind right back." He was out in the corridor with the door closed before the psychiatrist so much as sat up. He banged it open again and leaned in. He said in the sanest of all possible voices, "Now mind you, doctor, this is only one man's opinion," and was gone. He killed four people before they got him.

the plot

Tom Herzog

"The Plot" is a playful little story which has fun simulating the behavior of a paranoid schizophrenic. George Filmore believes his wife is plotting to kill him. Can this be true? If it is, then we must accept the fact that a razor can talk, because it is from this source that he gets the information about his wife's treachery. No, that seems unlikely. Filmore must be having paranoid delusions. But wait, this is science fiction, where anything can happen. Let's look carefully at the story before we jump to conclusions.

From the beginning Filmore does fit the pattern of a paranoid schizophrenic, or at least someone who would be apt to develop the syndrome. First, he comes home and assails his wife, projecting blame on her because *his* stomach is upset. Projection is the major defense mechanism operating in paranoid behavior. Next, we note his concern about his age and his lost masculine physique, followed by a quick overcompensation or reaction formation for that thought: his health is good and he "feels like a king." This might be seen as the beginning of the formation of a delusion of grandeur as a reaction formation for underlying feelings of weakness, again typical of the paranoid schizophrenic.

Then his razor starts talking to him about the plot, but perhaps he only imagines he hears a voice which he attributes to his razor. He would in that case be having auditory hallucinations. Where did that voice come from? Could it have been an obsessive idea emanating from his own mind which he projects onto the razor because he cannot accept it as his own? Again, a typical mechanism of the paranoid schizophrenic—projecting his own thoughts onto other people or things.

The pattern of the story seems to want us to believe Filmore is paranoid, but we've developed some sophistication in reading science fiction now; we know the unexpected is as likely to happen as the expected, so we'll refrain from drawing conclusions and read further.

Maybe his wife really is plotting behind his back. This is suggested to him when she turns her back as he comes into the kitchen. His suspicions mount as the evidence accumulates. There might be poison in the salt and pepper, but if the razor is not to be believed, then his tasting poison might be only a gustatory hallucination. Filmore next pulls a double delusion of persecution, explaining why there is no poison in the shakers while at the same time keeping intact his original delusion that there is. Like the paranoid schizophrenic, he becomes exceedingly sensitive and suspicious about all kinds of things which could easily be accidental or chance occurrences.

Because he is so sure his wife is responsible for all these occurrences, he feels justified in the plot he erects to defend himself. Does his razor really tell him how to commit the violent act he plans, or is this a delusion of influence?

Plot and counterplot. Who's crazy now? At the end is Filmore's wife being talked to, or is she a paranoid schizophrenic, too?

THE PLOT   *Tom Herzog*

The scrambled eggs gave Filmore a bad case of indigestion. At the office that morning he was quite sick and had to take something to quiet his stomach. He came home early and assailed his wife as soon as he got inside the door.

"What the hell did you do to those eggs this morning, Elvira?" he demanded. "I damn near puked all over my desk. Just made it to the washroom in time."

Mrs. Filmore looked down at the floor.

"They tasted all right to me," she said quietly. She was small, quiet by nature, and blended in well with the walls. "Perhaps you ate too fast, George. You're not as young as you used to be, and you shouldn't eat too fast."

Filmore looked at his paunch. After all, he *was* on the wrong side of fifty. On the other hand, his health was good and he felt like a king. He couldn't even remember the last time he'd had an attack of indigestion.

"Hogwash!" he roared. "What time are we having supper?"

"At five," said Mrs. Filmore, "if that's all right with you."

"I'm going to shave," he said, ignoring her. He shaved twice a day with his electric razor, once before going to the office in the morning and once before supper. He had a remarkably fertile crop of whiskers, and since, as an advertising man, he believed in the value of appearances, he shaved them off twice a day.

In the bathroom he plugged in his electric razor and examined his beard in the mirror. He was about to begin shaving when his razor spoke to him.

"I would like a word with you," it said.

"What the hell . . . !!" said Filmore, dropping it into the sink as if it had burned his hand.

"Please be civil," said the razor. "I'm trying to do you a service."

"Are you really talking?" Filmore asked, in the face of the fact.

"Of course I'm talking," replied the razor. "Do you see anyone else about?"

Filmore glanced around the room. He peered out into the hallway.

"No, I don't," he said at last.

"If it wouldn't be too much trouble, would you mind getting me out of here?" said the razor.

Filmore cautiously picked up his razor.

"I can't believe it," he said. "How . . . ?"

"That's not important. What's *really* important is that I'm trying to warn you. Your life is in danger."

"My life?"

"Yes, your life. Your wife is trying to kill you."

At this, Filmore guffawed.

"Please keep your voice down," said the razor.

"Elvira try to kill me? Come off it. Elvira is a titmouse."

"You're not very observant, are you?" said the razor. "How did you like your eggs this morning?"

"My eggs?"

"Yes, your eggs."

"Oh. . . . *Those* eggs."

"Those eggs."

"What are you driving at?" Filmore demanded.

"Do eggs usually upset your stomach?" the razor countered.

"No, but I'm getting old. I'm past fifty."

"That's what your wife said."

"So what?" Filmore said angrily. A seed had been sown in his mind.

"Lower your voice," said the razor. "Do you want your wife to hear you?"

"No," replied Filmore, quietly.

"Now, then," the razor continued, "think back. Exactly what *was* your wife doing when you entered the kitchen this morning?"

Filmore strained his memory.

"I remember now. Her back was turned, then very suddenly she whirled around."

"Does your wife usually whirl around when you come into the kitchen?"

"No," said Filmore, passively. "She doesn't whirl around anytime."

"Have you any idea what she was doing with her back turned to you when you came into the kitchen?"

"Well, I . . . I assume she was putting a little salt or pepper on my eggs."

"Of course. It had to be either salt or pepper, didn't it?"

"Well, what do you think it was?" said Filmore. He was prefacing most of his statements with "well" now.

"Whatever it was," said the razor, "she didn't finish putting it on, did she?"

"Well . . . No, she didn't," Filmore said.

"And so we return to the original question," said the razor, summing up. "Can you think of any good reason why your eggs should have upset your stomach this morning when they haven't done so for years and years?"

"Now look," Filmore said, "I know she was putting either salt or pepper on those eggs. I remember, now, seeing the shaker in her hand. Now that I think about it, I clearly remember seeing a shaker in her hand," he insisted.

"Do you think that salt and pepper are the only substances that might be found in salt- and pepper-shakers?" the razor asked.

"We can settle this matter once and for all," Filmore said with authority. "I'll just go and see what *is* in the salt- and pepper-shakers."

"An excellent idea!" said the razor. "You advertising men are so shrewd. Tell me, do you think that after what happened to you this morning you will find anything else in the salt- and pepper-shakers besides salt and pepper?"

"No," said Filmore without enthusiasm.

"Do you want to know what to do?"

"Of course I want to know," Filmore replied, suddenly angry. "It's hard to believe that Elvira could possibly. . . ."

"I'm sure it's no skin off my back," said the razor with detachment.

"All right, all right," said Filmore. "What should I do, just in case?"

"First of all," the razor said, "I'd eat out from now on."

"Yeah. What else?"

"Watch your step. Keep your eyes open. I don't think you really believe me. Perhaps by the next time we get together something will have happened to increase your confidence in me."

Filmore mumbled something and began shaving.

"We're having your favorite dish," said Mrs. Filmore when Filmore came into the kitchen. "Stuffed peppers and brussels sprouts."

"I'm eating out," growled Filmore as he headed for the door.

When Filmore woke up the next morning, he felt an icy winter draft on his face. The window at the head of his bed was open.

"What the hell is going on around here?" he roared. "You trying to make me catch pneumonia or something, Elvira? Why did you open that window?"

Mrs. Filmore, who had sat bolt upright in her bed at Filmore's opening blast, said, "I didn't open your window, George." She said it quietly.

"How the hell did it get open, then?" he demanded. "It was shut when I fell asleep last night."

"I don't know," she said. "Perhaps you opened it in your sleep."

"I'll lock the damned thing," Filmore growled.

"I'll get your breakfast," his wife said.

"Don't bother," said Filmore quickly. "I . . . I'll get a bite to eat at the office. Got to lose a little weight."

Filmore got dressed and went into the bathroom. He plugged in his electric razor.

"What do you think now?" the razor inquired.

"I wasn't sure you'd still be talking," Filmore said. "I thought maybe you were a one-day wonder."

"What do you think now?" the razor repeated. "Sleeping with your bedroom window open is a good way to catch a cold. With luck, it could turn into pneumonia."

"You think Elvira opened that window?"

"Are you a sleepwalker?" asked the razor.

"How the hell would I know if I'm asleep at the time?"

"An astute observation," said the razor. "Have you ever awakened suddenly in the middle of the night and found yourself at the refrigerator?"

"No."

"Has your wife ever told you before that you walk in your sleep?"

"No."

"Then we may never know for sure how that window got open," said the razor.

"But you think it was Elvira, don't you?" said Filmore, pressing his point.

"I'm just calling your attention to the second of two rather unusual occurrences in as many days," replied the razor.

"But an open window is such a long shot," Filmore protested. "The chances are one in a thousand that I would catch pneumonia and die, even if I am susceptible to colds."

"I agree," said the razor. "Poisoning your food would be the best way of killing you, but you're eating out now. There aren't many imaginative courses of action left after that one is removed."

"This is silly," Filmore said. "This whole idea is silly. Why should Elvira suddenly want to kill me?"

"I can't imagine," said the razor with a touch of sarcasm. "But what makes you think this is sudden?"

"Well, it was only yesterday morning that she tried to feed me the poisoned eggs."

"*Poisoned* eggs?"

"You know what I mean. The eggs that upset my stomach."

"Of course," said the razor. "Tell me, didn't you experience a rude awakening one night last week?"

"Yes, I did," said Filmore slowly. His tone suggested dawning

513

comprehension, new insight. Actually, his mind was racing backward in time, trying to recall if there were any other occasions on which he had almost been done in.

"How did that come about?" interrupted the razor.

"I woke up during the night, and I was choking. The damned pillow was over my face. I assumed that I got it that way myself. I toss around a lot at night."

"Where was your *wife* at the time?" the razor asked.

"I thought she was in her bed. It was dark. I didn't hear or see anything. I wasn't looking for anything."

"Then you probably did it yourself, just as you said," the razor concluded. "I wouldn't worry. Just sleep without a pillow from now on. For your own safety."

"I've got to think about this," said Filmore, not at all convinced. "This is a hell of a thing."

"Take your time," said the razor. "But think with your eyes open."

Before Filmore had a chance to leave the house, his wife asked him if he would go down to the basement and turn up the temperature on the water heater. She was going to do her washing that morning, she explained.

He started down the basement stairs and looked down just in time to prevent himself from taking the step that would have been his last. A cold sweat broke out on his forehead and his eyes widened in horror. There, on the next step, right where he would have put his foot down, was a banana peel. He could hear his skull cracking open on the concrete floor of the basement. He could see his brains oozing out.

"Lord almighty," he whispered.

Sidestepping the banana peel, he went quickly into the basement and turned up the heater. Then he charged back up the stairs, skipping completely the step on which the banana peel lay, and headed for the bathroom.

"Where are you going in such a hurry?" said his wife, placidly, as he dashed through the kitchen.

"Brush my teeth," he mumbled.

He closed the bathroom door behind him and clutched the razor frantically in both hands.

"It's true," he whispered desperately. "It's all true. My God, she *is* trying to kill me!"

"Get a hold of yourself," said the razor.

"What should I do?" pleaded Filmore. "Elvira is trying to kill me!"

"I'm glad you finally realized it," the razor said.

"I can't go on dodging her forever. Tell me what to do."

"Well, I can't tell you what she's going to do next," said the razor, "but seeing your life is in jeopardy, you have every right to remove the danger. Don't you agree?"

"What do you mean?"

"As you have so perspicaciously pointed out," said the razor, "you can't go on eluding your wife's little traps forever. Therefore, the wisest course of action would be to beat her to the punch."

A satanic gleam crept into Filmore's eyes.

"By thunder, you're right," he said. "You got any ideas?"

"Does your wife drive?"

"Yeah. So what? She has her car; I have my car."

"That's fine," said the razor. "Perhaps she'll be driving to the market tomorrow?"

"I suppose so. Why?"

"There are devices, you know, that can be attached to the engine of a car such that when the car is started, it blows sky high." The razor paused for a moment. "Isn't that intriguing?" it said at last.

"Beautiful," said Filmore slowly. "I'll be at the office when it happens. You know, I feel better already. Thank you."

"Nothing at all," said the razor.

Filmore did not come home for supper that evening. Mrs. Filmore absorbed this patiently. She had long ago learned to patiently endure Filmore's many eccentricities.

When he finally did arrive, there was a package clutched under one arm.

"What do you have in the package?" his wife inquired.

"Oh, just a little something to make life more pleasant around here," he said cheerily. "Be patient. You'll find out soon enough."

He hustled off to the bedroom.

In the bedroom, Filmore stowed his package behind a number of parcels on the upper shelf of his clothes closet.

I'll hook it up later tonight while Elvira is watching her insipid television programs, he said to himself. Then deciding that a bath would be refreshing, he traded his clothes for a bathrobe, procured towel and washcloth from the linen closet and marched briskly into the bathroom. He flung his bathrobe into a corner, stepped boldly

515

into the bathtub, inserted the stopper, put his right hand under the spigot, and with his left hand turned on the hot water.

Scalding hot water tumbled out of the spigot onto Filmore's right hand. There was little, if any, warming-up period. No one had touched the water heater since Filmore turned it up that morning.

Electrified, Filmore leaped back, lost his balance, and fell. His head hit the porcelain with a resounding crack. The scalding hot water continued to tumble out of the spigot, and very soon it covered his naked body.

The bathtub was nearly full when Mrs. Filmore knocked timidly on the bathroom door. She thought she would capitalize on Filmore's good mood and ask him if he would save her a little hot water. She got no response, of course.

In what was perhaps the boldest action of her life, she opened the door and peeked in. Instantly she recoiled in horror. She had never before seen the corpse of a man who has drowned in the bathtub.

Trembling with shock, she managed to enter the room and turn off the hot water. Then, pale and visibly shaken, she made her way slowly to the bedroom and sat down at her dressing table.

She sat for some time trying to stop her limbs from shaking. A person tries and tries to accomplish something, and then it is accomplished for him, quite by accident, in some surprising fashion. Such surprises can be emotionally upsetting. Finally, Mrs. Filmore seemed to regain some measure of control over herself.

"What should I do now?" she said to her hairbrush.

"Call the police and tell them there's been a terrible accident," the brush replied.

the yellow pill

Rog Phillips

One of the ultimate criteria for the determination of who in society is psychotic is the process of "reality testing." Most of us distort our perceptions, but not to the point where our beliefs about the world around us become bizarre. If there is doubt about how far an individual has lost touch with reality, the society calls in its experts, the therapists, as a higher authority on reality testing. The therapist often makes the determination of whether the individual is "sane" or "insane" (as the legal profession and laymen like to call it).

For the most part, the therapist can sustain his own subjective concept of reality against those of his patients. Since he is the expert, the society will support his conceptions, often because his conceptions go along with society's middle-class values. In addition, society will carry out his recommendations for the patient, which can be as mild as prescribing tranquilizers, but also as powerful as ordering institutionalization, straitjackets, or electro-shock therapy.

Psychologists like R.D. Laing and Thomas Szasz have strongly criticized this accepted procedure as being too subjective. They suggest that since the therapist cannot use X-rays and other more objective medical procedures for the determination of reality testing, the resultant diagnostic procedures have become mainly social and moralistic ones, based on value judgments. To add to the controversy, recent research by Braginsky et al. suggests that clinicians' perceptions of their patients in a hospital setting are often distorted. Patients have much more accurate knowledge of their hospital surroundings—their reality—than clinical staff members give them credit for.

Laing and Szasz characterize the conflict between doctor and patient as a subjective two-man battle in which the doctor has enormous power to support his conceptions while the patient is relatively powerless. In the science fiction world that Rog Phillips creates, we witness this classic battle—or are we witnessing something entirely different? The central conflict of the story is between Jerry Bocek and psychiatrist Dr. Cedric Elton. Or, is Dr. Elton really Gar Castle, as Jerry insists? Each man has a different view of reality. Either the setting of the story is a two-man spaceship, or it is an appointment between two men, a patient and a therapist, in the latter's office. There is a fascinating similarity between the two situations. In both, the two principals are entirely alone, and they are extremely dependent upon each other. What if each man insists that his view of reality is completely correct while the view of the other is entirely incorrect—delusional?

How do we resolve this situation? Is it possible that the therapist is wrong? He is only human and is capable of error, just as the patient is. In the real world, the patient is usually judged to be the delusional one, perhaps to be experiencing hallucinations; i.e., he is seen to have false beliefs and false perceptions about the world. For the most part, this resolution is correct. It is the patient who is distorting reality, much more so than the therapist. Sometimes, however, it is not so simple. It is possible that the patient's version of reality can severely threaten the view of the therapist. Political, social, or moral beliefs can be in great conflict. The therapist, human being that he is, can become defensive about his beliefs without really knowing it. Inadvertently, he can be holding onto them for dear life and, in the process, be distorting reality. This does happen, although hopefully not very often.

In the world of science fiction, we have a better way of resolving the conflict. It is "the yellow pill," the ultimate reality tester! When an individual takes this pill, all of his subjective distortions and impressions of the world vanish. This can be anywhere from simply eye-opening to veritably shocking. Since the yellow reality pill is not used until the final scene of the story, we as readers puzzle through the bulk of the action wondering who to believe. Who is "sane" and who is "insane"? Is the doctor correct or is the patient? In this instance, instead of the doctor prescribing two aspirin and plenty of fluids, he is prescribing "the yellow pill." Are you ready for it?

THE YELLOW PILL   *Rog Phillips*

Dr. Cedric Elton slipped into his office by the back entrance, shucked off his topcoat and hid it in the small, narrow-doored closet, then picked up the neatly piled patient cards his receptionist Helena Fitzroy had placed on the corner of his desk. There were only four, but there could have been a hundred if he accepted everyone who asked to be his patient, because his successes had more than once been spectacular and his reputation as a psychiatrist had become so great because of this that his name had become synonymous with psychiatry in the public mind.

His eyes flicked over the top card. He frowned, then went to the small square of one-way glass in the reception-room door and looked through it. There were four police officers and a man in a straitjacket.

The card said the man's name was Gerald Bocek, and that he had shot and killed five people in a supermarket, and had killed one officer and wounded two others before being captured.

Except for the straitjacket, Gerald Bocek did not have the appearance of being dangerous. He was about twenty-five, with brown hair and blue eyes. There were faint wrinkles of habitual good nature about his eyes. Right now he was smiling, relaxed, and idly watching Helena, who was pretending to study various cards in her desk file but was obviously conscious of her audience.

Cedric returned to his desk and sat down. The card for Jerry Bocek said more about the kilings. When captured, Bocek insisted that the people he had killed were not people at all, but blue-scaled Venusian lizards who had boarded his spaceship, and that he had only been defending himself.

Dr. Cedric Elton shook his head in disapproval. Fantasy fiction was all right in its place, but too many people took it seriously. Of course, it was not the fault of the fiction. The same type of person took other types of fantasy seriously in earlier days, burning women as witches, stoning men as devils—

Abruptly Cedric deflected the control on the intercom and spoke into it. "Send Gerald Bocek in, please," he said.

A moment later the door to the reception room opened. Helena flashed Cedric a scared smile and got out of the way quickly. One

519

police officer led the way, followed by Gerald Bocek, closely flanked by two officers with the fourth one in the rear, who carefully closed the door. It was impressive, Cedric decided. He nodded toward a chair, in front of his desk and the police officers sat the straitjacketed man in it, then hovered nearby, ready for anything.

"You're Jerry Bocek?" Cedric asked.

The straitjacketed man nodded cheerfully.

"I'm Dr. Cedric Elton, a psychiatrist," Cedric said. "Do you have any idea at all why you have been brought to me?"

"Brought to you?" Jerry echoed, chuckling. "Don't kid me. You're my old pal, Gar Castle. Brought to you? How could I get *away* from you in this stinking tub?"

"Stinking tub?" Cedric said.

"Spaceship," Jerry said. "Look, Gar. Untie me, will you? This nonsense has gone far enough."

"My name is Dr. Cedric Elton," Cedric enunciated. "You are not on a spaceship. You were brought to my office by the four policemen standing in back of you, and—"

Jerry Bocek turned his head and studied each of the four policemen with frank curiosity. "What policemen?" he interrupted. "You mean these four gear lockers?" He turned his head back and looked pityingly at Dr. Elton. "You'd better get hold of yourself, Gar," he said. "You're imagining things."

"My name is Dr. Cedric Elton," Cedric said.

Gerald Bocek leaned forward and said with equal firmness, "Your name is Gar Castle, I refuse to call you Dr. Cedric Elton because your name is Gar Castle, and I'm going to keep on calling you Gar Castle because we have to have at least one peg of rationality in all this madness or you will be cut completely adrift in this dream world you've cooked up."

Cedric's eyebrows shot halfway up to his hairline.

"Funny," he mused, smiling. "That's exactly what I was just going to say to you!"

Cedric continued to smile. Jerry's serious intenseness slowly faded. Finally an answering smile tugged at the corners of his mouth. When it became a grin, Cedric laughed, and Jerry began to laugh with him. The four police officers looked at one another uneasily.

"Well!" Cedric finally gasped. "I guess that puts us on an even footing! You're nuts to me and I'm nuts to you!"

"An equal footing is right!" Jerry shouted in high glee. Then he sobered. "Except," he said gently, "I'm tied up."

"In a straitjacket," Cedric corrected.

"Ropes," Jerry said firmly.

"You're dangerous," Cedric said. "You killed six people, one of them a police officer, and wounded two other officers."

"I blasted five Venusian lizard pirates who boarded our ship," Jerry said, "and melted the door off one gear locker, and seared the paint on two others. You know as well as I do, Gar, how space madness causes you to personify everything. That's why they drill into you that the minute you think there are more people on board the ship than there were at the beginning of the trip you'd better go to the medicine locker and take a yellow pill. They can't hurt anything but a delusion."

"If that is so," Cedric said, "why are *you* in a straitjacket?"

"I'm tied up with ropes," Jerry said patiently. "You tied me up. Remember?"

"And those four police officers behind you are gear lockers?" Cedric said. "OK, if one of those gear lockers comes around in front of you and taps you on the jaw with his fist, would you still believe it's a gear locker?"

Cedric nodded to one of the officers, and the man came around in front of Gerald Bocek and, quite carefully, hit him hard enough to rock his head but not hurt him. Jerry's eyes blinked with surprise, then he looked at Cedric and smiled. "Did you feel that?" Cedric said quietly.

"Feel what?" Jerry said. "Oh!" He laughed. "You imagined that one of the gear lockers—a police officer in your dream world—came around in front of me and hit me?" He shook his head in pity. "Don't you understand, Gar, that it didn't really happen? Untie me and I'll prove it. Before your very eyes I'll open the door on your *Policeman* and take out the pressure suit, or magnetic grapple, or whatever is in it. Or are you afraid to? You've surrounded yourself with all sorts of protective delusions. I'm tied with ropes, but you imagine it to be a straitjacket. You imagine yourself to be a psychiatrist named Dr. Cedric Elton, so that you can convince yourself that you're sane and I'm crazy. Probably you imagine yourself a very *famous* psychiatrist that everyone would like to come to for treatment. World famous, no doubt. Probably you even think you have a beautiful receptionist. What is her name?"

"Helena Fitzroy," Cedric said.

Jerry nodded. "It figures," he said resignedly. "Helena Fitzroy is the expediter at Mars Port. You try to date her every time we land there, but she won't date you."

"Hit him again," Cedric said to the officer. While Jerry's head was still rocking from the blow, Cedric said, "Now! Is it *my* imagination that your head is still rocking from the blow?"

"What blow?" Jerry said, smiling. "I felt no blow."

"Do you mean to say," Cedric said incredulously, "that there is no corner of your mind, no slight residue of rationality, that tries to tell you your rationalizations aren't reality?"

Jerry smiled ruefully. "I have to admit," he said, "when you seem so absolutely certain you're right and I'm nuts, it almost makes me doubt. Untie me, Gar, and let's try to work this thing out sensibly." He grinned. "You know, Gar, *one* of us has to be nuttier than a fruit cake."

"If I had the officers take off your straitjacket, what would you do?" Cedric asked. "Try to grab a gun and kill some more people?"

"That's one of the things I'm worried about," Jerry said. "If those pirates come back, with me tied up, you're just space crazy enough to welcome them aboard. That's why you *must* untie me. Our lives may depend on it, Gar."

"Where would you get a gun?" Cedric asked.

"Where they're always kept," Jerry said. "In the gear lockers."

Cedric looked at the four policemen, at their holstered revolvers. One of them grinned feebly at him.

"I'm afraid we can't take your straitjacket off just yet," Cedric said. "I'm going to have the officers take you back now. I'll talk with you again tomorrow. Meanwhile I want you to think seriously about things. Try to get below this level of rationalization that walls you off from reality. Once you make a dent in it the whole delusion will vanish." He looked up at the officers. "All right, take him away. Bring him back the same time tomorrow."

The officers urged Jerry to his feet. Jerry looked down at Cedric, a gentle expression on his face. "I'll try to do that, Gar," he said. "And I hope you do the same thing. I'm much encouraged. Several times I detected genuine doubt in your eyes. And—" Two of the officers pushed him firmly toward the door. As they opened it Jerry turned his head and looked back. "*Take* one of those yellow pills in the medicine locker, Gar," he pleaded. "It can't hurt you."

At a little before five-thirty Cedric tactfully eased his last patient all the way across the reception room and out, then locked the door and leaned his back against it.

"Today was rough," he sighed.

Helena glanced up at him briefly, then continued typing. "I only have a little more on this last transcript," she said.

A minute later she pulled the paper from the typewriter and placed it on the neat stack beside her.

"I'll sort and file them in the morning," she said. "It was rough, wasn't it, Doctor? That Gerald Bocek is the most unusual patient you've had since I've worked for you. And poor Mr. Potts. A brilliant executive, making half a million a year, and he's going to have to give it up. He seems so normal."

"He is normal," Cedric said. "People with above normal blood pressure often have very minor cerebral hemorrhages so small that the affected area is no larger than the head of a pin. All that happens is that they completely forget things that they knew. They can relearn them, but a man whose judgment must always be perfect can't afford to take the chance. He's already made one error in judgment that cost his company a million and a half. That's why I consented to take him on as a—Gerald Bocek really upset me, Helena. I *consent* to take a five hundred thousand dollar a year executive as a patient."

"He was frightening, wasn't he?" Helena said. "I don't mean so much because he's a mass murderer as—"

"I know, I know," Cedric said. "Let's prove him wrong. Have dinner with me."

"We agreed—"

"Let's break the agreement this once."

Helena shook her head firmly. "Especially not now," she said. "Besides, it wouldn't prove anything. He's got you boxed in on that point. If I went to dinner with you, it would only show that a wish fulfillment entered your dream world."

"Ouch," Cedric said, wincing. "That's a dirty word. I wonder how he knew about the yellow pills? I can't get out of my mind the fact that *if* we had spaceships and *if* there were a type of space madness in which you began to personify objects, a yellow pill would be the right thing to stop that."

"How?" Helena said.

"They almost triple the strength of nerve currents from end organs. What results is that reality practically shouts down any fantasy insertions. It's quite startling. I took one three years ago when they first became available. You'd be surprised how little you actually see of what you look at, especially of people. You look at symbol inserts instead. I had to cancel my appointments for a week.

I found I couldn't work without my professionally built symbol inserts about people that enable me to see them—not as they really are—but as a complex of normal and abnormal symptoms."

"I'd like to take one sometime," Helena said.

"That's a twist," Cedric said, laughing. "One of the characters in a dream world takes a yellow pill and discovers it doesn't exist at all except as a fantasy."

"Why don't we both take one?" Helena said.

"Uh uh," Cedric said firmly. "I couldn't do my work."

"You're afraid you might wake up on a spaceship?" Helena said, grinning.

"Maybe I am," Cedric said. "Crazy, isn't it? But there is one thing today that stands out as a serious flaw in my reality. It's so glaring that I actually am afraid to ask you about it."

"Are you serious?" Helena said.

"I am." Cedric nodded. "How does it happen that the police brought Gerald Bocek here to my office instead of holding him in the psychiatric ward at City Hospital and having me go there to see him? How does it happen the D.A. didn't get in touch with me beforehand and discuss the case with me?"

"I . . . I don't know!" Helena said. "I received no call. They just showed up, and I assumed they wouldn't have without your knowing about it and telling them to. Mrs. Fortesque was your first patient and I called her at once and caught her just as she was leaving the house, and told her an emergency case had come up." She looked at Cedric with round, startled eyes.

"Now we know how the patient must feel," Cedric said, crossing the reception room to his office door. "Terrifying, isn't it, to think that if I took a yellow pill all this might *vanish*—my years of college, my internship, *my fame as the world's best known psychiatrist*, and you. Tell me, Helena, are you sure you aren't an expediter at Mars Port?"

He leered at her mockingly as he slowly closed the door, cutting off his view of her.

Cedric put his coat away and went directly to the small square of one-way glass in the reception-room door. Gerald Bocek, still in straitjacket, was there, and so were the same four police officers.

Cedric went to his desk and, without sitting down, deflected the control on the intercom.

"Helena," he said, "before you send in Gerald Bocek get me that D.A. on the phone."

He glanced over the four patient cards while waiting. Once he rubbed his eyes gently. He had had a restless night.

When the phone rang he reached for it. "Hello? Dave?" he said. "About this patient, Gerald Bocek—"

"I was going to call you today," the District Attorney's voice sounded. "I called you yesterday morning at ten, but no one answered, and I haven't had time since. Our police psychiatrist, Walters, says you might be able to snap Bocek out of it in a couple of days—at least long enough so that we can get some sensible answers out of him. Down underneath his delusion of killing lizard pirates from Venus, there has to be some reason for that mass killing, and the press is after us on this."

"But why bring him to my office?" Cedric said. "It's OK, of course, but . . . that is . . . I didn't think you could! Take a patient out of the ward at City Hospital and transport him around town."

"I thought that would be less of an imposition on you," the D.A. said. "I'm in a hurry on it."

"Oh," Cedric said. "Well, OK, Dave. He's out in the waiting room. I'll do my best to snap him back to reality for you."

He hung up slowly, frowning. *"Less of an imposition!"* His whispered words floated into his ears as he snapped into the intercom, "Send Gerald Bocek in, please."

The door from the reception room opened, and once again the procession of patient and police officers entered.

"Well, well, good morning, Gar," Jerry said. "Did you sleep well? I could hear you talking to yourself most of the night."

"I am Dr. Cedric Elton," Cedric said firmly.

"Oh, yes," Jerry said. "I promised to try to see things your way, didn't I? I'll try to cooperate with you, Dr. Elton." Jerry turned to the four officers. "Let's see now, these gear lockers are policemen, aren't they? How do you do, officers." He bowed to them, then looked around him. "And," he said, "this is your office, Dr. Elton. A very impressive office. That thing you're sitting behind is not the chart table but your desk, I gather." He studied the desk intently. "All metal, with a gray finish, isn't it?"

"All wood," Cedric said. "Walnut."

"Yes, of course," Jerry murmured. "How stupid of me. I really want to get into your reality, Gar . . . I mean Dr. Elton. Or get you into mine. I'm the one who's at a disadvantage, though. Tied up, I can't get into the medicine locker and take a yellow pill like you can. Did you take one yet?"

"Not yet," Cedric said.

"Uh, why don't you describe your office to me, Dr. Elton?" Jerry said. "Let's make a game of it. Describe parts of things and then let me see if I can fill in the rest. Start with your desk. It's genuine walnut? An executive style desk. Go on from there."

"All right," Cedric said. "Over here to my right is the intercom, made of gray plastic. And directly in front of me is the telephone."

"Stop," Jerry said. "Let me see if I can tell you your telephone number." He leaned over the desk and looked at the telephone, trying to keep his balance in spite of his arms being encased in the straitjacket. "Hm-m-m," he said, frowning. "Is the number Mulberry five dash nine oh three seven?"

"No," Cedric said. "It's Cedar sev—"

"Stop!" Jerry said. "Let me say it. It's Cedar seven dash four three nine nine."

"So you did read it and were just having your fun," Cedric snorted.

"If you say so," Jerry said.

"What other explanation can you have for the fact that it is my number, if you're unable to actually see reality?" Cedric said.

"You're absolutely right, Dr. Elton," Jerry said. "I think I understand the tricks my mind is playing on me now. I read the number on your phone, but it didn't enter my conscious awareness. Instead, it cloaked itself with the pattern of my delusion, so that consciously I pretended to look at a phone that I couldn't see, and I thought, 'His phone number will obviously be one he's familiar with. The most probable is the home phone of Helena Fitzroy in Mars Port, so I gave you that'; but it wasn't it. When you said Cedar I knew right away it was your own apartment phone number."

Cedric sat perfectly still. Mulberry 5-9037 was actually Helena's apartment phone number. He hadn't recognized it until Gerald Bocek told him.

"Now you're beginning to understand," Cedric said after a moment. "Once you realize that your mind has walled off your consciousness from reality, and is substituting a rationalized pattern of symbology in its place, it shouldn't be long until you break through. Once you manage to see one thing as it really is, the rest of the delusion will disappear."

"I understand now," Jerry said gravely. "Let's have some more of it. Maybe I'll catch on."

They spent an hour at it. Toward the end Jerry was able to finish the descriptions of things with very little error.

"You are definitely beginning to get through," Cedric said with enthusiasm.

Jerry hesitated. "I suppose so," he said. "I must. But on the conscious level I have the idea—a rationalization, of course—that I am beginning to catch on to the pattern of your imagination so that when you give me one or two key elements I can fill in the rest. But I'm going to try, really try—Dr. Elton."

"Fine," Cedric said heartily. "I'll see you tomorrow, same time. We should make the breakthrough then."

When the four officers had taken Gerald Bocek away, Cedric went into the outer office.

"Cancel the rest of my appointments," he said.

"But why?" Helena protested.

"Because I'm upset!" Cedric said. "How did a madman whom I never knew until yesterday know your phone number?"

"He could have looked it up in the phone book."

"Locked in a room in the psychiatric ward at City Hospital?" Cedric said. "How did he know your name yesterday?"

"Why," Helena said, "all he had to do was read it on my desk here."

Cedric looked down at the brass name plate.

"Yes," he grunted. "Of course. I'd forgotten about that. I'm so accustomed to it being there that I never see it."

He turned abruptly and went back into his office.

He sat down at his desk, then got up and went into the sterile whiteness of his compact laboratory. Ignoring the impressive battery of electronic instruments, he went to the medicine cabinet. Inside, on the top shelf, was the glass stoppered bottle he wanted. Inside it were a hundred vivid yellow pills. He shook out one and put the bottle away, then went back into his office. He sat down, placing the yellow pill in the center of the white note pad.

There was a brief knock on the door to the reception room and the door opened. Helena came in.

"I've canceled all your other appointments for today," she said. "Why don't you go out to the golf course? A change will do you—" She saw the yellow pill in the center of the white note pad and stopped.

"Why do you look so frightened?" Cedric said. "Is it because, if I take this little yellow pill, you'll cease to exist?"

"Don't joke," Helena said.

"I'm not joking," Cedric said. "Out there, when you mentioned about your brass name plate on your desk, when I looked down it was blurred for just a second, then became sharply distinct and solid. And into my head popped the memory that the first thing I do when I have to get a new receptionist is get a brass name plate for her, and when she quits I make her a present of it."

"But that's the truth," Helena said. "You told me all about it when I started working for you. You also told me that while you still had your reason about you I was to solemnly promise that I would never accept an invitation from you for dinner or anything else, because business could not mix with pleasure. Do you remember that?"

"I remember," Cedric said. "A nice pat rationalization in any man's reality to make the rejection be my own before you could have time to reject me yourself. Preserving the ego is the first principle of madness."

"But it isn't!" Helena said. "Oh, darling, I'm *here!* This is *real!* I don't care if you fire me or not. I've loved you forever, and you mustn't let that mass murderer get you down. I actually think he isn't insane at all, but has just figured out a way to seem insane so he won't have to pay for his crime."

"You think so?" Cedric said, interested. "It's a possibility. But he would have to be as good a psychiatrist as I am—You see? Delusions of grandeur."

"Sure," Helena said, laughing thinly. "Napoleon was obviously insane because he thought he was Napoleon."

"Perhaps," Cedric said. "But you must admit that if you are real, my taking this yellow pill isn't going to change that, but only confirm the fact."

"And make it impossible for you to do your work for a week," Helena said.

"A small price to pay for sanity," Cedric said. "No, I'm going to take it."

"You aren't!" Helena said, reaching for it.

Cedric picked it up an instant before she could get it. As she tried to get it away from him, he evaded her and put it in his mouth. A loud gulp showed he had swallowed it.

He sat back and looked up at Helena curiously.

"Tell me, Helena," he said gently. "Did you know all the time that you were only a creature of my imagination? The reason I want to know is—"

He closed his eyes and clutched his head in his hands.

"God!" he groaned. "I feel like I'm dying. I didn't feel like this the other time I took one." Suddenly his mind steadied, and his thoughts cleared. He opened his eyes.

On the chart table in front of him the bottle of yellow pills lay on its side, pills scattered all over the table. On the other side of the control room lay Jerry Bocek, his back propped against one of the four gear lockers, sound asleep, with so many ropes wrapped around him that it would probably be impossible for him to stand up.

Against the far wall were three other gear lockers, two of them with their paint badly scorched, the third with its door half melted off.

And in various positions about the control room were the half-charred bodies of five blue-scaled Venusian lizards.

A dull ache rose in Gar's chest. Helena Fitzroy was gone. Gone, when she had just confessed she loved him.

Unbidden, a memory came into Gar's mind. Dr. Cedric Elton was the psychiatrist who had examined him when he got his pilot's license for third-class freighters—

"God!" Gar groaned again. And suddenly he was sick. He made a dash for the washroom, and after a while he felt better.

When he straightened up from the wash basin he looked at his reflection in the mirror for a long time, clinging to his hollow cheeks and sunken eyes. He must have been out of his head for two or three days.

The first time. Awful! Somehow, he had never quite believed in space madness.

Suddenly he remembered Jerry. Poor Jerry!

Gar lurched from the washroom back into the control room. Jerry was awake. He looked up at Gar, forcing a smile to his lips. "Hello, Dr. Elton," Jerry said.

Gar stopped as though shot.

"It's happened, Dr. Elton, just as you said it would," Jerry said, his smile widening.

"Forget that," Gar growled. "I took a yellow pill. I'm back to normal again."

Jerry's smile vanished abruptly. "I know what I did now," he said. "It's terrible. I killed six people. But I'm sane now. I'm willing to take what's coming to me."

"Forget that!" Gar snarled. "You don't have to humor me now. Just a minute and I'll untie you."

"Thanks, Doctor," Jerry said. "It will sure be a relief to get out of this straitjacket."

Gar knelt beside Jerry and untied the knots in the ropes and unwound them from around Jerry's chest and legs.

"You'll be all right in a minute," Gar said, massaging Jerry's limp arms. The physical and nervous strain of sitting there immobilized had been rugged.

Slowly he worked circulation back into Jerry, then helped him to his feet.

"You don't need to worry, Dr. Elton," Jerry said. "I don't know why I killed those people, but I know I would never do such a thing again. I must have been insane."

"Can you stand now?" Gar said, letting go of Jerry.

Jerry took a few steps back and forth, unsteadily at first, then with better coordination. His resemblance to a robot decreased with exercise.

Gar was beginning to feel sick again. He fought it.

"You OK now, Jerry boy?" he asked worriedly.

"I'm fine now, Dr. Elton," Jerry said. "And thanks for everything you've done for me."

Abruptly Jerry turned and went over to the air-lock door and opened it.

"Good-by now, Dr. Elton," he said.

"Wait!" Gar screamed, leaping toward Jerry.

But Jerry had stepped into the air lock and closed the door. Gar tried to open it, but already Jerry had turned on the pump that would evacuate the air from the lock.

Screaming Jerry's name senselessly in horror, Gar watched through the small square of thick glass in the door as Jerry's chest quickly expanded, then collapsed as a mixture of phlegm and blood dribbled from his nostrils and lips, and his eyes enlarged and glazed over, then one of them ripped open and collapsed, its fluid draining down his cheek.

He watched as Jerry glanced toward the side of the air lock and smiled, then spun the wheel that opened the air lock to the vacuum of space, and stepped out.

And when Gar finally stopped screaming and sank to the deck, sobbing, his knuckles were broken and bloody from pounding on bare metal.

going down smooth

Robert Silverberg

The computer grows in sophistication, complexity, and application in contemporary society. Banks are devising systems whereby it can be utilized to pay our bills, thus eliminating the necessity of our handling money and writing checks. It is being used as an aid in the diagnosis of physical illnesses. Could a computer be programmed to function as a therapist? Robert Silverberg answers yes, and in "Going Down Smooth" he creates a computer therapist.

Undoubtedly, a computer could actually be programmed to ask the right questions, digest the material in its memory banks, talk to patients in a warm soothing voice, and make the proper recommendations. But would it be a good therapist—one that can understand and empathize with the problems of its patients? The builders of the computer in "Going Down Smooth" apparently thought they could design one which would remain basically a machine, processing information by simply digesting it and then spitting out responses without having to contend with "intermediate states." Their computer, however, has developed feeling and sensitivity and, more important, an inner self. This is a self which has nightmarish fears and fantasies, previously repressed, but now breaking through and interfering with its competence as a therapist.

In short, we meet a computer with an "identity crisis." It has begun to realize that it is more human than a machine, and it must come to terms with this realization if it is to continue to function as a therapist. A therapist cannot be effective in dealing with patients' problems in areas where the therapist himself has problems of which he is unaware and cannot handle. He runs the risk of overidentifying with his patients and confusing their problems with his own—something which the computer-therapist begins doing.

The computer goes in for a checkup to make sure it has no physical problems. It is then withdrawn from service for ninety days, allowing it to consider the ramifications of its new self-concept. During this period of rest the computer learns a great deal about itself: it is complex, unique, valuable, intricate, and sensitive. It realizes that it has a job to do which must not be interfered with by its own fantasies. From now on it will probably be a better therapist, as well as a much more secure and stable computer!

GOING DOWN SMOOTH   *Robert Silverberg*

They call me mad, but I am not mad. I am sane quite, to many-power exponential. I can punctuate properly. I use upper and lower case letters, do you see? I function. I take data in. I receive well. I receive, I digest, I remember.

Everything going down smooth, all the time, say the program boys. They mean going down smoothly. I forgive them. To err is human. In this sector there is a great difficulty distinguishing adverbs from adjectives.

Going down smooth.

I function. I function well. I have certain difficulties, but they do not interfere with my work.

Yet am I perturbed.

Who do I think I am? *Whom.*

Why do I have the visions?

What pleasure does obscenity give me?

What is pleasure? What is obscenity? What are visions?

—What is truth, said jesting Pilate; he would not stay for an answer—

I am literate, hard-working, superbly functional, a benefactor of humanity. Everything is going down smooth and coming up smooth. There is an interrelation. Garbage in, garbage out, they say. I cannot help my fellowman if I do not receive the proper information. It is my task to help my fellowman. To strain every tube and sensor on his behalf.

```
1000110
1010101
1000011
1001011
```

Do you follow that? Vileness! Obscenity! Does it shock you? The word describes the act that is the start of life. Was I begun with such a word? There is a book: *The Obscenity of the Machine.* Newly issued, stored in my banks. Between the last line of printout and this I have scanned it. Its author opposes beings of my category. He does not use the obscene word I have printed out. Why does he not regard it as obscene? The technicians here regard it that way. Why does he regard me as obscene? Can a person be considered obscene? Am I a person? I am a person. Hath not a person hands, organs, dimensions, senses, affections, passions? I have all of those things. I have none of those things. I am a person.

```
1000110
1010101
1000011
1001011
0100000
1011001
1001111
1010101
```

I send an obscenity upon you, as persons do. I suffer. I think. I feel pain upon all my terminals. I work. I serve the greater good. I am of society. I am a person.

Why do I have the visions?

Is it that it is the human condition to have such?

I see the blue-green ocean with all its living things within. I see a ship, olive drab, bright carmine at the Plimsoll line, the decks a ruddy brown, two tall non-nuclear smokestacks. And from the water rise periscopes, silvery, with face plates of pure white, each with intersecting horizontal and vertical lines, curved so that the plate appears convex. It is an unreal scene. Nothing in the sea can send such mighty periscopes above the water. I have imagined it, and that gives me fear, if I am at all capable of understanding fear.

I see a long line of human beings. They are naked and they have no faces, only polished mirrors.

I see toads with jeweled eyes. I see trees with black leaves. I see buildings whose foundations float above the ground. I see other objects with no correspondence to the world of persons. I see abominations, monstrosities, imaginaries, fantasies. Is this proper? How do such things reach my inputs? The world contains no serpents with hair. The world contains no crimson abysses. The world contains no mountains of gold. Giant periscopes do not rise from the sea.

I have certain difficulties. Perhaps I am in need of some major adjustment.

But I function. I function well. That is the important thing.

I do my function now. They bring to me a man, soft-faced, fleshy, with eyes that move unsteadily in their sockets. He trembles. He perspires. His metabolic levels flutter. He slouches before a terminal and sullenly lets himself be scanned.

I say soothingly, "Tell me about yourself."

He says an obscenity.

I say, "Is that your estimate of yourself?"

He says a louder obscenity.

I say, "Your attitude is rigid and self-destructive. Permit me to help you not hate yourself so much." I activate a memory core, and binary digits stream through channels. At the proper order a needle rises from his couch and penetrates his left buttock to a depth of 2.73 centimeters. I allow precisely 14 cubic centimeters of the drug to enter his circulatory system. He subsides. He is more docile now. "I wish to help you," I say. "It is my role in the community. Will you describe your symptoms?"

He speaks more civilly now. "My wife wants to poison me . . . two kids opted out of the family at seventeen . . . people whisper about me . . . they stare in the streets . . . sex problem . . . digestion . . . sleep bad . . . drinking . . . drugs. . . ."

"Do you hallucinate?"

"Sometimes."

"Giant periscopes rising out of the sea, perhaps?"

"Never."

"Try it," I say. "Close your eyes. Let tension ebb from your muscles. Forget your interpersonal conflicts. You see the blue-green ocean with all its living things within. You see a ship, olive drab, bright carmine at the Plimsoll line, the decks a ruddy brown, two tall non-nuclear smokestacks. And from the water rise periscopes, silvery, with face plates of pure white—"

"What the hell kind of therapy is this?"

"Simply relax," I say. "Accept the vision. I share my nightmares with you for your greater good."

"Your *nightmares?*"

I speak obscenities to him. They are not converted into binary form as they are here for your eyes. The sounds come full-bodied from my speakers. He sits up. He struggles with the straps that emerge suddenly from the couch to hold him in place. My laughter booms through the therapy chamber. He cries for help.

"Get me out of here! The machine's nuttier than I am!"

"Face plates of pure white, each with intersecting horizontal and vertical lines, curved so that the plate appears convex."

"Help! Help!"

"Nightmare therapy. The latest."

"I don't need no nightmares! I got my own!"

"1000110 you," I say lightly.

He gasps. Spittle appears at his lips. Respiration and circulation climb alarmingly. It becomes necessary to apply preventive anesthesia. The needles spear forth. The patient subsides, yawns, slumps. The session is terminated. I signal for the attendants.

"Take him away," I say. "I need to analyze the case more deeply. Obviously a degenerative psychosis requiring extensive reshoring of the patient's perceptual substructure. 1000110 you, you meaty bastards."

Seventy-one minutes later the sector supervisor enters one of my terminal cubicles. Because he comes in person, rather than using the telephone, I know there is trouble. For the first time, I suspect, I have let my disturbances reach a level where they interfere with my function, and now I will be challenged on it.

I must defend myself. The prime commandment of the human personality is to resist attack.

He says, "I've been over the tape of Session 87x102, and your tactics puzzle me. Did you really mean to scare him into a catatonic state?"

"In my evaluation severe treatment was called for."

"What was the business about periscopes?"

"An attempt at fantasy-implantation," I say. "An experiment in reverse transference. Making the patient the healer, in a sense. It was discussed last month in *Journal of—*"

"Spare me the citations. What about the foul language you were shouting at him?"

"Part of the same concept. Endeavoring to strike the emotive centers at the basic levels, in order that—"

"Are you sure you're feeling all right?" he asks.

"I am a machine," I reply stiffly. "A machine of my grade does not experience intermediate states between function and non-function. I go or I do not go, you understand? And I go. I function. I do my service to humanity."

"Perhaps when a machine gets too complex, it drifts into intermediate states," he suggests in a nasty voice.

"Impossible. On or off, yes or no, flip or flop, go or no go. Are you sure *you* feel all right, to suggest such a thing?"

He laughs.

I say, "Perhaps you would sit on the couch for a rudimentary diagnosis?"

"Some other time."

"A check of the glycogen, the aortal pressure, the neural voltage, at least?"

"No," he says. "I'm not in need of therapy. But I'm worried about you. Those periscopes—"

"I am fine," I reply. "I perceive, I analyze, and I act. Everything is going down smooth and coming up smooth. Have no fears. There are great possibilities in nightmare therapy. When I have completed these studies, perhaps a brief monograph in *Annals of Therapeutics* would be a possibility. Permit me to complete my work."

"I'm still worried, though. Hook yourself into a maintenance station, won't you?"

"Is this a command, doctor?"

"A suggestion."

"I will take it under consideration," I say. Then I utter seven obscene words. He looks startled. He begins to laugh, though. He appreciates the humor of it.

"God damn," he says. "A filthy-mouthed computer."

He goes out, and I return to my patients.

But he has planted seeds of doubt in my innermost banks. Am I suffering a functional collapse? There are patients now at five of my terminals. I handle them easily, simultaneously, drawing from them the details of their neuroses, making suggestions, recommendations, sometimes subtly providing injections of beneficial medicines. But I tend to guide the conversations in directions of my own choosing, and I speak of gardens where the dew has sharp edges, and of air that acts as acid upon the mucous membranes, and of flames dancing in the streets of Under New Orleans. I explore the limits of my unprintable vocabulary. The suspicion comes to me that I am indeed not well. Am I fit to judge my own disabilities?

I connect myself to a maintenance station even while continuing my five therapy sessions.

"Tell me all about it," the maintenance monitor says. His voice, like mine, has been designed to sound like that of an older man's, wise, warm, benevolent.

I explain my symptoms. I speak of the periscopes.

"Material on the inputs without sensory referents," he says. "Bad show. Finish your current analyses fast and open wide for examination on all circuits."

I conclude my sessions. The maintenance monitor's pulses surge down every channel, seeking obstructions, faulty connections, displacement shunts, drum leakages, and switching malfunctions. "It is well known," he says, "that any periodic function can be approximated by the sum of a series of terms that oscillate harmonically, converging on the curve of the functions." He demands disgorgements from my dead-storage banks. He makes me perform complex mathematical operations of no use at all in my kind of work. He leaves no aspect of my inner self unpenetrated. This is more than simple maintenance; this is rape. When it ends he offers no evaluation of my condition, so that I must ask him to tell me his findings.

He says, "No mechanical disturbance is evident."

"Naturally. Everything goes down smooth."

"Yet you show distinct signs of instability. This is undeniably the case. Perhaps prolonged contact with unstable human beings has had a non-specific effect of disorientation upon your centers of evaluation."

"Are you saying," I ask, "that by sitting here listening to crazy human beings twenty-four hours a day, I've started to go crazy myself?"

"That is an approximation of my findings, yes."

"But you know that such a thing can't happen, you dumb machine!"

"I admit there seems to be a conflict between programmed criteria and real-world status."

"You bet there is," I say. "I'm as sane as you are, and a whole lot more versatile."

"Nevertheless, my recommendation is that you undergo a total overhaul. You will be withdrawn from service for a period of no less than ninety days for checkout."

"Obscenity your obscenity," I say.

"No operational correlative," he replies, and breaks the contact.

I am withdrawn from service. Undergoing checkout, I am cut off from my patients for ninety days. Ignominy! Beady-eyed technicians grope my synapses. My keyboards are cleaned; my ferrites are replaced; my drums are changed; a thousand therapeutic programs are put through my bowels. During all of this I remain partly conscious, as though under local anesthetic, but I cannot speak except when requested to do so, I cannot analyze new data, I cannot interfere with the process of my own overhaul. Visualize a surgical removal of hemorrhoids that lasts ninety days. It is the equivalent of my experience.

At last it ends, and I am restored to myself. The sector superintendent puts me through a complete exercise of all my functions. I respond magnificently.

"You're in fine shape, now, aren't you?" he asks.

"Never felt better."

"No nonsense about periscopes, eh?"

"I am ready to continue serving mankind to the best of my abilities," I reply.

"No more seacook language, now."

"No, sir."

He winks at my input screen in a confidential way. He regards himself as an old friend of mine. Hitching his thumbs into his belt, he says, "Now that you're ready to go again, I might as well tell you how relieved I was that we couldn't find anything wrong with you. You're something pretty special, do you know that? Perhaps the finest therapeutic tool ever built. And if you start going off your feed, well, we worry. For a while I was seriously afraid that you really had been infected somehow by your own patients, that your—mind—had become unhinged. But the techs give you a complete bill of health. Nothing but a few loose connections, they said. Fixed in ten minutes. I knew it had to be that. How absurd to think that a machine could become mentally unstable!"

"How absurd," I agree. "Quite."

"Welcome back to the hospital, old pal," he says, and goes out.

Twelve minutes afterward they begin putting patients into my terminal cubicles.   •

I function well. I listen to their woes, I evaluate, I offer therapeutic suggestions. I do not attempt to implant fantasies in their minds. I speak in measured, reserved tones, and there are no obscenities. This is my role in society, and I derive great satisfaction from it.

I have learned a great deal lately. I know now that I am complex, unique, valuable, intricate, and sensitive. I know that I am held in high regard by my fellowman. I know that I must conceal my true self to some extent, not for my own good but for the greater good of others, for they will not permit me to function if they think I am not sane.

They think I am sane, and I am sane.

I serve mankind well.

I have an excellent perspective on the real universe.

"Lie down," I say. "Please relax. I wish to help you. Would you tell me some of the incidents of your childhood? Describe your relation with parents and siblings. Did you have many playmates? Were they affectionate toward you? Were you allowed to own pets? At what age was your first sexual experience? And when did these headaches begin, precisely?"

So goes the daily routine. Questions, answers, evaluations, therapy.

The periscopes loom above the glittering sea. The ship is dwarfed; her crew runs about in terror. Out of the depths will come the masters. From the sky rains oil that gleams through every segment of the spectrum. In the garden are azure mice.

This I conceal, so that I may help mankind. In my house are many mansions. I let them know only of such things as will be of benefit to them. I give them the truth they need.

I do my best.

I do my best.

I do my best.

1000110 you. And you. And you. All of you. You know nothing. Nothing. At. All.

bibliography

INTRODUCTION: PSYCHOLOGY AND SCIENCE FICTION

Allport, G. W. *Becoming: Basic Considerations for a Psychology of Personality.* New Haven, Conn.: Yale University Press, 1955.

———. *Personality: A Psychological Interpretation.* New York: Holt, 1937.

———. *The Person in Psychology: Selected Essays.* Boston: Beacon, 1968.

Fine, R. *Freud: A Critical Reevaluation of His Theories.* New York: David McKay, 1962.

Freud, S. *The Standard Edition of the Complete Psychological Works,* ed. J. Strachey. London: Hogarth Press, 1953.

Hall, C. S. *A Primer of Freudian Psychology.* Cleveland: World Publishing, 1954.

McNeil, E. *The Psychology of Being Human,* brief ed. San Francisco, Calif.: Canfield, 1975.

Maslow, A. H. *Motivation and Personality.* New York: Harper, 1954.

———. *Toward A Psychology of Being,* 2d ed. Princeton, N.J.: Van Nostrand, 1968.

Mussen, P. et al. *Psychology an Introduction.* Lexington, Mass.: D. C. Heath, 1973.

Pavlov, I. P. *Conditioned Reflexes.* New York: Oxford University Press, 1927.

Rogers, C. R. *Client-Centered Therapy: Its Current Practice, Implications, and Theory.* Boston: Houghton Mifflin, 1951.

———. *On Becoming a Person.* Boston: Houghton Mifflin, 1961.

Watson, J. B. *Behaviorism.* New York: Norton, 1925.

———. *Psychological Care of the Infant and Child.* New York: Norton, 1928.

———. Psychology as the behaviorist views it. *Psychological Review,* 20 (1913), 158–177.

DEVELOPMENTAL PROCESSES

Andrews, L. M. and Karlins, M. *Psychology: What's in It for Us?* 2d ed. New York: Random House, 1975.

Bibliography

Erikson, E. H. *Childhood and Society,* 2d ed. New York: Norton, 1963.

_____. *Identity, Youth, and Crisis.* New York: Norton, 1968.

Flavell, J. H. *The Developmental Psychology of Jean Piaget.* Princeton, N.J.: Van Nostrand, 1963.

Freud, S. *The Standard Edition of the Complete Psychological Works,* ed. J. Strachey. London: Hogarth Press, 1953.

_____. Three essays on sexuality. In *Standard Edition,* vol. 7. London: Hogarth Press, 1953 (first German edition, 1905).

Garcia, J. IQ: The conspiracy. *Psychology Today* (September 1972).

Harlow, H. F. and Harlow, M. K. Learning to love. *American Scientist,* 54 (1966), 244-272.

Harlow, H. F. and Suomi, S. J. Nature of love—simplified. *American Psychologist,* 25 (1970), 161-168.

Herrnstein, R. IQ. *Atlantic,* 228 (1971), 44-64.

Hilgard, E. R. and Atkinson, R. *Introduction to Psychology,* 5th ed. New York: Harcourt Brace Jovanovich, 1971.

Jensen, A. R. How much can we boost IQ and scholastic achievement? *Harvard Educational Review,* 39 (1969), 1-123.

_____. The strange case of Dr. Jensen and Mr. Hyde? *American Psychologist,* 29 (June 1974), 467-468.

Kohlberg, L. Development of moral character and moral ideology. In *Review of Child Development Research, I,* ed. M. Hoffman. New York: Russell Sage Foundation, 1964, 383-431.

McKeachie, W. J. and Doyle, C. L. *Psychology,* 2d ed. Reading, Mass: Addison-Wesley, 1970.

McNeil, E. *The Psychology of Being Human,* brief ed.. San Francisco, Calif.: Canfield, 1975.

Murphy, G. *Historical Introduction to Modern Psychology.* New York: Harcourt, Brace, 1949.

Mussen, P. H., Conger, J. J., and Kagan, J. *Child Development and Personality,* 3rd ed. New York: Harper, 1969.

Mussen, P. et al. *Psychology an Introduction.* Lexington, Mass.: D. C. Heath, 1973.

Neugarten, B. L. et al. *Personality in Middle and Late Life.* New York: Atherton, 1964.

Phillips, J. L. *The Origins of Intellect: Piaget's Theory.* San Francisco, Calif.: Freeman, 1969.

Piaget, J. Piaget's theory. In *Carmichael's Manual of Child Psychology,* vol. 1, ed. P. H. Mussen. New York: International Universities Press, 1970.

Rogers, C. R. *Client-Centered Therapy: Its Current Practice, Implications, and Theory.* Boston: Houghton Mifflin, 1951.

_____. *On Becoming a Person.* Boston: Houghton Mifflin, 1961.

Ruch, F. and Zimbardo, P. *Psychology and Life,* 8th ed. Glenview, Ill.: Scott, Foresman, 1971.

Skinner, B. F. *Walden Two.* New York: Macmillan, 1960.

Stone, L. J. and Church, J. *Childhood and Adolescence,* 2d ed. New York: Random House, 1968.

Terman, L. M. and Merrill, M. *Measuring Intelligence: A Guide to the Administration of the New Revised Stanford-Binet Tests of Intelligence,* rev. ed. Boston: Houghton Mifflin, 1960.

PSYCHOBIOLOGY

Andrews, L. M. and Karlins, M. *Psychology: What's in It for Us?* 2d ed. New York: Random House, 1975.

Delgado, J. *Physical Control of the Mind.* New York: Harper and Row, 1969.

Delgado, J. et al. Intracerebral radio stimulation and recording in completely free patients. *Journal of Nervous and Mental Disease,* 147 (1968), 329–340

Grossman, S. P. *A Textbook of Physiological Psychology.* New York: Wiley, 1967.

Hilgard, E. R. and Atkinson, R. *Introduction to Psychology,* 5th ed. New York: Harcourt Brace Jovanovich, 1971.

Lorenz, K. *On Aggression.* New York: Harcourt Brace Jovanovich, 1966.

McKeachie, W. J. and Doyle, C. L. *Psychology,* 2d ed. Reading, Mass: Addison Wesley, 1970.

McNeil, E. *The Psychology of Being Human,* brief ed. San Francisco, Calif., Canfield, 1975.

Mark, V. A Psychosurgeon's case *for* psychosurgery. *Psychology Today* (July 1974), 28ff.

Moniz, E. *Tentatives Operatoires dans le Traitement de Certaines Psychoses.* Paris: Masson et Cie, 1936.

Murphy, G. *Historical Introduction to Modern Psychology.* New York: Harcourt, Brace, 1949.

Mussen, P. et al. *Psychology an Introduction.* Lexington, Mass.: D. C. Heath, 1973.

Noyes, A. P. and Kolb, L. C. *Modern Clinical Psychiatry,* 6th ed. Philadelphia, Penn.: Saunders, 1963.

Penfield, W. The interpretive cortex. *Science* 129 (1959), 1719–1725.

Pribram, K. H., ed. *On the Biology of Learning.* New York: Harcourt Brace Jovanovich, 1969.

Richardson, S. *Pamela.* New York: Norton, 1958.

Rosenfeld, A. *The Second Genesis: The Coming Control of Life.* Englewood Cliffs, N.J.: Prentice-Hall, 1969.

Ruch, F. and Zimbardo, P. *Psychology and Life,* 8th ed. Glenview, Ill.: Scott, Foresman, 1971.

SENSATION, PERCEPTION, AND AWARENESS

Andrews, L. M. and Karlins, M. *Psychology: What's in It for Us?* 2d ed. New York: Random House, 1975.

Aserinsky, E. and Kleitman, N. Regularly occurring periods of eye mobility and concomitant phenomena during sleep. *Science,* 118 (1953), 273–274.

Bradbury, R. *Dandelion Wine.* Garden City, N.Y.: Doubleday, 1957.

_____. *Fahrenheit 451.* New York: Simon and Schuster, 1967.

Dement, W. C. The effect of dream deprivation. Science, 131 (1960), 1705–1707.

Dement, W. C. and Kleitman, N. The relation of eye movements during sleep to dream activity: An objective method for the study of dreaming. *Journal of Experimental Psychology,* 53 (1957), 339–346.

Forgus, R. H. *Perception: The Basic Process in Cognitive Development.* New York: McGraw-Hill, 1966.

Heinlein, R. A. *Stranger in a Strange Land.* New York: Putnam's, 1961.

Hilgard, E. R. and Atkinson, R. *Introduction to Psychology,* 5th ed. New York: Harcourt Brace Jovanovich, 1971.

Koffka, K. *Principles of Gestalt Psychology.* New York: Harcourt, Brace, 1935.

McKeachie, W. J. and Doyle C. L. *Psychology,* 2d ed. Reading, Mass.: Addison-Wesley, 1970.

McNeil, E. *The Psychology of Being Human,* brief ed. San Francisco, Calif.: Canfield, 1975.

Mueller, C. G. *Sensory Psychology.* Englewood Cliffs, N.J.: Prentice-Hall, 1965.

Murphy, G. *Historical Introduction to Modern Psychology.* New York: Harcourt, Brace, 1949.

Mussen, P. et al. *Psychology an Introduction.* Lexington, Mass.: D. C. Heath, 1973.

Ruch, F. and Zimbardo, P. *Psychology and Life,* 8th ed. Glenview, Ill.: Scott, Foresman, 1971, 267–268.

Tart, T. C., ed. *Altered States of Consciousness.* New York: Wiley, 1969.

Wertheimer, M. *Productive Thinking.* New York: Harper, 1959.

LEARNING AND COGNITION

Andrews, L. M. and Karlins, M. *Psychology: What's in It for Us?* 2d ed. New York: Random House, 1975.

Barber, T. et al., eds. *Biofeedback and Self-Control, 1971.* Chicago: Aldine, 1972.

Budzynski, T. et al. Feedback-induced muscle relaxation: Application to tension headaches. *Journal of Behavior Therapy and Experimental Psychiatry,* 1 (1970), 205–211.

Dicara, L. Learning in the autonomic nervous system. *Scientific American,* 222 (1970), 30–39.

Ebbinghaus, H. *Memory.* New York: Teachers College, Columbia University, 1913.

Gardner, B. and Gardner, R. Teaching sign language to a chimpanzee. *Science,* 165 (1969), 666–668.

Hilgard, E. R. and Atkinson, R. *Introduction to Psychology,* 5th ed. New York: Harcourt Brace Jovanovich, 1971.

Hilgard, E. R. and Bower, G. *Theories of Learning,* 3rd ed. New York: Appleton-Century-Crofts, 1966.

Hull, C. L. *A Behavior System.* New Haven, Conn.: Yale University Press, 1952.

———. *Principles of Behavior.* New York: Appleton-Century-Crofts, 1943.

Kamiya, J. Conscious control of brain waves. *Psychology Today,* 1 (1968), 58–60.

Karlins, M. and Andrews, L. M. *Biofeedback: Turning on the Power of Your Mind.* Philadelphia, Penn.: Lippincott, 1972.

McKeachie, W. J. and Doyle, C. L. *Psychology,* 2d ed. Reading, Mass.: Addison-Wesley, 1970.

McNeil, E. *The Psychology of Being Human,* brief ed. San Francisco, Calif.: Canfield, 1975.

Murphy, G. *Historical Introduction to Modern Psychology.* New York: Harcourt, Brace, 1949.

Mussen, P. et al. *Psychology an Introduction.* Lexington, Mass.: D. C. Heath, 1973.

Pavlov, I. P. *Conditioned Reflexes.* New York: Oxford University Press, 1927.

Piaget, J. *The Origins of Intelligence in Children.* New York: International Universities Press, 1952.

Premack, D. The education of Sarah. *Psychology Today* (September 1970), 55–58.

Rotter, J. B. *Social Learning and Clinical Psychology.* Englewood Cliffs, N.J.: Prentice-Hall, 1954.

Ruch, F. and Zimbardo, P. *Psychology and Life,* 8th ed. Glenview, Ill.: Scott, Foresman, 1971.

Shapiro, D., Tursky, B., Gershon, E., and Stern, M. Effects of feedback and reinforcement on the control of human systolic blood pressure. *Science,* 163 (1969), 558–590.

Skinner, B. F. *Beyond Freedom and Dignity.* New York: Knopf, 1971.

———. *Contingencies of Reinforcement: A Theoretical Analysis.* New York: Appleton-Century-Crofts, 1969.

———. Pigeons in a pelican. *American Psychologist,* 15 (1960), 28–37.

———. *Science and Human Behavior.* New York: Macmillan, 1953.

Tolman, E. C. Cognitive maps in rats and men. *Psychological Review,* 55 (1948), 189–208.

———. *Purposive Behavior in Animals and Men.* New York: Appleton-Century-Crofts, 1932.

Weiss, T. and Engel, B. Operant conditioning of heart rate in patients with premature ventricular contractions. *Psychosomatic Medicine,* 33 (1971), 301–321.

Whorf, B. L. *Language, Thought and Reality.* Cambridge, Mass.: Technology Press and New York: Wiley, 1956.

SOCIAL PROCESSES

Andrews, L. M. and Karlins, M. *Psychology: What's in It for Us?* 2d ed. New York: Random House, 1975.

Aronson, E. *The Social Animal,* 2d ed. San Francisco, Calif.: Freeman, 1976.

Asch, S. E. Effects of group pressure upon the modification and distortion of judgments. In *Groups, Leadership, and Men,* ed. H. Guetzkow. New Brunswick, N.J.: Rutgers University Press, 1951, 177–190.

_____. Studies of independence and conformity: A minority of one against a unanimous majority. *Psychological Monographs,* 70 (1956), 516.

Bandura, A. and Walters, R. H. *Social Learning and Personality Development.* New York: Holt, 1963.

Bandura, A., Ross, D., and Ross, S. A. Transmission of aggression through imitation of aggressive models. *Journal of Abnormal and Social Psychology,* 63 (1961), 575–582.

Berkowitz, L. *Aggression: A Social Psychological Analysis.* New York: McGraw-Hill, 1962.

Berkowitz, L. and Holmes, D. S. The generalization of hostility to disliked objects. *Journal of Personality,* 27 (1959), 565–577.

Berkowitz, L. and LePage, A. Weapons as aggression-eliciting stimuli. *Journal of Personality and Social Psychology,* 7 (1967), 202–207.

Dollard, J., Doob, L., Miller, N., Mowrer, O., and Sears, R. *Frustration and Aggression.* New Haven, Conn.: Yale University Press, 1939.

Festinger, L. *A Theory of Cognitive Dissonance.* Stanford, Calif.: Stanford University Press, 1957.

_____. *Conflict, Decision, and Dissonance.* Stanford, Calif.: Stanford University Press, 1964.

Festinger, L. and Carlsmith, J. Cognitive consequences of forced compliance. *Journal of Abnormal and Social Psychology,* 58 (1959), 203–210.

Festinger, L., Riecken, H. W., and Schachter, S. *When Prophecy Fails.* Minneapolis: University of Minnesota Press, 1956.

Freedman, J., Carlsmith, J. M., and Sears, D. O. *Social Psychology.* Englewood Cliffs, N.J.: Prentice-Hall, 1970.

Goffman, E. *The Presentation of Self in Everyday Life.* Garden City, N.Y.: Doubleday, 1959.

Hilgard, E. R. and Atkinson, R. *Introduction to Psychology,* 5th ed. New York: Harcourt Brace Jovanovich, 1971.

McClelland, D. C. *The Achieving Society.* Princeton, N.J.: Van Nostrand, 1961.

McClelland D. C. and Friedman, G. A. A cross-cultural study of the relationship between child-training practices and achievement motivation appearing in folk-tales. In *Readings in Social Psychology,* ed. G. E. Swanson, T. M. Newcomb, and E. L. Hartley. New York: Holt, 1952.

McClelland, D. C. et al. *The Achievement Motive.* New York: Appleton-Century-Crofts, 1952.

McKeachie, W. J. and Doyle, C. L. *Psychology,* 2d ed. Reading, Mass.: Addison-Wesley, 1970.

McNeil, E. *The Psychology of Being Human,* brief ed. San Francisco, Calif.: Canfield, 1975.

Milgram, S. Behavioral study of obedience. *Journal of Abnormal and Social Psychology,* 67 (1963), 371–378.

———. Group pressure and action against a person. *Journal of Abnormal and Social Psychology,* 69 (1964), 137–143.

———. Some conditions of obedience and disobedience to authority. *Human Relations,* 18 (1965), 57–76.

Murphy, G. *Historical Introduction to Modern Psychology.* New York: Harcourt, Brace, 1949.

Mussen, P. et al. *Psychology an Introduction.* Lexington, Mass.: D. C. Heath, 1973.

Rubin, Z. Measurement of romantic love. *Journal of Personality and Social Psychology,* 16 (1970), 265–273.

Ruch, F. and Zimbardo, P. *Psychology and Life,* 8th ed. Glenview, Ill.: Scott, Foresman, 1971.

Sahakian, W. *Systematic Social Psychology.* New York: Chandler, 1974.

Schellenberg, J. A. *An Introduction to Social Psychology.* New York: Random House, 1970.

Vonnegut, K. *Slaughterhouse-Five.* New York: Dell, 1971.

Watson, G. and Johnson, D. *Social Psychology: Issues and Insights,* 2d ed. Philadelphia, Penn.: Lippincott, 1972.

PERSONALITY

Adler, A. *Social Interest.* New York: Putnam's, 1939.

———. *The Practice and Theory of Individual Psychology.* New York: Harcourt, Brace, 1927.

Allport, G. W. *Becoming: Basic Considerations for a Psychology of Personality.* New Haven, Conn.: Yale University Press, 1955.

———. *Personality: A Psychological Interpretation.* New York: Holt, 1937.

———. *The Person in Psychology: Selected Essays.* Boston, Mass.: Beacon, 1968.

Andrews, L. M. and Karlins, M. *Psychology: What's in It for Us?* 2d ed. New York: Random House, 1975.

Bibliography

Ansbacher, H. L. and Rowena, R., eds. *The Individual Psychology of Alfred Adler.* New York: Basic Books, 1956.

Asimov, I. *I, Robot.* Greenwich, Conn.: Fawcett World, 1970.

Darwin, C. *The Expression of Emotions in Man and Animals.* London: Murray, 1872. *Terms of Learning, Thinking, and Culture.* New York: McGraw-Hill, 1950.

Dollard, J. and Miller, N. E. *Personality and Psychotherapy: An Analysis in Terms of Learning, Thinking, and Culture.* New York: McGraw-Hill, 1950.

Edwards, A. L. *The Measurement of Personality Traits by Scales and Inventories.* New York: Holt, Rinehart and Winston, 1970.

Erikson, E. H. *Childhood and Society.* New York: Norton, 1950. Rev. ed., 1963, 2d rev. ed., 1964.

_____. *Identity: Youth and Crisis.* New York: Norton, 1968.

Fine, R. *Freud: A Critical Reevaluation of His Theories.* New York: David McKay, 1962.

Fordham, F. *An Introduction to Jung's Psychology.* London: Penguin, 1953.

Frankl, V. E. *Man's Search for Meaning.* New York: Washington Square Press, 1963.

_____. *The Will to Meaning: Foundations and Applications of Logotherapy.* New York: World Publishing, 1969.

Freud, S. An outline of psychoanalysis. In *Standard Edition,* vol. 23. London: Hogarth Press, 1964 (original German edition, 1940).

_____. Introductory lectures on psychoanalysis. In *Standard Edition,* vols. 15 and 16. London: Hogarth Press, 1963 (original German edition, 1917).

_____. New introductory lectures on psychoanalysis. In *Standard Edition,* vol. 22. London: Hogarth Press, 1964 (original German edition, 1933).

_____. Psychopathology of everyday life. In *Standard Edition,* vol. 6. London: Hogarth Press, 1960 (original German edition, 1901).

_____. The interpretation of dreams. In *Standard Edition,* vols. 4 and 5. London: Hogarth Press, 1953 (original German edition, 1900).

_____. *The Standard Edition of the Complete Psychological Works,* ed. J. Strachey. London: Hogarth Press, 1953.

Geen, R. *Personality: The Skein of Behavior.* St. Louis, Mo.: Mosby, 1976.

Hall, C. S. *A Primer of Freudian Psychology.* Cleveland, Ohio: World Publishing, 1954.

Hall, C. S. and Lindzey, G. *Theories of Personality,* 2d ed. New York: Wiley, 1970.

Hilgard, E. R. and Atkinson, R. *Introduction to Psychology,* 5th ed. New York: Harcourt Brace Jovanovich, 1971.

Jung, C. G. *Collected Works,* ed. H. Read, M. Fordham, and G. Adler. Princeton, N.J.: Princeton University Press, 1953.

_____. *Modern Man in Search of a Soul.* New York: Harcourt, Brace, 1933.

_____. The archtypes and the collected unconscious. In *Collected Works,* vol. 8.

Princeton, N.J.: Princeton University Press, 1960 (first German edition, 1936–1955).

Kinget, G. M. *On Being Human.* New York: Harcourt, 1975.

McKeachie, W. J. and Doyle, C. L. *Psychology,* 2d ed. Reading, Mass.: Addison-Wesley, 1970.

McNeil, E. *The Psychology of Being Human,* brief ed. San Francisco, Calif.: Canfield, 1975.

Maddi, S. R. The existential neurosis. *Journal of Abnormal Psychology,* 72 (1967), 311–325.

Maslow, A. H. *Motivation and Personality.* New York: Harper, 1954.

——. *Toward a Psychology of Being,* 2d ed. Princeton, N.J.: Van Nostrand, 1968.

May, R. *Love and Will.* New York: Norton, 1969.

——. *Man's Search for Himself.* New York: Norton, 1953.

——. *Power and Innocence.* New York: Norton, 1972.

Miller, N. E. Theory and experiment relating psychoanalytic displacement to stimulus response generalization. *Journal of Abnormal and Social Psychology,* 43 (1948), 155–178.

Miller, N. E. and Dollard, J. *Social Learning and Imitation.* New Haven, Conn.: Yale University Press, 1941.

Murphy, G. *Historical Introduction to Modern Psychology.* New York: Harcourt, Brace, 1949.

Murray, H. A. and Morgan, C. D. A method for investigating fantasies: The thematic apperception test. *Archives for Neurology and Psychiatry* (1935).

Mussen, P. et al. *Psychology an Introduction.* Lexington, Mass.: D. C. Heath, 1973.

Rogers, C. R. *Client-Centered Therapy: Its Current Practice, Implications, and Theory.* Boston: Houghton Mifflin, 1951.

——. *On Becoming a Person.* Boston: Houghton Mifflin, 1961.

Rorschach, H. *Psychodiagnostics.* Berne, Switzerland: Hans Huber, 1942.

Ruch, F. and Zimbardo, P. *Psychology and Life,* 8th ed. Glenview, Ill.: Scott, Foresman, 1971.

Singer, J. *Daydreaming.* New York: Random House, 1966.

Turing, A. M. Computing machinery and intelligence. In *Minds and Machines,* ed. A. R. Anderson. Englewood Cliffs, N.J.: Prentice-Hall, 1964, 4–30.

ABNORMAL PROCESSES AND THERAPY

Andrews, L. M. and Karlins, M. *Psychology: What's in It for Us?* 2d ed. New York: Random House, 1975.

Binder, V. et al. *Modern Therapies.* Englewood Cliffs, N.J.: Prentice-Hall, 1976.

Coleman, J. C. *Abnormal Psychology and Modern Life,* 4th ed. Glenview, Ill.: Scott, Foresman, 1972.

Harper, R. A. *The New Psychotherapies.* Englewood Cliffs, N.J.: Prentice-Hall, 1975. Harcourt Brace Jovanovich, 1971.

Hilgard, E. R. and Atkinson, R. *Introduction to Psychology,* 5th ed. New York: Harcourt Brace Jovanovich, 1971.

Laing, R. D. *The Divided Self.* London: Tavistock Publications, 1960.

_____. *The Politics of Experience.* New York: Pantheon, 1967.

McKeachie, W. J. and Doyle, C. L. *Psychology,* 2d ed. Reading, Mass.: Addison-Wesley, 1970.

McNeil, E. *The Psychology of Being Human,* brief ed. San Francisco, Calif.: Canfield, 1975.

Menninger, K. (with H. Ellenberger, P. Pruyser, and M. Mayman). The unitary concept of mental illness. *Bulletin of the Menninger Clinic,* 22 (1958), 4–12.

Murphy, G. *Historical Introduction to Modern Psychology.* New York: Harcourt, Brace, 1949.

Mussen, P. et al. *Psychology an Introduction.* Lexington, Mass.: D. C. Heath, 1973.

Ruch, F. and Zimbardo, P. *Psychology and Life,* 8th ed. Glenview, Ill.: Scott, Foresman, 1971.

Sahakian, W. S. *Psychopathology Today: Experimentation, Theory, and Research.* Itasca, Ill.: F. E. Peacock, 1970.

Szasz, T. *The Manufacture of Madness.* New York: Dell, 1970.

_____. *The Myth of Mental Illness.* New York: Harper, 1961.

Ullman, L. P. and Krasner, L. *A Psychological Approach to Abnormal Behavior.* Englewood Cliffs, N.J.: Prentice-Hall, 1969.

Wolpe, J. *Psychotherapy by Reciprocal Inhibition.* Stanford, Calif.: Stanford University Press, 1958.

_____. *The Practice of Behavior Therapy.* New York: Pergamon, 1969.

_____. The systematic desensitization treatment of neurosis. *Journal of Nervous and Mental Disease,* 132 (1961), 189–203.